Mastering Adobe Photoshop 2026

Second Edition

Enhance your digital imagery skills with advanced photo editing and visual design workflows

Gary Bradley

‹packt›

Mastering Adobe Photoshop 2026
Second Edition

Copyright © 2025 Packt Publishing

Portfolio Director: Pavan Ramchandani
Relationship Lead: Mohd Riyan Khan
Program Manager: Divij Kotian
Content Engineer: Akanksha Gupta
Technical Editor: Vidhisha Patidar
Copy Editor: Safis Editing
Indexer: Pratik Shirodkar
Proofreader: Akanksha Gupta
Production Designer: Jyoti Kadam
Growth Lead: Nivedita Singh

First published: January 2024
Second published: December 2025

Production reference: 1281125

Published by Packt Publishing Ltd.
Grosvenor House
11 St Paul's Square
Birmingham
B3 1RB, UK.

ISBN 978-1-80602-171-0
www.packtpub.com

For Luka and Alfie.

May you never lose the curiosity and joyful mischief that make every day an adventure.

— Gary Bradley

Foreword

When I created my first photo composite of my grandfather standing arm in arm with his younger self back in the early 2000s, I quickly realized something important: Photoshop's basic tools could produce compelling results, but truly professional work required mastering the deeper workflows and hidden capabilities that most users never discover on their own.

That moment of creative possibility sparked a passion that would define my career path. What began as experimentation grew into formal graphic design training and eventually teaching Photoshop to professionals through courses and at events like Adobe MAX and CreativePro Week. Along the way, I met many professionals who found it challenging to move beyond the basics. Online tutorials offered scattered tips, but they rarely connected into complete workflows that could be applied in daily practice.

This book is exactly the kind of comprehensive resource I wish had existed during my own journey from curious experimenter to professional trainer. Photoshop is endlessly fascinating because its countless functions can be combined in infinite ways. Your learning journey truly never ends, since there is always someone discovering a new combination of tools that makes tasks easier or produces better results. Gary Bradley's *Mastering Adobe Photoshop 2026* does that by gathering proven techniques into one place, so you do not have to search for them yourself.

What makes this book particularly valuable is how Gary integrates cutting-edge AI workflows alongside established techniques. While Photoshop has incorporated intelligent features for years, the recent explosion of generative AI has changed how we approach complex tasks such as advanced retouching, seamless compositing, and brand mockup creation. Gary provides clear guidance on when and how to use these new capabilities effectively.

Whether you're a seasoned designer looking to work more efficiently, a marketing professional seeking stronger visual results, or a content creator ready to expand your skills, this book offers workflows that will help you get much more out of Photoshop. It saves you the search for scattered information and brings together the best of both traditional and modern techniques.

What I love most about Photoshop is how it continues to grow with you. Whether you are just beginning with composites or already know every tool in the program, there are always new combinations to discover. The excitement you feel when a technique suddenly makes everything click is the same experience this book will give you, as you uncover methods you did not know existed.

Rob de Winter

Trainer, Author, and International Speaker

Foreword

It is a true privilege to introduce you to Mastering Adobe Photoshop 2026, and to the brilliant mind of experienced professional and seasoned educator, Gary Bradley.

I first met Gary in 2004, after starting as a 3D artist and animator at an agency in Sheffield. From week one, I knew Gary as "the Photoshop guy." If you needed help with anything Adobe, Gary was an absolute fountain of knowledge. He didn't just know the tools; he mastered the workflows. His workstation was packed with custom shortcuts, automations, and asset libraries he'd configured to support our intense production workflows, ensuring efficiency was always at the heart of the creative process.

I learned so much from Gary in those early days of finding my feet in a fast-paced, professional creative environment. He had a natural, supportive teaching style and always made time to guide you. And when he wasn't on client work, he was busy building new templates and how-to guides for the design team or leading a training course for some of our clients. Following those 3D agency days, we followed different career paths—mine into customer experience and digital agency land, and Gary, unsurprisingly, moved heavily into the teaching field, quickly making a big name for himself in the Adobe circuit.

This background is exactly why I can speak with confidence about the critical value of this book today. Our industry has undergone immense technological shifts in the last twenty years, yet the fundamentals of human connection, creative ideas, and execution remain central to any successful project.

In my current leadership role, focused on delivering world-class customer experiences at UNRVLD, AI has become a powerful accelerator – and an equally powerful challenge. We champion an approach that maintains the 'human at the core,' where technology serves, but never replaces, human creativity and judgment. The philosophy is simple: Start with the customer, not the AI. The technology must accelerate your vision and should be woven across all systems – from CMS to analytics and experimentation - to provide maximum context and deliver tangible business outcomes.

The human element is paramount. When an AI generates an image or executes an action, it operates based on learned logic and training data. It cannot, however, discern the ultimate creative quality needed for your specific assignment, nor can it supply the empathy, humor, and authenticity crucial for brand consistency in an accelerating, automated world. The human touch is what elevates the work, ensuring creativity and brand integrity remain intact. You are the creative director; the AI is your tireless assistant.

This brings us directly to the core of Gary's expertise. *Mastering Adobe Photoshop 2026* is far more than a guide to the latest features - including the powerful AI functionalities mentioned in *Chapter 12*. It is a foundation in the proven best practices required to truly leverage new technology. This book demonstrates how to use new tools to increase confidence, accelerate your workflow, and free up time and energy to focus on creative strategy and vision. Ultimately, Gary's training provides the technical skills needed to command the Photoshop toolkit, ensuring that this cutting-edge technology serves your creative vision, and not the other way around.

I encourage you to turn the page and dive in. You are in the hands of a true master and a generous teacher.

James Carrington

Commercial Director at UNRVLD

Contributors

About the author

Gary Bradley is an award-winning graphic designer, creative director, author, and dedicated educator with over 25 years of industry experience and a passion for nurturing creative talent. Throughout his career, Gary has led multidisciplinary design teams across four continents and delivered innovative projects for clients such as Virgin Atlantic, the London Science Museum, Guinness, and Hugo Boss. His expertise spans print, interactive media, web design, visual effects, 3D visualization, and motion graphics.

Gary founded Creative Frontiers, a mentoring business that has supported thousands of designers across 26 countries, helping enhance the creative capabilities of companies including Microsoft, Burberry, and Walmart. In education, he serves as a Graphic Design Lecturer at University Campus Doncaster. Gary holds a BA in Graphic Design from Leeds Beckett University, a Postgraduate Certificate in Higher Education from Falmouth University, and professional certifications in Creative Thinking from King's College London. He is also an Adobe Master Instructor, with over forty Adobe Expert Certifications in applications such as Photoshop, InDesign, and Illustrator.

I hope you found valuable tips and guidance on using Adobe Photoshop 2026 for your daily digital design work in this book. I want to express my deepest gratitude to all the people who were part of putting this book together: my long-suffering family, who supported me throughout and never complained during long evenings and missed walks in the Peaks. My good friends Steve Askey, Dave Ellis, and Neil Roebuck, who always make time to lend an ear. Special thanks to James Carrington for somehow finding time to write the foreword to this book, along with Rob de Winter. And of course, the Packt Team, Akanksha Gupta, Mohd Riyan Khan, and Vidhisha Patidar, for their patience and invaluable support, along with the technical reviewers Iain Anderson and Matthew Gibbon.

About the reviewers

Iain Anderson is the author of *Final Cut Pro Efficient Editing* and the upcoming book, *AI for Creative Production*. Based in Brisbane, Australia, Iain is an Apple Certified Trainer, a regular writer for ProVideoCoalition, a co-creator of the current Apple Certified FCP Training exam and curriculum, a plug-in developer for FxFactory, a lead trainer and writer for macProVideo.com, a regular conference speaker, a videographer, an editor, an animator, a designer, a photographer, a retoucher, and sometimes an app developer for iPad, Apple Watch, and Apple Vision Pro. He's created animations and live videos for clients including Microsoft and CoreMelt, designed virtual islands in Second Life for the government, and made screensavers for fun.

Matthew Gibbon is a Mac systems trainer and Apple Certified Support Professional with over 33 years of experience in advertising, desktop publishing, and design. Based in South Africa, he specializes in supporting and maintaining Mac IT environments, managing deployments, diagnostics, repairs, upgrades, and data recovery. Matthew provides comprehensive macOS and Repro training across Apple hardware, iPadOS and iOS apps, and leading creative tools including Illustrator, InDesign, Photoshop, Lightroom, Camera Raw, Bridge, and Acrobat. A longtime Mac beta tester and technical coordinator, he delivers hands-on guidance to end-users and creative teams alike. Matthew has served as a technical reviewer for Mastering Adobe Photoshop 2024 and Mastering Adobe Photoshop 2026.

Dedicated to my family, Yolanda, Bianca, and Ryan, for their support and guidance and love.

Table of Contents

Preface   xiii

Free Benefits with Your Book xviii

Part 1: Raising Your Photoshop Game   1

Chapter 1: What's New in Photoshop 2026?   3

Technical requirements 4

What's new in Photoshop 2026 on the desktop 4

Creating and applying adjustment presets • 4

The all-new Adjustment Brush Tool • 5

Adjust colors • 7

Color and Vibrance • 8

Remove background • 9

Harmonize • 11

Generate image • 13

Contextual Task Bar updates • 15

The new Photoshop app on iOS and Android 16

Summary 18

Chapter 2: Making Photoshop Work Harder and Smarter   19

Technical requirements 20

Creating a bespoke workspace 20

Modifying panels • 21

Customizing the Tools panel • 25

Saving a custom workspace • 28

Modifying keyboard shortcuts and menus • 29

Modifying preferences • 31

Defining color settings • 38

Quality-first approach **40**

Image quality • 41

Resolution • 42

Pixels per inch • 42

Vector graphics • 42

Calculating PPI in Photoshop • 43

Online resources **44**

Unsplash • 45

Pexels • 46

Adobe Stock • 46

Other notable stock resources on the web • 48

An introduction to image usage and copyright • 48

Creative Commons licensing • 48

CC BY • 49

CC BY-SA • 49

CC BY-ND • 49

CC BY-NC • 49

CC BY-NC-SA • 49

Attribution, non-commercial, no derivatives (CC BY-NC-ND) • 50

CC0 • 50

Model release • 50

Property release • 50

Summary **51**

Chapter 3: Non-Destructive Healing and Retouching 53

Technical requirements 54

Cropping and straightening images and extending the canvas 54

Straightening a crooked image • 54

Cropping images • 56

Extending the canvas with content-aware cropping • 58

Quick cropping tips • 61

Content-aware scaling • 63

Healing and retouching 64

Removing cables from a photo • 66

Removing large blemishes with Content-Aware Fill • 68

Bending subjects with Puppet Warp • 71

Using the Clone Stamp tool to remove unwanted content • 76

Adding smiles to portraits with Face-Aware Liquify • 79

Portrait retouching • 81

Eliminating glare from glasses • 83

Color and tonal editing with adjustment layers 88

How adjustment layers work • 88

Quick tonal editing with adjustment layers and blend modes • 89

Removing color casts • 90

Altering the hue of multiple subjects • 92

The simplest method for color matching • 95

Matching subjects to new backdrops • 97

Summary 101

Chapter 4: Masking and Cutouts 103

Technical requirements 104

Applying and editing a basic layer mask 104

Masking power shortcuts • 107

Using masks to cut out image backgrounds • 107

Applying masks to adjustment layers • 110

Retouching with a layer mask • 113

Working with gradient masks • 116

Creating distressed photo edges • 119

Masking with Blend If • 121

Masking hair 124

Making detailed adjustments to layer masks • 128

Unlinking images and masks 130

Masking layer groups • 132

Working with vector masks 136

Creating an editable vignette with a vector mask • 136

Creating a typographic mask effect • 138

Summary 141

Part 2: Bringing Brands Front and Center   143

Chapter 5: Building Brand Mock-Ups and Prototypes   145

Technical requirements 146

Considerations for developing mock-ups 146

Applying branding to perspective 147

Adding a logo to a bag in perspective • 148

Creating a mural mock-up • 151

Wrapping artwork around curved surfaces 159

Applying a cylinder warp • 159

Warping artwork across book designs • 162

Replacing device screens with your own artwork 172

Creating an iPad mock-up • 172

Creating a smartphone mock-up • 174

Adding screen reflections • 177

Creating clothing and soft furnishing mock-ups 180

Applying original designs to clothing • 180

Adding pattern designs to a cushion • 183

Creating the cushion displacement map • 183

Applying the pattern artwork • 185

Finessing the rippled surface details • 187

Summary 192

Chapter 6: Creating Printed Marketing Collateral 193

Technical requirements 194

Creating new print projects 194

Color • 194

Printers' marks • 194

Folds • 196

Setting up a Photoshop grid system 197

Building a new A4 poster document • 198

Creating a new business card template • 201

Building a new Z-fold brochure • 203

Importing artwork and formatting types 205

Creating a business card design using only vector assets • 206

Synchronizing fonts from Creative Cloud • 209

Adding type to the Z-fold brochure • 210

Creating and applying paragraph styles • 214

Adding artwork to the brochure • 216

Exporting documents for professional print 220

Exporting to Adobe PDF • 221

Exporting to the Tagged Image File Format • 221

Saving as a JPG • 222

Summary 223

Chapter 7: From Pixels to Post: Images for Social Media   225

Technical requirements 226

Creating new documents for screen and web 226

Examining artwork specs for Facebook • 228

Examining artwork for X • 230

Examining artwork for Instagram • 232

Examining artwork specs for Pinterest • 234

Examining artwork for LinkedIn • 235

Social media sizes • 238

Working with artboards 239

Adding a header image • 244

Creating an X post template • 245

Adding text to the artboard • 251

Duplicating artboards 252

Exporting and scheduling posts 256

Batch export artboards • 257

Scheduling posts with Adobe Express • 259

Summary 260

Chapter 8: Creating Animated GIFs and Videos   263

Technical requirements 264

The Timeline panel 264

Video groups 266

AV file formats accepted by Photoshop 268

Video and GIF limitations on social media 269

Creating animated GIFs 271

Defining a new animation document • 271

Adding brand colors, logos, and text • 272

Creating frame animations • 275

Creating tween animations • 278

Working with video and audio in Photoshop **283**

Creating a new document intended for video • 283

Adding media to the timeline • 284

Applying transitions to footage • 286

Animating an Adobe Illustrator logo in the timeline • 287

Adding a soundtrack to the timeline • 291

Creating videos from still images and text **292**

Setting up a duplicate document • 292

Importing and animating an image • 292

Copying and pasting keyframes onto the second clip • 294

Copying and pasting keyframes onto the third clip • 295

Adding titles to the sequence • 297

Exporting animations and video from Photoshop **300**

Exporting animated GIFs • 300

Export Video • 302

Summary **303**

Part 3: Building Visual Components   305

Chapter 9: Bringing Typography to Life with Effects and Styling   307

Technical requirements **308**

Understanding typographic terms and principles **308**

Synchronizing Adobe fonts **312**

Creating cut and fold effects **314**

Creating sliced text • 314

Creating an embossed type • 317

Creating cut and fold effects • 323

Applying ink and paint effects **332**

Creating dripping paint • 333

Creating and applying the paint displacement map • 334

Refining the paint effect • 336

Creating a graffiti typographic effect • 337

Formatting the underlying type layer • 338

Creating long shadows • 339

Adding spray paint effects to the text and shadows • 341

Summary 343

Chapter 10: Creating Textures, Patterns, and Backdrops   345

Technical requirements 346

Creating new textures, gradients, and patterns 346

Creating a texture from scratch • 346

Creating an atmospheric gradient backdrop • 353

Creating pop-art-inspired artwork with custom patterns • 355

Managing backdrop assets 359

Adding assets with Creative Cloud libraries • 359

Importing and exporting assets • 361

Simulating environments with filters and effects 362

Summary 369

Chapter 11: Creating and Applying Brushes   371

Technical requirements 372

Creating and managing brush tip presets 372

Creating a custom bird brush • 373

Modifying brush properties 377

Creating the large Art History Brush • 379

Creating the medium Art History Brush • 381

Creating a small Art History Brush • 383

Creating a reconstruction Art History Brush • 384

Creating and backing up a brush preset group • 386

Applying brushes for creative effect 388

Using brushes for retouching 392

Creating a snowflake brush • 392

Creating a stubble brush • 396

Summary 401

Part 4: World Building   403

Chapter 12: Integrating Artificial Intelligence   405

Technical requirements 405

Handy tips for text prompts 406

How to structure effective prompts • 407

Describing the medium and subject • 407

Describing actions, the environment, and props • 408

Going deeper with your prompt • 408

Generating images with Adobe Firefly 410

About Firefly image models • 410

Getting to know the Firefly interface • 411

Creating an image in Firefly • 414

Generative retouching 416

Replacing drab skies • 416

Replacing content with Generative Fill • 419

Removing distractions • 420

The Remove Tool • 421

Partner models 423

Upscaling images with AI • 423

Everyone is Bananas for Gemini 2.5 • 424

Replacing and expanding backgrounds 427

Extending the canvas • 427

Generating new backgrounds 429

Summary 431

Chapter 13: Blending and Collaging Images　　　433

Technical requirements 434

Creating seamless panoramas 434

Building collages with texture and paint 439

Posterizing the source photo • 439

Selecting and masking posterized regions • 442

Adding texture and paint to the posterized sections • 444

Creating double-exposure compositions 449

Blending unrelated images • 449

Blending two exposures of the same image • 455

Working with HDR images 458

Advice for shooting HDR source images • 458

Installing Adobe Bridge • 458

Creating an HDR image with HDR Pro • 460

Summary 467

Chapter 14: Creating Surrealist Artwork　　　469

Technical requirements 470

How to approach a surrealist art project 470

Creating simple yet effective surrealist art 471

Transferring the Moon artwork • 471

Scaling and distorting the Moon • 473

Turning the pink balloon into grayscale • 476

Replacing chair shadows • 478

Creating moonlight effects • 490

Creating and editing project-specific assets 497

Isolating the hands from the shot • 497

Creating smoke effects with brushes and filters 507

Summary 512

Chapter 15: Unlock Your Exclusive Benefits 513

Unlock this Book's Free Benefits in 3 Easy Steps 513

Other Books You May Enjoy 519

Index 523

Preface

Mastering Adobe Photoshop 2026 will guide you step-by-step through the in-demand skills required by the industry. This book will build on your existing Photoshop knowledge, helping you become a more productive image editor and improve the quality of your work. It will teach you about essential resources for graphic designers or marketers seeking transformative career growth, including the knowledge and skills to achieve jaw-dropping results with AI tools built into Photoshop and Adobe Firefly.

As a digital content creator, whether you're working on projects for print, screen, or social media, having a solid understanding of Photoshop is essential. So, if you are ready to hone your skills and expand your capabilities, *Mastering Adobe Photoshop 2026* will guide you there.

This book takes a step-by-step approach, breaking down each technique into easily understandable terms, which makes it accessible even to those who are new to advanced editing. Then, through a series of hands-on exercises, you'll have the opportunity to practice these techniques and learn about each tool's strengths and limitations.

In the book's final section, you'll bring everything together and learn how to produce your digital media projects from start to finish. You'll learn how to plan your projects, maintain flexibility throughout the editing process, and prepare artwork for a range of outputs.

From creating captivating visuals for social media to mastering retouching and compositing, this book focuses on the knowledge and skills that will help you achieve a stronger workflow and a more refined approach to producing professional-quality visuals.

Who this book is for

This book is for people with a basic working knowledge of Adobe Photoshop who are determined to enhance their skills to a professional standard with proven industry techniques and workflows. Understanding digital media file types will be an advantage to help you gain the most value from this book.

If you're a designer or marketer looking to build upon a basic working knowledge of Adobe Photoshop, gain invaluable insights into professional editing techniques, and take your career to the next step, this book is for you.

What this book covers

Chapter 1, What's New in Photoshop will guide you through the most impactful updates since the 2026 release, including innovative AI tools and streamlined workflows.

Chapter 2, Making Photoshop Work Harder and Smarter, provides you with new ways of working with familiar tools that will build upon and enhance your basic knowledge of Adobe Photoshop.

Chapter 3, Non-Destructive Healing and Retouching, teaches you how to hide unwanted content from images and apply essential color and tonal edits non-destructively, meaning that your edits can be edited multiple times without losing quality. This will first require quick and accurate selections with a variety of tools.

Chapter 4, Masking and Cutouts, showcases powerful tools for concealing and revealing layer content without permanent deletion. These skills enable you to extract intricate details such as hair from backgrounds and create montages.

Chapter 5, Building Brand Mock-Ups and Prototypes, teaches you how to bring ideas and concepts to life by creating realistic mockups. You will learn how to apply graphics to a series of surfaces, such as walls, device screens, t-shirts, and cushions, using smart workflows that allow you to re-edit your assets without losing quality.

Chapter 6, Creating Printed Marketing Collateral, provides an in-depth look at how to prepare new documents for print output for flyers, posters, and business cards, and how to create grid systems and print characteristics like bleed to expertly manage content such as text layers, branding, and photos.

Chapter 7, From Pixels to Post: Images for Social Media, takes you through a streamlined process for creating social media images. You will learn how to use artboards to manage multiple images in a single document, protect text and logos in smart object layers, and text styles for rapid type formatting. Then, you will see how to export your branded images with ease to multiple file formats and sizes, ready for posting online.

Chapter 8, Creating Animated GIFs and Videos, looks at how to create and edit video and animated GIFs in Photoshop. We will be using familiar tools to import video clips, add transitions and audio to a simple yet powerful timeline, and export animated GIFs or render video to common file formats ready for posting online or on platforms such as YouTube.

Chapter 9, Bringing Typography to Life with Effects and Styling, takes you through a series of typographic effects to make your text stand out. We will use editable layer effects to create paper folds, slices, dripping paint, graffiti art, and embossed paper, all while keeping your text layers editable. You will learn how to change characters, words, font families, and font size without compromising your final designs.

Chapter 10, Creating Textures, Patterns, and Backdrops, teaches how to create your own backdrops, from realistic textures to geometric gradients, pop art, and science fiction space scenes. All will be created from scratch without any source images so you can build visually captivating backdrops anytime.

Chapter 11, Creating and Applying Brushes, introduces you to the immense power and flexibility of Photoshop brushes. You will learn how to create your own brush tip shapes, from a flock of birds and snowflakes to sampled paint strokes and facial hair for retouching.

Chapter 12, Integrating Artificial Intelligence, explores the generative image technology built into familiar tools and the Photoshop interface, as well as the online platform, Adobe Firefly, to create an array of visuals from simple text prompts.

Chapter 13, Blending and Collaging Images, combines many of the professional-grade techniques in this book to successfully create image montages, seamless panoramas, collage self-portraits, double-exposure effects, and beautifully lit scenes using high dynamic range images that blend the lighting data of multiple shots.

Chapter 14, Creating Surrealist Artwork, challenges you and your new skills with two surrealist art projects. You will draw upon the techniques covered throughout this book to produce visually captivating, surreal artwork.

To get the most out of this book

Software/hardware covered in the book	Operating system requirements
Adobe Photoshop	Windows, macOS, or Linux
Adobe Bridge	
Adobe Express	

Download the example files

You can download the example files for this book from `https://packt.link/gbz/9781806021710`. If there's an update to the files, it will be updated at the link.

We also have other code bundles from our rich catalog of books and videos available at `https://github.com/PacktPublishing/`. Check them out!

Download the color images

We also provide a PDF file that has color images of the screenshots/diagrams used in this book. You can download it here: `https://packt.link/gbp/9781806021710`.

Conventions used

There are a number of text conventions used throughout this book.

`CodeInText`: Indicates code words in text, folder names, filenames, file extensions, pathnames, dummy URLs, and user input. For example: "Open `Shoreline.jpg` from the `03-Retouch` folder."

Bold: Indicates a new term, an important word, or words that you see on the screen. For instance, words in menus or dialog boxes appear in the text like this. For example: "**Zoom with Scroll Wheel** allows you to avoid activating the **Zoom** tool altogether, while **Animated Zoom** and **Flick Panning** make the motion of panning and zooming less jarring on the eye."

> Warnings or important notes appear like this

> Tips and tricks appear like this.

Get in touch

Feedback from our readers is always welcome.

General feedback: If you have questions about any aspect of this book or have any general feedback, please email us at customercare@packt.com and mention the book's title in the subject of your message.

Errata: Although we have taken every care to ensure the accuracy of our content, mistakes do happen. If you have found a mistake in this book, we would be grateful if you reported this to us. Please visit http://www.packt.com/submit-errata, click **Submit Errata**, and fill in the form.

Piracy: If you come across any illegal copies of our works in any form on the internet, we would be grateful if you would provide us with the location address or website name. Please contact us at copyright@packt.com with a link to the material.

If you are interested in becoming an author: If there is a topic that you have expertise in and you are interested in either writing or contributing to a book, please visit http://authors.packt.com/.

Share your thoughts

Once you've read *Mastering Adobe Photoshop 2026*, we'd love to hear your thoughts! Scan the QR code below to go straight to the Amazon review page for this book and share your feedback.

https://packt.link/r/1806021714

Your review is important to us and the tech community and will help us make sure we're delivering excellent quality content.

Free Benefits with Your Book

This book comes with free benefits to support your learning. Activate them now for instant access (see the "*How to Unlock*" section for instructions).

Here's a quick overview of what you can instantly unlock with your purchase:

PDF and ePub Copies

Next-Gen Web-Based Reader

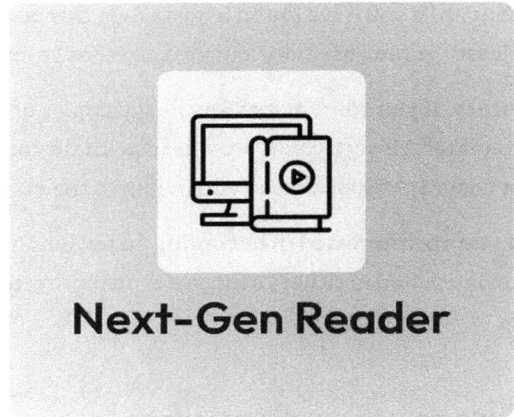

Free PDF and ePub versions

Next-Gen Reader

Access a DRM-free PDF copy of this book to read anywhere, on any device.

Use a DRM-free ePub version with your favorite e-reader.

Multi-device progress sync: Pick up where you left off, on any device.

Highlighting and notetaking: Capture ideas and turn reading into lasting knowledge.

Bookmarking: Save and revisit key sections whenever you need them.

Dark mode: Reduce eye strain by switching to dark or sepia themes.

How to Unlock

Scan the QR code (or go to packtpub.com/unlock). Search for this book by name, confirm the edition, and then follow the steps on the page.

Note: Keep your invoice handy. Purchases made directly from Packt don't require one.

Part 1

Raising Your Photoshop Game

We all discover Photoshop differently, often learning about tools and features that are relevant to our work. However, this can lead to knowledge gaps that may hold us back. *Part 1* of this book will focus on essential skills and how to build upon them, starting with *Chapter 1*, which brings you bang up to speed with the latest features and updates announced at Adobe Max.

This part of the book includes the following chapters:

- *Chapter 1, What's New in Photoshop*
- *Chapter 2, Making Photoshop Work Harder and Smarter*
- *Chapter 3, Non-Destructive Healing and Retouching*
- *Chapter 4, Masking and Cutouts*

1

What's New in Photoshop 2026?

As a young designer in the late 1990s, I greeted new versions of Adobe Photoshop like a kid in a candy store. Updates were shipped on a CD-ROM every two years, so there was a fair amount of anticipation. In between, little was known about how Adobe's digital tools would evolve until they were installed.

These days, things are very different. Social media provides a constant drip feed of teasers and posts covering features that haven't even appeared in the full application, thanks to Beta versions. Updates can now pass you by, often installed automatically without your knowledge, which could lead you to miss out on valuable time-saving enhancements to your workflow.

In this chapter, we'll examine updates and new features in the desktop version of Photoshop 2026 (version 27.0) and the recently launched smartphone version of the application.

In this chapter, we'll cover the following topics:

- What's new in Photoshop 2026 on the desktop
- The new Photoshop app on iOS and Android

Free Benefits with Your Book

Your purchase includes a free PDF copy of this book along with other exclusive benefits. Check the *Free Benefits with Your Book* section in the Preface to unlock them instantly and maximize your learning experience.

Technical requirements

The project files for this chapter can be found at `https://packt.link/gbz/9781806021710`.

What's new in Photoshop 2026 on the desktop

In October 2023, Adobe implemented the first of several changes to the **Adjustments** panel and the methods for editing color and tone in Photoshop. These modifications mimic some of the editing concepts found in **Adobe Camera Raw (ACR)**, where multiple edits can be applied simultaneously and saved for future use. Let's explore how this works in principle, starting with an updated **Adjustments** panel.

Creating and applying adjustment presets

You can now add layer adjustments to an image and save one or more of them as a preset for later use. This can be particularly handy if, for example, you need to boost color and enhance contrast in your images quickly. To achieve this, click on the text tab named **Single adjustments**, apply one or more adjustments to your image, and edit their respective settings. As in previous versions of Photoshop, every single adjustment is added as a separate layer in the **Layers** panel.

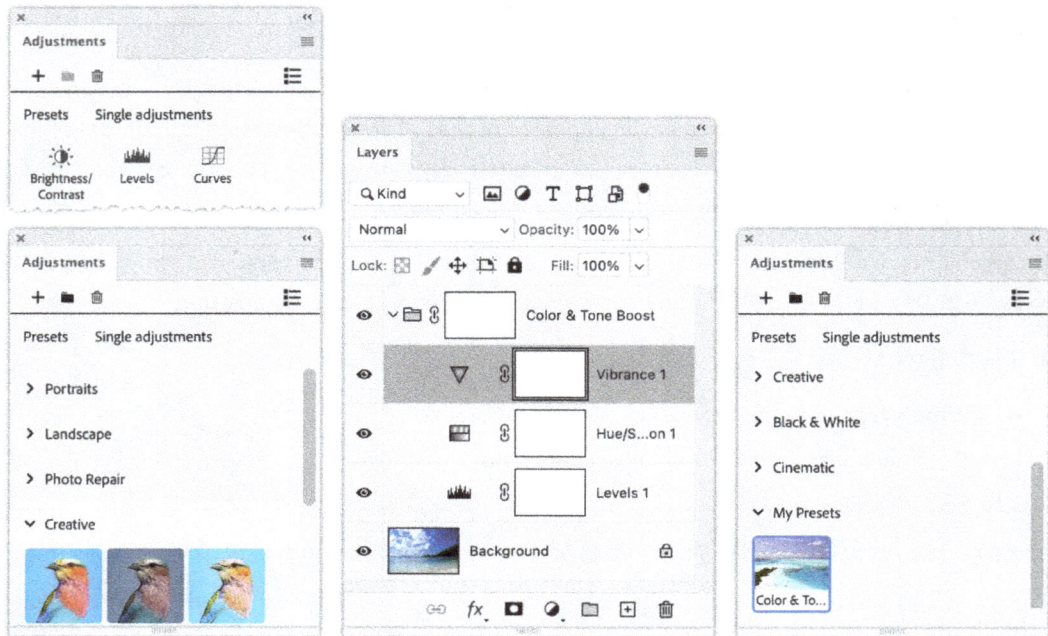

Figure 1.1: Creating presets in the Adjustments panel

When you want to save them as a preset, head to the **Layers** panel and target (make active) the adjustment layers you wish to include in your preset by clicking on them in the **Layers** stack. Alternatively, hold *Ctrl* (Windows) or *Cmd* (macOS) as you click the layer name to add additional layers. Then, click on **Create Adjustment Preset**, which is shown as a plus icon at the top of the **Adjustments** panel.

The new adjustment preset will be automatically added to the active preset group in the **Adjustments** panel. If, like me, you prefer to keep your presets organized into specific sets, I recommend creating a new preset group. It's possible to accidentally add a new preset group to an existing group, which can be frustrating. Ensure that no existing preset group is active by clicking in an empty space at the bottom of the **Adjustments** panel. Then, click on the **Create Group** icon, represented by a folder icon at the top of the **Adjustments** panel. Name your group and click **OK**. You will then be able to drag and drop the presets and groups as necessary at the bottom of the **Adjustments** panel.

To apply an adjustment preset, click on the thumbnail of the corresponding preset. You can also hover your cursor over a preset thumbnail to reveal an on-image preview of what the edits would look like on your active image before applying them.

The all-new Adjustment Brush Tool

If you've worked with adjustment layers in Photoshop, you'll know that not every edit to color and tone is required across an entire image. The addition of a layer mask is often necessary to conceal edits where they are not needed. The new **Adjustment Brush Tool** aims to expedite the masking part of this process. In previous versions of Photoshop, you'd often have to create a selection of the region you needed to affect, then add an adjustment layer, which subsequently used your active selection as a layer mask.

Select **Adjustment Brush Tool**, located in the lower half of the **Tools** panel. Next, from either the **Options** bar or the contextual task bar, choose an adjustment from the **Adjustment Type** drop-down menu. There are 16 adjustments available that replicate those found in the main **Adjustments** panel. Since this is a painting tool, you can then adjust the size, hardness, or brush tip shape from the **Options** bar before applying brush strokes.

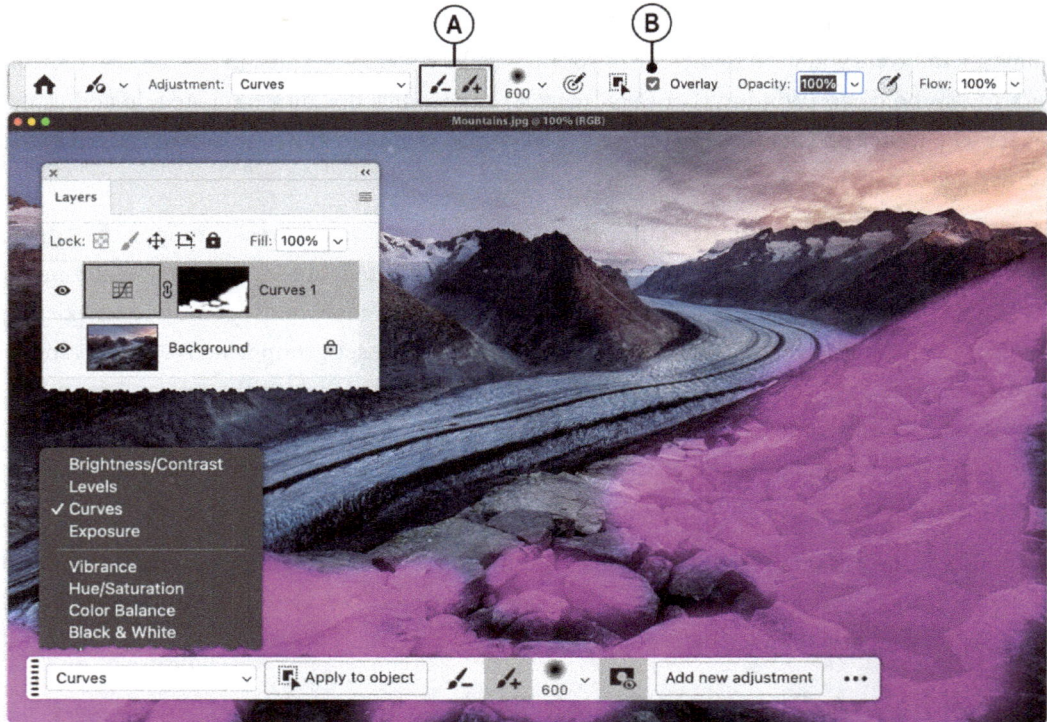

Figure 1.2: The new Adjustment Brush Tool with settings in the Options bar and Contextual Task Bar

As you drag the Adjustment Brush Tool across your image, a magenta overlay will appear, indicating where your edits will be visible, with the adjustment's default settings applied in a new adjustment layer in the **Layers** panel. The **Properties** panel will also appear, where you can fine-tune the adjustment settings once you release the mouse. You find it necessary at this point to deactivate the colored overlay (**B** in *Figure 1.2*) so that you can see the impact of your edits on the image.

To edit the adjustment layer mask, choose either the **Add to Mask** or **Subtract from Mask** modes in the **Options** bar/Contextual Task Bar (**A** in *Figure 1.2*) and drag in the region of the image you wish to edit with the Adjustment Brush Tool.

You can change the adjustment type by selecting a different option from the **Adjustment Type** dropdown. To add more adjustments, click the **Add new adjustment** button in the contextual task bar, select your adjustment type, and begin dragging the Adjustment Brush Tool over the image. Alternatively, you can click on the **Apply to Object** button in the contextual task bar. Then, hover your cursor over an object in your image to reveal the overlay, and click to create a new adjustment layer with the object masked.

Adjust colors

The **Hue/Saturation** adjustment panel now identifies the six most prominent colors in your image to simplify editing, replacing the fixed color ranges once available in a drop-down menu. You can access the **Adjust colors** feature from the contextual task bar when you have a pixel-based layer or smart object active in the **Layers** panel. Click on the **Adjust colors** button.

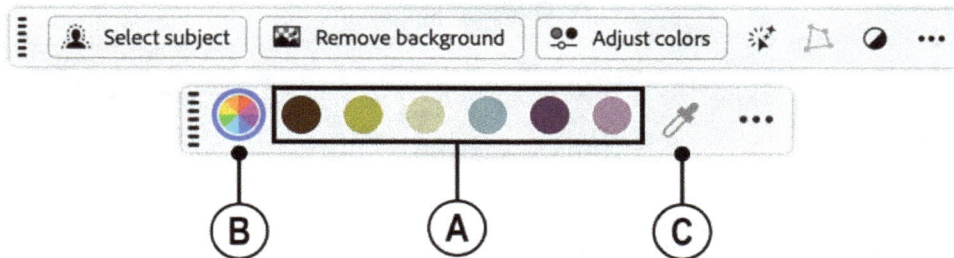

Figure 1.3: The Adjust colors option in the Contextual Task Bar

Once **Adjust colors** is activated, Photoshop will detect the six most prominent colors (**A** in *Figure 1.3*) in the image and display them in the contextual task bar. In addition, a **Hue/Saturation** adjustment layer will be added to the layer stack. By default, all colors are active for editing in the image, and by clicking on the far-left icon in the contextual task bar (**B** in *Figure 1.3*), you can edit the hue, saturation, and lightness.

To change a prominent color for an alternative of your choice, click on an unused color slot (**A** in *Figure 1.3*). Then, click on the **Sample color** icon (**C** in *Figure 1.3*) in the contextual task bar, hover your cursor over the desired color in the image, and click.

To change the appearance of a prominent color, click on it in the contextual task bar to reveal a pop-up containing the **Hue**, **Saturation**, and **Lightness** sliders. Then, drag the sliders accordingly to make the necessary changes.

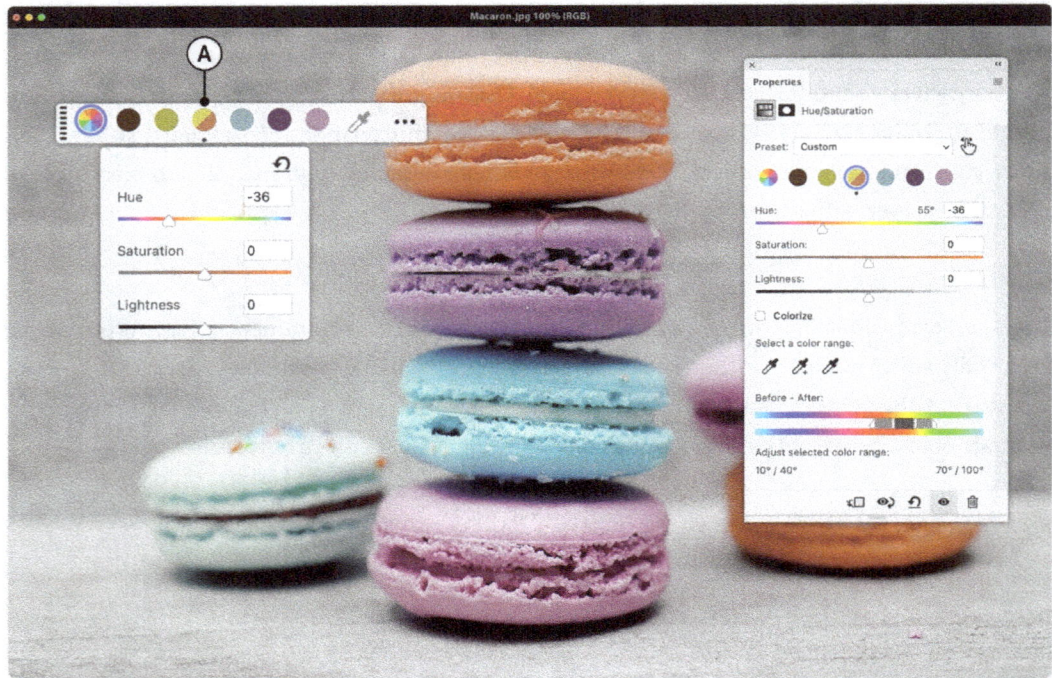

Figure 1.4: Adjusting the six most prominent colors in your image with Adjust colors

Edited colors display a dot under their swatch icon (**A** in *Figure 1.4*) with a split showing the original color and the edited color. The same settings can be found in an updated version of the **Adjustments** panel.

Color and Vibrance

Another adjustment to undergo a boost is **Vibrance**. Now renamed **Color and vibrance**, it includes controls for **Temperature** and **Tint** in addition to **Vibrance** and **Saturation** for non-destructive editing. **Temperature** allows you to adjust the warmth of an image; negative values result in a cooler blue/cyan appearance, whilst positive values give a warmer yellow/orange appearance. The **Tint** slider lets you change the balance between green and magenta, with negative values giving a green cast, and positive values a magenta cast.

Alternatively, you can select the **White Balance** tool (**A** in *Figure 1.5*) next to the **White Balance** drop-down menu to set **Temperature** and **Tint** automatically. Once active, hover the **White Balance** tool over a neutral region of the image containing no color, such as the shaded white window surrounds (**B**). Then, click to set the white balance.

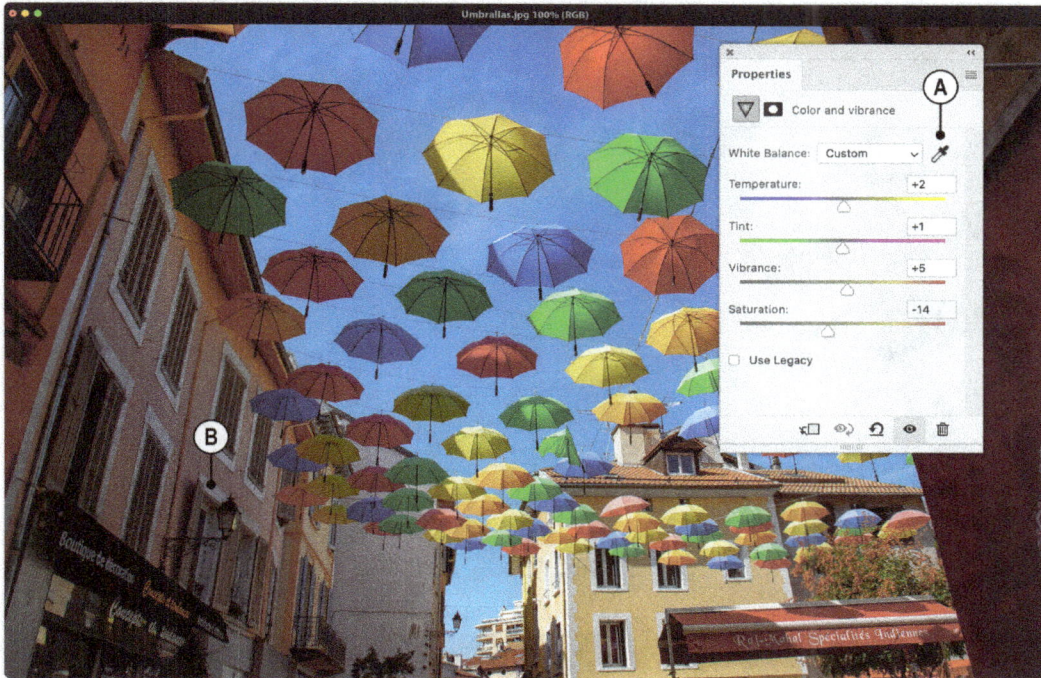

Figure 1.5: Color and vibrance allows non-destructive editing for Temperature and Tint

Remove background

First introduced in 2019, the **Remove background** feature sped up masking by detecting a subject and adding a layer mask that concealed the rest of the image, thereby removing the background. In later versions, selecting a subject could be processed either in the cloud for better results, which took longer, or on the active device for faster processing but with less reliable results.

In Photoshop 2026, the results of both cloud and device masking have taken an enormous leap forward in quality. You can now use either the cloud or device method to achieve high-quality cut-outs. In the example shown in *Figure 1.6*, the device produced a better-quality mask than the cloud version:

Figure 1.6: Remove background now produces far better masking results

Even with a background color that was similar to the subject, Photoshop could correctly identify the foreground object and keep fine details such as the spokes intact. Only a feathered edge around the chain would have required me to make further refinements to the mask.

To remove the background in an active image, click on the **Remove background** button in the contextual task bar (Window → Contextual Task Bar).

You can set a default method for processing selections when using **Select subject** and **Remove background**. Go to **Edit → Preferences → Image Processing** (Windows) or **Photoshop → Preferences → Image Processing** (macOS). Click the **Select Subject and Remove Background** dropdown, then choose **Cloud** or **Device** (default) from the list of options.

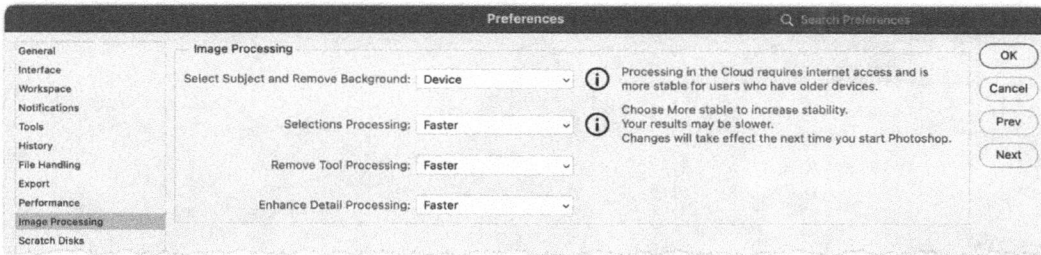

Figure 1.7: Choosing a default method for selecting and removing backgrounds in Preferences

Photoshop's **Preferences** settings allow you to modify the application's appearance, performance, and behavior. From the painting cursors to units of measure, we'll take an in-depth look at **Preferences** in *Chapter 2*.

Harmonize

In *Chapter 3*, we'll look at a technique for merging a subject into a new backdrop, a process that can be time-consuming and require editing the color, tone, shadows, and reflections to achieve a convincing result. Now, **Harmonize** promises to do this in one click.

In each instance, you'll need to remove the background of your subject and then juxtapose it with a new background.

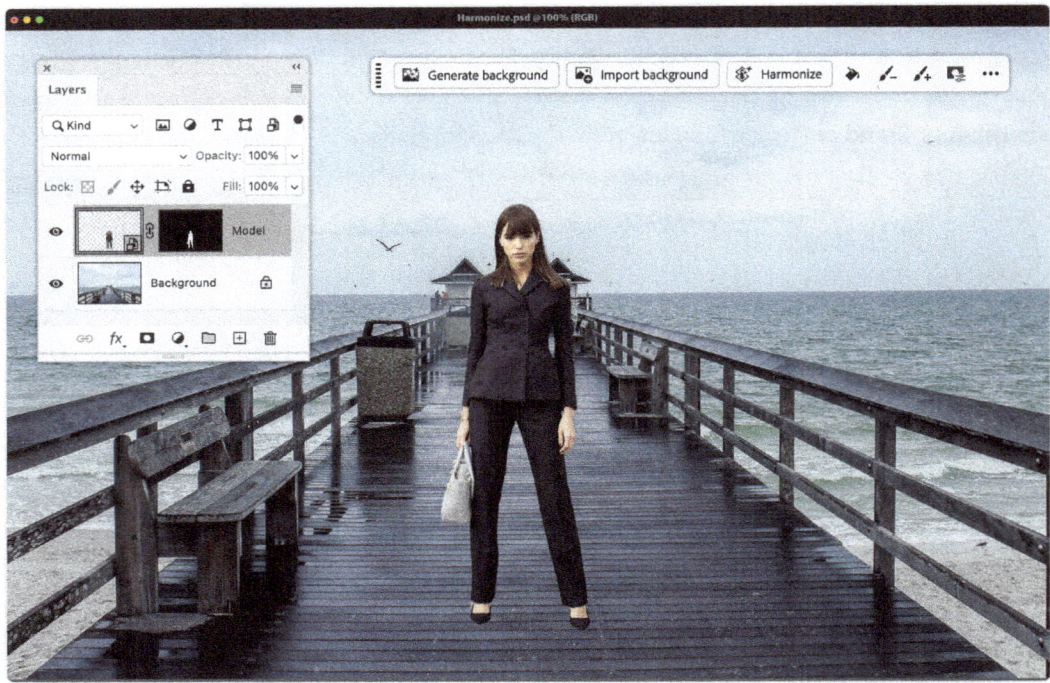

Figure 1.8: Juxtaposing the subject within a new background

With your subject placed accordingly, click on **Harmonize** from the contextual task bar. Photoshop will then analyze the background and create a copy of it and the subject, merging them into a new layer. Generative AI will match the color and lighting, as well as create shadows and reflections cast by the subject.

Once complete, the **Properties** panel then displays three variations that you can click on and choose your final composition from. The original background and subject layers will be maintained lower in the layer stack, with the new **Harmonized** layer at the top. This allows you to delete the **Harmonized layer** and refine the placement of the original assets, if needed.

Harmonize tends to add shadows and reflections as though the subject were touching the surface, which may be problematic if your subject is leaping in the air, for example. It might take a few attempts to achieve the desired look, but for a one-click solution, this could be a dramatic time saver.

Figure 1.9: The subject and background blended with Harmonize

Generate image

A simplified version of **Adobe Firefly** is now available within the Photoshop interface, used for creating new AI-generated images for use in your project work. Go to **Edit → Generate image** to open the dialog.

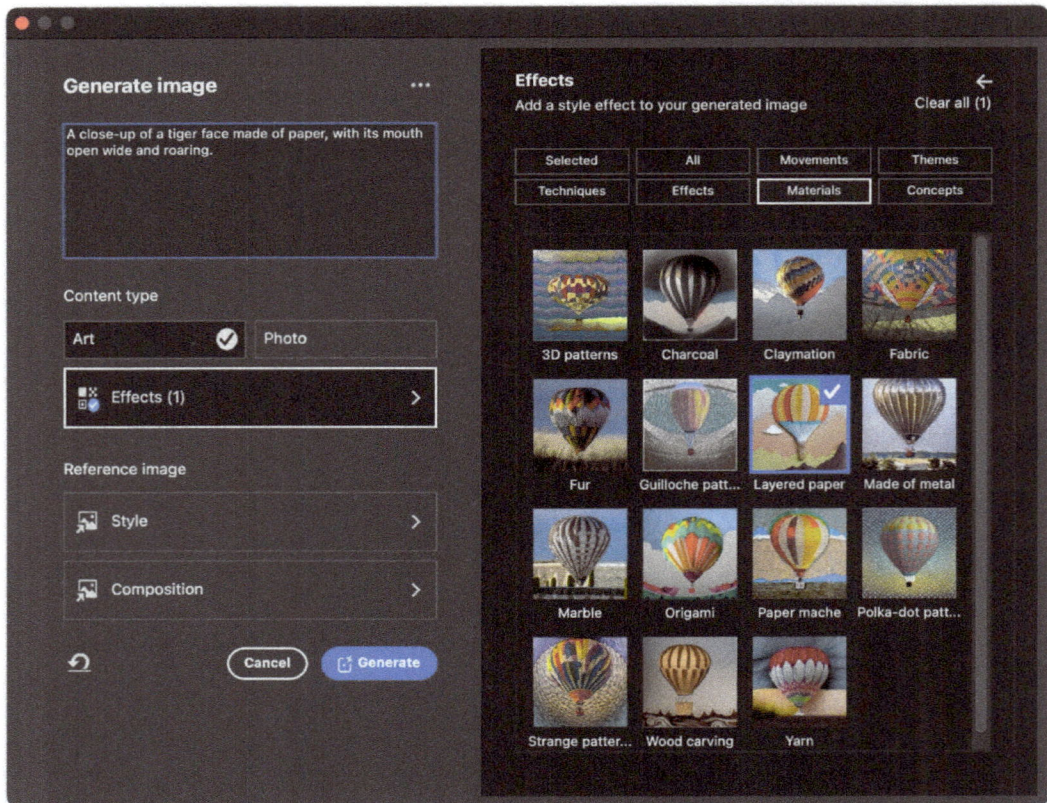

Figure 1.10: Creating AI-generated images in Photoshop

When the **Generate image** dialog appears, enter a description of the image you want to create in the **Prompt** field. Choose whether the image should look like a photo or art by clicking on the corresponding button under **Content type**.

You can also specify an effect from one of the eight topics shown on the right of the dialog, such as **Materials**, **Technique**, **Themes**, and **Concepts**. Like the web version of Adobe Firefly, you can upload an image for a **Style** and **Composition** reference. **Style** will attempt to match a visual theme from the uploaded photo or the pre-supplied library. **Composition** will try to match the angles and overall structure of the reference image.

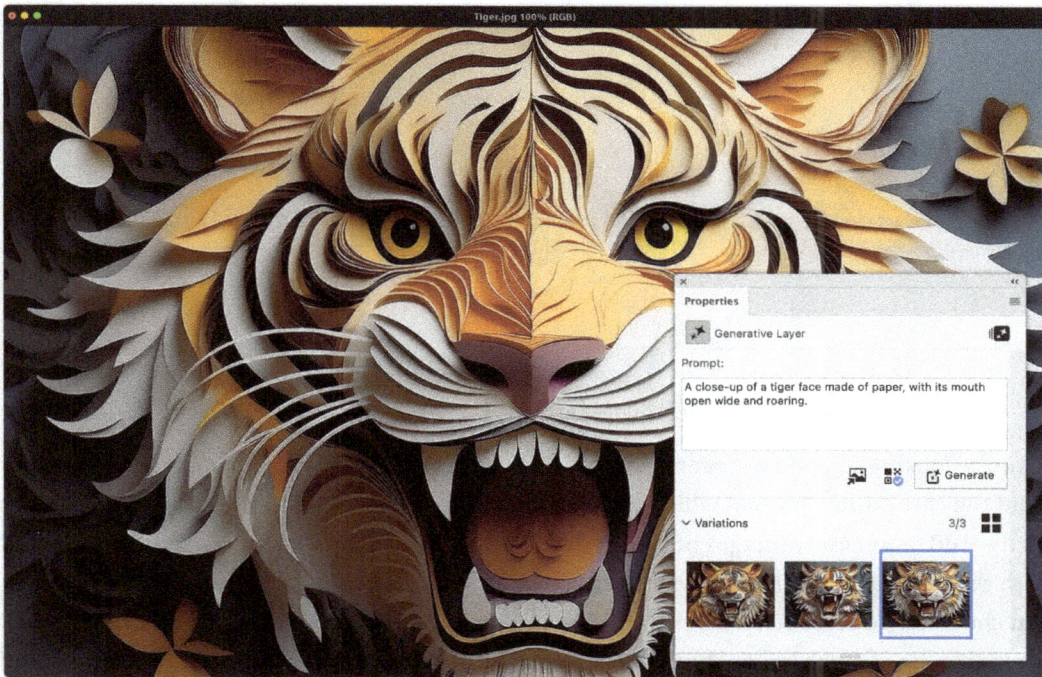

Figure 1.11: An example AI-generated image

Generated images are inserted into your active image in Photoshop at a maximum resolution of 2048 x 2048 px. The **Properties** panel will display three variants. Click on each thumbnail to display the variant in the image window. You will learn more about Photoshop's generative AI features in *Chapter 12*.

Contextual Task Bar updates

Since its first appearance in the 2023 Photoshop release, the **Contextual Task Bar** has expanded to include new, convenient options. Along with features already discussed in this chapter that can be edited via the contextual task bar, such as **Harmonize** and **Adjust colors**, you'll now find more **Type** options (**A** in *Figure 1.12*), including **Leading**, **Tracking**, **Faux Bold**, **Faux Italics**, and **Faux Underline**. You can also toggle **Dynamic Text** on or off (**B**).

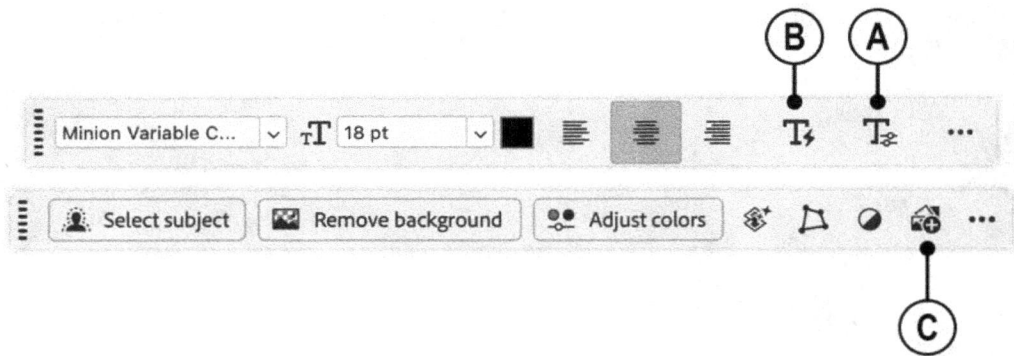

Figure 1.12: New and updated features found in the Contextual Task Bar

If you're looking to add new content to your image, you can now add or generate new images from the contextual task bar, which includes access to Adobe's free-to-use stock images. Click on the **Add or generate images** button in the contextual task bar (**C**), and you will be presented with three options: **Add from device, Add free Adobe Stock images**, or **Generate image**. When you choose to add Adobe Stock, you will be taken to an in-app browser window. You can scroll through a list of stock image thumbnails displayed in categories such as **Animals, Fabric**, and **Celestial**, or use the search field to perform your own keyword search. Click the image you want to use, then click the **Add** button to add it to your active document.

> Turn on **Always Create Smart Objects When Placing** to prevent a loss in quality when scaling layers, including those downloaded from Adobe Stock, by going to **Edit → Preferences → General** (Windows) or **Photoshop → Preferences → General**.

The new Photoshop app on iOS and Android

Adobe released Photoshop for mobile for iOS in February 2025, with the Android version following in June 2025. Photoshop for mobile is available in both free and premium versions. The free version includes access to over 64,000 free Adobe Stock images, selection tools, unlimited layers, **Spot Healing** tools, **Generative Fill**, and **Generative Expand**, as well as limited color and tonal adjustments.

Figure 1.13: Examples of the Photoshop for mobile interface and tools

The **Welcome** screen behaves much like the desktop version. You'll find a series of handy video explainers for getting started with the app. Jump back into previous files, create new documents, or start with Adobe Stock content and generative images from the **Let's get started** section.

The Premium plan for the Photoshop mobile version also includes the web browser version with full access to all features on both platforms. Edits to your files automatically sync between the mobile and web versions. You can benefit from familiar tools such as **Object Selection Tool**, **Magic Wand**, **Remove Tool**, **Clone Stamp**, and **Content-Aware Fill**.

I found that the touch-screen gestures took a while to get used to, especially when using the retouching tools. I often found myself accidentally brushing across the image rather than panning, pinching, and zooming. But what surprised me the most was the speed and simplicity of the user experience. I was afraid it might feel fiddly working on a small screen, but it felt intuitive quickly, and edits such as retouching worked quicker than on the desktop. A simple, scrollable menu system at the bottom of the screen allows you to jump between selections, color and tonal editing, retouching, actions such as remove background, text editing, and paint. The only downside is the limited screen space, which means having to pan more to view different parts of the image to inspect my edits.

The layer features are also impressive and relatively simple to access. You can lock, duplicate, mask, and transform content and alter the stacking order. You can export to a range of formats, including PSD, TIFF, JPG, and PNG.

I think the mobile version of Photoshop, in particular, will be a welcome addition for people accustomed to working on their mobile devices, perhaps managing social media accounts on the go. This is an impressive first release.

Summary

In this first chapter, we have taken a look at the most significant updates and new features across the Photoshop editing ecosystem. Changes to the desktop application included an enhanced workflow for painting color and tonal adjustments with the new **Adjustment Brush Tool**, which acts as a masking tool to restrict the region you edit. We also explored **Adjust colors**, which identifies the six most prominent colors in your image to simplify editing their hue and saturation. We then looked at AI-enhanced tools and features such as **Harmonize**, which blends the active layer with the document's background; **Remove background,** for rapid, high-quality masking of a subject; and **Generate image**, bringing the Firefly experience directly into the desktop application. Finally, we took a first look at the new Photoshop for mobile app.

In the next chapter, we'll look at setting up Photoshop's interface, tools, and preferences to maximize their use.

2

Making Photoshop Work Harder and Smarter

We all learn Photoshop in our own unique way, discovering the tools and features that work best for us. But here's the thing: sometimes we might miss out on certain things that could really boost our skills. *Part 1* of this book, *Raising Your Photoshop Game*, not only focuses on new and updated features but also essential skills and builds upon them, starting with *Chapter 2*, which establishes a streamlined interface and tools setup.

First, we'll customize the interface, modifying panels and tools so that they're easier to locate, putting the most effective features front and center in your interface while keeping less frequently used features just a mouse click away. We'll reorder the **Tools** panel, stripping away redundant tools in place of your favored go-to, high-impact tools, and set up keyboard shortcuts that make little-known features easy to activate or modify a tool with ease.

Then we'll explore digital imaging 101 to ensure you've got a clear understanding of key industry terminology and image quality, as well as the resources available online to source your project artwork. Finally, we'll look at copyright and gaining the appropriate permission to include images in your published projects.

As with many concepts in this book, the first chapter focuses on attaining the best possible quality from the outset while leveraging time-saving techniques whenever possible, essential for today's busy digital image editors. In this chapter, we'll cover the following topics:

- Creating a bespoke workspace
- Modifying preferences
- Quality-first approach
- Online resources
- An introduction to image usage and copyright

Technical requirements

The project files for this chapter can be found at - `https://packt.link/gbz/9781806021710`.

Creating a bespoke workspace

It's one thing to know your Photoshop tools and features, but quite another to make them more accessible. Delving into a rabbit hole of sub-menus to find a time-saving tool burns valuable time, diminishing its effectiveness. At first, the extra mouse clicks might seem inconsequential, but over the course of a year, that could amount to dozens of hours wasted when you could have been meeting deadlines faster. I would suggest thinking about which tools and panels you use most frequently and prioritizing your screen real estate.

In the following exercises, we'll look at customizing panels, tools, and shortcuts. You can adjust these techniques to suit your individual workflow.

Modifying panels

Photoshop panels are arranged into **workspaces**, with the default, called **Essentials**, active when you open it for the first time, an option that Adobe believes is important to all Photoshop users. This workspace is arranged into two columns on the right-hand side of the interface; the right-hand column is expanded for high-use options, while the left-hand column is collapsed into a thin set of icons for less frequently used features. The **Layers** panel is core to almost everything we do in Photoshop; therefore, it's omnipresent and requires space. We will arrange other panels around it. Here's how to do this:

1. Click on the **Workspace Switcher** menu located at the top-right-hand side of the interface (**A** in *Figure 2.1*) and choose **Essentials** from the list of options. Then, return to the same menu and choose **Reset Essentials**:

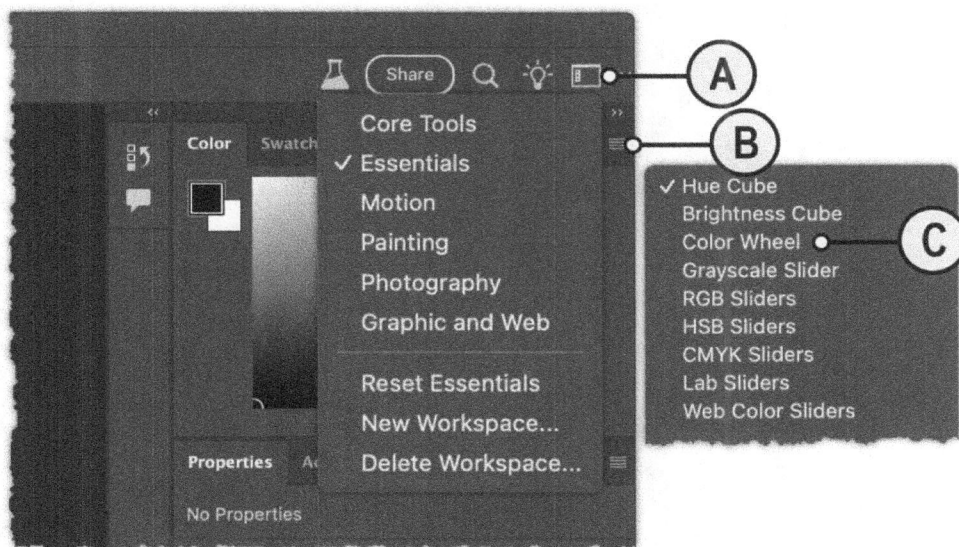

Figure 2.1: The Workspace Switcher menu

2. Click on the **Color** panel tab to make it active, then click on its panel fly-out menu in the top-right corner (**B**). From the list of options, choose **Color Wheel** (**C**). This can make visualizing new colors easier. If you need to create a specific color value, you can simply click on the foreground icon located at the top of the **Color** panel.

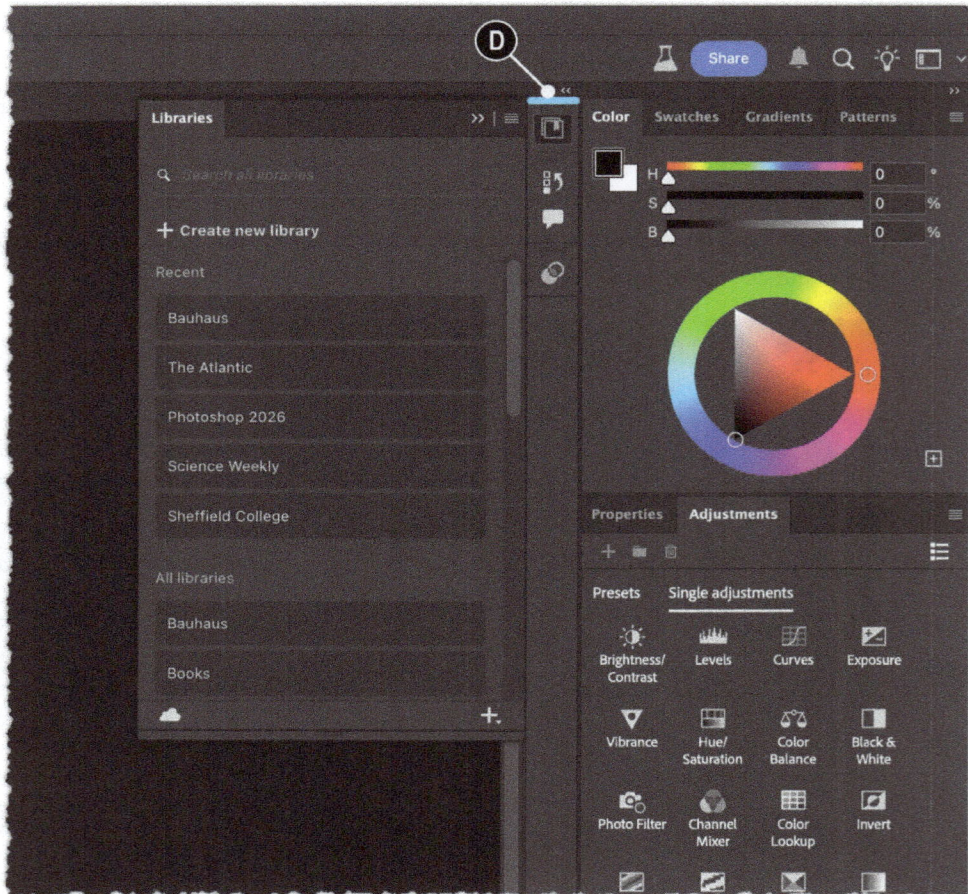

Figure 2.2: Repositioning the Libraries panel above the History panel

3. Next, hover your cursor over the **Libraries** panel tab and drag it over to the image window to undock it. This panel often requires lots of height to browse through assets, and the best place I've found for it is in the left-hand column, collapsed into icons with the **History** and **Comments** panels. To add the **Libraries** panel to this column, drag the **Libraries** panel tab above the icon for the **History** panel, at which point you will see a pale blue line appear. Release the mouse to dock it at the top of the column (**D** in *Figure 2.2*).

4. The **Libraries** panel now appears in icon mode; click on it to expand it. Hover your cursor over its bottom edge to reveal the scaling symbol, a double-headed arrow, and drag the panel edge downward to extend its height so that more content will be visible when needed. Then, click on the **Libraries** panel icon to minimize. Use the same technique to expand the height of the other panels in the column to reduce the amount of scrolling that is required with small panels:

5. I added the **Brushes** panel within the collapsed column, which also appears with the **Brush Settings** panel (**Window → Brushes**). Both are handy. Using the same technique, you can add any other infrequently used panels to the collapsed column. In the example shown, and my personal preference, I also dragged the **Patterns** and **Gradient** panels, originally adjacent to the **Color** panel, into the collapsed column, along with the **Shapes** panel and **Styles** panel, found under the **Window** menu:

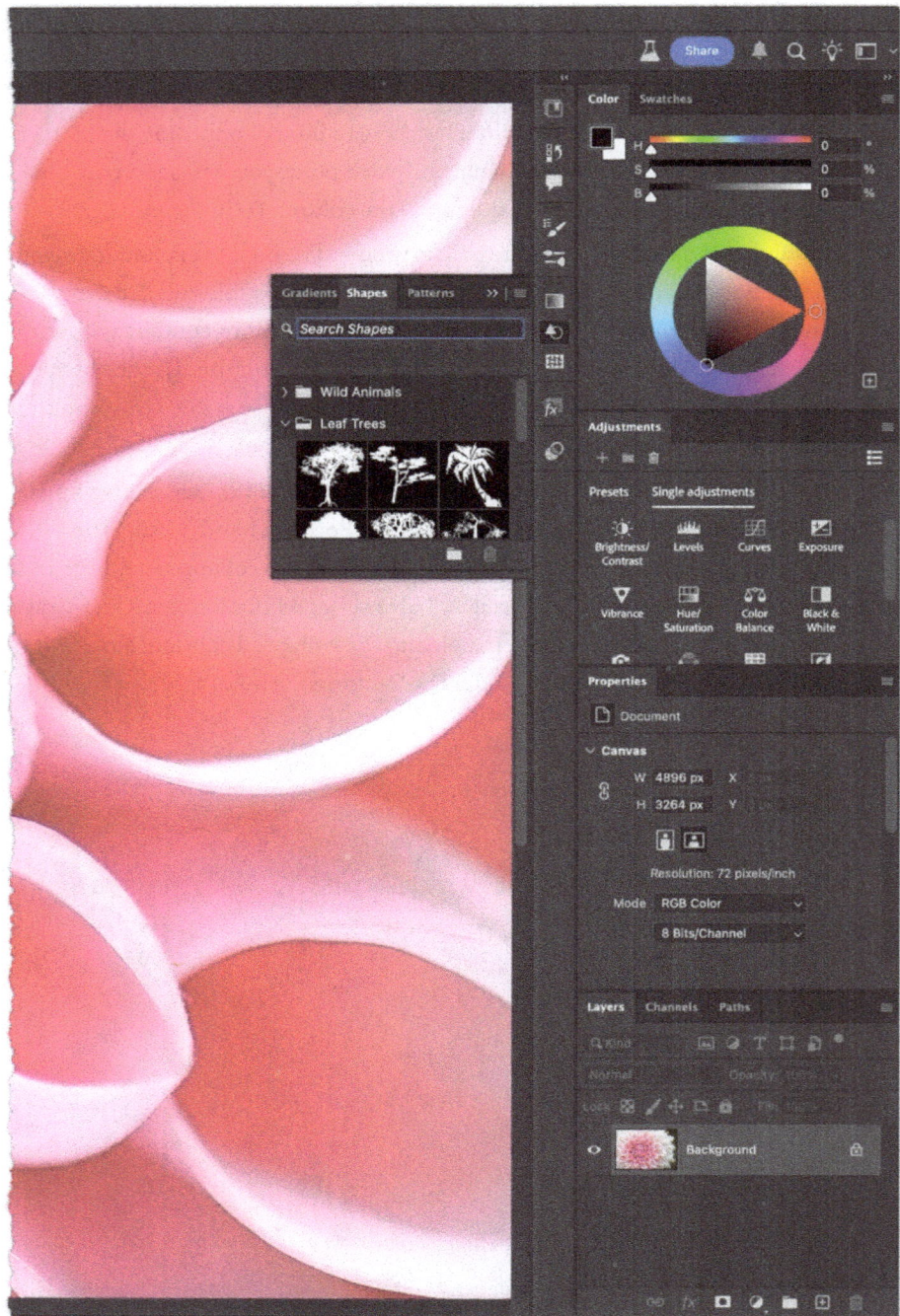

Figure 2.3: The workspace after reconfiguration

Customizing the Tools panel

The Photoshop **Tools** panel contains more than 70 tools; only 21 are visible at any one time, and the majority are hidden. This is another of those scenarios where Adobe can make a best guess as to the tools appropriate to your workflow, but never exactly. This leaves room for improvement and a little simplification. You can start by modifying the default set of tools, or you can create a fresh **Tools** panel with just a handful of specialist tools; the choice is yours. We'll start with the former:

1. Click and hold down on the **Edit Toolbar** button in the lower section of the **Tools** panel (**A**, in *Figure 2.4*). From the pop-out menu that appears, click on the only option, also called **Edit Toolbar**.

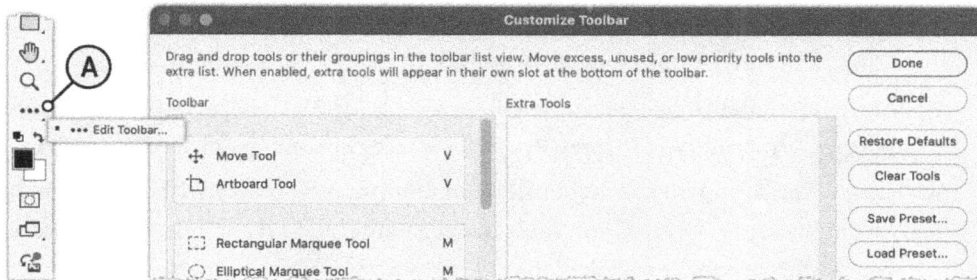

Figure 2.4: The Customize Toolbar dialog

2. This opens the **Customize Toolbar** dialog, where you'll be presented with two columns. The left-hand column, named **Tools** panel, lists tools included in the **Tools** panel, and there is an **Extra Tools** column on the right-hand side for tools you wish to hide. It's likely there will be no tools listed on the right at this point.

3. The list of tools on the left is grouped; each group represents a "slot" on the **Tools** panel. Take the second group down in the list, starting with the **Rectangular Marquee Tool**, currently visible in the **Tools** panel in the second slot down, under the first slot of tools that include the **Move Tool**. The remaining three selection tools in the group, **Elliptical Marquee**, **Single Row**, and **Single Column**, are hidden under it.

4. Start by dragging the **Single Row** and **Single Column** selection tools to the right-hand column. I can honestly say I've used them twice in the last 20 years. Repeat the same step for the **Slice** tool and the **Slice Selection** tool.

5. As the **Frame** tool behaves like a clipping mask within which you can place images, it can be associated with the crop tools. Drag the icon for the **Frame** tool under the **Perspective Crop** tool to add it to the same group of tools.

6. Focusing on the next group down, drag the **3D Material Eyedropper, Ruler, Notes**, and **Count** tools to the right-hand column.

7. Hover your cursor over the edge of the tool group containing the eraser tools. This will allow you to drag the entire group across to the right-hand column.

8. Drag the **Red Eye Tool, Color Replacement Tool, 3D Material Drop Tool, Vertical Type Mask**, and **Horizontal Type Mask** tools to the right-hand column.

9. Although not entirely necessary, you can combine all the brush tools by dragging the **History Brush** and **Art History Brush** tools into the same group as the **Brush** tool.

10. Having removed what I would call redundant tools, you may wish to click on the **Save Preset** button, give your new **Tools** panel a name, and save it in the folder presented to you by Photoshop. Then, click **Done**.

Naturally, this is how I alter the **Tools** panel, but you may need to adjust this layout to better suit your own needs by using the same techniques covered in the exercise:

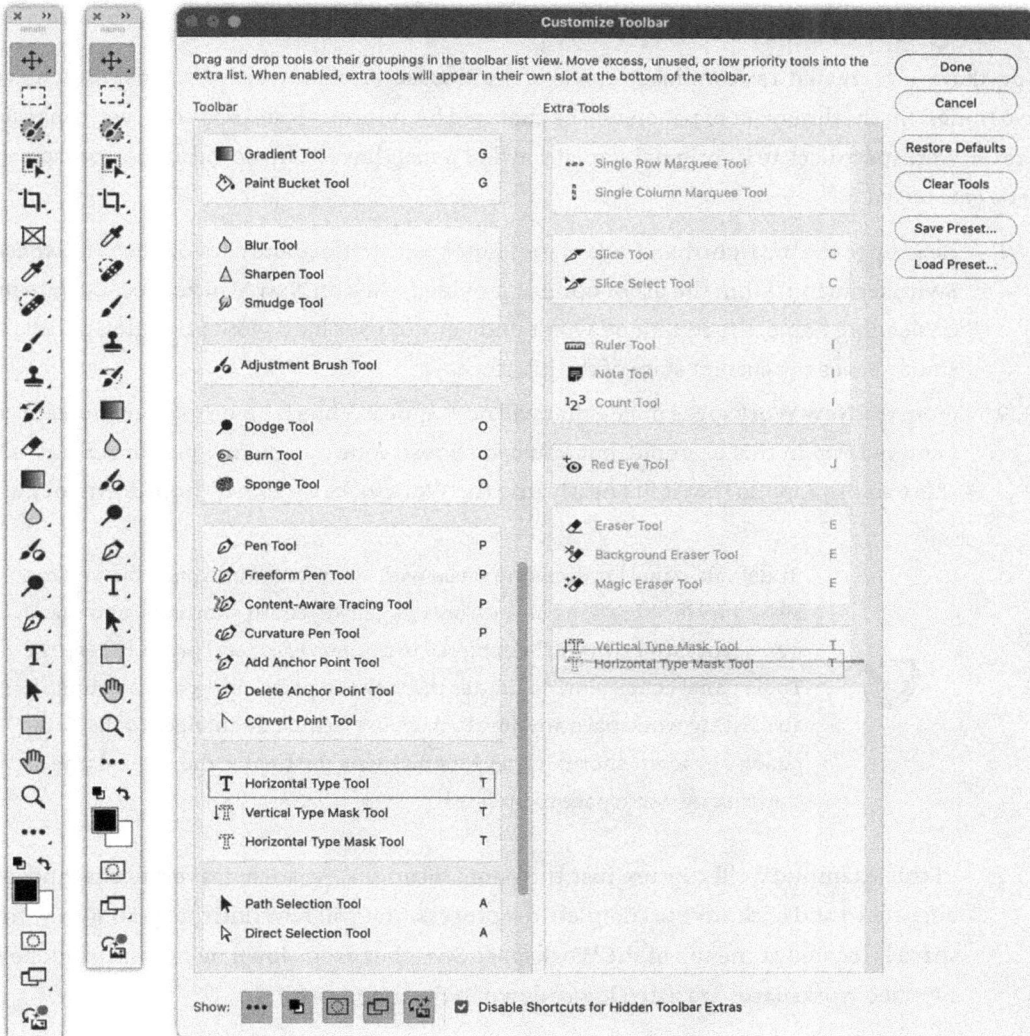

Figure 2.5: The Customize Toolbar dialog alongside the edited Tools panel

Saving a custom workspace

Now that we've created a streamlined version of the interface, it's time to save it. This will achieve two things: firstly, the layout of panels will be captured for future use, and secondly, you can reset a saved workspace back to its original state if you find panels have been moved around on-screen. Let's get started:

1. Head up to the top right-hand side of the Photoshop interface and click on the **Workspace Switcher** menu. From the list of options provided, click on **New Workspace**. Despite its misleading name, the command won't undo any of your hard work arranging panels; it simply saves the current state of the interface.

2. From the **New Workspace** dialog that will now appear, enter a name for your workspace. I entered Pro in this example, but you can choose your own name. Just make sure it's short and snappy so that it fits neatly into the **Workspace Switcher** drop-down menu.

    > By default, panel locations are saved with every new workspace, but you can also capture alterations to the **Tools** panel, keyboard shortcuts, and menu items. The latter two will be explored in the next exercise. I prefer to keep the **Tools** panel consistent, no matter the task I'm performing. You can update an existing workspace anytime and choose to include changes to the **Tools** panel, keyboard shortcuts, and menu items. Just enter the same name as the existing workspace to update it.

3. In this example, we'll capture just the panel locations. As such, leave the checkboxes unchecked and click **Save** to complete the process. You will now find that your new workspace is located at the top of the **Workspace Switcher** drop-down menu, while Adobe's supplied workspaces are listed lower down in the dropdown:

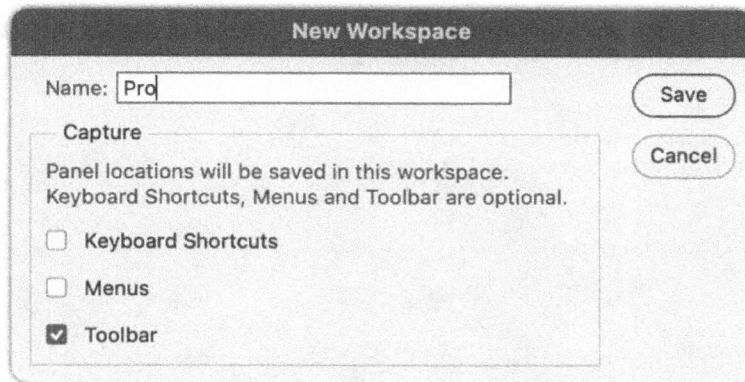

Figure 2.6: The New Workspace dialog captures panel locations, shortcuts, and menus

Modifying keyboard shortcuts and menus

Keyboard shortcuts can save you invaluable time and help avoid navigating through convoluted sub-menus, from more rudimentary tasks such as copying to applying warps. You can also hide redundant menu commands, found in the application dropdowns at the top of the screen. In this exercise, you will explore techniques for assigning a custom shortcut and hiding a menu option:

1. Go to **Edit** → **Keyboard Shortcuts and Menus**. Ensure the **Shortcuts For** drop-down menu is set to **Application Menus** (**A** in *Figure 2.7*). Scroll down the list to **Window** and expand the toggle to reveal the sub-categories.

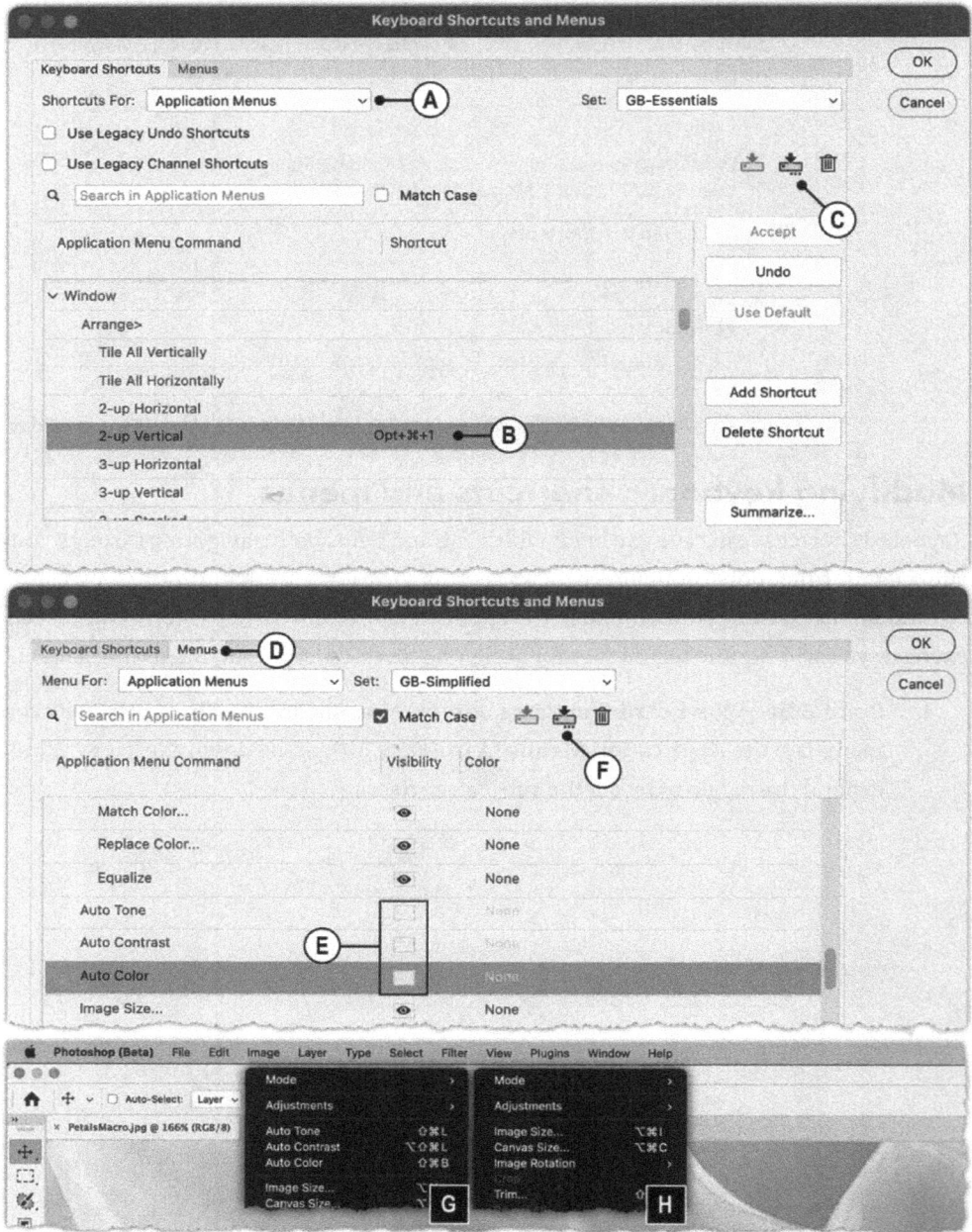

Figure 2.7: The Keyboard Shortcuts and Menus dialog

2. Under the right-hand column, labeled **Shortcut**, click in the empty space adjacent to **2-up Vertical** (**B** in *Figure 2.7*) to open the type entry field. Type into the field Ctrl+Alt+1 (Windows) or Cmd+Option+1 (macOS). If the shortcut is already assigned elsewhere, click on the **Accept** button in the upper right-hand side of the dialog.

3. Once you have all other remaining shortcuts, click on the **Create New Set** button (**C** in *Figure 2.7*). Enter a name for the set of shortcuts and click **Save** when done.

4. Then, click on the **Menus** tab (**D** in *Figure 2.7*), scroll down the list until you reach **Image**, and click on the toggle to expand and open a list of sub-categories. Turn off the visibility icons for **Auto Tone, Auto Contrast**, and **Auto Color** (**E** in *Figure 2.7*). This will hide those destructive editing options in the **Image** menu.

5. Once you have altered the visibility settings of all other menus of your choosing, click on the **Create New Set** button (**F** in *Figure 2.7*). Enter a name for the set of menus and click **Save**. Then, click on **OK** to close the **Keyboard Shortcut and Menus** dialog. Click on the **Image** menu, and you'll notice the items have been hidden (**H**). To temporarily reveal them (**G**), you can click on the **Show Menu Items** at the bottom of the list.

As we've discussed, Adobe can only make educated guesses regarding which tools and features are suitable for our needs. Therefore, refining the interface is a crucial first step to speeding up day-to-day editing by ensuring the tools we require are easy to find. In the next section, we'll adjust preference settings.

Modifying preferences

It is possible to modify the behavior and appearance of some Photoshop features and tools through the **Preferences** settings, from the brightness of the **user interface** (**UI**) to painting cursors and auto-save. In the following steps, I'll highlight settings that could offer high value to your editing workflow:

1. **Preferences** can be found on macOS via **Photoshop → Settings → General**, or on Windows via **Edit → Preferences → General**. Alternatively, you can press *Ctrl + K* (Windows) or *Cmd + K* (macOS) to launch the **Preferences** settings and reveal **General** settings.

2. Turn on the checkbox for **Auto-Update Open File-based Documents**. Contrary to the option's name, **Auto-Update** won't automatically update your active document, but it will inform you that someone else has edited and saved changes to the file you are working on. Photoshop will then give you the option to keep editing your active version or dispense with your edits and update to reflect the other user's latest saved changes. This is handy when editing project files that are accessible to several users simultaneously on a server:

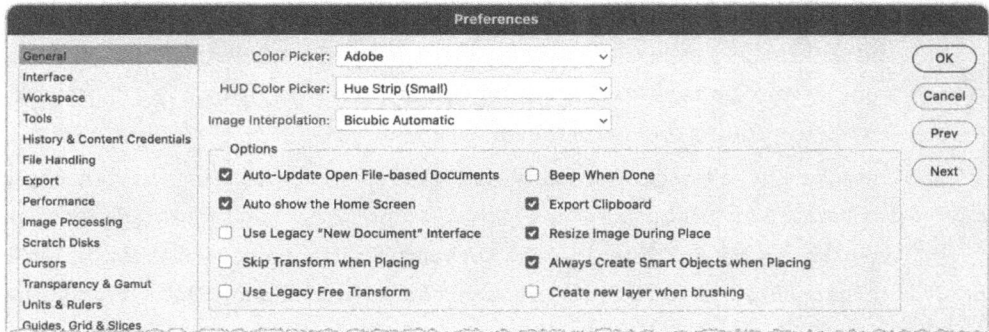

Figure 2.8: General preferences

3. Next, click on **Interface** from the list on the left-hand side. You can change the **UI Color Theme** option from the default of **Medium Dark** to three other variations. You can also alter the style of the image border shown in the image window, as well as the background color that surrounds your images.

I find that if the UI brightness is high, this often contributes to eye strain. As such, I tend to set the UI theme to **Dark** or leave it set to **Medium Dark** to compensate. Turning on the **Neutral Color Mode** checkbox removes distracting color from interface buttons and icons. I don't find lines or shadows around images' edges helpful; I set it to **None**. You may wish to alter the brightness of the image window background to **Black**, **Dark**, **Medium**, **Light Gray**, or a **Custom** color of your choice. I prefer the less distracting **Default** option of mid-tone gray:

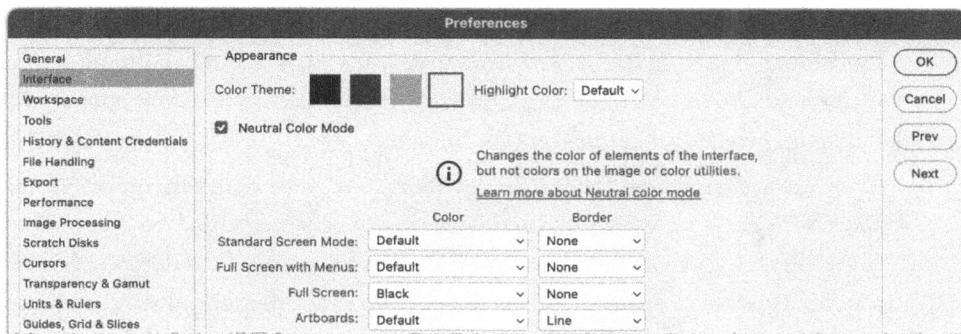

Figure 2.9: Interface preferences

4. Click on **Tools** from the list on the left-hand side. With the exception of **Show Rich Tooltips**, you can turn on all checkboxes in this section:

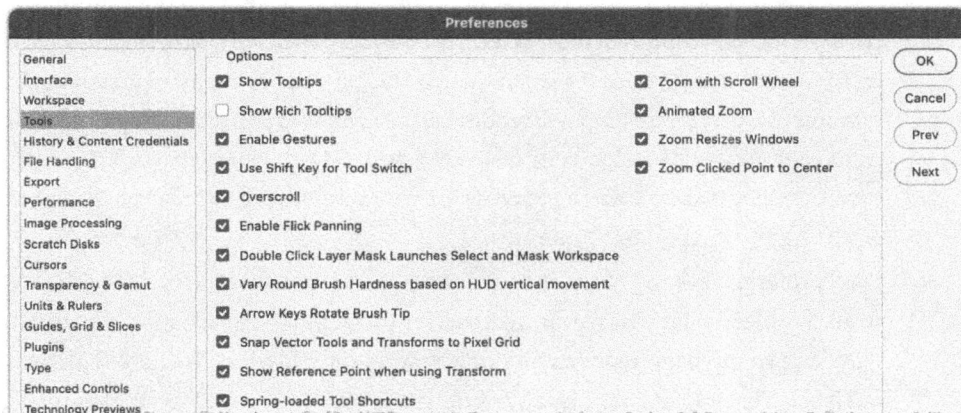

Figure 2.10: Tools preferences

Tool preferences

Rich Tooltips is the animated video explainer that appears every time you hover your cursor over a tool in the **Tools** panel, which can become tedious very quickly. Other features in this section generally enhance the usability of a tool or the ease with which you accomplish tasks. **Zoom with Scroll Wheel** allows you to avoid activating the **Zoom** tool altogether, while **Animated Zoom** and **Flick Panning** make the motion of panning and zooming less jarring on the eye. **Overscroll** allows you to position the edges of an image anywhere in the image window, making edge editing easier to accomplish.

5. Click on **File Handling** from the list on the left-hand side. Under **File Saving Options**, I recommend setting **Image Previews** to **Always Save**. Saving an image preview and a thumbnail allows you to quickly check an image's contents before opening it through Finder on macOS or Explorer on Windows.

6. If you are accustomed to saving files in Photoshop, you could turn on the **Enable legacy "Save As"** checkbox, which also activates **Do not append "copy" to filename when saving a copy**. This will allow you to save your active document in a different format slightly quicker. However, you will need to take care not to accidentally overwrite an existing file with the same name in the same folder due to the **Do not append "copy" to filename when saving a copy** option being deactivated.

7. Turn on the **Save in Background** checkbox. This will allow you to edit a different Photoshop document while another is saving.

8. Next, decide how much work you want to risk losing by defining the **Automatic Save Recovery** interval dropdown to **5**, **10**, **15**, **30**, or **60** minutes. I prefer to set the **Save Recovery** increment to every **5** minutes so that when I do experience a crash, I lose a maximum of 5 minutes of work. Photoshop will reboot and ask whether you want to open each document from your previous session at its last saved point. If you experience a lag in performance each time Photoshop saves a recovery file, you might have to balance the pros and cons of setting the interval to **10** minutes.

9. I still prefer to save my Photoshop documents in a dedicated network folder along with related project assets. However, you can set the default save location to **Creative Cloud**. There are many benefits to saving on Creative Cloud, which include a file history and, not least, a backup of your file. The option to save to Creative Cloud is also available each time you save a document.

10. Turn on the **Prefer Adobe Camera Raw for Supported Raw Files** and **Use Adobe Camera Raw to Convert Documents from 32 bit to 16/8 bit checkboxes**. Turn on the **Ask Before Saving Layered TIFF Files** checkbox and set **Maximize PSD and PSB File Compatibility** to **Always** (*Figure 2.11*):

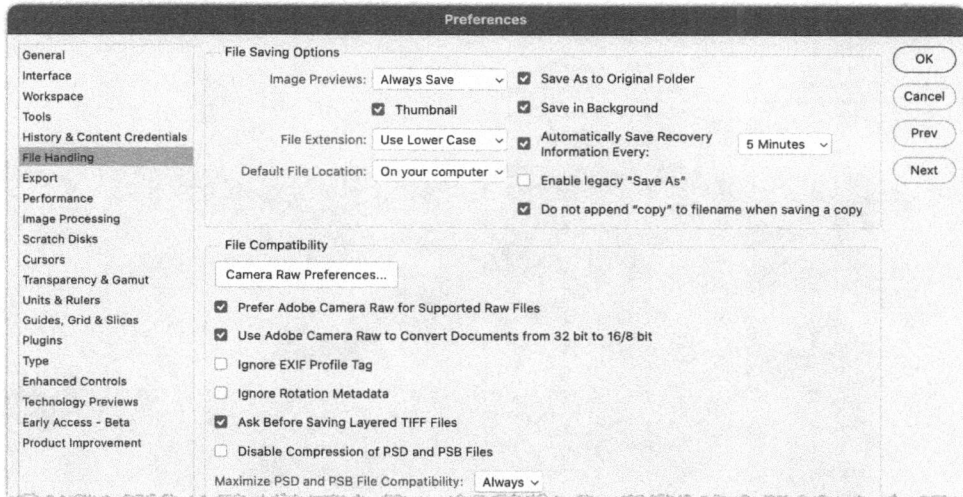

Figure 2.11: File Handling preferences

Camera Raw

Adobe Camera Raw offers fantastic tools and features for editing digital negatives; as such, I recommend utilizing it rather than Photoshop for such tasks. Maximizing the compatibility of your **Photoshop Document (PSD)** files means that when you share files with colleagues who have older versions of Photoshop, they will be able to open and edit them.

11. Click on **Cursors** from the list on the left-hand side. Set **Painting Cursors** to **Normal Brush Tip** and turn on the **Show Crosshair in Brush Tip** checkbox. Set the **Other Cursors** option to **Precise**. Preview images in the dialog update accordingly to visualize changes to brush tips and icons (*Figure 2.12*):

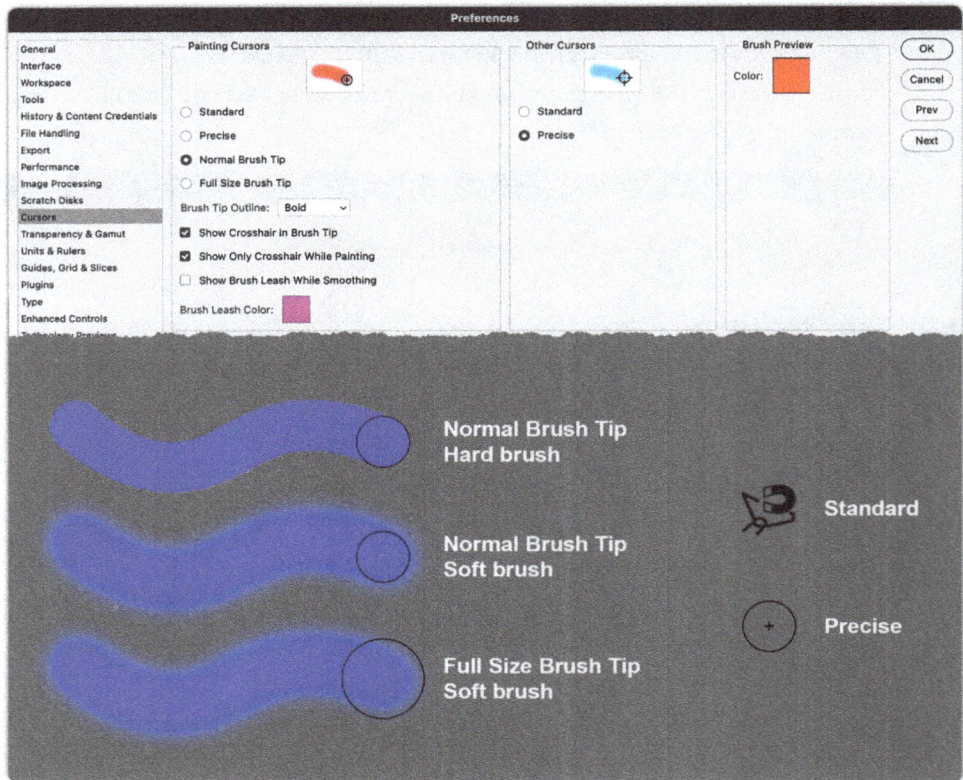

Figure 2.12: Cursors preferences

Painting tools

Painting cursors are integral to editing in Photoshop, so it's important to understand how each of the cursor appearances might affect the way you use them. The size of a brush tip is indicated by an outline, shown in the preferences as a circle for simplicity, with a red paint stroke. A normal brush tip indicates only the area that receives a full coverage of red, while a full-size brush tip indicates full coverage of red and soft brush marks. I find the normal brush tip size more intuitive to work with. The crosshair inside a brush tip is mainly used for alignment. The section labeled **Other Cursors** includes selection tools. **Standard** will make the cursor appear as the icon of the tool itself, while the far more intuitive, precise version includes features that make the **Magic Wand** selection tool far easier to use.

12. Click on **Type** from the list on the left-hand side (*Figure 2.13*).

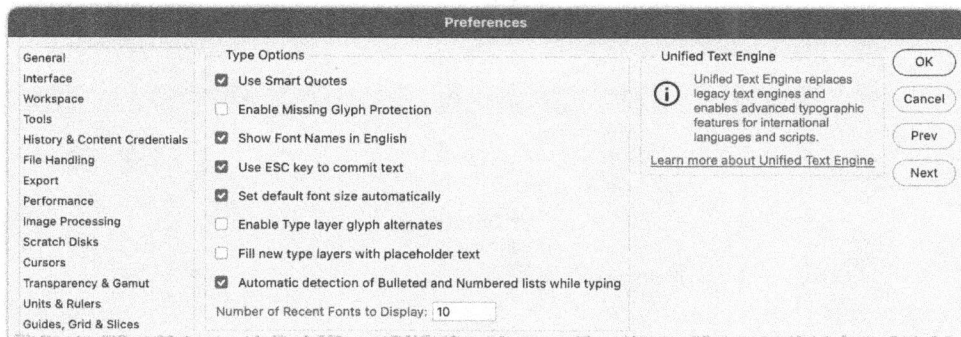

Figure 2.13: Type preferences.

13. Photoshop's **Smart Quotes** feature automatically replaces unappealing straight quotes, similar to inch marks. I strongly suggest you keep **Smart Quotes** active. However, it is worth noting that Photoshop sometimes ignores existing smart quotes, so it's essential to check your copy carefully and manually replace any straight quotes wherever necessary.

14. Photoshop now automatically replaces missing fonts or glyph characters with the most suitable match available on your computer. The trouble is that you might not notice this. By turning off **Glyph Protection** (*Figure 2.13*), this issue should highlight missing characters, allowing you to manually correct the issue with a font of your choice:

15. You can now exit **Type** editing mode in Photoshop by pressing the *Esc* key, matching the behavior of Illustrator and InDesign. For this reason, I activate the **Use ESC key to commit text** checkbox.

16. Photoshop will now highlight alternative characters when editing text; however, the pop-up tooltip related to this feature can make editing smaller text frames frustrating. For this reason, I deactivate it and go to the **Glyphs** panel instead (**Window → Glyphs**).

> Photoshop's **Glyphs** panel allows you to insert special type characters, such as symbols, superscript, and currencies, that would otherwise be challenging to add using just a keyboard.

17. When you create new text frames, Photoshop fills them with copy using the last known type settings. I find this to be a hindrance and suggest deactivating **Fill new type layers with placeholder text**.

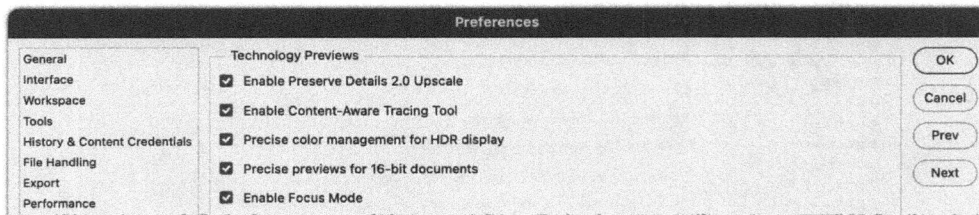

Figure 2.14: Technology preferences

18. Finally, click on **Technology Previews** from the list on the left-hand side. I suggest that you turn on all checkboxes (as shown in *Figure 2.14*). All the features in this section enhance my experience with Photoshop. **Preserve Details 2.0 Upscale** allows for better-quality image enlargements. The **Content-Aware Tracing** tool detects edges when creating a path, which can save valuable time compared to manually creating a vector path with the **Pen** tool. By enabling **Focus Mode**, you can minimize the number of non-essential pop-ups that appear in the interface, minimizing distractions.

19. Finally, click **OK** to accept all changes in the dialog. Preference settings are only saved when you close Photoshop, so as soon as you complete your preference changes, close Photoshop and launch it once more.

If you experience persistent Photoshop crashes, it could be related to a corrupt preference file. To resolve this, delete preferences and redo them by going to **General** from the list on the left-hand side of the **Preferences** dialog and choosing **Reset Preferences on Quit**.

Now that we have modified Photoshop preferences, I recommend evaluating them for a week or two. Over time, you will no doubt modify them further to better suit your needs. Next, we need to define **Color Settings** to ensure that Photoshop displays color consistently across all images and projects.

Defining color settings

For us humans, color is processed by the wonders of biology as we observe the world around us, almost without being conscious of it. Sadly, the same cannot be said for digital technology, where data is captured on **digital single-lens reflex cameras** (**DSLRs**) and smartphones and then passed from one application to another before ultimately being viewed in print and on screen.

To ensure that each device and application recreates color consistently, we need a method by which our technology speaks the same language of color. It's like traveling to a country where the language differs; we learn to communicate in the same tongue to understand one another. And so, we use color management to achieve this. It's relatively simple to set up, can be synchronized across all Adobe Creative Cloud desktops, and only takes a few moments – a small price to pay for relatively consistent color across our projects. Here's how to do it:

1. You define a color management policy for your artwork by going to **Edit → Color Settings.** Click on the **Settings** drop-down menu in the upper left-hand corner of the dialog. Depending on which region of the world you're based in, the default setting displayed will differ.

2. If you are based in the US, choose **North American Prepress 2**, which is often recommended for creating artwork intended for onscreen, web, and consumer-level printing (for example, a USB-connected printer) and professional printing at a third-party provider. In Europe, the equivalent is **European Prepress 3**.

3. If you want to avoid warning messages popping up on a regular basis, turn off the three checkboxes under **Color Management Policies.** Photoshop will still do all of the color synchronizing required; it just won't tell you about it every time it does!

4. Once you have defined the appropriate settings, click on the **Save** button located at the top right of the dialog. You should be prompted to save the file in the Settings folder presented to you. This is where Adobe looks for the settings file (CSF). Enter a filename of MyColor and click on the **Save** button.

5. A message in the middle of the **Color Settings** dialog reads **Not Synchronized**. This indicates that your other Adobe applications are not using the same settings. We will resolve this in the next step. Click **OK** to exit. To complete the final stage, you will need to install **Adobe Bridge** from the **Creative Cloud** desktop application.

6. To sync the color settings across Creative Cloud desktop apps, we need to open Adobe Bridge. In Photoshop, go to **File → Browse in Bridge**. Once Bridge opens, go to **Edit → Color Settings**. Select **MyColor** from the list of available color settings and click on **Apply**. Bridge will apply the same settings across any desktop applications you have already installed:

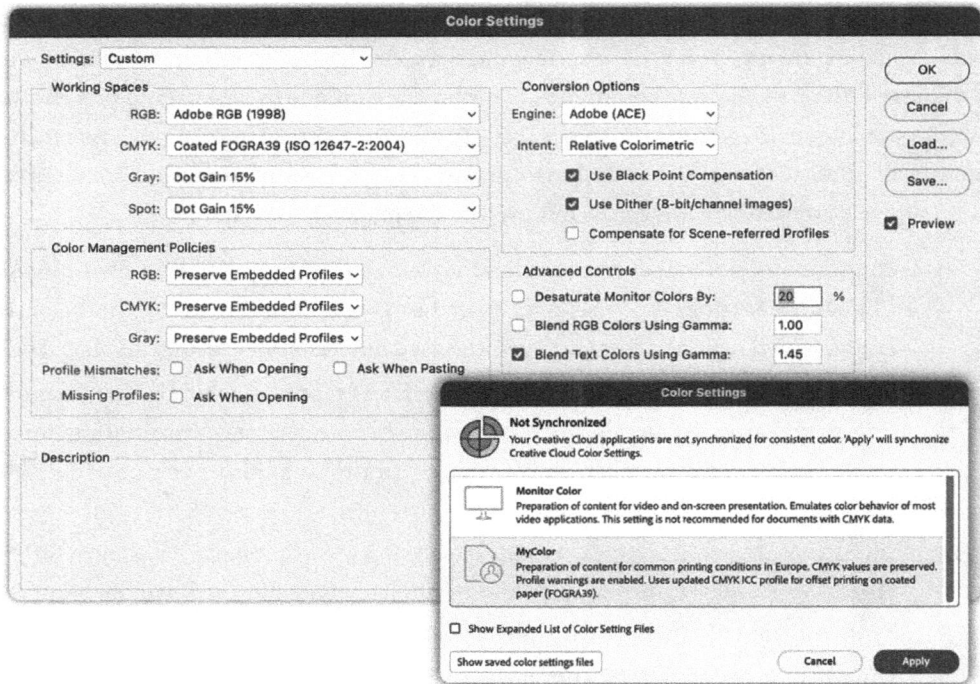

Figure 2.15: Color settings, defined in Photoshop and synchronized in Adobe Bridge

In this section, we've modified preference settings and color management. As the feature suggests, some settings are simply down to your personal preference, such as the brightness of the interface, while others, such as changing the appearance of cursors, should now make editing with tools such as brushes simpler and feel more precise. Color management helps ensure color consistency across Creative Cloud applications. The final part of the chapter explores the building blocks of digital images. The better we understand how images are composed, the easier it will be to deconstruct them and attain the best possible quality.

Quality-first approach

You've probably heard the saying, *garbage in, garbage out*. Well, this holds true in Photoshop as well. Just because an image looks fantastic on screen, it doesn't guarantee it will when printed. Trust me – the last thing you want to experience is the horror of unboxing thousands of prints containing pixelated or blurred images.

PSD is by far the most powerful image format, offering tremendous flexibility within the application. The PSD format supports up to 250,000 layers in a single document, allowing you to scale, rotate, or reposition each component of your design with ease. Or, if you prefer, you can hide or even delete a layer without it affecting the rest of the composition.

Layers are a common facet of nearly all Adobe desktop applications and are especially critical to saving time. Because of the tight integration between other Adobe products, such as Illustrator, InDesign, Premiere, and After Effects, you can directly import layered PSD files and preserve many of the Photoshop features. So, before you save your project artwork in a flattened JPEG format, which can only store a single background layer and no transparency, consider using PSD instead.

This is a critical step to saving production time, as you can edit and reuse the same document, rather than resaving an updated version in a different format each time you edit your artwork. Most applications will auto-update or prompt you to update your imported PSD rather than insist on importing again.

When saving a PSD and setting it to maximize file compatibility, it will include a composite version of a layered image so that other applications, including previous versions of Photoshop, can read it.

Layered image files mean your text layers stay editable, and if you export from Illustrator, you can choose to create a layered PSD and keep text frames made in Illustrator editable in Photoshop, too.

Common edits that you make to the color or brightness of your image, for example, can be stored in adjustment layers. They affect any layer below them in the stack and can be turned off/on and re-edited at any point by double-clicking on the layer's adjustment icon thumbnail in the **Layers** panel.

You can apply layer effects to specific layers to add a drop shadow or glow. Then, re-edit the effect at any time by double-clicking on the effect name. If you wish to move the effect to a different layer, you can simply drag it from the source layer and onto the destination layer. Or, you could even create a duplicate by holding down the *Alt/Option* key as you drag and drop a layer effect.

Image quality

All digital photos are mosaics composed of tiles called **pixels**, an amalgamation of two words: *picture* and *element*. These tiny squares each contain just a single color. If you magnify an image in Photoshop beyond a zoom factor of 500%, those pixels become more apparent. But at first glance, at 100% magnification, they are indistinguishable, and our brains resolve those tiny patterns of color into a seamless representation of what the camera captured.

Resolution

Resolution has long been established and leveraged by artists over the centuries. Monet painted with short brush strokes known as **daubs** to create small clusters of colors. Standing close to the canvas, they have no apparent structure, but walk further back, and our eyes resolve these paint marks to create an image. Therefore, the distance and the size of the color marks are significant. This is as true for pixels as it is for paint.

Pixels per inch

In the industry, we refer to our formula as **pixels per inch** (PPI), a method for calculating image size in relation to the number of pixels in a given region, such as an inch. Magazines, read at a distance of 18 inches, require images with 300 pixels vertically and horizontally within every inch, which are then converted into **dots per inch** (DPI) when printed. A billboard ad viewed from several meters away requires only 30 PPI, while web graphics require 72 to 144 PPI to attain the appropriate quality.

Vector graphics

As with photographs, **vector graphics** are used in abundance in print, online, and on screen. When you see a logo, a road sign, or wayfinding graphics in a supermarket, those are almost certainly made from vector graphics. Unlike digital photographs, vectors typically contain a dozen or so colors and are composed of anchor points and segments that form shapes, not pixels. This means vector graphics are resolution-independent and capable of being used at any size, and capable of being printed and manufactured without losing quality.

Digital text is a form of vector art, but it could be simple shapes such as circles, rectangles, and lines. Photoshop provides a set of vector-editing tools and several shape libraries that can retain their vector quality. By storing vector art in its own shape layer, Photoshop can preserve the quality of the graphics, allowing them to be modified without losing quality.

In the following example, the photo of the pumpkin (**A** in *Figure 2.16*), opened in Adobe Photoshop at a magnification of 12,800%, reveals the underlying structure of the image as a series of colored pixels. In contrast, the vector logo (**B**) displayed at 64,000% in Adobe Illustrator, the application in which it was created, remains smooth at this high level of scrutiny.

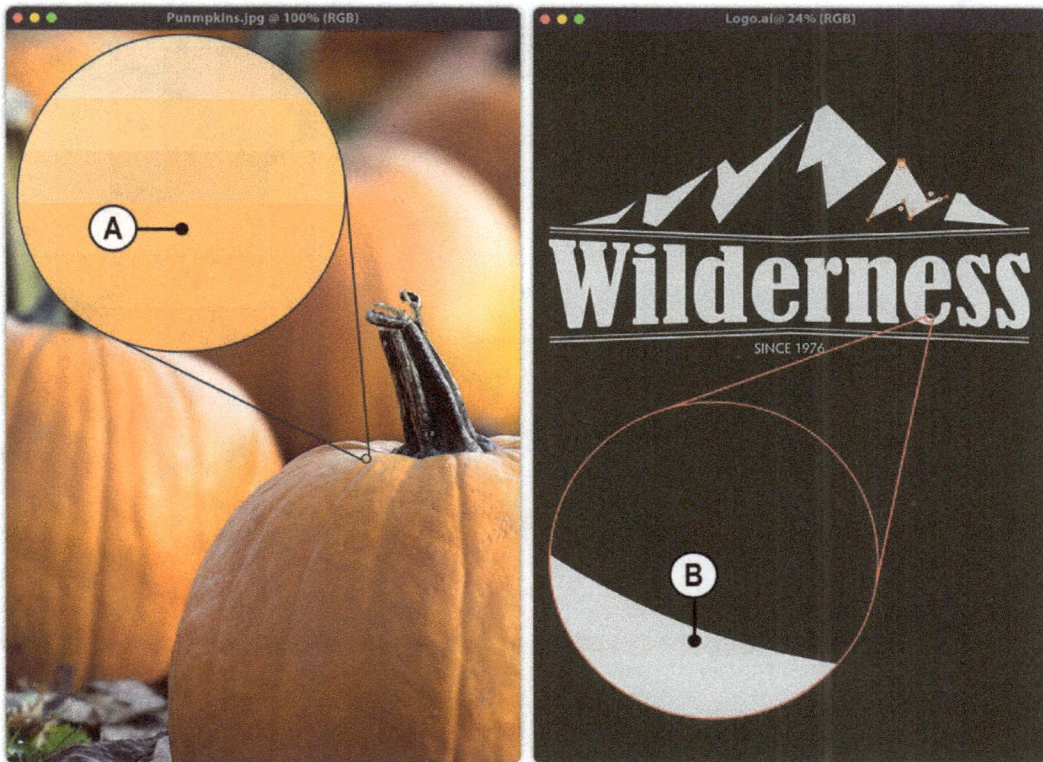

Figure 2.16: A comparison between pixel-based images (A) and vector graphics (B)

Calculating PPI in Photoshop

Image Size isn't the most exciting Photoshop feature, but it is essential to determine the maximum size an image can be in print and on screen. Here's how to use it:

1. Go to **Image → Image Size**. When the dialog appears, set the **Width** and **Height** units to **Millimeters** (or whichever unit of measurement you are accustomed to) by clicking on the drop-down menu.

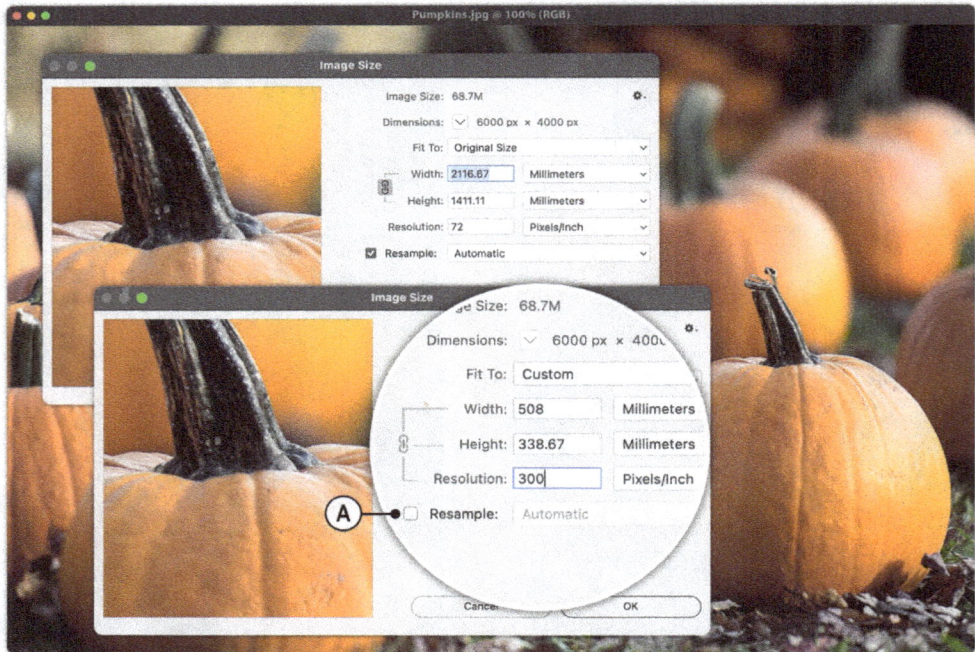

Figure 2.17: The Image Size dialog

2. Turn off the **Resample** checkbox (**A** in *Figure 2.17*) to create a link between the image's width and height and the resolution.

3. It is normal that when you download an image from a stock site or your digital camera, it will possess a large width and height (for example, 2,116 mm x 1,411 mm) but a very low resolution of 72 PPI. With the image size and the resolution now linked, enter the desired PPI into the **Resolution** field. For professional print, this is 300 PPI. Click **OK** when done.

In this section, we have learned the importance of defining quality from the outset by measuring the resolution of pixel-based images. In the final section, I'll share with you some of the free online resources I've used over the years to support my project work.

Online resources

One of the toughest challenges in creating great-looking projects is capturing and acquiring high-quality assets. If, unlike me, you are a fantastic photographer and possess the necessary equipment to take your own photographs, some images remain out of reach due to their geographical location, making it too costly to shoot in person. Online resources and stock images can bridge that gap.

In this section, I want to share some resources I regularly use for my projects, which save valuable time and money. I've focused primarily on free content, but I also included a handful of sites that offer incredible high-end paid stock content.

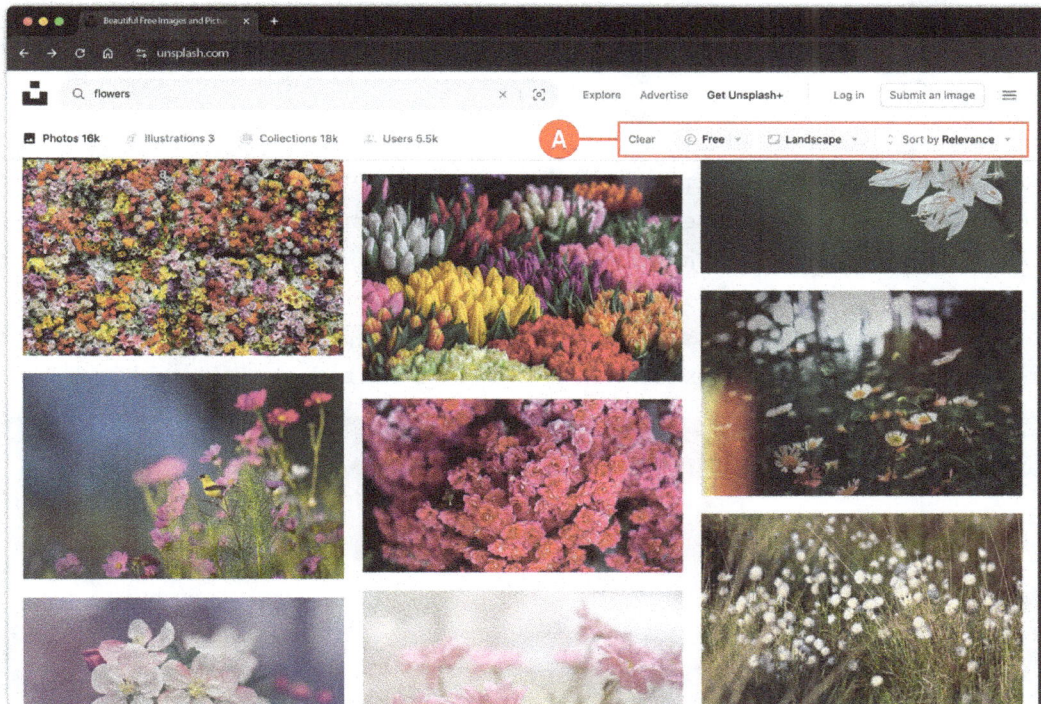

Figure 2.18: Unsplash offers over 6 million free images

Unsplash

Back in 2013, Unsplash was a humble Tumblr blog offering just 10 images, but it has grown to over 6 million images thanks to a global community of creators who contribute their work, from freelance photographers to NASA. What makes the images on Unsplash useful is their straightforward copyright policy. You can download and use any free image for both personal and commercial use without attribution if you choose. The site also offers a paid subscription called Unsplash+, and images under the paid plan are clearly labeled in the search results. You might find it helpful to change the filter settings to show only free images, along with your choice of orientation from the navigation bar (**A** in *Figure 2.18*). You can find the site at www.unsplash.com.

Pexels

Pexels offers photographs and videos, all free of charge and without attribution. Video content ranges from standard definition to 4K. Interestingly, Pexels does not permit users to contribute content generated with AI technology. You can find the site at `www.pexels.com`.

Adobe Stock

In May 2013, Adobe launched the Creative Cloud, representing a seismic shift in delivering flagship programs such as Photoshop and transitioning to a cloud-based subscription model. This move aimed to enhance online services, foster greater collaboration among creative teams, and improve desktop integration. Within a year, Adobe acquired Fotolia, the stock image company, for $800 million as the foundation for its reimagined digital stock offering. Adobe Stock now includes over 450 million digital assets, encompassing PSDs, InDesign templates, and After Effects projects. It also features a vast number of free assets in addition to the available paid stock plans.

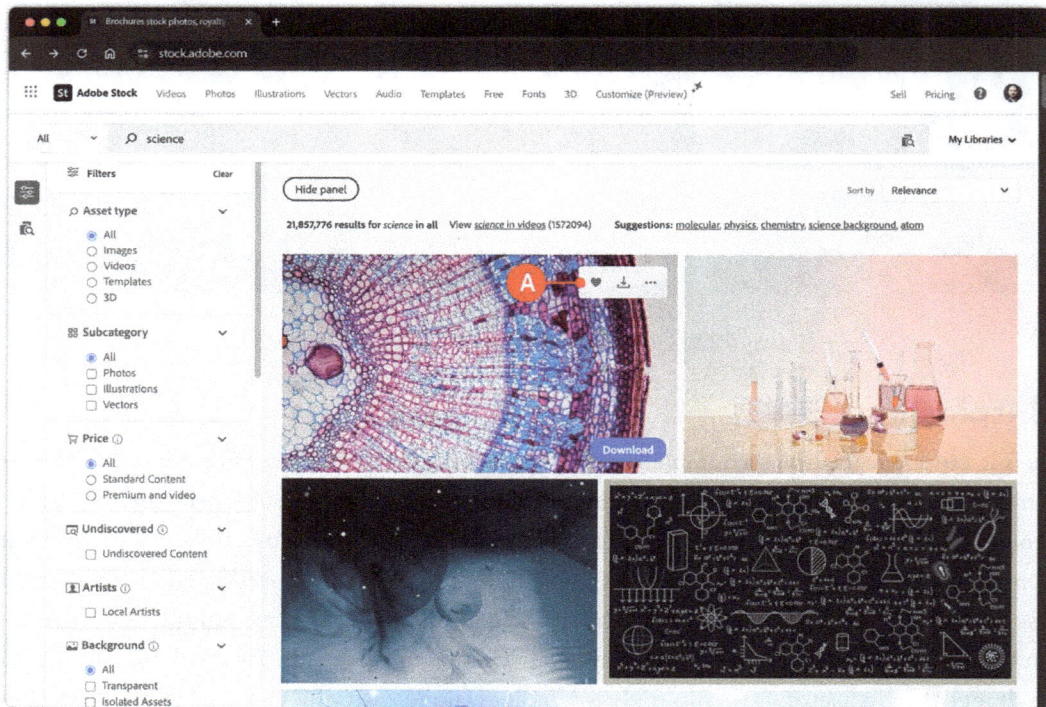

Figure 2.19: Adobe Stock provides unrivaled integration with the Creative Cloud

Visit Adobe's free stock assets at `https://stock.adobe.com/uk/free`, where you can further filter the results by **Asset type** and **Subcategory** and even exclude generative AI content. You can also browse with **Undiscovered Content** active to view assets that have never been downloaded. Click on the **Save to Library** icon (**A** in *Figure 2.19*) to download an unlicensed version to your **Libraries** panel in Photoshop for use in your projects.

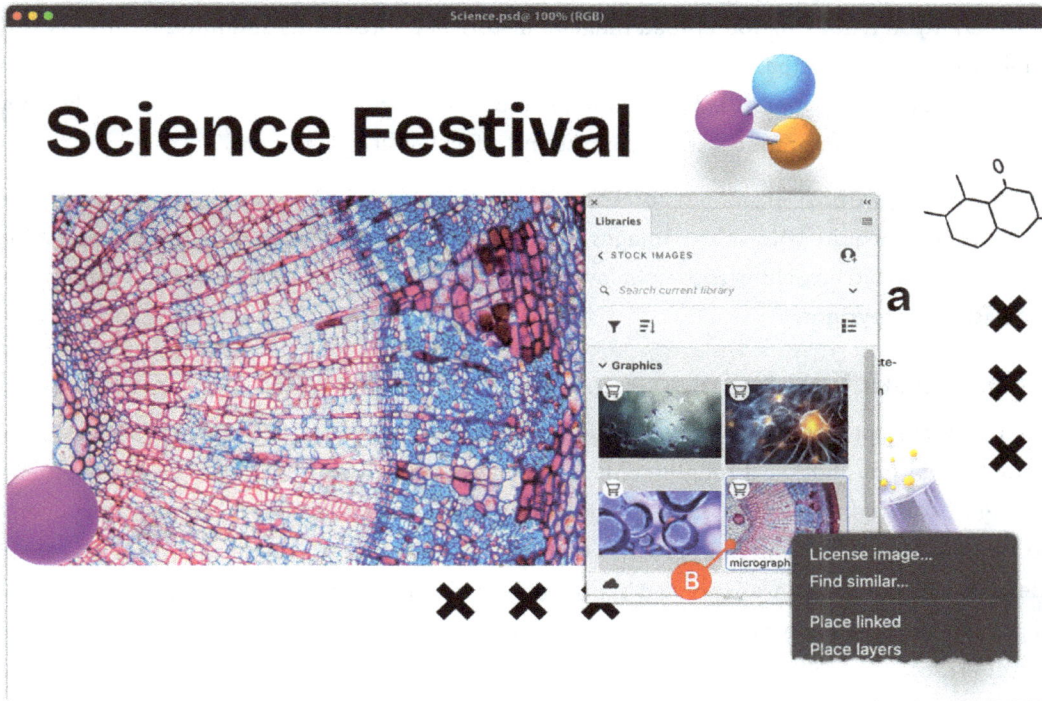

Figure 2.20: Integrate preview versions of assets in Photoshop before licensing

Once added to a library of your choice, you can drag and drop assets into your Photoshop layouts from the **Libraries** panel to assess their suitability, including making basic edits such as adding layer masks. Once you're ready to buy the asset, right-click on it in the **Libraries** panel and choose **License Image** from the list of options (**B** in *Figure 2.20*). You must have an active Adobe Stock account and available credits to license assets. Subscriptions start at around $29.99 per month for 10 standard images or 1 video. Compared to other online stock subscriptions, Adobe Stock is certainly at the higher end. As much as anything, you're paying for convenience and integration.

Other notable stock resources on the web

There are too many online resources and stock sites to mention here, but the following are additional sites that I'm certain you will find incredibly useful. Freepik (`www.freepik.com`) offers a wide range of stock assets, including PSD templates, many of which are free. Alternatively, you can get a paid subscription for around $6.00 per month, which includes up to 84,000 downloads per year. If you're looking for a broad range of historical photographs and illustrations, try the Public Domain Archive (`pdimagearchive.org`) or the British Library at `www.imagesonline.bl.uk`. Wikipedia Commons contains over 117 million images at `commons.wikimedia.org`. Finally, for a mix of images, vector graphics, music, and sound effects, visit `www.pixabay.com`.

In this section, we have examined notable online resources for finding project assets. Wherever you choose to acquire your source images, please ensure you check the licensing agreement for each asset to avoid breaching copyright law. Speaking of which, in the next section, we'll explore the basics of copyright.

An introduction to image usage and copyright

Pablo Picasso once said, "*Good artists copy, great artists steal.*" While artists have undoubtedly been influenced by one another throughout history and even copied as a method of self-development, infringing copyright is a serious matter that can result in an unlimited fine and even imprisonment. So, what is copyright? Copyright protects the rights of an author or creator to control how their ideas are used once they are expressed in a tangible form. In most countries, copyright protection is granted automatically without the need for registration. Copyright covers several forms of tangible artifacts, such as literary works, software, film, music, art, and architecture.

Copyright and the use of images can vary. Therefore, it is essential to check the specific usage rights of each image before considering it for your projects. This often requires contacting the author directly or an agent representing them to discuss, for instance, the context in which the works will be used, the duration, and the number of copies that will be created, as well as national and international restrictions.

Creative Commons licensing

Creative Commons allows authors of original works to be flexible about how their work can be reused. Developed by a nonprofit organization, it provides six straightforward forms of licensing that stipulate attribution, remixing, sharing, and commercial use.

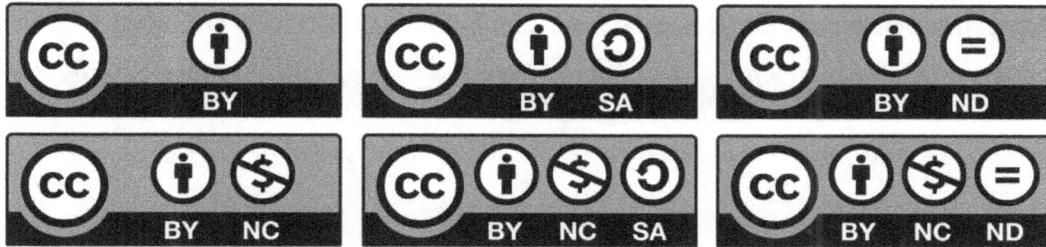

Figure 2.21: Creative Commons license types

CC BY

This license allows people to share, remix, adapt, and use the author's work for both commercial and non-commercial purposes, provided credit is given to the author.

CC BY-SA

This license lets you share, remix, adapt, and build on the original material in any medium or format you deem necessary, provided you credit the creator. You can use it for commercial purposes. If you remix, adapt, or build upon the original work, you must license the new material under the same terms, which means you must credit the original creator.

CC BY-ND

Under this license, original works can be copied and shared in any format for personal or commercial use. However, you cannot make changes. You must also give credit to the creator.

CC BY-NC

This license lets you share, modify, and build on the material in any way you deem necessary, provided you give credit to the original creator and don't use it for commercial purposes.

CC BY-NC-SA

Like BY-NC, this license allows you to share, remix, adapt, and build upon the material in any medium or format, provided you give credit to the original creator and don't use it for commercial purposes. The modified material must be licensed under identical terms if the original work is remixed, adapted, or built upon.

Attribution, non-commercial, no derivatives (CC BY-NC-ND)

Of all the Creative Commons licenses, this is the most restrictive, only allowing others to download, share, and reuse the work in its original form while ensuring they give credit to the author. The original work cannot be altered or used for commercial purposes.

CC0

Often referred to as CC Zero, CC0 is a public dedication license that allows creators to give up their copyrights and put their works into the worldwide public domain. CC0 enables reusers to distribute, remix, adapt, and build upon the material in any medium or format with no conditions.

If you want to learn more about Creative Commons and the available licenses, please visit www. creativecommons.org. Additionally, you can learn more about international copyright at www. wipo.int.

Model release

A model release, also known as a liability waiver, is a legal document signed by the subject of a photograph, granting permission for its publication. While a release is not required to take a photograph, it becomes necessary if the image is to be used for commercial purposes, such as advertising a product or service.

Property release

When photographs feature identifiable locations, buildings, artworks, vehicles, animals, or other privately owned property, permission from the owner is usually required. This consent is typically granted through a signed property release that authorizes the image's use and distribution. This is an important aspect to consider when downloading assets from stock image sites to ensure that you don't use recognized brands, products, or landmarks without permission.

In this section, we have examined the importance of copyright, how it protects the original creator, and the necessity of identifying the usage rights and permissions for every image you intend to publish in your projects.

Summary

In this chapter, we customized the Photoshop interface to better suit our needs. We simplified the panel arrangement to make tools easier to find while providing ample space for images. The **Tools** panel was tailored by hiding redundant tools and highlighting popular ones. We also explored keyboard shortcuts for easier access and concealed nonessential menu options, all in a workspace that can be saved for future use.

We saw how preference settings can significantly impact how we interact with cursors and tool behavior in general.

We then examined image quality concepts such as PPI and resolution that define pixel artwork quality, ensuring it meets necessary standards before editing. In the next chapter, we will learn how to crop images, remove blemishes, and correct colors with non-destructive workflows.

We also looked at online resources for acquiring both free-to-use and paid project assets. Finally, we explored the importance of copyright and gaining permission to use images in your projects.

In the next chapter, we'll get to work in Photoshop, opening images, cropping unwanted content, and learning how to correct color and tonality.

Get This Book's PDF Version and Exclusive Extras

UNLOCK NOW

Scan the QR code (or go to `packtpub.com/unlock`). Search for this book by name, confirm the edition, and then follow the steps on the page.

Note: Keep your invoice handy. Purchases made directly from Packt don't require one.

3

Non-Destructive Healing and Retouching

The size and quality of source images can vary greatly, and they often end up being integrated into compositions that bear no resemblance to the original artwork. This process starts by removing unwanted content. This involves trimming peripheral details, fixing imperfections, and correcting tone and colors to ensure our source imagery is in good shape for further editing or integration elsewhere.

In this chapter, we'll focus on cropping techniques, which allow us to trim unwanted edge details precisely and correct crooked photos. We'll extend the canvas using techniques that allow us to transform image orientation while seamlessly filling new regions with image content.

Blemishes, or unwanted content, that are often captured in the original photo can be removed with a combination of retouching tools. We'll look at scenarios in which each of these tools provides quick, high-quality results with a combination of precise selections, painting cursors, and dedicated retouching workspaces.

With blemishes concealed, we'll then move on to color and tonal edits. This will include simple edits to alter image brightness and contrast, through to detailed color matching. We'll achieve all this without permanently changing the source image by using non-destructive adjustment layers.

In this chapter, we'll cover the following topics:

- Cropping and straightening images and extending the canvas
- Working with the healing and spot healing tools and content-aware technology
- Color and tone editing with adjustment layers

Technical requirements

The project files for this chapter can be found at `https://packt.link/gbz/9781806021710`.

Cropping and straightening images and extending the canvas

In *Chapter 1*, we established that the first task when working with new images is to verify their maximum output size and quality. The next step is to review the composition. Does the image appear level, and are the subjects framed appropriately? Cropping is ideal for addressing this issue.

Straightening a crooked image

Crooked images are commonplace. Even mounting a camera on a tripod to capture a photo won't guarantee that the horizon line is level. Fortunately, the **Crop** tool comes with a straightening feature that makes fixing a crooked horizon a breeze. Let's take a look:

1. Go to **File → Open**, browse to the `03-Retouch` folder, and select `Horizon.jpg`. Ensure that the entire canvas is visible in the image window by going to **View → Fit on Screen** and then zooming out slightly so that you can see the region beyond the edge of the canvas.

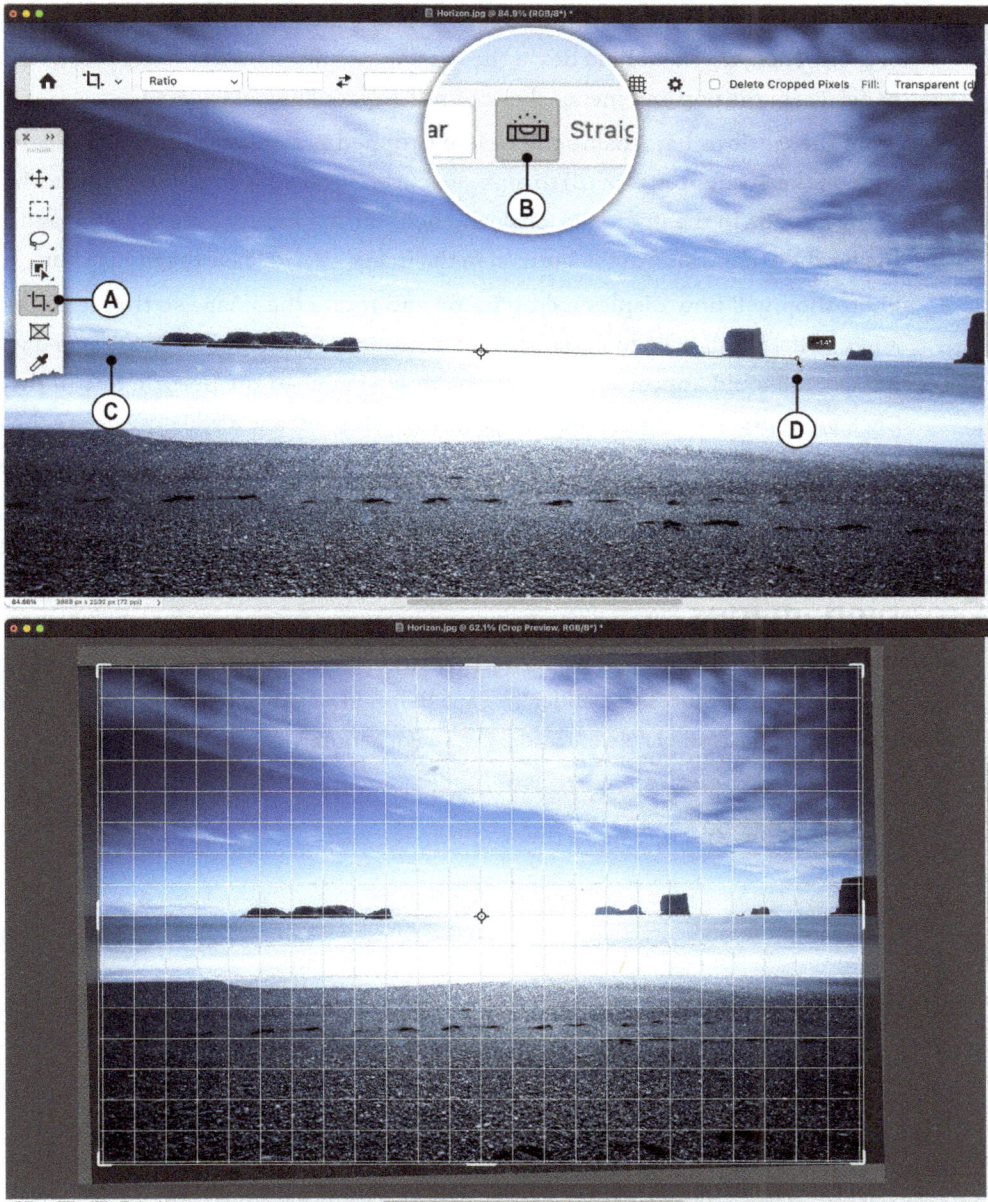

Figure 3.1: Using the Straighten tool to correct crooked images

2. Switch to the **Crop** tool (**A** in *Figure 3.1*) by pressing the *C* key to activate the correct group of tools. Then, click and hold down the left mouse button on the active tool in the **Tools** panel. From the pop-out menu, click on the **Crop** tool to make it active.

3. From the **Options** bar, ensure the **Delete Cropped Pixels** checkbox is turned on. Then, click on the **Straighten** tool (**B**) to make it active. Hover your cursor over the far-left edge of the horizon in the photo (**C**), click and hold the left mouse button down, and drag to the far right-hand side of the horizon in the image (**D**). Release the mouse button.

4. Photoshop will now display a crop frame and rotate the image so that it matches the angle of the **Straighten** tool, set between the start and end points you dragged with the mouse. It should appear level if you accurately matched the horizon line in the photo. Click on **Apply** to complete the straightened edit; Photoshop will now delete the region of the image that falls outside of the crop frame (the shaded region), leaving you with a straightened photo.

5. Save the file as a PSD in the 03-Retouch folder and close the document when you're done.

Cropping images

Traditionally, cropping is the act of removing content from one or more edges of an image. The image in our example requires the subjects – two ladies in our case – to be cropped tighter and conform to the compositional rule of thirds. Let's take a look:

1. Open Shoreline.jpg from the 03-Retouch folder. When the image appears, go to **View** → **Fit on Screen** to make the whole image visible.

Figure 3.2: Using the rule of thirds grid to create more visually interesting compositions

2. Switch to the **Crop** tool and, from the **Options** bar, set the crop preset to **Ratio**. Ensure both the **Width** and **Height** fields are blank, set the overlay menu (**A** in *Figure 3.2*) to **Rule of Thirds**, and make sure that the **Delete Cropped Pixels** checkbox is turned off.

3. Hover your cursor over the top-left point on the crop frame (**B**) and drag it to the right-hand side. As you drag, you will notice that a grid composed of nine squares will appear in the crop frame. Drag the crop frame until the left dividing line of the grid, which marks a third of the width, is positioned between the ladies (**C**).

4. Click on the **Commit** button in the **Options** bar to apply the crop. This will crop the image but not delete the region outside of the crop frame. To reveal the region in the future, go to **Image → Reveal All**.

5. With the edits now complete, go to **File → Save As**, keeping the filename the same. However, you will need to save the document in PSD format to keep the cropped region of the photo within the file (JPG format flattens the artwork and dispenses with any content outside the canvas). Save the document in the 03-Retouch folder and go to **File → Close** when done.

> **Rule of thirds**
>
> The rule of thirds is a technique for creating more engaging compositions by dividing an image into nine equally spaced sections with intersecting horizontal and vertical lines. By placing a subject along one of the imagined intersecting lines, one-third of the way into the image instead of at the center, the viewer is often drawn to explore the image more thoroughly and for longer.

In this section, we saw how to use Photoshop's cropping features. You can trim unwanted content from the edges of the image and improve the composition with a rule-of-thirds grid. Next, we will look at ways to extend the canvas.

Extending the canvas with content-aware cropping

Historically, cropping has almost always reduced the size of an image, partly due to the once-popular method of "digitizing" print images via a scanner and trimming away the unwanted background. However, with the advances of Photoshop's AI-enhanced features, we can also extend the canvas.

The process is almost identical to the previous exercise, but instead, we will drag one or more crop frame handles beyond the edge of the existing canvas. Content-aware technology will use existing image content to extend the artwork and fill a new region for us. This is especially handy when you need to alter the orientation of an image or extend its width to create an extra-wide web banner for social media. Let's get started:

1. Open `Waves.jpg` from the `03-Retouch` folder. This image calls for an extension to the canvas to convert its ratio from square to portrait.

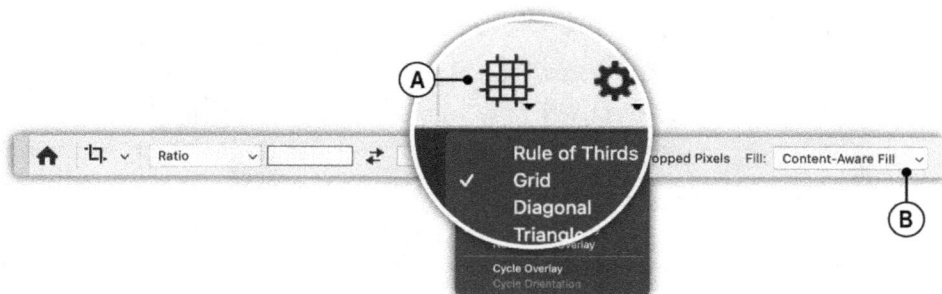

Figure 3.3: Set up the Options bar for extending the canvas

2. Switch to the **Crop** tool. From the **Options** bar, click on the **Overlay** button menu, which appears as a grid, to reveal the drop-down menu (**A** in *Figure 3.3*). Choose **Grid** from the list. Then, choose **Content-Aware Fill** from the **Fill** drop-down menu (**B**).

Figure 3.4: Use the Crop tool to extend the canvas and fill new regions with repurposed pixels

3. Hover your cursor over the top point on the crop frame (**A** in *Figure 3.4*) and drag upward until you reveal approximately 5 additional grid rows above the image. These should extend the height of the image to 3000 pixels, as shown in the tooltip adjacent to your cursor.

4. Click on the **Commit** button in the **Options** bar. This will extend the canvas to the point where you dragged the frame handles. Photoshop will fill in the new region using parts of the existing image, blending it in with the original pixels.

5. Save the file as a PSD in the 03-Retouch folder and close the document when you're done.

Quick cropping tips

Buried away in a Photoshop sub-menu is an auto-cropping feature that was once intended for extracting photos from scanned backgrounds. However, auto-crop is brilliant for extracting thumbnail images or logos from a plain background. With your image open, go to **File → Automate → Crop & Straighten Photos**. Photoshop will detect any items surrounded by a plain background, and then copy, straighten, and paste them into a new file.

There may be occasions when, after cropping, you notice unwanted rows and columns of pixels along the edges of an image. By default, the crop tool snaps to the edge of the canvas, making cropping a few pixels a tedious task. Instead, zoom above 500% zoom level so that you can see the pixel grid appear and estimate the number of rogue pixels. Then, go to **Image → Canvas Size**. Set the units to pixels, then set a negative value for the pixels you wish to remove (-7, for example). Anchor the canvas at the opposite side from the one you are trying to remove pixels from. Then, click **OK** to remove those troublesome pixels.

If you need to crop away transparent pixels or contrast-colored pixels from any edge of an image, you can use **Image → Trim**. By default, Photoshop will search for transparent pixels along all four edges of an image and crop them away. You can change this behavior and instead search for any pixel color that matches that of the top-left pixel color or the bottom-right pixel color, and crop those away from each edge. You can also choose which edge is trimmed by turning off one or more of the **Trim Away** checkboxes.

You can avoid the **Crop** tool altogether by using the selection tool. Create a selection using any method or tool you prefer. Then, with your selection active, go to **Image → Crop**. Photoshop will crop the image down to the four edges of your selection, leaving you with a rectangular region. Any pixels outside of your original selection will be deleted.

It is possible to crop one image to the dimensions of another. Open both images in Photoshop and ensure that the image you wish to reference the size of is active. Then, switch to the **Crop** tool. From the **Options** bar, click on the **Crop Preset** drop-down menu and choose **Front Image** from the list. Photoshop will populate the **Width**, **Height**, and **Resolution** fields in the **Options** bar with sampled canvas data. Click on the tab of the document that requires cropping and press *Enter* to apply cropping to the image:

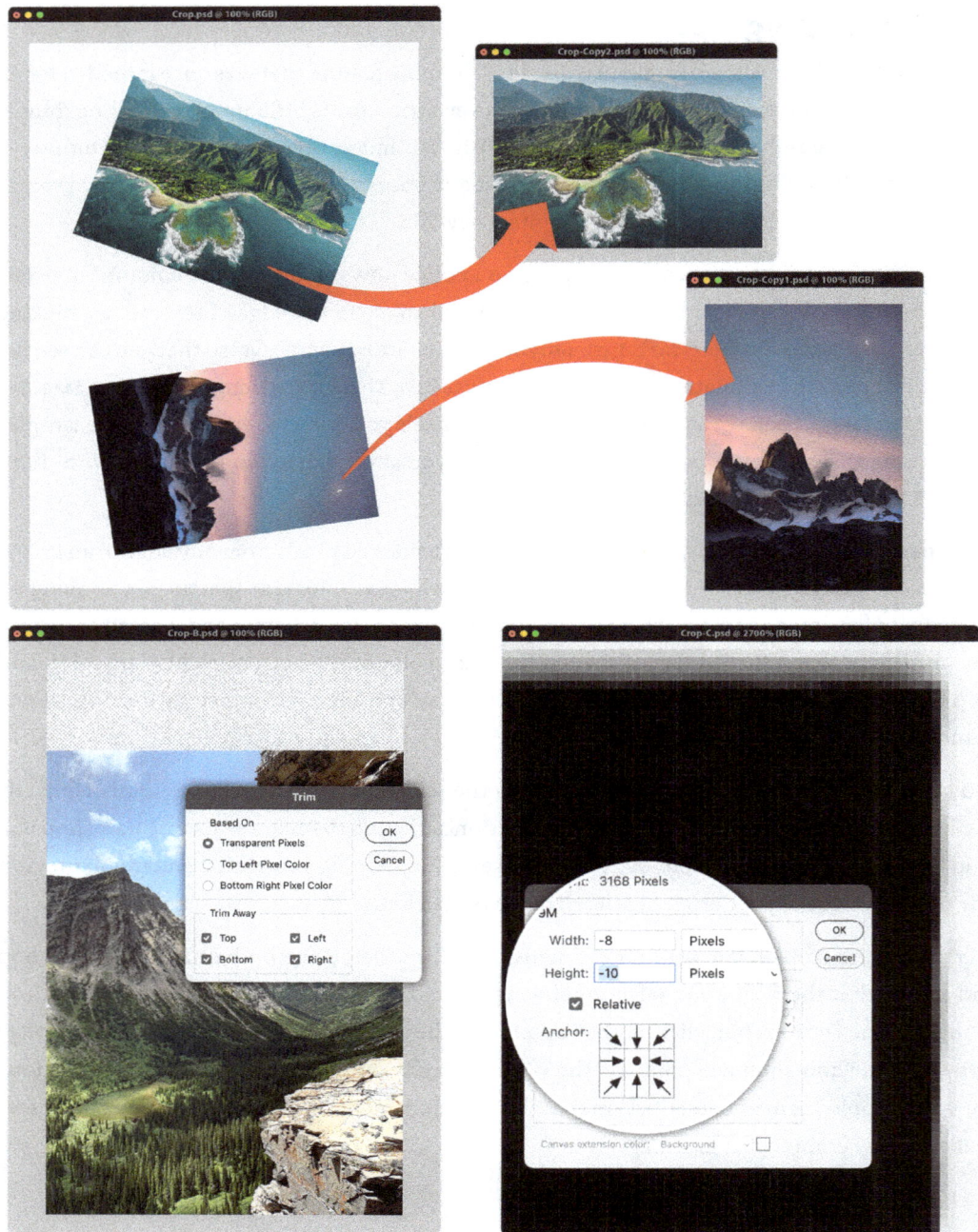

Figure 3.5: Cropping and straightening photos (top), trimming (bottom left), and canvas size (bottom right)

Content-aware scaling

There may be occasions when you need to extend your canvas, but due to the complex content in your image, you cannot use content-aware cropping. If this is the case, you can always try content-aware scaling to stretch your image without obvious distortions. Let's take a look:

1. Open Boats.jpg from the 03-Retouch folder. This image is required as a web banner and must be widened. However, the challenge here is that the background contains lots of details, which can be too complicated for content-aware cropping.

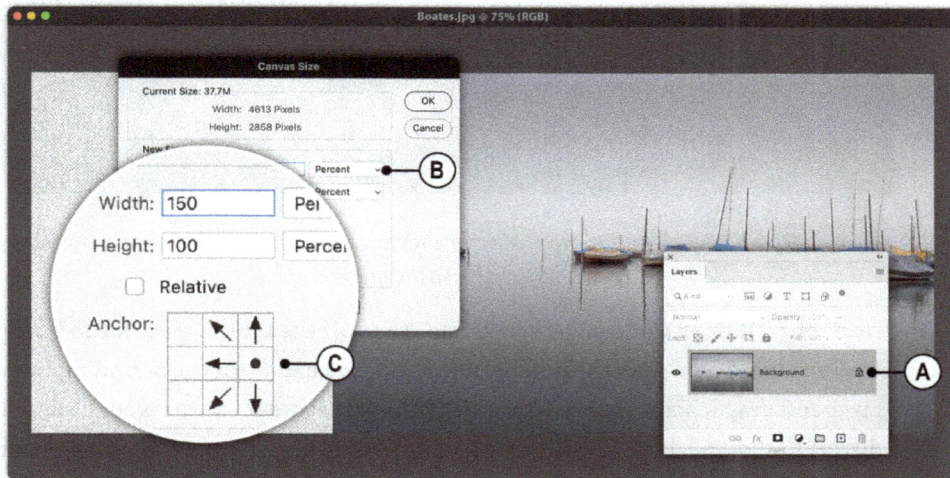

Figure 3.6: Extend the canvas before extending the photo with content-aware scaling

2. Go to the **Layers** panel and click on the padlock icon associated with the background layer (**A** in *Figure 3.6*) to unlock the content. This will allow the photo to be edited with a feature called **Content-Aware Scale** in a follow-up step. You will also notice that by unlocking the layer, the name has been replaced with the default of Layer 0. Rename the layer Panorama.

3. Next, go to **Image → Canvas Size**. When the dialog appears, ensure that the **Relative** checkbox is turned off. Then, set the unit of measurement to **Percentage** for the **Width** and **Height** drop-down menus (**B**). Click on the center-right anchor point icon (**C**) in the **Anchor** section of the dialog.

4. Enter 150 into the **Width** field and click **OK** to apply the edit. This will double the canvas's width, but crucially, the extended region will be transparent (empty), as shown by the checkered region.

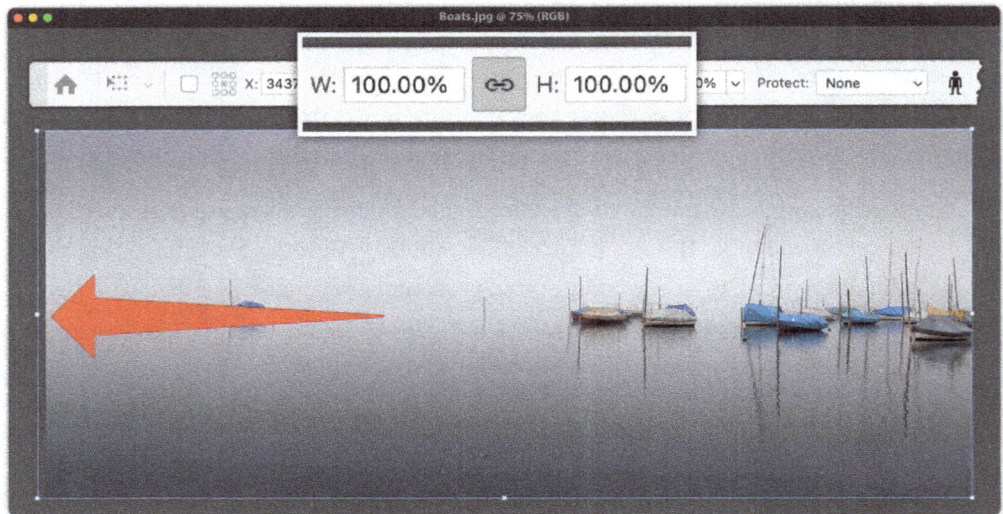

Figure 3.7: Content-Aware Scale stretches low-detail areas whilst protecting details like the boats

5. Next, go to **Edit → Content-Aware Scale**. Turn off the **Link Aspect Ratio** button in the **Options** bar. Then, grab the middle-left-hand side handle of the bounding box over the layer and drag it across to the left until all the transparent canvas is concealed. This will distort low-detailed areas such as the sky but leave important detailed areas untouched. Click on the **Commit** button to apply the changes.

6. Switch to the **Zoom** tool and click to a magnification of at least 100% to quickly examine the image for distortions.

7. Save the file as a PSD in the 03-Retouch folder and close the document when you're done.

In this section, we saw how Photoshop's suite of cropping tools can be used to extend the canvas and repurpose the original pixels in the image to add AI-generated content. Next, we will take a look at healing and retouching techniques.

Healing and retouching

In the following exercises, we'll explore two different approaches to removing unwanted content, referred to as blemishes, either by applying brush strokes or filling selections. Both techniques replicate parts of the existing image and paste them over the desired region.

In recent editions of Photoshop, we have seen the introduction of AI-enhanced retouching features, such as the **Remove** tool and **Generative Fill**. Both are powerful additions and are covered in detail in *Chapter 12, Integrating Artificial Intelligence*.

Some of Photoshop's long-established retouching tools, such as the **Spot Healing Brush** tool, also utilize AI-powered technology by sampling "blemish-free" parts of an image that contain similar colors to the blemish and repurposing them precisely to blend them in seamlessly. Photoshop decides which parts of the image to sample, pasting them into the brush tip as you drag across the image. This makes the **Spot Healing Brush** tool a popular choice. However, the trade-off in speed is that it sometimes results in smudged or blurred details on the edges of the brush stroke.

Alternatively, if you require precise control over which portions of the image you want Photoshop to sample, consider using the **Clone Stamp** or **Healing Brush** tool. Hover your cursor over the region you wish to sample, hold down *Alt* (Windows) or *Option* (macOS), and click to define the starting point for your sample. Head to the blemished pixels and drag across them. The **Healing Brush** tool samples the textures in the sampled region of the image and replaces the blemished textures while preserving the original color and luminosity.

The **Clone Stamp** is essentially a copy-and-paste tool that samples and pastes pixels via the brush tip. This can be used to your advantage on highly detailed images, such as landscapes. This helps you avoid small details becoming smudged or blurred. The challenge here is to modify the brush tip so that it does the blending for you.

Non-destructive workflows

Photoshop is a wonderfully powerful application, but it can be unforgiving as a linear image editor. Wherever possible, avoid edits and features that are permanent and incapable of being removed, reset, or edited. Several commands found in the application menus apply permanent edits, but there are two features related to layers that have revolutionized editing in Photoshop over the last 20 years: **Smart Objects** and **adjustment layers**. Both techniques will be explored extensively in the following section. Both are relatively quick and simple to use and can save hours of precious production time.

Removing cables from a photo

Great-looking images can be ruined by cables and other unsightly elements, some of which may not seem very noticeable at the time of capturing the image. Let's take a look at how to remove such objects:

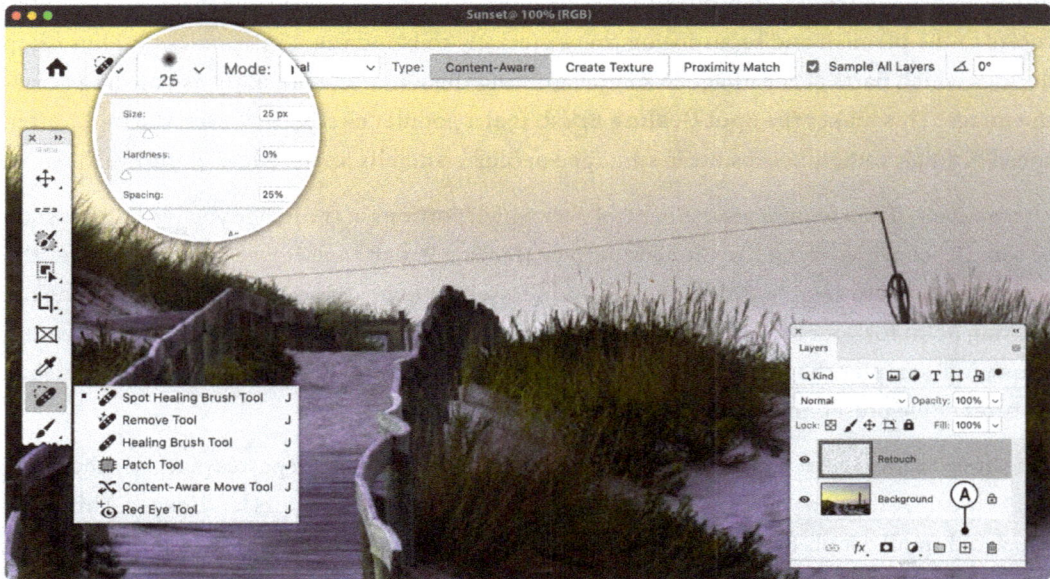

Figure 3.8: Activate and set up the Spot Healing Brush tool

1. Open Sunset.jpg from the 03-Retouch folder. The cable runs across this image, ruining the view of the sunset.

2. Click on the **New Layer** icon (**A** in *Figure 3.8*) at the bottom of the **Layers** panel and name the new empty layer retouch. Ensure the new layer is active.

3. Press the *J* key and hold down the left mouse button on the active tool in the **Tools** panel. From the pop-out menu, click on the **Spot Healing Brush** tool. In the **Options** bar, set the brush tip **Size** value to 25 px, **Mode** to **Normal**, and **Type** to **Content-Aware**. Then, turn on the **Sample All Layers** checkbox.

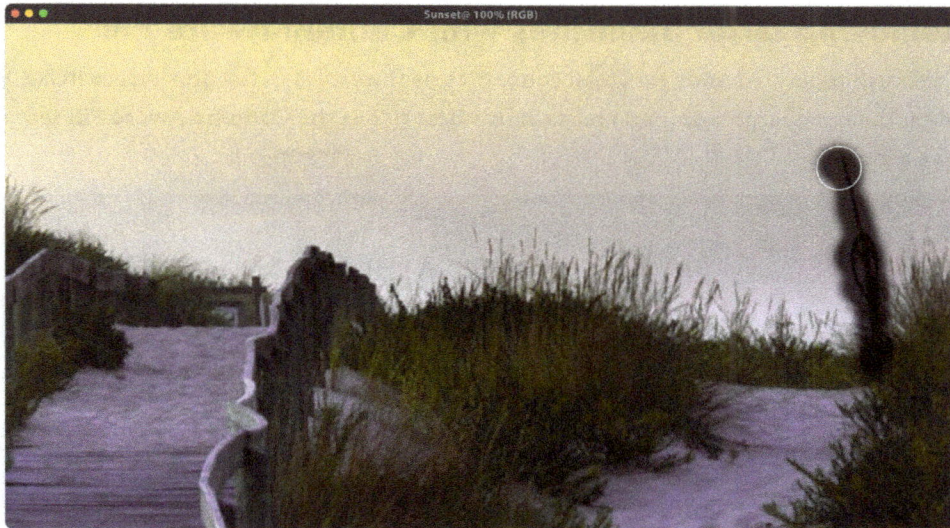

Figure 3.9: Drag the Spot Healing Brush tool across the cable to remove it

4. Hover your cursor over the left edge of the cable and then hold the left mouse button down as you drag across the cable to the right-hand side. This will remove the cable once you release the left mouse button.

5. Then, with the **Spot Healing Brush** tool still active, click and drag over the pole from top to bottom. You can run your cursor through the greenery to ensure all of it has been removed.

Painting straight lines

Although dragging Photoshop's painting tools across an image to apply edits feels natural, you can also paint in straight lines. Click in the region where you wish to start your straight paint mark and release the left mouse button. Then, hover your cursor over the region where you wish to end the straight line, hold down *Shift*, and then click again. Release the mouse button and the *Shift* key. This technique can be used for a variety of painting and retouching tools, such as the **Spot Healing Brush** tool.

Removing large blemishes with Content-Aware Fill

The brush tools are handy for small edits, such as the cables in the previous exercise. However, when there are large regions to retouch, it's best to use the **Content-Aware Fill** feature. Let's take a look:

Figure 3.10: Remove unwanted regions to prevent them from being sampled by Content-Aware Fill

1. With the **Spot Healing Brush** tool active, click and drag over small details such as the orange light and the mast on top of the tower to ensure they are not sampled when using **Content-Aware Fill**.

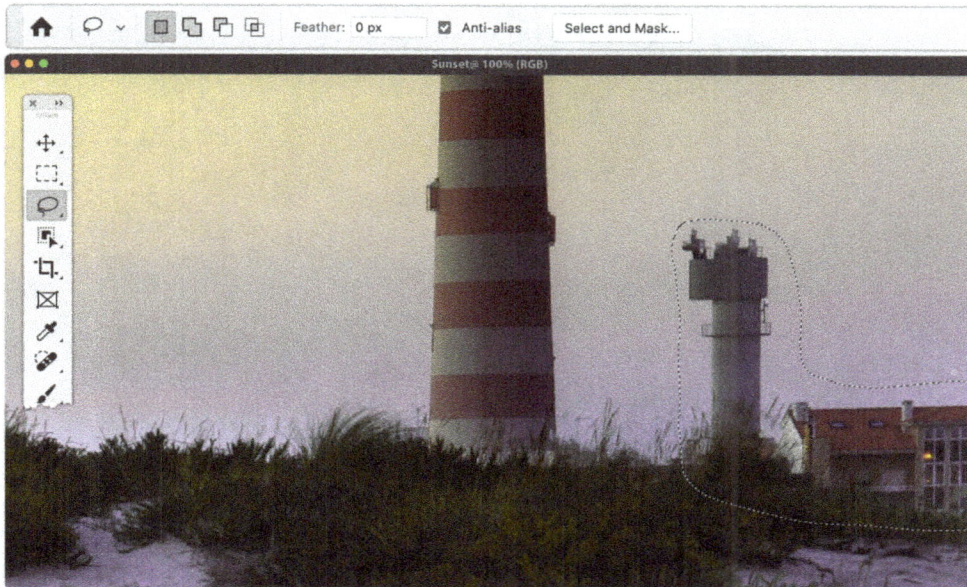

Figure 3.11: Select the buildings to the right of the lighthouse with the Lasso tool

2. Switch to the **Lasso** tool by pressing *L*. Set the selection mode to **New** and set the **Feather** value to 0. Click and drag around the tower with the masts attached to it and the adjacent building to the right, leaving a generous region around it. Once you have reached the place where you started, release the left mouse button. If necessary, you can add or subtract from the original selection by changing the selection mode and then using the same click-and-drag technique.

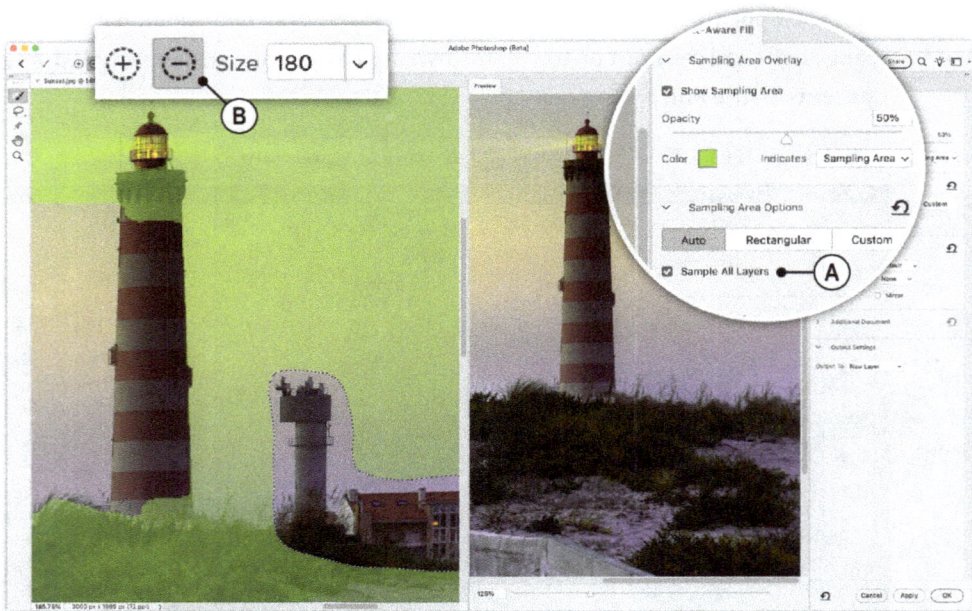

Figure 3.12: Use Content-Aware Fill to remove significant blemishes or unwanted content

3.   Go to **Edit → Content-Aware Fill** to enter the dedicated workspace. Photoshop will use the green highlighted region in the left half of the editor to denote the regions of the image from which it will sample pixel content. It will replace the original content with matching pixels, the previewed results for which can be seen in the right-hand window.

4.   Turn on the **Sample All Layers** checkbox and ensure the **Auto** mode is active under **Sampling Area Options** (**A** in *Figure 3.12*).

5.   The **Sampling Brush** tool will be active by default. Change **Mode** to **Subtract** from the **Options** bar (**B**)and increase the brush size to 180 px. If necessary, paint over any regions that are not suitable, such as the lighthouse, to remove them from sampling and prevent those parts from being duplicated. Once complete, you will see the preview update. Click **OK** when you're done to apply the edits and close the dialog. Then, choose **Select → Deselect** to deactivate the selection.

6.   Once all the edits are complete, go to **Select → Deselect**.

7.   Save the file as a PSD in the 03-Retouch folder and close the document when you're done.

Bending subjects with Puppet Warp

The **Free Transform** tool is handy for making rectangular transforms, such as scaling and rotating. However, in the following example, we need a more "organic" way of manipulating a tree to straighten it so that it doesn't distract from the rest of the composition:

1. Open Palm.jpg from the 03-Retouch folder.

Figure 3.13: Concealing the original palm tree with Content-Aware Fill

2. Press *W* to activate the **Object Selection** tool (**A** in *Figure 3.13*). Long-press the tool icon in the **Tools** panel to reveal the popout and ensure the correct tool is active.

3. Ensure the selection mode is set to **New** from the **Options** bar (**B**). Then, hover your cursor over the large palm tree to reveal a pink selection highlight and click to select only the palm tree.

4. Next, press *Ctrl + J* (Windows) or *Cmd + J* (macOS) to copy and paste the selected pixels onto a new layer. Double-click on the layer name and rename it Tree. Hover your cursor over the layer's name and right-click to reveal the context menu. Choose **Convert to Smart Object** to protect the layer's content and make **Puppet Warp** re-editable.

Figure 3.14: Concealing the original palm tree with Content-Aware Fill

5. Hover your cursor over the **Tree** layer thumbnail, press *Ctrl* (Windows) or *Cmd* (macOS), and click. This will create a selection of all the pixels in a layer – in this case, all the large palm tree pixels.

6. Click on the **Background** layer to make it active. The selection of the large palm tree should still be active. Go to **Select → Modify → Expand**. Set the amount to 20 pixels and click **OK** to enlarge the selection size.

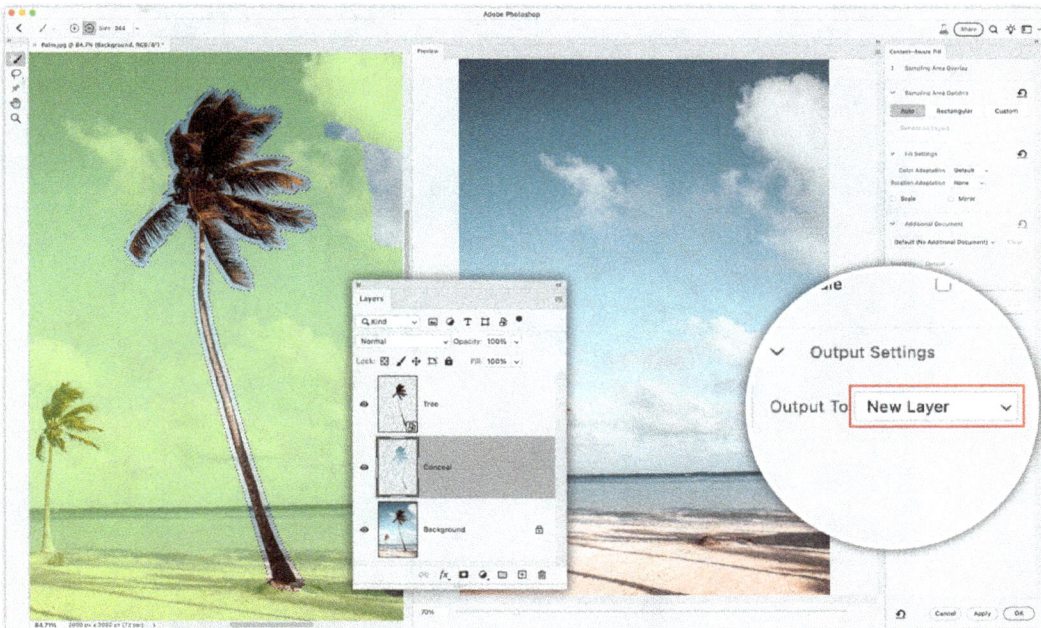

Figure 3.15: Concealing the original palm tree with Content-Aware Fill

7. Next, go to **Edit → Content-Aware Fill**. When the dialog appears, you will see two windows. On the left will be the regions used to sample parts of the image, and on the right will be a preview of the edits.

8. Set the mode to **Auto** from the settings on the right-hand side of the interface.

9. Ensure the **Output To** dropdown is set to **New Layer** (highlighted in *Figure 3.15*) and then click on **OK** to apply the edits. Rename the new layer `Conceal`. Click on the **Lock All** icon in the upper portion of the **Layers** panel to prevent it from moving accidentally.

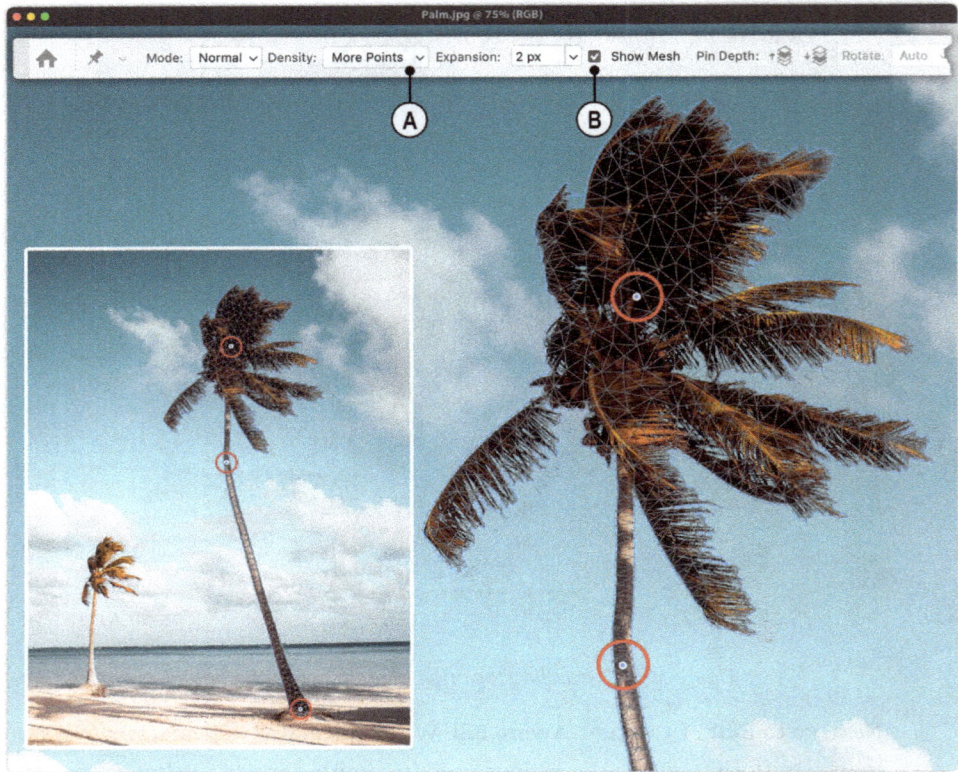

Figure 3.16: Alter the Puppet Warp settings before manipulating the tree

10. Next, go to **Edit → Puppet Warp**. When the options appear at the top of the screen, set **Mode** to **Normal** and **Density** to **More Points** (**A** in *Figure 3.16*), leave **Expansion** set to the default of **2 px**, and turn on the **Show Mesh** checkbox (**B**).

11. Hover your cursor over the base of the tree trunk and click to add a pin. Add a second pin on the trunk where it bends, and a third pin in the middle of the palm leaves (circled in *Figure 3.16*). There will be no need to move the bottom pin – we're only adding it to stop the bottom of the tree from moving.

12. You can turn off the **Show Mesh** checkbox to see your edits more clearly now that all the pins have been added. Drag the top pin to the left and the middle pin to the right to straighten the palm tree. Click on the tick in the **Options** bar to apply the edits when you're done.

13. You will notice that the edits have been added to the layer. You can edit them at any point by double-clicking on the **Puppet Warp** text label, which appears under the **Tree** layer as a smart filter.

14. Save the file as a PSD in the 03-Retouch folder and close the document when you're done.

Figure 3.17: The completed Puppet Warp edits

Creative Cloud mesh advice

When it comes to mesh objects within Creative Cloud, it's best to start simply and add more complexity as needed. In the case of the **Puppet Warp** mesh, which is controlled by pins, you can add them once you begin warping your pixels. Hover over the area of the mesh where you need more control and click to add an additional pin. You can also delete pins by clicking on them and then pressing the *Delete* key on your keyboard.

Using the Clone Stamp tool to remove unwanted content

Almost all images contain imperfections or distracting elements. In this exercise, you will utilize a series of retouching tools to enhance a panorama:

1. Open BeachPano-01.jpg from the 03-Retouch folder.

2. Zoom into the image to around 100%, navigating to the sign located on the far right-hand side of the panorama so that you have a clear view of it in the center of the image window.

3. Go to the **Layers** panel and click on the **Create New Layer** icon at the bottom of the **Layers** panel to add a new empty layer. Double-click on the current layer's name to open the type entry field in the layer in the stack, enter a new name of Retouch, and press *Enter* to apply the name change.

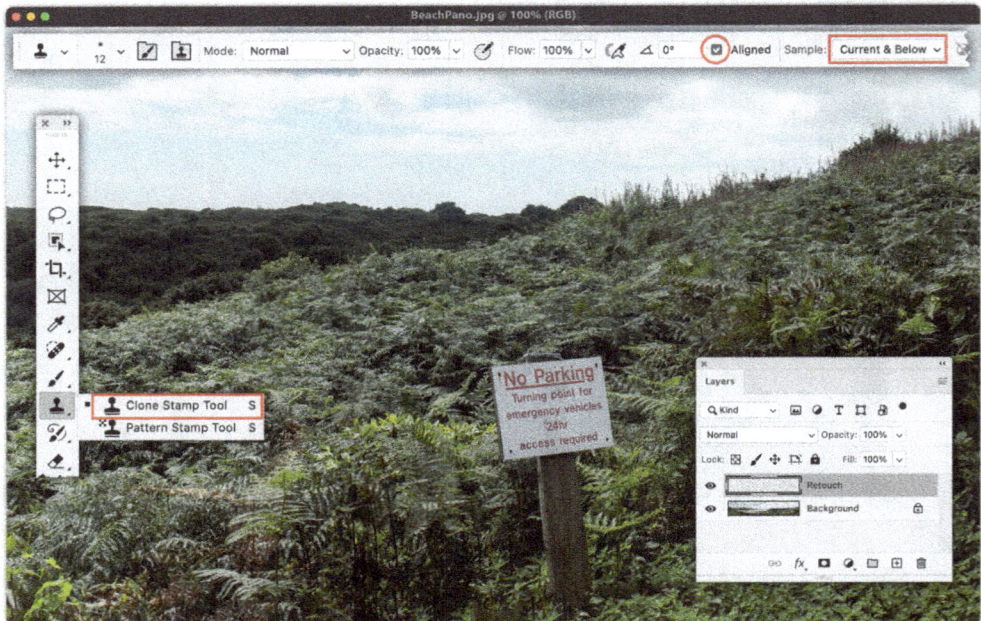

Figure 3.18: Create a new, empty layer to add your clone edits into

4. Switch to the **Clone Stamp** tool by pressing *S*. Click and hold on the active tool in the **Tools** panel to ensure you have the correct tool active – **Clone Stamp** and **Pattern Stamp** look almost identical.

5. From the **Options** bar, ensure that **Mode** is set to **Normal** and **Opacity** and **Flow** are set to 100%. From the sampling settings, turn on the **Aligned** checkbox and set the **Sample** drop-down menu to **Current & Below**.

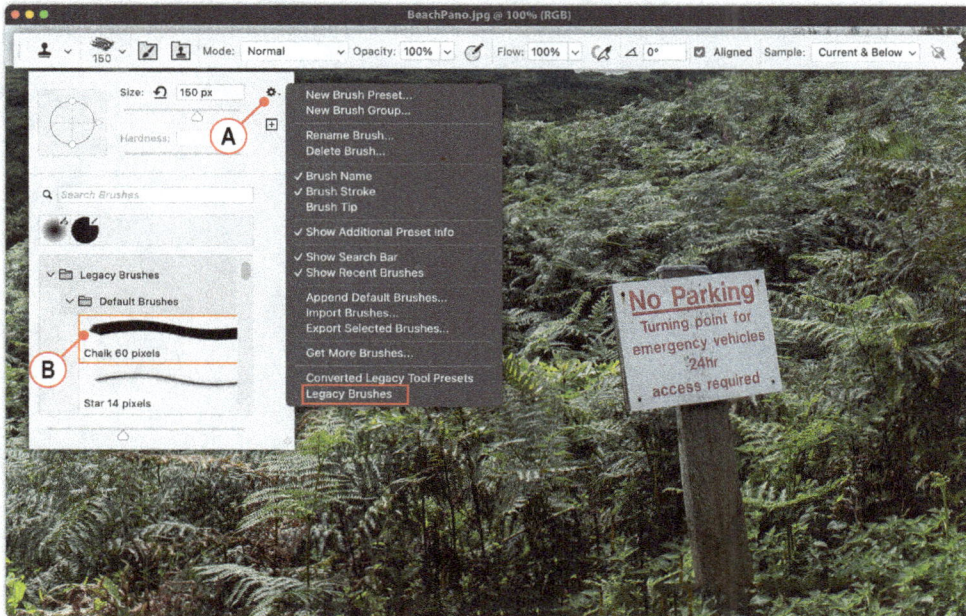

Figure 3.19: Choose a rough-edged brush tip to blend your edits

6. Click on the panel menu icon, shown as a cog in the upper right-hand side of the popout (**A** in *Figure 3.19*), and choose **Legacy Brushes** from the list. Legacy brushes contain a wealth of shapes and styles; some are especially effective when retouching organic content in photos.

7. From the **Options** bar, change the shape of the brush tip by expanding the folder named **Legacy Brushes** and then **Default Brushes**. Scroll down the list and select **Chalk 60 (B)**. Change the brush tip size to 150 px, then press *Enter* to close the brush tip popout.

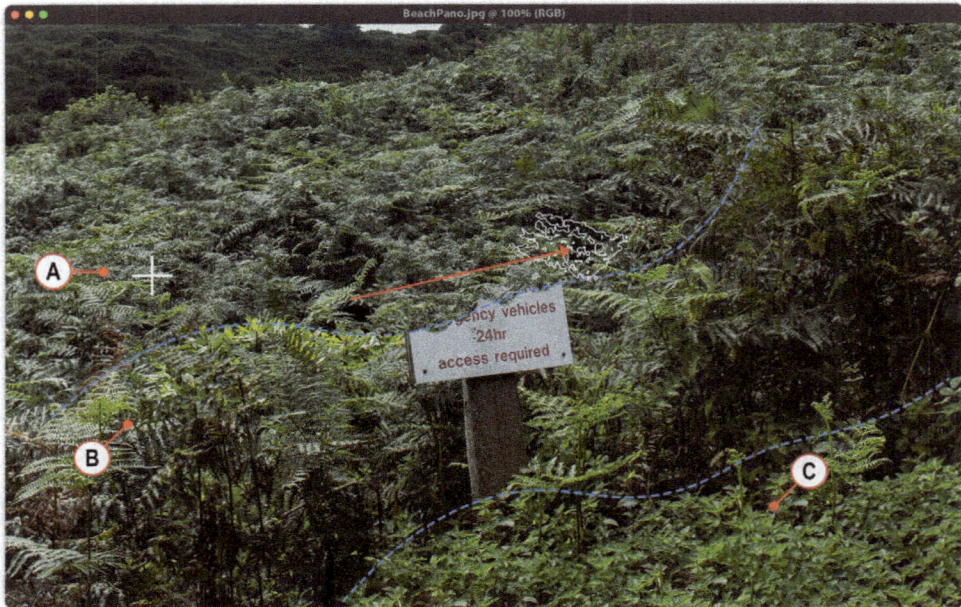

Figure 3.20: Sample suitable areas of the image to conceal the sign

8. The **Clone Stamp** tool acts like a copy-and-paste brush, copying from a sampled part of the image and then pasting it into your cursor as you perform brush strokes. Hover your cursor over the background, the region above the sign (**A** in *Figure 3.20*), and sample by pressing *Alt* (Windows) or *Option* (macOS) and, simultaneously, clicking. Release the key and the left mouse button once you have captured your sample.

9. Hover your brush tip cursor to the left of the sign, then click and hold the left mouse button and drag across the top of the sign and beyond its right edge to conceal it (shown as a red arrow in *Figure 3.20*).

Sampling with the Clone Stamp tool

The sample, shown as a small target, will be visible as you apply a cloned brush mark and always starts at the point where you sampled. The sample target moves in perfect synchrony with your brush tip. Avoid sampling close to the edge of the canvas, as Photoshop may run out of images to sample if the target runs off the edge of the canvas. It is also worth considering how long your brush strokes will take and ensuring that your sample target doesn't pick up unwanted content. I would also recommend resampling before each new brush stroke to avoid patterns emerging in your artwork.

10. Repeat the same technique to remove the middle of the sign. Sample a slightly different patch of bracken from the mid-ground (**B**) before each brush stroke to avoid repeating the duplicate content.

11. To conceal the sign's upright post, sample the image's foreground (**C**), using a mixture of nettles and bracken stalks. Once the sign has been concealed, save the file as a PSD in the 03-Retouch folder and close the document when you're done.

Adding smiles to portraits with Face-Aware Liquify

It can be frustrating to capture the image you want, only to find that someone wasn't smiling. But you can now change facial expressions thanks to Photoshop's liquify tools. Let's take a look:

1. Open Smile.jpg from the 03-Retouch folder. Right-click on the **Background** layer in the **Layers** panel and choose **Convert to Smart Object** from the list of options. Rename the layer Smile.

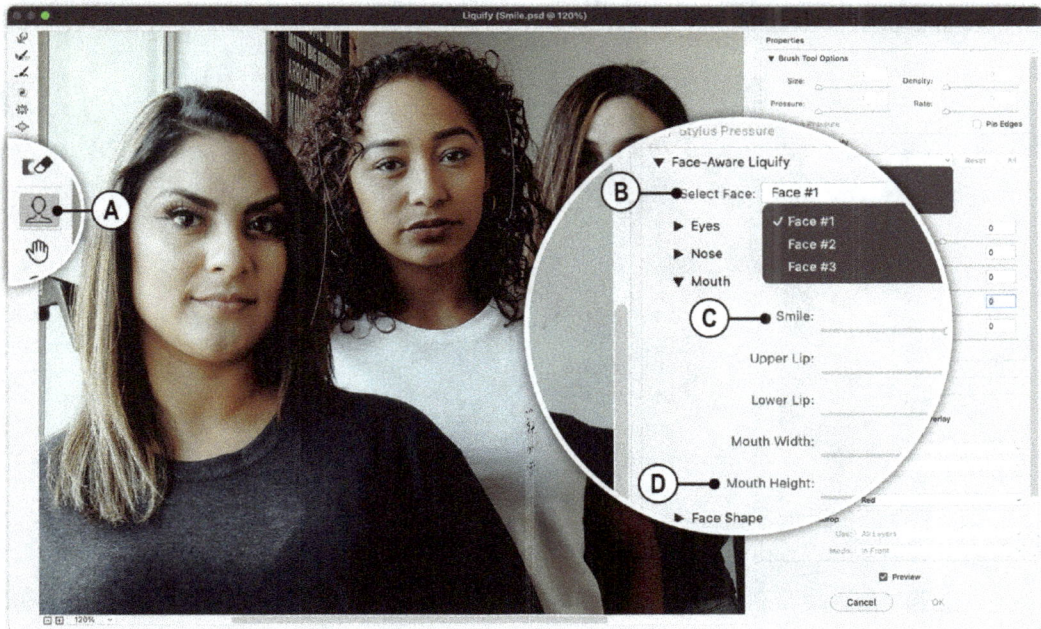

Figure 3.21: The Face-Aware Liquify dialog

2. Then, go to **Filter → Liquify**. Activate the **Face** tool (**A** in *Figure 3.21*). Then, choose a face to edit from the **Face-Aware Liquify** settings on the right-hand side. Photoshop will detect all human faces. It will start on the left with **Face #1**, **Face #2** in the middle, and **Face #3** on the right.

3. You will see the **Smile** slider (**C**) under the **Mouth** sliders and settings on the right-hand side. Like all the others, the slider is set to the center at a neutral value of 0. In this case, dragging to the left will apply a negative effect, which is frowning, while dragging to the right will increase the smile effect.

4. If you want to create a more convincing smile effect, try reducing the value of the **Mouth Height** slider (**D**). It can make the lips appear pursed like a real smile would tend to appear.

5. Once you have finished, click **OK** to exit the **Liquify** dialog. Save the file in 03-Retouch folder as a PSD file with the same name.

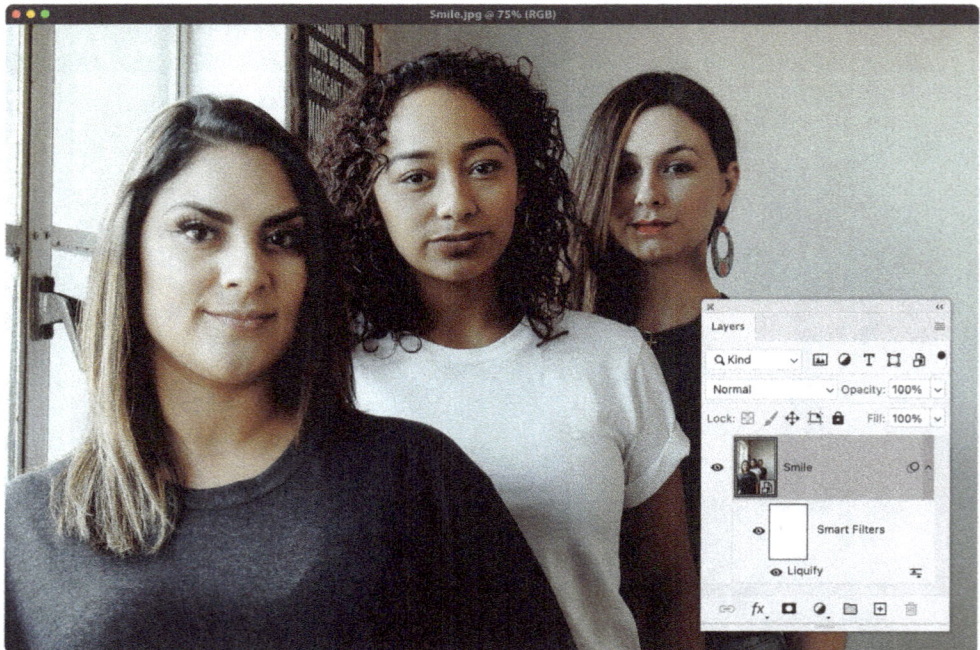

Figure 3.22: The completed image with editable liquify effects in the Layers panel

Portrait retouching

The **Patch** and **Spot Healing Brush** tools excel at editing skin tones and textures, softly blending in edits automatically with their surrounding pixels for a more natural finish. We'll take a closer look at them in this section:

1. Open Snowboarder.jpg from the 03-Retouch folder. The photo requires some edits to the man's face and clothing using retouching tools.

2. Go to the **Layers** panel and click on the layer named **Snowboarder**, which should be at the top of the stack. Then, click on the **Create New Layer** icon at the bottom of the **Layers** panel. Name the layer Heal and make sure it is active.

3. Zoom into the right-hand eye to around 600%, which contains visible blood vessels. Switch to the **Patch** tool by pressing the *J* key to activate one of the retouching tools in the **Tools** panel, and then click and hold down the left mouse button to reveal a pop-out menu. Click on **Patch Tool** to make it active (**A** in *Figure 3.23*):

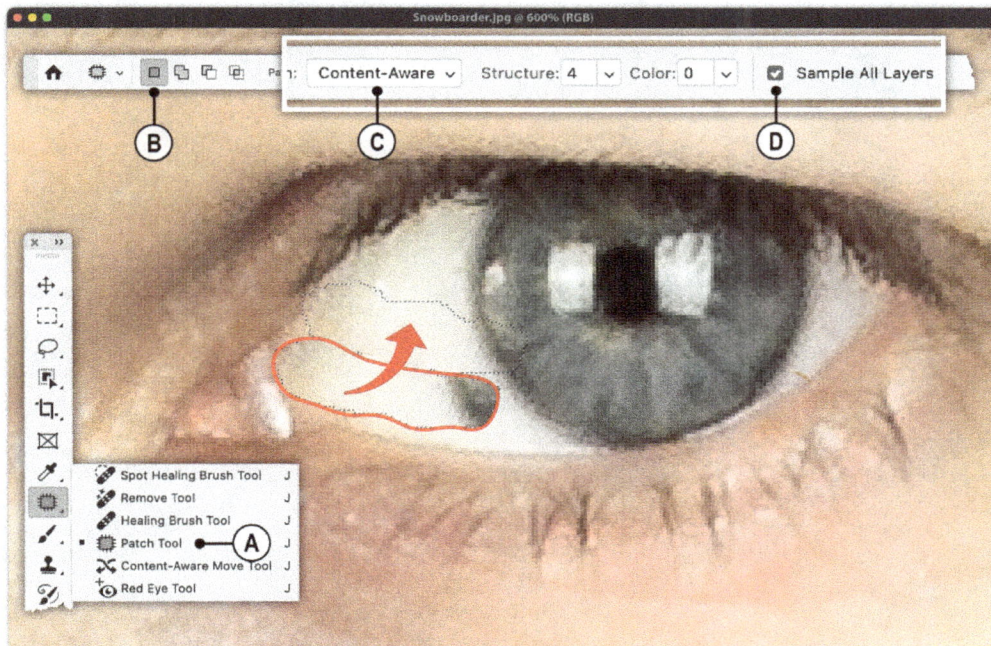

Figure 3.23: The initial selection, shown in red, is used to sample desirable pixels

4. The **Patch** tool allows you to create a **Lasso** tool-style selection around the pixels you wish to repair. From the **Options** bar, set the selection mode to **New (B)** and **Patch** mode to **Content-Aware (C)**. Turn on the **Sample All Layers** checkbox (**D**) to ensure that the **Patch** tool has pixel content to sample from the underlying layers in the stack, rather than the empty new layer you just created.

5. The **Patch** tool has a lasso selection mode built into it. You can use this tool to create a selection of the blood vessel in the right-hand eye or use a different selection tool. In the example shown, the **Patch** tool was used. With the **Patch** tool active, click and hold down the left mouse button and create a tight selection around the blood vessel. Then, hover your cursor inside the selection to reveal the **Patch** tool symbol. Click and hold down the left mouse button and then drag the selection to a region of white in the eye immediately above. Release the mouse button to apply the patch.

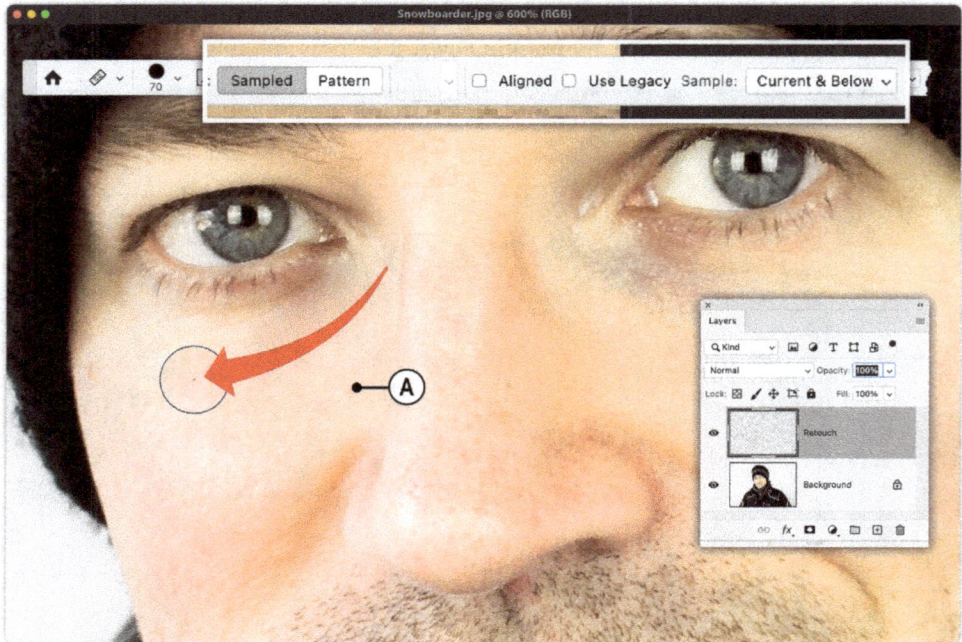

Figure 3.24: The Healing Brush tool

6. Go to **Select** → **Deselect**. Then, switch to the **Healing Brush** tool by holding the left mouse button down on the **Patch** tool icon in the **Tools** panel to reveal it in the pop-out menu. Set the brush tip's size to 80 px. Ensure that **Mode** is set to **Normal**, **Source** is set to **Sampled**, the **Aligned** checkbox is on, **Sample** is set to **Current & Below**, and **Diffusion** is set to 4.

7. Hover the cursor over a portion of skin under the eye (**A** in *Figure 3.24*), click to sample. Hover your cursor over one end of the dark mark on the lower eyelid and then click and drag across the blemishes to remove them. Photoshop will automatically blend your edits with the surrounding pixels. Repeat the same technique for the other eye.

8. To finish off the retouching work, switch to the **Spot Healing Brush** tool, which can be found in the same set of sub-tools in the **Tools** panel. Set the brush size to 70 px, set **Mode** to **Content-Aware**, and turn on **Sample All Layers**. Click on any of the pimples on the skin or pieces of white fluff on the clothing to remove them. Turn the **Heal** layer's visibility back on.

9. Save the file as a PSD in the 03-Retouch folder and close the document when you're done.

Eliminating glare from glasses

Reflections on spectacles can often obscure the subject's eyes and detract from an otherwise excellent portrait. In this exercise, we will eliminate reflections using color and luminance adjustment layers, apply generative fill, and spot retouching to fine-tune the final result. Let's take a look:

1. Open Spectacles.jpg from the 03-Retouch folder. The image contains green reflections (**A** in *Figure 3.25*) and several blown-out details along the lower and upper eyelids (**B**).

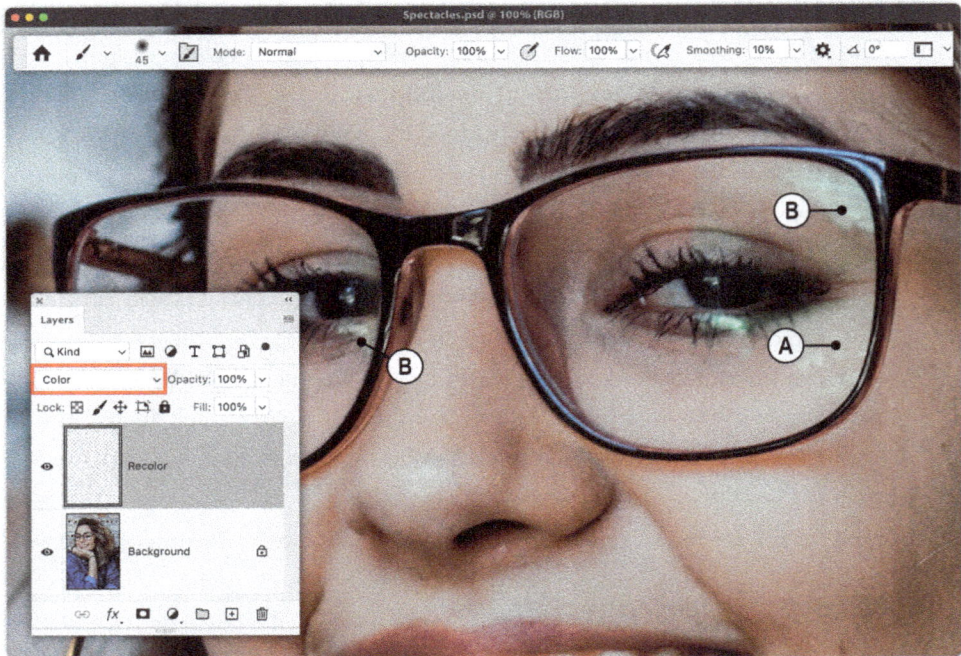

Figure 3.25: Add a new layer with blend mode set to Color

2. Add a new layer by clicking the **Create a New Layer** button at the bottom of the **Layers** panel, then name it Recolor and set the **Blend Mode** dropdown to **Color** (highlighted in *Figure 3.25*).

3. Press the *B* key to switch to the **Brush** tool. Select the **Soft Round** brush tip from the brush tip menu and set **Size** to approximately 45 px with a **Hardness** value of 0 px.

4. Start by eliminating the subtle green reflection color to the right of the right-hand-side eye (**A** in *Figure 3.25*). Hover the **Brush** tool over a region of unaffected skin and hold *Alt* (Windows) or *Option* (macOS) to activate the color sampler. Then, click to sample the color before releasing the key on the keyboard.

5. Ensure the **Recolor** layer is active, then carefully paint the warm skin color over the green reflection area in the glass to remove it. This is because the layer blend mode is set to **Color**. Make sure to keep resampling lighter and darker shades of unaffected skin tone to keep the edits looking convincing.

6. Repeat the same process to eliminate the subtle green reflection from the left-hand-side eye, ensuring you sample regularly.

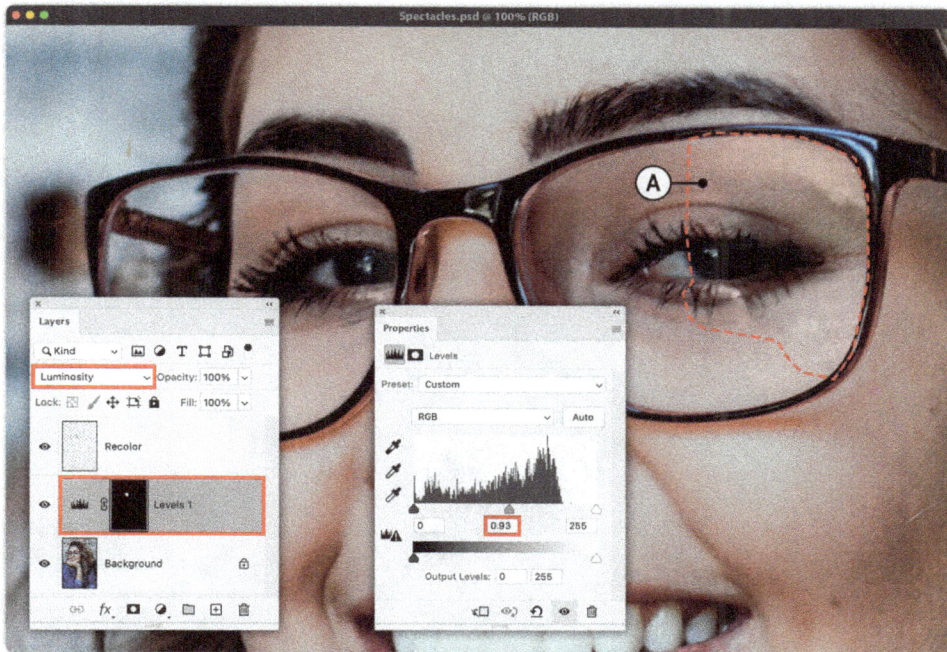

Figure 3.26: Apply a Levels adjustment to correct the skin's brightness

7. Press the *L* key, then click and hold the active tool icon to reveal the other **Lasso** tools and select the **Polygonal Lasso** tool. Set the selection mode to **New**.

8. Create a selection around the right-hand side of the spectacles that includes all of the reflection (**A** in *Figure 3.26*).

9. Then go to **Image → Adjustment → Levels**.

10. When the **Levels** dialog appears, change the midpoint slider to approximately 0.93 (highlighted in *Figure 3.26*). This should correct the highlight and make all the skin behind the glass consistent.

11. If you notice an edge along the boundary of your levels edit, click on the **Levels 1** layer mask in the **Layers** panel and go to **Filter → Blur Gaussian → Blur**. When the dialog appears, set the amount to between 0.5 and 1.0 px. This should blend the boundary of your levels edit.

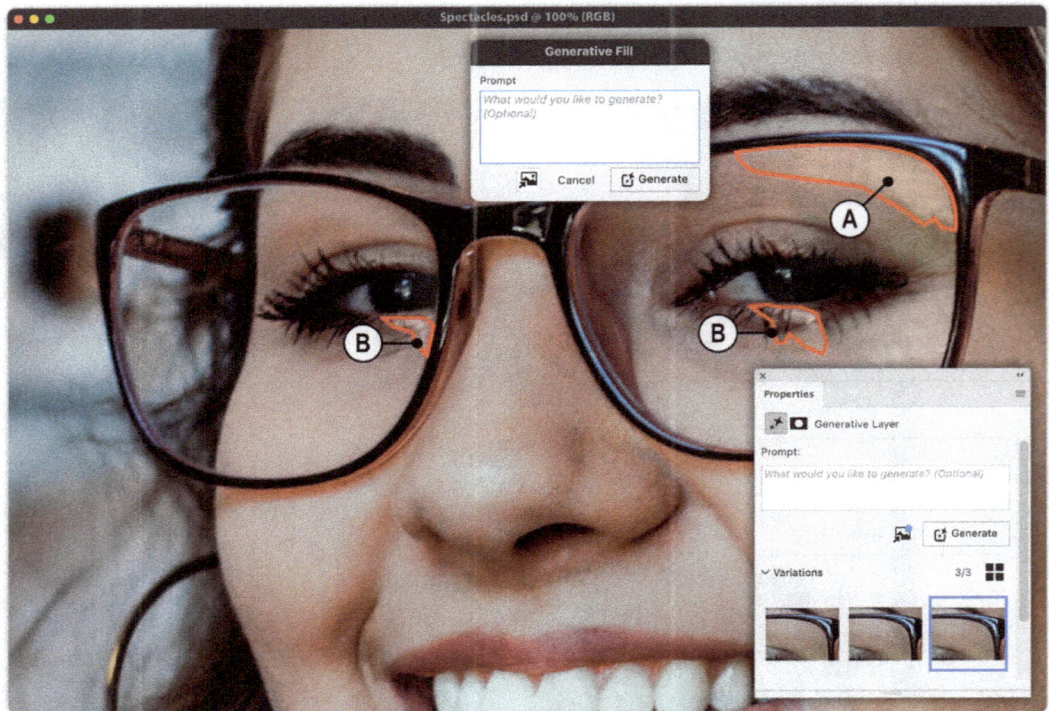

Figure 3.27: The brightest highlights will need to be eliminated with Generative Fill

12. The bright highlight on the upper right-hand side of the right glass is almost too distinct to edit quickly with color and tonal editing alone. It needs retouching. Create a selection around the highlight (**A** in *Figure 3.27*) with the **Polygonal Lasso** tool, ensuring you include a region of unaffected pixels to ensure the edit removes all the highlight.

13. Click on the **Background** layer in the **Layers** panel to make it active. Then go to **Edit →
Generative Fill**. When the dialog appears, click on **Generate** to start the edit. After a few seconds, Photoshop will display three variations in the **Properties** panel. Click on each to view and then decide which version is best.

14. Repeat the same technique. Select bright highlights on the lower eyelids (**B**) and go to **Edit → Generative Fill**.

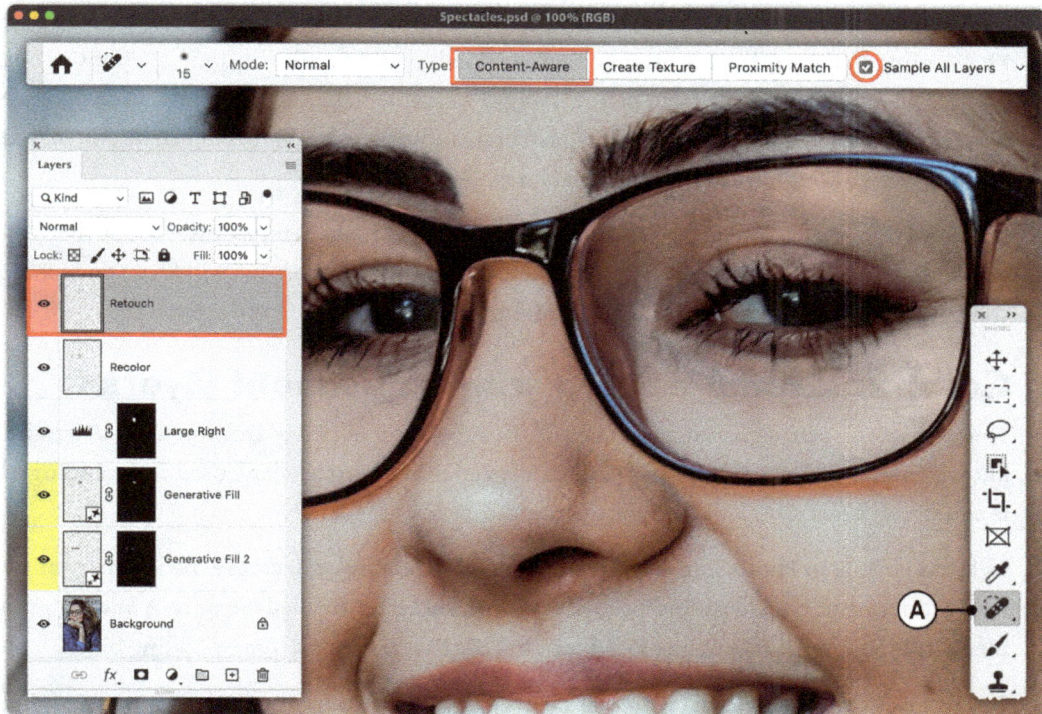

Figure 3.28: Touch up small imperfections with the Spot Healing Brush tool

15. If minor blemishes or borders remain, switch to the **Spot Healing Brush** tool, set **Size** to 15 px and **Hardness** to 0 px, and turn on the **Sample All Layers** checkbox from the **Options** bar.

16. Create a new layer at the top of the layer stack and name it Retouch (highlighted in *Figure 3.28*). Hover your cursor over any affected areas and drag across them to remove blemishes or visible borders.

17. Save the document as a PSD in the 03-Retouch folder and close the document when done.

In this section, we explored techniques that allow us to conceal undesirable content and blemishes captured in the original shot. The **Spot Healing Brush** tool has become one of the most popular retouching tools due to its simplicity, requiring you to simply drag across an image to replace unwanted pixels.

Content-Aware Fill is ideal for replacing larger regions of an image. Starting with a loose selection of a region, the AI-powered **Content-Aware** feature hand-picks the best parts of the existing image to remove subjects from their background.

The **Healing Brush** tool can be used to remove skin blemishes, allowing you to choose a healthy part of the image to sample from before using the sample to blend away unwanted pixels. Next, we'll correct colors and tones with non-destructive adjustment layers that can be edited, hidden, or removed without harming the original image.

In this section, we used an array of healing and retouching tools, in many cases to conceal unwanted content, but also to enhance the appearance of the image. Next, we will focus on techniques that allow you to alter colors and image brightness.

Color and tonal editing with adjustment layers

The term *color* is self-explanatory, if not a little vague. After all, there are more than 18 quadrillion known colors. When we need to reference a specific color, such as one used for branding, there is usually an exact CMYK or RGB formula that describes it visually.

As far as editing in Photoshop is concerned, we can increase or decrease the intensity of a color with *saturation* or boost low-intensity colors with something called *vibrance*. A *hue* is a pure pigment, unaltered by white to create a *tint* or a *shade* that darkens a hue by adding black.

Tone is a less commonly used term that means light. Photoshop commonly characterizes light in 256 grayscale steps from pure black to pure white. Regarding RGB, black has a value of 0 (red 0, green 0, blue 0), while white is defined as 255 (red 255, green 255, blue 255). It's important to be aware of these numbers because Photoshop's selection tools use them as a method for selecting colors, including the **Magic Wand** tool and the **Color Range** dialog, both of which will be covered in this chapter.

How adjustment layers work

Adjustment layers have been around for decades in Photoshop and remain one of the most popular features because of their ability to edit color and tone non-destructively. Believe it or not, these kinds of edits once had to be applied permanently to pixel layers, making the editing process far more tedious, not to mention frustrating.

Photoshop offers 16 color and tonal editing adjustments that can be added to a document layer stack, within which all the edits are stored. This means their visibility can be turned off, or the opacity altered, like all other layer types. Adjustments only affect the appearance of layers lower down in the stack. It's typical to see two or three adjustments in a document, and you can add as many adjustments as necessary, although any more than a dozen can become confusing.

To re-edit an adjustment layer, double-click on the adjustment layer thumbnail in the **Layers** panel. The settings for altering adjustment layers can be found in the **Properties** panel, which appears automatically when a new adjustment is added or re-edited. Adjustment layers come equipped with a layer mask by default to control which parts of a composition they affect.

Quick tonal editing with adjustment layers and blend modes

The simplest adjustments within Photoshop allow you to make edits with just a couple of sliders, which is ideal for a quick, effective edit without any fuss. In this exercise, you will boost the contrast in an image to give it more impact:

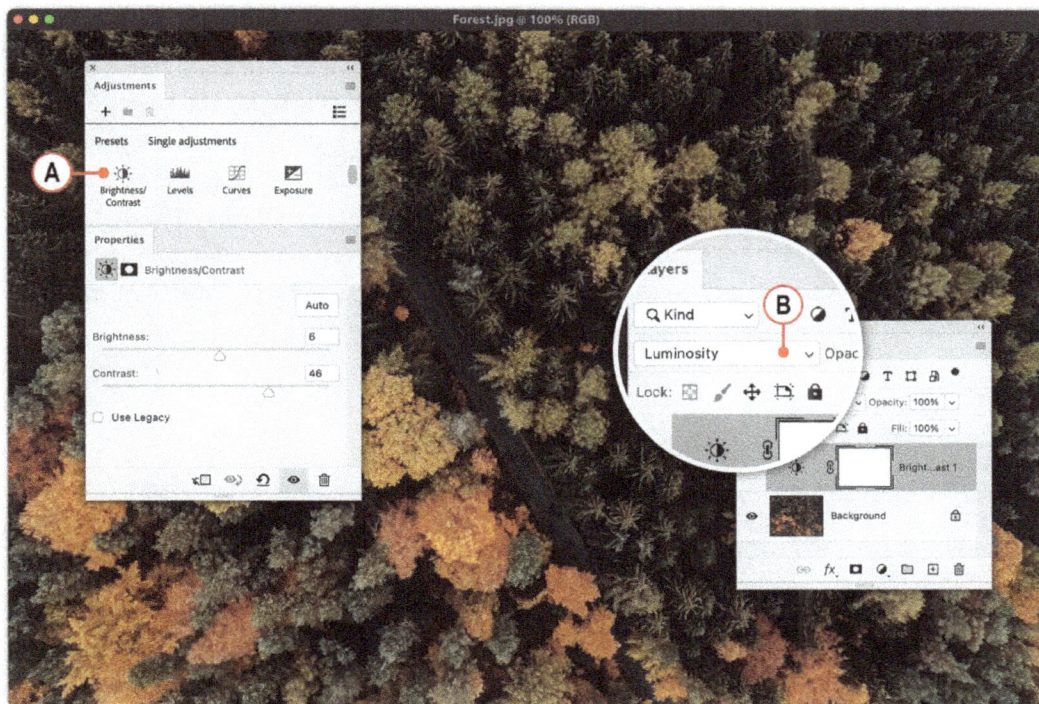

Figure 3.29: The Brightness/Contrast adjustment, set to alter only tonal values

1. Open Forest.jpg from the 03-Retouch folder. This image could benefit from a boost in contrast. Click on the **Brightness/Contrast** icon (**A** in *Figure 3.29*), located in the **Adjustments** panel's top-left corner.

2. The **Properties** panel will display two sliders – one to control **Brightness** and another to alter **Contrast**. Click on the **Auto** button on the top right-hand side of the panel; Photoshop will attempt to improve the image. I scaled back the edits by lowering the **Brightness** slider to 6 and the **Contrast** slider to 46. You can show/hide the layer adjustment visibility by clicking the visibility icon at the bottom of the **Properties** panel.

3. Increasing the image contrast usually intensifies colors. If you show/hide the adjustment layer, you will notice that the autumnal reds and oranges of the treetops have been intensified. With the adjustment layer still active, click on the **Blend Mode** drop-down menu at the top left-hand side of the **Layers** panel (**B**) and choose **Luminosity** from the list. This will ensure that only the brightness levels, referred to as tone, are altered, not the colors.

4. Save the file as a PSD in the 03-Retouch folder and close the document when you're done:

> **Blend modes**
>
> You can think of **blend modes** as transparency effects between the layer you edit and the layers behind it in the composition, or lower down in the layer stack. Divided into six sections, blend modes are set to **Normal** by default and perform no blending. Other blending groups hint toward their purpose by the name of the first mode in each group, such as **Darken** and **Lighten**. **Overlay** provides contrast, while **Difference** inverts the colors in overlapping layers. As you work down each item in a blend group, the result becomes more pronounced.

Removing color casts

A **color cast** is an unwanted wash of color that affects an image. Certain types of light can cause digital cameras to capture a color cast. Outdoor photos are prone to blue color casts, while in indoor photos, yellow is often captured due to artificial lighting. Let's take a look:

1. Open Clifftop.jpg from the 03-Retouch folder.

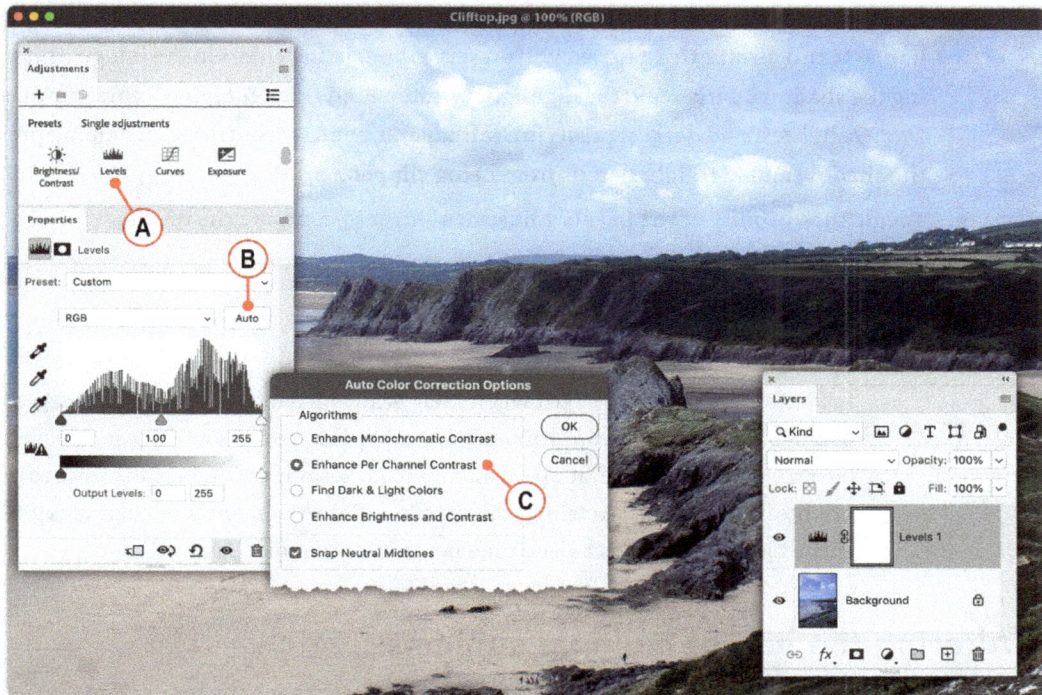

Figure 3.30: The Levels adjustment

2. Go to the **Adjustments** panel and click on the **Levels** adjustment icon (**A** *in Figure 3.30*) to add a new adjustment layer to the **Layers** panel and display the **Levels** settings in the **Properties** panel.

3. Then, press *Alt* (Windows) or *Option* (macOS) and then click on the **Auto** button (**B**) to open the **Auto Color Correction Options** dialog. Click on the **Enhance Per Channel Contrast** radio button (**C**). This will edit the red, green, and blue channel data, enhancing the contrast while removing the blue color cast.

4. Turn on **Snap Neutral Midtones**, and Photoshop will find the average color in the image, referred to as a midtone, and make it a perfect gray. In turn, this will cause other colors to shift and appear more accurate.

5. Experiment with each of the different algorithms to see how they affect the image. **Enhance Monochromatic Contrast** will preserve the existing colors in the image while making the shadows darker and the highlights whiter. **Find Dark & Light Colors** samples the average lightest and darkest pixels in the image, enhancing contrast and helping prevent the shadow and highlight details from being clipped.

6. Toggle the visibility of the **Levels** adjustment layer to compare the results.

7. Save the file as a PSD in the 03-Retouch folder and close the document when you're done.

How Photoshop removes a color cast

In Photoshop, color casts exist when there is an imbalance or loss of the red, green, or blue values that make up an image. Photoshop knows that a healthy image should have an even data distribution for all three colors, from the darkest shadows to the brightest highlights. Stretching the data for all three channels of color along the entire histogram creates balance and neutralizes the color cast.

Altering the hue of multiple subjects

The **Magic Wand** tool selects by color, which is handy for images where, for example, the same color is found throughout, and you want to avoid selecting lots of elements individually. Let's take a closer look:

1. Open Tulips.jpg from the 03-Retouch folder. This image contains dozens of red tulips that need recoloring.

Chapter 3   93

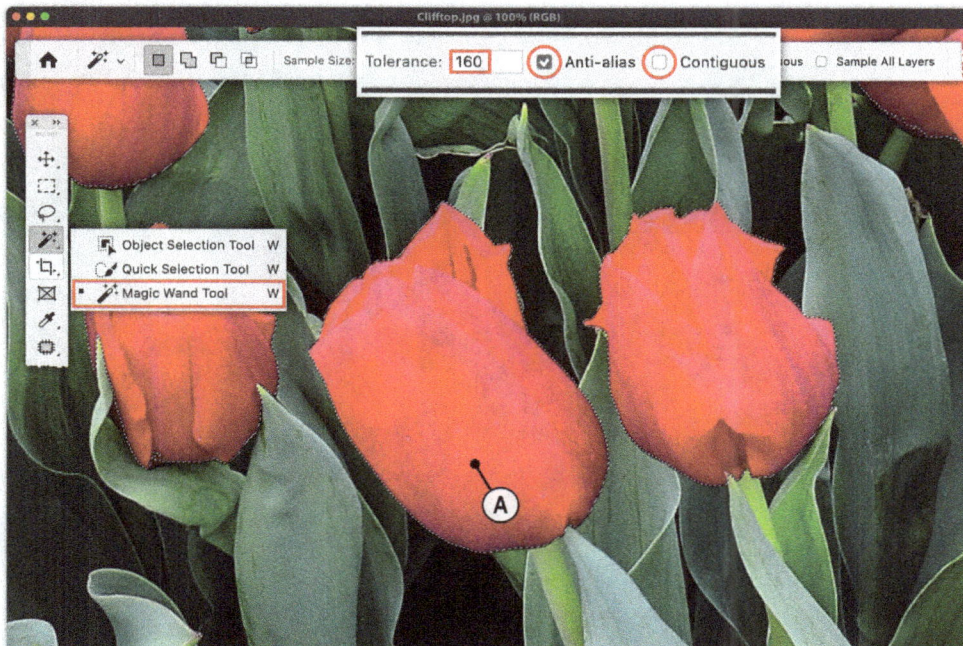

Figure 3.31: Prepare the Magic Wand tool to select the red tulips

2. Press the *W* key. Then, long-press the active tool in the **Tools** panel to reveal the popout to select the **Magic Wand** tool.

3. From the **Options** bar, set the selection mode to **New** and **Tolerance** to 160. Ensure the **Anti-alias** checkbox is active and then turn off the **Contiguous** checkbox so that you can select all the red tulips in the image rather than just the one you click on.

4. Hover your cursor over a red tulip in the center of the image (**A** in *Figure 3.31*). Ensure that your cursor hovers over a mid-range red rather than a very bright or very dark red in the tulip – this will give you a better chance of selecting all the reds in the image. Click to make your selection.

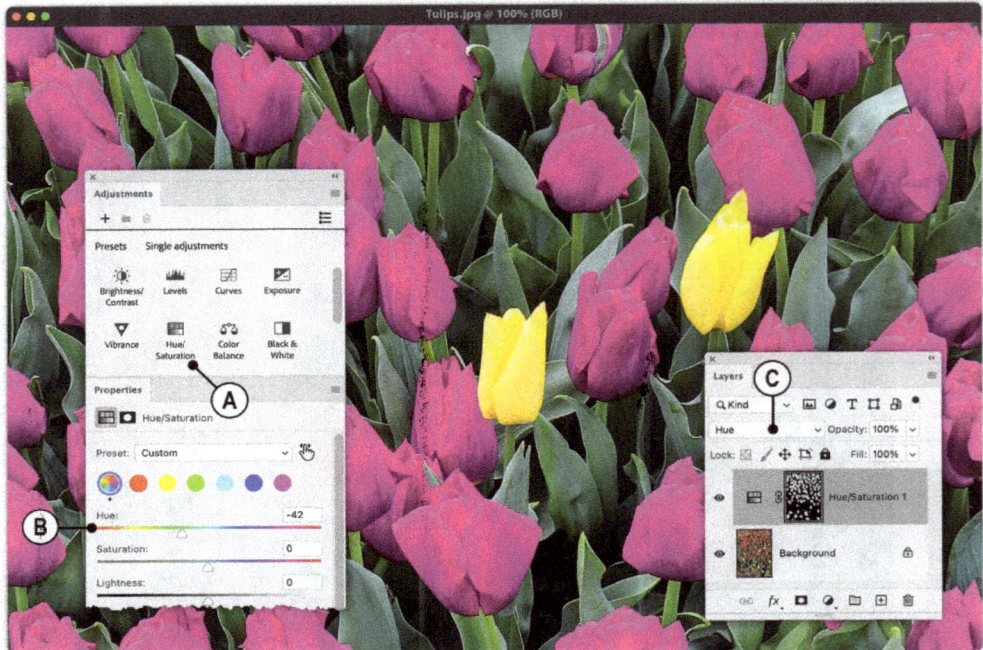

Figure 3.32: Alter the hue of the tulips

5. Click on the **Hue/Saturation** icon (**A** in *Figure 3.32*) in the **Adjustments** panel. Change the **Hue** value to -42 by dragging the slider (**B**) to the left. The red tulips should now appear closer to magenta.

6. Change the blend mode (**C**) of the **Adjustment** layer to **Hue** to make the color edits appear more natural.

7. Save the file as a PSD in the 03-Retouch folder and close the document when you're done.

Magic Wand insider tips

The **Tolerance** value controls how similar a selected color should be to the original pixel you click on. The higher the value, the broader the range of similar colors you'll select. Try doubling or halving the **Tolerance** value to find the appropriate selection quickly. When **Contiguous** is active, Photoshop searches for similar colors from the point where you click with the **Magic Wand** tool, but when it is inactive, Photoshop searches the entire image for similar colors.

The simplest method for color matching

On the face of it, changing one color to look exactly like another should be simple. However, it often proves to be the opposite. Avoid getting bogged down by a bewildering array of adjustment layers and instead try this technique:

1. Open `Respray.jpg` and `Porche_Blue.jpg` from the `03-Retouch` folder. The paintwork of this car needs to be altered from orange to a client-specified blue.

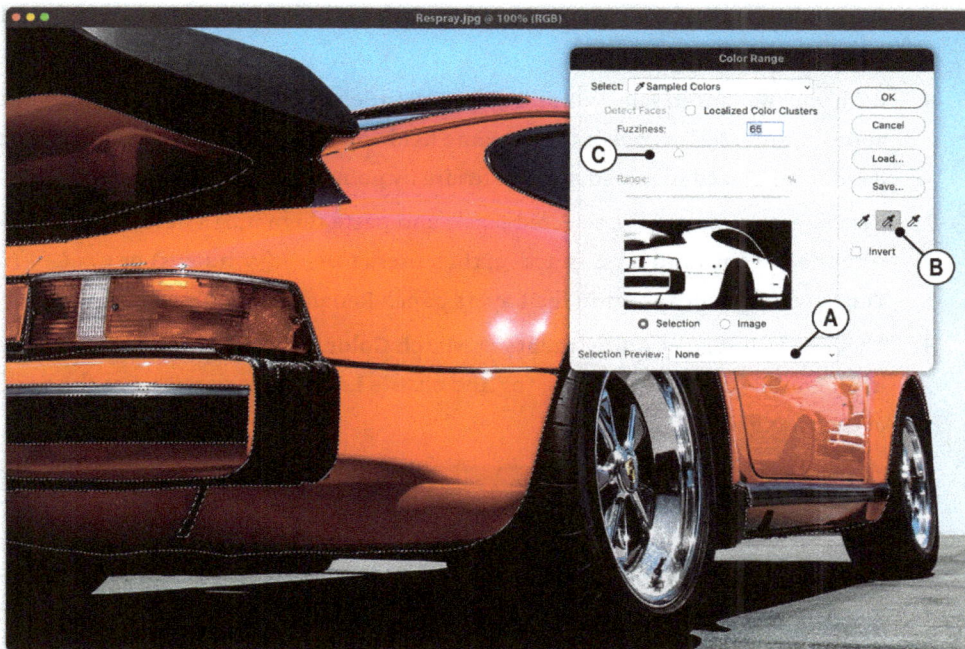

Figure 3.33: Create a selection of the orange paintwork

2. Ensure the `Respray.jpg` file is active. Switch to the **Lasso** tool by pressing *L*. From the **Options** bar, set the selection mode to **New** and leave the **Anti-alias** checkbox turned on. Then, create a very loose selection of the car that includes the orange paintwork but excludes details such as the tires and ground. This should help make the next stage of the selection process more accurate.

3. With the selection in place, go to **Select → Color Range**. When the dialog appears, ensure that the **Invert** checkbox is inactive and the selection preview is set to **None** from the drop-down menu at the bottom of the dialog (**A** in *Figure 3.33*).

4. Hover your cursor over a mid-range orange in the car's paintwork in the image window and click to set the sample. The small preview in the dialog will display the white regions that have been selected. Switch to the **Add to Sample** tool (**B**). Hover your cursor over the rear end of the car in a patch of orange paintwork, then click and drag through only a variety of oranges in the car. As you do, the preview window will show the selected regions grow.

5. When you are happy that a large portion of the orange has been selected, drag the **Fuzziness** slider (**C**) to increase or decrease the number of similar colors you have selected. When almost all of the oranges have been selected, click **OK**. You can always refine the missing portions later.

6. With your enhanced selection still active, go to **Select → Save Selection**. When the dialog appears, enter `Paintwork` into the **Name** field and click **OK**. Saving a selection can prove handy if you need to reload it in the future by going to **Select → Load Selection**.

7. Next, create a copy of the selected pixels and paste them into a new layer. To do this, ensure the **Background** layer is active, then press *Ctrl + J* (Windows) or *Cmd + J* (macOS). The new layer will appear in the **Layers** panel. Rename it `Recolor`.

8. Then, go to **Image → Adjustments → Match Color**. Set the **Source** drop-down menu (**A** in *Figure 3.34*) to `Porche_Blue.jpg` and ensure **Layer** is set to reference the background of that same file. Click **OK**.

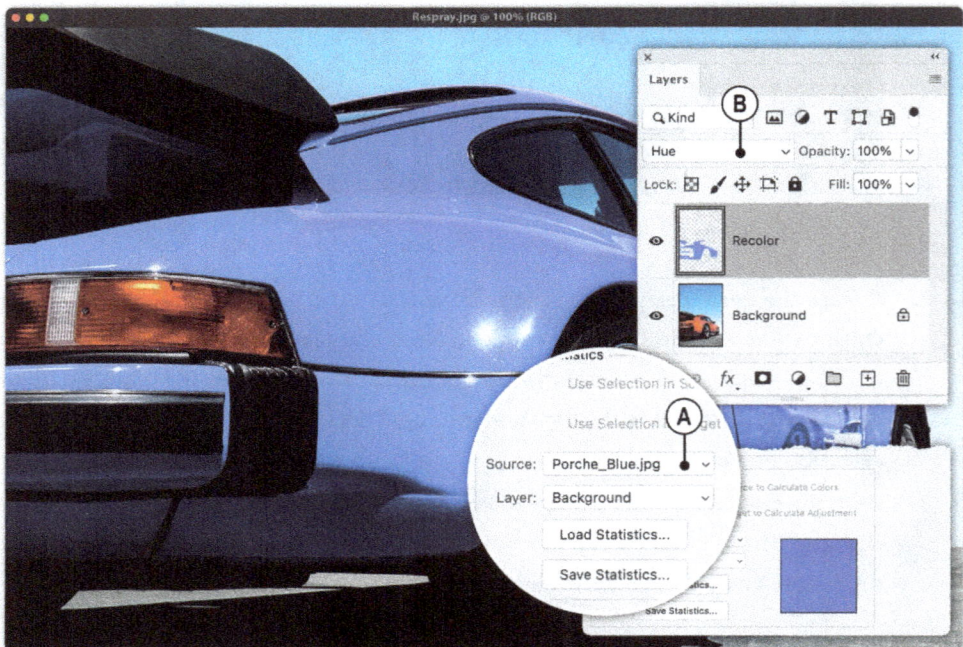

Figure 3.34: The Match Color feature is a highly effective method for altering colors

9. Finally, change the blend mode of the **Recolor** layer to **Hue (B)**.

10. Save the file as a PSD in the 03-Retouch folder and close the document when you're done.

This is the simplest method I've discovered for color matching in Photoshop. It does come with one downside, however: it requires a permanent edit in the form of the **Match Color** feature. **Match Color** won't work with smart objects, which is one of the reasons why the original selection was saved. If you need to match a different color, you can go to **Select → Load Selection** and choose the saved selection from the **Channel** drop-down menu.

Matching subjects to new backdrops

Removing an unwanted background from a subject and placing it in a new photographic environment can be challenging. Daylight, shadows, and color temperature often differ; even subtle differences can make a photomontage appear unconvincing. In this exercise, we'll explore a proven technique for tackling all of these challenges:

1. Open Subject.psd and Boardwalk.jpg from the 03-Retouch folder.

2. Right-click on the **Model** layer name in the **Layers** panel to reveal the context menu. Choose **Duplicate Layer** from the list.

3. When the dialog appears, ensure the **As** field reads Model, select Boardwalk.jpg from the **Document** drop-down menu, and click **OK**. This will create a copy of the image and transfer it to the other document open in Photoshop.

4. Click on the **Document Tab** for Boardwalk.jpg to ensure the image is transferred across. Then, close the Subject.psd document.

5.   Go to **Edit → Free Transform**; from the **Options** bar, reduce the scale of **Width** and **Height** to 60.00% (*Figure 3.35*). Then, drag the image of the woman to the center of the image, with her shoulders just above the horizon line.

Figure 3.35: Transfer the subject to the new composition

6.   Click on **Black & White** from the **Adjustments** panel (**A** in *Figure 3.36*) to make the image appear grayscale. This helps to judge whether the subject's highlights and shadows (brightest and darkest regions) match the new background.

Figure 3.36: A Black & White adjustment helps judge highlights and shadows

7.   Ensure the **Model** layer is active in the **Layers** panel, then click on the **Levels** adjustment. Then click the **Apply Clipping Layer** button at the bottom of the **Properties** panel (circled in *Figure 3.36*) to make the **Levels** edits only affect the **Model** layer.

8.   In the **Properties** panel, increase the **Black Point** slider to 6 and reduce the **White Point** slider to 245 to increase the intensity of shadows and highlights to better match those in the background image.

9.   Delete the **Black & White** adjustment in the **Layers** panel when done.

10. Rename the **Levels** adjustment Lighting and change its **Blend Mode** setting to **Luminosity**. This will restrict edits to the layer's brightness and maintain the layer's colors.

11. Click on **Curves** from the **Adjustments** panel (**A** in *Figure 3.37*). Then click the **Apply Clipping Layer** button at the bottom of the **Properties** panel.

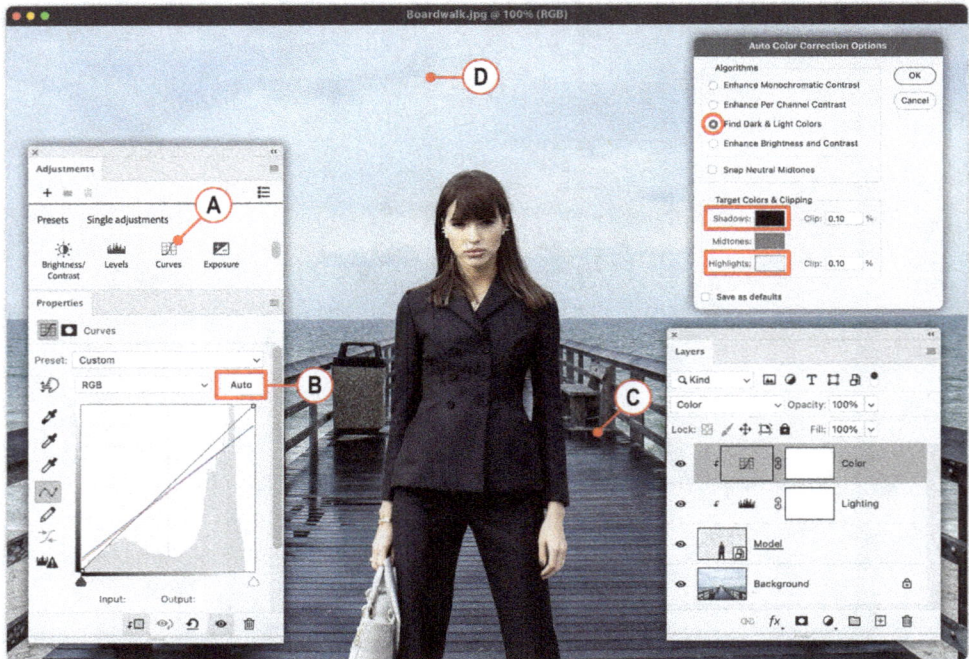

Figure 3.37: Adjust the color of the subject with a Curves adjustment

12. Hold *Alt* (Windows) or *Option* (macOS) and click on the **Auto** button (**B**) in the **Properties** panel to open the **Auto Color Correction Options** dialog.

13. Click the **Find Dark & Light Colors** radio button, then select the **Shadows** swatch and hover your cursor over a dark area of the background, such as the shadows under a bench (**C**). Click to sample. This will adjust the black/shadow content of the **Model** layer to match the background better. Click **OK** to close the **Color Picker** dialog.

14. From the **Auto Color Correction Options** dialog, click on the **Highlights** swatch, hover your cursor over a white region of the clouds in the background layer (**D**), and click to sample. Click **OK** to close the **Color Picker** dialog and then click **OK** to close the **Auto Color Correction Options** dialog.

15. Rename the **Curves** adjustment Color and change its **Blend Mode** setting to **Color**, restricting edits to the **Model** layer's colors.

16. Click on **Hue/Saturation** from the **Adjustments** panel. From the **Properties** panel, decrease the **Saturation** slider to -15 (**A** in *Figure 3.38*).

Figure 3.38: Desaturate the subject's original skin tones (inset)

17. Click the **Apply Clipping Layer** button at the bottom of the **Properties** panel, rename the **Hue/Saturation** adjustment to Desaturate, and change its **Blending Mode** setting to **Color**.

18. Save the file as a PSD in the 03-Retouch folder and close it when done.

In this final section, we utilized adjustment layers, smart objects, and precise selections to accurately modify image colors, eliminate color casts, and enhance image tonality. We also explored a technique for transferring a subject to a new background while matching the color and tone.

Summary

In this chapter, we edited the canvas by straightening crooked images, trimming away unwanted content, and extending the size of an image with content-aware technology. This is a crucial step to reduce file size and progress with only the content you need.

Then, we explored several techniques to conceal blemishes or unwanted content in photos with tools such as **Spot Healing Brush** and **Clone Stamp**. Both are well equipped to conceal smaller details such as cables. We also looked at **Content-Aware Fill** when the regions we need to conceal are larger. The **Healing Brush** tool is adept at repairing skin blemishes that seamlessly blend in with their surrounding pixels. Most of these techniques utilize multiple layers, with new layers being created to separate edits from the original image for flexibility.

Finally, we used adjustment layers to perform non-destructive color and tonal edits, such as brightening an image, boosting contrast, and altering hues. In the next chapter, we will become familiar with a wide range of masking techniques to reveal and conceal layers rather than delete them.

Get This Book's PDF Version and Exclusive Extras

UNLOCK NOW

Scan the QR code (or go to packtpub.com/unlock). Search for this book by name, confirm the edition, and then follow the steps on the page.

Note: Keep your invoice handy. Purchases made directly from Packt don't require one.

4

Masking and Cutouts

As we have already seen, Photoshop is a powerful and versatile application. However, it can be unforgiving if you make permanent edits, such as erasing layer content. In this chapter, we'll explore masking techniques to reveal and conceal layer content, rather than deleting it. Masks can be applied to almost any layer type in Photoshop and are commonly used when applying adjustment layers to control the parts of an image that the adjustment affects.

We'll start by removing a background from an image and then placing the "masked" subject into a new background. This will allow you to experience how an accurate selection is used as the basis for a **layer mask** intended to conceal the background while revealing the subject.

Using this masking technique, we'll apply it in the context of an adjustment layer to create a black-and-white isolation, with the subject in color and the background in grayscale. Then, you'll have the opportunity to edit the layer mask with painting tools to fine-tune its accuracy.

Masks can also blend the best parts of two or more images, which is ideal when you have a group photo and one person is looking the wrong way or has their eyes closed. You'll create the complete masked version by combining each source image.

After accomplishing these fundamental masking techniques, you'll learn how to extract hair from a background using a dedicated masking workspace, enhance fine details, and remove rogue background colors to create a high-quality cutout.

We'll then experiment with different applications of layer masks, including using text as a mask, layer effects that use luminance to conceal parts of an image, and masks composed of vector shapes. In this chapter, we'll cover the following topics:

- Applying and editing a basic layer mask
- Unlinking images and masks
- Masking hair
- Working with vector masks

Technical requirements

The project files for this chapter can be found at `https://packt.link/gbz/9781806021710`.

Applying and editing a basic layer mask

Layer masks control the visibility of image content in Photoshop and can be applied to nearly any layer type. One benefit of using a mask is that it eliminates the need to delete image content, allowing for re-editing at any stage during the production process. Masks come in various forms, including standard layer masks, clipping masks, vector masks, and **Blend If** masks.

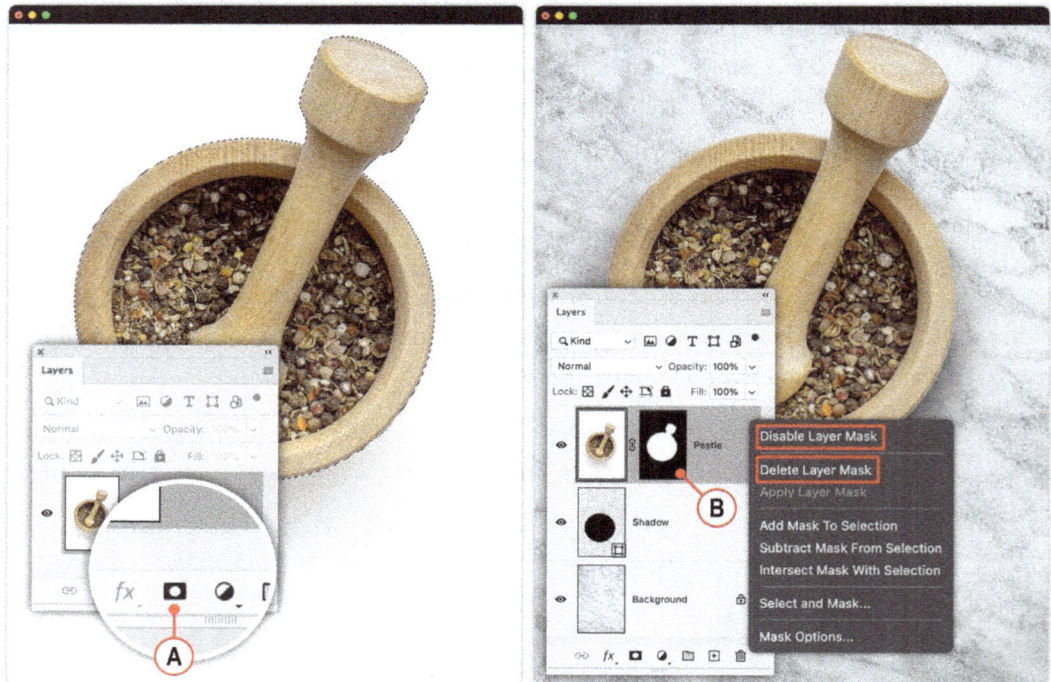

Figure 4.1: Examples of selection used as the basis for layer masks in Photoshop

As shown in *Figure 4.1*, layer masks are commonly applied with an active selection in place, and by clicking the **Add a Mask** button at the bottom of the **Layers** panel (**A**). Once assigned, a layer mask denotes concealed regions in black and revealed portions of a layer in white (**B**) that were previously selected. As such, they are commonly composed of pixels and can be edited with any number of painting tools by painting with black to conceal pixels or white to reveal layer content.

Layer masks can be deactivated or deleted at any time. Right-click on a layer mask thumbnail and select **Disable Layer Mask** or **Delete Layer Mask** from the context menu (shown in *Figure 4.1*). Disabled layer masks are indicated by a red cross on the layer mask thumbnail, which temporarily reveals all layer content. When deleting a layer mask, you can choose to apply it first. However, any regions hidden by the mask will be permanently removed as you delete the layer mask, so be certain you won't need this content in the future.

Photoshop allows you to store multiple layers within a layer group. This offers several benefits, including the ability to add a single group mask that affects anything within it (**A** in *Figure 4.2*):

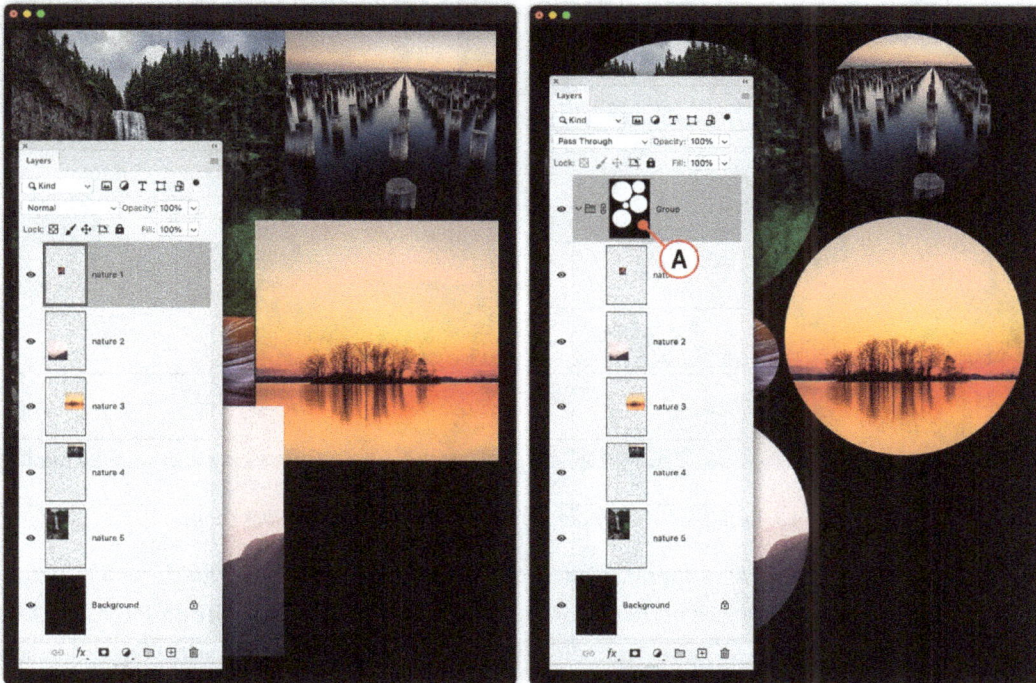

Figure 4.2: Masks can also be applied to layer groups

This allows for further flexibility in the editing process as you can reposition, scale, and rotate individual layers in a group independently from each other. For challenging masking projects, you can even add a layer mask to a layer within a group containing a group mask.

Clipping masks use the content of an underlying layer to determine which parts of that layer remain visible. For example, you can use an editable text layer as a clipping mask, position a photo above it in the layer stack, and *clip* the photo to the text layer. The photo would only be visible where text is present in the underlying layer. This allows for text to be edited and the photo to be repositioned relatively easily.

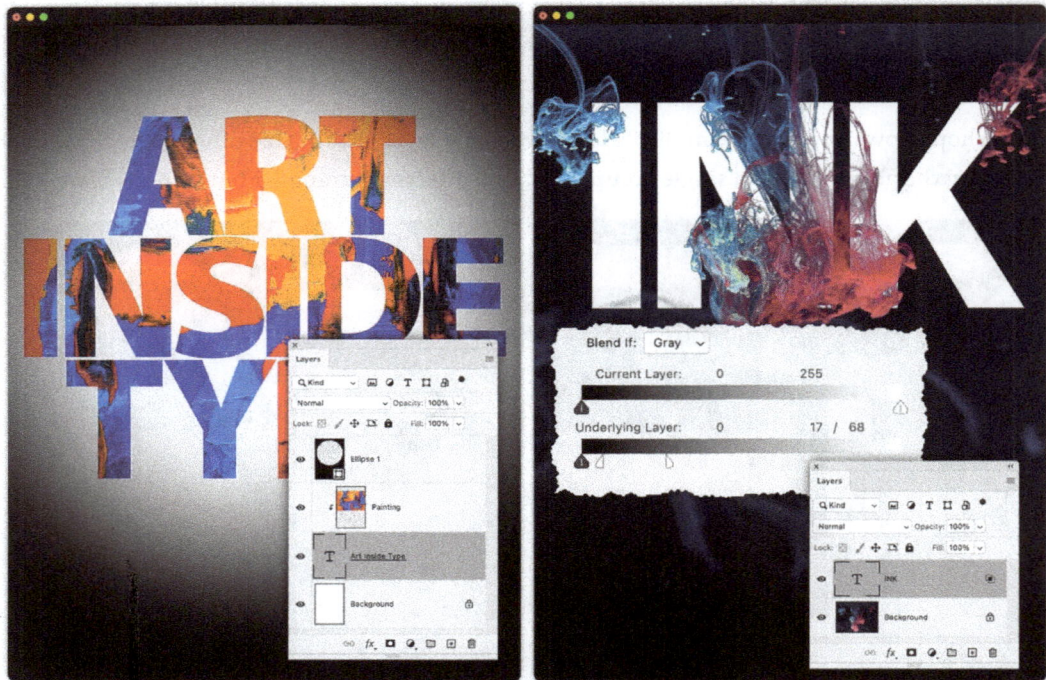

Figure 4.3: Examples of a clipping mask (left) and a Blend If mask (right)

Blend If is a type of mask that is applied from the **Effects** dialog box. It analyzes the active source layer and determines which part of that layer to display, based on whether the underlying pixels in other layers in the stack are darker than those in the source layer. As a scenario, you could use a blend on an active layer containing a logo that is black with a layer below it in the layer stack that contains a photo of clouds. By altering one of the **Blend If** sliders, you can make lighter portions of the cloud show through the logo to give the impression that the logo is in the sky.

As you can see, the variety of masks is vast and offers incredible flexibility to the editing process. Documents saved in PSD format can be imported into applications such as Adobe InDesign, which can detect the presence of a layer mask to apply features such as text wrap. You will find the ability to mask in almost any Adobe application, and the principles remain similar.

Masking power shortcuts

You can include the following shortcuts in your masking workflow to save valuable time:

- **Quick Masks**, which has been in Photoshop for decades, lets you preview an active selection as a red overlay by pressing Q, and return to your selection by pressing Q again. You can also achieve a similar outcome by pressing backslash (|) with a layer mask thumbnail active.

- Temporarily disable a layer mask to reveal all layer content by holding *Shift* as you click on the layer mask thumbnail and repeat to enable the layer mask again.

- You can load a layer mask as a new selection by holding *Ctrl* (Windows) or *Cmd* (macOS) as you click on the layer mask thumbnail. Press *Ctrl + Alt* (Windows) or *Cmd + Option* (macOS) as you click to load the layer mask and subtract it from an active selection. Hold *Ctrl + Alt + Shift* (Windows) or *Cmd + Option + Shift* (macOS) as you click to load the layer mask and intersect an active selection, which leaves only the regions where they overlap as an active selection.

- With a layer active and no selection active, press *Alt* (Windows) or *Option* (macOS) as you click on the layer mask icon to conceal all layer content.

- Invert an active layer mask by pressing *Ctrl + I* (Windows) or *Cmd + I* (macOS). Press *Alt + Backspace* (Windows) or *Option + Delete* (macOS) to fill an active layer mask with the foreground color. Conversely, press *Ctrl + Backspace* (Windows) or *Cmd + Delete* (macOS) to fill the active layer mask with the background color.

- Copy a layer mask by pressing *Alt* while dragging (Windows) or *Option* while dragging (macOS) the layer mask thumbnail to a different layer or layer group.

Using masks to cut out image backgrounds

In this first exercise, you will create an accurate selection of a subject in a photo and then hide the region beyond the selection with a mask:

1. Open `Pestle.jpg` and `Marble.jpg` from the `04-Masking` folder.

2. Ensure the pestle image is active. Switch to the **Object Selection** tool. Click on the **Select Subject** button in the options bar to create a selection of the pestle.

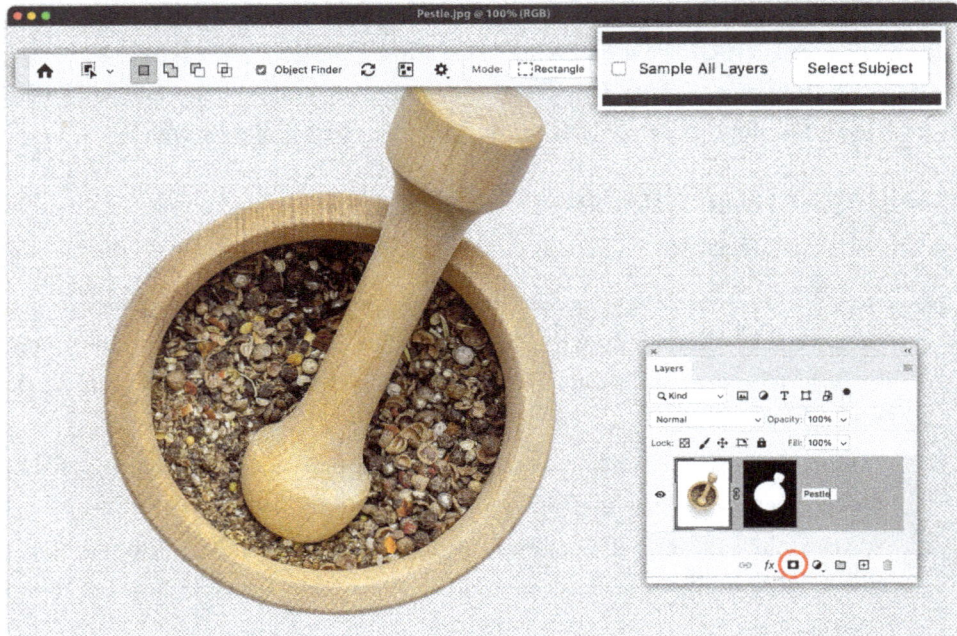

Figure 4.4: The original image with the layer mask added

3. Next, click the **Add a Mask** icon at the bottom of the **Layers** panel (circled in *Figure 4.4*) to hide the white background, which is not part of the current selection. The mask will now appear adjacent to the layer thumbnail in the **Layers** panel.

4. Double-click on the layer name to open the type entry field. In the field, enter Pestle as the new name. Press *Enter* to confirm the name change.

5. Next, right-click on the layer name in the **Layers** panel to reveal the context menu. Choose **Duplicate Layer...** from the list:

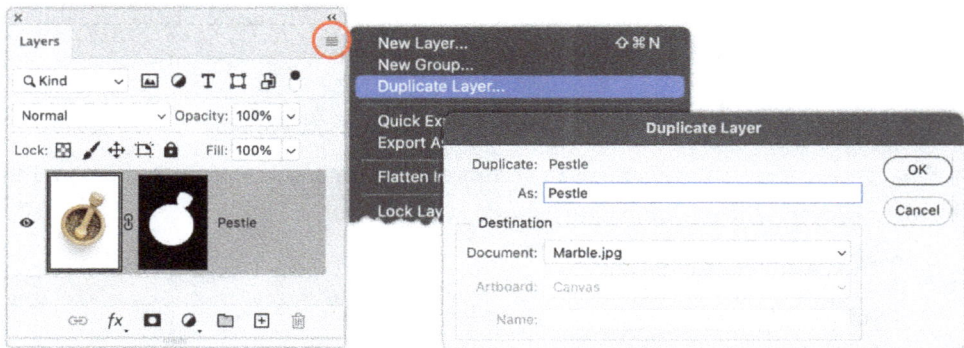

Figure 4.5: Duplicate the pestle layer and transfer it to the marble image

6. When the dialog appears, ensure the **As** field reads `Pestle`, select `Marble.jpg` from the **Document** drop-down menu, and click **OK**. This will create a copy of the pestle image and transfer it to the other document open in Photoshop.

7. Click on the **Document** tab for `Marble.jpg` and switch to the **Move** tool. Reposition the **Pestle** layer centrally.

8. Click on the **Background** layer in the **Layers** panel to make it active. Next, select the **Ellipse** tool from the **Tools** panel by pressing the *U* key and then long-press on the active tool icon to reveal the popout. Click on the **Ellipse** tool.

9. From the options bar, set **Mode** to **Shape**, click on the **Fill** icon, and set the color to black (red `0`, green `0`, blue `0`). Click on the **Stroke** icon and choose **None** from the pop-out menu.

10. Hover your cursor over the top-left edge of the pestle bowl, click and hold down the left mouse button, and drag down to the left-hand side of the pestle bowl, matching its overall width and height before releasing the left mouse button:

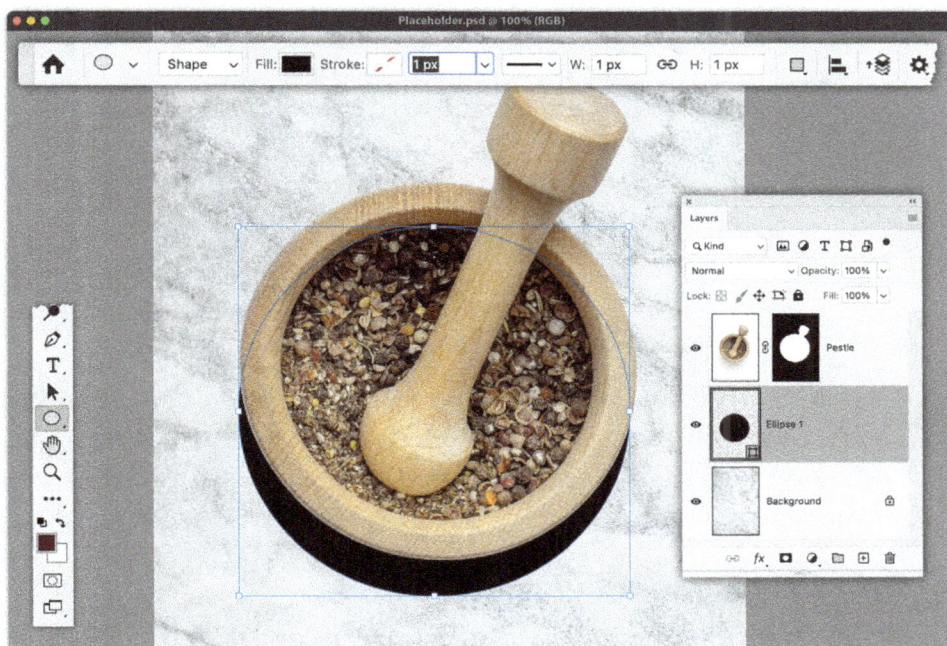

Figure 4.6: Add a black ellipse under the Pestle layer

11. Change the new shape layer name to Shadow.

12. Switch to the **Move** tool and reposition the black elliptical shape to the lower left-hand side of the bowl. Go to the **Properties** panel and click on the **Mask Properties** icon (**A** in *Figure 4.7*) to reveal the settings. Increase the **Feather** to 90 px:

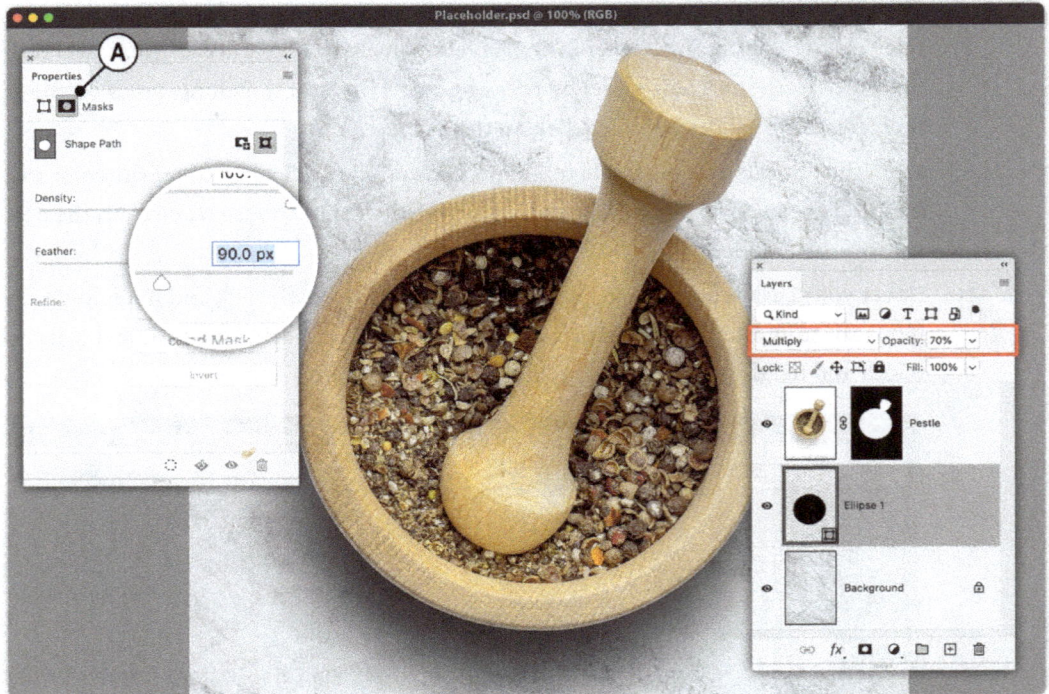

Figure 4.7: The completed image cutout shown on a new backdrop

13. Finally, change the **Shadow** layer blend mode to **Multiply** from the **Blend Mode** menu in the **Layers** panel and reduce the layer's **Opacity** value to around 70% (highlighted in *Figure 4.7*). Go to **File → Save** and name the file Food-A as a PSD file in the working folder. Close both documents when done; there is no need to save the Pestle.jpg image.

Applying masks to adjustment layers

In this masking exercise, you will use a selection of a pumpkin as the basis for a black-and-white effect that is controlled by a layer mask:

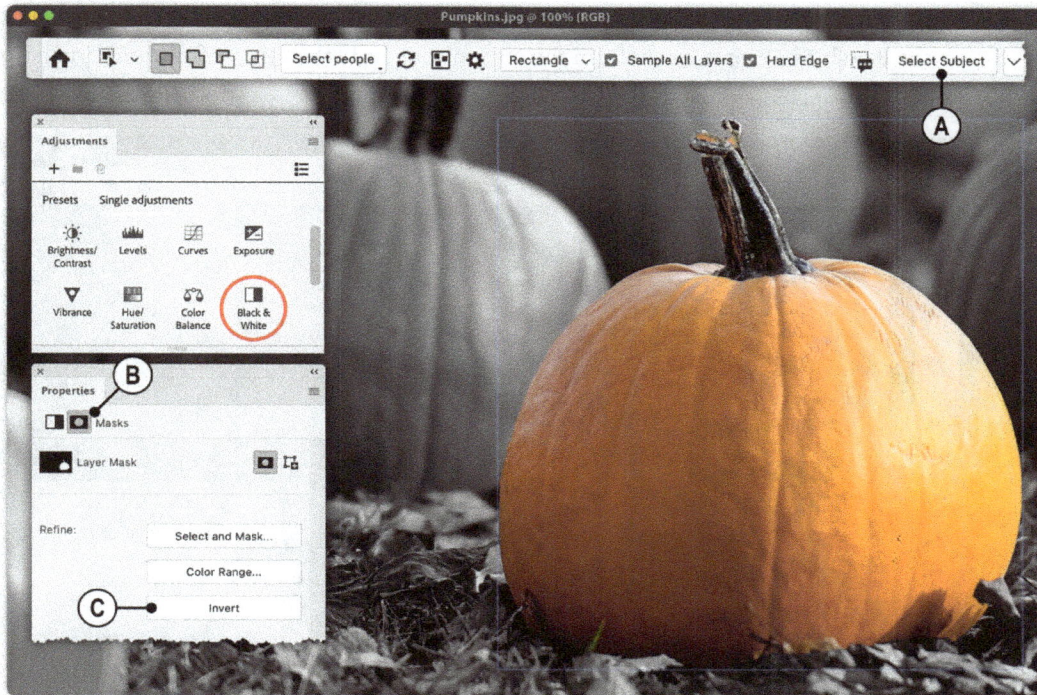

Figure 4.8: Select the pumpkin and apply a black and white adjustment

1. Open Pumpkins.jpg from the 04-Masking folder. Switch to the **Object Selection** tool. Click on the **Select Subject** button (**A** in *Figure 4.8*) in the options bar to create a selection of the pumpkin.

2. With the selection in place, go to the **Adjustments** panel and click on the **Black & White** adjustment icon to add a new adjustment layer. By default, this will make the pumpkin appear grayscale.

3. Click on the **Masks** icon in the **Properties** panel (**B**), and then click on the **Invert** button (**C**); it will display only the selected pumpkin in color and the rest of the image in grayscale.

4. You can now fine-tune the layer mask. Switch to the **Brush** tool by pressing the *B* key. Click on the **Brush Tip Preset** menu from the options bar and select the **Soft Round** brush tip from the preset list. Adjust the brush's **Size** value to around 35 px and set **Hardness** to 90%:

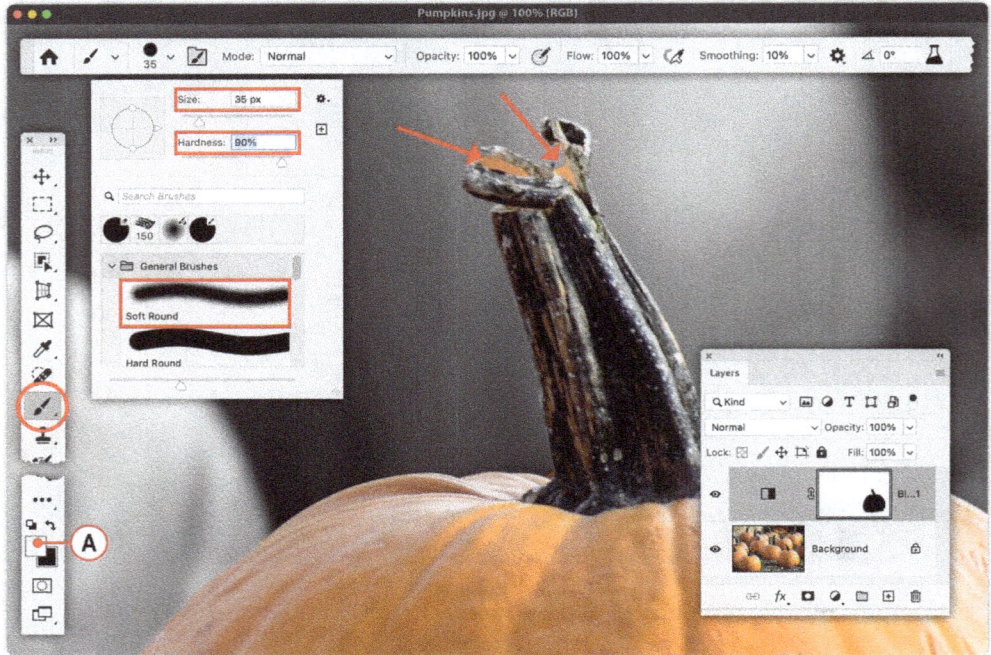

Figure 4.9: Select the pumpkin and apply a black and white adjustment

5. Then, press the *D* key to reset the **Foreground** and **Background** colors to black and white, with white now being the **Foreground** color you will paint with (**A** in *Figure 4.9*). Paint with white around the pumpkin's stem to reveal the grayscale effect.

6. Press the *X* key to *exchange* (swap) the foreground color to black and paint to remove the grayscale effect from the leaves around the pumpkin's base.

7. Once completed, go to **File** → **Save**, navigate to the 04-Masking folder, and name the document Pumpkins.psd. Then, close all the documents.

Retouching with a layer mask

Imagine this scenario: you take a photo, only to realize later that someone had their eyes closed or someone else is in the shot that you want to remove. By combining two images, you can get the best of both with layer masks:

1. Go to **File → Scripts → Load Files into Stack....**

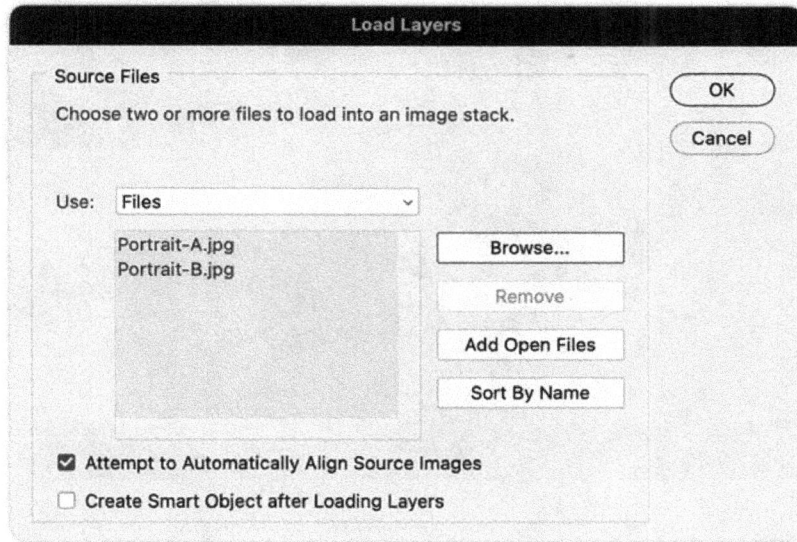

Figure 4.10: Combine separate files into a single document

2. When the dialog appears, click on **Browse...** and navigate to the 04-Masking folder. Select Portrait-A.jpg and Portrait-B.jpg. Turn on the **Attempt to Automatically Align Source Images** checkbox and click **OK** when done. The **Layers** panel will now be populated with the two original photos.

3. Click on **Portrait-B.jpg** layer's **Visibility** icon in the **Layers** panel to hide it (**A** in *Figure 4.11*) to reveal the transparent edges that need trimming away:

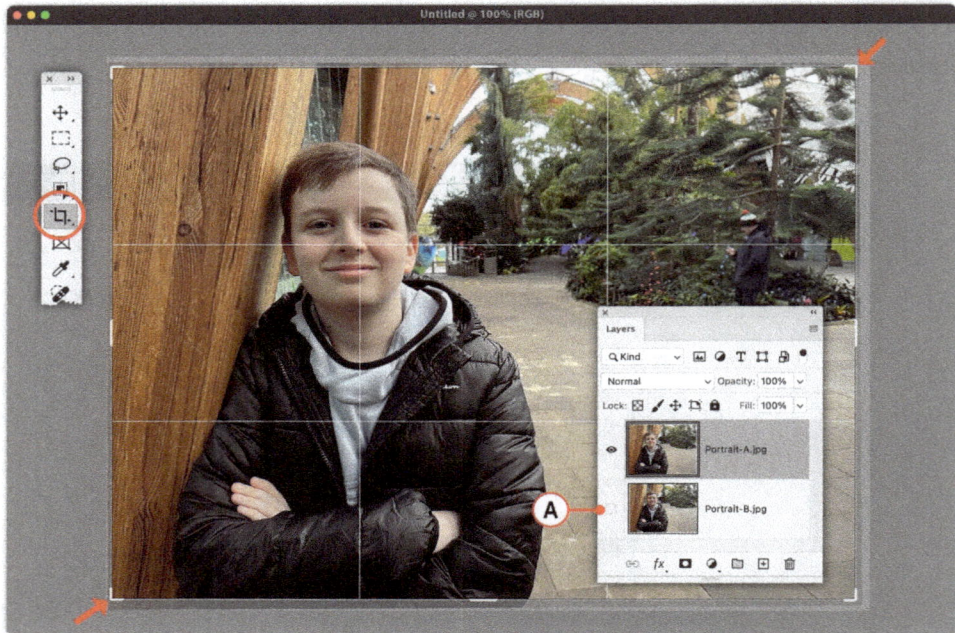

Figure 4.11: Trim the transparent regions along the edge of the image

4. Click on the **Crop** tool (circled in *Figure 4.11*), then drag the bottom-left corner of the crop frame toward the center of the canvas until all the transparency is outside the crop frame.

5. Use the same technique for the top-right corner of the crop frame, dragging it toward the center of the image until all transparent pixels are outside of the crop frame. Click on the **Commit** icon in the **Options** bar to apply the edits.

6. Turn on the visibility of the **Portrait-B.jpg** layer. Then, click on the **Portrait-A.jpg** layer in the **Layers** panel to ensure it is active.

7. Click the **Add Layer Mask** icon at the bottom of the **Layers** panel. When you add a layer mask without an active selection, the mask appears white, revealing all content in that layer, allowing you to paint black in the layer mask and hide parts of the layer.

8. Press the *B* key to switch to the **Brush** tool. From the **Options** bar, click on the **Brush Trip Preset** menu. Set the brush's **Size** value to 300 px, **Hardness** to 0%, and **Opacity** to 100% (**A** in *Figure 4.12*):

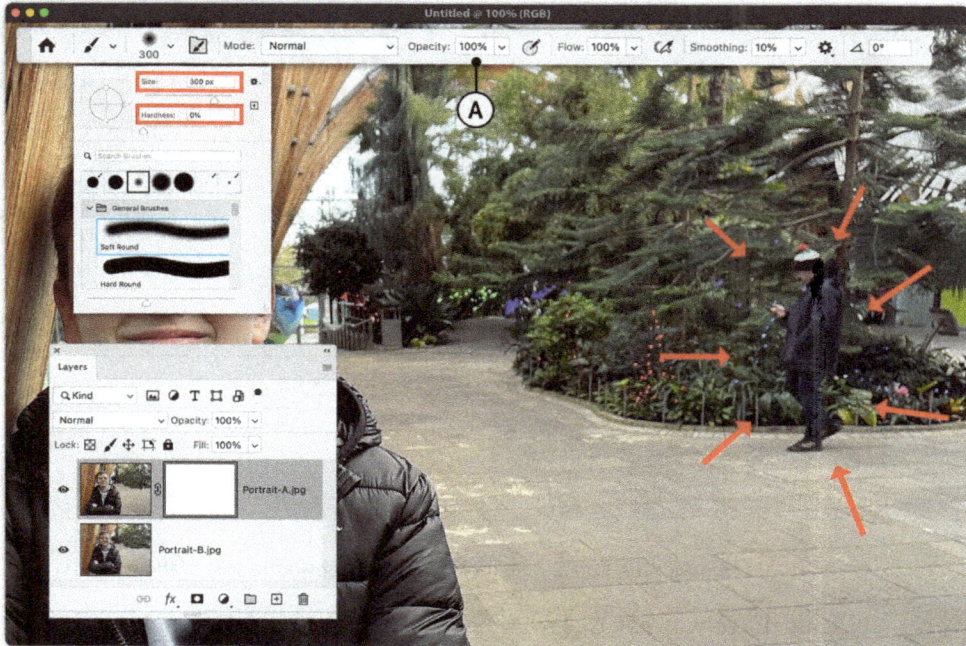

Figure 4.12: Add a Layer mask to hide parts of the front-most layer in the image

9. Then, press the *D* key to reset the default colors and set black as the active color, and then press the *X* key to set black as the foreground color. Painting black in the layer mask will conceal parts of the image in that layer and, in turn, reveal parts of the layer below in the layer stack.

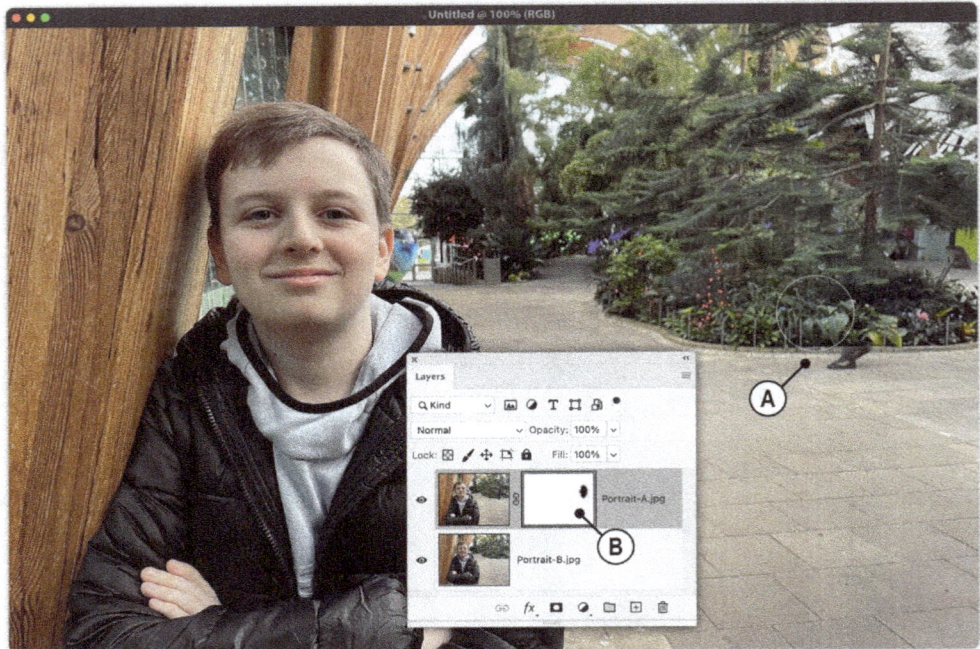

Figure 4.13: Conceal the person on the right-hand side of the image

10. Click and drag the **Brush** tool over the person on the far right-hand side of the image to conceal them (**A** in *Figure 4.13*). This will reveal the **Portrait-B.jpg** layer below it, containing no people. In the layer mask thumbnail, you will also notice a black region where your brush marks have been added (**B**).

11. Once the person on the right-hand side of the image has been completely removed, go to **File → Save** and browse to the 04-Masking folder. Name the file Merge-Portrait, click **Save** when done, and close the document.

Working with gradient masks

We have now established through several exercises that masks can be edited with a painting tool, such as the **Brush** tool. However, you can also use the **Gradient** tool to create smooth transitioning masks. In this exercise, you'll blend a landscape with a night sky:

1. Open Mountain.jpg from the 04-Masking folder.

2. Press the *C* key to activate the crop tools. Then, long-press on the active tool icon to reveal the sub-list and click the **Crop** tool to make it active.

3. Choose **Generative Expand** from the **Fill** drop-down menu in the options bar (highlighted in *Figure 4.14*). This will use a generative credit if you are not on the All Apps Creative Cloud plan:

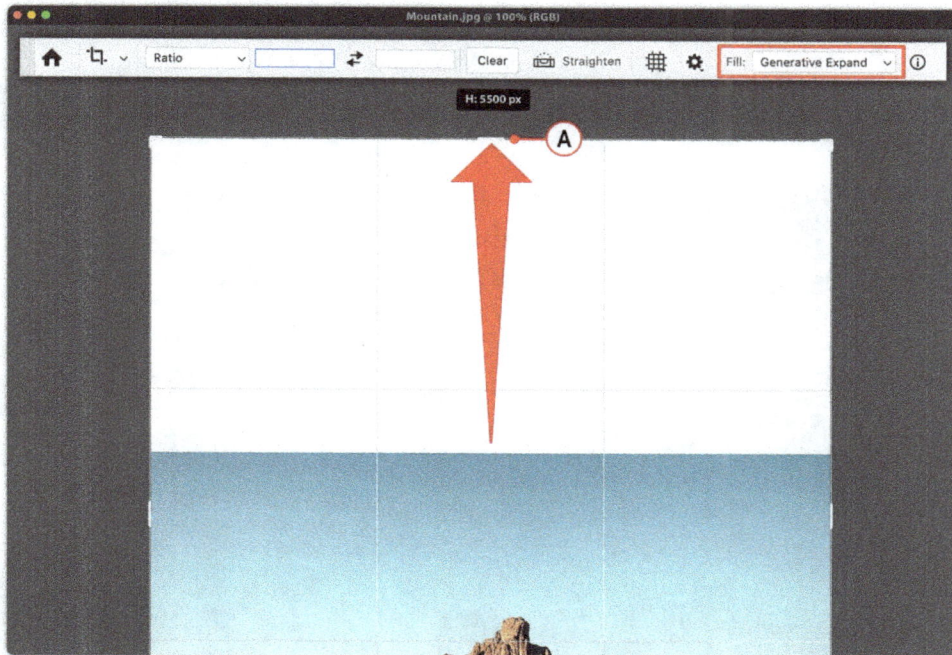

Figure 4.14: Extend the landscape with the Crop tool and Generative Expand

4. Hover your cursor over the top point on the crop frame (**A** in *Figure 4.14*) and drag upward until approximately 5500 pixels are shown in the tooltip adjacent to your cursor.

5. Click on the **Commit** button in the **Options** bar. This will extend the canvas, revealing a white background. When the **Generative Expand** dialog appears, click on the **Generate** button. Photoshop will extend the sky.

6. Go to **File → Place Embedded**. Navigate to the 04-Masking folder and select Sky.jpg. Click **Place**.

7. When the image appears within the canvas, scale the artwork's width and height up to 124%. Then, drag the bottom of the image just below the bottom edge of the canvas before pressing *Enter* (Windows) or *Return* (macOS) to apply the changes:

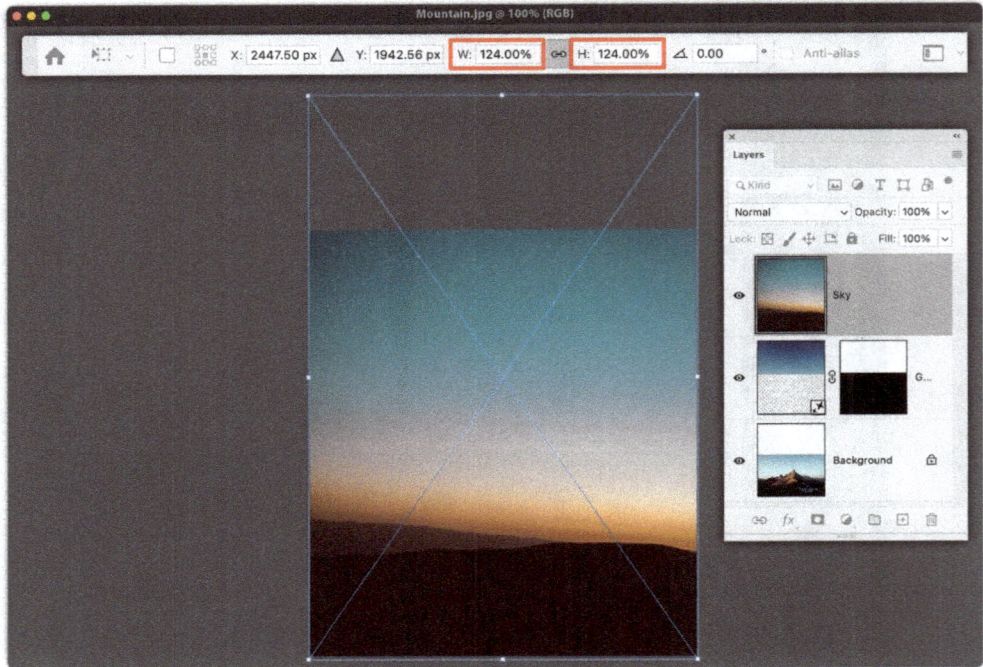

Figure 4.15: Place the new sky into the composition

8. Go to **Image → Reveal All**.

9. Press the *G* key to activate the paint tools. Then, long-press on the active tool icon to reveal the sub-list and click the **Gradient** tool to make it active.

10. From the **Options** bar, choose **Gradient** from the **Mode** menu. Then, click on the **Gradient Preset** dropdown (**A** in *Figure 4.16*), expand the **Basics** folder, and select the **Foreground to Background** preset (**B**). Click the **Linear Gradient** button, which is on the left-most side of the set of five in the **Options** bar:

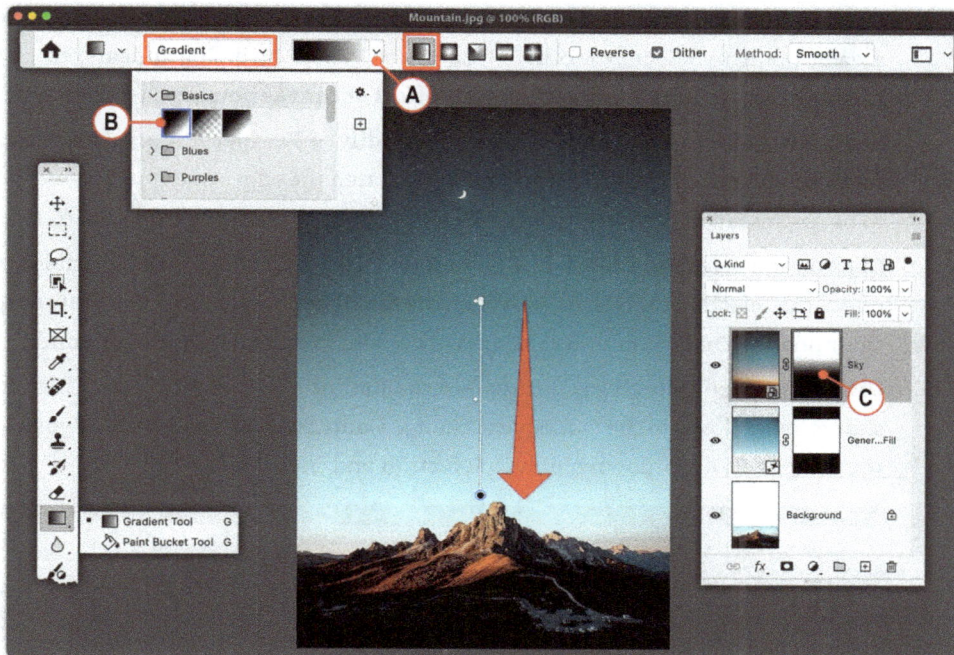

Figure 4.16: Add a smooth gradient mask to the sky

11. Press the *D* key to reset the colors at the bottom of the **Tools** panel, then click on the **Sky** layer mask thumbnail in the **Layers** panel.

12. Hover your cursor over the center of the canvas, one-third of the way down the image. Then drag the **Gradient** tool down the image and release it once you reach the top of the mountain summit. The sky should now blend seamlessly with the mountain sky. You can redraw the gradient as required until satisfied with the result.

13. Switch to the **Crop** tool and trim away any white edges made visible when the canvas was expanded.

Go to **File → Save As** and save the document as Mountain.psd in the 04-Masking folder. When you're done, close all documents.

Creating distressed photo edges

The **Select & Mask** workspace settings are often used to enhance fine masking details, such as hair. However, it can also be used to create an intriguing border around your images:

1. Go to **File → Open**. Browse to the 04-Masking folder and select the document named Edges.jpg.

2. Create a selection of the entire canvas by going to **Select → All**. Then shrink the selection area by going to **Select → Modify → Contract**. When the dialog appears, enter 200 into the **Contract By** field. Turn on the **Apply effect at canvas bounds** checkbox and click **OK**.

3. Soften the selection by going to **Select → Modify → Feather**. Enter 20 into the **Feather Radius** field and click **OK**. This will not only soften the edges of the selection, allowing it to be distressed in the next step, but also round the corners of the selection.

4. Click on the **Select and Mask** button in the options bar, which will be visible whenever one of the selection tools is active. When the dialog appears, change the **View** drop-down thumbnail to **On Layers** to set the artwork against a transparent background.

5. Under the **Edge Detection** settings, set the **Radius** slider to 71 pixels. Then, from the sliders lower down in the workspace, change **Contrast** to 60% and **Shift Edge** to +70%. Set the **Output To** drop-down menu to **Selection** and click **OK**:

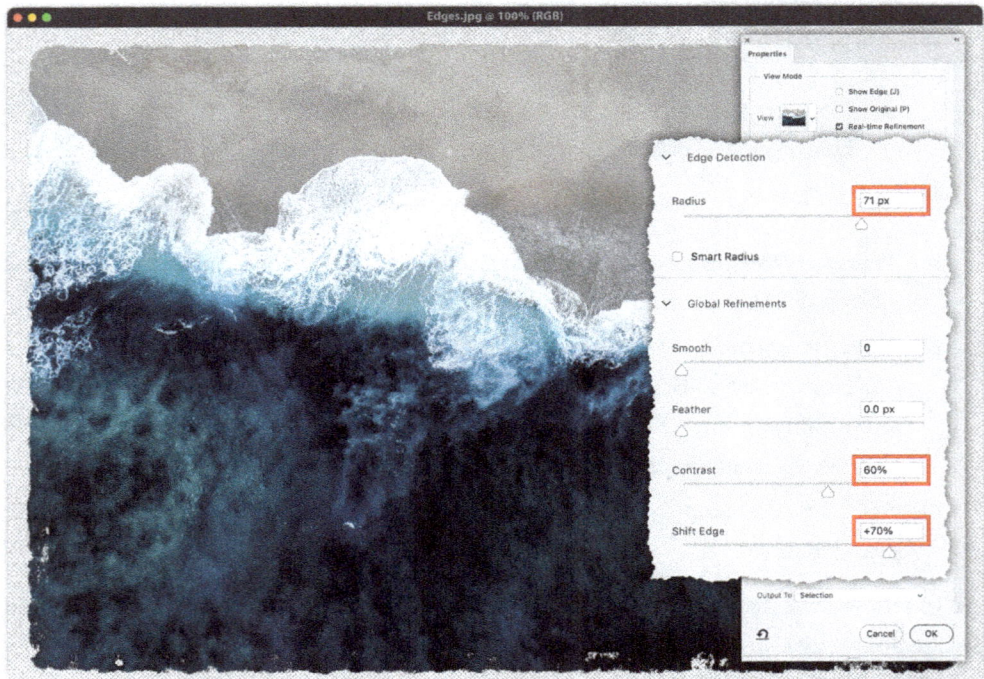

Figure 4.17: Use Refine Edge to create a roughened edge effect

6. Click the **Add a Mask** button at the bottom of the **Layers** panel and rename the layer Edges.

7. Click on the **Create new fill or adjustment layer** button at the bottom of the **Layers** panel (circled in *Figure 4.18*), and then click on **Solid Color...** (**A**) to create a new layer containing a single color. Set the color to white and click **OK** to generate the layer.

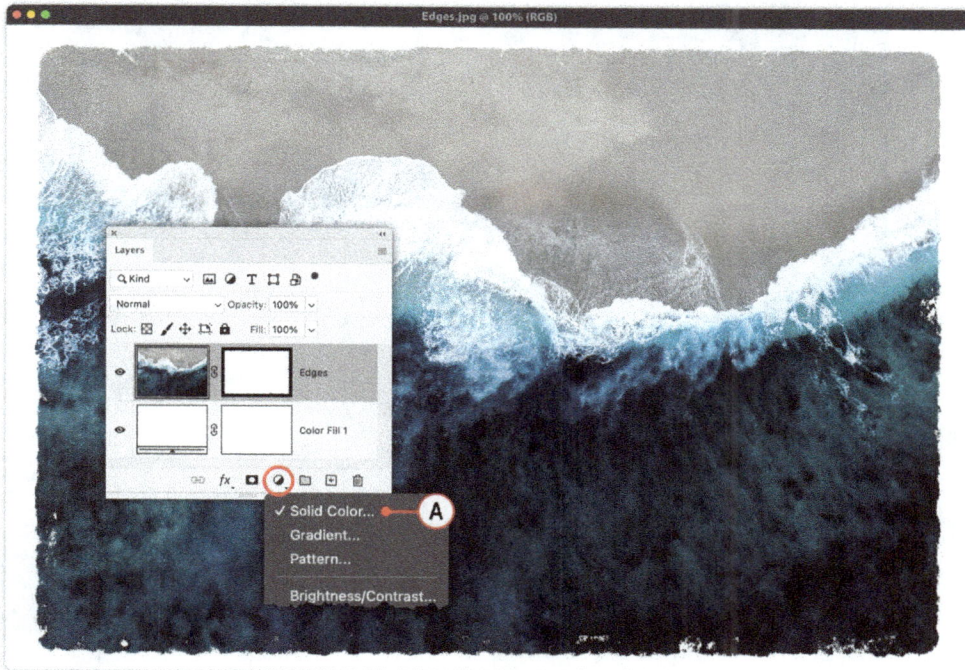

Figure 4.18: The finished frame effect

8. Drag the new color fill layer underneath the **Edges** layer in the stack.

9. Go to **File → Save As** and save the document in the 04-Masking folder with the same name and in the PSD format. Then go to **File → Close**.

Masking with Blend If

Blend If settings are one of those mysterious, hard-to-discover features that can offer incredible value. When used correctly, they can perform highly detailed masking without the need for a single selection or layer mask:

1. Go to **File → Open** and navigate to the 04-Masking folder. Select InkDive.psd and click **Open** when done.

2. Hover your cursor over the **INK** text layer and double-click on the empty space to the right of the layer name (**A** in *Figure 4.19*) to open the **Layer Style** blending options. The **Blend If** settings are at the bottom:

Figure 4.19: Blend If layer style settings can create intricate masks based on luminance

3. The two grayscale strips allow you to hide part of the active layer using the luminance of the underlying layers. Reduce the **Underlying Layer** slider to 17 (**B**), making any pixels in the **Background** layer that are lighter than a luminance level of 17 appear through the **INK** layer's editable text.

4. To eliminate the hard transition around the ink, hold your cursor over the white point slider, and hold down *Alt* (Windows) or *Option* (macOS) as you drag the right half of the slider, splitting the slider to create a fall-off. Stop when you reach a value of 68 (**C**). Click **OK** when done to apply the edits.

5. Click on the **Create new layer** icon at the bottom of the **Layers** panel, name the layer Shadows, and change **Blend Mode** to **Darken** (**A** in *Figure 4.20*):

Figure 4.20: Add a new layer and change Blend Mode to Darken

6. Right-click on the **Shadows** layer name in the **Layers** panel and again choose **Create Clipping Mask** to make it affect only the text layer.

7. Press the *B* key to switch to the **Brush** tool. From the **Brush Tip** Preset menu, choose a soft round brush tip. Set **Size** to 500 px, lower **Opacity** to 10%, and set black as the foreground color from the **Tools** panel.

8. Apply brush strokes over the regions where the ink appears in front of the text to make it appear to cast a faint shadow across the text:

Figure 4.21: Add shadow effects by painting black with the Brush tool

9.   Once complete, go to **File → Save** and close the document.

In this section, we have looked at various scenarios where several layers or images require blending to achieve a desired outcome. Hiding unwanted parts of one layer to reveal another underlying layer; or, in the case of the ink image, we used a form of masking that uses the luminance levels of one layer to hide portions of our text in a separate layer. Next, we will look at masking hair.

Masking hair

One of the more challenging aspects of masking is being confronted with fine details such as hair, which require Photoshop's powerful mask refinement tools. Let's see how we can use them via an exercise:

1.   Go to **File → Open** and navigate to the 04-Masking folder. Select Cutout.jpg and click **Open** when done.

Figure 4.22: Use the Select Subject feature to make your base selection

2. Switch to the **Object Selection** tool. In the **Options** bar, click the **Process Selection** drop-down (**A** in *Figure 4.22*) and select **Cloud (Detailed results)** from the list of options. This may take slightly longer to process the selection, but the results should be more accurate.

3. Then click the **Select people** button to reveal all detected people and click on the woman's face (**B** in *Figure 4.22*) to create a selection of the woman. Once Photoshop generates the selection, click the **Select and Mask…** button.

4. When the **Select and Mask** dialog appears, click on the **View** drop-down thumbnail (**A** in *Figure 4.23*) and change it to **Overlay**:

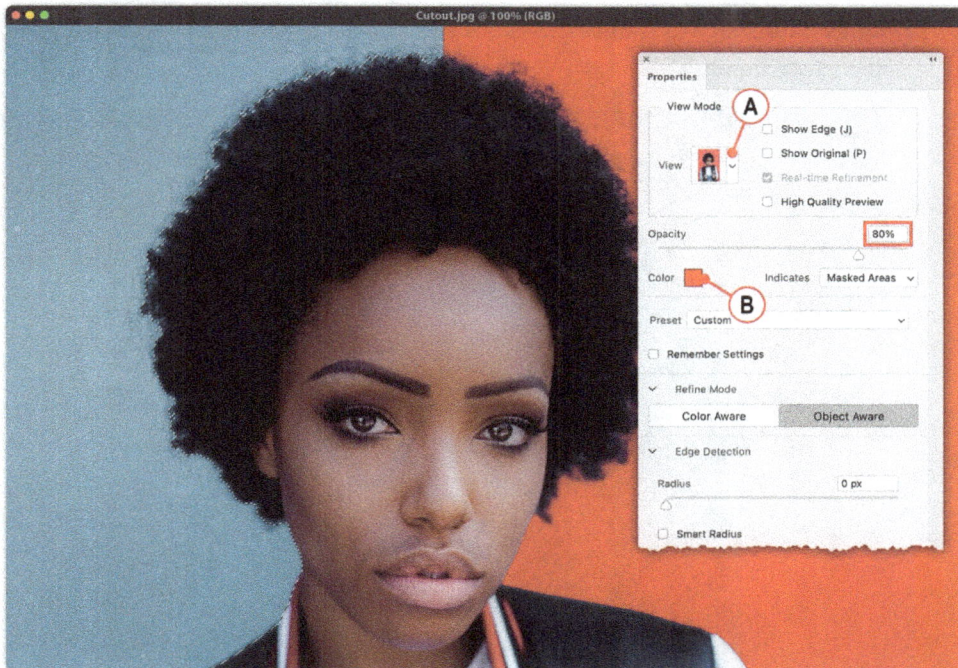

Figure 4.23: The original selection (left) compared to the initial, enhanced edge selection (right)

This will allow you to preview the region outside of your selection in a temporary color of your choosing.

5. Change the overlay color to one that contrasts with the hair and the photo's original background. Click on the color picker (**B**), select a bright red, and click **OK**.

6. Set the **Opacity** slider to 80% to increase the visibility of the red overlay. I've found from experience that this can help discern fine hair details.

7. Under **Refine Mode**, choose **Object Aware**, better suited to complex details such as hair and fur.

8. Click on the **Refine Radius** brush in the **Tools** panel. Then click on the **Refine Hair** button in the **Options** bar. This will search for hair details and refine them.

9. You can enhance hair details by painting with the **Refine Radius** brush if necessary. From the **Options** bar, set the brush's **Size** value to 60 px.

10. Click and drag the brush from the recolored background toward the visible pixels of the hair until you overlap a small portion of visible hair. When you release the mouse button, the brush will reveal colors similar to those of the hair while hiding the background colors.

11. From the right-hand side of the workspace, where you will find **Global Refinements**, adjust **Shift Edge** to -10% to shrink the selection edge and help conceal stray colors from the background:

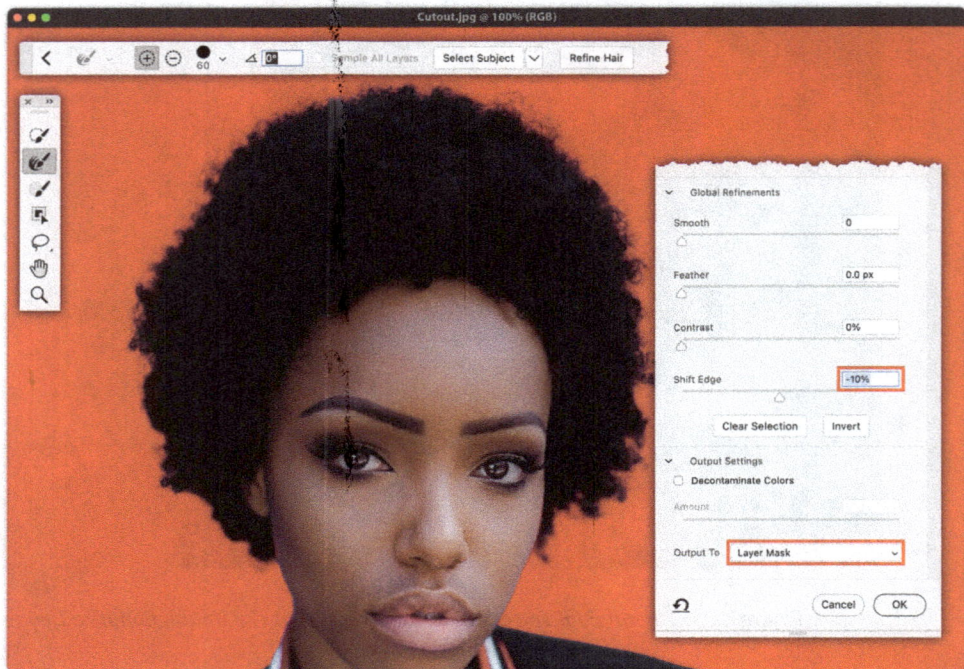

Figure 4.24: Enhance the hair details with the Refine Radius brush

12. Ensure the **Output To** dropdown is set to **Layer Mask**, then click **OK** to apply the changes. When the dialog closes, you will notice that the **Background** layer, now given a default name of **Layer 0**, has a mask assigned to it, which hides the original backdrop.

13. Rename the layer Subject:

Figure 4.25: The subject with a layer mask assigned, hiding the original background

14. Click on the **Create new fill or adjustment layer** button at the bottom of the **Layers** panel to create a new layer containing a single color. Enter cac816 into the **Hexadecimal** field and click **OK**. Drag the new layer to the bottom of the **Layers** stack behind the image of the woman.

15. Assess the quality of the mask, looking for rogue colors around the hair.

Making detailed adjustments to layer masks

When further refinement of a layer mask is required, you can take the following optional steps:

1. Hide the visibility of the **Color Fill 1** layer.

2. Ensure that the **Subject** layer is active in the **Layers** panel. Then, click the **Create a new layer** icon at the bottom of the **Layers** panel. Name the new layer Hair, then change **Blend Mode** to **Darken**:

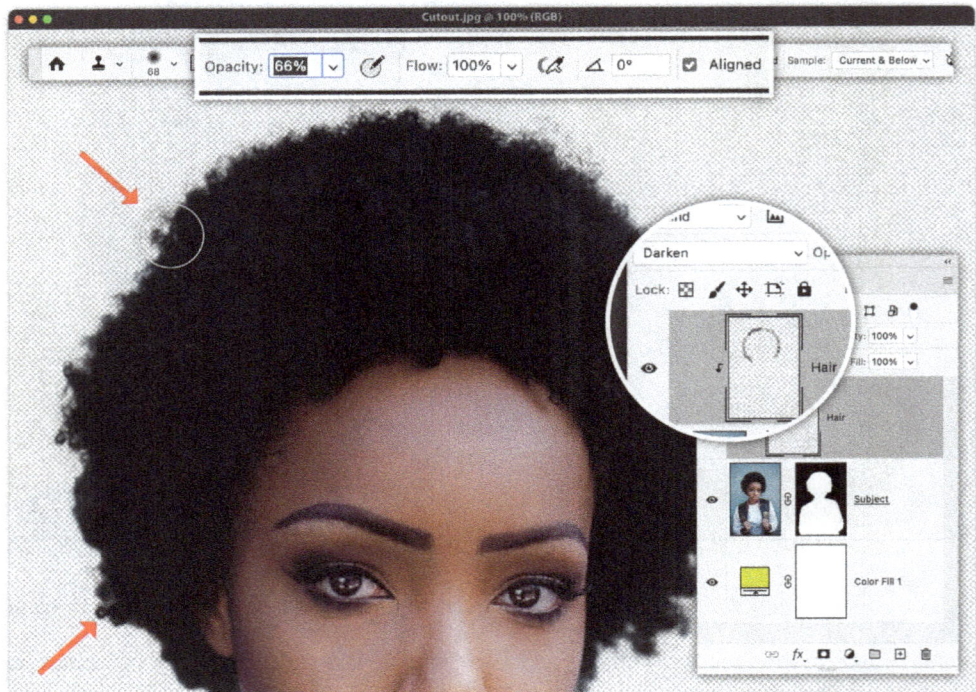

Figure 4.26: Remove unwanted colors around the hair with the Clone Stamp tool

3. Go to the **Layers** panel fly-out menu and choose **Create Clipping Mask** to ensure that any edits only appear where pixels in the **Subject** layer exist in the layer below it.

4. Switch to the **Clone Stamp** tool by pressing *S*. Go to the **Brush Presets** menu and select a **Soft Round** brush tip from the list. Set the brush's **Size** value to 80 px and **Hardness** to 0%. From the **Options** bar, enable the **Aligned** checkbox and set the **Sample** dropdown to **Current & Below**.

5. Hover your cursor over a region of hair in the subject and hold *Alt* (Windows) or *Option* (macOS) as you click to sample a region of black hair in the center of the head. Stay away from the edges of the hair as you need a solid hair texture.

6. With the sample now captured, hover the **Clone Stamp** tool cursor over the edges of the hair details that still contain blue from the original backdrop and drag the clone stamp across them. Work in small clusters and remember to resample new hair textures before cloning a new hair region. Once complete, you can turn the **Color Fill** layer visibility back on.

7. Go to **File → Save** to save the image in the 04-Masking folder. Close all documents when done.

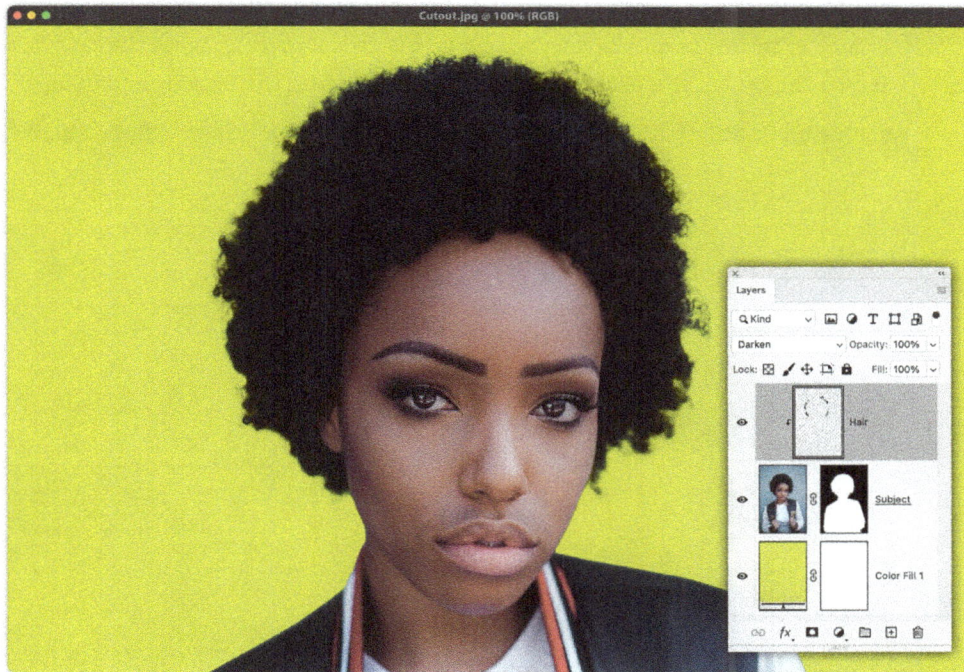

Figure 4.27: The completed masking project

In this section, we have used the **Select and Mask** workspace and the **Refine Radius** brush to extract fine details, such as hair, from a background. Next, we will focus on the advantages of separating an image from its layer mask.

Unlinking images and masks

The ability to unlink a layer mask from the layer content can be a critical time-saver, as it avoids the need to remove and reposition a layer mask. In this exercise, you will fill an empty picture frame to create a mockup of an exhibition space and unlink the image from the layer mask to juxtapose the photo within the frame:

1. Go to **File → Open**. Select `PictureFrame.jpg` from the `04-Masking` folder and click **Open**. Once open, go to **File → Place Embedded** and select `Ravine.jpg` from the same folder.

2. When the image appears in the canvas, go to the options bar and change the **Width** field to a scale of 17%. When you're done, click on the tick in the options bar to apply the edits.

3. Reduce the **Ravine** layer's **Opacity** to 70% in the **Layers** panel (highlighted in *Figure 4.28*). Switch to the **Move** tool, hover your cursor over the **Ravine** image in the canvas, and drag it over the center of the largest, empty picture frame in the background image:

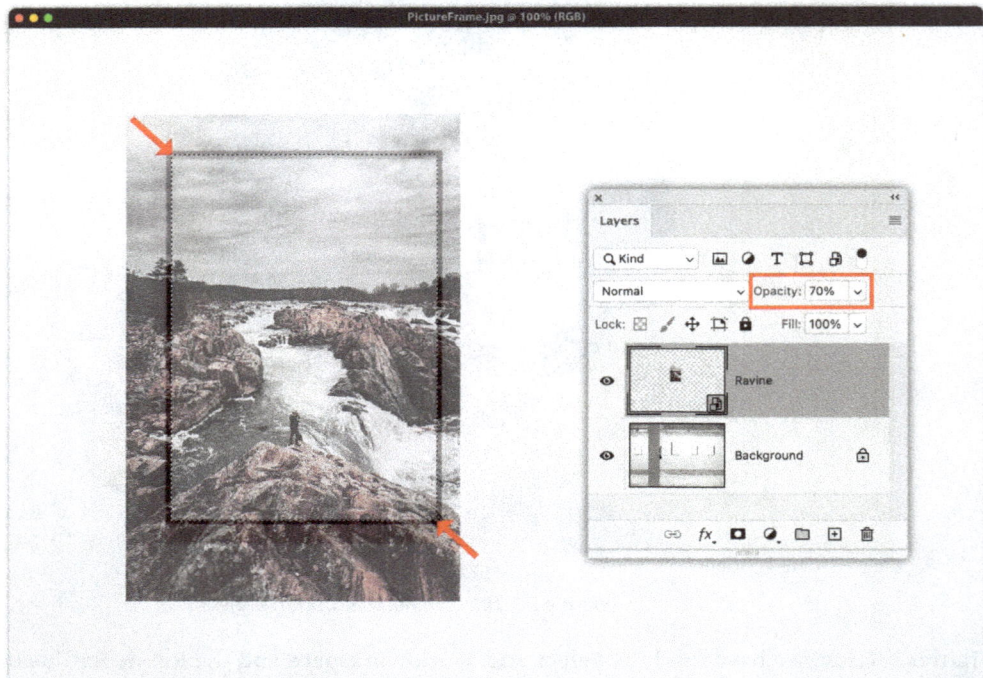

Figure 4.28: Scale and position the photo over the frame

4. Zoom into the middle picture frame so that it occupies most of the image window. Press the *M* key to switch to the **Rectangular Marquee** tool.

5. Hover your cursor inside the top-left edge of the plain black picture frame. Then, click and drag diagonally down to the bottom-right corner of the black picture frame to create a rectangular selection that includes all the white space inside the frame. Release the mouse button when done to complete the selection.

6. Click on the **Ravine** layer in the **Layers** panel once to ensure it is active. Then click the **Add a Mask** button at the bottom of the **Layers** panel and change **Blend Mode** to **Multiply** to reveal the shadows around the original picture frame, making the effect more convincing:

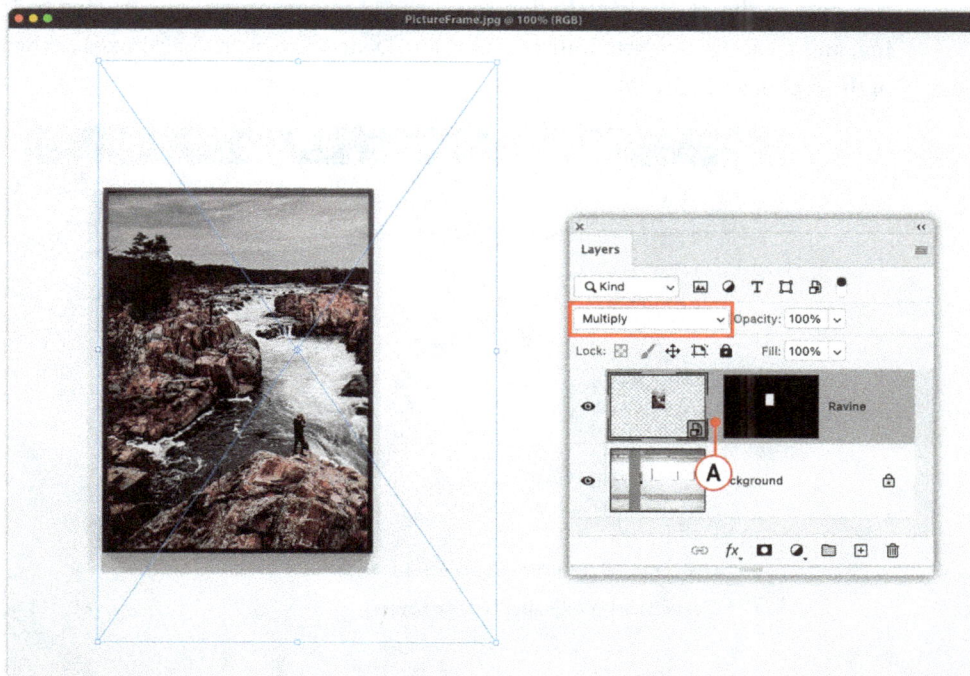

Figure 4.29: Unlinking the layer mask from the image

7. Click on the link between the image and the layer mask thumbnail (**A** in *Figure 4.29*). Then click on the image thumbnail to make it active. You can now reposition or scale the ravine photo by dragging it around the image window while keeping the layer mask static.

8. Once you have positioned the photo in the picture frame to your liking, link the image and the layer mask again by clicking in the space between both thumbnails in the **Layers** panel.

9. Go to **File → Save As**, browse to the 04-Masking folder, name the file PictureFrame.psd, and close the document when done.

Masking layer groups

Copying and arranging images into a grid can be time-consuming but there are some sneaky scripts, cropping features, and group masking techniques that you can use to save time:

1. Go to **File → Open**, select Poster_A4_01.psd from the 04-Masking folder, and click **Open** when done.

2. Go to **File → Scripts → Load Files into Stack...** and click **Browse** when the dialog appears. Navigate to the 04-Masking folder, select the 14 images from Trek_01.jpg to Trek_14. jpg, and click **Open** when done to add them. Deactivate both checkboxes at the bottom of the dialog and click **OK**.

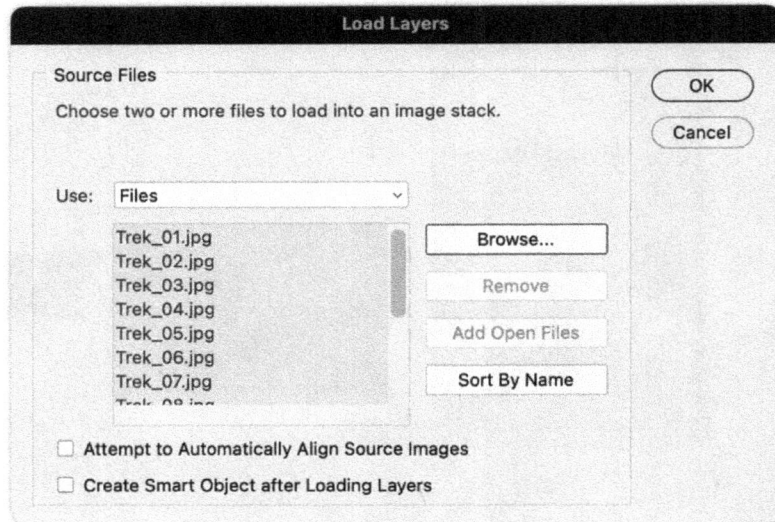

Figure 4.30: Combine separate files into a single layer stack

3. Photoshop will now copy all 14 images into a new document (**A** in *Figure 4.31*). Go to **Select → All Layers**. Then press *Ctrl + G* (Windows) or *Cmd + G* (macOS) to add all the active layers into a new group, named **Group 1** by default (**B**). Rename the layer group Images (**C**).

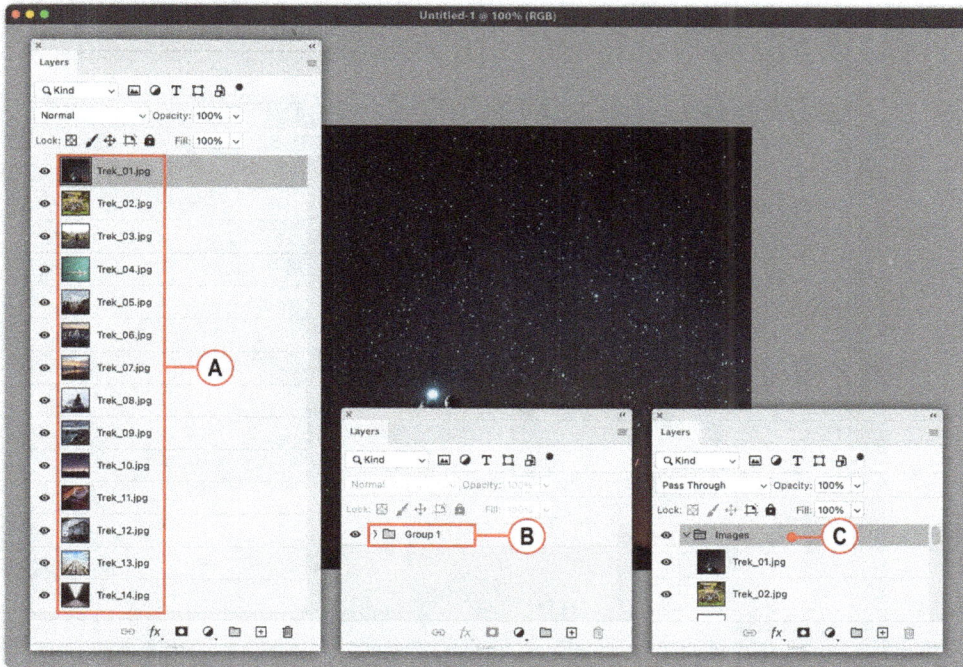

Figure 4.31: Merge separate files into a single layer and store them in a layer group

4. Right-click on the layer group name in the **Layers** panel and choose **Duplicate Group...**
    from the context menu (*Figure 4.32*). Set the **Destination** dropdown to Poster_A4_01.psd
    and click **OK**. Click on the Poster_A4_01.psd document tab to make it active.

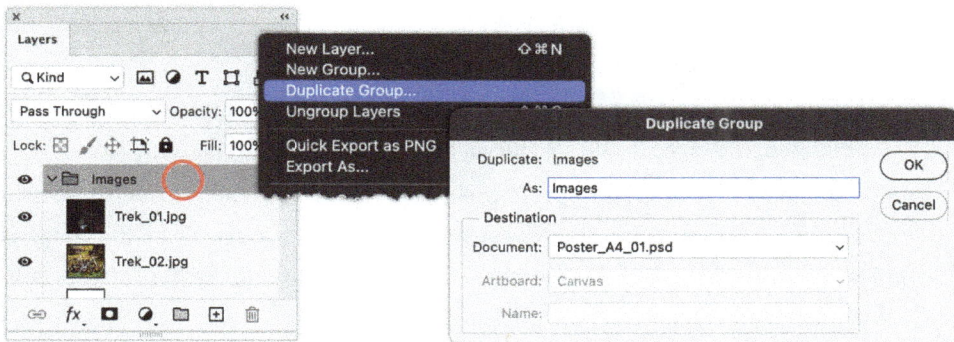

Figure 4.32: Duplicate the group and send it to the poster document

5. Click on the toggle next to the **Images** group in the **Layers** panel. Then, turn off the visibility of the **BKG** layer (circled in *Figure 4.33*) to make the red guides easier to see:

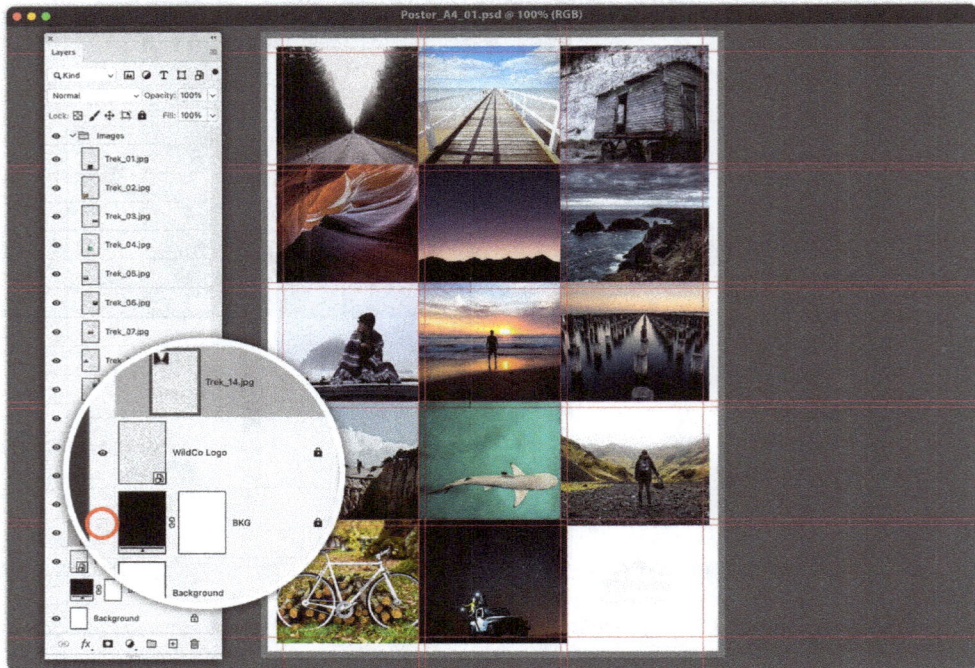

Figure 4.33: Duplicate the group and send it to the poster document

6. Ensure that **View → Snap to Guides** is active before moving the artwork.

7. Switch to the **Move** tool. Click on the **Trek_01** layer and drag it down the canvas to align centrally with the empty grid cell adjacent to the logo.

8. Repeat the same technique to reposition all 14 images into each of the red grid cells. Once completed, the logo should still be visible on the bottom right-hand side of the image.

9. Press the *M* key, then long-press the active tool in the **Tools** panel to reveal the pop-out. Click on the **Rectangular Marquee** tool to make it active. From the **Options** bar, set **Selection Mode** to **Add to Selection**. Create a selection for each of the 14 grid squares containing images:

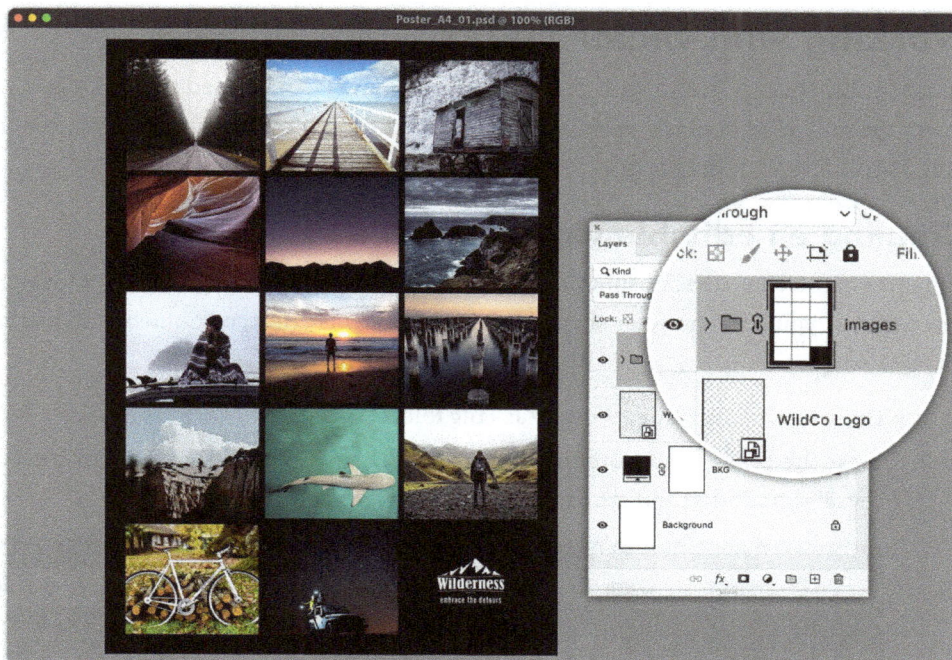

Figure 4.34: Create rectangular selections of each grid cell to create the layer mask

10. Double-check that the **Images** layer group is active in the **Layers** panel. Then click the **Add a Mask** button at the bottom of the **Layers** panel to hide the regions that appear in the grid's margin and gutter. If necessary, reposition individual layers in the **Images** layer group.

11. Go to **File → Save** and close the document when you're done. You can close the Untitled file without saving the changes as it is no longer required.

In this section, we have looked at techniques for unlinking layer masks to provide more flexibility. Firstly, a photo can be scaled and repositioned without affecting the mask. Secondly, we've seen a similar technique with the mask applied to a layer group. This allows each layer within the group to be repositioned and edited as required while keeping the mask unaffected. Next, we'll look at using vector content as the basis for a mask.

Working with vector masks

So far in this chapter, we've seen how pixel-based masks can be used to good effect, but they aren't the only kind of mask available to us in Photoshop. Vector masks can be used to create pin-sharp edges with shapes or even text.

Creating an editable vignette with a vector mask

Vignettes can create an atmospheric darkened edge around an image or add a focal point. In this exercise, you'll use a vector shape as the basis for this effect, combined with feathering of its mask properties:

1. Open Ravine.jpg from the 04-Masking folder.

2. Press the *U* key to activate the vector tools. Then, long-press on the active tool icon to reveal the sub-list and click the **Ellipse** tool to make it active.

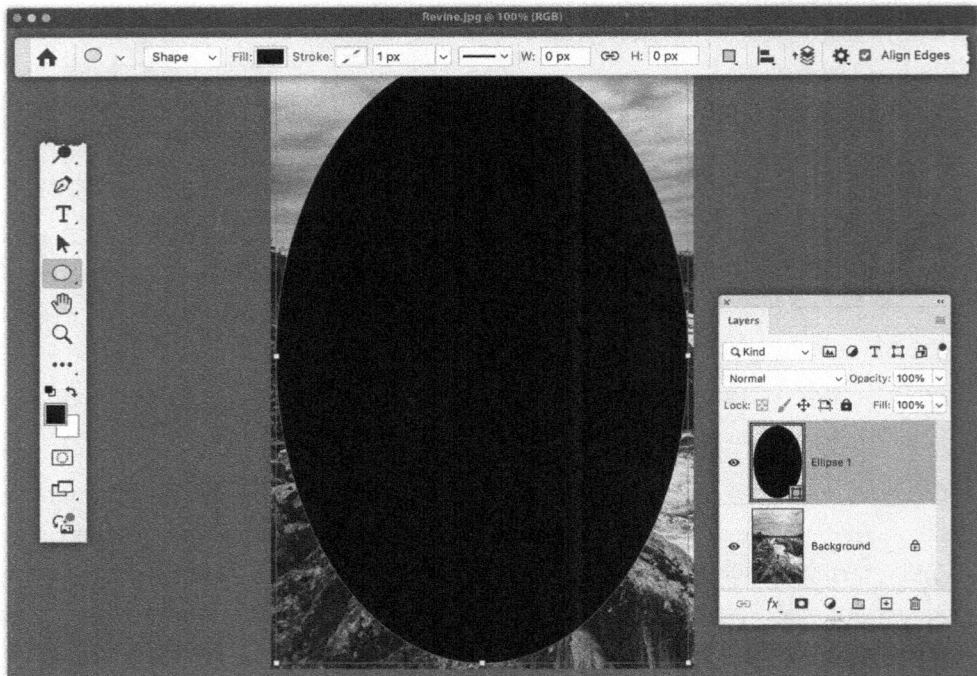

Figure 4.35: Create a black elliptical shape with the Ellipse tool

3. Go to the **Options** bar and ensure that the **Mode** drop-down menu is set to **Shape**. Set the **Fill** color to black.

4. With the **Ellipse** tool active, hover your cursor over the top-left corner of the canvas and drag it down to the bottom right-hand corner to create an ellipse that is approximately the same size as the canvas:

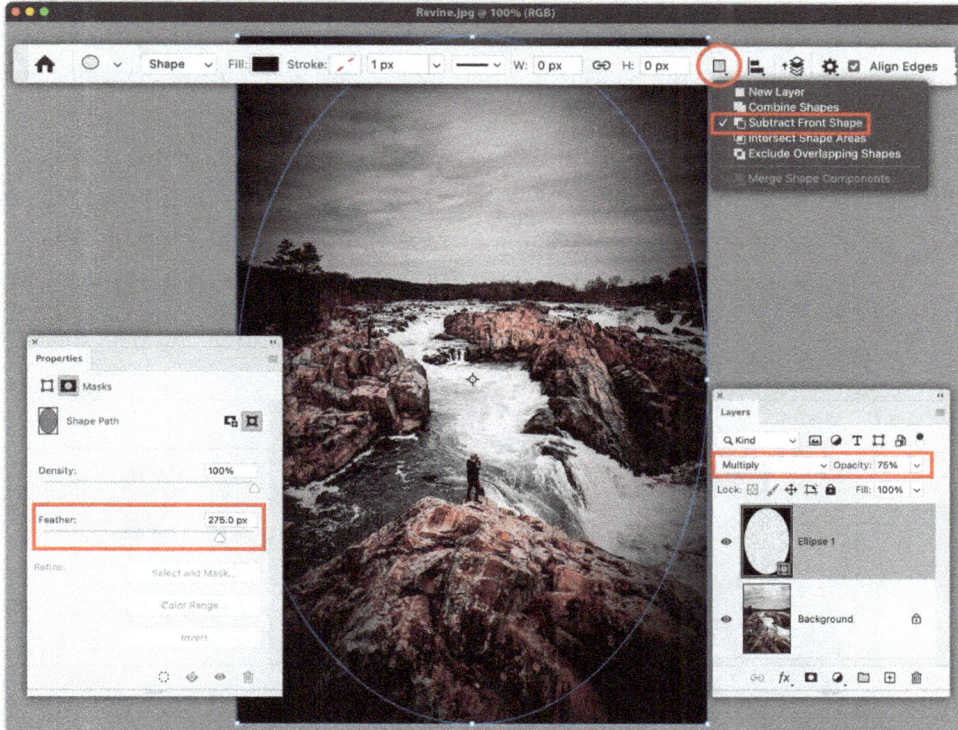

Figure 4.36: The vignette effect, created by using the feather value

5. With the **Ellipse 1** layer active, invert the shape so that black appears around the outside rather than inside by clicking on the **Path Operations** dropdown in the options bar and selecting **Subtract Front Shape**.

6. Click on the **Mask** icon at the top of the **Properties** panel to reveal the masking options in the same panel. Change the **Feather** slider to 275 to soften the ellipse and create the vignette.

7. Change the **Ellipse 1** layer's **Blend Mode** setting to **Multiply**, then lower the **Opacity** value to 75%. You can adjust the **Feather** and **Opacity** values to your liking at any point without affecting the quality of the final image.

8. Go to **File → Save As**, saving the file as Ravine.psd. Then go to **File → Close** when done.

Creating a typographic mask effect

Clipping masks offer a flexible method for masking underlying layers such as photos, and can be edited with ease, especially when composed of editable text:

1. Go to **File → Open** and select the ParagraphClipping.jpg document from the 04-Masking folder. To ensure that you can see the whole image and some of the region beyond the canvas, go to **View → Zoom Out**.

2. Go to the **Layers** panel and click once on the padlock located on the right-hand side of the **Background** layer (circled in *Figure 4.37*). Double-click on the layer name and enter a new name of Face Left. Press *Return* or *Enter* when done to apply the name change:

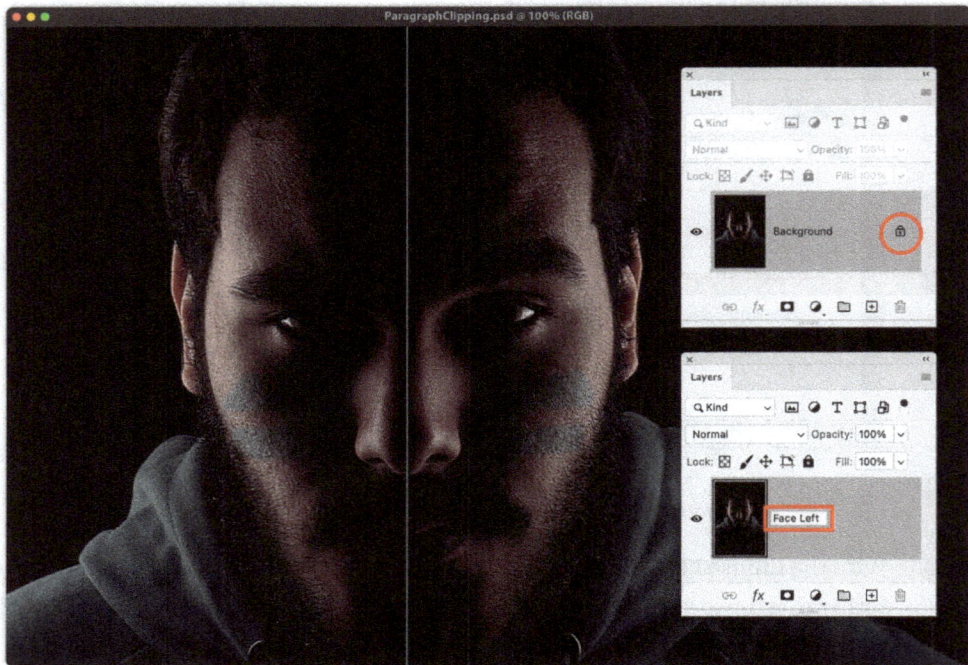

Figure 4.37: Rename the Background layer

3. If you do not see any guides in the document, go to **View → Show Guides**. You should now see a guide in the center of the canvas.

4. Press the *M* key to switch to the **Rectangular Marquee** tool, activating the correct group of tools. Then, hold down the left mouse button on the active tool icon to reveal the list of hidden tools. Click on the **Rectangular Marquee** tool icon to make it active.

5. Hover your cursor outside the top-middle of the canvas. Then, click and drag down to the bottom right-hand side of the canvas. Release the mouse to generate the selection:

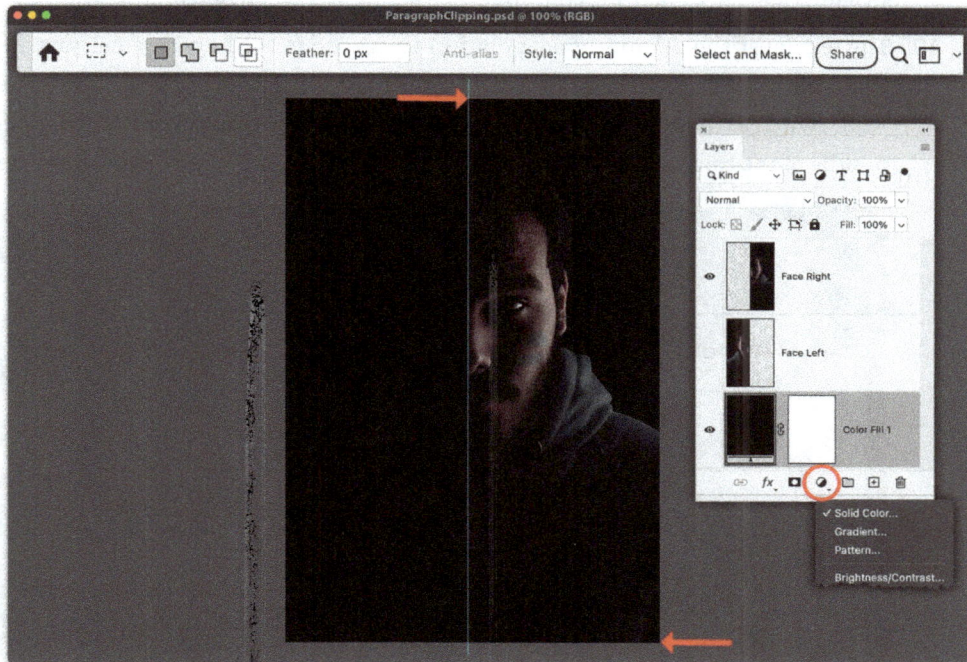

Figure 4.38: Use the guide to split the face into two separate layers

6. Ensure the **Face Left** layer is active, then navigate to **Layer → New → Layer via Cut** to cut and paste the selected content into a new layer. Double-click the new layer name to edit it, type Face Right, and press *Enter* or *Return* to confirm the name change.

7. Next, click on the **Create New Fill or Adjustment Layer** icon at the bottom of the **Layers** panel and select **Solid Color** from the top of the list. When the layer is generated, enter 5 into the **Red, Green,** and **Blue** fields to match the dark backdrop in the photo, then click **OK**.

8. Then, drag the color fill layer to the bottom of the layer stack.

9. You will need to add text to the document. Fortunately, this has been prepared in advance. Go to **File → Open** and select the document named Text.psd from the 04-Masking folder. Once open, click on the only layer in that document, the text layer, and right-click on the layer name in the **Layers** panel to reveal the context menu. Choose **Duplicate Layer** from the list of commands. Set the document **Destination** dropdown to ParagraphClipping. jpg and then click **OK**. Close the Text.psd document when done.

10. The text layer should now appear on the canvas and in the **Layers** panel, just above the **Face Left** layer. Turn off layer visibility for the **Face Right** layer by clicking on its **Visibility** icon. Switch to the **Move** tool and drag the left edge of the text artwork to the guide in the middle of the canvas, leaving a roughly equal gap at the top and bottom of the text layer.

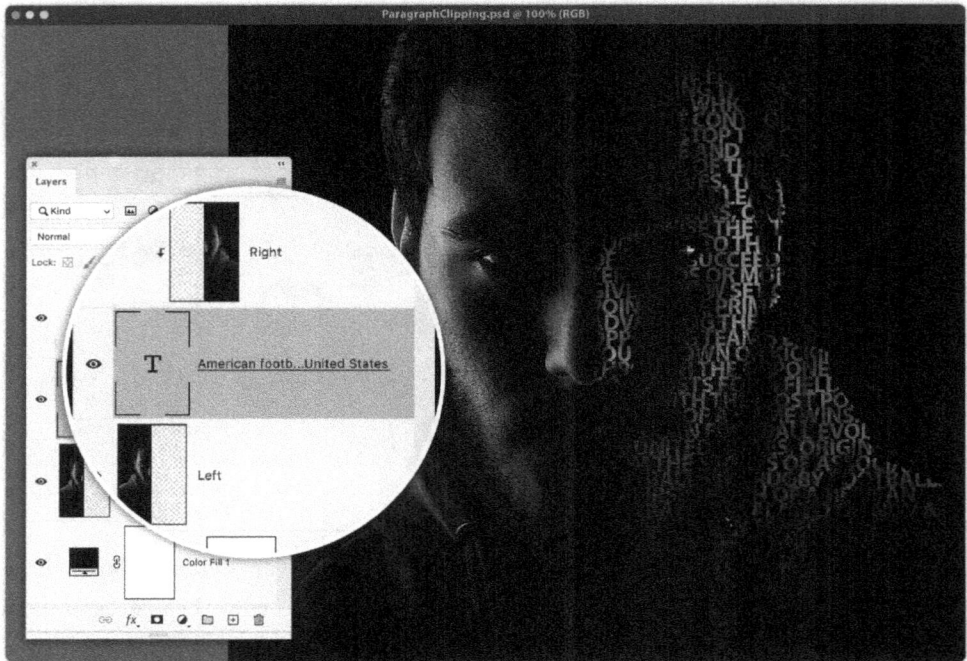

Figure 4.39: Editable text can be used as a clipping mask that affects the underlying layer

11. Turn on the **Layer Visibility** for **Face Right** and click on the layer in the **Layers** panel to make it active.

12. Go to the **Layers** panel fly-out menu and choose **Create Clipping Mask** from the list of commands. This will make any visible content in the text layer act as a mask and hide portions of the **Face Right** layer where there is no text in that layer. Go to **File → Save As** and save the document in the 04-Masking folder as ParagraphClipping.psd.

You don't always require a pixel-based layer to mask in Photoshop. Vector masks and clipping masks are just two examples covered in this section that are highly effective masking techniques that don't require a pixel-based layer.

Summary

In this chapter, we have seen how masking plays a fundamental role in controlling the visibility of layers: firstly, to remove an unwanted background while keeping a subject visible and combining it with a new backdrop; and secondly, in conjunction with a black-and-white adjustment layer, excluding the subject from the effect to maintain its color. We then used the **Brush** tool to edit the mask, painting black in the mask to conceal the adjustment layer and white to reveal it.

We have seen how masks provide a unique method for extracting hair from a background. Specialist masking tools detect image colors to hide background details and preserve a subject's hair.

In contrast to the previous techniques, we have also seen how disconnecting a mask from image content has advantages. It allows images to be scaled or rotated independently of a mask to juxtapose the photo better without affecting it.

We leveraged vector tools as the basis for a mask, using editable text as a clipping layer to create the effect of a typographic portrait and then using basic shapes and their masking properties to form a vignette.

In the next chapter, we will build branded prototypes in various scenarios, such as clothing, vinyl wall graphics, and website prototypes on device screens.

Get This Book's PDF Version and Exclusive Extras

Scan the QR code (or go to packtpub.com/unlock). Search for this book by name, confirm the edition, and then follow the steps on the page.

Note: Keep your invoice handy. Purchases made directly from Packt don't require one.

Part 2

Bringing Brands Front and Center

All brands exist to be seen in print, onscreen, and on the web. The process of bringing brands to life is iterative and often calls for mock-ups of logos, websites, and products, and feeding the constant demands of social media. In *Part 2* of this book, you will create realistic mockups, print assets such as flyers and posters, and social media templates for images, posts, videos, and animated GIFs.

This part of the book includes the following chapters:

- *Chapter 5, Building Brand Mock-Ups and Prototypes*
- *Chapter 6, Creating Printed Marketing Collateral*
- *Chapter 7, From Pixels to Post: Images for Social Media*
- *Chapter 8, Creating Animated GIFs and Videos*

5

Building Brand Mock-Ups and Prototypes

Brands aim to be visible in print, onscreen, and on the web. This process is iterative and often calls for mock-ups of logos, websites, and products before committing to the final product, aiming to reduce costs associated with manufacturing the actual product. This is especially pertinent as we should also endeavor to reduce our carbon footprint and consider the use of natural materials.

In this chapter, you will create mock-ups for various scenarios, from devices such as iPads and smartphones to bottles, T-shirts, and murals. Most of these can be edited using **smart objects**, **group masks**, and **linked assets**.

We'll start by reviewing the key characteristics of source images and the environment within which your mock-ups will be brought to life. We will scrutinize aspects such as angles, depth of field, and content obscuring a mock-up's focal point.

Then, we'll consider placing artwork into a perspective grid, either to put a logo on a product or to prototype large-format graphics such as murals in real-world environments.

After that, we'll use **transforms** and **warps** to distort artwork into a composition, with the additional benefit of being able to edit or replace the prototype artwork, when necessary, without starting from scratch. Many of the techniques in this chapter aim to create a "surface" within which artwork is stored.

Finally, we'll cover the most challenging form of mock-ups—irregular surfaces where artwork needs to conform to the folds and creases of products such as cushions and T-shirts, using displacement maps and **Liquify**.

In this chapter, we'll cover the following topics:

- Considerations for developing mock-ups
- Applying branding to perspective
- Wrapping artwork around curved surfaces
- Replacing device screens with your own artwork
- Creating clothing and soft furnishing mock-ups

Technical requirements

The project files for this chapter can be found at: `https://packt.link/gbz/9781806021710`.

Considerations for developing mock-ups

When sourcing photos of walls, devices, and other surfaces to apply your design, there are a few factors to consider. You'll want your designs to look convincing, authentic, and clearly communicate the intended messaging or visual, so avoid acute angles wherever possible, as it can be incredibly challenging to make content "look right" under these contexts. Anything that obscures your design will add to its authenticity but will probably require masking. So, take a moment to think about how time-consuming it will be to mask those regions before purchasing stock content.

As an Adobe Creative Cloud subscriber, you can access over 70,000 free assets, including ready-made mock-ups. If you need to save time and money, these can be a valuable resource, and the techniques covered in this chapter will allow you to edit them with confidence or become an official Adobe Stock contributor so that you can sell your mock-ups. Head to `https://stock.adobe.com/uk/free` to access free stock assets.

Depth of field can be a highly effective facet to make mock-ups look authentic, but motion blur is challenging to mask and time-consuming. Equally, having a pedestrian walking in front of your bus shelter advert mock-up, for example, might seem like an authentic visual addition, but think about how you would go about masking the individual that obscures the region where your mock-up will appear. You'll want to avoid surfaces that are out of focus as your pin-sharp artwork will either need to be blurred and become illegible or stand out like a proverbial sore thumb.

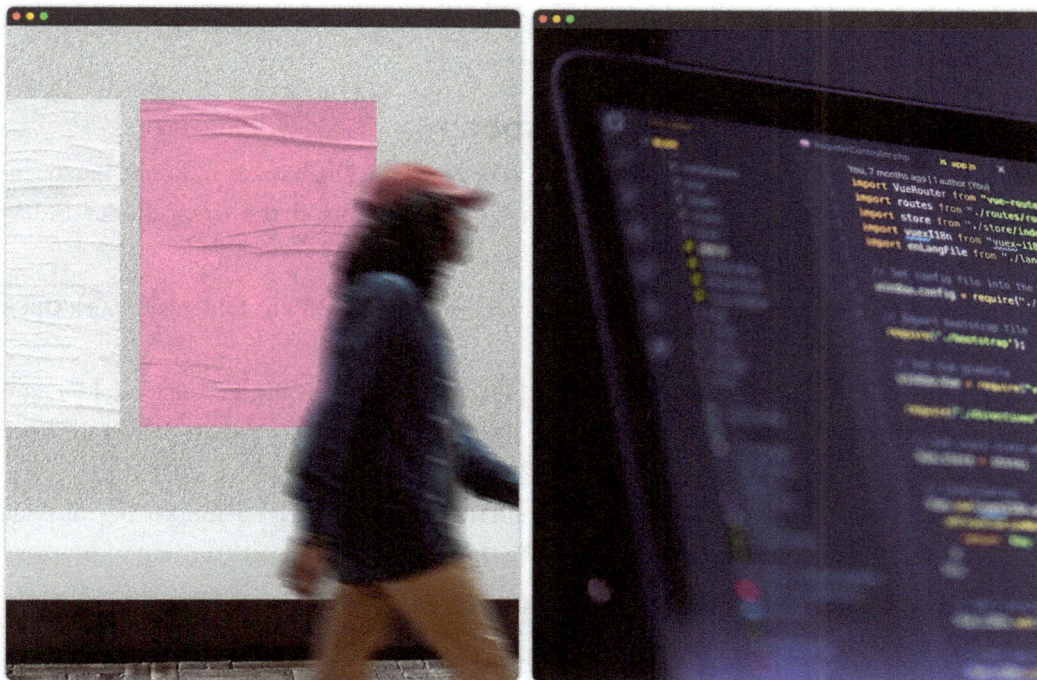

Figure 5.1: If possible, avoid obstructions and shallow depth of field in your source images

The colors of the source image play a significant role. From my experience, white tends to be more forgiving as a backdrop to apply logos or other types of artworks onto than dark backgrounds, but it's all about context.

In this section, we have explored some of the challenges involved in creating convincing mockups. In the next section, we will examine these as we incorporate branding into surfaces that present challenging perspectives.

Applying branding to perspective

There are two popular methods for adding artwork to perspective in Photoshop: using a transform and using the **Vanishing Point** filter effect. Transforms can be applied to smart objects, making them ideal for repeat editing, but the mesh points that control a transform can sometimes be challenging.

Vanishing Point has been around for decades, providing a relatively simple method for adding artwork to a perspective grid and healing and retouching in perspective to good effect. The downside is that it can't be applied to smart objects, and the workflow needs modernization.

In this chapter, we'll look at both techniques so that you can experiment with each workflow for yourself and judge their strengths and weaknesses.

Adding a logo to a bag in perspective

In this example of perspective editing, you will take an original logo made in Adobe Illustrator and place it in a photo to create a realistic mock-up. Then, you'll match the perspective of the bag using Vanishing Point and a blend mode:

1. Go to **File → Open**, select ShoppingBag.jpg from the 05-Mockup folder, and click **Open** when done.

2. Go to **File → Place Embedded**, select WildCo_Logo.ai from the 05-Mockup folder, and click **Place** when done. When the image appears, drag the placed artwork over the front of the bag.

3. Ensure that the link between the **Width** and **Height** fields is active before setting the scale to 40%. Click on the **Commit** button in the **Options** bar to complete the import process:

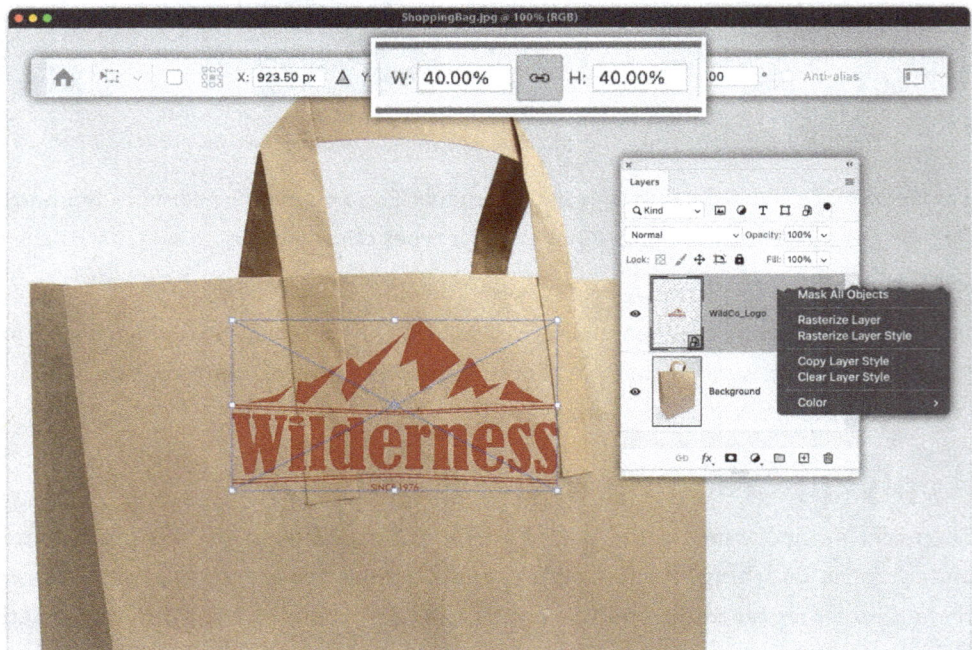

Figure 5.2: The imported logo, shown here at 40% of its original size

4. Adobe Illustrator artwork is automatically converted to a smart object. However, smart objects cannot be used in Vanishing Point. Therefore, you must hover your cursor over the imported layer name in the **Layers** panel, right-click, and choose **Rasterize Layer** from the list of options.

5. Rename the layer Logo, and press *Enter* (Windows) or *Return* (macOS).

6. Ensure that the **Logo** layer is active in the **Layers** panel by clicking on it once. Then, go to **Select → All** and choose **Edit → Cut**.

7. To launch the Vanishing Point interface, go to **Filter → Vanishing Point**. The **Create Plane** tool (circled in *Figure 5.3*) will be active by default when you enter Vanishing Point. Photoshop needs to work with a perspective plane, one that you will create and usually trace from the image that appears in the **Vanishing Point** image window.

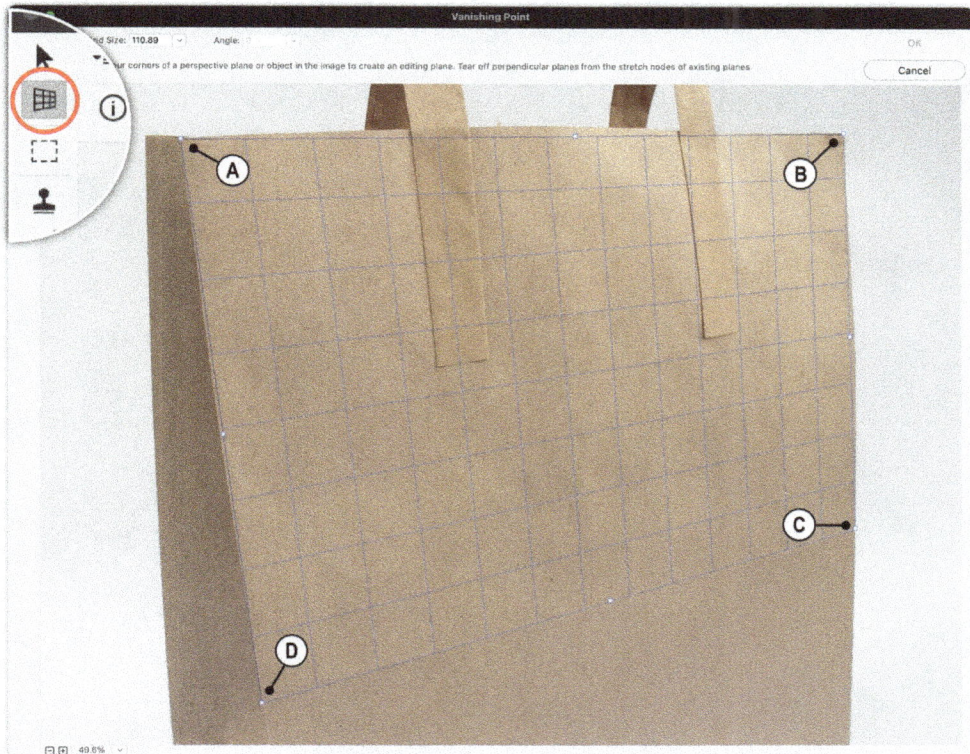

Figure 5.3: The Vanishing Point dialog showing the perspective grid

8. Hover your cursor over the front top-left corner of the bag (**A** in *Figure 5.3*) and click to add the first grid point. Then, hover your cursor over the top right-hand side of the bag (**B**) and click to add a second grid point. Place a third grid point at the bottom right-hand side of the bag (**C**) and a last grid point in the bottom-left corner of the bag (**D**). The grid should now appear and will be one of three colors: red (inaccurate grid), yellow (requires improvement), or blue (accurate grid).

9. If your grid is not blue, it will require editing; try dragging each corner point slightly until the grid turns blue. Often, only the slightest of tweaks is required to enhance the grid. You can switch to the **Zoom** tool or the **Hand** tool, both of which are located on the top left-hand side of the dialog, if zooming into each of the grid points is necessary.

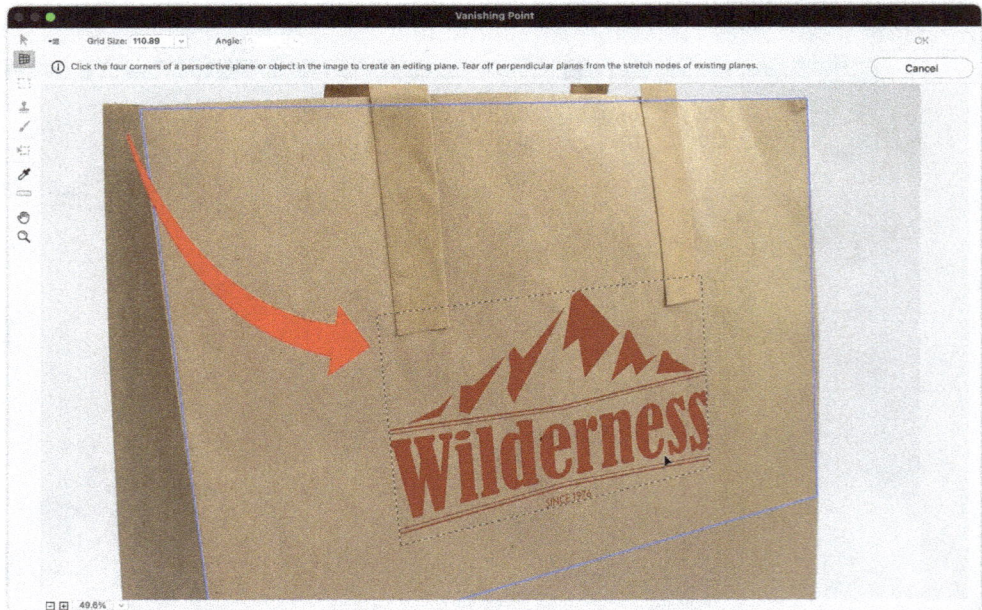

Figure 5.4: Once pasted, drag the logo onto the perspective plane

10. Once you have a blue grid, press *Ctrl + V* (Windows) or *Cmd + V* (macOS) to paste the logo into the interface. This will always appear in the top-left corner of the image window. Hover your cursor over the middle of the logo and drag it down into the grid, central to the front of the bag; the logo will conform to the grid's perspective. Click **OK** when you have fine-tuned the position of the logo.

11. Finally, save the file as a PSD named ShoppingBag.psd in the 05-Mockup folder. Then, close the document.

> **The limitations of Vanishing Point**
>
> As useful as the Vanishing Point feature is, sadly, it doesn't accept smart objects, and you can't repeat-edit a raster layer using this feature in the same way you can with a layer effect such as **Drop Shadow**. If you are looking for a more flexible workflow for perspective editing, I recommend transform warps, which will also be covered in this chapter.

Creating a mural mock-up

One of the hidden gems of the Vanishing Point feature is its ability to wrap artwork around corners. This is ideal for creating murals, as you can use a single image and let Vanishing Point do the rest of the work:

1. Open Walls.jpg and Mural-A.jpg from the 05-Mockup folder.

2. Ensure that the Mural-A.jpg document is active, then go to **Select → All**. Then, go to **Edit → Copy** and close the document as it is no longer needed.

3. With Walls.jpg active, click the **Create a New Layer** icon at the bottom of the **Layers** panel. Name the new layer Mural Art and ensure that it is targeted.

4. Go to **Filter → Vanishing Point**. When the dialog appears, the **Create Plane** tool will already be active. You will create a perspective grid covering the far right-hand side wall and the wall behind the cushions.

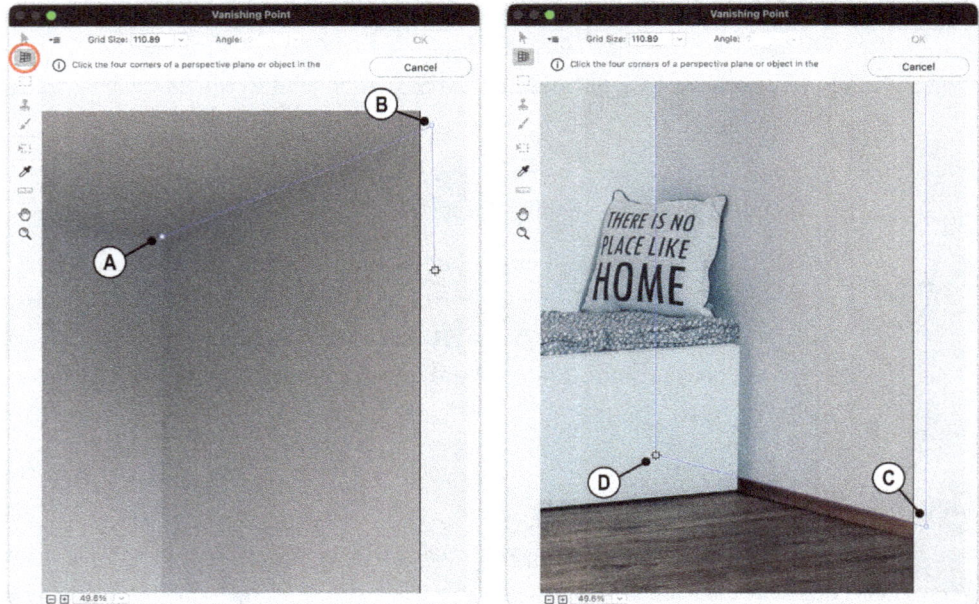

Figure 5.5: Create a new perspective grid plane that matches the right-hand wall

5. Start by clicking in the room's top-left corner of the right-hand side wall (**A** in *Figure 5.5*). Then, hover your cursor over the top-right edge of the wall where it meets the ceiling and the edge of the image, and click to add a second plane point (**B**). Add a third point where the right-hand wall meets the wooden skirting along the right edge of the image (**C**). Add a fourth point approximately where the corner of the wall would finish behind the cushions (**D**) to complete the plane.

6. Fine-tune the positions of the points by zooming in on them individually and dragging them to align with the four corners of the wall. It is preferable to make the Vanishing Point plane larger than the walls, as they can be masked later; you won't end up with a section of the wall lacking mural art because the grid didn't cover the entire area.

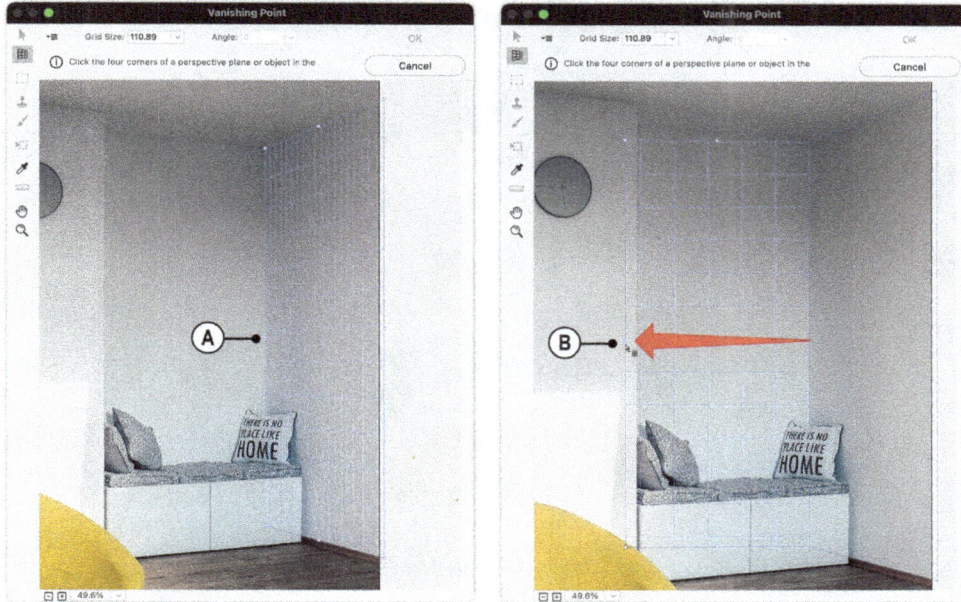

Figure 5.6: Extend the plane onto a second wall

7. With the grid fine-tuned, hover your cursor over the center-left handle of the grid (**A** in *Figure 5.6*). Then, hold *Ctrl* (Windows) or *Cmd* (macOS) as you drag the handle to the left-hand side and across the other wall that runs behind the cushions until you reach slightly further than the edge of that wall (**B**). Once you've done that, release the left mouse button and the *Ctrl/Cmd* key on the keyboard. This will create a perspective corner that the artwork will wrap around.

8.   The second plane will no doubt require adjusting. Drag the top-left and bottom-right handles to match the wall (circled in *Figure 5.7*), ensuring that the grid runs to the floor.

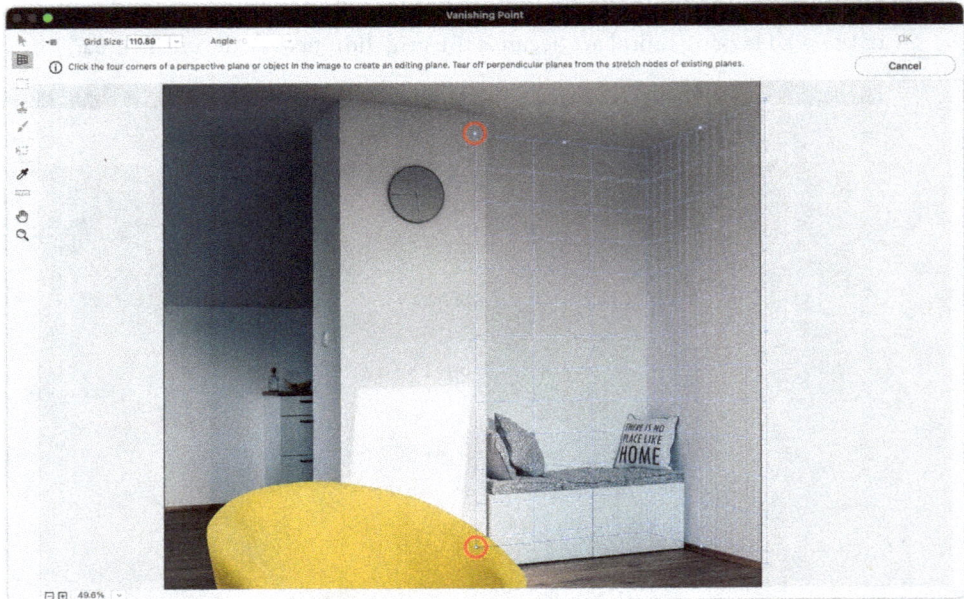

Figure 5.7: Some fine-tuning of the grid will be necessary

9.   With the perspective grid in place, press *Ctrl + V* (Windows) or *Cmd + V* (macOS) to paste the mural art you copied from the Mural-A.jpg file earlier in this exercise.

10. Hover your cursor over the middle of the artwork and drag it into the grid. It has been sized slightly larger than the grid. You will need to ensure that both walls are covered with artwork:

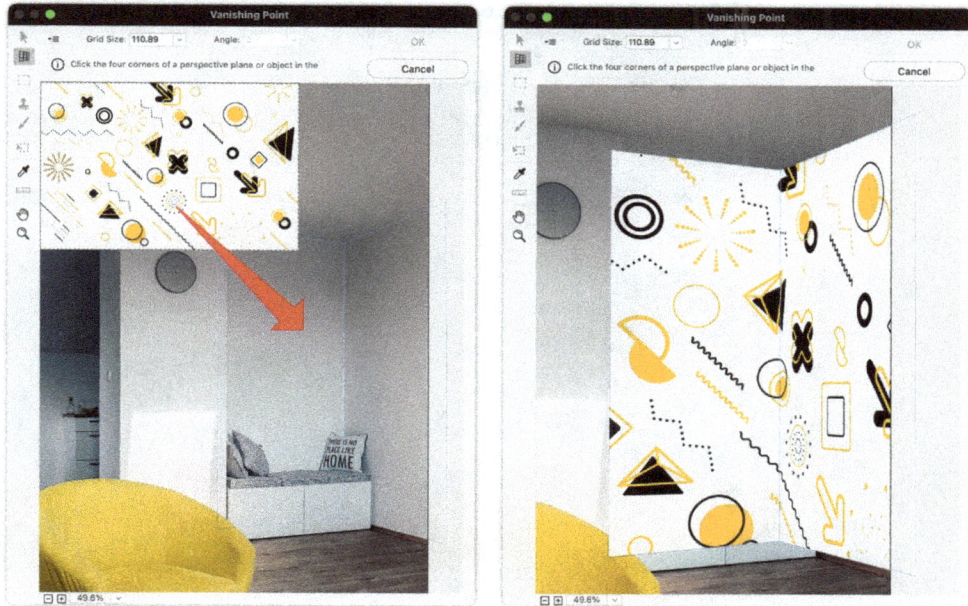

Figure 5.8: Drag the pasted mural artwork onto the perspective grid

11. Click **OK** to apply the edits and return to the main Photoshop interface. You will see that the edits have been applied to the **Mural Art** layer, which requires masking. Ensure that the **Mural Art** layer is active, then click on the **Add Layer Mask** icon at the bottom of the **Layers** panel.

12. Switch to the **Polygonal Lasso Tool** from the **Tools** panel. From the **Options** bar, set the selection mode to **New**.

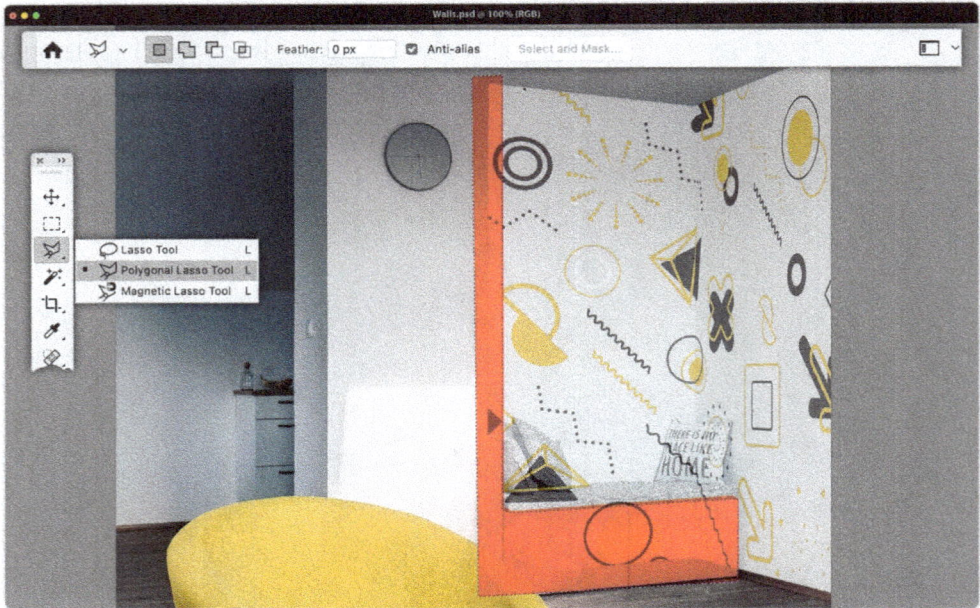

Figure 5.9: Create a new selection of the wall and cabinet

13. Select all mural art extending onto the wall containing the clock and the cabinet under the seat (highlighted in *Figure 5.9*).

14. With the selection in place, press the *D* key to reset the **Foreground** and **Background** colors and then press *Ctrl + Delete* (Windows) or *Cmd + Backspace* (macOS) to paint black in the layer mask and hide the mural where the selection is active.

15. Switch to the **Magnetic Lasso** tool from the **Tools** panel. From the **Options** bar, set the selection mode to **New**.

16. Create a new selection of the cushions (highlighted in *Figure 5.10*):

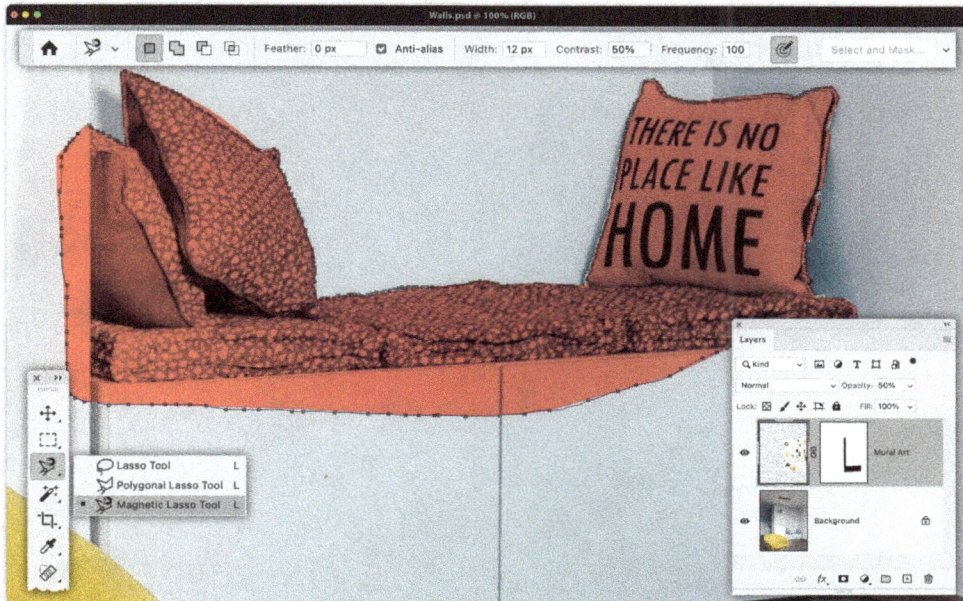

Figure 5.10: Create a new selection of the cushions

17. With the selection in place, hide the wall mural where the selection is active by pressing *Ctrl* + *Backspace* (Windows) or *Cmd* + *Delete* (macOS).

Figure 5.11: The completed mural mock-up

18. Change the **Mural Art** layer **Blend Mode** option to **Color Burn** from the **Blend Mode** menu.

19. You can desaturate the mural's colors by going to the **Adjustments** panel and adding a **Hue/Saturation** adjustment layer above the **Mural Art** layer in the stack. Click on **Create Clipping Layer** from the bottom of the **Properties** panel (circled in *Figure 5.11*).

20. Decrease the **Saturation** value to -30 to make the colors of our artwork more natural and match the contrast in the photo. Change the **Hue/Saturation** adjustment layer **Blend Mode** option to **Saturation**.

21. Save the document as Mural.psd in the 05-Mockup folder and close the document when you're done.

In this section, we explored how to use the Vanishing Point feature to add artwork to a perspective grid. This process requires you to draw a grid that accurately matches the flat surface before pasting artwork into the perspective grid. We also observed that grids can consist of one or multiple planes, as needed. For the mural, we extended the first grid to wrap artwork along two walls. The downside of Vanishing Point is that it lacks editability. Next, we will explore techniques for applying artwork around curved surfaces.

Wrapping artwork around curved surfaces

The Photoshop warp transform features provide practical techniques for bending and distorting artwork to match curved surfaces. In the following two exercises, you will apply 2D artwork to a bottle and a page within a book. In doing so, you will match the surface of both products.

Applying a cylinder warp

In the following exercise, you will apply 2D artwork to an unbranded bottle, utilizing a relatively recent addition to the warp feature that specifically addresses cylindrical distortions.

1. Open `Bottle.jpg` from the `05-Mockup` folder.

2. Then, go to **File → Place Linked**, select `Bottle-Label.jpg` from the `05-Mockup` folder, and click **Open** when done to import the artwork.

3. The logo will appear in a **Transform** box in the center of the canvas. Link the **Width** and **Height** fields in the **Options** bar and increase the scale to 115%. Click on the **Commit** button in the **Options** bar to complete the import process:

Figure 5.12: Import and scale the label art

4. Switch to the **Move** tool and drag the label down the bottle, aligning the bottom edge of the label with the bottom edge of the bottle.

5. Right-click on the imported **Bottle-Label** layer and choose **Convert to Smart Object** from the list of commands.

6. Go to **Edit → Transform → Warp**. The warp settings will then appear in the **Options** bar. Click on the **Warp** drop-down menu and choose **Cylinder**.

7. When the cylinder warp becomes active, the artwork will distort considerably, requiring you to pull the design back toward the bottle in the photograph. Start by dragging the bottom-left corner of the warp grid (**A** in *Figure 5.13*) to the bottom-left corner of the bottle, above the lip of the bottle:

Figure 5.13: Begin curving the artwork with a cylinder warp

8. Next, drag the top-right corner of the warp grid (**B**) to the top-right edge of the bottle at the point before the bottle tapers inward. This will set a rough size for the warp grid.

9. Now, you will need to alter the top edge curve (**C**) to match the bottle's curve; it should have a slight downward curve. Then, drag the bottom edge curve (**D**) upward to match the bottle's lower lip. The photo contains a slight distortion that can be corrected in a layer step. For now, ensure that the label curves to match the bottle as closely as possible.

10. Click on the **Commit changes** button in the **Options** bar to apply the edits.

11.   Then, go to **Edit → Transform → Distort**. When the transform frame appears, zoom in closely to each corner (circled in *Figure 5.14*) and drag the corner points as close to the edge of the bottle as possible:

Figure 5.14: Apply a transform distortion to the artwork to match the sides of the bottle

It's better to make the artwork slightly larger than the bottle so that any white edges of the bottle can be concealed; these will be noticeable if the label doesn't cover them.

12.   Click on the **Commit changes** button in the **Options** bar to apply the edits.

13. To help blend the artwork into the bottle, change the blend mode to **Multiply** from the **Blend Mode** menu in the **Layers** panel:

Figure 5.15: Changing the blend mode of the Bottle-Label layer

14. Save the document as a PDF in the 05-Mockup folder and name the file Bottle.pdf. Close the document when you're done:

Warping artwork across book designs

The warp transform features in Photoshop allow for granular editing using a grid. In the following exercise, you will use a rectangular grid to morph the contents to match a page curl in a photo:

1. Open Book.jpg from the 05-Mockup folder.

2. Go to **File → Place Linked** and select Page-Left.psd from the 05-Mockup folder. Click **Open** to import the artwork onto the canvas.

3. The artwork will appear in a **Transform** box in the center of the canvas. Move the top-left corner of the grid in the imported artwork to align with the top-left corner of the left-hand side page in the photo.

4. Go to **Edit → Free Transform**. Click on the checkbox in the **Options** bar to activate the **Reference Point** grid and click on the top-left corner point in the **Reference Point** grid (circled in *Figure 5.16*):

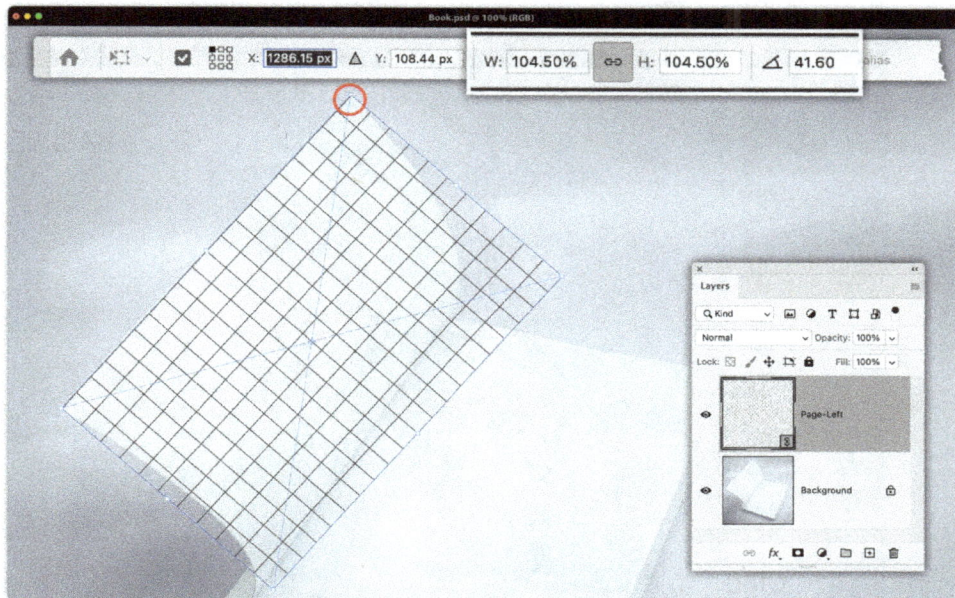

Figure 5.16: Align the imported grid image to the left-hand page

5. Increase **Scale** to 104.5% and set **Rotation** to 41.6°. This should align the left edge of the imported grid with the left edge of the page. Click on the **Commit changes** button in the **Options** bar to apply the edit.

6. Go to **Edit → Transform → Warp**. When the settings appear in the **Options** bar, click on the **Grid** drop-down menu and choose **Custom** from the list. When the **Custom Grid Size** dialog appears, change **Column** and **Row** to 1 and click **OK** when you're done, as shown in *Figure 5.17*:

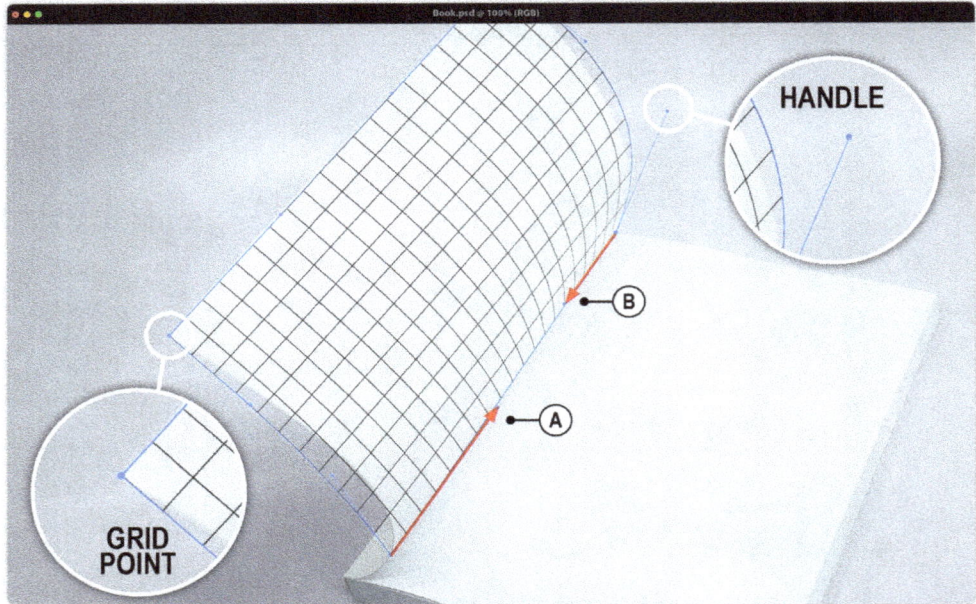

Figure 5.17: Use the corner handles to curve the edges of the grid to match the book

7. Click on the cog icon to reveal the **Guide Options** popout; click the **Never Show Guides** radio button to hide them. As we have our own grid, hiding these guides will simplify things a little onscreen.

8. With the warp grid visible, drag the bottom-right corner of the grid to the lowest visible portion of the page. Then, drag the top-right corner of the warp grid to the highest right-hand portion of the page turn.

9. Next, you will need to drag the handles of the top-right and bottom-right grid points to match the angle of the page edges. To do this, I often refer to the angle of these handles as hands around a clock face. Odd, I know, but if you think of the grid point as the center of a clock face, the handles that emanate from it act like the hands on a clock pointing to numbers on the imaginary clock face.

10. Starting with the bottom-right corner of the warp grid, hover your cursor over the right-hand side handle end (**A** in *Figure 5.18*) and drag it to the right edge of the page to point to a 2 o'clock position. The handle should also point to the top-right-hand corner of the grid now:

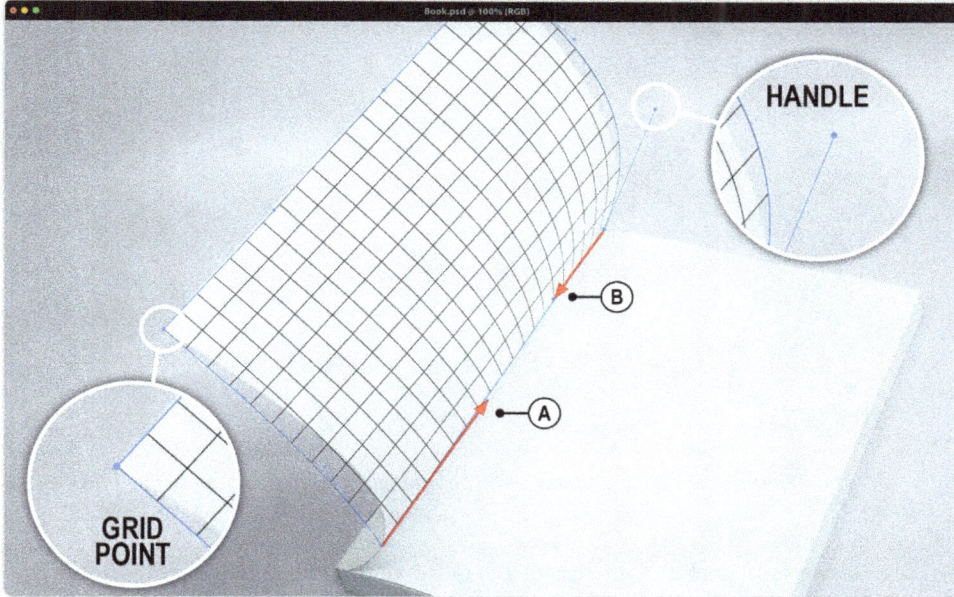

Figure 5.18: Drag the handles at the top of the placed image to match the page curl

11. Next, focus on the top-right grid point (**B**) and drag the lower-left handle down to point to a 7 o'clock position. This should also result in the handle pointing to the bottom-right-hand side of the grid.

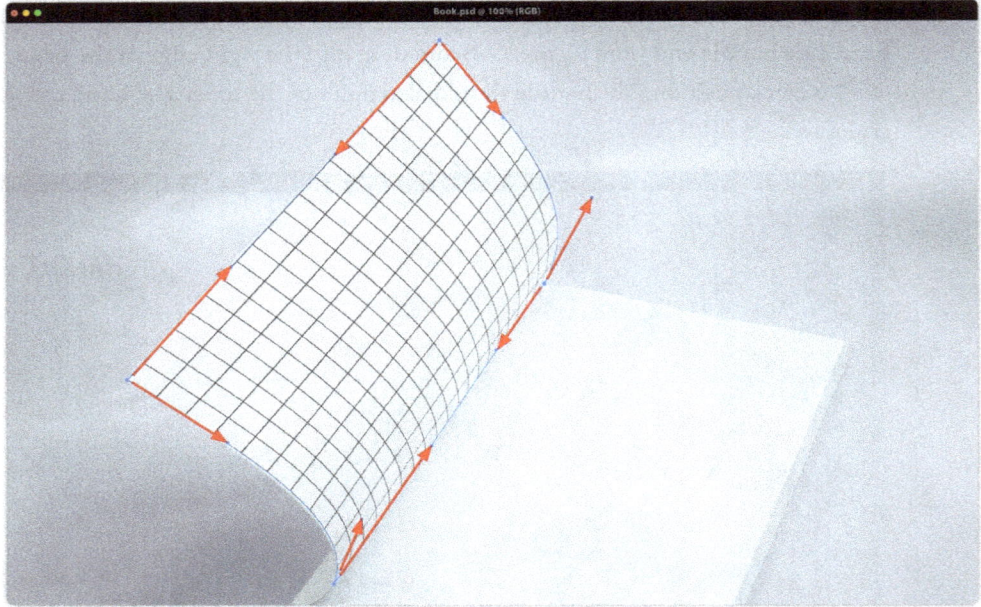

Figure 5.19: The red arrows indicate the length and direction of each handle you need to edit

12. Use the same technique to drag each of the remaining six handles to match the diagram (*Figure 5.19*), where the angle and length of each handle are shown as a red arrow. Once all the handles have been repositioned, click the **Commit changes** button in the **Options** bar to apply the edits.

13. Now that the grid artwork has been suitably matched to the curves of the page, it's time to reveal the magazine design. Hover your cursor over the **Page-Left** layer thumbnail in the **Layers** panel and double-click on it to open the file.

14. When the document opens, turn off the layer visibility of the **Grid-Left** layer, and then turn on layer visibility for the **Page-Left** layer. Go to **File → Save** and close the document. The edits will now be updated in the book mock-up:

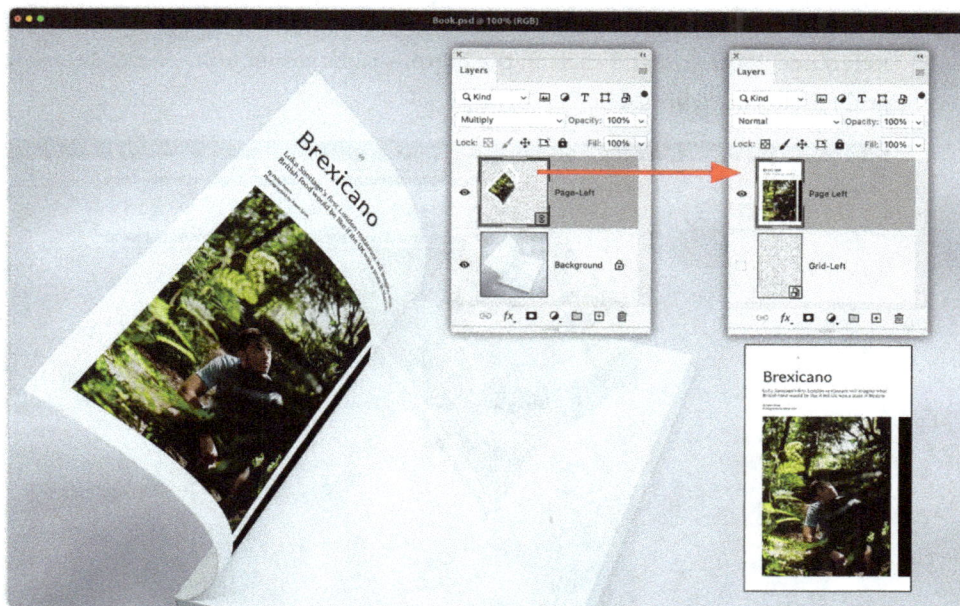

Figure 5.20: The imported page design is now visible over the photo

15. To help blend the artwork into the page, change **Blend Mode** to **Multiply** from the **Layers** panel.

16. Save the document in the 05-Mockup folder as Book.psd. Next, we need to add the right-hand page artwork to the mock-up.

17. Go to **File → Place Linked**, choose Page-Right.psd from the 05-Mockup folder. Click **Open** to import the artwork onto the canvas.

18. The artwork will appear in a **Transform** box in the center of the canvas. Move the bottom-right corner of the grid in the imported artwork to align with the bottom-right corner of the right-hand page in the photo.

19. Go to **Edit** → **Free Transform**. Click on the checkbox in the **Options** bar to activate the **Reference Point** grid and click on the bottom-right corner point in the **Reference Point** grid (circled in *Figure 5.21*):

Figure 5.21: The imported right-hand grid

20. Increase **Scale** to 96.5% and set **Rotation** to 22.48°. This should align the right edge of the imported grid with the right edge of the page. Click on the **Commit changes** button in the **Options** bar when you're done to apply the edits.

21. Go to **Edit → Transform → Warp**. When the settings appear in the **Options** bar, click on the **Grid** drop-down menu and choose **Custom** from the list. When the **Custom Grid Size** dialog appears, change **Column** and **Row** to 2 and click **OK**. This imported grid requires an additional warp point in the center to match the curve along the top edge of the page:

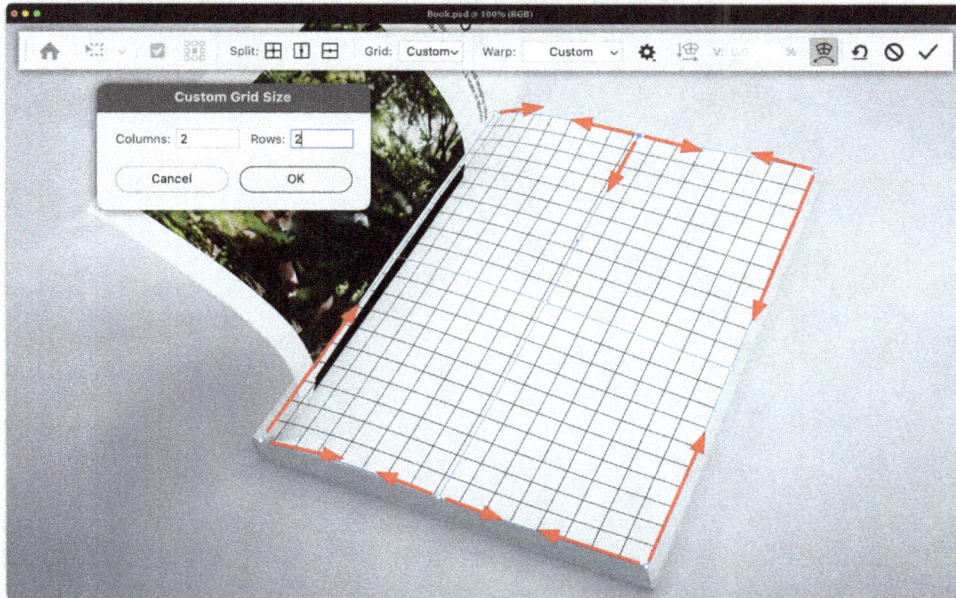

Figure 5.22: The grid points and handles have been edited to match the curve of the page

22. Repeat the same technique you used in the previous steps to move the warp grid points into each corner of the right-hand page of the photo and then adjust each of the handles so that they match the curve of the page. Click on the **Commit changes** button to apply the edits.

23. Hover your cursor over the **Page-Left** thumbnail, then press *Ctrl* (Windows) or *Cmd* (macOS) and click to create a selection of the layer content.

24. Switch to the **Polygonal Lasso Tool** from the **Tools** panel. Set the selection mode to **Add to Selection** and **Feather** to 0 px. Create a selection around the small portion of the book cover that can be seen in the lower-left-hand side of the photo. Then, go to **Select → Inverse**.

25. With the selections combined and the **Page-Right** layer active, click on the **Add a mask** icon at the bottom of the **Layers** panel to apply the mask. Change the **Page-Right** layer's **Blend Mode** option to **Multiply**:

Figure 5.23: The right-hand side grid artwork with a mask applied

26. Hover your cursor over the **Page-Right** layer thumbnail in the **Layers** panel and double-click on it to open the file.

27. When the document opens, turn off the layer visibility of the **Grid-Right** layer, and then turn on the layer visibility for the **Page-Right** layer.

28. Save and close the document. The edits will now be updated in the book mock-up. Then, save and close all documents.

Figure 5.24: The completed book mock-up

In this section, we used Photoshop's perspective editor, Vanishing Point, to create a perspective grid where our artwork was aligned with surfaces in existing photographs, such as the front of a bag and a wall. We refined the results using a combination of masking and blend modes. Next, we worked with transform warps and distortion tools to curve our designs, creating the impression that our original designs were wrapped around a bottle and a double-page spread within a book.

In the following exercises, we will substitute device screens with our own artwork and merge the designs with the original photograph, overlaying custom reflections and inner shadows onto our screen artwork.

Replacing device screens with your own artwork

It is important to note that all good mock-ups require designs that have been created to fit the content they will be added to. Therefore, if you intend to replace an iPhone screen with a website mock-up, you must find out the screen size of the iPhone in the photo and build the website mock-up to that size and ratio. High-quality effects such as reflections, shadows, and textures cannot hide a badly formatted design.

Creating an iPad mock-up

This exercise focuses on replacing an existing iPad display with a website mock-up from a top-down view while applying an inner shadow effect to make the design appear as though it is behind the glass screen. In reality, the screen on modern devices is much closer to the glass, with minimal shadows; however, a little creative license can sometimes make your mock-up more convincing. Let's get started:

1. Go to **File → Open** and pick the Tablet.jpg document from the 05-Mockup folder. Click **Open** when you're done and ensure that the entirety of the image is visible within the image window to make positioning the new screen easier.

2. Go to **File → Place Linked**, browse to the 05-Mockup folder, select the Website_iPad.psd file, and click **Place**. When the image appears, drag the placed artwork so that the bottom-left corner aligns with the bottom-left corner of the iPad screen in the background. Click on the **Commit changes** button in the **Options** bar to complete the import process. You should notice a link icon inside the imported layer thumbnail in the **Layers** panel, indicating that the artwork has been linked to the original PSD and that any edits you make to the website design will be automatically reflected in this file.

3.   Next, go to **Edit → Free Transform**. In the **Options** bar, pin the bottom-left **Reference Point** grid, which can be found on the far left-hand side. Then, enter a rotation value of -23.6° to match the iPad screen angle. After that, click on the **Maintain Aspect Ratio** button. Change the **Width** field to a scale of 95% to make the new screen fit appropriately to the iPad screen. Click on the **Commit changes** button in the **Options** bar to apply the edits:

Figure 5.25: Scale and rotate the placed artwork to match the screen

4.   With the **Website_iPad** layer still active, click on the **Fx** icon at the bottom of the **Layers** panel and choose **Inner Shadow** from the list of effects to launch the **Layer Styles** dialog (*Figure 5.26*). I used the following settings to fine-tune the effect, but feel free to experiment. I set **Angle** to -45˚, **Distance** to 0 px, **Spread** to 0%, **Size** to 46 px, and **Opacity** to 33%. Click **OK** when you're done.

Figure 5.26: Add an inner shadow effect to the imported artwork

5. Save the document in the 05-Mockup folder, as Device.psd, and close the document when done.

Creating a smartphone mock-up

The previous exercise only required a flat, top-down view of a device screen. In this example, the screen display is angled and requires masking to fit the screen. It will also require you to re-create reflections to make the mock-up look convincing:

1. Go to **File → Open** and pick the Smartphone.jpg document from the 05-Mockup folder. Click **Open** when you're done and zoom into the image, making the smartphone occupy most of the image window to make positioning the new screen easier.

2. Go to **File → Place Linked**, select Website_iPhone.ai from the 05-Mockup folder, and click **Place**.

3. Increase the scale of the placed artwork to 136% from the **Options** bar.

4. Drag the placed artwork, aligning its top-right corner with the top-right corner of the smartphone's screen in the photo. Click the **Commit changes** button in the **Options** bar to complete the import process.

5. To skew and distort the artwork you've placed, you need to convert it into a smart object. Right-click on the **Website_iPhone** layer's name in the **Layers** panel and choose **Convert to Smart Object** from the list of commands.

6. Then, lower the layer's **Opacity** value to 25% so that when you distort the artwork, you can see the original screen through the artwork for accuracy:

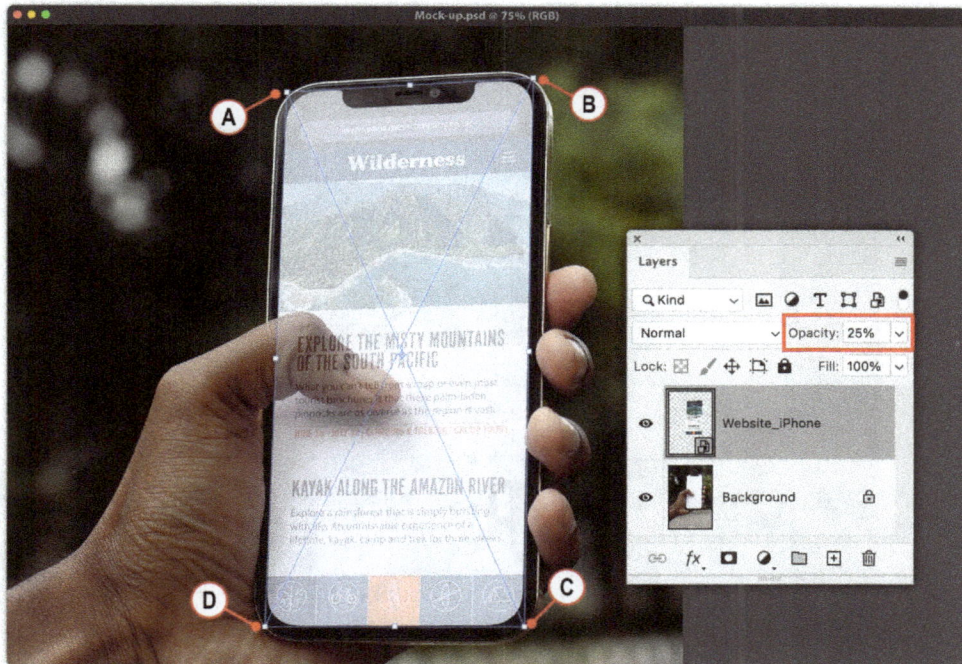

Figure 5.27: Scale the imported artwork to match the screen size

7. Next, go to **Edit → Free Transform → Distort**, where the transform frame will appear around the website artwork. Drag each bounding box corner point to the outer edges of the original screen (shown as **A–D** in *Figure 5.27*). Ensure that the artwork is slightly larger than the screen to conceal the white backdrop.

8. In the **Layers** panel, turn off the visibility of the **Website_iPhone** layer and click on the **Background** layer to make it active.

9. Switch to the **Magic Wand** tool from the **Tools** panel. From the **Options** bar, set the selection mode to **New Selection**, **Sample Size** to **Point Sample**, and **Tolerance** to 50. Ensure that the **Anti-alias** and **Contiguous** checkboxes are active.

10. Hover your cursor over the white region of the original phone screen toward the upper half and click to select that region. Then, change the selection mode to **Add to Selection** and click on the white screen regions under the thumb to add them to the current selection.

11. If parts of the thumb become selected, switch to the **Magnetic Lasso Tool**. Then, from the **Options** bar, set the selection mode to **Subtract Selection**, **Width** to 20, **Contrast** to 10, and **Frequency** to 100. Ensure that the **Anti-alias** checkbox is active.

12. Hover your cursor over the top of the thumb where it meets the phone's left edge and click to start the selection (*Figure 5.28*). Trace along the entire thumb to remove it from the selection, leaving just the white screen selected:

Figure 5.28: Create a selection of the original white screen as the basis for a layer mask

13. Go to the bottom of the **Layers** panel and click on the **Create a New Group** button. With the selection still active and the new layer group, click on **Add a Mask** at the bottom of the **Layers** panel to apply the mask to the group.

14. Double-click on the layer group's name in the **Layers** panel, change it to Mockup, then press *Enter* to accept the change. Drag the **Website_iPhone** layer into the **Mockup** layer group in the **Layers** pane, and in doing so, mask the corners of the artwork to fit the screen.

15. Increase the **Website_iPhone** layer's **Opacity** to 100% and change **Blend Mode** to **Multiply** from the **Blend Mode** drop-down menu in the **Layers** panel. Changing the blend mode will reveal the shadow in the photo. Keep the document open.

Adding screen reflections

In the example we covered in the previous exercise, prototype artwork was applied to an original smartphone screen. However, this often conceals highlights from the photo, making the result look less than convincing. Let's look at some techniques that can help with this:

1. With the **Website_iPhone** layer active in the **Layers** panel, click on the **Fx** icon at the bottom of the **Layers** panel and choose **Gradient Overlay** from the list of effects.

2. When the dialog appears, ensure that **Blend Mode** is set to **Screen** and enter 50% for **Opacity**. Click on the **Gradient Preset** dropdown, expand the Basic folder, and click on the thumbnail named **Foreground to Transparent**. Tooltips will reveal the name of each preset when you hover over it with the cursor.

3. Turn on the **Align with Layer** checkbox and set the gradient's **Style** setting to **Linear**, **Angle** to -77, and **Scale** to 100%:

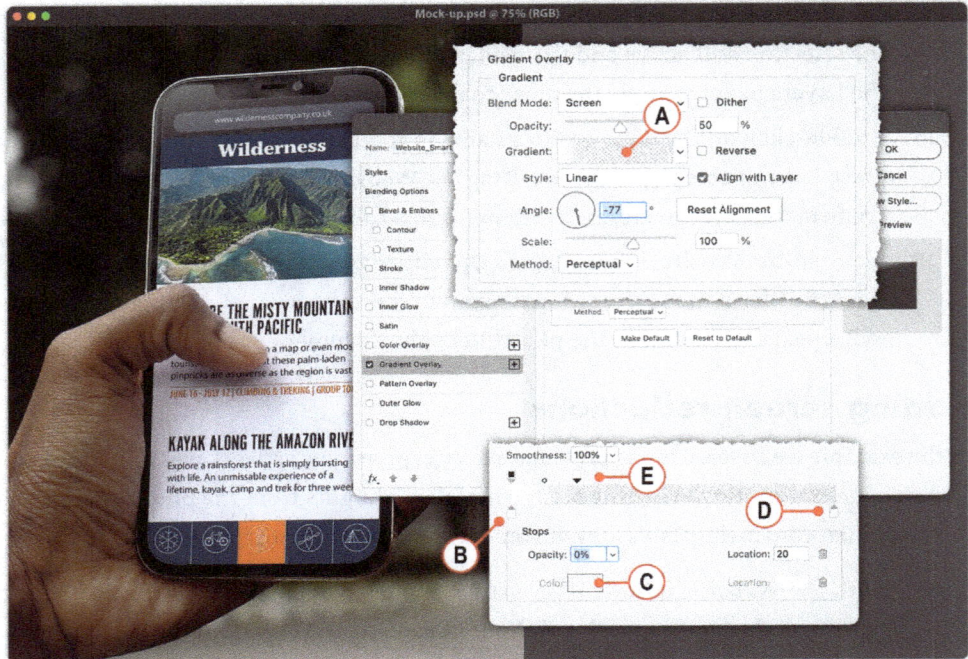

Figure 5.29: Add a gradient overlay to give the impression of reflected glass

4. To fine-tune the gradient's appearance, click on **Gradient Preview** (**A** in *Figure 5.29*).

5. When the **Gradient Editor** area appears, click on the bottom-left color stop (**B**) and change it to white by clicking on the **Color** picker (**C**). Enter 255 into each of the **Red**, **Green**, and **Blue** numerical fields. Repeat the same step for the right-hand color stop (**D**).

6. Finally, change the top-right transparency stop's (**E**) **Location** value to 20%. This should create the appearance of a white highlight that starts in the top-left corner of the website artwork and slowly disappears a quarter of the way down the screen. Click **OK** to apply the effect.

7. Next, go to **File → Place Linked**, browse to the 05-Mockup folder, select the Reflection-A.jpg file, and click **Place**. Increase the scale of the placed artwork to 130% from the **Options** bar. Press *Enter* to import the image.

8. Change **Blend Mode** to **Lighter Color** and reduce the layer's **Opacity** value to 5% from the **Layers** panel. Then, go to **Filter → Blur → Gaussian Blur**. When the dialog appears, adjust **Radius** so that it blurs the trees where they can be seen over the website's artwork. In this example, **Radius** was set to 5.0. Click **OK** when you're done to apply the settings:

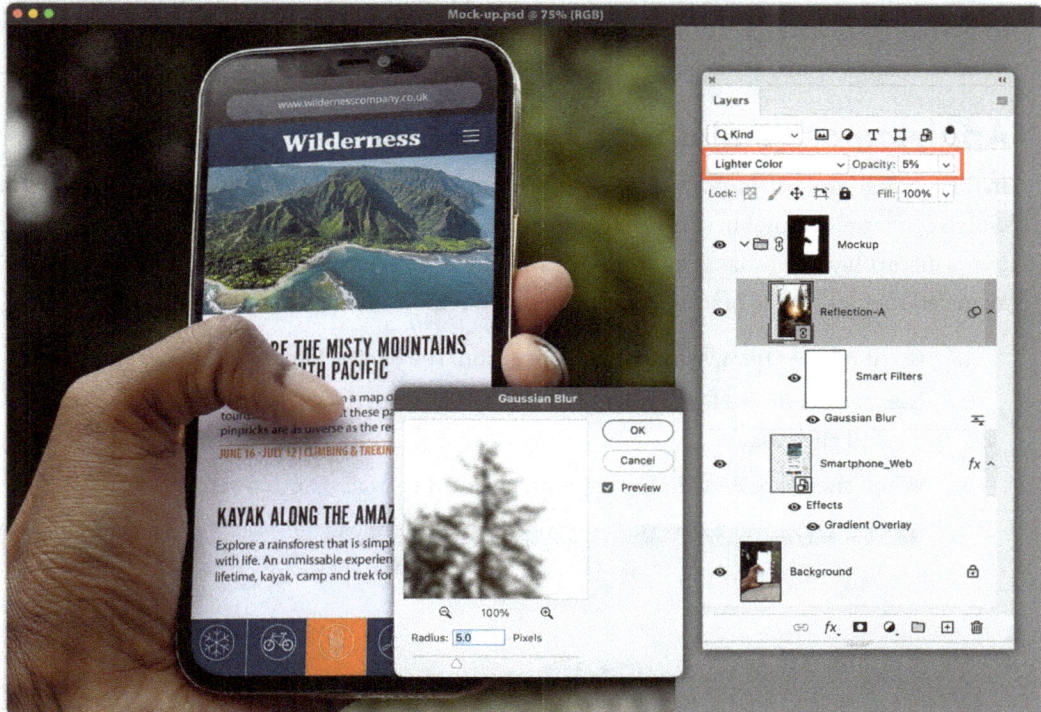

Figure 5.30: Import an image of trees to enhance the illusion of a screen reflection

9. With all the edits now complete, go to **File → Save As**, browse to the 05-Mockup folder, name the file Smartphone.psd, and close the document.

In this section, we looked at techniques for replacing device screens that account for the angle, obstructions, and glass, where necessary, recreating reflections and highlights to create a more realistic mock-up. Each of the techniques we have covered allows for every component to be edited or replaced without recompositing. Live-linked artwork can be edited in the original PSD or Adobe Illustrator file and updated in Photoshop mock-ups. The gradients, reflections, and effects can be edited by double-clicking with the mouse. Next, we will apply designs across fabric surfaces, such as clothing and soft furnishings.

Creating clothing and soft furnishing mock-ups

As we have seen in this chapter, applying designs to flat or curved surfaces presents numerous challenges. Applying designs to fabric with irregular surfaces poses additional difficulties. Firstly, how can we match our designs to the curved, rippled, or distorted surface of the fabric? Most importantly, how can we accomplish this without engaging in unproductive work when we need to change or update a design? In the following exercises, we will overcome both challenges.

Applying original designs to clothing

In this section, you will import original designs onto a photo of a hoodie using **displacement maps**, which can mimic ripples in soft surfaces such as fabric. Created as grayscale images, displacement maps distort layer content to produce the illusion of raised or indented surfaces. White appears as raised regions, while black indicates indented regions. Let's see how:

1. Go to **File → Open**, select Hoodie.jpg from the 05-Mockup folder, and click **Open**.

2. Next, go to **File → Place Embedded**. Then, browse to the 05-Mockup folder, select LogoType.ai, and click **Place**.

3. When the **Place PDF** dialog appears, click **OK** to place the artwork.

Figure 5.31: Import and position the logo over the hoodie

4. Switch to the **Move** tool and center the motif over the center of the hoodie. Then, go to **Filter → Distort → Displace**. When the dialog appears, accept the default options, as they are a good starting point, and click **OK**.

5. Choose `Displace.psd` from the `05-Mockup` folder. This image contains a black-and-white version of the hoodie image, with the ripples in the hoodie exaggerated. Black regions denote low or no raised regions, while white regions denote raised areas. In a later exercise, you'll create your own displacement map.

6. With the **Detours-A** layer still active, click the **Add a Mask** icon at the bottom of the **Layers** panel. Zoom into the logo type at a magnification level of around 350%. Switch to the **Brush** tool and set the foreground color to black. Click on the **Brush Preset Picker** tool from the **Options** bar and select the **Soft Round** brush tip. Set its **Size** value to 15 px and **Hardness** to 95 px:

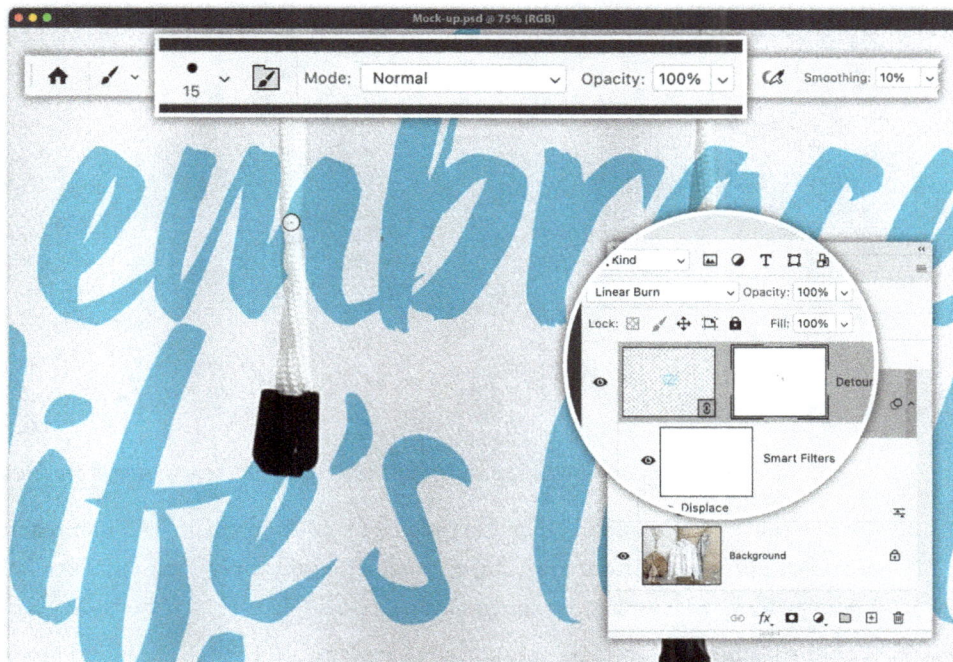

Figure 5.32: Hide the motif with a layer mask where it overlaps the hoodie ties

7. Paint black in the layer mask where the pull-strings of the sweater hood overlap the region where the **Detours-A** layer appears, concealing the design.

8. Switch to the **Rectangular Marquee** tool and click on the **Background** layer in the **Layers** panel to make it active. From the **Options** bar, set the selection mode to **New Selection**, **Feather** to 0 px, and **Style** to **Normal**.

9. Create a selection of the hoodie that is slightly larger than the region the type design occupies (shown in *Figure 5.33*). With the selection in place, go to **Layer → New → Layer via Copy**. Drag the new layer to the top of the layer stack, then change **Blend Mode** to **Multiply**.

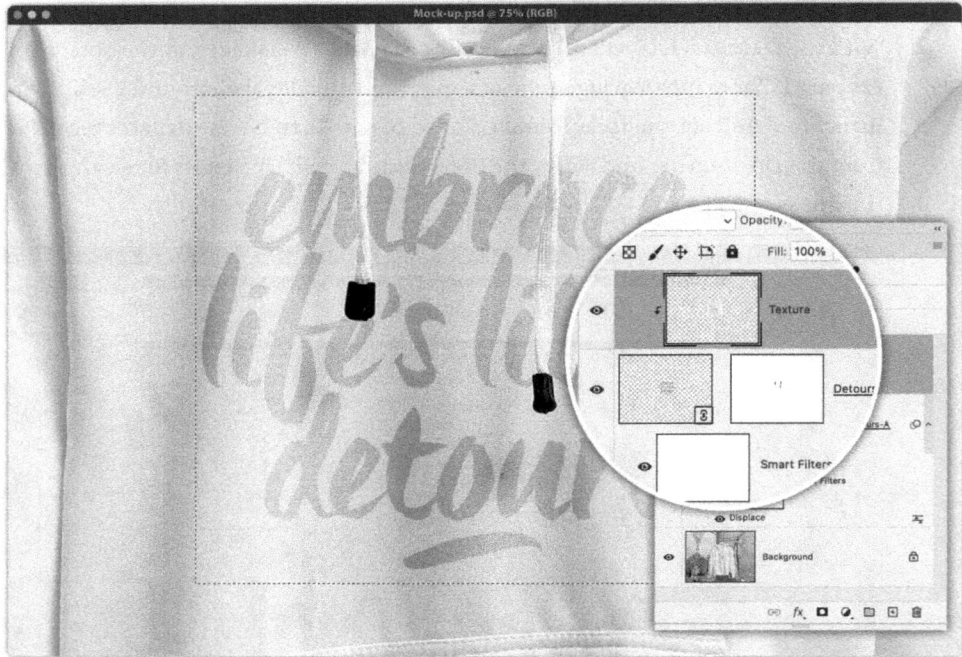

Figure 5.33: Copy a section of the hoodie photo into a new layer at the top of the stack

10. Change the layer's name to Texture, then right-click on the layer's name and choose **Create Clipping Mask** from the list of options. This will apply the hoodie's texture to the logo type to make it look more convincing.

11. With the **Detours-A** layer still active in the **Layers** panel, change the **Blend Mode** setting to **Linear Burn** to emphasize the fabric texture.

12. Save the document as Hoodie.psd in the 05-Mockup folder and close the document when you're done.

Figure 5.34: A displacement map creates the effect of rippled or uneven surfaces

Adding pattern designs to a cushion

In this section, you will import original designs onto a photo of a cushion. However, on this occasion, you will not only create the displacement map but also exaggerate the distortion to match the contours of the cushion using the **Liquify** feature.

Creating the cushion displacement map

In a previous exercise, you applied a displacement map to create the illusion of a raised surface. In the following steps, you will make your own displacement map:

1. **Open** Cushion.jpg from the 05-Mockup folder.

2. Go to **Image** → **Duplicate**. When the dialog appears, name the duplicate Cushion-Displace and click **OK**.

3. Go to **Filter → Convert for Smart Filters**. When the dialog appears informing you that the selected layer will be converted into a smart object, click **OK**. Rename the layer Photo in the **Layers** panel.

4. Next, go to **Filter → Blur → Surface Blur**. This type of blur maintains edge details but smoothens surfaces and similar color regions, such as the texture of a cushion. This will help prevent tiny details from distorting the appearance of the artwork once they're applied to a cushion while maintaining the large creases and folds. Set **Radius** to 10 px and **Threshold** to 15 px:

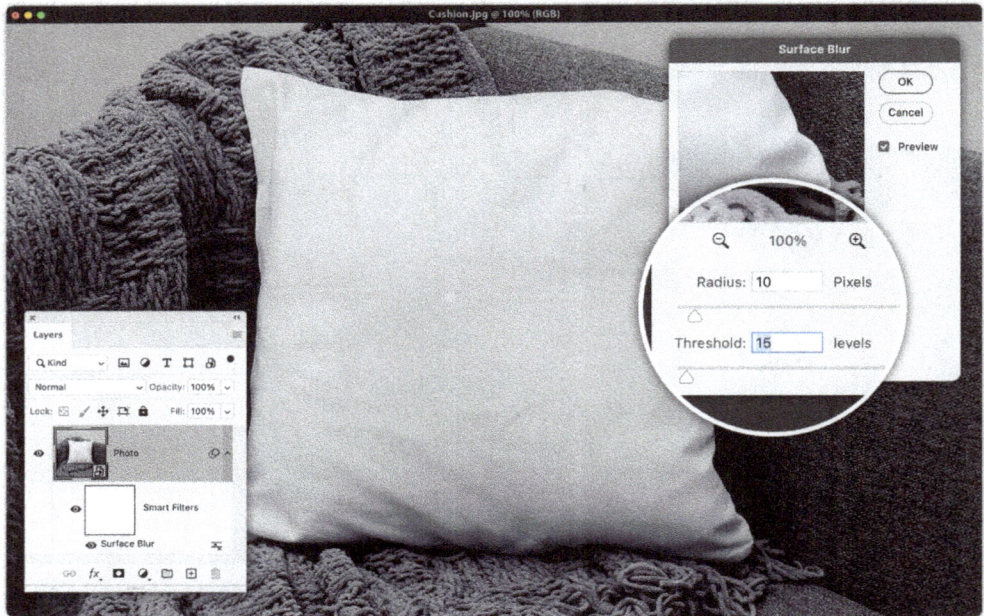

Figure 5.35: Blur the displacement artwork to eliminate fine textures

5. Then, go to the **Adjustments** panel and add a **Levels** adjustment. When the **Properties** panel displays the **Levels** settings, enter 33 in the black point field, 0.75 in the mid-tone field, and 237 in the white point field at the bottom of the **Properties** panel:

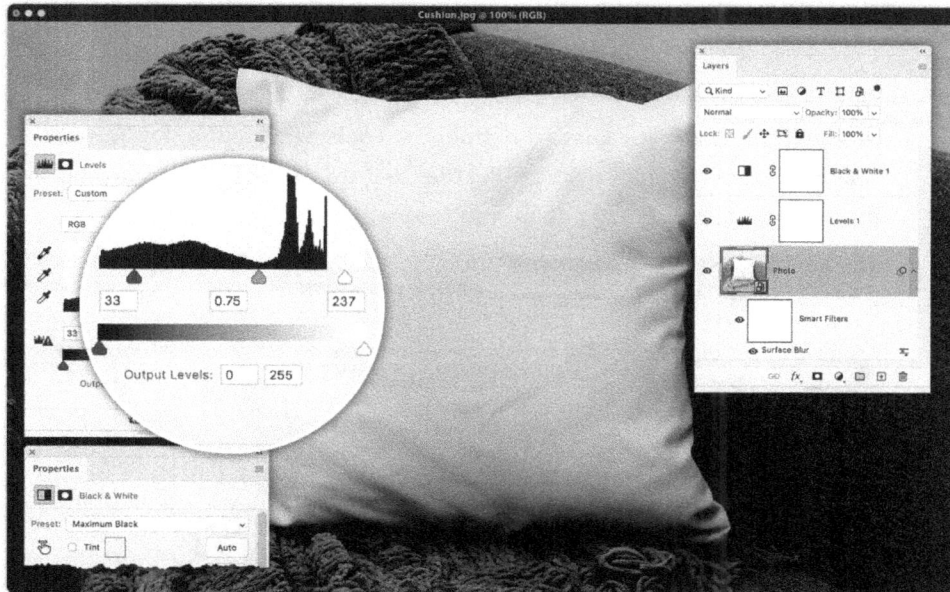

Figure 5.36: Add a Black & White adjustment

6. Next, add a **Black & White** adjustment from the **Adjustments** panel. When the settings appear in the **Properties** panel, select **Maximum Black** from the **Preset** drop-down menu.

7. With both adjustment layers now added to the **Layers** stack, change the blend mode of the **Black & White** adjustment layer to **Color** and the **Levels** adjustment layer to **Luminosity**.

8. Go to **File → Save As**, browse to the 05-Mockup folder, and name the file Cushion-Displace. psd. Leave the file open for now in case any further edits are required.

Applying the pattern artwork

With the displacement map now generated and saved, you can focus on the pattern artwork and apply it to the cushion in the photo:

1. Switch to the **Document** tab for the Cushion.jpg file. Go to **File → Place Linked**. Choose Pattern-A.ai from the 05-Mockup folder. When the **Place PDF** dialog appears, click **OK** to place the artwork.

2. From the **Options** bar, change the pattern's **Scale** value to 90%, then click the **Commit changes** button to complete the placing process.

3. Switch to the **Move** tool and move the pattern artwork to the center of the cushion. In the **Layers** panel, turn off the visibility of the **Pattern-A** layer and click on the **Background** layer to make it active.

4. Switch to the **Magnetic Lasso** tool from the **Tools** panel. From the **Options** bar, set the selection mode to **New Selection**, **Feather** to 0, the **Anti-alias** checkbox on, **Width** to 30 px, **Contrast** to 10%, and **Frequency** to 100:

Figure 5.37: Create a selection around the cushion

5. Hover your cursor over the top-left edge of the cushion in the photo and click to start the selection. Guide the cursor around all the cushion's edges until you return to the selection start point, then click to complete the selection.

6. Go to the bottom of the **Layers** panel and click on the **Create a New Group** button. With the selection still active and the new layer group targeted, click on **Add a Mask** at the bottom of the **Layers** panel to apply the mask to the group. Name the group Design. Drag the **Pattern-A** layer into the layer group to apply the mask to it.

7. With the **Pattern-A** layer still active in the **Layers** panel, change the blending mode to **Linear Burn** from the **Blend Mode** drop-down menu. This will help show the shadow and highlight details throughout the design:

Figure 5.38: Use the selection to create a layer mask that hides the pattern edges

Finessing the rippled surface details

As we have already witnessed, displacement maps provide a subtle yet effective level of detail to irregular surfaces. However, when a more aggressive form of distortion is required, **Liquify** is ideal:

1. With the **Pattern-A** layer active, go to **Filter → Distort → Displace**. When the dialog appears, accept the default options and click **OK**.

2. Then, browse to the 05-Mockup folder, select Cushion-Displace.psd, and click **Open**. You will notice that the pattern design matches the contours of the cushion's creases.

3. Ensure that the **Pattern-A** layer is active and visible in the **Layers** panel. Then, go to **Filter → Liquify** to launch the dedicated editor.

4. When the dialog appears, expand the **View Options** section on the right-hand side and turn on the **Show Image** checkbox. Lower down in the same set of options, turn on the **Show Mask** checkbox, and set **Mask Color** to **Red**. Turn on the **Show Backdrop** checkbox and set the **Use** mode to **Background**, **Mode** to **Behind**, and **Opacity** to 10:

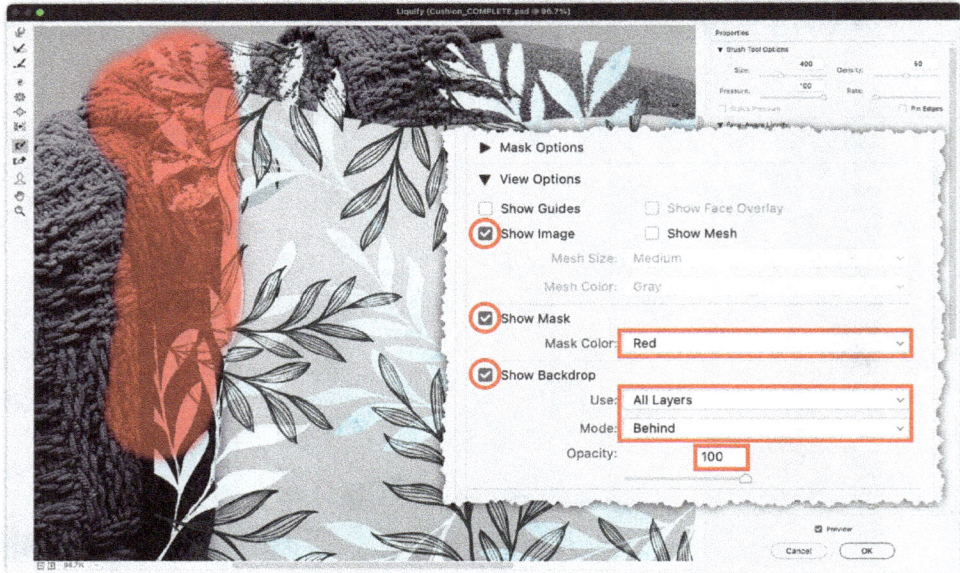

Figure 5.39: Configure the viewing options in Liquify before making edits

5. The next stage involves "freezing" sections of the pattern artwork, so they are unaffected by **Liquify**. Switch to the **Freeze Mask** tool by pressing the *F* key. Hover your cursor over the **Liquify** image window to reveal the circular brush tip. To increase/decrease its size, you can change the **Size** slider on the top right-hand side of the interface.

6. Paint along the left edge of the fold in the top-left corner of the cushion, where a long fold can be seen. By painting over it, you will need to freeze that portion from the fold to the edge of the cushion:

Freezing and thawing a Liquify mask

The masking tools in Liquify allow you to dictate which portions of an image can be affected or protected from warping edits. The Freeze Mask tool protects image areas, while the Thaw Mask tool removes masked regions. This is similar to painting black or white in a regular Photoshop layer mask.

Figure 5.40: Freeze the outer edges of the cushion to prevent it from being affected by Liquify

7. Then, switch to the **Forward Warp** tool (**A** in *Figure 5.41*), located at the top left-hand side set of tools, by pressing the *W* key. You will need to make the brush size considerably larger than you might first expect. In this case, start by setting the **Size** slider to 300 px:

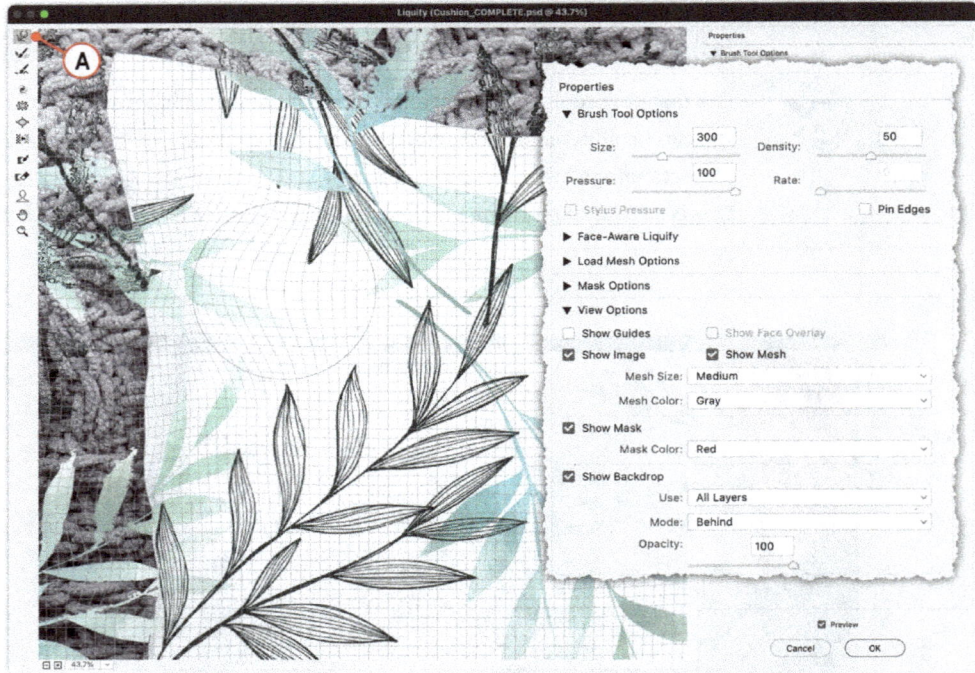

Figure 5.41: Use the Forward Warp tool to distort the pattern so it matches the cushion folds

8. Then, hover your cursor over the right-hand side of the fold you just froze. Very gently, click and drag toward the fold on the left to create the impression that some of the pattern has disappeared behind the fold.

9. Repeat the same technique with other significant folds on the cushion where you feel it will provide value. Freeze one side of a fold, then warp the other. In places where the indentation changes, you can also distort the pattern so that it matches the changes in the cushion's surface.

10. Click **OK** when you're done to apply the changes and exit the **Liquify** dialog. Notice that the edits have been added to the **Pattern** layer's smart filters in the **Layers** panel. You can edit the Liquify edits whenever necessary.

Figure 5.42: The completed mock-up

11. Save the document in the 05-Mockup folder as Cushion.psd and close the document when done.

Replacing pattern artwork

We used a smart object to protect our artwork. This means that whenever you change pattern artwork with surface details applied to it, such as displacement maps and Liquify distortion, those edits remain intact. This makes mock-ups of this nature incredibly flexible. You can also replace the pattern layer artwork. Simply right-click on the layer name of the pattern or placed artwork and choose **Replace Contents** from the context menu, where you'll be prompted to choose a different file. You can also double-click on the layer thumbnail. The layer artwork will appear in a separate window, or, in the case of artwork from Adobe Illustrator, open in a different application where you can make edits. Save the edits, and they will update in your master file back in Photoshop.

In this section, we applied original designs to fabric, matching the irregular contours of the material to make the mock-up look convincing enough to be used for marketing or as a tool to drive further design decision-making.

Summary

In this chapter, we examined the multifaceted challenges of creating branded mock-ups that must appear convincing and legible for marketing purposes or to aid in decision-making during the design process. Sometimes, the mock-up may only need to suggest a look or approximation of the final product, but there are also situations where the visuals must feel real and convincing.

To tackle these challenges, we identified the traits that define a suitable source photograph and the scene or scenario where our prototype will be displayed.

Then, we applied the methods that are required to match a surface, whether it be a wall, a bottle, or a fabric such as a T-shirt, using Vanishing Point, transforms and warps, and displacement maps. Apart from Vanishing Point, which doesn't accommodate smart object layers, each technique could be edited, or the source artwork replaced with ease.

Finally, we looked at techniques for recreating reflections and highlights or leveraging existing glass properties using blend modes.

In the next chapter, we will continue with the theme of mock-ups and prototypes by creating print collateral such as business cards and flyers.

6

Creating Printed Marketing Collateral

Applications such as InDesign are adept at creating multi-page publications; however, this doesn't mean you can't create single-page or front-and-back designs for print within Adobe Photoshop. In this chapter, you will create common print collateral, such as flyers and posters, that can be used internally or sent to a professional print provider for mass production.

We'll start by defining new document characteristics appropriate for print, ensuring PPI and color modes have been considered. Then, we'll look at how to add bleed to a print file using **Canvas Size** to ensure our projects are printed from edge to edge on the destination paper stock.

Guides will play an essential role in setting up our print files. They will indicate the edges where our artwork will be trimmed and identify a safe zone where type and other important content are kept clear from the paper edges when printed.

Photoshop isn't viewed as a tool for editing extensive amounts of text; however, its features and controls for one- or two-page projects are extremely powerful, offering the same detailed control as its sister applications, InDesign and Illustrator, for basic character formatting.

It is possible to export to various file formats for print when working in Photoshop. These include **Joint Photographic Experts Group (JPG)**, **Tagged Image File Format (TIFF)**, and Adobe **Portable Document Format (PDF)**. We will carefully review each to ensure our projects are sent in the best possible quality for professional print output. In this chapter, we will explore the following topics:

- Creating new print documents
- Setting up a Photoshop grid system

- Importing artwork and formatting types
- Exporting documents for professional print

Technical requirements

The project files for this chapter can be found at `https://packt.link/gbz/9781806021710`.

Creating new print projects

Unlike images intended for screen or use on the web, print projects require additional steps for managing the process from a digital desktop to ink and paper on a multitude of stock types. Mistakes in print can be costly; you don't have the luxury of simply replacing a print image as you would with a web graphic. In the following subsections, we will examine the challenges of managing color, the need for printer marks, and how folds need to be accommodated in the setup of our digital files. By understanding these challenges, you will be better able to avoid common mistakes related to print output and save valuable time and money.

Color

It is common for artwork to consist of **red**, **green**, and **blue** (**RGB**) pixels displayed on a backlit RGB display. When your RGB document is printed, those pixels appear as tiny dots of ink using combinations of **cyan**, **magenta**, **yellow**, and **black** (**CMYK**). These are the four inks utilized by a commercial print bureau during a standard print run. This process can lead to a shift in color appearance as they are converted, so managing this process with screen and printed proofs is essential. Photoshop can simulate printed colors onscreen (soft proof), approximating what your RGB colors might look like when printed. However, the most accurate way to approximate print colors is to print them on a locally connected print device (hard proof). Additionally, the print provider should supply their own hard proof before the final print run.

Printers' marks

Printers' marks play an essential role in the world of print. They are required for almost every print project. They help the print provider understand what to do with the document (see *Figure 6.1*). Two common elements of print output are crop marks (**A** in *Figure 6.1*) and bleed marks (**B**):

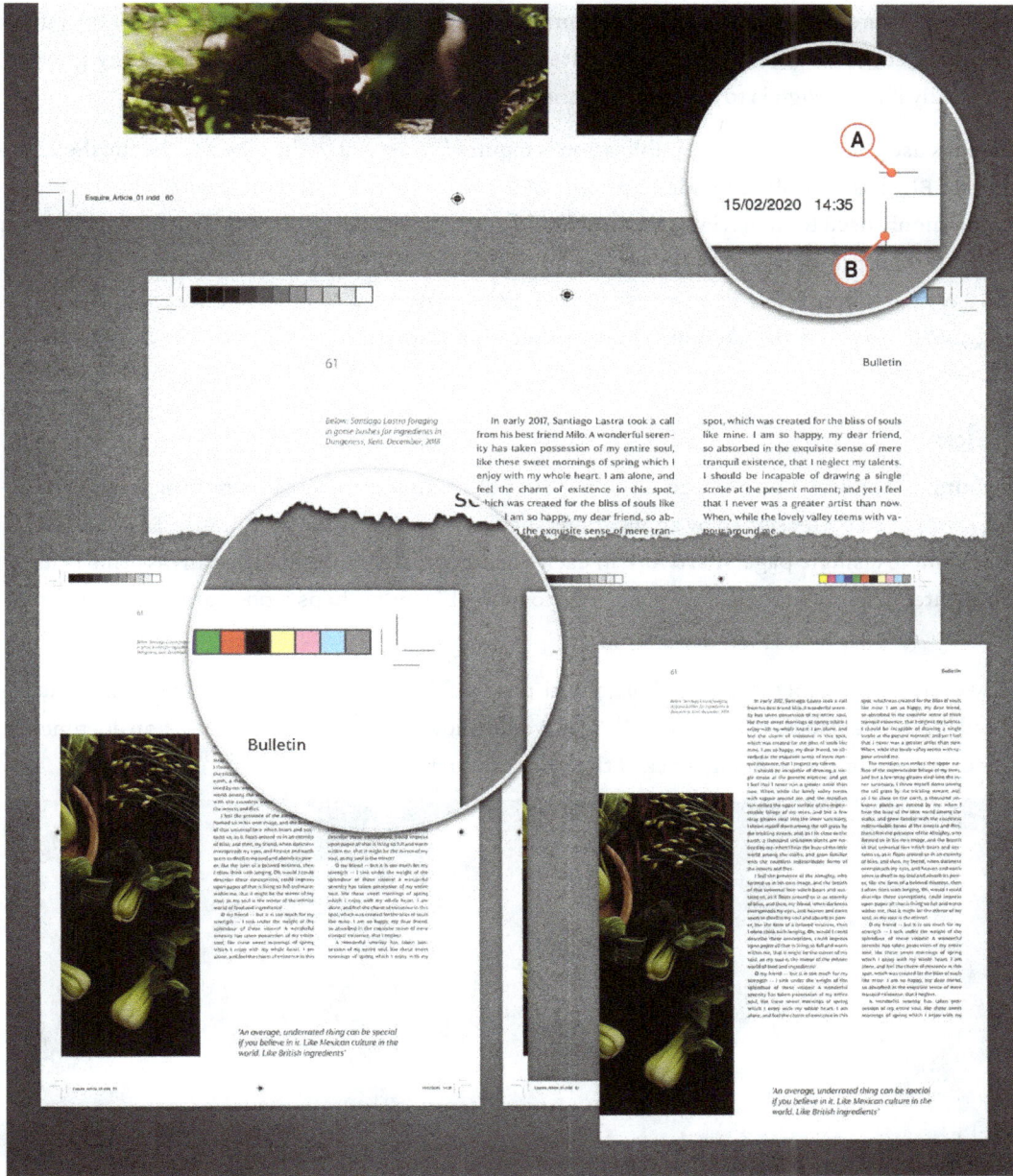

Figure 6.1: The printers' marks used to create professional print collateral

Crop marks are thin lines placed on the corners of a print design that indicate where the paper should be cut to make it the correct size after printing. Crop marks are essential for any artwork, especially if the design is to be printed to the edge of the trimmed paper.

Bleed is used when the printed publication is required to extend to the edges of the finished document. Bleed is typically extended 3 mm/0.125 inches or more beyond the edge of your media. It is commonly used for materials you would hold at a typical reading distance, such as magazines. Large-format print projects, such as pop-up stands and banners, will typically require a bleed of 10 mm or more. This will ensure that the finished, trimmed product is printed from edge to edge. Without bleed, the likelihood of white, unprinted strips along one or more edges increases significantly.

Folds

If your print project is an ambitious multi-page publication, such as a brochure or a bound booklet, it would be better served by applications such as InDesign. By its very nature, Photoshop can only handle a single page of artwork in each document, stored within the canvas. This is ideal for printed posters that need only one side to be visible, or perhaps a postcard made up of two separate documents, one for each side.

However, it is possible to create short, multi-page publications that contain no binding and instead incorporate folds (see *Figure 6.2*). This would allow for two separate Photoshop documents to be created for the front and back of the print product.

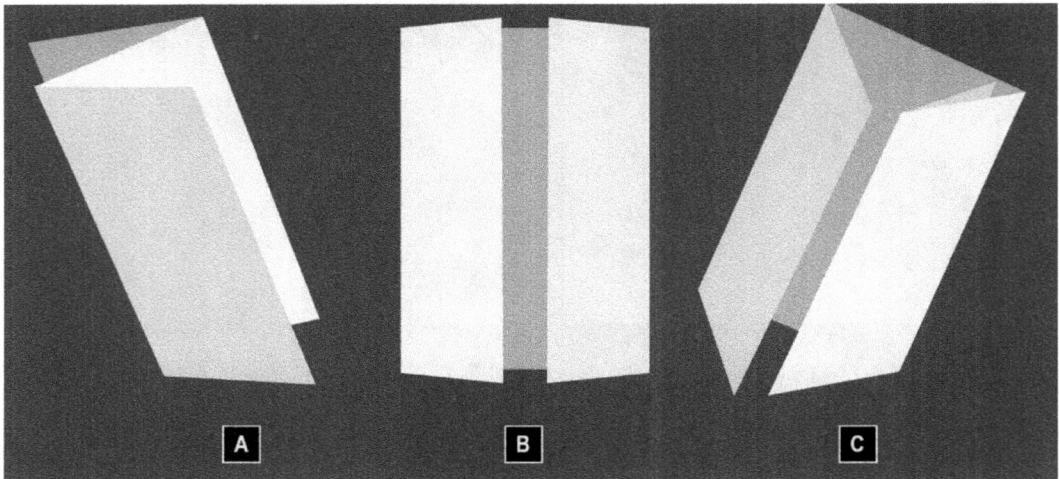

Figure 6.2: From left to right, a Z-fold, an open gate-fold, and a roll-fold brochure

One of the most common folds will undoubtedly be those used for greeting cards. A *tent fold* is simply folded in half horizontally to create four pages: the front cover, back cover, and two internal pages. A tent fold can be produced in either portrait or landscape format.

A *tri-fold* brochure is a great example of a common format used in print collateral, and it is cost-effective to print since it typically fits a standard A4 or letter size. Interestingly, its name is misleading because it features only two folds, not three. The result is a three-panel design printed on both sides, offering a total of six pages.

Tri-fold brochures feature one page that is slightly narrower than the others, allowing it to be tucked inside the two. In A4 format, two pages measure 99 mm x 210 mm, while the shorter page measures 97 mm x 210 mm.

A *Z-fold* (**A** in *Figure 6.2*) consists of two creases that create six pages, all of which are identical in width and height. For A4, that's 99 mm x 210 mm. The pages do not fold into one another but form a Z shape when opened, resembling an accordion.

An *open gate-fold* (**B** in *Figure 6.2*) is creased twice to give six pages but contains a center page twice the size of the left and right page panels. This is ideal for adding arresting imagery to the inside center page. As the smaller panels are opened, they provide a dramatic reveal of the inner pages.

A *roll fold* (**C** in *Figure 6.2*) features three creases that form eight pages. As the first page is opened, rather like a book, the inner pages tucked inside fold out in the opposite direction to the right-hand side, creating a rolling motion.

Photoshop isn't intended for large, multi-page projects. However, multi-page designs can be generated from just two image files in Photoshop and combined with a combination of folds to form an interesting print product.

In this section, we reviewed the challenges of working with RGB screen colors, which are ultimately converted to CMYK inks for printing. We also covered various print terms and considerations for creating and managing print projects, from printers' marks to the types of documents suitable for Photoshop. Next, we will create print templates with grid systems.

Setting up a Photoshop grid system

Not every project begins with a digital photograph. Sometimes, it's smarter to start with a blank canvas and make sure you're working toward the intended output size with all the right quality settings from the get-go, including a grid system and bleed. Using a grid system can help create well-structured, consistent layouts and manage white space, resulting in a more professional final product.

Building a new A4 poster document

In this first exercise, we will define document characteristics for a relatively simple one-page print file that includes bleed, trim guides, and a safe zone for your copy:

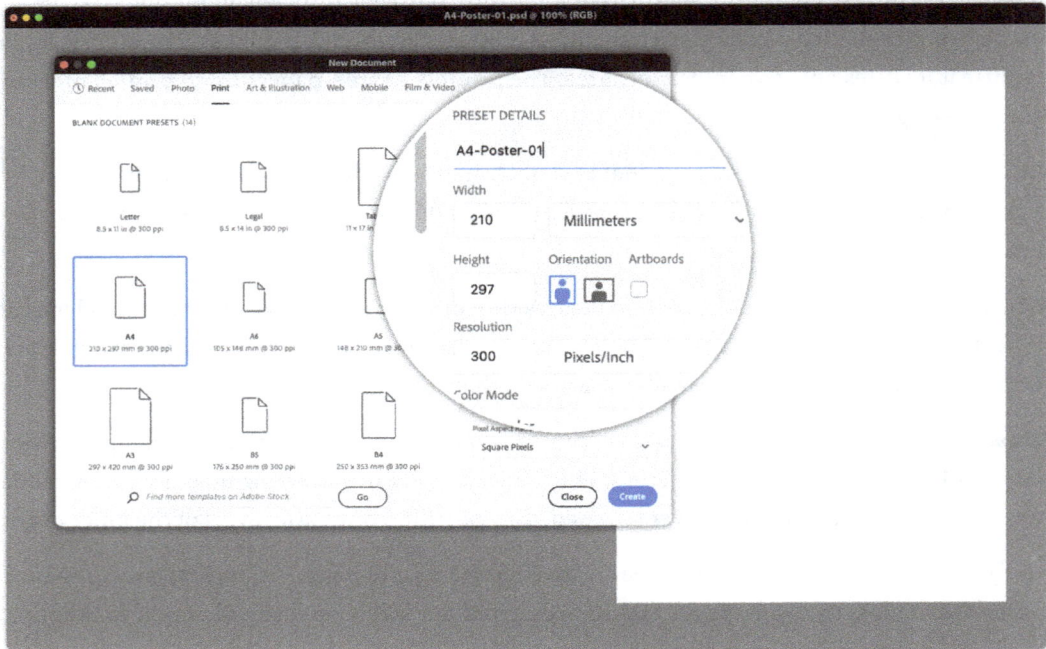

Figure 6.3: Create a new document

1. Go to **File → New**.

2. When the **New Document** dialog appears, click on the **Print** tab at the top to display a series of page thumbnail presets. Click on the **A4** thumbnail. The word **Untitled** will be highlighted within the **Name** field on the right-hand side of the dialog. This will become the filename when saved. Change the name to A4-Poster-01.

3. Set **Units** to **Millimeters**, orientation to **Portrait**, and **Resolution** to 300 ppi. Set **Color Mode** to **RGB Color, 8-bit**, and then change **Background Content** to **White**.

4. In **Advanced Options**, change **Color Profile** to **Adobe RGB (1998)**. The recommended workflow is to create artwork in RGB and then convert to CMYK before printing, when necessary. Click **OK** when you're done.

5. With the new document now open and active, ensure the units are set to millimeters by going to **View → Rulers**. If a tick can be seen adjacent to the Rulers command in the menu, they are active and visible in the **Image** window; if not, click on the command to activate them. Then, right-click on either the vertical or horizontal ruler found around the edge of the **Image** window and click on **Millimeters** from the list.

6. Go to **View → Guides → New Guide Layout** (*Figure 6.4*). Set the guide color to **Cyan** from the drop-down menu. Turn on the **Columns** checkbox, enter 4 into the **Number** field, leave **Width** blank, and set **Gutter** to 5 mm. Turn on the **Rows** checkbox, enter 6 into the **Number** field, leave **Height** blank, and set **Gutter** to 5 mm. Turn on the **Margin** checkbox and enter 10 mm into all four fields. Click **OK** when done.

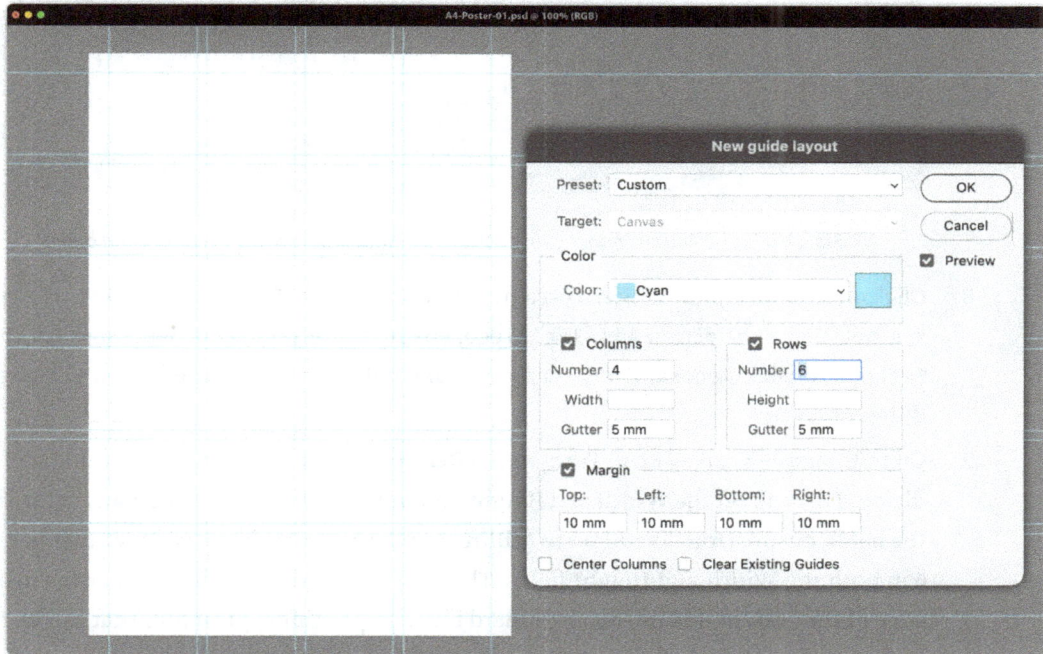

Figure 6.4: Create a new guide layout window

7. Most print files created in Photoshop will require identical bleed settings, which can be recorded and used on any document in the future. Go to **Window → Actions**. When the panel appears, click on the folder icon at the bottom to create a new action set. Name it Document Setup and click **OK**:

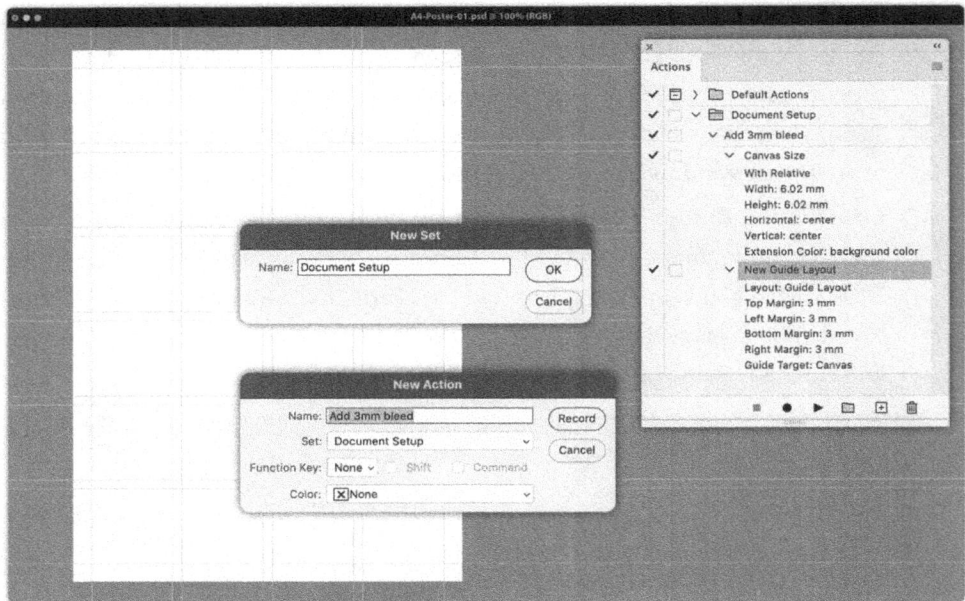

Figure 6.5: The Actions panel can record your Photoshop edits, such as adding bleed

8. Click on the create new action icon at the bottom of the **Actions** panel, shown as a circle symbol. Name the action Add 3mm bleed, ensure the action **Set** is defined as Document Setup, and click **Record**. Every edit you make will now be recorded, even clicking on different layers.

9. Go to **Image → Canvas Size**. Turn on the **Relative** checkbox found in the middle of the dialog. This will set the **Width** and **Height** amounts to 0. Before you enter any values into the fields, ensure **Units** is still set to **Millimeters (mm)** from the drop-down menu. Enter 6 in both the **Width** and **Height** fields. This will add 3 mm of additional canvas to each edge of the current document, a standard bleed size for most print files that can be held in the hand at reading distance. Then, click **OK** when done to apply the edits.

10. Next, we need to add trim lines to visualize where the document will be trimmed after printing. Go to **View → Guides → New Guide Layout**. Set the guide **Color** to **Red** from the drop-down menu. Turn off the **Columns** and **Rows** checkboxes to deactivate them. Turn on the **Margin** checkbox and enter 3 mm in each field. Ensure that the **Center Columns** and **Clear Existing Guides** checkboxes are deactivated before clicking **OK**:

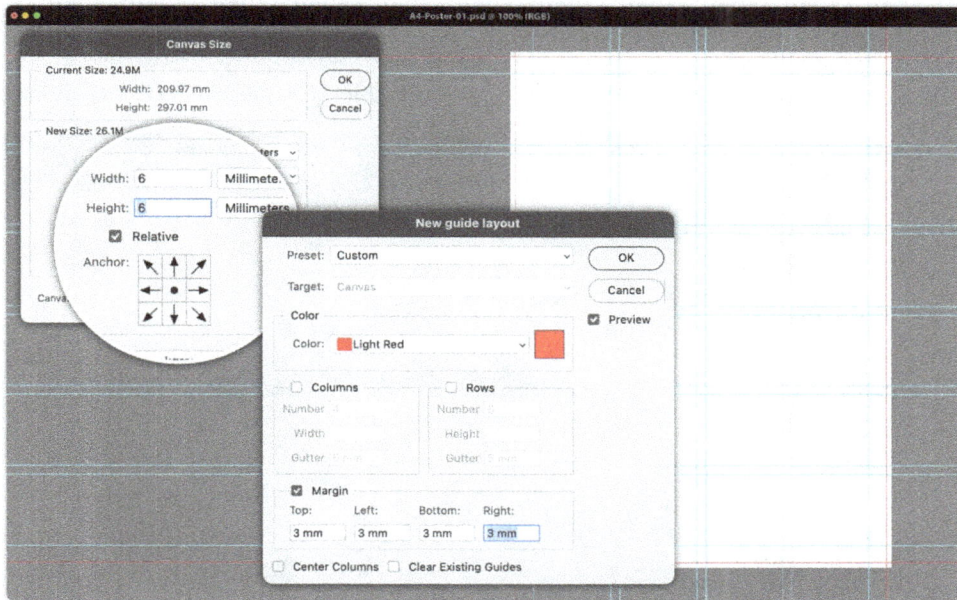

Figure 6.6: Add bleed marks

11. Go to **View → Guide → Lock Guides**. This will prevent you from unintentionally repositioning the guides as you edit the document.

12. Finally, click on the stop recording icon, which appears as a square symbol at the bottom of the **Actions** panel. You will now have a quick way of adding bleed and trim lines to a print file.

13. Save the document in the 06-Print folder as a PSD.

Creating a new business card template

In the previous exercise, we saw how a relatively simple A4 poster could be set up, accounting for bleed, trim lines, and a document grid. In this exercise, you will create a single document intended for creating a front and back design for a business card, but this time using layers to combine both designs:

1. Go to **File → New**.

2. When the **New Document** dialog appears, click on the **Print** tab and the **A4** preset thumbnail. Change **Name** to BizCards-01.

3. Change the document width to 85 mm and the height to 55 mm. Set the orientation to land-scape, enter a **Resolution** value of 300 ppi, and set **Color Mode** to **RGB color, 8-bit**. Change **Background Contents** to **White**. Set **Color Profile** to **Adobe RGB (1998)** and click **OK**.

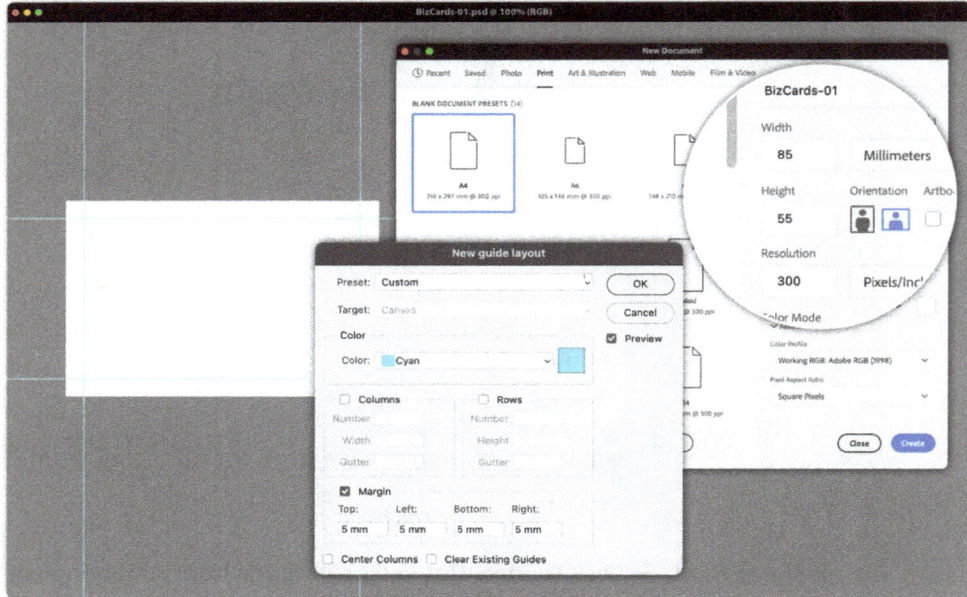

Figure 6.7: Add margins to the business card

4. Go to **View → Guides → New Guide Layout** (see *Figure 6.7*). Set the guide **Color** to **Cyan** from the drop-down menu. Turn off the **Columns** and **Rows** checkboxes to deactivate them. Turn on the **Margin** checkbox and enter 5 mm into all fields. Click **OK** when done.

5. Now, you will play the action created in the previous exercise. In the **Actions** panel, click on the **Add 3mm bleed** action. Then click on the **Play Action** icon at the bottom of the panel to run the action:

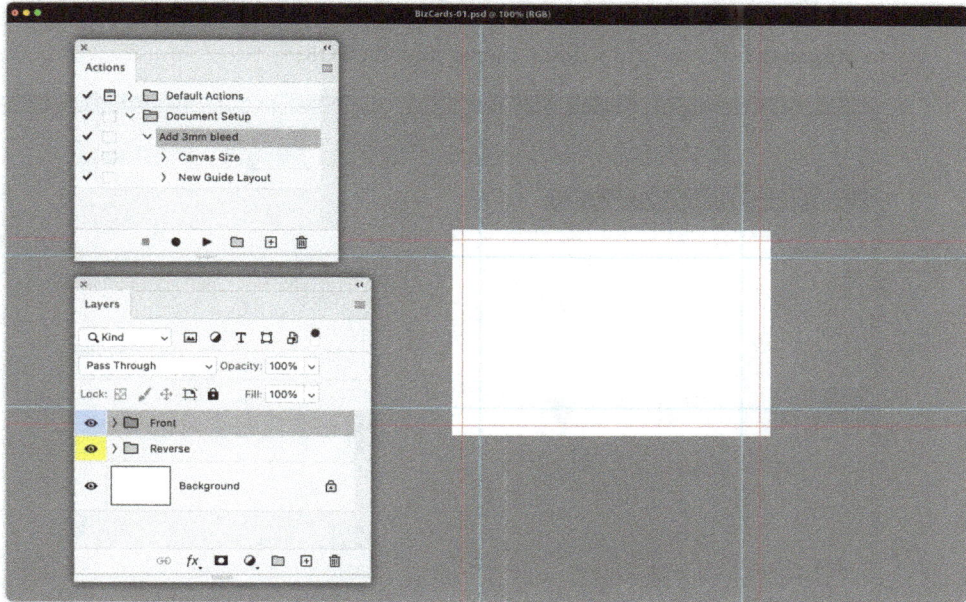

Figure 6.8: Add guides and layer groups to the document

6. Navigate to the **Layers** panel and click the **New Group** icon at the bottom of the panel. When the group appears in the layer stack, change the name to Reverse and press *Enter*. Hover your cursor over the layer group visibility icon and right-click to reveal the context menu of color labels. Choose **Yellow** from the list. Repeat the same technique to create a second folder, but this time name it Front and set the group color to **Blue**.

7. Save the document in the 06-Print folder as a PSD.

Building a new Z-fold brochure

In the last of our document-building exercises, we will set up a Z-fold brochure template. This example will follow similar steps to the previous files, except we need to account for two folds within our grid system:

1. Go to **File → New**. When the **New Document** dialog appears, click on the **Print** tab, and then click on the **A4** preset thumbnail. Change the name to Zfold-01.

2. Set the orientation to landscape, enter a **Resolution** value of 300 ppi, and set **Color Mode** to **RGB color, 8-bit**. Change **Background Contents** to **White**. Set **Color Profile** to **Adobe RGB (1998)** and click **OK**.

3. Go to **View → Guides → New Guide**. Add a **Vertical** guide at 99 mm, set the guide **Color** to **Magenta** from the drop-down menu, and click **OK**:

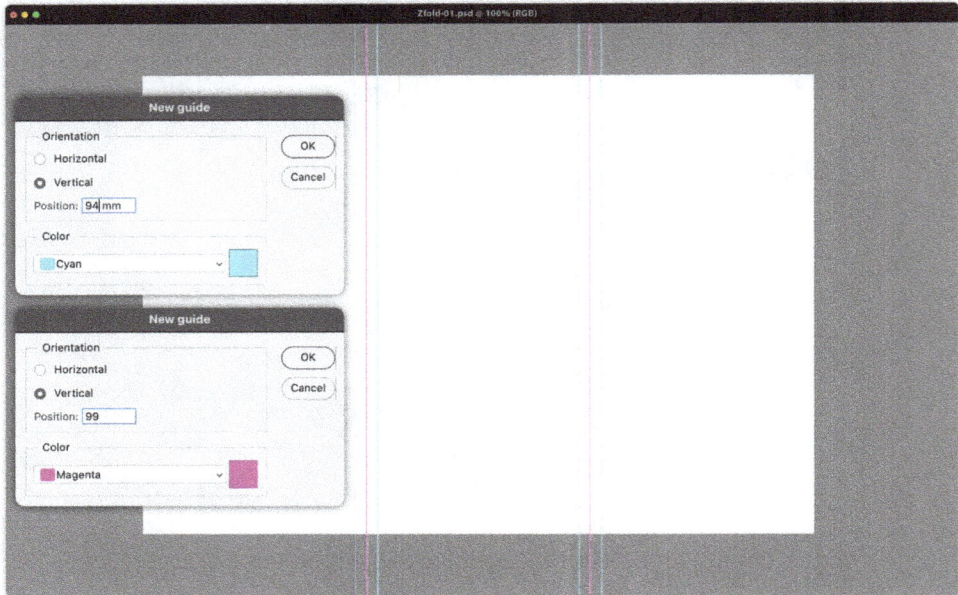

Figure 6.9: Add guides to indicate the location of folds

4. Repeat the same step, adding a second **Magenta** guide at 198 mm. These guides will both indicate folds.

5. More guides! Add four **Cyan** guides at 94 mm, 104 mm, 193 mm, and 203 mm. These guides will indicate the inside margins for each of the three panels.

6. Go to **View → Guides → New Guide Layout**. From the drop-down menu, set the guide **Color** to **Cyan**. Turn on the **Margin** checkbox and enter 5 mm into all fields. Click **OK** when done:

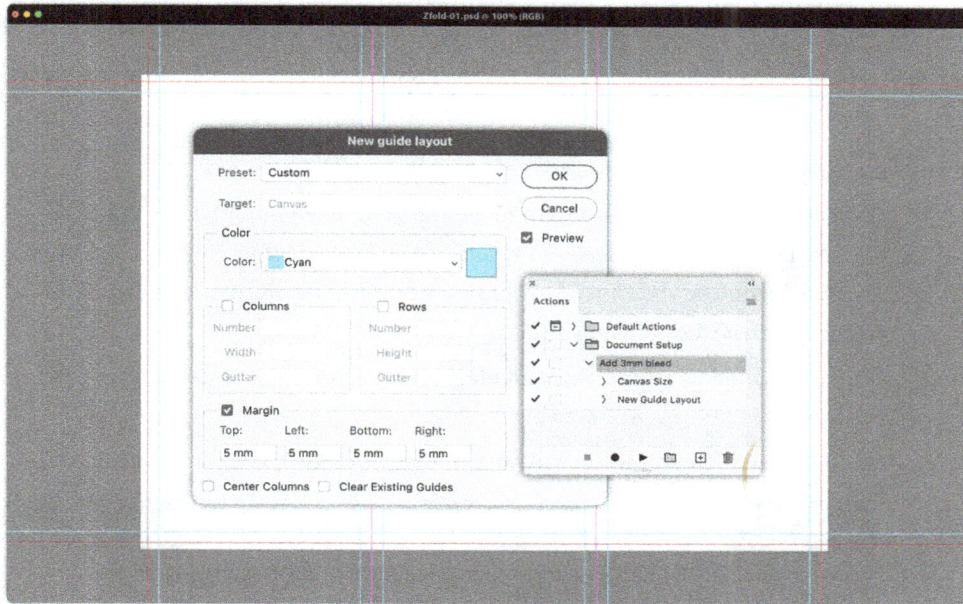

Figure 6.10: Add bleed and trim guides

7. Click on the **Add 3 mm bleed** action. Then, click on the **Play Action** icon at the bottom of the panel to apply the edits to the tri-fold document.

8. Save the document in the 06-Print.

In this section, we have used several methods for adding guides to a print file that indicate safe zones, trim lines, and bleed. As we have seen, guides can be added with great precision to create layout grids that assist in juxtaposing content. In the next section, we will add images, logos, and text to these templates.

Importing artwork and formatting types

We created three print templates in previous exercises, featuring grid systems and other suitable print settings. They now need compelling imagery and text. There are best practices for importing assets, which we will address in the upcoming exercises.

Creating a business card design using only vector assets

Not everything in Photoshop must involve photographic content. In the following steps, you will add a vector logo and editable text to the business card template:

1. Open `BizCards-01` from the `06-Print` folder.

2. Click on the **Front** layer group to make it active. Then go to **File → Place Linked**, select `WildCo_Logo.ai` from the `06-Print` folder, and click **Place** when done. The vector artwork imported from Adobe Illustrator offers incredible flexibility, as it can be scaled to any required size without losing quality.

3. When the **Open as smart object** dialog appears, press **OK** to accept the default options to import the first page of artwork.

4. Ensure the **Width** and **Height** fields are linked before setting the scale to 11%:

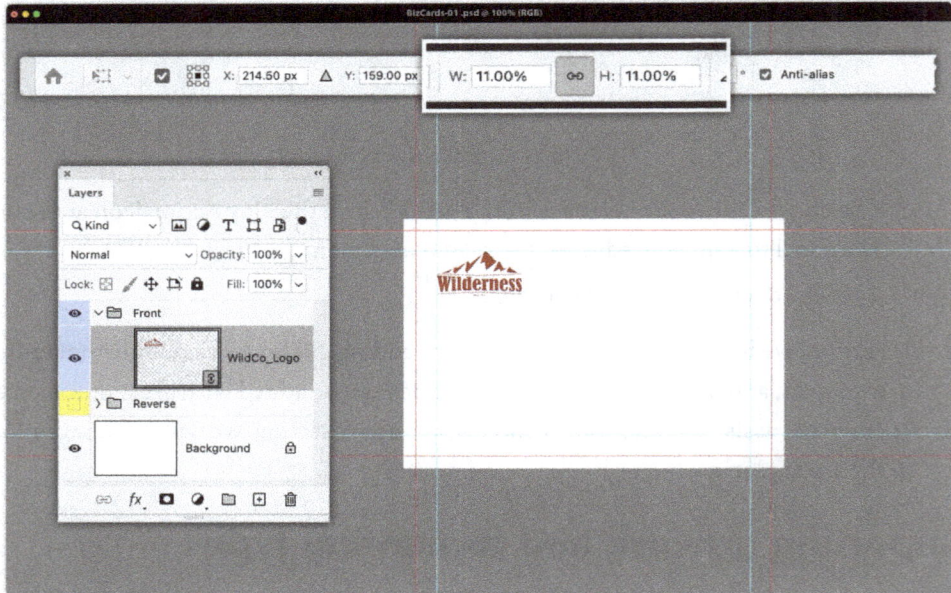

Figure 6.11: The completed front side of the business card design

Then, click the **Commit** button in the **Options** bar to complete the import process.

5. Switch to **Move Tool** and drag the placed artwork to the top-left corner of the cyan-colored guides that denote the safe zone. If the imported artwork was not added to the **Front** layer group, drag it into the folder in the **Layers** panel.

6. Photoshop doesn't allow you to import text from a saved document, so unfortunately, you will need to use your operating system's file browser to locate the `BizCard-Copy.txt` file in the `06-Print` folder and open it. When the document opens, copy the text and return to Photoshop.

7. Switch to the **Horizontal Type** tool from the **Tools** panel by pressing the *T* key. Position your cursor level with the left set of cyan guides on the canvas, beneath the imported logo. Then, click and drag the cursor to the right set of cyan guides to create a new text frame.

8. Go to **Edit → Paste** to add the copy into the frame.

9. Highlight all text in the frame to make it active. Then, from the **Properties** panel (see *Figure 6.12*), change **Font** to **Myriad Pro**, set **Size** to **9 pt**, and set **Paragraph Alignment** to left-align.

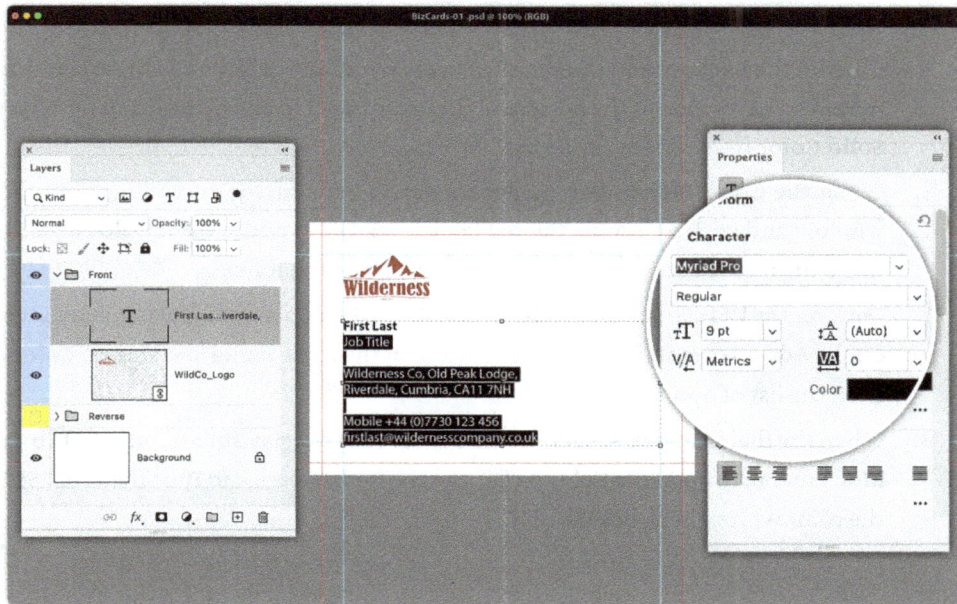

Figure 6.12: Add text to the composition

10. Click on the **Set Text Color** box in the **Properties** panel, and enter 0 into the **Red**, **Green**, and **Blue** fields to make the text black, then click **OK**.

11. As a final touch, highlight the characters **First Last** within the text frame and change **Font Style** to **Bold**. With the complete text edits, press *Esc* to exit type editing mode and apply all edits to the text layer.

With the front side of the business card now complete, we'll focus on the reverse side, featuring just the company logo.

1. Right-click on the layer named WildCo_Logo in the **Layers** panel and choose **Duplicate Layer** from the list of commands. When the dialog appears, change the layer name to WildCo_Logo LARGE from the **As** field and ensure **Destination** is set to the current document, BizCard-01.psd. Then, click **OK**.

2. Drag the WildCo_Logo LARGE layer into the **Reverse** layer group folder in the **Layers** panel. Then, turn off the **Front** layer group visibility.

3. Go to **Edit → Free Transform**. Ensure the link between the **Width** and **Height** fields is linked before setting the scale to 20%. Click on the **Commit** button in the **Options** bar.

4. Next, drag the logo to the center of the canvas, at which point Smart Guides will appear when the logo is aligned with the **Background** layer.

5. Click on the **Background** layer in the **Layers** panel and click on the **Create new fill or Adjustment Layer** icon at the bottom of the same panel to reveal the list of options. Choose **Solid Color** from the top of the list.

6. When the **Color Picker** dialog appears, hover your cursor over the logo in the **Image** window and click to sample the red logo. Click **OK** to add the **Fill Color** layer. This will make the logo disappear briefly, but we will correct that next.

7. Click on the WildCo_Logo LARGE layer in the **Layers** panel to make it active. Then click on the **Add a layer style** icon at the bottom of the same panel and choose **Color Overlay** from the list of options.

8. When the dialog appears, click on the **Set color of overlay** square, adjacent to the **Blend Mode** menu, to open the Color Picker. Set the **Red**, **Green**, and **Blue** fields to 255, making the color white, then click **OK**.

9. Go to **File → Save** to capture all edits. Then close the document.

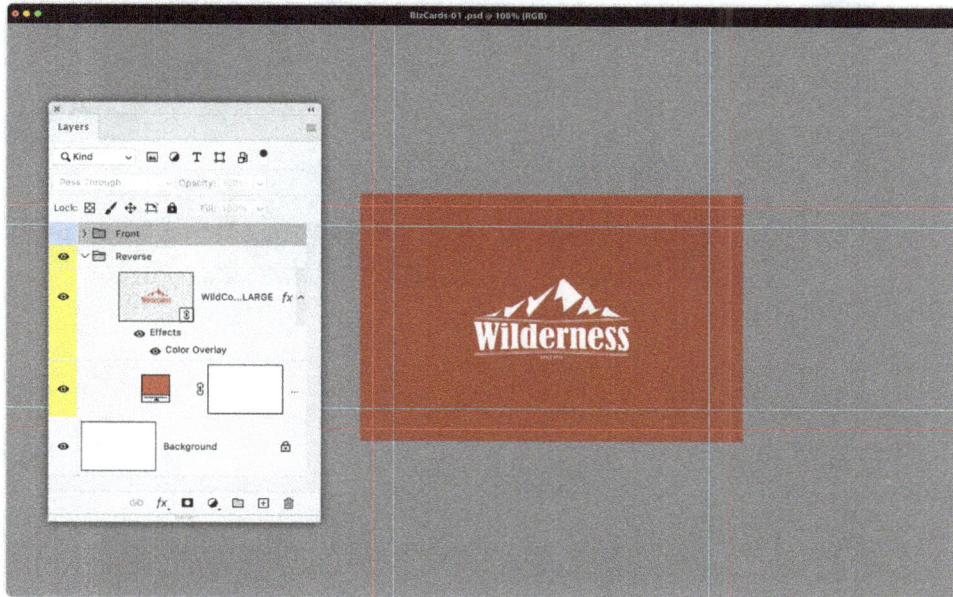

Figure 6.13: The completed reverse side of the business card design

In these layer groups, you can now generate designs for the front and back of the business card in a single document. Make each visible when they need to be exported for print.

Synchronizing fonts from Creative Cloud

Your monthly subscription to Creative Cloud includes access to over 20,000 fonts. You sync them at any time to automatically install them. Here's how to synchronize fonts from Creative Cloud:

1. You can access Adobe Fonts from the **Font Family** drop-down menu within Photoshop, the Creative Cloud desktop app, or the website at www.fonts.adobe.com.

2. Use the search field in the upper-right corner of the site to find the **Amatic Bold** and **Flood Std** fonts. Once you reach the corresponding font page, scroll down the list of available font styles and click the **Add Family** button on the right (**A** in *Figure 6.14*). After a moment, the font will download, install, and become available in Photoshop.

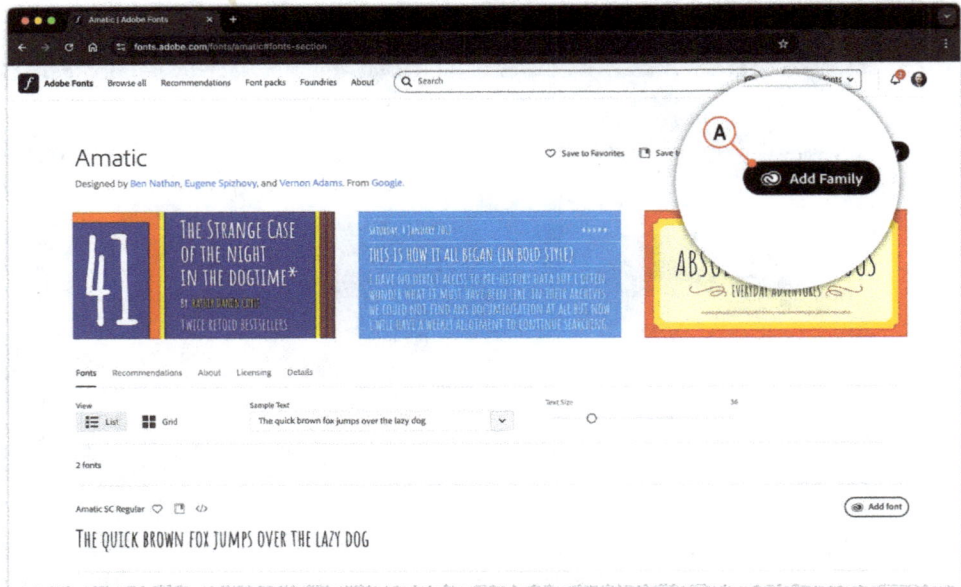

Figure 6.14: Sync fonts on the Adobe website by clicking on the Add Family button

Adding type to the Z-fold brochure

After experimenting with importing type and brand logos in the previous exercise, it's time to tackle a more challenging aspect of the project and finalize the Z-fold brochure. You will edit a revised version of the brochure we created:

1. Open `Zfold-Inner-01.psd` from the `06-Print` folder.

2. Using the same technique as in the previous exercise, use your file browser to locate the `ZFold-Copy-A.txt` file in the `06-Print` folder and open it. When the document opens, copy the text and return to Photoshop.

3. Switch to the **Horizontal Type** tool from the **Tools** panel by pressing the *T* key. Hover your cursor over the center panel design in the middle of the canvas, level with the top cyan guides. Then, click and drag the cursor across to the right-hand cyan guides of the center panel design to create a new text frame. Then go to **Edit → Paste** to insert the text you copied.

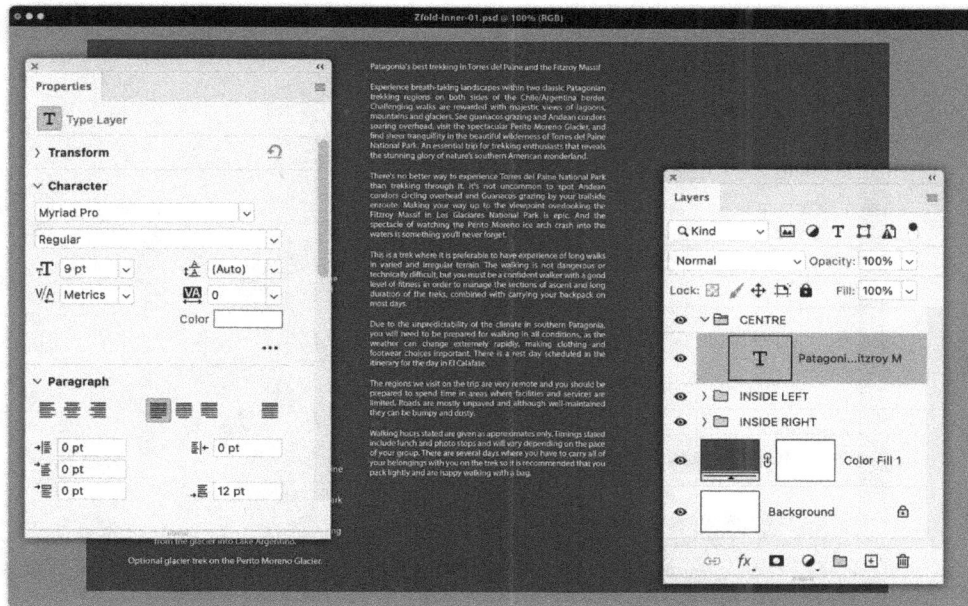

Figure 6.15: Paste the supplied text into the document and apply type formatting

4. Highlight all text in the frame to make it active. From the **Properties** panel (see *Figure 6.15*), change **Font** to **Myriad Pro** and set **Size** to **9 pt**. Then, click the **Set Text Color** box and enter 255 into the **Red, Green**, and **Blue** fields to set the color to white. Click **OK** when you're done.

5. From the **Paragraph** options, set the alignment to **Justify last left**. This will force the text to use the full width of the text frame, creating a stronger regular text region. However, the last line of the paragraph should be left-aligned to avoid unsightly spaces between words.

6. Increase **Space After Paragraph** to **12 pt** to help indicate to the reader where new paragraphs start and finish.

7. Highlight all of the title text in the first line of the text frame. Change the **Font** to **Amatic SC** and **Bold** from the **Properties** panel and set the **Size** to **24 pt**. Click on **Set Text Color** in **Properties** and enter 238 into the **Red** field, 200 into the **Green** field, and 50 into the **Blue** field to set the color to yellow. Click **OK** when done. Click on the **Commit** button under **Options** to apply the text edits.

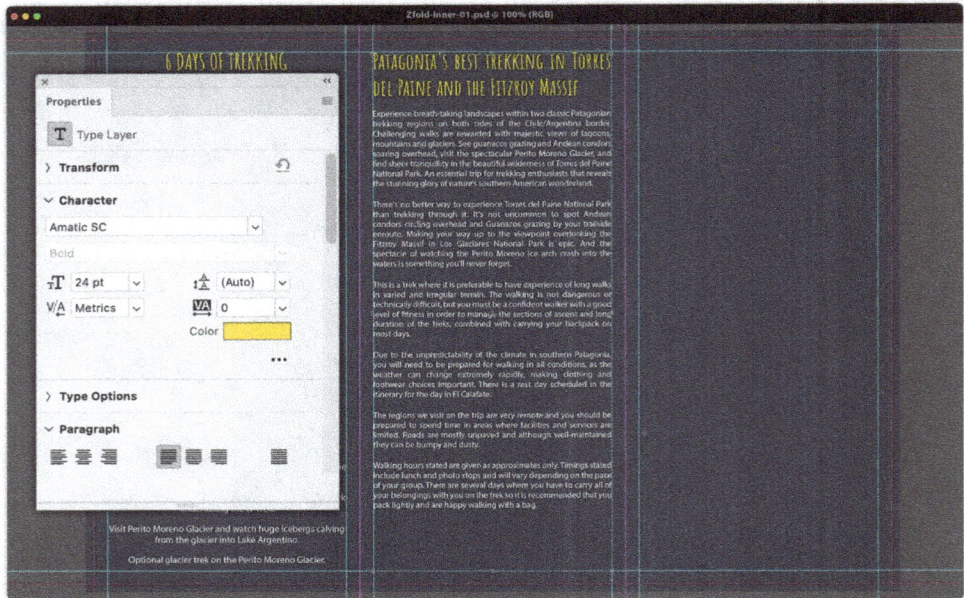

Figure 6.16: Format the heading

8. Before finishing the type edits, ensure the text frame itself is the same size as the region within the cyan guides in the center panel. You can resize a text frame by hovering over one of the corner bounding box points of the frame and dragging it to the desired position. Press the *Esc* key to exit type editing mode and apply all edits to the text layer.

9. Open `Zfold-Outer-01.psd` from the `06-Print` folder.

10. Switch to the **Horizontal Type** tool from the **Tools** panel. Create a new text frame at the center of the canvas. Type `Patagonia` into the text frame.

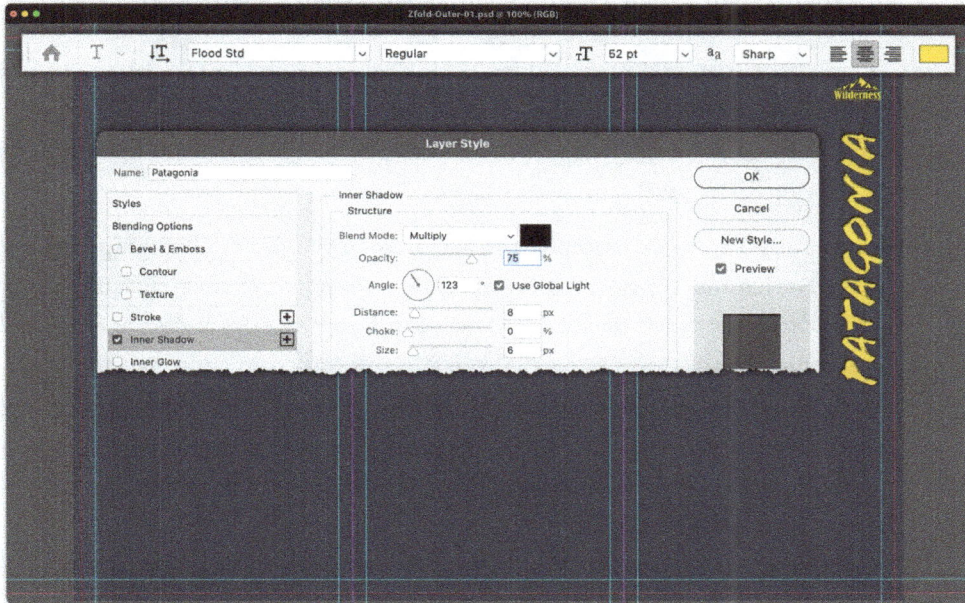

Figure 6.17: Add text and effects to the outer flyer design

11. Highlight all text in the frame to make it active. From **Properties**, change the **Font** to **Flood Std** and set the **Size** to **52 pt**. Click on **Set Text Color** under **Properties** and enter 238 into the **Red** field, 200 into the **Green** field, and 50 into the **Blue** field to set the color to yellow. Click **OK** when done. Click on the **Commit** button under **Options** to apply the text edits.

12. Then go to **Edit → Free Transform**. Enter -90 into the **Angle** field under **Options** to rotate the text so that the letter P is at the bottom and the letter A is at the top of the frame. Press *Enter* when done to apply the edits.

13. Switch to the **Move** tool. Drag the Patagonia text frame to the right side of the canvas so that it is centered underneath the logo.

14. With the text layer still active, click on the **Fx** icon at the bottom of **Layers** and choose **Inner Shadow** from the list of effects to launch the **Layer Styles** dialog. Set **Angle** to 125˚, **Distance** to 8 px, **Choke** to 0%, **Size** to 6 px, and **Opacity** to 75%. Click **OK** when done.

15. Save the document and keep both files open for the next exercise.

Creating and applying paragraph styles

If there is one repetitive and tedious task, it's formatting text repeatedly with the same settings. Thankfully, paragraph styles let you save text formatting and apply it throughout your Photoshop document. When needed, any changes to the paragraph style automatically update all text using that style, altering their appearance accordingly:

1. With `Zfold-Inner-01.psd` open and active, go to **Window → Paragraph Styles**. Switch to the **Horizontal Type** tool by pressing the *T* key. Then, double-click on the text frame you added in the center panel of the flyer containing the titles and paragraphs of the copy. Ensure the type cursor is active in the first line of text containing the title.

2. Then click on the **Create New Paragraph Style** icon at the bottom of **Paragraph Styles** to add a new style, which will appear higher in the same panel, named **Paragraph Style 1**. This style must be renamed by clicking on **Paragraph Styles** and going to the **Panel** fly-out menu at the top right.

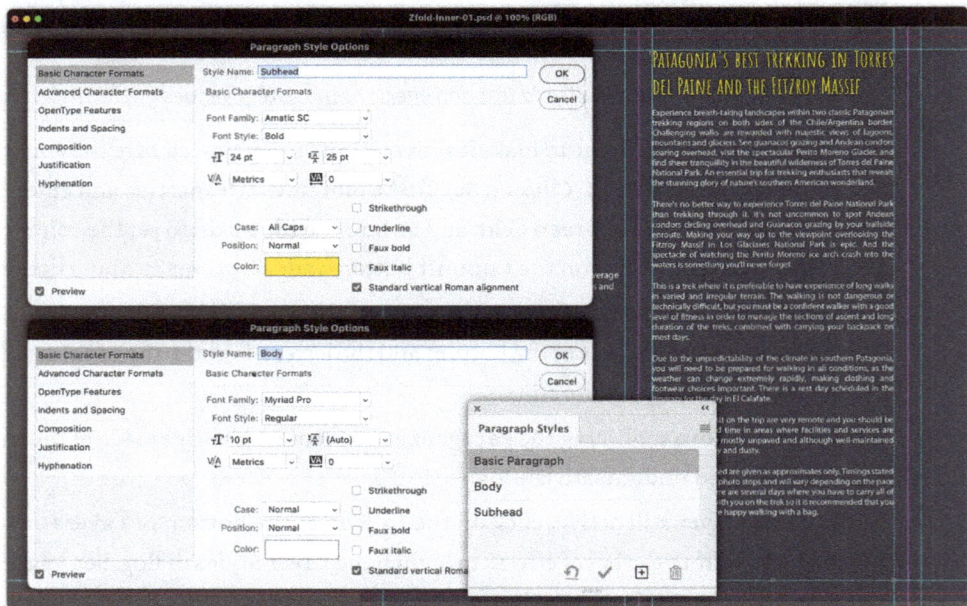

Figure 6.18: Create paragraph styles

3. Choose **Style Options** from the list. When the dialog appears, change the name to Subhead and click **OK**.

4. Repeat the same technique to create a new paragraph style, but this time select all the paragraphs of white text lower down in the text frame first. Once the style has been made, rename it by going to the **Panel** fly-out menu and entering Body into the **Style Name** field. Click **OK** when done.

5. Click on the document tab for Zfold-Outer-01.psd.

6. Next, you will apply this style to the new copy. Using your file browser, open the ZFold-Copy-B.docx file in the 06-Print folder with any text editor you prefer. When the document opens, copy the text and then return to Photoshop.

7. Switch to the **Horizontal Type** tool under **Tools** by pressing the *T* key. Create a new text frame in the center panel that is the same size as the previous one you made. Then go to **Edit → Paste** to insert the copied text.

8. Select all text in the frame to make it active, then click on the **Body** paragraph style in the **Paragraph Styles** panel.

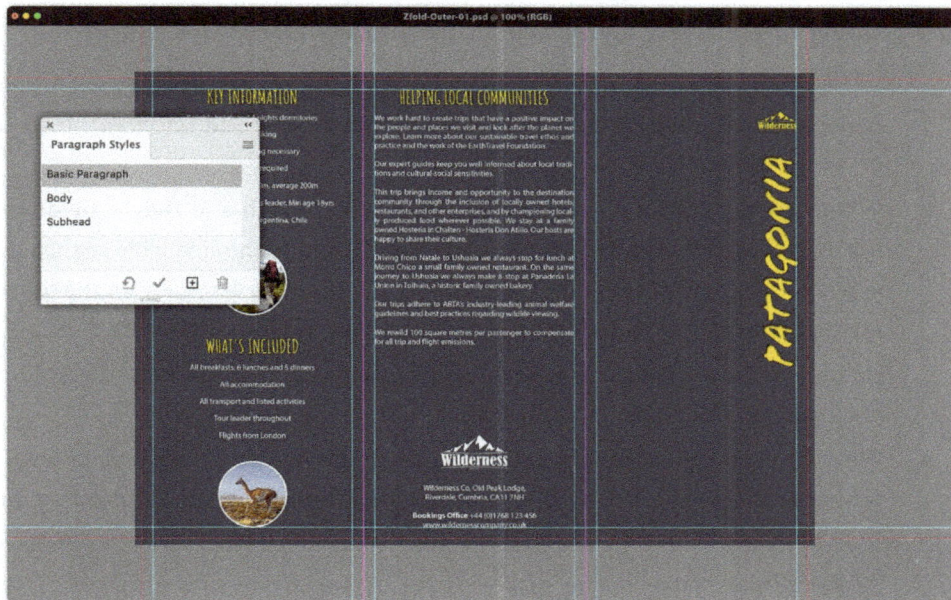

Figure 6.19: Add and apply the paragraph styles to text in the outer Z-fold file

You should now see that the formatting matches that of the first text frame you edited. Then, select all text in the first paragraph and click on the **Subhead** style to apply it to the selected text. Press the *Esc* key to exit type editing mode and apply all edits to the text layer.

9. Save both documents before moving on to the next exercise.

About paragraph styles and character styles

To save time, Photoshop styles can be used to capture the appearance of existing layer content. In the case of type, Photoshop can capture the type formatting of an active text layer or highlighted paragraph to create a paragraph style. The style can then be applied to other text layers, matching the original formatting. If you need to apply a style to just a single word or sequence of characters, then character styles can be used in the same way. To both capture and apply a character style, the desired text must be highlighted with the type tool.

Adding artwork to the brochure

With the text edits now complete, you can add the finishing touches to the outer flyer design. First, add a featured image to the front cover, and then add a map to the reverse:

1. With Zfold-Outer-01.psd open, click on the layer group named **Front** in the **Layers** panel to make it active. Then go to **File → Place Linked** and select Paint.ai from the 06-Print folder.

2. When artwork appears on the canvas, ensure the **Width** and **Height** fields are linked before setting the scale to 100%. Drag the paint marks to the right side so that half of the artwork is hidden off the edge of the canvas and centered vertically on the canvas. Click on the **Commit** button under **Options** to complete the import process.

3. Go back to **File → Place Linked** and select Hiker.jpg from the 06-Print folder. When you're done, click **Place**.

4. When artwork appears on the canvas, ensure the **Width** and **Height** fields are linked before setting the scale to 14%. Then drag the image of the hiker into a position directly in front of the paint marks on the right side of the canvas. Click on **Commit** under **Options** when done.

5. Right-click on the layer named Hiker.jpg and select **Create Clipping Mask** from the list of options. This will use the paint layer directly beneath the photo as a mask. Adjust the photo so that the entire hiker is visible and no gray paint strokes are visible.

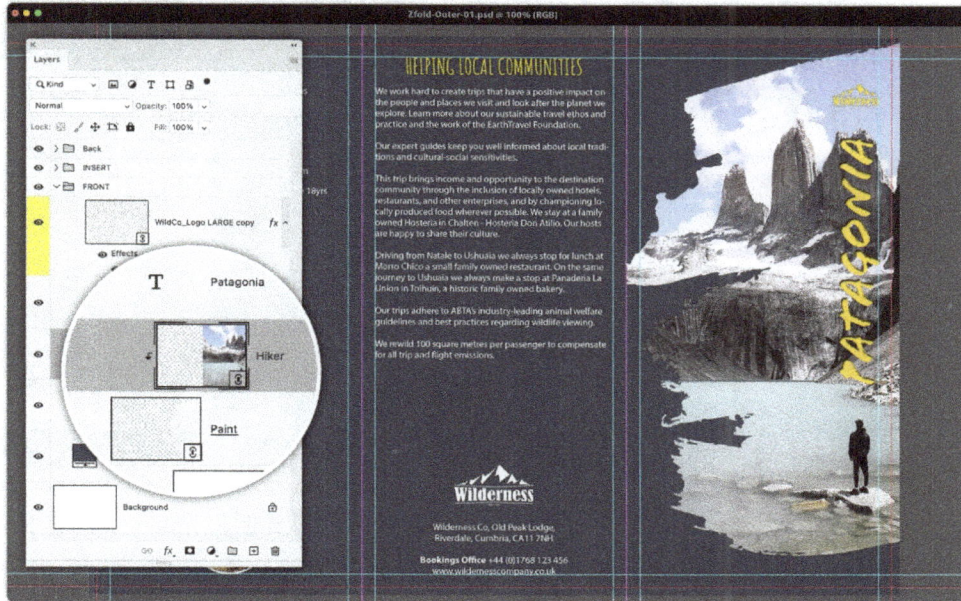

Figure 6.20: Add the paint and photo artwork

6. With Zfold-Inner-01.psd active, expand the layer group named **Inside Left** in the **Layers** panel and click on one of the text layers.

7. Press the *U* key to switch to the **Ellipse** tool under **Tools**. Then click and hold the active tool to reveal the popup. Click on the **Ellipse** tool icon.

8. Hover your cursor over the left panel of the brochure, where the space appears between the two text frames, and click to launch the **Ellipse** dialog. Enter a **Width** and **Height** value of 30 mm and then click **OK**.

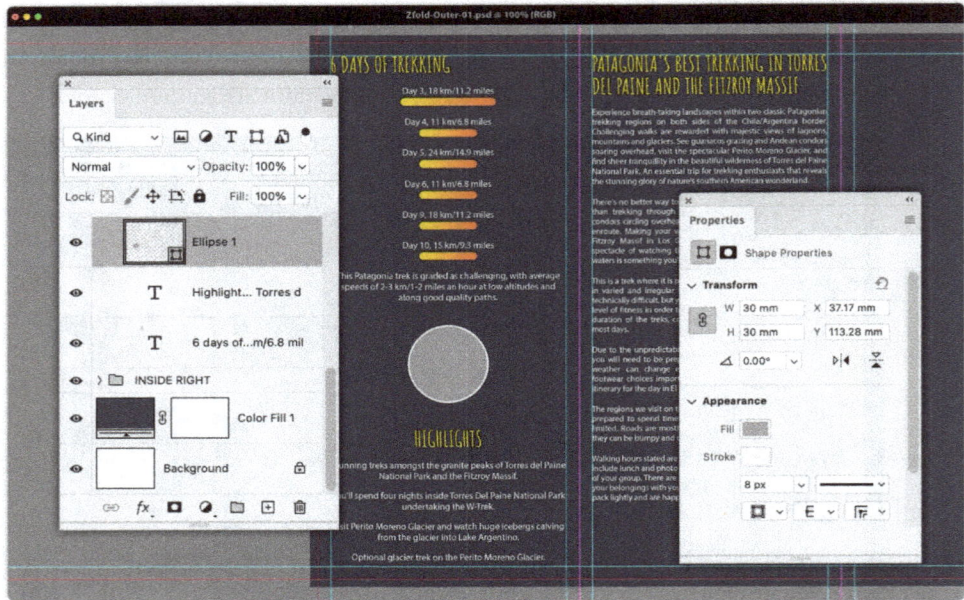

Figure 6.21: Create an elliptical shape

9. When the shape appears, go to the **Properties** panel and set the stroke to white by clicking on the **Set Shape Stroke Type** icon adjacent to the word **Stroke**. When the dialog appears, click on the **Color Picker** icons located in the top-right corner and set the **Red**, **Green**, and **Blue** values to 255, then click **OK**. Enter 8 pt into the **Stroke Width** field. Set the circle's **Fill** to anything you wish; it will be hidden shortly, but a fill color is required.

10. Switch to the **Move** tool and reposition the ellipse horizontally, centered to the text in the center of the empty space between the two text frames.

11. Go to **File → Place Linked**, select Hiker-Small-A.jpg from the 06-Print folder, and click **Place** when done.

12. Switch to the **Move** tool and reposition the placed image so it is central to the circle you created.

13. Right-click on the layer named Hiker-Small-A.jpg and choose **Create Clipping Mask** from the list of options. This will use the circle's fill as a mask but keep the stroke white.

14. When artwork appears on the canvas, ensure the **Width** and **Height** fields are linked before setting the scale to 52%. Drag the photo to appear in the same place as the circle you just made. Click on the **Commit** button under **Options** to complete the import process.

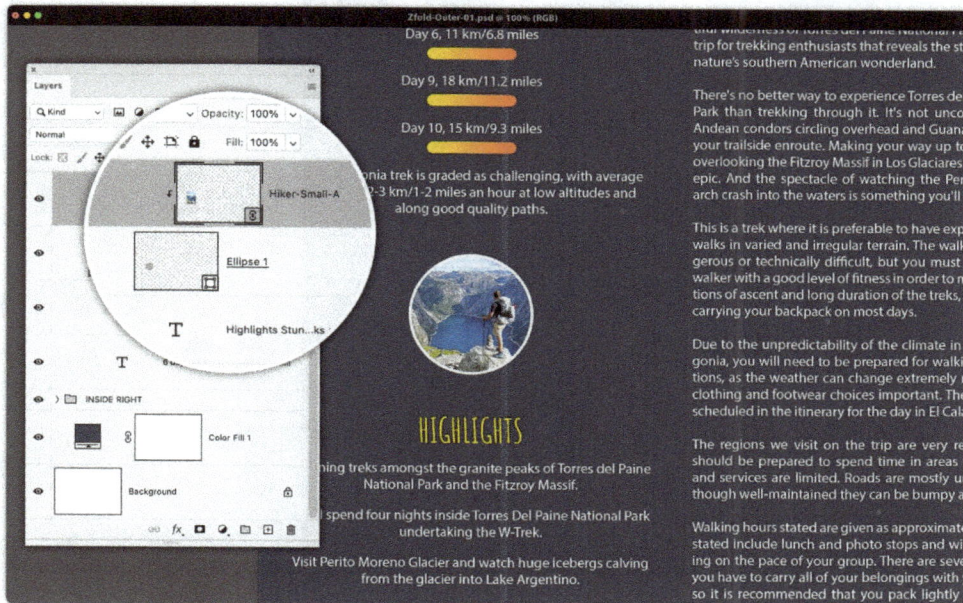

Figure 6.22: Clip the hiker artwork to the elliptical shape

15. Click on the layer group named `Inside Right` in the **Layers** panel to make it active. Go to **File → Place Linked**, browse to the `06-Print` folder, select the file named `Map.ai`, and click **Place** when done.

16. When artwork appears on the canvas, ensure that the **Width** and **Height** fields are linked before setting the scale to 100%. Drag the map to the right-hand edge of the canvas, central to the canvas. Click on the **Commit** button under **Options** to complete the import process.

17. Save and close all documents.

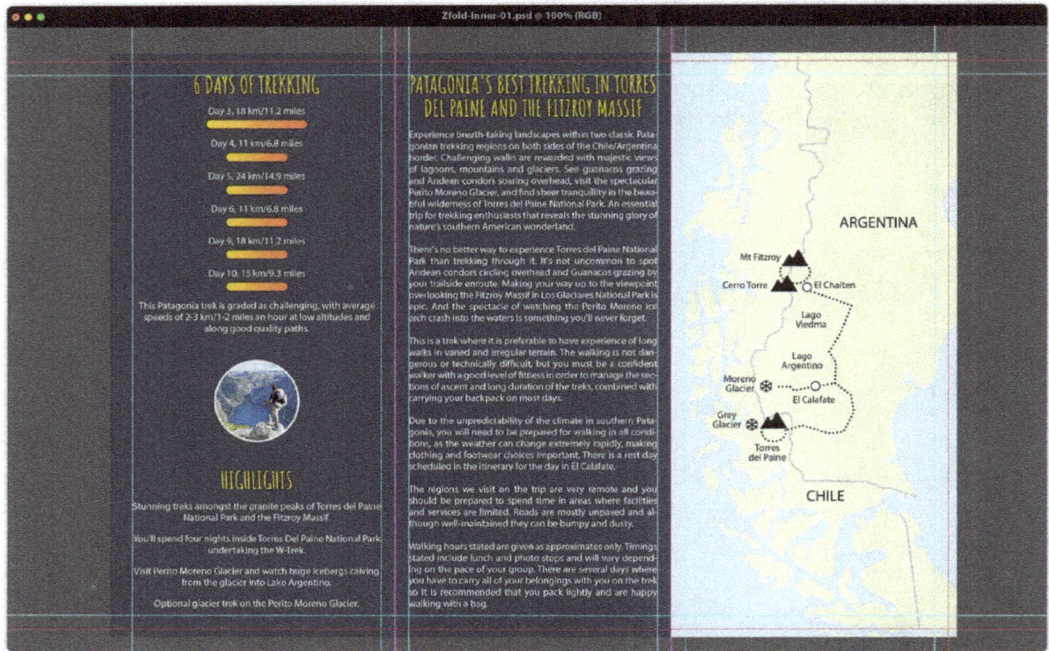

Figure 6.23: Import the map to complete the project

In this section, we have used techniques for greater flexibility when editing project assets. We have seen how logos created in Adobe Illustrator can be placed into a Photoshop document and linked live to the source file. This means that any edits made to the logo in Illustrator will be reflected in the Photoshop file. Text can be edited at any time by double-clicking to enter type editing mode, where all text editing features remain available despite the addition of layer styles and effects. Color overlays and fill layers that accurately match brand colors can also be edited by double-clicking the layer thumbnail in the **Layers** panel. In the next section, we will export artwork in various formats for professional print.

Exporting documents for professional print

When outputting your artwork for hand-off to a print bureau, there are so many things to account for. Managing the output process for this option is far more critical than output to the web, as mistakes here often cost time and money. It is essential that you supply your final artwork in an appropriate file format to ensure the highest possible quality in print.

Exporting to Adobe PDF

By far the most flexible format to pass to a third-party print provider, PDF has been the industry standard for many years. It preserves vector shapes and text layers. Let's take a look at this process in the following exercise:

1. With the `Zfold-Inner-01.psd` document open, go to **File → Save** to ensure the master file (PSD) captures the latest edits. Then go to **File → Save a Copy** and choose **Photoshop PDF** from the format menu. Change the filename to `Trifold-ProPRINT` and browse to the `06-Print` folder. Click **Save**.

2. When the **Save Adobe PDF** dialog box appears on screen, change the Adobe PDF preset to **[PDF/X-4:2001]** from the drop-down menu. This is the recommended option when sending your artwork to a print bureau. Then, turn on the **View PDF after Saving** checkbox.

3. Go to the **Image Compression** heading on the left to reveal the options. Set **Bicubic Downsampling** to 300 and ensure that **Image Quality** is set to **Maximum**.

4. Go to **Output** from the list on the left-hand side and ensure that **Color Conversion** is set to **Convert to Destination**. Your document CMYK should be set to the destination prescribed by your print provider (or working CMYK), which is taken from Photoshop's color settings, as defined in *Chapter 1*.

5. When done, click on the **Save PDF** button. Your PDF will shortly launch for you to review. If you have not installed Acrobat Pro or Acrobat Reader, the PDF may launch in an alternative third-party application. Review the exported document and print a hard copy to a locally connected printer to evaluate any color shifts that may have occurred.

Exporting to the Tagged Image File Format

Many print providers, especially magazines, still accept TIFF for supplying images for an advert. Like the PDF format, TIFF can preserve all of the same things PSD can, including layers. Let's see how in the next exercise:

1. With the `Trifold-01` document open, go to **File → Save a Copy** and choose **TIFF** from the format menu. Change the filename to `Trifold-ProPRINT` and turn off the **Layers** checkbox. Browse to the `06-Print` folder and click **Save**.

2.   When the **TIFF Options** dialog appears, set **Image Compression** to **None**. This will avoid compatibility issues when it is opened on other devices. Turn off the **Image Pyramid** checkbox and leave **Pixel Order** as the default setting of **Interleave**. **Byte Order** can be set to either **IBM PC** or **Macintosh** to address a historical issue with shared files between different platforms. If you didn't turn off the **Layers** checkbox in the previous dialog, choose **Discard Layers and Save a Copy** from the **Layer Compression** settings. Click **OK** when done.

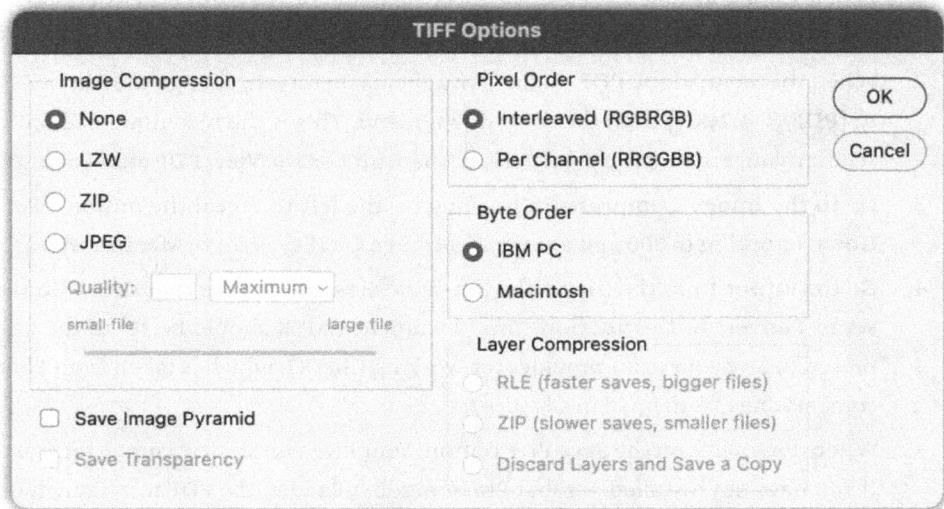

Figure 6.24: The TIFF Options dialog box

Saving as a JPG

The JPG format is incredibly flexible for continuous tone images, such as photos with millions of colors. The truth is that the human eye cannot detect the subtle differences between a printed PSD, TIFF, or JPG. If you are printing a high-end photographic project where fine quality is of paramount importance, then I would suggest avoiding JPG and instead using PDF or TIFF. But for many other use cases, JPG is a suitable alternative to PDF and TIFF:

1.   With the `Trifold-01` document open, go to **File → Save a Copy** and choose **JPG** from the format menu. Change the filename to `Trifold-ProPRINT`, browse to the `06-Print` folder, and click **Save**.

2.   When the **JPG Options** dialog appears, ensure **Quality** is set to **Maximum**. You can ignore the format options as they relate to web and screen output. Click **OK** when done.

File formats that should be avoided when printing

If there is one file format that I've most seen used wrongly for print projects over the years, it must be the **Portable Network Graphics (PNG)** format. It was created as a free alternative to GIF and is only intended for screen and web output. Like the GIF format, it is most effective when saving images that possess 256 colors or fewer. For similar reasons, GIFs should also be avoided when dealing with print.

In this chapter's final section, we reviewed techniques for exporting artwork from Photoshop to pass on to a print provider, ensuring that all our diligent work to build files fit for print is not undermined by choosing an inappropriate file format. Where necessary, we have also discussed the strengths and the limitations of those image formats so that you can make informed choices about which format to use in each scenario.

Summary

In this chapter, we created Photoshop documents that were specifically for print. We've used various techniques that minimize the costly errors that are common in print projects.

We have built new documents characterized by the appropriate resolution and size to match common ISO paper sizes. We extended the canvas to account for bleed and added a series of grid systems and guides that indicate critical parts of print artwork, such as trim lines and safe zones. In doing so, we ensured that important visuals and text were kept clear of the document edges.

Time-consuming, repetitive tasks were recorded using actions, which we then applied in other projects at lightning-fast speeds.

We built flexibility into each project, from logos linked to an original Illustrator document to text that could be edited at any point. We also applied color overlays that allow a single logo to contain different brand colors that can be turned on or off at the click of a mouse.

These techniques will be built upon in the next chapter, as we will create social media templates.

Get This Book's PDF Version and Exclusive Extras

UNLOCK NOW

Scan the QR code (or go to packtpub.com/unlock). Search for this book by name, confirm the edition, and then follow the steps on the page.

Note: Keep your invoice handy. Purchases made directly from Packt don't require one.

7

From Pixels to Post: Images for Social Media

According to an analysis by **Kepios** (`https://datareportal.com/social-media-users`), approximately 5.31 billion social media users worldwide were active at the start of April 2025, equating to 64.7% of the world's population. On average, an online user will spend 151 minutes daily on social media platforms. With that kind of reach, you can understand the attraction of brands engaging online with their audience.

Businesses often pay a consultancy to manage their social media accounts. Given that over 30 platforms boast 100 million active users monthly, you can understand why. Where do you begin? If you've had to manage content for a small business with a modest customer base, you'll appreciate that it is a monumental task.

Over the years, I've worked with in-house design teams managing brand accounts. In that time, I've realized that this type of work must respond to changing events within minutes rather than hours to be effective. Your artwork must be simple to edit with as few repetitions of tasks as possible and adapt to a plethora of output sizes for each platform.

There are several features built into Photoshop that, when combined, provide a highly efficient workflow for creating and exporting visuals for the web and social media. These are tools that, although not initially intended for generating social media images, have proven essential to my Photoshop workflow.

In this chapter, I'll share my unique workflow for creating robust project files built for the demands of a fast-paced social media ecosystem, focusing on the following topics:

- Creating new documents for screen and web
- Working with artboards
- Duplicating artboards
- Exporting and scheduling posts

Technical requirements

The project files for this chapter can be found at https://packt.link/gbz/9781806021710.

Creating new documents for screen and web

In the previous chapter, we looked at the challenges of managing print projects. While we don't have to include bleed, trim, and other print characteristics in our web projects, we must manage several images, each with specific sizes for several platforms. The challenge here is the impact of repetition. The same artwork you use for X must be adapted for LinkedIn, Pinterest, Facebook, and so on. What might seem like a minor text edit in a single file for print now becomes a time-consuming ripple effect across dozens of graphics. This calls for an organized approach and smart workflows.

Historically, Photoshop could only produce a single page of artwork in each document, limited by its canvas. However, with the release of CC2015, Adobe introduced **artboards**, allowing for multiple pages. Initially, artboards were intended to address the growing number of screen sizes available in the growing smartphone and tablet market.

However, artboards can be adapted for social media campaigns where output sizes vary considerably.

Figure 7.1: Artboards allow for multiple pages in Photoshop

Each artboard is labeled to distinguish it (**A** in *Figure 7.1*), and adding or duplicating artboards is made simple with **plus widgets** (**B** in *Figure 7.1*). Create an additional blank artboard by clicking a plus widget or pressing *Alt* (Windows) or *Option* (macOS) to duplicate the artboard along with its corresponding artwork.

When exporting images for posting online, we'll avoid having to save each artboard separately, thanks to scripts built into Photoshop that automate the process. Don't be put off by the term *scripts*; you'll interact with them via dialog that looks like any other in Photoshop.

Throughout this chapter, I'll share crucial time-saving tips such as protecting imported images as **smart objects** and applying gradient effects to make text legible (**A** in *Figure 7.2*):

Figure 7.2: Save time with color overlay effects and linked artwork

Gradient effects can be edited from the **Layers** panel and adapted to suit the specific image and text colors. Imported logos will have multiple color overlays (**B** in *Figure 7.2*) applied, making it easier to switch brand colors by revealing and concealing the appropriate overlay rather than reimporting artwork. Text in our social posts will be linked to the original files as smart objects. This means that when we change the text, they update wherever we need them to, reducing the amount of repetitive work.

Examining artwork specs for Facebook

According to **Statista** (https://www.statista.com/statistics/264810/number-of-monthly-active-facebook-users-worldwide), Facebook has over 2.9 billion monthly active users and is the world's largest social network. In October 2020, 13.1% of users on the platform were women between the ages of 25 and 34, and male users aged between 25 and 34 accounted for 19.3%. This might be useful information to refer back to as you create your business profile.

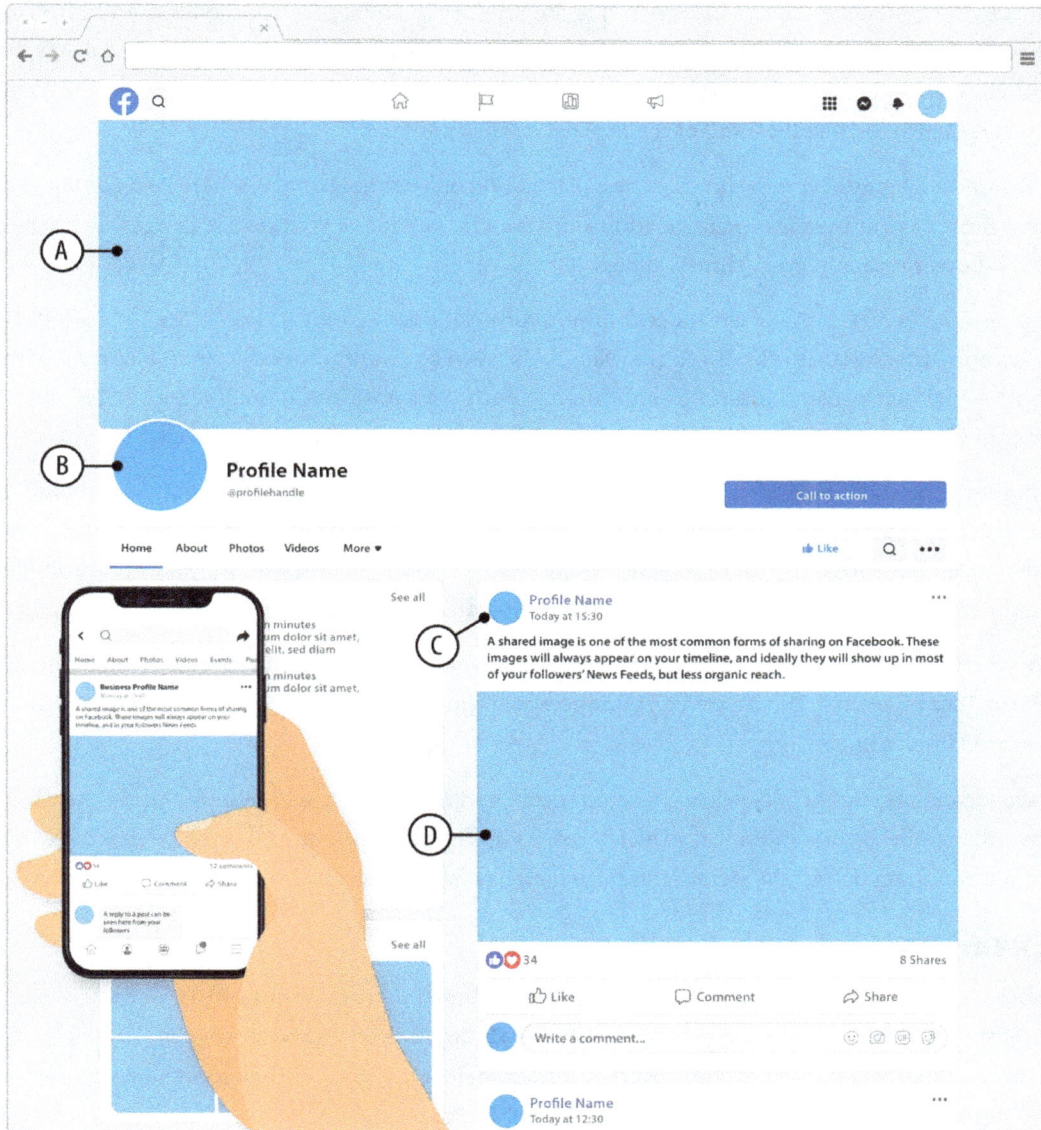

Figure 7.3: A Facebook profile page and the accompanying mobile app

Your *Facebook cover photo* (**A** in *Figure 7.3*) will only appear on your Facebook timeline, and like many social media sites, it's far bigger than your profile picture at 851 × 315 px. If you upload artwork smaller than this, it will be stretched. Your profile picture is an appropriate place for a picture of you or a brand logo. Use your cover photo to post something that encapsulates your brand or mission.

Your *business profile photo* (**B** in *Figure 7.3*) is the primary image representing you, your brand, or your organization across the network. It will be seen across the platform in several places by numerous people, so, as I'm sure you have guessed by now, ensure that your artwork is free from clutter, easily recognizable, and of the highest quality possible!

The largest display of your profile picture can be found on your home page, where it can be viewed by visitors to your business page. In addition, a smaller version of your profile image will appear in a follower's stream every time you post (**C**).

A *shared image* (**D**) is one of the most common forms of posting on Facebook. Your posts will always appear on your timeline, and they should be seen by your followers in their feeds. As with most social platforms, the more people engage with your post, the more likely your followers and their followers will also see it.

Another great technique to use on Facebook is sharing a link (shared link image). It's very similar to posting a shared photo, but this method provides more opportunities to add data. You can create *shared links* with two different types of layout styles: a shared link with a small square image on the left and your copy on the right, or a larger rectangular image on top with text underneath.

Do you have something to shout out about? You can also celebrate a milestone with a *highlighted image*. This image will be situated on your personal timeline, but it will occupy more space than a shared link or image.

Facebook *event posts* help capture users' attention and rise above the Facebook chatter. Reminders will be sent to your audience, so make sure your post has adequate space for an eye-catching image and that you use the right image size for a Facebook event cover photo.

Examining artwork for X

Since its inception in July 2006, X has witnessed a surge in its active monthly user base, which now stands at 415 million (https://sproutsocial.com/insights/twitter-statistics/). As a result, it has become one of the most frequented social networks and a place where customers will converse about your brand or mission.

Let's take a look at the different image assets required to manage an X account:

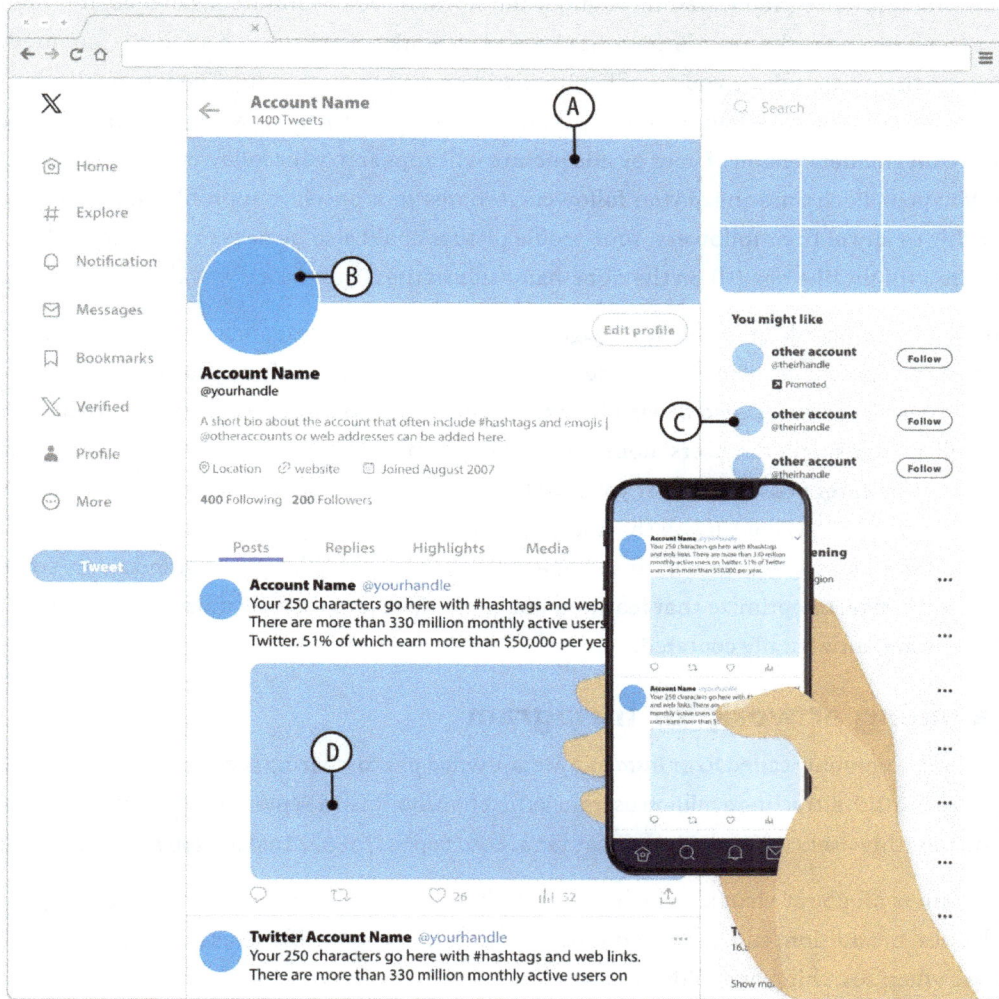

Figure 7.4: X profile page and the accompanying mobile app

Your *header photo* (**A** in *Figure 7.4*) is the panoramic image that runs across the top of your X profile page. It should encapsulate your brand message and inform the visitor of your services or cause. It's going to be a good deal larger than your other profile imagery, so make sure to create and export your artwork at the best possible resolution. Services such as X will often apply aggressive compression levels to reduce image file size and decrease download times. Depending on the content in your images, this may have a negative impact on image quality. Uploading to X will likely compress your image to a lower-quality JPG file.

Your X *profile photo* (**B** in *Figure 7.4*) is the primary image that represents you or your brand across the network. It will be replicated throughout the site and seen by numerous people. It is fair to say that it is be one of the most important pieces of artwork you will use, so quality is paramount. These are the places where your profile photo will be visible on the site. The largest display of your profile picture can be found on your profile page, where it can be viewed by anyone using the platform. A smaller version of your profile picture will appear in your followers' X streams every time you post. Each time one of your followers reshares your posts, your profile picture will also be visible to any of their followers. Your profile picture could also be next to a link to your page in the **You might like** box (**C**) on the right-hand side of the X interface.

Your posts can include an *embedded image* (**D**) without counting against your character limit. Like your profile image, pictures included in your posts will be visible to your followers. When shared, these images will also be visible to the followers of your followers. Your embedded images will appear smaller in users' home feeds, which may result in some of your artwork being cropped. Whenever possible, center your content horizontally so the most important elements of the image remain visible. If you share a link with a featured image on X, it can be displayed as part of a *"rich" X card*. Remember, this image will be slightly smaller than a standard in-stream photo. Therefore, to optimize that featured image for X, ensure that the most essential parts of the image are horizontally centered.

Examining artwork for Instagram

Instagram, commonly called *IG* or *Insta*, is a Meta-owned photo-sharing social network. Instagram launched in 2010, attracting a million users in its first two months. In September 2020, it reached two billion monthly users (`https://www.statista.com/topics/1882/instagram/#editorsPicks`).

Instagram is all about visuals, which should indicate the importance of following image size guidelines. In addition, ensure that your profile image is recognizable so users can find you even quicker when searching or exploring.

When posting to Instagram, it is worth trying to use the native app on your smartphone to generate a higher-resolution photo. The resolution will be lower if you upload an image or video from any other device, such as a desktop. Unlike Facebook and X, which rely on text and pictures, Instagram relies solely on sharing unique and engaging visuals with its audience.

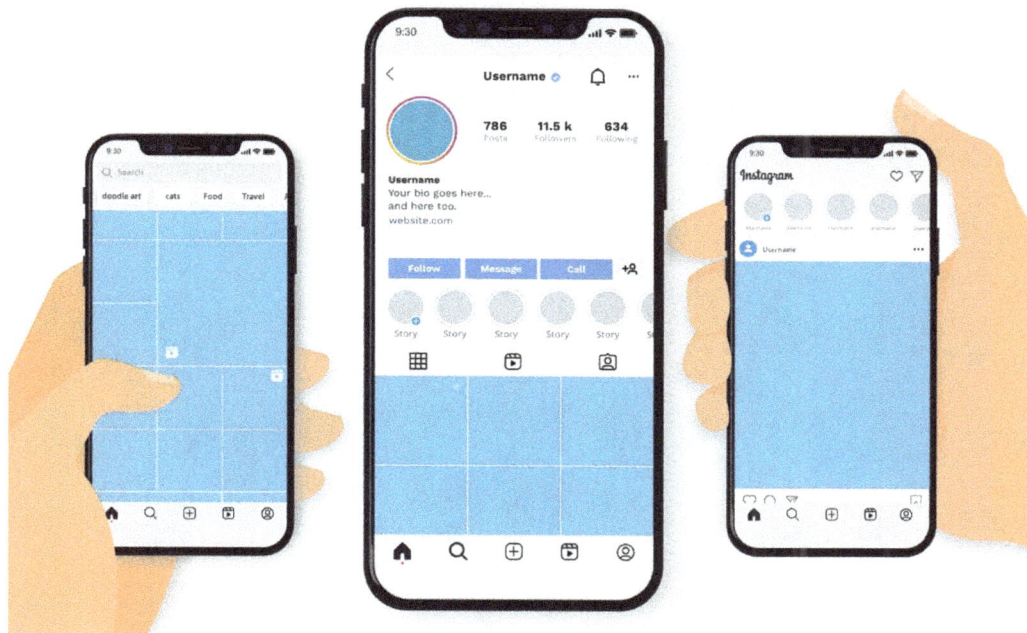

Figure 7.5: Instagram shown in its various modes via the mobile app

While sharing numerous images on Facebook might be acceptable, you must be ruthless with your Instagram posts. Why? Firstly, posting once a day is typical for an Instagram account, so hold off on bulk posting once a week and instead post daily. Be selective about how many images you post on a single event or post. Instagram isn't the platform where you post several similar photos. Post only your best images and focus on quality.

It is essential to keep your Instagram feed consistent. This can often be more challenging when managing a personal or freelance account, as the topics can be broad and go off-topic. But when it comes to a business account, your posts will likely be based on a singular topic or brand; you should make every effort to keep your image feed consistent in style and brand. Think ahead of time and plan how your images will work together. After all, it isn't just about posting great disparate visuals that lead to sales. Still, your audience will also be drawn to your *Instagram bio* to see how your posts build into a mosaic image gallery (referred to as a puzzle post) when viewed side by side.

Released in August 2016, *Instagram Stories* was intended to rival a similar feature on Snapchat. Stories allow users to post sequential content that followers can only access for 24 hours. According to Instagram, stories let you "*share all the moments of your day, not just the ones you want to keep on your profile.*" This feature lets you share multiple photos and videos in a *slideshow* format.

They are often used to create more informal or candid posts. Some brands leverage them to create a series of behind-the-scenes videos for an upcoming product release to build anticipation.

Examining artwork specs for Pinterest

Pinterest has 553 million monthly active users, but it was only the 14th most-used social platform in 2022, according to the 2025 Sprout Social Index (`https://sproutsocial.com/insights/pinterest-statistics/`).

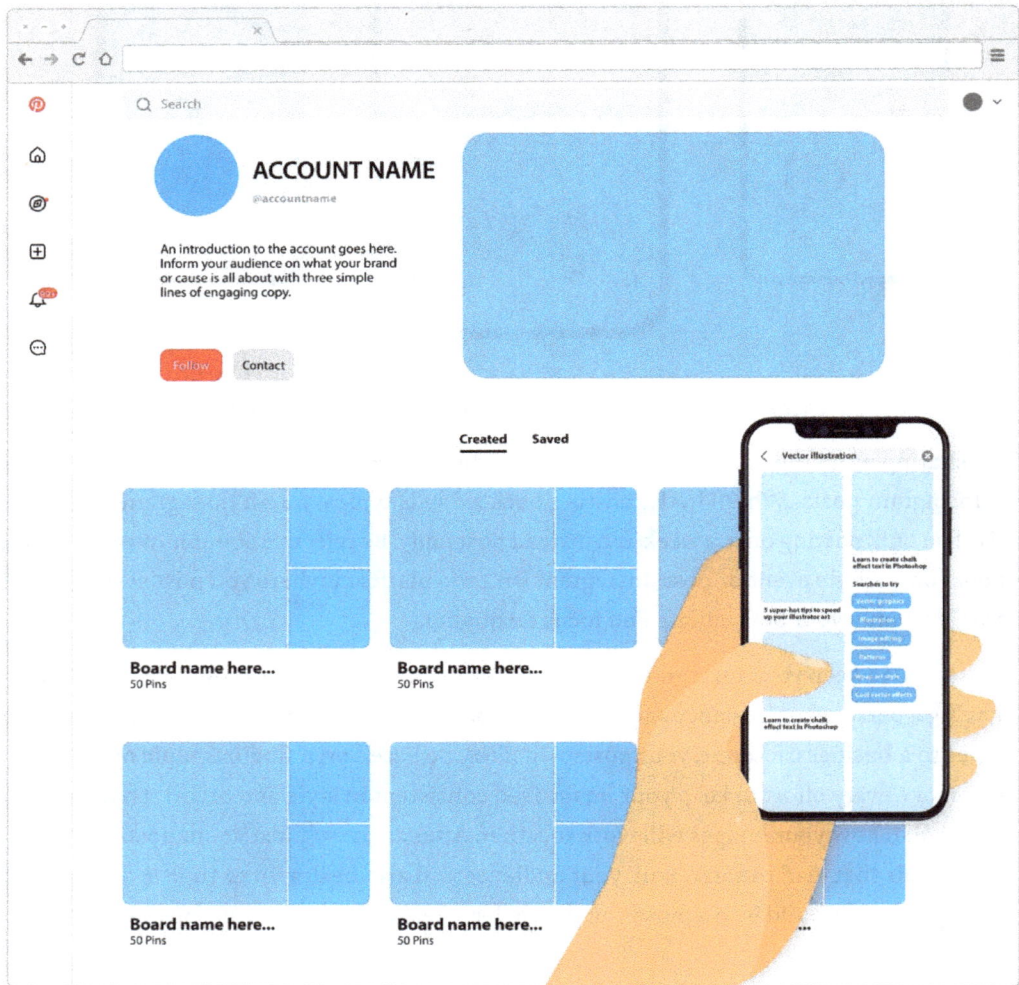

Figure 7.6: Pinterest shown on the desktop and mobile

Pinterest is one of the most popular *visual search platforms*, and it shouldn't be underestimated, since, according to the company, 62% of Gen Z and Millennials say they'd like to be able to search by image.

Your *profile image* should be square (1:1 ratio). The larger, the better, but it is recommended to be at least 165 x 165 px. Pinterest will resize it to fit proportionally. Like other social sites, your profile picture should be closely tied to your brand or service.

Pinterest is a vertically oriented browsing experience, meaning that you are limited to the width of your *image pins* but not the height. This allows you to add a square photo or one that will scale to be even taller, but if a photo is of a ratio larger than 2:3, your pin will be scaled to fit a width of 238 pixels or possibly truncated, which can affect the performance of your pin.

Long infographics have been popular on Pinterest for many years. The almost limitless height of a pin has allowed for rich visuals, but this is changing. Pinterest has a name for sprawling pins that the platform deems too high: giraffe pins. Since June 2018, Pinterest's algorithm has been favoring pins that are approximately 2:3 in proportion. You may struggle to get traction if you deviate far from that golden ratio. The maximum size your pin can be posted at without cropping is 1000 x 2100 pixels.

Creating Pinterest boards is one of the most important things you can do on the platform. It's essential to ensure you're using an image that fits the size criteria perfectly. Large thumbnail images should be 222 x 150 pixels, and small board thumbnails should be 55 x 55.

Examining artwork for LinkedIn

With 1.2 billion monthly active users (`https://sproutsocial.com/insights/linkedin-statistics/`), LinkedIn is not only the place to grow your professional network but also an effective means of raising brand awareness and marketing your goods and services. Users can follow your company page to keep updated with news and events you post, which can be seen on a user's home feed.

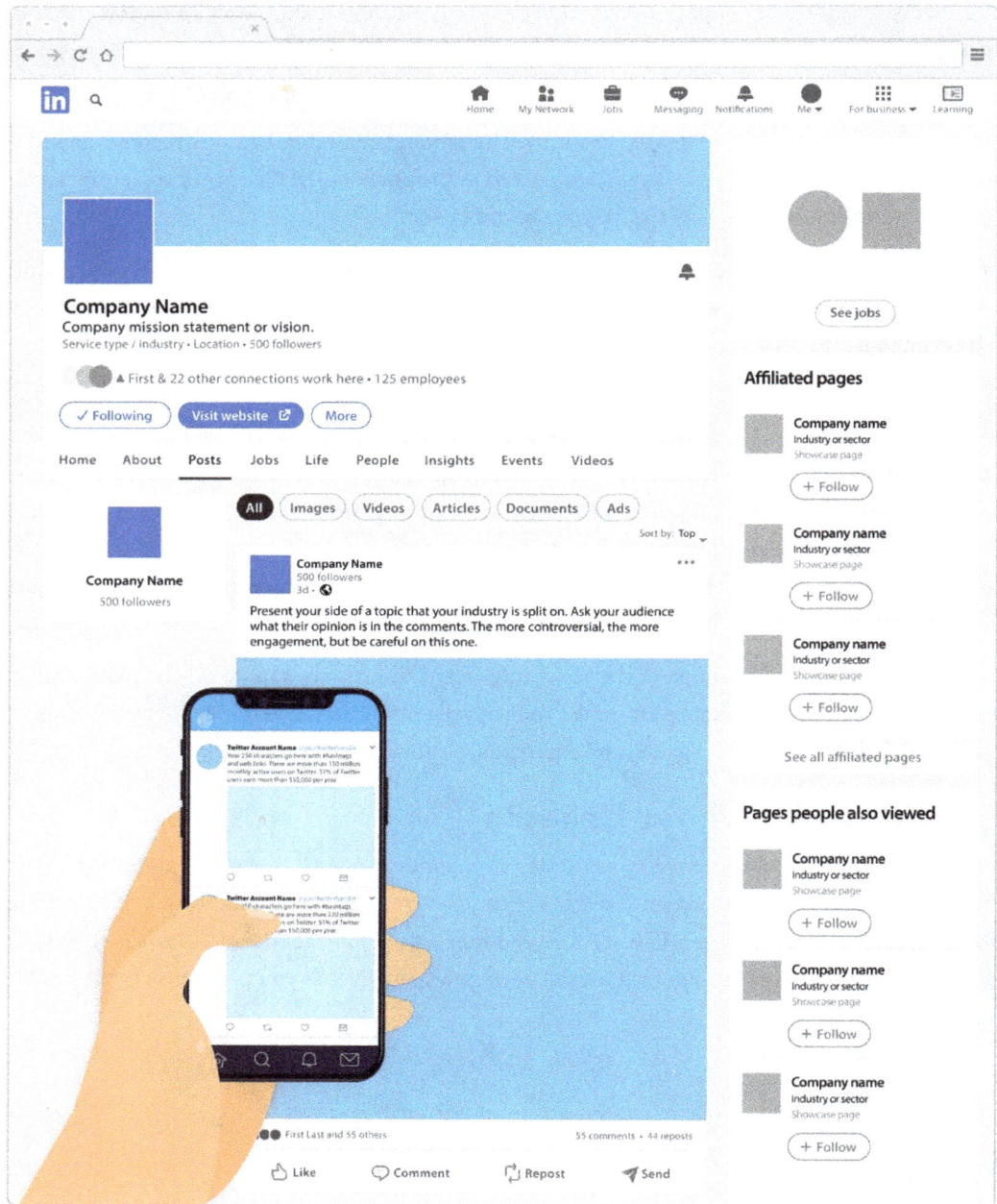

Figure 7.7: LinkedIn shown on the desktop and mobile

LinkedIn company pages feature a *logo* and a slim *cover image* at the top. There's also space for a brief company mission statement and geographical location, as well as a number of employees. The page will also highlight any followers in a user's network who follow the company.

Due to the slimline size of 1128 x 191 px, it can be challenging to juxtapose a prominent subject within the company cover and still provide context to the page visitor. Some companies instead use a pattern or abstract art in this space. For example, Adobe uses its own logo as a pattern, while Apple uses an aerial shot of its headquarters, Apple Park, in California:

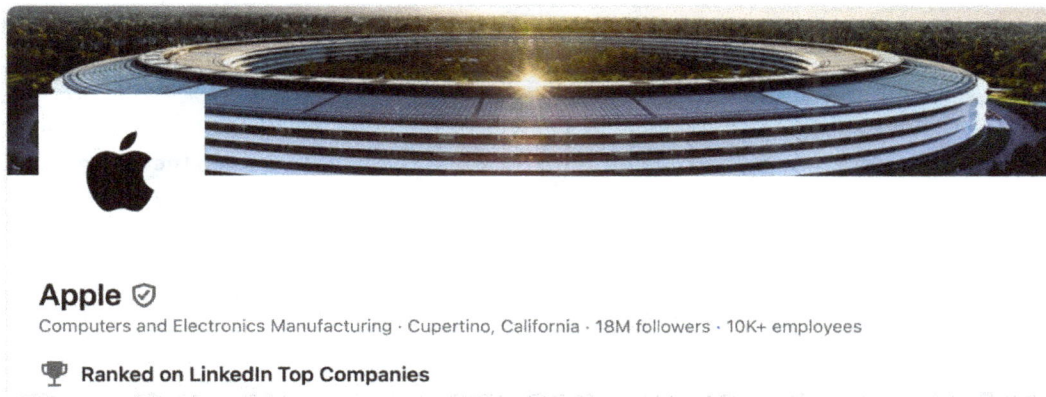

Figure 7.8: The Apple company page on LinkedIn

Along the header of a company page are quick links where a user can explore further information by navigating to the **About** or **Jobs** pages. It also provides a *Life* section, where visitors can learn more about the company culture and staff success stories. This presents another opportunity to add artwork, and at 1128 x 376 px, you have more space to work with than the company cover.

When it comes to posting on LinkedIn, you are spoilt for choice by supported file types, from the standard JPG, GIF, and PNG formats to multi-page presentations such as PowerPoint, Word, and PDF. All of these are accommodated well with simple navigational icons to click through each page, rather like slides. A PDF is best suited to this format, with an aspect ratio of 1:1 and 1080 x 1080 px or a 16:9 ratio and a size of 1920 x 1080 px tall. PDFs are limited to 300 pages and cannot exceed 100 MB.

Native videos up to 4K in resolution and in portrait or landscape orientations are also supported on LinkedIn. Unlike videos posted to LinkedIn via a link and hosted on YouTube, videos uploaded directly to the LinkedIn platform play automatically in a user's feed, making them more engaging. A native video is limited to 10 minutes in length and 5 GB.

Event posts, such as demonstrations, how-tos, or product launches, are great ways of attracting engagement. You can broadcast live on LinkedIn, where viewers can post questions in chat. You can also create *event pages* where users can find further details and register. Event pages are branded with a *banner* 1600 x 900 pixels in size.

In the first part of this section, we examined the assets required to brand popular social media platforms with examples of how they are displayed. Next, we'll look at the technical specifications for each image type.

Social media sizes

One of the most challenging aspects of creating images for use online, and especially for social media, is considering the sizes required by each platform. In the following table, I've included common image sizes required by platforms that have a focus on business and the strong use of visuals:

	Recommended size	Accepted file formats	Recommended maximum file size
Facebook			
Profile	320 x 320	PNG/JPG	5 MB
Cover	851 x 315	PNG/JPG	
Shared image	1080 x 1350	PNG/JPG	
Shared link with image	1080 x 1350	PNG/JPG	
Event image	1920 x 1005	PNG/JPG	
Fundraiser image	800 x 300	PNG/JPG	
X			
Profile	400 x 400	PNG/JPG/GIF	5 MB/15 MB (GIF)
Header	1500 x 500	PNG/JPG/GIF	5 MB/15 MB (GIF)
Single shared image	1600 x 900	PNG/JPG/GIF	5 MB/15 MB (GIF)
Two shared images	700 x 800	PNG/JPG/GIF	5 MB/15 MB (GIF)
Instagram			
Profile	110 x 110	PNG/JPG	
Photo thumbnails	161 x 161	PNG/JPG	

	Recommended size	Accepted file formats	Recommended maximum file size
Photo feed	1080 x 1080	PNG/JPG	
Stories (portrait)	1080 x 1350	PNG/JPG	
LinkedIn			
Company logo	400 x 400	PNG/JPG	3 MB
Company cover photo	1128 x 191	PNG/JPG	3 MB
Shared image or link	1200 x 627	PNG/JPG/GIF	
Main image and company photos (the **Life** tab)	1128 x 376	PNG/JPG	
Pinterest			
Profile	165 x 165	PNG/JPG	10 MB
Pin	735 x 1102	PNG/JPG	
Board display (large)	222 x 150	PNG/JPG	
Board display (small)	55 x 55	PNG/JPG	

Table 7.1: Image specifications for posting to popular social media platforms

In this section, we have previewed the principles of the tools and techniques that will be deployed to create our social media projects. We have also reviewed the various platform characteristics and image sizes required for branding your organization's home pages and posts. Next, we will create a web document and its corresponding artboard.

Working with artboards

In this first exercise, we will create a new document, define the artboard properties, and add brand assets such as logos, colors, and aspirational photos:

1. Go to **File → New**. When the **New Document** dialog appears, click on the **Web** tab at the top of the dialog to display the presets. Click on the **Web Most Common** thumbnail. Enter SM26, an abbreviation of the project name and year, into the **Name** field in the top-right corner of the dialog.

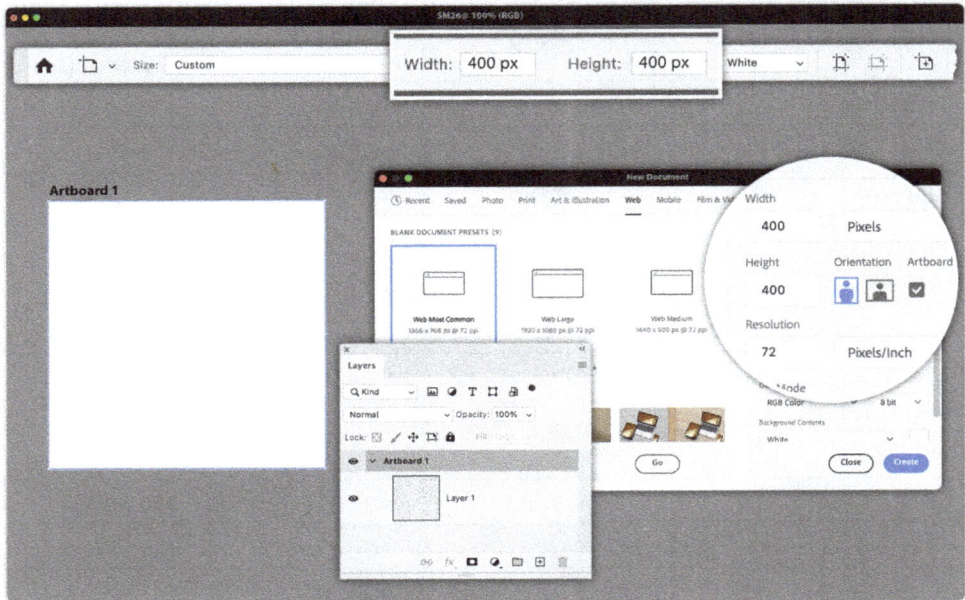

Figure 7.9: Creating a new document

2. Change the **Width** value to 400 px and the **Height** value to 400 px. This will match the
    profile image size on X. Ensure the **Artboards** checkbox is active, **Color Mode** is set to **RGB
    Color** and **8 bit**, and **Background Contents** is **White**. Click **OK** when done to generate
    the document.

3. Hover your cursor over **Artboard 1** in the **Layers** panel and double-click to open the type
    entry field. Type X-Profile and press *Enter* to apply the name change. Notice that the
    label above the top-left corner of the artboard in the **Image** window has also updated.

4. Next, we will add a branded color to the background. Click on the **New Fill and Adjust-
    ment layer** icon (circled in *Figure 7.10*) at the bottom of the **Layers** panel and choose **Solid
    Color...** from the list of options. When the **Color Picker** dialog appears, enter 142 into the
    R (red) field, 58 into **G** (green), and 42 into **B** (blue) to create a burnt red color. Click **OK**.

Figure 7.10: Adding a background color and logo

5. Go to **File → Place Linked**, browse to the 07-Social folder, and select the file named WildCo_Logo.ai. Click **Place** when done. When the dialog appears, click on the *page 7* thumbnail, which contains a white version of the logo. Then, click **OK** to import the artwork.

6. When the logo appears, it will be scaled to fit the artboard. Ensure the **Width** and **Height** fields are linked in the **Options** bar, change the **Scale** to 60%, and click on the **Commit Changes** button in the **Options** bar to finish the import process.

7. With the logo layer still active in **Layers**, click on the **Fx** icon at the bottom of the same panel and choose **Color Overlay** from the list. When the dialog appears, the overlay setting should be visible. Click on the **Color Picker** icon (**A** in *Figure 7.11*), and when the **Color Picker** dialog appears, enter 142 into the **R** (red) field, 58 into **G** (green), and 42 into **B** (blue)to create a burnt red color. Click **OK** when done to dismiss the **Color Picker** dialog.

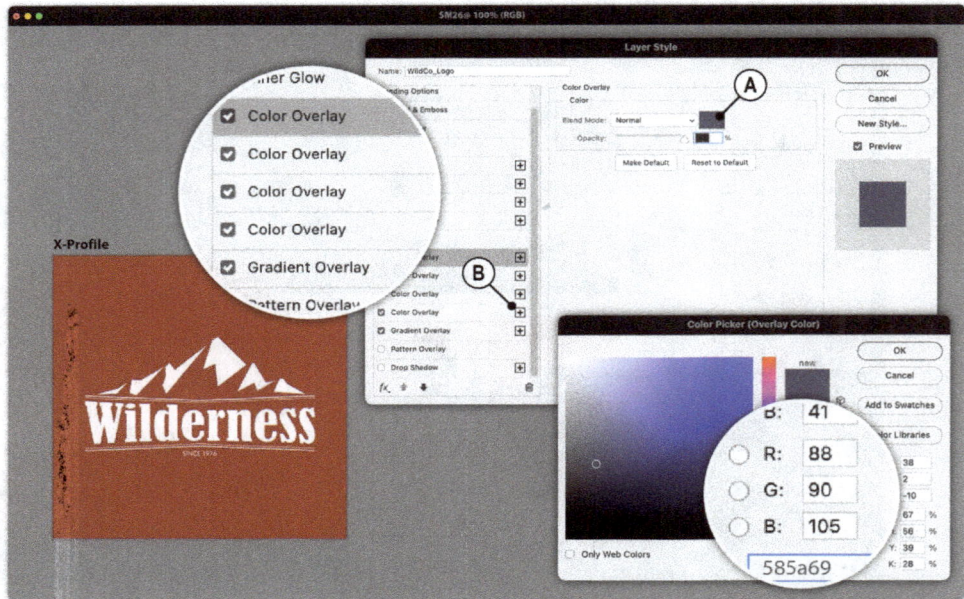

Figure 7.11: Adding a background color and logo

8. From the list on the left-hand side of the **Layer Effects** dialog, click on the plus icon adjacent to **Color Overlay** (**B** in *Figure 7.11*) to add an additional color. Click on the **Color Picker** icon. When the **Color Picker** dialog appears, enter 101 into the **R** (red) field, 39 into **G** (green), and 86 into **B** (blue) to create a deep magenta color. Click **OK** when done to dismiss the **Color Picker** dialog.

9. Repeat the same technique to create a further two colors: a dark green composed of **R** 65, **G** 72, and **B** 43, and a dark blue composed of **R** 88, **G** 90, and **B** 105.

10. Once all the colors have been added, click on **Drop Shadow** from the list in the **Layer Effects** dialog. Set **Opacity** to 30%, **Angle** to 90, **Distance** to 0%, **Spread** to 0%, and **Size** to 18 px. Then, click **OK** to close the **Layer Effects** dialog. Turn off the visibility for all **Color Overlay** effects and **Drop Shadow**. These will be needed on other artboards.

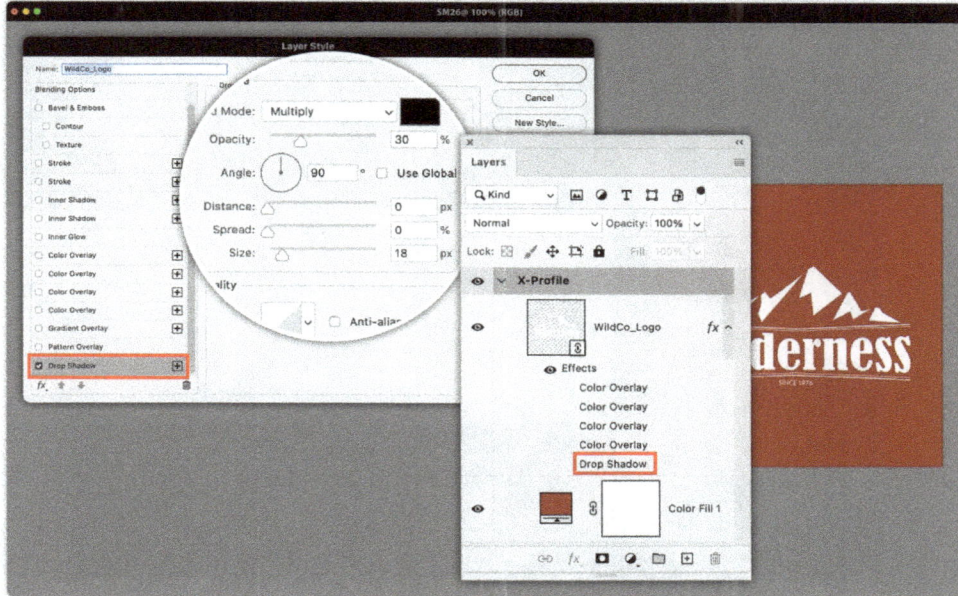

Figure 7.12: Adding a drop shadow effect to the logo

Adding a header image

With the first artboard and two editable brand assets created, you will now build on this to create an X header graphic:

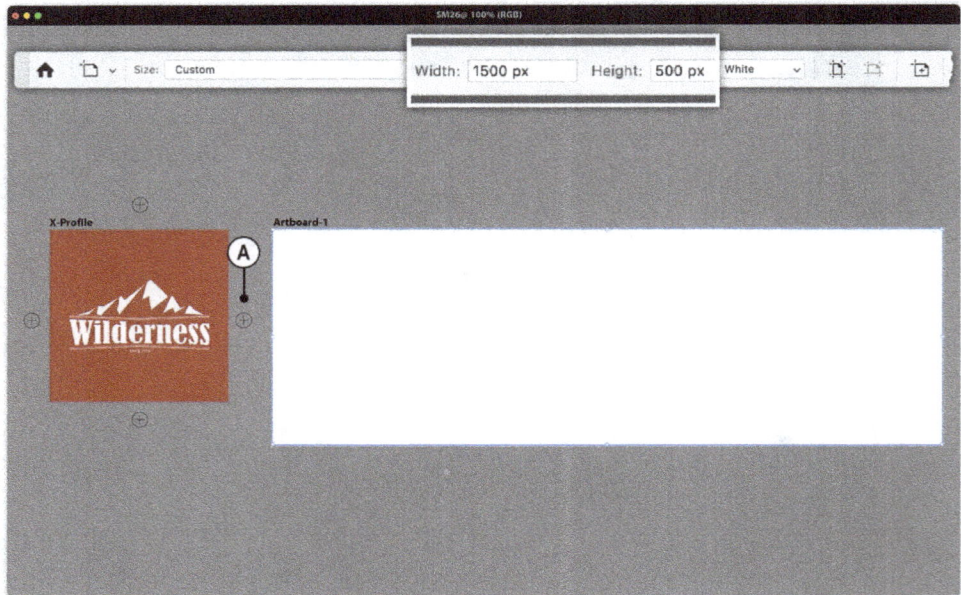

Figure 7.13: Creating a second artboard for the X header

1. Switch to the **Artboard** tool by clicking on the artboard name X-Profile located in the top-left corner of the artboard in the **Image** window. You should now see plus widgets along each side of the artboard, shown as circles with a plus symbol within them. These plus widgets allow you to copy or duplicate existing artboards. Click on the right-hand plus widget (**A** in *Figure 7.13*) to create a second artboard.

2. Double-click the artboard name Artboard-1 in the **Layers** panel to open its type entry field. Enter a new name of X-Header and press *Enter* to apply the name change. Ensure that the **Artboard** tool is still active. From the **Options** bar, change the **Width** of the active artboard to 1500 px and the **Height** to 500 px. Press *Enter* to apply the changes.

3. Go to **File → Place Linked**, browse to the 07-Social folder, and select the file named Trek-A.jpg. Click **Place** when done.

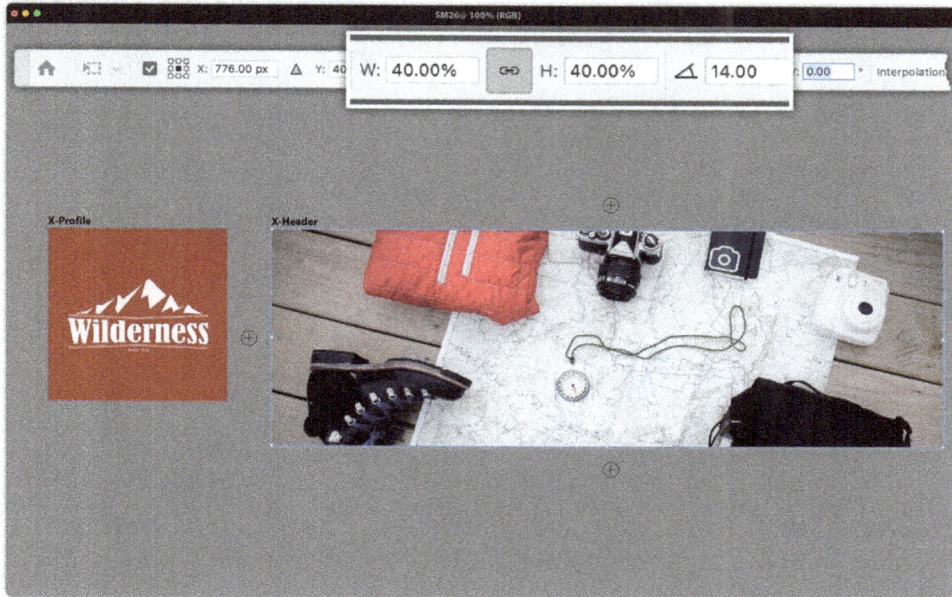

Figure 7.14: Adding a background image to the new artboard

4. From **Options,** change **Scale** to 40% and **Rotate** to 14% to make the composition more interesting. Click on the **Commit Changes** button. Reposition the artwork to include as many items from the flat-lay photo as possible within the artboard.

Creating an X post template

This type of image will require flexibility built into it to account for different backgrounds, colors, and contrast with the logo. The number of images you add in a post will influence the size. Next, you will create a template for an X post containing a single image:

1. Click on the artboard named **X-Header** to activate the **Artboard** tool. When the plus widgets appear along each side of the artboard, click on the right-hand plus widget (**A** in *Figure 7.15*) to create a third artboard:

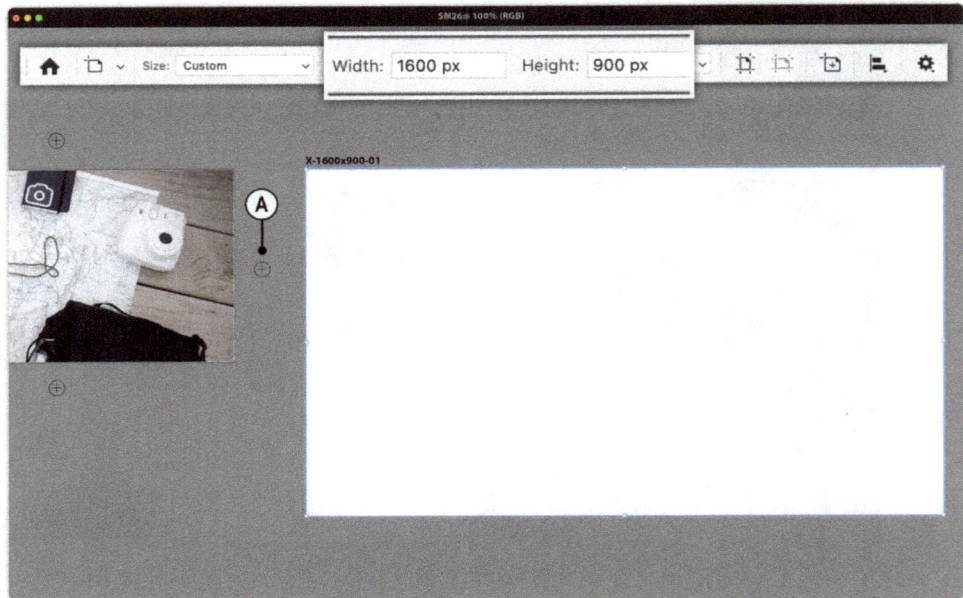

Figure 7.15: Creating a third artboard

2. Double-click the artboard named **Artboard-1** in the **Layers** panel. Enter a new name of
    X-1600x900-01 and press *Enter* to apply the name change. Ensure that the **Artboard** tool
    is still active. From the **Options** bar, change the **Width** of the active artboard to 1600 px
    and the **Height** to 900 px. Press *Enter* to apply the changes.

3. Go to **File → Place Linked**, browse to the 07-Social folder, and select the file named Trek-B.jpg. Click **Place** when done.

Figure 7.16: Importing and scaling artwork to fill the third artboard

4. Change **Scale** to 36% from the **Options** bar and click the **Commit Changes** button. Reposition the artwork so that the hikers and the mountain's peak are visible on the artboard.

5. With the hiking photo still active in the **Layers** panel, press the *D* key to reset the foreground and background colors in the **Tools** panel. This will ensure that black is active when we set the following gradient.

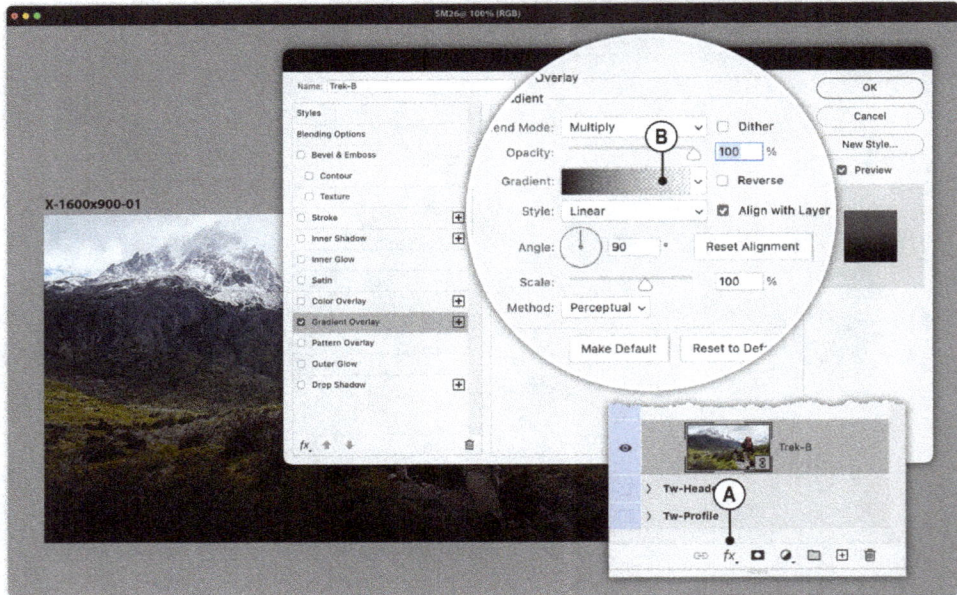

Figure 7.17: Adding a gradient overlay to the hiker image

6. Click on the **Fx** icon at the bottom of the same panel (**A** in *Figure 7.17*) and choose **Gradient Overlay** from the list.

7. When the dialog appears, the gradient setting should be visible. Set **Blend Mode** to **Multiply**, **Opacity** to **100**, **Angle** to **90**, and **Scale** to **100%**. Choose **Linear** from the **Style** dropdown menu, turn off the **Reverse** checkbox, and activate the **Align with Layer** checkbox.

8. Click on the **Gradient** preview (**B** in *Figure 7.17*) to open the editor.

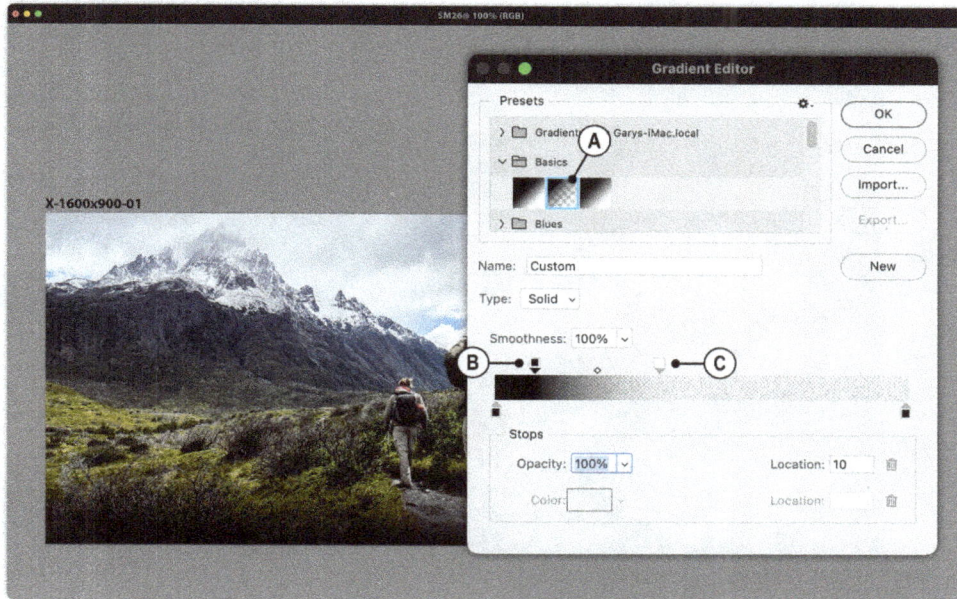

Figure 7.18: Modifying the gradient properties

9. Expand the Basics folder and click on the gradient named Foreground to Transparent (**A** in *Figure 7.18*). Then, click on the top-left **Transparency Stop** icon (**B**) to make it active. Change the values lower down in the dialog. Set **Location** to 10% and **Opacity** to **100%**.

10. Click on the top-right **Transparency Stop** icon (**C**). Change **Location** to 40% and **Opacity** to **0%**. This should create a black fade along the bottom of the photo, making any text or logo stand out when necessary. Click **OK** to close the editor, then click **OK** to close the **Layer Styles** dialog.

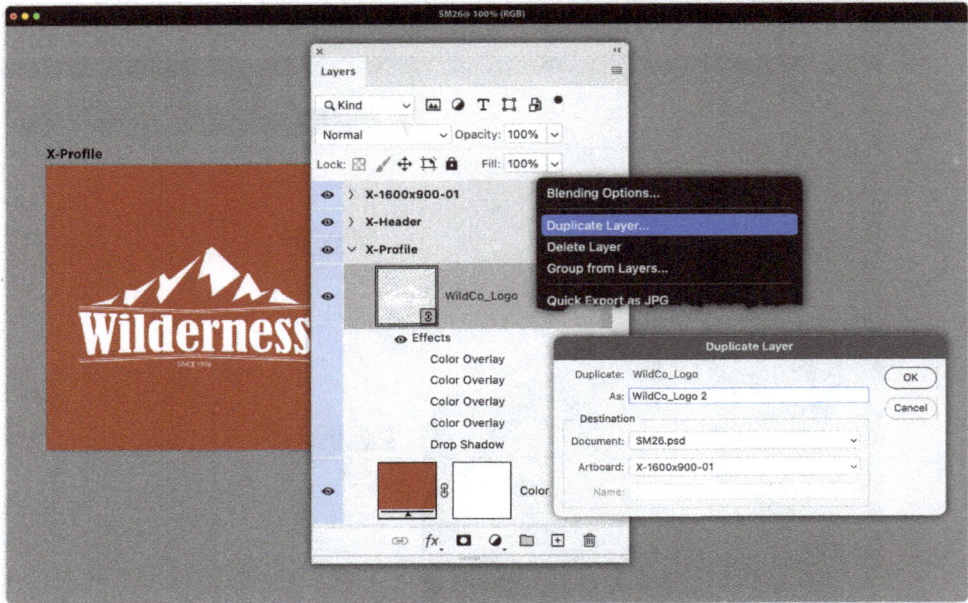

Figure 7.19: Adding a gradient overlay to the hiker image

11. Hover your cursor over the layer containing the logo in the **Layers** panel, imported in a previous exercise (which can be found by right-clicking on the layer name), and choose **Duplicate Layer** from the list of options. When the **Duplicate layer** dialog appears, rename the layer WildCo_Logo 2, set the **Destination Document** to **SM26.psd** (the file you are editing), and set **Artboard** to **X-1600x900-01**. Click **OK** when done.

12. Ensure the newly duplicated **WildCo_Logo 2** layer is active in the **Layers** panel. Then, go to **Edit → Free Transform** and scale the logo to 30% from the **Options** bar. Press *Enter* to apply the changes. Drag the logo to the left-hand side of the artboard. Keep the logo layer active in the **Layers** panel.

13. Go to **File → Save** and keep the document open.

Adding text to the artboard

With the main part of the design created, it is now time to add a text heading to promote the holiday destination. The fonts used in all the exercises in this book can be installed from the Adobe Fonts website. Alternatively, you can use a different font already installed on your system. Here is how to add text to the artboard:

1. Switch to the **Horizontal Type** tool by pressing the *T* key. Hover the tool over the left-hand side of the **X-1600x900-01** artboard. Click and drag to the right to draw a text frame approximately half the artboard's width. Release the left mouse button to generate the text frame. Inside, you will see the active type cursor.

> Introduced in Photoshop 2026, **Dynamic Text** automatically resizes and reflows text within a bounding box, potentially making it easier to create multiple posts in varying sizes. See *Chapter 1, What's New in Photoshop 2026*, to learn more about this brilliant time-saving feature.

Figure 7.20: Adding text to the artboard

2. Type Patagonia into the text frame and highlight all characters in the frame with the **Horizontal Type** tool. From the **Properties** panel, set **Font** to **Flood Std**, **Size** to **60 pt**, **Leading** to **Auto**, and **Tracking** to **350**.

3. Set the alignment to **Center** from the **Paragraph** options. Set the text **Color** option to white by clicking on the color swatch to open **Color Picker**. Enter 255 into the **R, G,** and **B** fields. Click **OK** to apply the color change and close **Color Picker**. Press *Esc* to apply the text and exit type editing mode.

4. Ensure that both the text layer and the logo are active in the **Layers** panel. Click on **Align Horizontal Centers** from the **Options** bar to align them with one another. Switch to the **Move** tool and reposition them in the lower left-hand side of the artboard.

5. Save the document in the 07-Social folder as a PSD and keep the document open.

In this section, we have added key assets to our social media templates, including an aspirational photo, company logo, brand colors, and text. In the next section, we will use these template designs to create additional designs in varying sizes for other platforms.

Duplicating artboards

In the following exercise, you will duplicate the initial artboards, such as the profile, header, and shared image X post. Then, using these original designs, you will modify them to create artwork for a different platform:

1. Switch to the **Artboard** tool by clicking on the **X-Profile** artboard name. You should now see plus widgets along each side of the artboard. Press *Alt* (Windows) or *Option* (macOS) as you click on the bottom plus widget to duplicate the artboard. The duplicate will now appear under the original.

2. Repeat the same technique of pressing *Alt* (Windows) or *Option* (macOS) and clicking on the bottom plus widget of the two remaining artboards, **X-Header** and **X-1600x900-01**, to duplicate them under the originals. You should now have six artboards in total in the document.

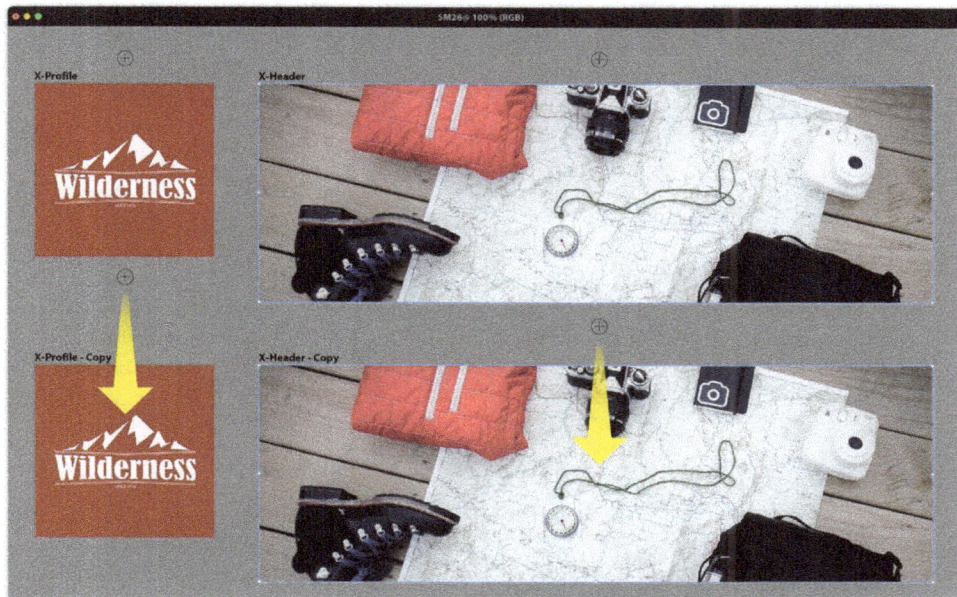

Figure 7.21: Duplicating the profile and header artboard

3. Go to the **Layers** panel and double-click the **X-Profile-Copy** artboard to open the type entry field. Enter a new name of Fb-Profile and press *Enter* to apply the name change.

4. Double-click the artboard named **X-Header-Copy** to open the type entry field. Rename it Fb-Cover and press *Enter* to apply the change.

5. Then, double-click the artboard named **X-1600x900-01-Copy** and rename it Fb-1920x1005-01. Press *Enter* to apply the name change:

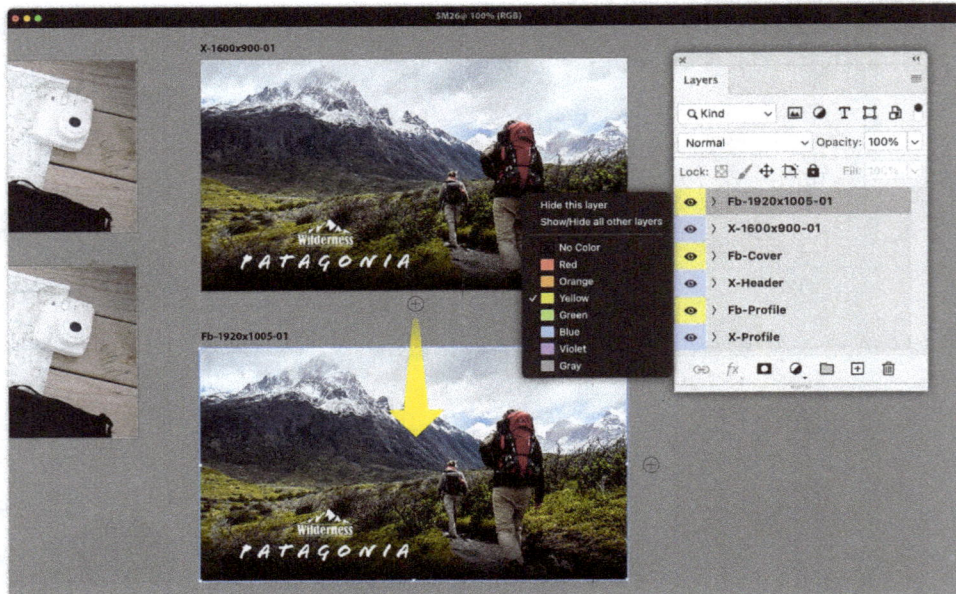

Figure 7.22: Renaming and color-coding the layer groups

6. Right-click on each of the newly duplicated artboards' **Visibility** icons in the **Layers** panel and change the color highlight to **Yellow** from the list of options. Any remaining artboards created for X in the **Layers** panel should be recolored to blue to distinguish them from each other.

7. Switch to the **Move** tool, click on the **WildCo_Logo** layer inside the **Fb-Profile** artboard, and drag the logo to the top-left corner. Go to **Edit → Free Transform**. Change the photo **Scale** value to 25% and click on the **Commit** button under **Options**.

8. Click on the **Fb-Profile** artboard label in the **Image** window (see *Figure 7.23*) to switch to the **Artboard** tool and make the artboard active. From **Options**, change the **Width** value of the active artboard to 320 px and the **Height** value to 320 px. Press *Enter* to apply the changes.

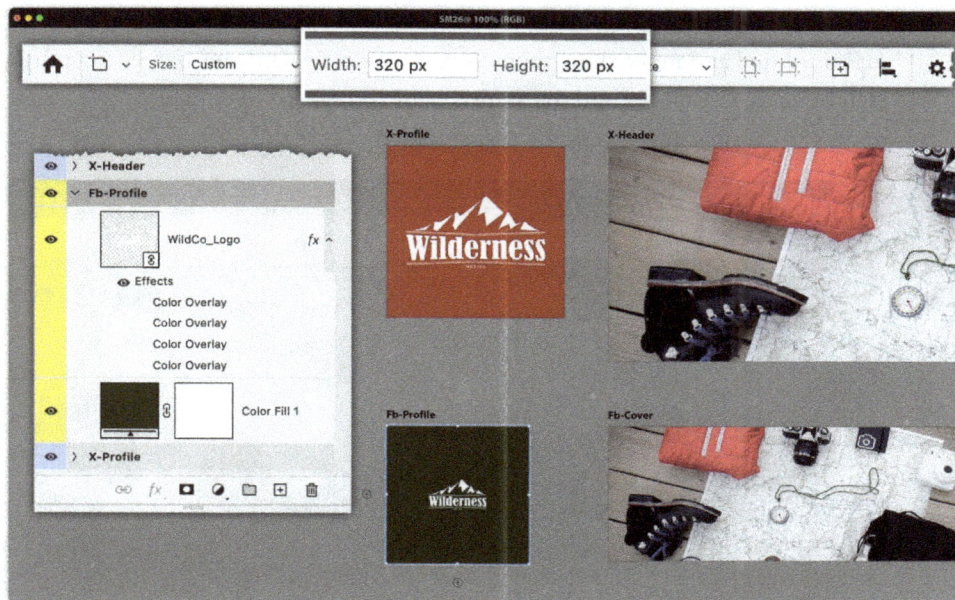

Figure 7.23: Scaling the Facebook logo and artboard and changing the background color

9. Switch to the **Move** tool, click on the **WildCo_Logo** layer in the active artboard, and drag the logo to the center of the artboard.

10. Next, click on the **Color Fill** layer inside the newly created **Fb-Profile** artboard. To change the color, double-click on the layer thumbnail in the **Layers** panel, shown as a swatch. When the **Color Picker** dialog appears, set **R** to 65, **G** to 72, and **B** to 43 for a dark green color. Click **OK** when done to apply the change.

11. Click on the **Fb-Cover** artboard label in the **Image** window to switch to the **Artboard** tool and make the artboard active. From **Options**, change the **Width** of the active artboard to 851 px and the **Height** value to 315 px. Press *Enter* to apply the changes.

12. Click on the photo inside **Fb-Cover**. Switch to the **Move** tool and then go to **Edit → Free Transform**. Change the **Scale** value of the photo to 58% and click on the **Commit** button in the **Options** bar. Reposition the photo as required within the artboard.

13. Click on the **Fb-1920x1005-01** artboard name in the **Image** window to switch to the **Artboard** tool and make the artboard active. From the **Options** bar, change the artboard **Height** value to 1005 px and the **Width** value to 1920 px (see *Figure 7.24*). Press *Enter* to apply the change. Reposition the text and logo within the artboard as required.

Figure 7.24: Altering the size of the duplicated artboards

14. Go to **File** → **Save** when done and keep the document open.

In this section, we have duplicated existing artboards and repurposed their designs for other social platforms in various sizes. Next, we'll export artwork to the appropriate formats for posting online.

Exporting and scheduling posts

When social media demands are time-sensitive, the last thing you want is to waste valuable time saving artboards as separate files, choosing a directory to save them to, and naming them every time. The following techniques seek to avoid the time-consuming challenge of exporting to the web.

Batch export artboards

Photoshop has provided batch export options for decades, but with the advent of artboards, these long-standing features could not process these new multi-page designs. Thankfully, Adobe eventually added a set of scripts that could export all artboards in a single document:

1. With the SM26 document open, go to **File → Export → Artboards to Files**. When the dialog appears, click the **Browse** button, select the 07-Social folder, and click **Open**. The location will default to the folder the document has been saved to each time.

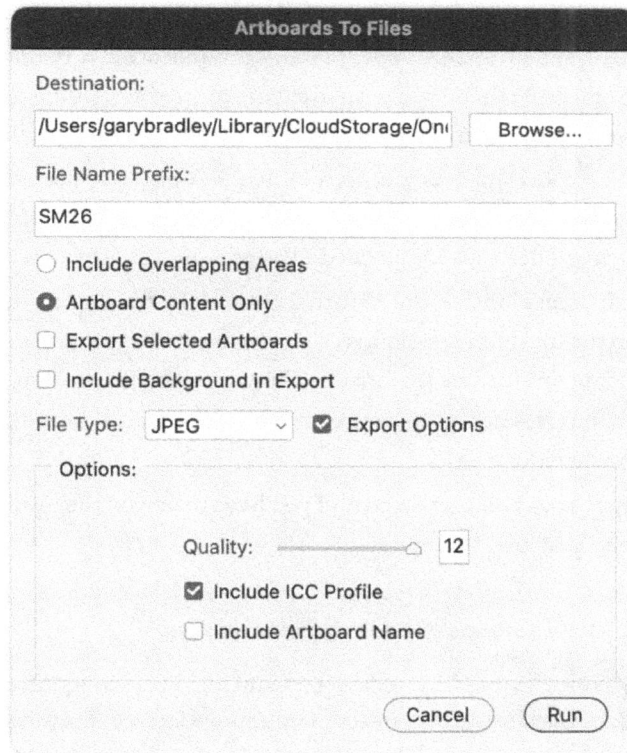

Destination:
/Users/garybradley/Library/CloudStorage/On(Browse...

File Name Prefix:
SM26

○ Include Overlapping Areas
● Artboard Content Only
☐ Export Selected Artboards
☐ Include Background in Export

File Type: JPEG   ✓   ☑ Export Options

Options:

Quality: ──────○ 12
☑ Include ICC Profile
☐ Include Artboard Name

Cancel   Run

Figure 7.25: Exporting one or more artboards ready for posting online

2. Under **File Name Prefix**, set the current file to **SM26**, an abbreviation of "social media 2026." This name will default each time you enter the dialog box, so saving your files with short names is worth considering.

3. Under the dialog, you have a choice of two radio buttons. Choose **Artboard Content Only**.

4. The **Export Selected Artboards** checkbox is useful when you've just made an edit to an artboard and wish to export an updated version, but it is irrelevant in our scenario. If you decide to use this feature later, you must click on the artboard you wish to export before returning to this dialog box.

5. **Include Background in Export** is useful for artboards containing a standard white background or another color that you wish to include in the exported artwork. In most cases, your artwork will hide the background and make it irrelevant. We will leave this deactivated.

6. Under the **File Type** drop-down menu, you can choose from **BMP, JPEG, PDF, PSD, Targa, TIFF, PNG-8**, and **PNG-24**. Choose **JPEG**, as the bulk of our artwork contains photographic content. Remember that if you wish to export content containing 256 or fewer colors, such as a logo for a profile, you can alternatively use **PNG-8** for a smaller file size.

7. Turn on the **Export Options** checkbox. When the options appear, ensure the **Quality** value is set to 12, which is the maximum. Turning on **Include ICC Profile** is helpful when color modes such as Adobe RGB 1998 need to be honored, but this is not the case with our files.

8. You can add a text label to the exported artwork by turning on **Include Artboard Name**. Located in the top-left of the image, the canvas of the exported image will be extended to accommodate this feature. Historically, this was useful for proofing images and referencing each asset, but it is not appropriate for our final artwork. Leave this option deactivated. Click **Run** when done.

9. Once all files have been exported and you have reviewed the results, you can go to **File →** **Save**. Then, close the document.

Which file formats should I use when posting?

If your image contains mostly text and plain colors, try using the PNG format to reduce the file size. This offers more appropriate compression and is built for images with 256 colors or fewer. Use JPEG for continuous tone images, such as photos, where you are managing thousands of colors. You can post animated GIFs to your Facebook timeline up to 8 MB in size, but they should contain less than 20% text and not have grainy content or flashes; these posts may not be approved by Facebook if you try to boost them.

Scheduling posts with Adobe Express

Adobe Express continues to expand its online editing and creation tools, including a social media scheduler with access to Adobe's free stock collection. Here's how to schedule posts with Adobe Express:

1. From your web browser, head to `https://express.adobe.com/`, where you may need to log in to your Creative Cloud account.

2. Once logged in, click on the **Schedule** button from the list on the left (**A** in *Figure 7.26*). When the calendar appears, click the **+New** button at the top right and choose **New Post** (**B**).

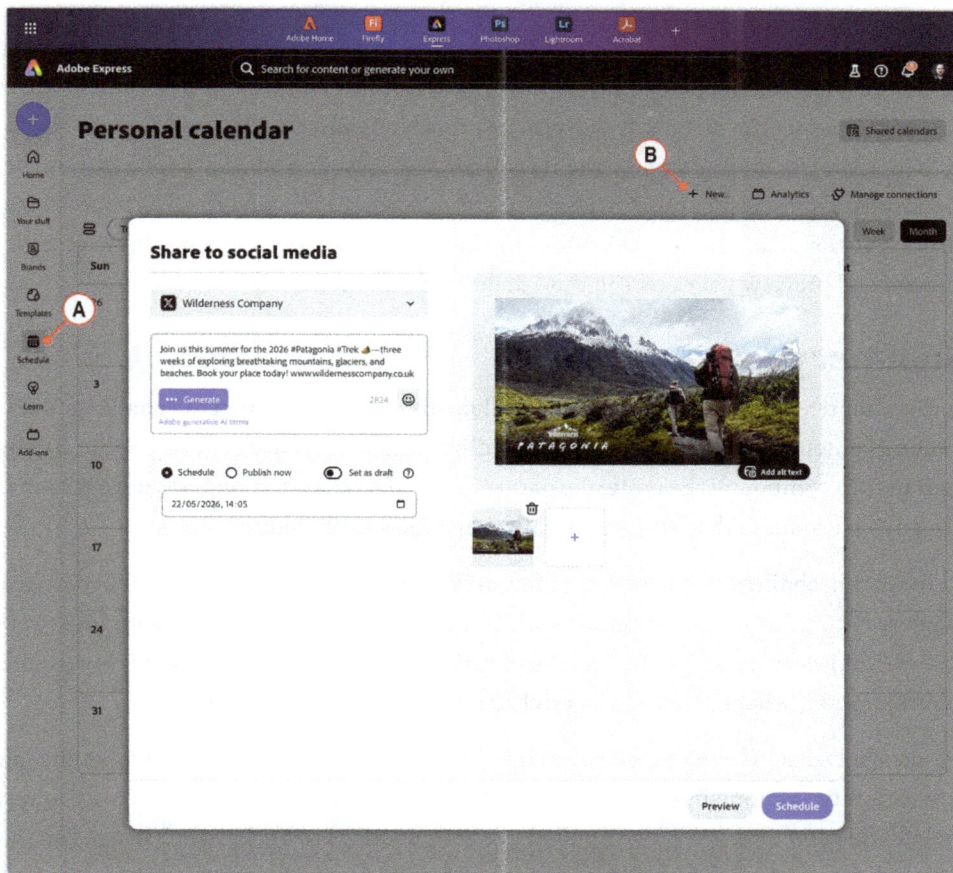

Figure 7.26: Scheduling social media posts from Adobe Express

3. You can drag and drop SM26X-1600x900-01.jpg from the 07-Social folder. Once the image preview is displayed, click **Upload**.

4. In the **Share to social media** window, you can compose your post just as you would on X. You can access emojis and add URLs and hashtags. Under **Select Channels**, click on **X**.

5. Choose a **Publish date** and **Time** option from the corresponding drop-down menus to the right of the interface and click **Schedule**. Your post will then appear in the calendar.

> You can schedule and publish posts across all your platforms using the **content scheduler** tool built into Adobe Express. Just ensure that you post the correct image size to the corresponding platform.

In the final section of the chapter, we looked at the methods for exporting images from Photoshop for use on social media platforms. By utilizing scripts for this task, we can batch process every artboard or select the artboards we wish to export beforehand. This avoids us having to export each image separately and name them each time. We also introduced Adobe Express, an online social media management tool, where you can take source images edited in Photoshop and add responsive text, animations, and videos to adapt them to each platform. Once created, you can prepare and preview your posts in the Adobe Express scheduler.

Summary

In this chapter on creating images for social media, we first outlined the challenges involved in creating content for multiple platforms and different sizes for each type of graphic, depending on their use. To compound the issue, the nature of social media often requires us to respond quickly to evolving events so that we can capitalize on public engagement.

To meet this challenge, we looked at features built into Photoshop that deliver high-quality imagery with short project timescales while managing dozens of images with identical content that are subject to constant changes. First, artboards allow us to create a single document with multiple pages, where assets are just a click away and easy to duplicate.

We also looked at infusing brand colors into layers, such as logos, to provide flexibility and maintain legibility. By applying multiple layer effects, such as color overlays, we can simply turn a specific color on or off. We also applied gradient overlays to background images so that when required, those same logos and text can be made legible against a soft vignette, fading from black to transparent. Each of these layer effects can be edited quickly.

As we have seen in many chapters, smart objects are invaluable for protecting the quality of original photos. They can be easily replaced for future projects or scaled for different artboards according to the use case. Finally, we used scripts to batch export our social media images to a specific file format and directory, avoiding the need to complete this process manually for each image.

In the next chapter, we will continue with the theme of social media, focusing on motion in the form of animated GIFs and videos.

Get This Book's PDF Version and Exclusive Extras

UNLOCK NOW

Scan the QR code (or go to packtpub.com/unlock). Search for this book by name, confirm the edition, and then follow the steps on the page.

Note: Keep your invoice handy. Purchases made directly from Packt don't require one.

8

Creating Animated GIFs and Videos

Photoshop is one of the most powerful image editors around, and since the 2007 release of Creative Suite 3, it has also been possible to import and edit videos. You might be wondering why you would choose to edit videos in Photoshop when there are dedicated applications such as Premiere Pro and After Effects. If you edit large projects containing several assets, it would be prudent to look at Adobe's flagship video editing applications. However, if you need to combine a video clip with some text and an audio file to create a short sequence, you may find comfort in Photoshop's simplified workflows and familiar tools.

In the late '90s, Photoshop introduced the **History** panel, which is like an *undo* panel, and leveraging the same technology, it also became possible to capture layer states that included visibility, position, and opacity. Much like the hand-drawn frame animation of the early 20th century, Photoshop frames could be turned into an animation sequence and saved as a GIF. Animated GIFs might be an "old-timer" file format, but they have survived through the birth and death of Flash. Today, animated GIFs still have a place across the spectrum of social media platforms.

In this chapter, you will use familiar tools and techniques to create video and frame animations for use on social media. You'll characterize new documents, work with a timeline to organize and edit your footage and export files in suitable formats for posting online.

You will explore the following topics:

- Creating new motion projects in Photoshop
- Creating animated GIFs
- Working with video and audio in Photoshop
- Creating videos from still images and text
- Exporting animations and video from Photoshop

Before creating new motion projects, we must cover two fundamental features to manage the timing and arrangement of **audiovisual (AV)** content in Photoshop.

Technical requirements

The project files for this chapter can be found at `https://packt.link/gbz/9781806021710`.

The Timeline panel

A standard workflow in Photoshop involves editing still images where time is of no concern. However, when working with sequences or sets of frames that need to appear on the canvas at specific times, we need a way to arrange assets accordingly. That's where the aptly named **Timeline** panel comes in, a central part of the **motion workspace**, where you can work with frame animations or a video timeline. Frame animation typically lets you create animated GIFs, while the video timeline is used for working with video. It provides a linear editing system where you can see the start of the sequence on the far left-hand side, starting at frame 1 (**A** in *Figure 8.1*):

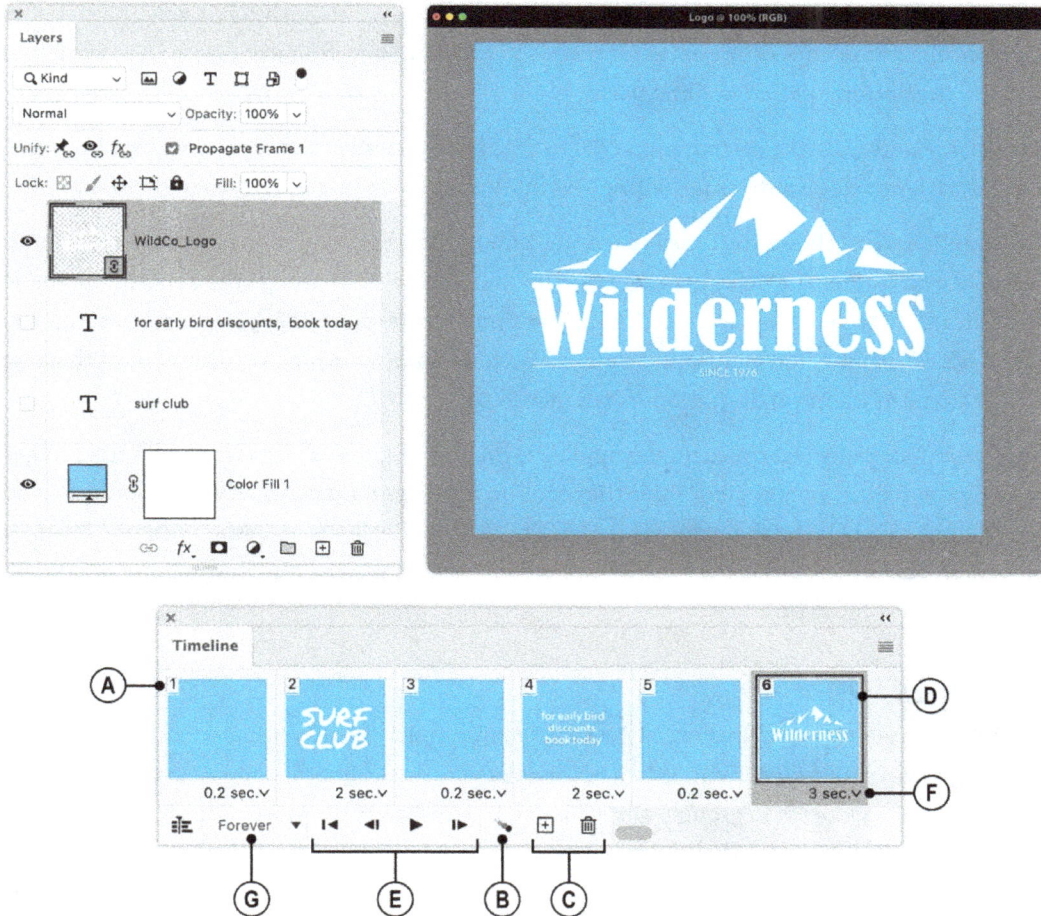

Figure 8.1: Animated GIFs can be created and managed in the Timeline panel

You start by changing the appearance of the first frame, then add more frames to the right-hand side to build up a sequence. In traditional hand-drawn animation, a sheet of paper would represent one frame, and approximately 24 sheets of paper would provide 1 second of animation.

You don't have to create every frame of animation in Photoshop; instead, use tweening. Start by defining the appearance of an active frame, such as a plain colored background. Then, insert an additional frame with a different appearance, such as a logo in front of the colored background. Then, select both frames, click the **Tweens animation frames** button (**B**), and have Photoshop create additional frames between them, making the logo appear gradually over several frames.

The appearance of each frame can be controlled from the **Layers** panel by changing the visibility, position, opacity, or style of one or more layers. You can add a new frame or delete an active frame (**C**) from the bottom of the **Timeline** panel.

You can navigate from the current frame (**D**) to the previous or next frames in the **Timeline** panel using the frame select buttons (**E**) or preview the animation by pressing the **Play** button.

The **Timeline** panel allows you to set a frame delay (**F**), where the animation pauses before moving on to the next frame. The delay is set to a default of **0**, but you can change the delay of the active frame from 0.1 seconds to 5 seconds. This is handy for frames containing logos or titles that you may wish to keep on-screen longer. You can also loop animations by a set number of times or forever from the **Loop Settings** drop-down menu (**G**).

The regular "stacking" feature of layers applies to motion sequences just as it does in still images. Imagine the scenario of opening titles that contain a background, such as video footage, a still image, or a plain color with text in front of it. This would ideally be achieved with two layers: a background layer containing the color or footage, and then, further along the timeline, a separate layer where text fades in.

Video groups

In the previous chapter, we extensively used artboards and artboard groups to create several artwork pages in a single document. When editing video assets in Photoshop, we use video groups, which act like regular layer groups, allowing you to store multiple assets within them. The difference with video groups is that they work in conjunction with the **Timeline** panel, where they appear in the same stacking order as the **Layers** panel, allowing you to arrange text layers in front of colored backgrounds to create, for example, a title sequence. These layers are independent of each other in the **Layers** and **Timeline** panels so that they can appear when needed:

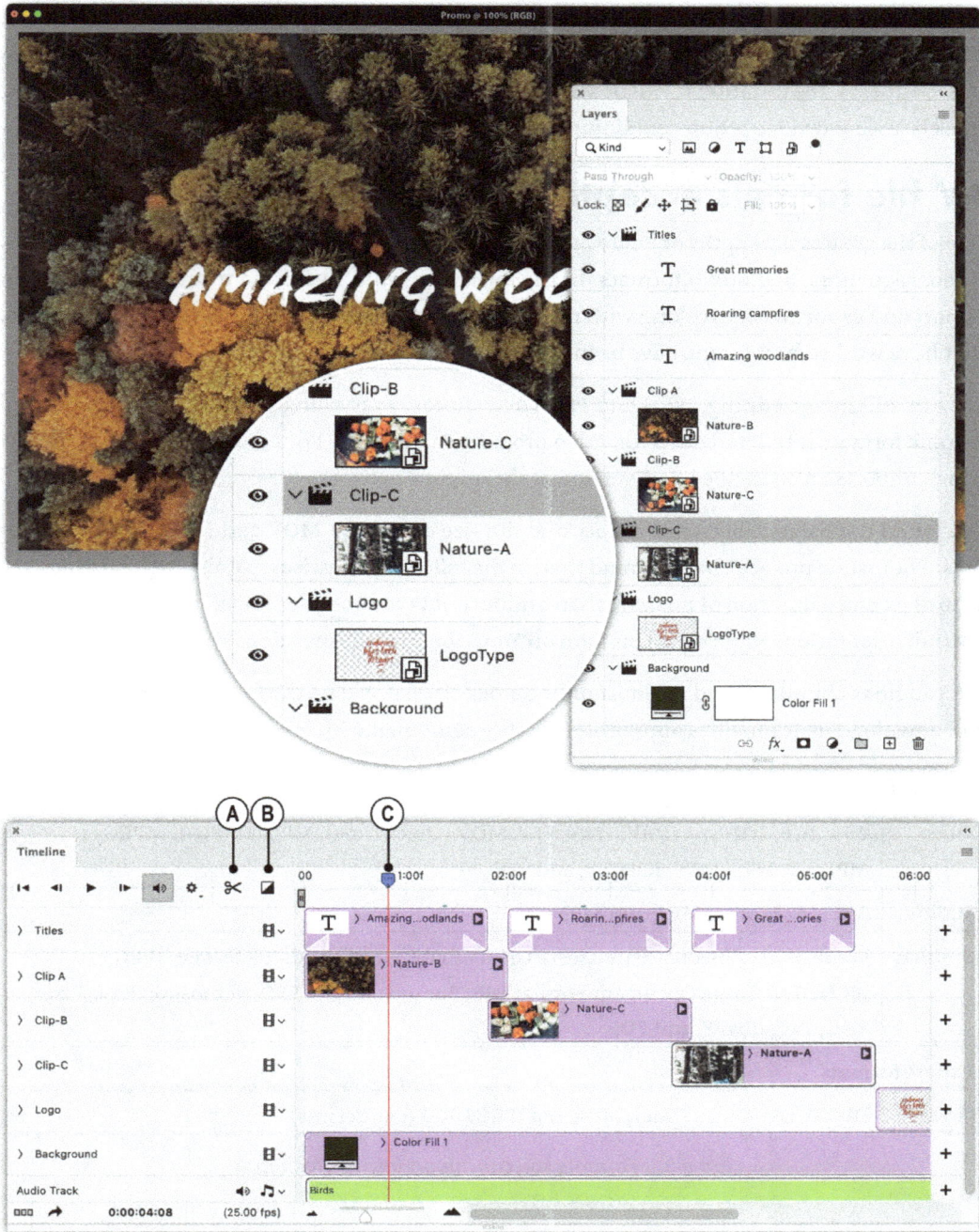

Figure 8.2: The video timeline supports video (A), audio, transitions (B). (C) is the Playhead

If your video requires several titles that need to appear one at a time, they can be created as separate text layers in a video group named `Titles`. This will allow you to control when each text frame appears, the duration it will be visible, and when it disappears. At the bottom of the layer stack is a second video group containing the background.

AV file formats accepted by Photoshop

One of the greatest strengths of Photoshop is its ability to work with a wide range of still images, video, sequences, and audio formats. In the following table, I've listed most formats you can import and export when working with motion projects in Photoshop. However, the file formats that have worked best for me have been highlighted in bold.

As with still image editing, JPEG and PSD cover almost everything you need when importing graphic formats into Photoshop for video projects. In addition, I often use Adobe Illustrator AI, which imports an embedded PDF version of the original artwork.

I've found the balance between quality and file size offered by MOV and MPEG-4 suitable for most Photoshop projects. Bear in mind that, in the following exercises, we aim to publish at 1920 x 1080 px and a duration of no more than 1 minute; it is common for social media posts to be in portrait orientation, while 4K is common on YouTube, and the duration is often much longer.

MP3 audio is abundant, and for most online stock sites, it will be the format of choice that you will download in. It provides appropriate quality combined with low data sizes:

Import formats	
Video	**.264**, 3GP, 3GPP, AVC, AVI , F4V, FLV, MOV (QuickTime), MPE, MPEG-1, **MPEG-4**, MPEG-2, MTS, MXF, R3D, TS, and VOB
Audio	AAC, M2A, M4A, MP2, and MP3
Graphic	WebP, BMP, Cineon, CompuServe GIF, DICOM, HEIF/HEIC, IFF format, JPEG, JPEG2000, Large Document Format PSB, Photoshop EPS, PSD, Photoshop Raw, Pixar, PNG, Targa, TIFF, and PDF
Export formats	
Video	DPX, MOV (QuickTime), MP4, and JPEG2000 (QuickTime)

Table 8.1: Formats you can import into Photoshop.

Video and GIF limitations on social media

Video is one of the best methods for generating higher engagement on social media. Both MOV and MPEG format videos are supported online, with animated GIFs supported on many platforms. The following table provides specifications for posting video files to popular social media platforms; however, you can exceed these minimum resolution standards if you wish, where it is possible to upload at 1920 x 1080 px:

Social media video and animation guide	
Facebook	
Supported file types	MP4, MOV, and GIF
Recommended video dimensions	1080 x 1920 px
Minimum video dimensions	1200 pixels wide (portrait/landscape)
Aspect ratio	16:9
Maximum data size	4 GB (8 MB for GIF)
Maximum duration	240 minutes
X	
Supported file types	MP4, MOV, GIF
Recommended video dimensions	1280 x 720 or 720 x 720 px
Minimum video dimensions	32 x 32 pixels
Aspect ratio	16:9 or 1:1
Maximum data size	512 MB (5 MB for GIF when uploaded from a smartphone or 15 MB on a desktop)
Duration	0.5–140 seconds
Instagram	
Supported file types	MP4, MOV
Recommended video dimensions	1920 x 1080 px
Minimum video dimensions	1080 x 1080 px
Aspect ratio	16:9 or 1:1 or 4:5
Maximum data size	4 GB
Duration	3–140 seconds

Social media video and animation guide	
TikTok	
Supported file types	MP4, MOV, and GIF
Recommended video dimensions	1080 x 1920 px
Minimum video dimensions	1080 x 1080 px
Aspect ratio	9:16 or 1:1
Maximum data size	287.6 MB
Duration	15–60 seconds
YouTube	
Supported file types	AVI, AVI, FLV, MOV, MPEG-1, MPEG-4, MP4, MKV, WMV, 3GPP, WebM, and GIF
Recommended video dimensions	1920 x 1080 px
Minimum video dimensions	426 x 240 px
Aspect ratio	9:16 or 4:3
Maximum data size	128 GB
Duration	15 seconds–12 hours
LinkedIn	
Supported file types	ASF, AVI, FLV, MOV, MPEG-1, MPEG-4, MP4, MKV, and WebM
Recommended video dimensions	1080 x 1920 px
Minimum video dimensions	1080 x 1080 px
Aspect ratio	16:9 or 1:1 or 9:16
Maximum data size	5 GB
Duration	3 seconds–10 minutes
Pinterest	
Supported file types	MP4, MOV, and M4V
Aspect ratio	16:9 or 1:1 or 2:3 or 4:5
Maximum data size	2 GB
Duration	6–15 minutes

Table 8.2 – Output settings best suited for popular social platforms

In this section, we reviewed the key tools and features that are used in Photoshop to create and manage motion projects, and the file types you can import and export from the application. This section also included a guide on the recommended specifications for posting videos and animated GIFs to popular social media platforms. Next, we will create a new web document for an animation project.

Creating animated GIFs

In this first exercise, we will define document characteristics for a short and simple GIF animation to become familiar with the techniques surrounding frame animation. When exporting animated GIFs, it is prudent to limit the number of colors you use to keep the file size low.

Defining a new animation document

I've come to think of animation files as containing three crucial elements that could be likened to a theatrical performance. You have the canvas, which is the stage, the cast, which are the individual layers, and the scenes, which are the arrangement of content in the **Timeline** panel. I should point out that I don't get out much! So, the first step is to set up a suitable stage with a new document (*Figure 8.3*):

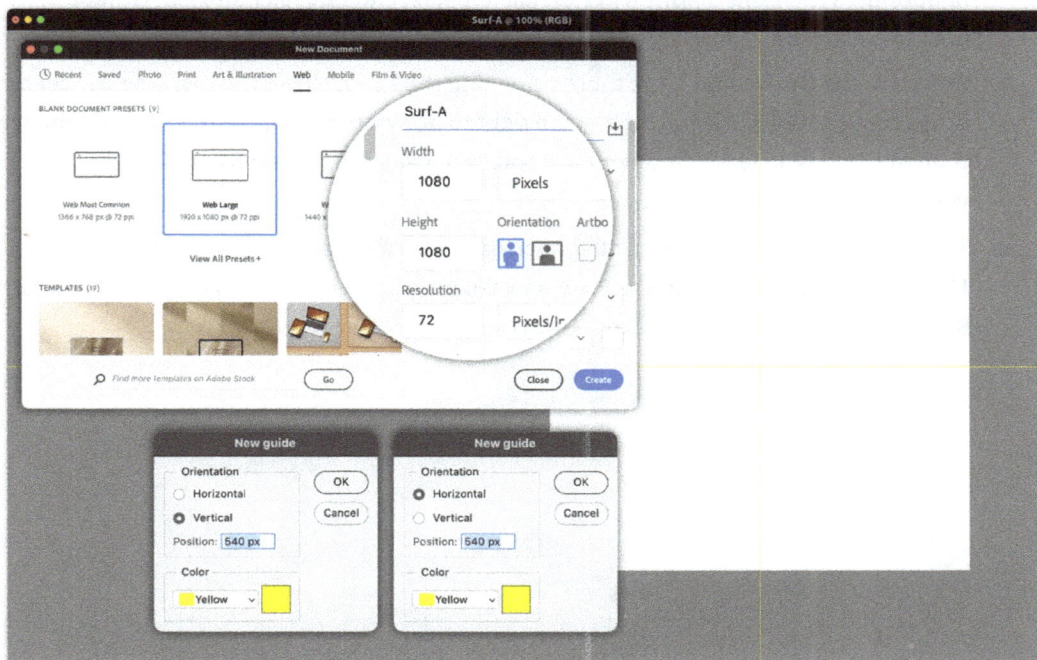

Figure 8.3: Creating a new file with guides added across the center of the canvas

1. Go to **File → New**. When the **New Document** dialog appears, click on the **Web** tab at the top to display the presets. Click on the **Web Large Common** thumbnail. Enter Surf-A into the **Name** field at the top right-hand side of the dialog.

2. Change **Width** to 1080 px and **Height** to 1080 px. Turn the **Artboards** checkbox off as we only need a single image; then, set **Color Mode** to **RGB Color, 8-bit**, and **Background Contents** to **Transparent**. Click **OK** when you're done, to generate the document.

3. Go to **View → Guides → New Guide**. Add a **Vertical** guide at 540 px, set the guide's **Color** option to **Yellow** from the drop-down menu, and click **OK**.

4. Next, head back to **View → Guides → New Guide**. Add a **Horizontal** guide at 540 px, set the guide's **Color** option to **Yellow** from the drop-down menu, and click **OK**. These two guides will help with centering content visually in the canvas (*Figure 8.3*).

Adding brand colors, logos, and text

Sticking with our theater theme, next, we need to add the cast in the form of layers:

1. Here, we will add a branded color to the background. Click on the **New Fill and Adjustment layer** icon at the bottom of the **Layers** panel and choose **Solid Color** from the list of options. When the **Color Picker** dialog appears, enter 0db0d9 into the **Hexadecimal** field to create cyan. Click **OK**.

2. Switch to the **Horizontal Type** tool by pressing the *T* key. Hover the tool over the center of the canvas, then click and drag to the right to draw a text frame that is slightly smaller than the canvas. Release the left mouse button to generate the text frame, inside of which you will see the active type cursor.

3. Type SURF CLUB into the text frame, then highlight all characters in the frame with the **Horizontal Type** tool. From the **Properties** panel, set **Font Style** to **Permanent Marker**, **Size** to 350 pt, **Leading** to 250 pt, and **Tracking** to -20:

Figure 8.4: Adding a text frame using the Permanent Marker Creative Cloud font

4. Set the alignment to **Center** from the **Paragraph** options. Set the text's **Color** option to white by clicking on the color swatch to open the color picker. Enter `ffffff` into the **Hexadecimal** field. Click **OK** to apply the color change and close the color picker.

5. With all copies formatted, reduce the size of the text frame so that it is just large enough to show all text. Press *Esc* to apply the text and exit type editing mode. Then, turn the visibility of the text layer you just created off.

6. Hover your cursor over the top-left region of the canvas and click and drag to create another text frame that is around the same size as the one you just created.

7. From the **Properties** panel, set **Font** to **Myriad Pro**, **Style** to **Bold**, **Font Size** to 128 pt, **Leading** to 133 pt, and **Tracking** to -25. Then, type for early bird discounts, book today into the text frame (*Figure 8.5*):

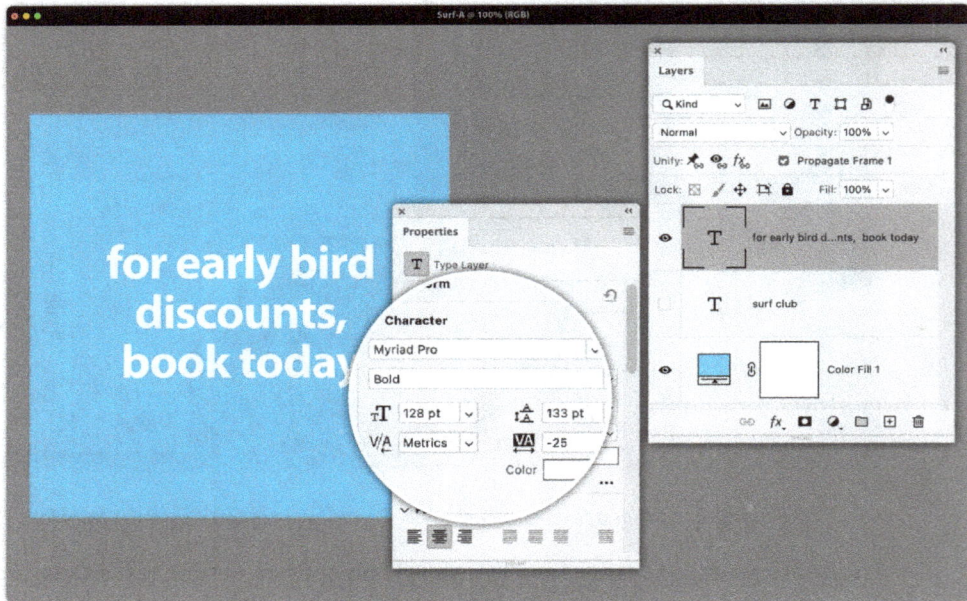

Figure 8.5: Adding a second text frame to the document

8. Set the alignment to **Center** from the **Paragraph** options. Set the text's **Color** option to white by clicking on the color swatch to open the color picker. Enter ffffff into the **Hexadecimal** field. Click **OK** to apply the color change and close the color picker. Again, reduce the size of text frame so that it fits the text. Press *Esc* to apply the text and exit type editing mode. Turn the visibility of the text layer off.

9. Go to **File → Place Linked**, browse to the 08-Motion folder, select the WildCo_Logo.ai file, and click **Place**. When the dialog appears, click on the page 7 thumbnail, which contains a white version of the logo. Then, click **OK** to import the artwork.

10. When the logo appears, it will be scaled to fit the artboard. Ensure that the **Width** and **Height** fields are linked in the **Options** bar, then change **Scale** to 160% and click on the **Commit Changes** button in the **Options** bar to finish the import process (*Figure 8.6*):

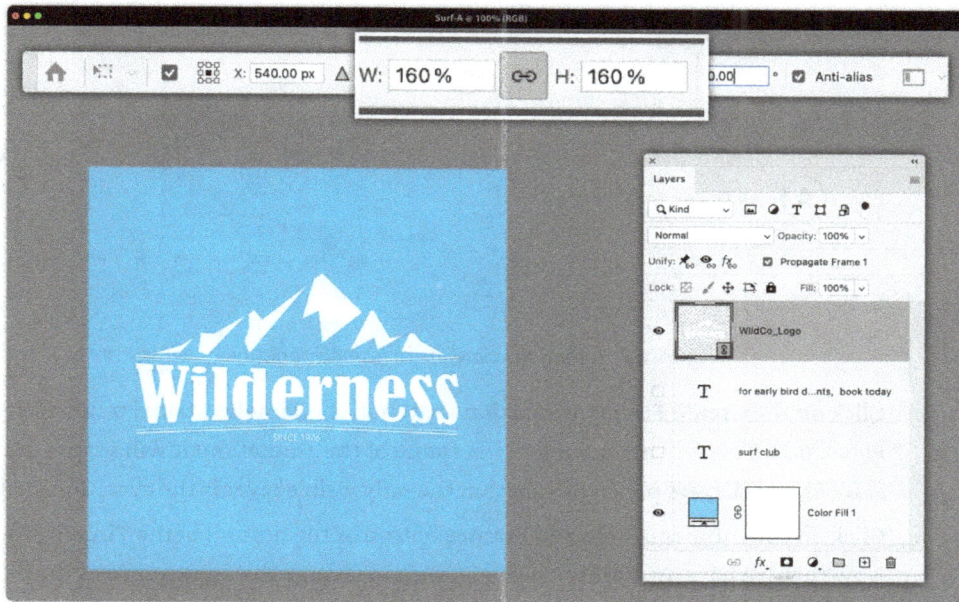

Figure 8.6: Placing a vector logo in the document and increasing the original scale to 150%

11. Switch to the **Move** tool and reposition the logo to the center of the canvas using the guides to help you. Turn the visibility of the logo layer off, then turn the visibility for each text layer on, one at a time, and center them on the canvas visually. When using the align tools, the size of the text frame will be taken into account, often leaving text looking off-center. Once all the layers have been aligned to the center of the canvas, hide all layers except for the cyan **Color Fill** layer.

Creating frame animations

Act one, scene one! Now, we can start making our animated GIF frames using the **Timeline** panel. We'll start with frame pauses to generate the animation timing:

1. Open the **Timeline** panel by going to **Window → Timeline**. It will appear docked at the bottom of the interface. In this position, it takes up far too much room. Undock it by dragging the **Panel** tab containing the **Timeline** panel's name upward. I suggest placing it adjacent to your canvas:

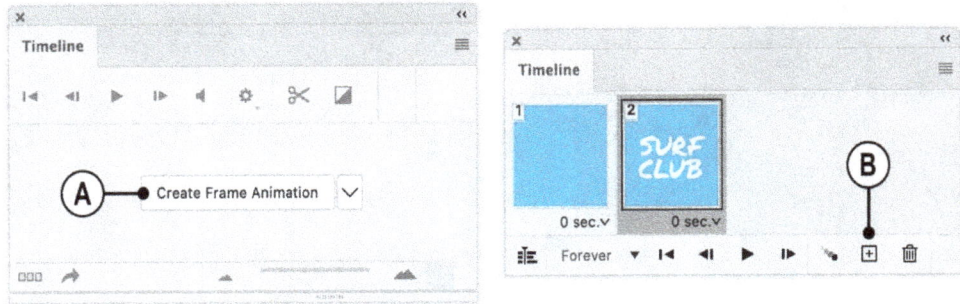

Figure 8.7: Setting the timeline to frame animation to get started

2. Click on the **Create Frame Animation** button in the **Timeline** panel to get started (**A** in *Figure 8.7*). This will generate the first frame of the animation; it will match the current state of your **Layers** panel. Ensure that the only visible layer is the cyan **Color Fill** layer.

3. Click on the **Duplicate Selected Frames** button at the bottom of the **Timeline** panel (**B**). Now that we have an additional frame, we can change the appearance of the document canvas through the **Layers** panel. Turn the visibility of the **SURF CLUB** layer on.

4. Click on the **Duplicate Selected Frames** button once more to create a third frame. Turn the visibility of the **SURF CLUB** layer off.

5. Click on the **Duplicate Selected Frames** button to create a fourth frame. Turn the visibility of the **for early bird...** text layer on in the **Layers** panel:

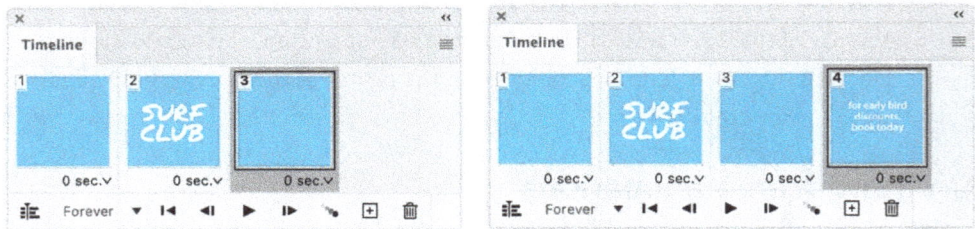

Figure 8.8: Adding new frames and making changes to the Layers panel to build the animation

6. Click on the **Duplicate Selected Frames** button once more to create a fifth frame. Turn the visibility of the **for early bird...** layer off.

7. Click on the **Duplicate Selected Frames** button to create a sixth frame. Turn the visibility of the **WildCo_Logo** layer off in the **Layers** panel. We've created the required number of frames to generate our animated GIF.

8. Next, click on the **Frame 1** thumbnail to make it active. You will notice that the image changes appearance to match the thumbnail. Click on the **Select Frame Delay** drop-down menu under the **Frame 1** thumbnail (**A** in *Figure 8.9*), which currently reads **No delay**. Choose **0.2 sec.** from the list:

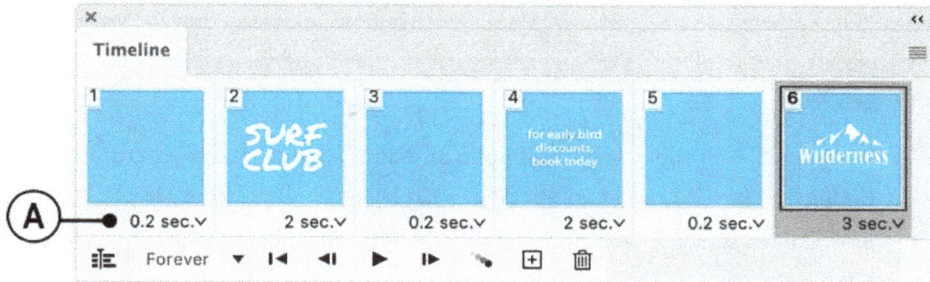

Figure 8.9: The completed six-frame animation, created with frame pauses

9. Click on **Frame 3** and **Frame 4** in turn and apply the same edit to pause the frames for 0.2 sec.

10. Next, click on the **Frame 2** thumbnail to make it active. This will reveal the **SURF CLUB** text. Change **Frame Delay** to **2 sec.** from the list. Then, click on the **Frame 4** thumbnail to make it active. This will reveal the **early bird** text. Change its **Frame Delay** value to **2 sec.** from the list.

11. Finally, click on the **Frame 6** thumbnail to make it active and reveal the logo. Change its **Frame Delay** value to **3 sec.** from the list. Then, ensure that the **Loop** option is set to **Forever** from the bottom-left corner of the **Timeline** panel.

12. Now, you can sit back and watch your animation by clicking on the **Play Animation** button at the bottom of the **Timeline** panel. Press the **Stop Animation** button once you have checked the animation.

13. Go to **File → Save**, browse to the 08-Motion folder, save the file as a PSD file called Surf-A, and keep the document open for the next exercise. You will learn how to export animated GIFs at the end of this chapter.

Creating tween animations

Traditional animation required an artist to draw each frame to capture movement, a process that I imagine would have required considerable patience. Similarly, in Photoshop, when we want to create the impression of movement, we need to generate every frame of that animation. Fortunately, we can use a technique called **tweening**, where we define the start and end of the animation after which Photoshop generates the frames in between, hence the name tweening! Let's take a look:

1. With the Surf-A document still open and active, go to **Image → Duplicate**. When the dialog appears, name the duplicate file MotionSurf-A and click **OK**.

2. Save the MotionSurf-A document in the 08-Motion folder as a PSD, then close the original Surf-A file.

3. Click on frames 2 to 6 in the timeline and delete them by pressing the *Del* or *Backspace* key, leaving you with a single frame.

4. Double-click on the **Color Fill** layer thumbnail in the **Layers** panel and change the **Hexadecimal** value to 32838C to create a vibrant turquoise. Click **OK** when you're done.

5. Turn on the visibility of all layers in the **Layers** panel. Click on the **WildCo_Logo** layer and then press *Shift* and click on the **Surf Club** layer to make all three layers active in the **Layers** panel.

6. Switch to the **Move** tool from the **Options** bar and enable the **Show Transform Controls** checkbox. Drag all the active layers off the bottom of the canvas until they disappear, holding *Shift* to prevent horizontal movement. Then, set the **Opacity** value of all active layers to **0%**:

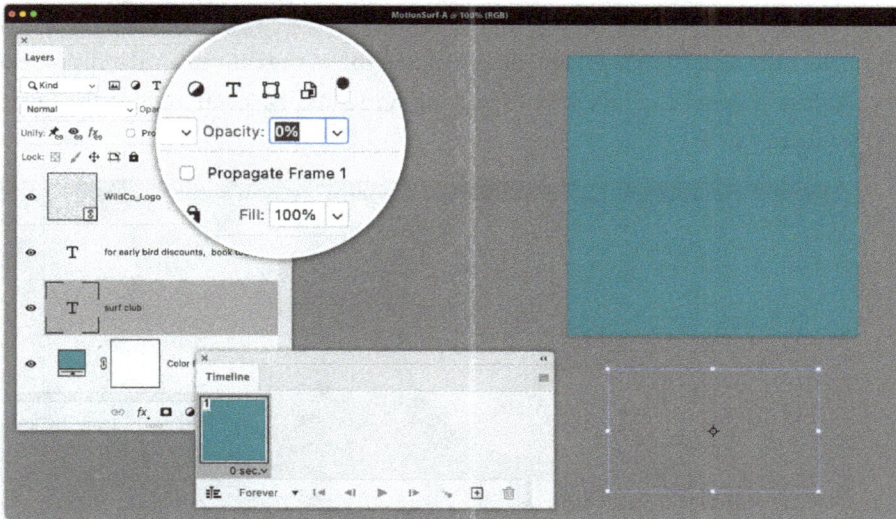

Figure 8.10: Each new keyframe defines the start and end of the final animation

7. Click on the **Duplicate Selected Frames** button at the bottom of the **Timeline** panel to create a second frame.

8. Click on the **Surf Club** layer to make it active. Increase the **Surf Club** layer's **Opacity** value to 100%. Then, drag the active layer to the center of the canvas, again holding *Shift* as you do so to prevent the layer from moving horizontally:

Figure 8.11: Moving each layer back onto the canvas and increasing the opacity

9. Click on the **Duplicate Selected Frames** button to create a third frame.

10. Select the **Surf Club** layer and drag it off the top of the canvas until it disappears, holding *Shift* to prevent the layers from moving horizontally. Then, reduce the layer's **Opacity** value to 0%:

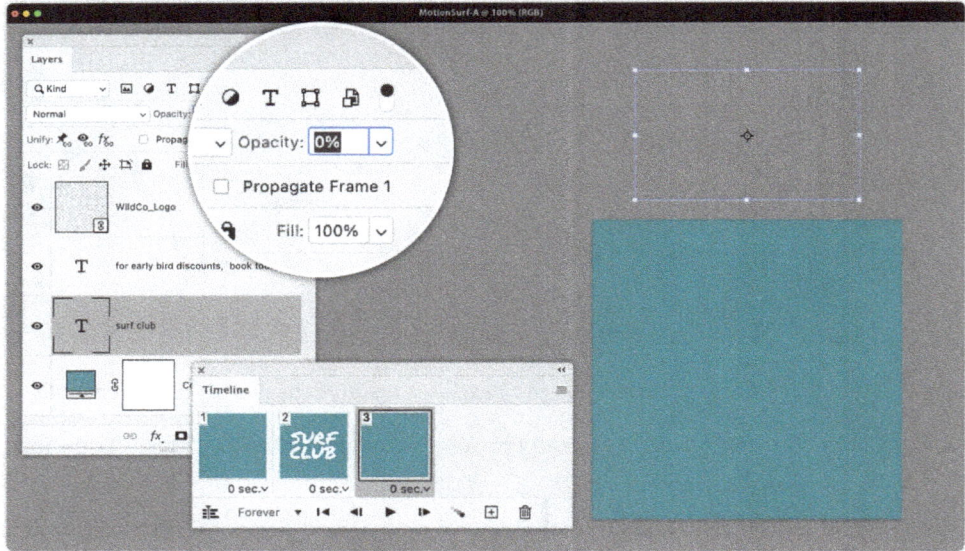

Figure 8.12: Reducing the opacity of each layer and moving them beyond the top of the canvas

11. Click on the **Duplicate Selected Frames** button to create a fourth frame.

12. Click on the **for early bird...** layer in the **Layers** panel to make it active and increase the layer's **Opacity** value to **100%**. Then, drag the active layer to the center of the canvas, again holding *Shift* as you do so to prevent the layer from moving horizontally.

13. Click on the **Duplicate Selected Frames** button to create a fifth frame.

14. With the **for early bird...** layer active, drag it off the top of the canvas until it disappears, holding *Shift* to prevent the layers from moving horizontally. Then, reduce the layer's **Opacity** value to 0%.

15. Click on the **Duplicate Selected Frames** button to create a sixth frame.

16. Click on the **WildCo_Logo** layer in the **Layers** panel to make it active and increase its **Opacity** value to 100%. Then, drag the active layer to the center of the canvas, again holding *Shift* to prevent it from moving horizontally.

17. Click the **Duplicate Selected Frames** button to create a seventh frame.

18. With the **WildCo_logo** layer active, drag it off the top of the canvas until it disappears, holding *Shift* to prevent the layers from moving horizontally. Then, reduce the layer's **Opacity** value to 0%.

19. Click on **Frame 1** in the **Timeline** panel and then press *Shift* and click on **Frame 2** to make both frames active. Click on the **Tween animation frames** button at the bottom of the **Timeline** panel (circled in *Figure 8.13*):

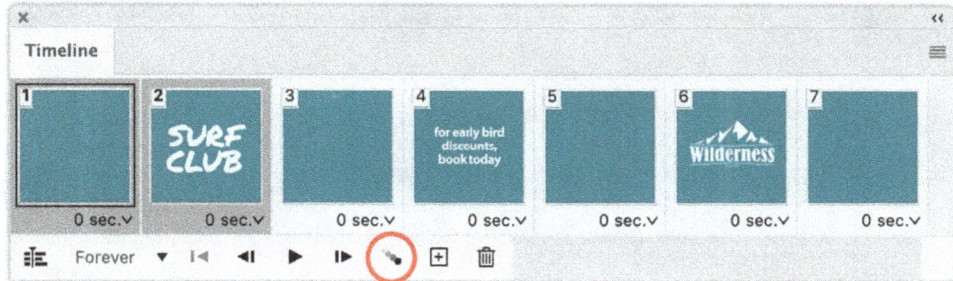

Figure 8.13: With all keyframes created, a pair of frames can be tweened

20. When the dialog appears, set **Tween with** to **Selection**, **Frames to Add** to 5, include **All Layers**, and leave all the **Parameters** checkboxes active. Click **OK** when you're done, to add the additional frames.

21. Click on **Frame 7** in the **Timeline** panel and then press *Shift* and click on **Frame 8** to make both frames active. Click on the **Tween animation frames** button at the bottom of the **Timeline** panel. The settings should be identical to the ones you defined previously. As such, click **OK**.

22. Click on **Frame 13** in the **Timeline** panel and then press *Shift* and click on **Frame 14** to make both frames active. Click on the **Tween animation frames** button and click **OK** when the dialog appears.

23. Click on **Frame 19** in the **Timeline** panel and then press *Shift* and click on **Frame 20** to make both frames active. Click on the **Tween animation frames** button and click **OK** when the dialog appears.

24. Click on **Frame 25** in the **Timeline** panel and then press *Shift* and click on **Frame 26** to make both frames active. Click on the **Tween animation frames** button and click **OK** when the dialog appears.

25. Click on **Frame 31** in the **Timeline** panel and then press *Shift* and click on **Frame 32** to make both frames active. Click on the **Tween animation frames** button and click **OK** when the dialog appears. This completes the tweening process!

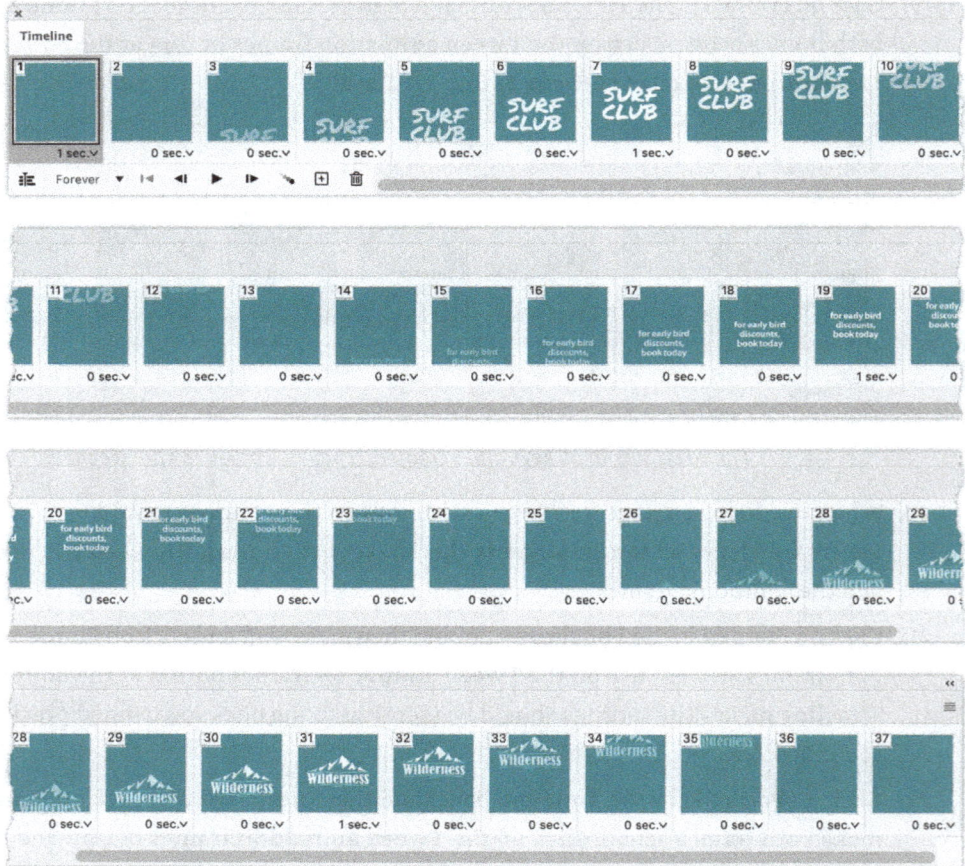

Figure 8.14: Every frame of the animation after tweening

26. In turn, select frames 1, 7, 19, and 31 and change the frame delay to 1.0 sec.. This will allow the text and the logo to pause onscreen before disappearing.

27. Press the **Play** button in the **Timeline** panel to preview the animation and press **Stop** when you're done. Go to **File → Save** and close the document.

In this section, we explored two types of animated GIF techniques. The first required creating frames and pauses in the form of frame delays. The second technique required us to create keyframes to capture the position and opacity changes. Then, we tasked Photoshop with tweening, a process in which the additional frames are generated, and in doing so, create the final animation. Next, we will create a new video project, where we'll be importing MPEG-4 video and audio.

Working with video and audio in Photoshop

Believe it or not, Photoshop was created by John Knoll to facilitate motion picture special effects while working with a company called Industrial Light & Magic. Some 20 years later, Photoshop allowed for editing and rendering of video footage with the launch of Creative Suite 3 in 2007, and its features have strengthened since. While you could use applications such as After Effects and Premiere Pro, Photoshop offers a simple, familiar interface with powerful features for creating videos.

Creating a new document intended for video

When you open video footage in Photoshop, it creates a document based on the source video characteristics. Alternatively, you can create a new document and import the source footage, like the example in the next exercise:

1. Go to **File → New**. When the **New Document** dialog appears, click the **Video** tab and click on the **HDTV 1080p** preset. Enter VideoWoodland-A into the **Name** field at the top right-hand side of the dialog and click **Create**.

2. Ensure that the **Timeline** panel is visible (**Window → Timeline**). You will notice that the **Timeline** panel is empty. Click on the **Create** drop-down menu in the center of the **Timeline** panel (**A** in *Figure 8.15*) and change the timeline option to **Create Video Timeline** from the list to make it visible. Then, click on the **Create Video Timeline** button to generate the timeline. This will add one media group containing a generic white background, reflecting the visibility of the **Layers** stack. In addition, safe frames appear around the edges of the canvas.

> Some video document presets include **safe frames**, which appear as guides around the edges of the canvas. These are intended for broadcast video displayed on a TV and are not relevant when creating web content. Where relevant, important action should not extend beyond the *Action* safe area (outer guides), while important text such as titles should not extend beyond the *Title* safe area (inner guides).

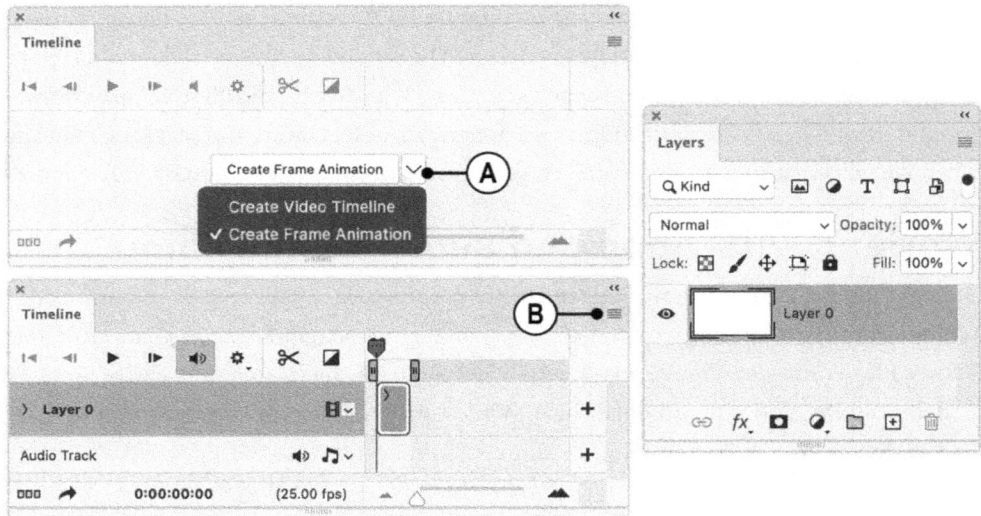

Figure 8.15: Creating a new video timeline to get started

3. Click on the **Timeline Panel** fly-out menu (**B** in *Figure 8.15*), choose **Set Timeline Frame Rate** and **25 frames per second**, and click **OK**.

> **Frames per second (fps).** 25 fps is standard in Europe and Australia, while 29.97 fps is common in North America and elsewhere. Matching the frame rate to the footage you're using is important to avoid stutters.

Adding media to the timeline

You will start by adding footage to the active timeline and then edit its position, duration, and audio settings:

1. Click on the **New Fill and Adjustment layer** icon at the bottom of the **Layers** panel and choose **Solid Color** from the list of options. When the **Color Picker** dialog appears, enter 41472C into the **Hexadecimal** field to create a dark green. Click **OK**.

2. Click on **Layer 0** in the **Layers** panel to make it active and press the *Del* or *Backspace* key to delete the layer. This will leave just the color fill you created in the **Layers Stack** area.

3. Go to the **Timeline** panel, click the **Media** button, which looks like a film strip, and select **New Video Group from Clips** from the list of options. Drag the **Color Fill** layer into the new video group in the **Layers** panel.

4. Double-click on the video group's name from the **Layers** panel to open the type entry field. Rename it Background and press *Enter*.

5. Head back to the **Timeline** panel, click the **Media** button again, and choose **New Video Group**. Rename the media group Footage using the technique you used in the previous step:

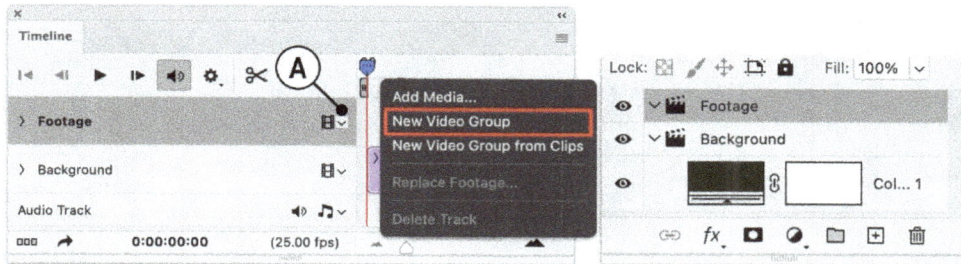

Figure 8.16: Replacing the background and creating new media groups

6. In the **Timeline** panel, click the **Add Media** button (**A** in *Figure 8.17*) adjacent to the **Footage** video group and choose **Add Media** from the list. Select Forest_01.mp4 from the 08-Motion folder and click **Open** to import the footage.

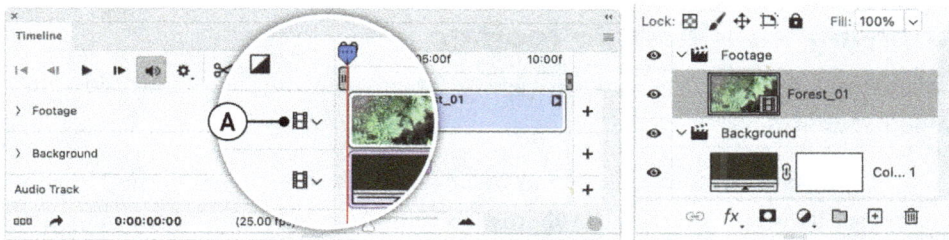

Figure 8.17: Importing video footage into the timeline

7. If the content in the timeline appears too small or is not entirely visible, try using either the **Zoom Out Timeline** or **Zoom In Timeline** icons at the lower left-hand side of the **Timeline** panel, represented as small and large mountain icons, so that the entire sequence can be seen.

8. We do not require the full 11-second sequence. Drag the playhead to *frame 04:00* and click on **Split at Playhead** (**A** in *Figure 8.18*) to cut the footage into two sections. Click on the right-hand portion and press the *Del* or *Backspace* key to delete the unwanted footage.

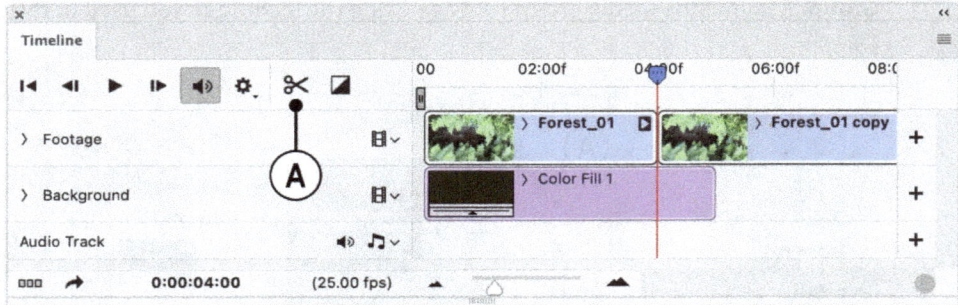

Figure 8.18: Splitting the footage at frame 4, and deleting the footage to the right of the playhead

9. Ensure that the Forest_01.mp4 footage is active in the timeline, click on the **Add Media** icon in the **Timeline** panel, and choose **Add Media**. Select Forest_02.mp4 and Forest_03. mp4 from the 08-Motion folder and click **Open** to import the footage.

Applying transitions to footage

Rather than leaving an abrupt cut between each piece of footage, we'll next add a cross-fade for smoother transitions:

1. Click on the **Transitions** icon (**A** in *Figure 8.19*) at the top left of the **Timeline** panel to reveal the pop-out menu. In Photoshop, transitions are added by dragging them from the pop-up menu onto or between two pieces of footage.

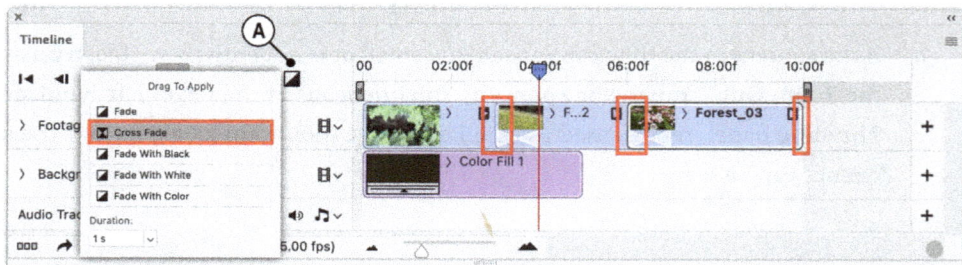

Figure 8.19: Dragging and dropping transitions between each piece of footage

2. Drag the **Cross Fade** transition icon from the pop-up and over to the region where the Forest_01.mp4 and Forest_02.mp4 footage meet, at which point you will see a bold black box appear, indicating you can release the mouse button to add the **Cross Fade** transition. Adding a cross-fade will shorten the footage because it overlaps the two pieces of video to be created.

3. Drag a second **Cross Fade** transition between the Forest_02.mp4 and Forest_03.mp4 footage.

4. The Forest_03.mp4 footage will also need a **Fade** transition added to it so that it fades to the background color. Click on the **Transitions** icon and drag the **Fade** transition icon onto the end of the Forest_03.mp4 clip in the timeline. When the black outline box appears, release the mouse.

Animating an Adobe Illustrator logo in the timeline

To reinforce the company brand, we will place the logo in the timeline and then animate the scale of the logo:

1. click on the **Footage** video group in the **Timeline** panel to make it active, and then click on the Forest_03.mp4 clip. This can help prevent new footage from appearing in an undesirable position in the timeline.

2. Go to **File → Place Linked**. Browse to the 08-Motion folder and select LogoType.ai. Click **Open** to import the footage; it will appear adjacent to the Forest_03.mp4 footage.

3. Click on the **Maintain Aspect Ratio** button in the **Options** bar to link the **Width** and **Height** values and then change the scale to 280% (*Figure 8.20*). Click on the **Commit Changes** button in the **Options** bar to apply the edits.

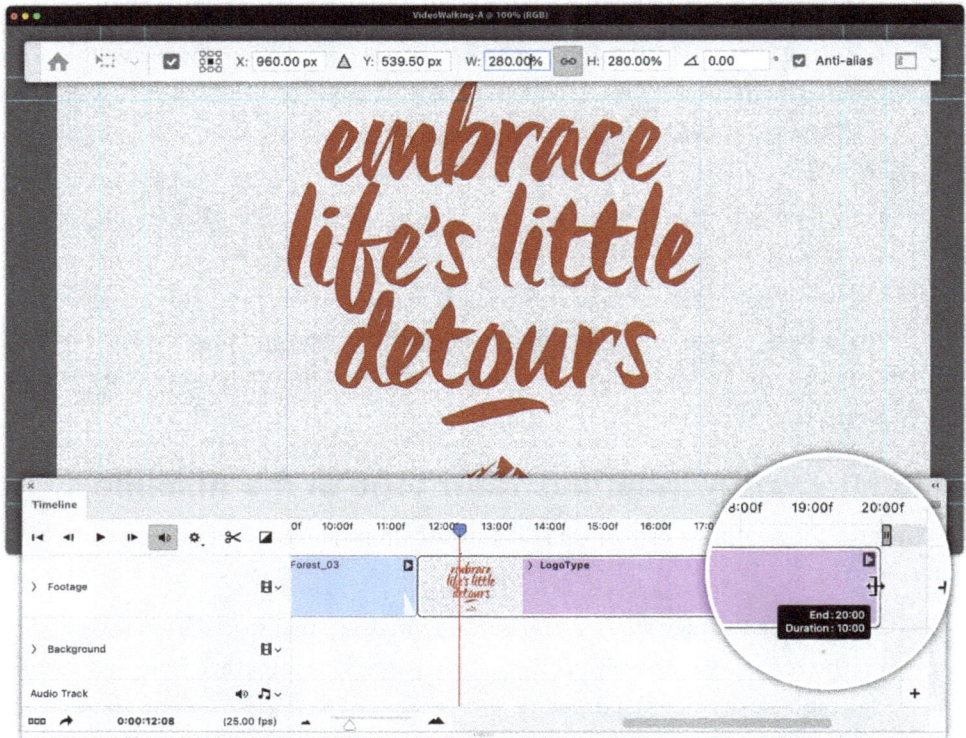

Figure 8.20: Extending the length of the logo footage in the timeline

4. Right-click on the **LogoType** layer's name in the **Layers** panel and choose **Convert to Smart Object**. This will allow the layer to be animated.

5. Hover your cursor over the end of the **LogoType** clip in the **Timeline** panel to reveal the clip editing icon, then click and drag the end of the clip to the 20-frame mark in the timeline.

6. Drag the playhead to the start of the **LogoType** clip. Expand the **Footage** video group toggle in the **Timeline** panel to reveal the **Transform**, **Opacity**, and **Style** animation properties. Click on the **Enable Keyframe Animation** button (**A** in *Figure 8.21*), which is adjacent to **Transform** and **Opacity** and shown as a stopwatch icon. This will add a keyframe for **Transform** (**B**) and **Opacity** (**C**) where your playhead resides in the timeline.

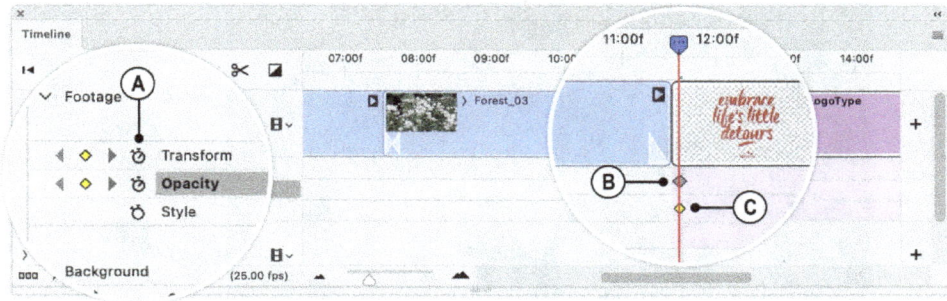

Figure 8.21: The transform, opacity, and style properties of smart objects can be animated

7. Reduce the **Opacity** value of the **LogoType** layer to 0% from the **Layers** panel. Then, drag the playhead to **Frame 14** and increase **Opacity** to 100%. This should add a second keyframe.

8. Go to **Edit** → **Free Transform** and, in the **Options** bar, link the **Width** and **Height** values. You will notice that because we turned the **LogoType** layer into a smart object, the scale now reads 100%. Reduce the scale to 75%. Click on the **Commit Changes** button in the **Options** bar to apply the edits. This will add a second keyframe under the **Transform** section of the animation properties in the **Timeline** panel.

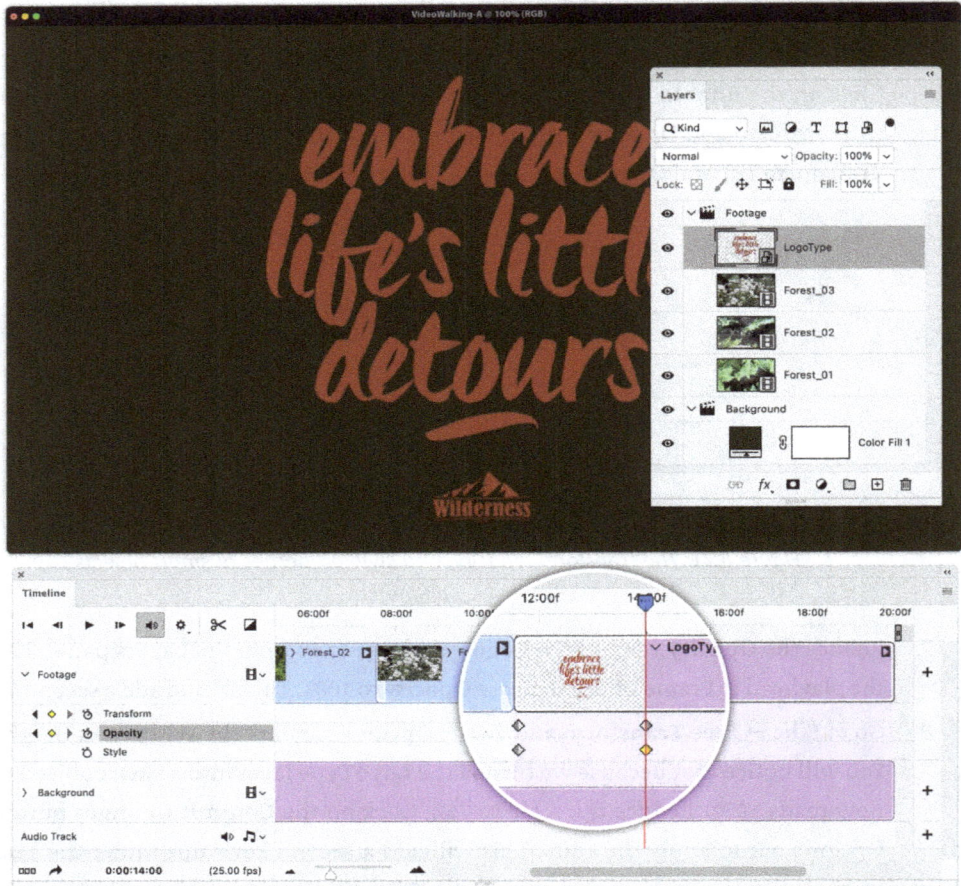

Figure 8.22: Reducing the scale of the logo will automatically add a keyframe

9. The background behind the logo is currently transparent. Locate the **Color Fill** layer, which can be found in the **Background** video group. Hover your cursor over the end of the clip and drag it to **Frame 20** (*Figure 8.22*).

10. The **LogoType** clip also needs a **Fade** transition added. Click on the **Transitions** icon and drag the **Fade** transition icon onto the start of the **LogoType** clip in the timeline. When the black outline box appears, release the mouse.

11. Drag the playhead back to the start of the clip and press **Play**. You should now see the logo appear and zoom in on the canvas's center. Press **Stop** when you have reviewed the animation and keep the document open.

Adding a soundtrack to the timeline

You can add audio files to the timeline, which can be edited like video clips. This allows you to add a music backing track of your choice to the timeline for dramatic effect:

1. Click on the musical note icon in the lower left-hand side of the **Timeline** panel and choose **Add Audio** from the list of commands. Browse to the 08-Motion folder and select Birds. wav. Then, click **OK** to import the audio.

2. In the **Timeline** panel, zoom out to find the end of the audio clip. Hover your cursor over the end of the clip to reveal the **Trim** icon, drag it to the left-hand side to the 20-frame mark so that it matches the length of the sequence, and then release the mouse button.

3. Now that we have shortened the audio, we must fade it. Right-click on the Birds.wav clip at the bottom of the **Timeline** panel to reveal the **Audio** options pop-up (*Figure 8.23*). Change the **Fade Out** value to 1 s, and then the **Fade Out** value to 1 s. Click away from the pop-up to make it disappear.

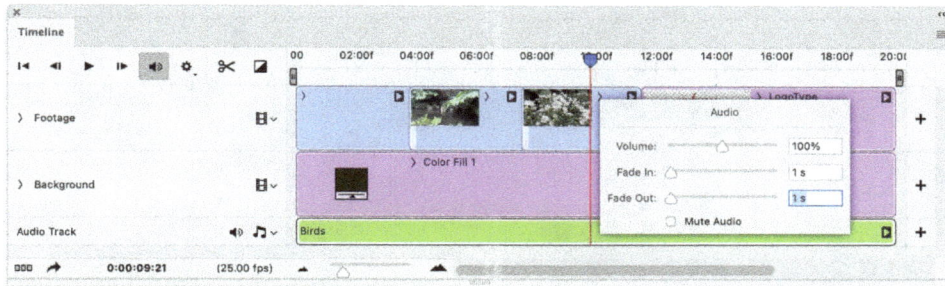

Figure 8.23: Right-clicking audio clips to access the fade-in and fade-out controls

4. Drag the playhead back to the start of the timeline and press **Play** to check the sequence. Press **Stop** when you're done and then go to **File → Save**. Keep the document open for the next exercise.

In this section, we have worked with motion footage and audio to create a new video sequence, but you might not have the luxury of video footage at hand to create your projects, and that's where animating still images comes in handy.

Creating videos from still images and text

You may find yourself in a situation where you need to post videos but are without video footage. This exercise will take you through the process of adding motion to still images to create the illusion of motion.

Setting up a duplicate document

Follow these steps:

1. With the VideoWoodland-A document still open and active, go to **Image → Duplicate**. When the dialog appears, name the duplicate file StillWoodland-A and click **OK**.

2. Go to **File → Save As**, browse to the 08-Motion folder, and save the document as a PSD file. Then, close the original file, VideoWoodland-A.

3. Click on each of the MPEG-4 video clips in the timeline and delete them by pressing the *Del* or *Backspace* key.

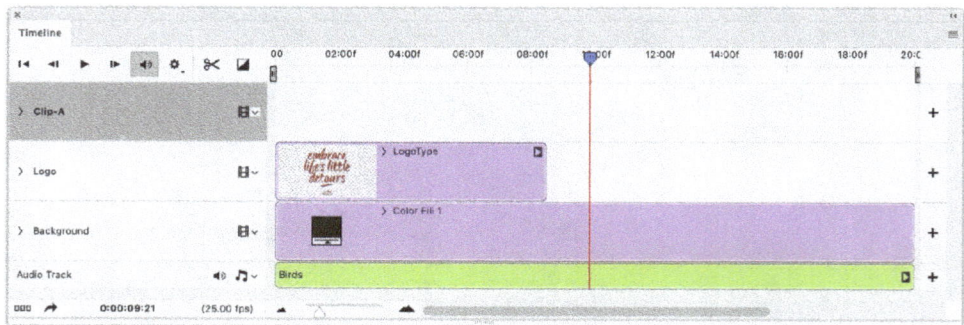

Figure 8.24: Deleting all the unwanted clips in the timeline

4. Change the name of the **Footage** video group to Logo from the **Layers** panel. Then, click on the **Media** button adjacent to the **Logo** group in the **Timeline** panel and select **New Video Group**. Change the name of the new group to Clip-A.

Importing and animating an image

You will be animating three still images in total. However, the hard work of animating the images only needs to be done once, after which they can be copied to subsequent clips:

1. Click on the **Media** button adjacent to the **Clip-A** group in the **Timeline** panel and select **Add Media**. Browse to the 08-Motion folder and select Nature-1.jpg. Click **Open** when you're done.

2. Once the images appear in the timeline, right-click on the layers and choose **Convert to Smart Object** to enable animation features.

3. Next, shorten the length of the imported clip so that its duration is 2 frames. Ensure that the clip starts at **Frame 0**, the beginning of the timeline.

4. Go to **Edit → Free Transform** and link the **Width** and **Height** fields in the **Options** bar. Reduce **Scale** to 41%. Click on the **Commit Changes** button in the **Options** bar to apply the edits.

5. Drag the playhead to the start of the Nature-1 clip. Expand the **Clip-A** video group toggle in the **Timeline** panel to reveal the **Transform, Opacity**, and **Style** animation properties. Click on the **Enable Keyframe Animation** button adjacent to **Transform**.

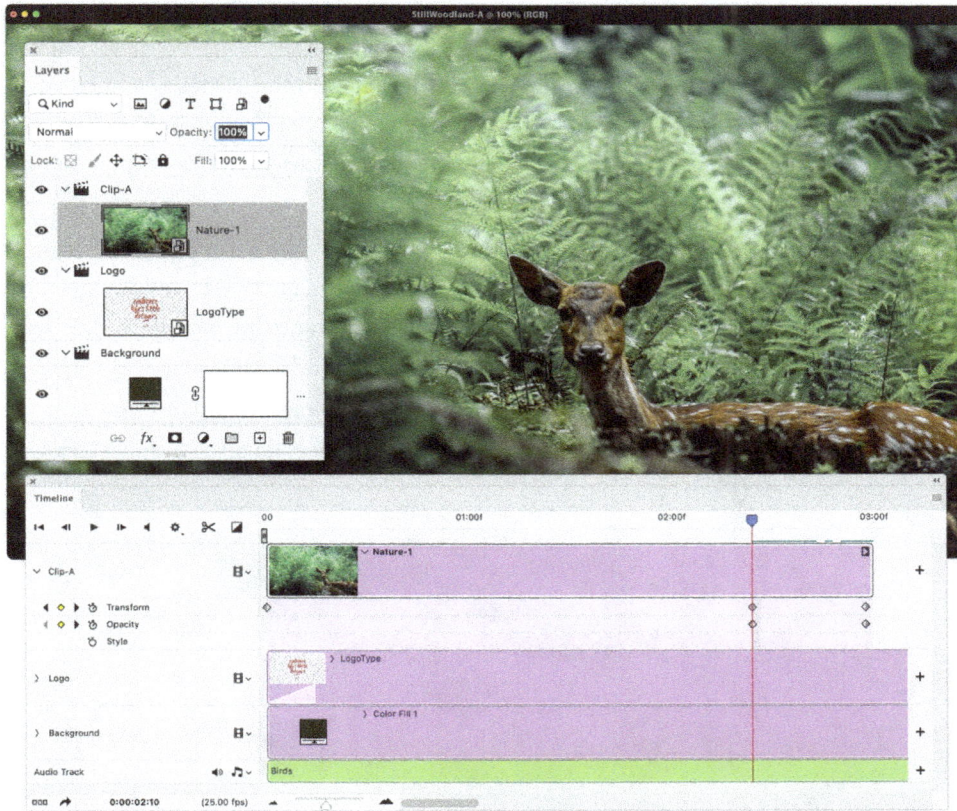

Figure 8.25: Adding scale, rotation, and opacity keyframes to the still image

6.   Drag the playhead to **Frame 2.10**. Go to **Edit → Free Transform** and increase **Scale** to **44%**. Click on the **Commit Changes** button in the **Options** bar to apply the edits and create a new keyframe. Click on the **Enable keyframe animation** button adjacent to **Opacity** to add an opacity keyframe.

7.   Drag the playhead to **Frame 2.24**. Go to **Edit → Free Transform** and increase **Scale** to 74% and **Rotation** to -18. Click on the **Commit Changes** button in the **Options** bar to apply the edits and create a new keyframe. Then, lower the **Opacity** value of the layer to **0%** from the **Layers** panel.

Copying and pasting keyframes onto the second clip

Now that the hard work of animating the first clip is complete, we will copy and paste the animation onto a new media clip:

1.   Click on the Nature-1 clip in the timeline, then go to the **Timeline** panel's flyout menu and choose **Keyframes → Select all** from the list of options. Then, return to the same fly-out menu once more and choose **Keyframes → Copy**. The keyframes should now be highlighted in yellow in the timeline.

2.   Click the **Media** button adjacent to the **Logo** group in the **Timeline** panel and select **New Video Group**. Change the name of the new group to Clip-B. This will create a new group under the **Clip-A** group so that when the images transition, they will fade and become visible.

3.   Click on the **Media** button adjacent to the **Clip-B** group in the **Timeline** panel and select **Add Media**. Browse to the 08-Motion folder and select Nature-2.jpg. Click **Open** when you're done (*Figure 8.26*).

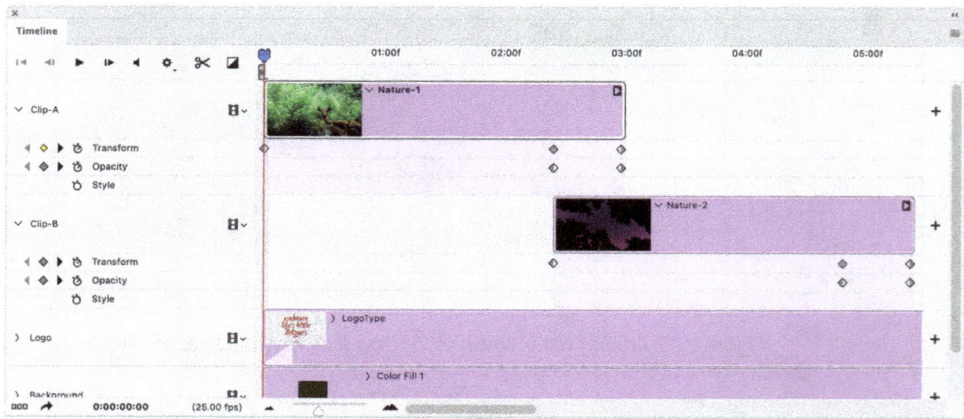

Figure 8.26: Copying and pasting keyframes from the first clip onto the second clip

4. Once the images appear in the timeline, right-click on the layers and choose **Convert to Smart Object** to enable animation features. As we did previously, shorten the length of the imported clip so that the duration is 3 frames in length.

5. Go to **Edit → Free Transform** and link the **Width** and **Height** fields in the **Options** bar. Reduce **Scale** to 41%. Click on the **Commit Changes** button in the **Options** bar to apply the edits.

6. Click on the Nature-2 clip in the timeline, then go to the **Timeline** panel's fly-out menu and choose **Keyframes → Paste** from the list of options. This will add the same scale, rotation, and opacity transformations.

7. Then, drag the clip so that it starts at **Frame 2.10** in the timeline, at the point where the previous clip begins to rotate and fade:

Copying and pasting keyframes onto the third clip

In the following steps, you will repeat the same process you used for the second clip to paste animation keyframes. This will finish the animation for the document:

1. In the **Timeline** panel, click on the **Media** button adjacent to the **Logo** group and select **New Video Group**. Then, change the name of the new group to Clip-C.

2. Click the **Media** button adjacent to the **Clip-C** group in the **Timeline** panel and select **Add Media**. Browse to the 08-Motion folder and select Nature-3.jpg. Click **Open** when you're done.

3. Once the images appear on the timeline, right-click on the layers, select **Convert to Smart Object**, and shorten the clip to 3 frames in length.

4. Go to **Edit → Free Transform** and link the **Width** and **Height** fields in the **Options** bar. Reduce **Scale** to 41%. Click on the **Commit Changes** button in the **Options** bar to apply the edits.

5. Click on the Nature-3 clip in the timeline, then go to the **Timeline** panel's fly-out menu and choose **Keyframes → Paste** from the list of options.

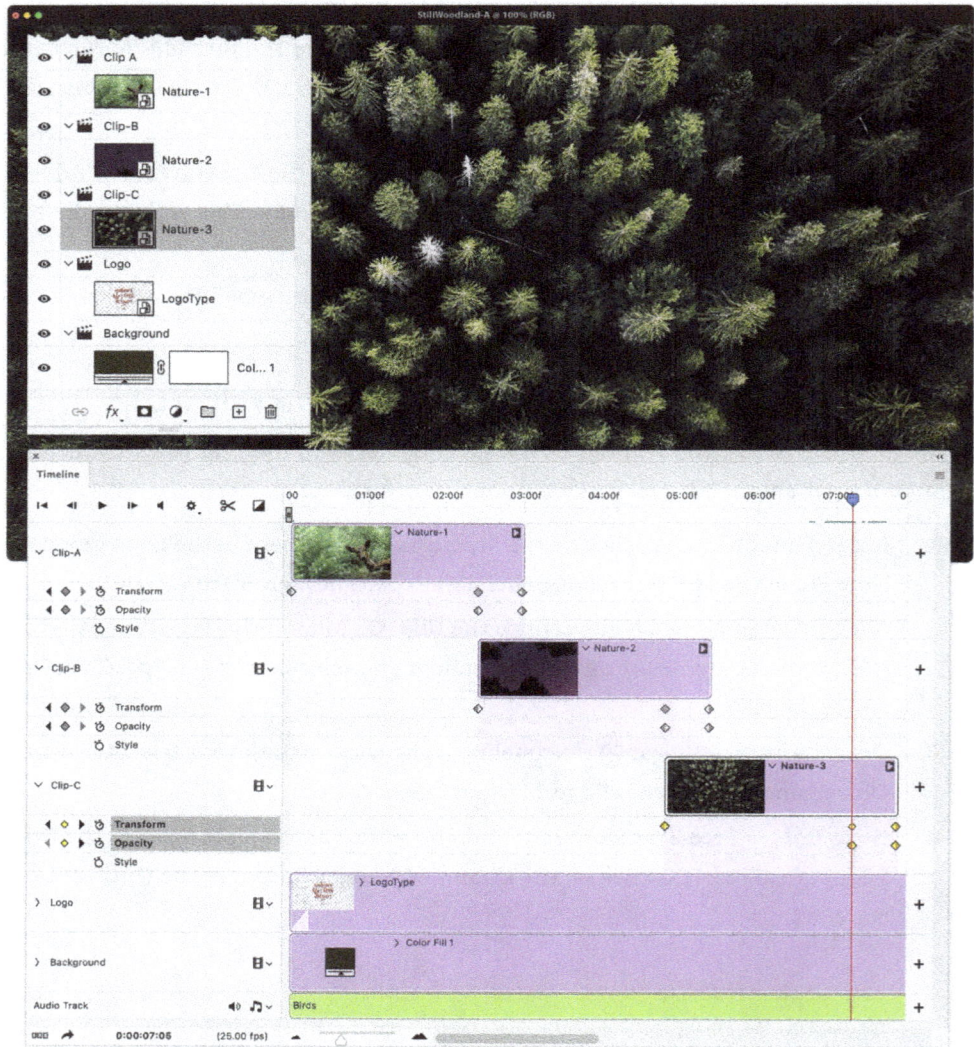

Figure 8.27: Each of the three images with keyframes pasted on clips two and three

6. Then, drag the clip so that it starts at **Frame 4.20** in the timeline, at the point where the previous clip begins to rotate and fade.

Adding titles to the sequence

Now that the images have been arranged and animated, we can create the title text to accompany them:

1. Click on the **Media** button adjacent to the **Clip A** group in the **Timeline** panel, select **New Video Group**, and rename it to `Titles`.

2. Switch to the **Horizontal Type** tool by pressing the *T* key. Hover the tool over the left-hand side of the canvas. Click and drag to the right to draw a text frame almost the full width of the canvas. Release the left mouse button to generate the text frame, inside of which you will see the active type cursor.

3. Type `Amazing Woodlands` into the text frame, then highlight all characters in the frame with the **Horizontal Type** tool. From the **Properties** panel, set **Font** to `Flood Std`, **Font Size** to `128 pt`, **Leading** to `Auto`, and **Tracking** to `20`.

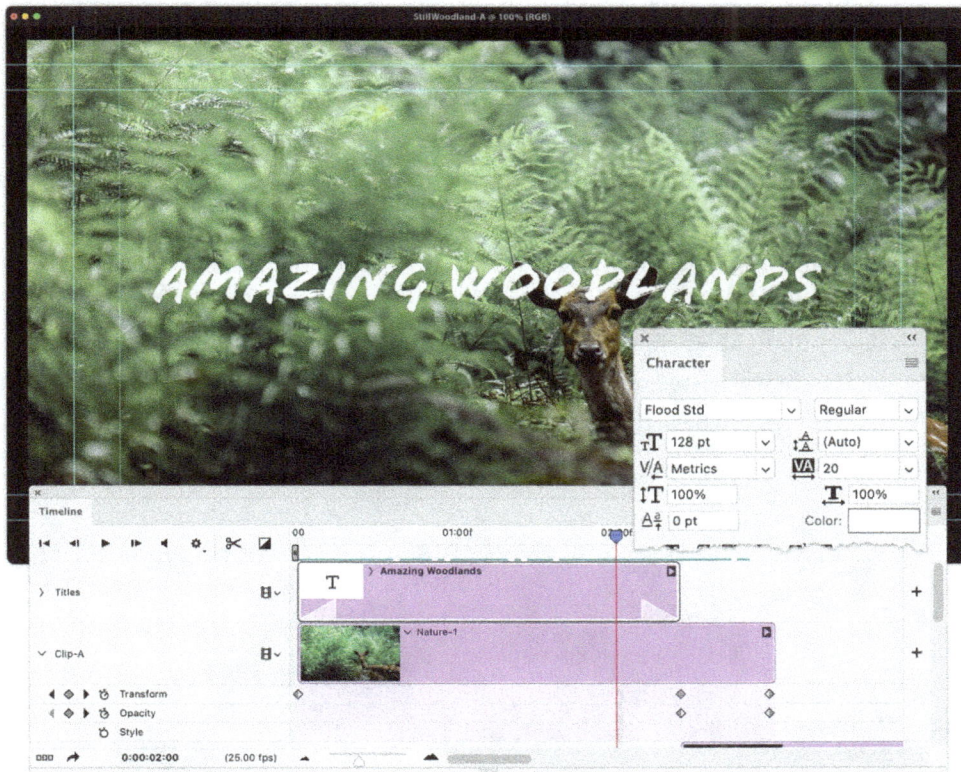

Figure 8.28: Adding a text layer with fades applied to the start and end of the clip

4. Set the alignment to **Center** from the **Paragraph** options. Set the text's **Color** option to white by clicking on the color swatch to open the color picker. Enter `ffffff` into the **Hexadecimal** field. Click **OK** to apply the color change and close the color picker.

5. Press *Esc* to apply the text and exit type editing mode, switch to the **Move** tool, and position the text frame in the center of the canvas. Finally, ensure that the text layer you just created is in the **Titles** layer group.

6. In the **Timeline** panel, ensure that the **Amazing Woodlands** clip starts at **Frame 00:00** and extends to **Frame 02:10**, ending at the point where the **Nature-A** image begins to rotate and fade.

7. From the **Transitions** pop-out menu in the **Timeline** panel, drag a **Fade** transition, lasting 0.25 seconds, onto the start and end of the **Amazing Woodlands** clip.

8. Ensure that the **Amazing Woodlands** clip is active in the **Timeline** panel and press *Ctrl + C* (Windows) or *Cmd + C* (macOS). After that, press *Ctrl + V* (Windows) or *Cmd + V* (macOS) to paste a copy of the clip to the right of the original in the timeline.

9. Drag the new clip so that it starts at **Frame 03:00** and shorten the clip by dragging the end to **Frame 04:20**. Drag the playhead to the middle of the new text layer clip in the **Timeline** panel. Switch to the **Horizontal Type** tool and click on the text in the canvas to enter type editing mode. Replace the current text with `Starry night skies`, press *Esc* to apply the text, and exit type editing mode:

10. Copy and paste the **Starry night skies** text clip from the **Timeline** panel to create a third text frame clip on the right-hand side. You may find that Photoshop moves the original **Starry night skies** clip to the left-hand side of the timeline. If that does happen, move it and the newly pasted text frame to the right-hand side. Then, move the start of the **Starry night skies** clip back to **Frame 03:00**.

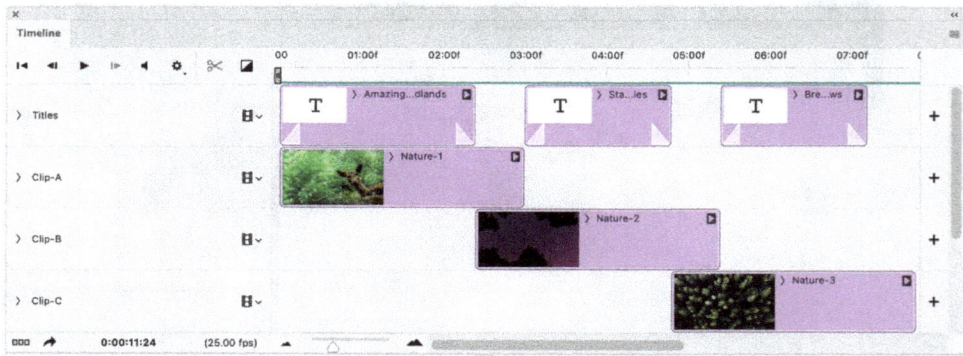

Figure 8.29: Duplicating text frames with fades already applied saves valuable time

11. Drag the new clip so that it starts at **Frame 05:10**, without changing the length of the clip. Drag the playhead to the middle of the new text layer clip in the **Timeline** panel. Switch to the **Horizontal Type** tool and double-click on the text in the canvas to enter type editing mode. Replace the current text with Breathtaking views, press *Esc* to apply the text, and exit type editing mode.

12. Ensure that the **LogoType** clip starts at **Frame 07:20** and ends at **Frame 12:00**. You must drag the green **Color Fill** clip and the **Birds** audio clip endpoints to **Frame 12:00** so that all footage finishes simultaneously.

13. Rewind the playhead to the start of the timeline and press **Play** to preview the animation. Press **Stop** when done, then go to **File → Save**.

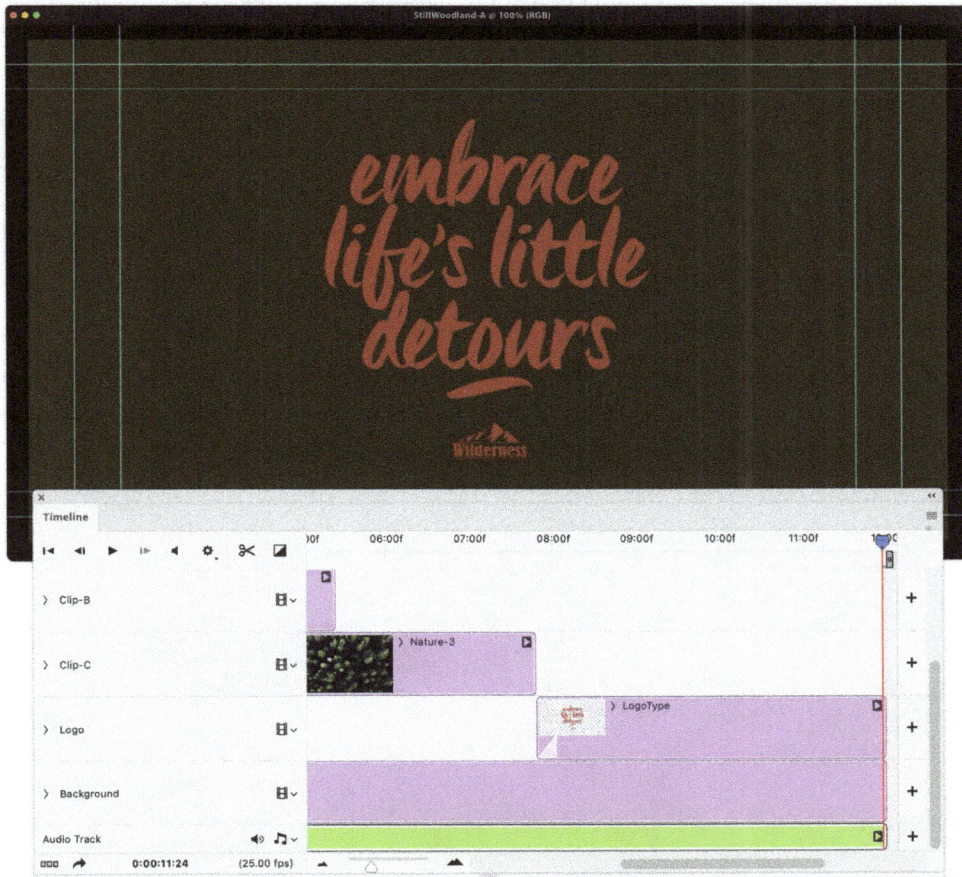

Figure 8.30: The completed sequence

In this section, we created a new document specifically for a video sequence. We set up video groups in the **Layers** and **Timeline** panels to organize our media clips. Then, we imported a series of MPEG-4 video files into the timeline, where they were trimmed and arranged into a sequence. We added cross-fade transitions between the clips to blend them seamlessly. We also added an MP3 audio track to the timeline to accompany the visuals. Next, we'll export the video so that it's ready to be used on YouTube, X/Twitter, and Facebook.

Exporting animations and video from Photoshop

In this final section, you will export the PSDs using Photoshop's built-in rendering tools. In the case of animated GIFs, you have the ancient **Save for Web** dialog, which remains the only method for exporting animated GIFs from Photoshop that provides a preview of your file and data size before you export.

Exporting animated GIFs

Having created several animations, it would be a shame to ruin that hard work by exporting GIF animations that will be rejected by social media platforms because the data size is too large, or the looping options are not set to forever. The following workflow will help strike a balance between low file size and high quality:

1. Go to **File → Export → Save for Web (Legacy)**.

2. When the dialog appears, select **GIF** from the **Optimized File Format** drop-down menu. Set the **Colors** value to 16 and choose Selective from the **Color Reduction Algorithm** dropdown. Finally, turn off the **Transparency** checkbox.

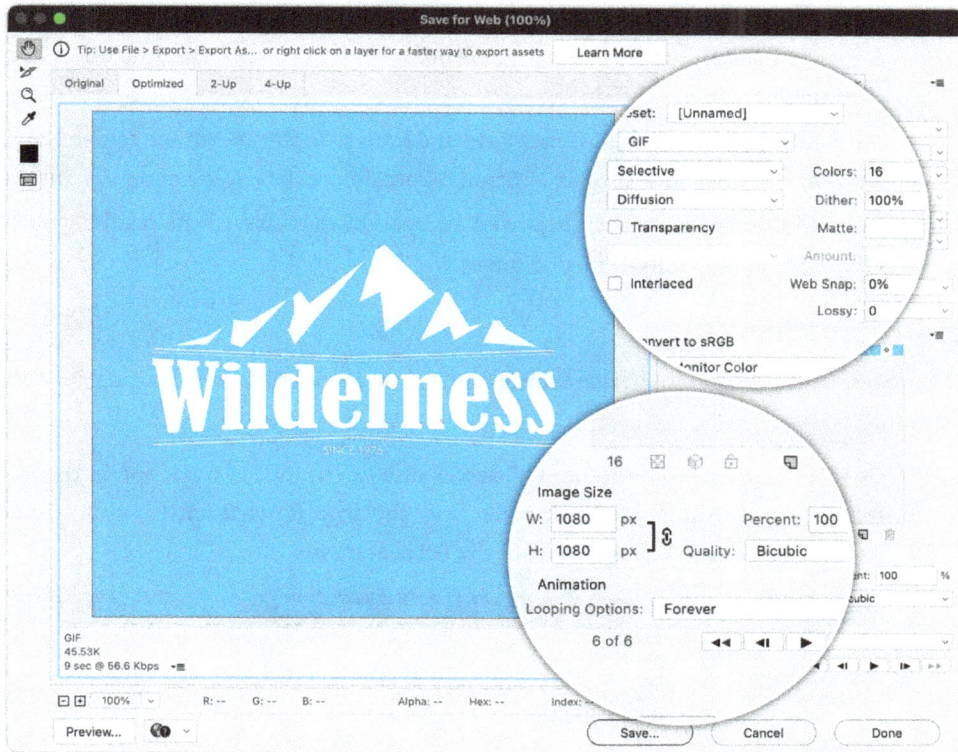

Figure 8.31: The Save for Web (Legacy) dialog remains the best method for exporting GIF animations

3. The remaining drop-down menus and fields in the **Preset** section at the top of the dialog, such as **Matte, Amount, Web Snap**, and **Lossy,** can be left blank or set to 0. However, ensure that the **Convert to sRGB** checkbox is active.

4. You can choose to include data about copyright and your organization's contact details by choosing **Copyright and Contact Info** from the **Metadata** dropdown. This information will need to be added to the file, ideally before you export from Photoshop via **File → File Info**, but in this case, we will press on and export without that additional information.

5. Under **Image Size** (*Figure 8.31*), set the dimensions to their original **Width** of 1080 px and **Height** of 1080 px. If the file size is a little large, you can always use the **Percent** field to experiment with different sizes where available. However, we will leave the scale at **100%** in this example.

6.   Under **Animation Settings**, ensure that **Looping Options** is set to **Forever**. If you wish to preview the animation one last time before exporting, use the controllers in the same section.

7.   With all the settings in place, click **Save** and browse to the 08-Motion folder. Name the file Surf-A, and then click the **Save** button. Photoshop will now generate the animated GIF.

8.   Once all the files have been exported and you have reviewed the results, you can go to **File → Save**. Then, close the document.

Export Video

The process of exporting video from Photoshop is called rendering. In this scenario, we'll output video for YouTube:

1.   Go to **File → Export → Render Video**. Name the file SurfPromo.mp4 in the 08-Motion folder. Choose **Adobe Media Encoder** from the drop-down menu to export the sequence as a video. Then, select **H.264** from the **Format** menu:

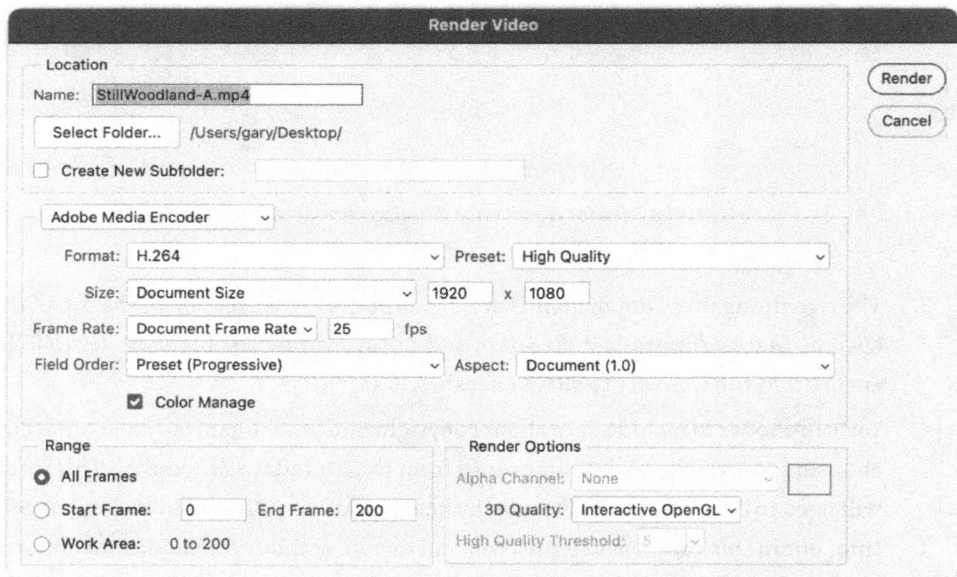

Figure 8.32: You can render video sequences from within Photoshop

2.   Ensure that **Frame Rate** is set to 25 fps. Set **Range** to **All Frames**. Click on the **Render** button when you're done.

3. Photoshop will display a progress bar to indicate the rendering task. Once complete, browse the 08-Motion folder via your operating system and watch the video. When you return to Photoshop, go to **File → Save** and close the document.

In this section, we examined two contrasting methods for exporting video and animation from Photoshop. Both allow us to create ready-to-post files on several online platforms. The fact that we can create, edit, and export from Photoshop and thereby avoid using third-party applications is a real plus.

Summary

In this chapter, we have seen Photoshop's intuitive yet straightforward features for creating and editing motion files.

First, we explored some key concepts related to motion files (namely, time, in the form of frames), and how they relate to the duration of our animations and videos. We also explored some of the specifications to be aware of when posting videos online, such as maximum file size, duration, and loop settings for animations.

Then, we created new documents to house our motion projects, complete with safe frames and a dedicated timeline for adding assets, all of which can be saved as PSD files. Starting with just a logo and layers that we created from scratch, such as color fills and text layers, we organized them in the **Layers** panel specifically for animating.

We used the **Timeline** panel to capture the current state of a file as individual frames to create simple animations with pauses and loops for GIFs. By turning the layer visibility of layers on or off, we can change the appearance of the animation and capture new frames.

We also used keyframes to capture movement in our animations, allowing us to specify a start and end point. Then, using tweening, we tasked Photoshop with the job of creating individual frames between them to form an animation.

For complex motion projects, we turned to video and audio. This is managed in a video timeline, where content is stored in video groups in the **Layers** panel. This allows content to appear in the **Timeline** panel so that it can be arranged and trimmed to the desired duration or have transitions applied to it. We saw how MP3 audio can be added to the timeline, where the volume can be modified or faded where necessary.

Finally, we used two methods for exporting motion files from Photoshop. We exported animated GIFs with a visually led dialog box that accurately previews what the file will look like before exporting, along with the predicted file size. We rendered our timeline to create MPEG-4 and QuickTime video.

In the next chapter, we will dive deep into typography and use a series of layer styles and special effects to bring our copy to life, all while keeping the text editable.

Get This Book's PDF Version and Exclusive Extras

UNLOCK NOW

Scan the QR code (or go to packtpub.com/unlock). Search for this book by name, confirm the edition, and then follow the steps on the page.

Note: Keep your invoice handy. Purchases made directly from Packt don't require one.

Part 3

Building Visual Components

Not all Photoshop projects start with a stunning stock image or a professional photo shoot. You can create amazing visuals with just the tools and features within the application. This part looks at techniques for creating impactful type effects and custom backdrops with patterns and textures. Finally, by mastering the immense power of Photoshop brushes, you'll complete artwork with your own custom brush tips to create snowflakes, retouch hair, and leverage sampled real brush strokes to create a portrait.

This part of the book includes the following chapters:

- *Chapter 9, Bringing Typography to Life with Effects and Styling*
- *Chapter 10, Creating Textures, Patterns, and Backdrops*
- *Chapter 11, Creating and Applying Brushes*

9

Bringing Typography to Life with Effects and Styling

Type effects can range from a simple drop shadow to help text stand out against a busy background to complex combinations that create effects resembling molten lava. When applied correctly, effects can keep the original type layers editable. In this chapter, you'll explore various effects and workflows that can vivify your designs.

We'll start by slicing editable type using smart objects and layer masks. Then, we'll create paper effects, such as embossing and 3D cut-outs.

In the second half of this chapter, we will focus on painterly effects, starting with a displacement technique to create a dripping paint effect and a graffiti spray paint effect using blend modes and a field blur. We will cover the following topics:

- Understanding typographic terms and principles
- Synchronizing Adobe fonts
- Creating cut and fold effects
- Applying ink and paint effects

Figure 9.1: Examples of the projects you will undertake in this chapter

Technical requirements

The project files for this chapter can be found at `https://packt.link/gbz/9781806021710`.

Understanding typographic terms and principles

To achieve effective type formatting, it is essential to be aware of the various characteristics and terminology. Type characters rest upon an invisible baseline – below it extend descenders, such as the tail of the letter *y*. Between the baseline and the top of lowercase characters is a region referred to as the *x-height*. The region above the *x-height* contains ascenders, such as the top of the lowercase *k*:

Figure 9.2: Typographic terms that are also utilized in Photoshop

A *serif* is an accent or embellishment that's found at the end of the central vertical and horizontal portions of a character, such as a lowercase *n* and *u* or the *foot* of a capital *T*. Its counterpart, *sans serif*, where sans is French for *without*, does not contain the same decorative strokes or accents in the main sections of the type:

Figure 9.3: A comparison of serif (lighter shade) and sans serif typefaces

Typefaces come in a multitude of weights, thicknesses, and styles, all of which control the text's slant or posture. It is common to find several weights in a single font, such as normal, italic, and bold, while some typefaces offer dozens of weights:

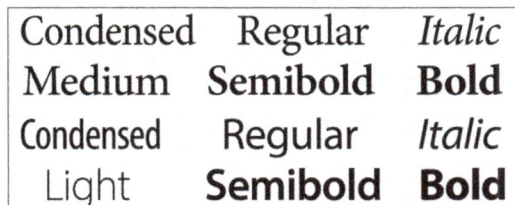

Figure 9.4: Some of the weights or styles that can be found in typefaces

Many of the buttons and features relating to typography throughout Creative Cloud originate from fifteenth-century printing presses, which used an assortment of metal type blocks that could be arranged as required. **Leading** (pronounced led-ing) is the space between two lines of text, from one baseline to another, and was originally formed of strips of lead that could be inserted between lines of text:

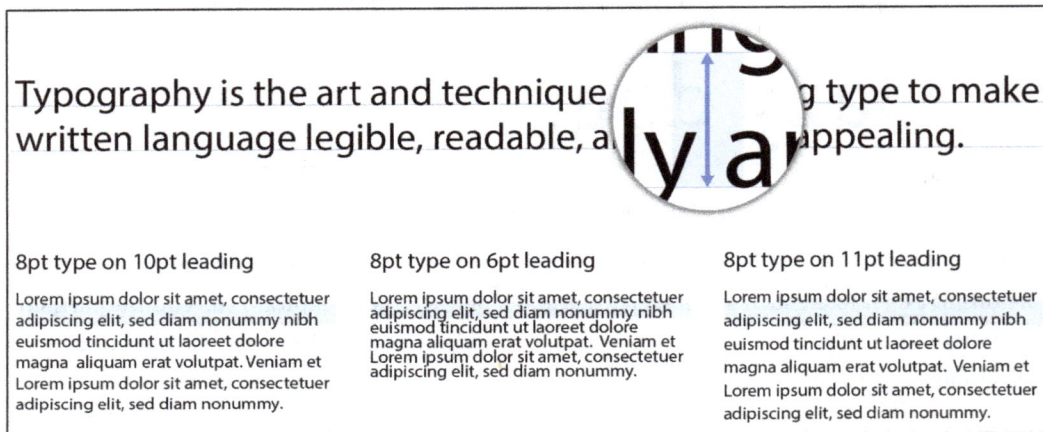

Figure 9.5: Leading controls vertical line spacing

Many Creative Cloud applications import or create text at 12 points in size with 14.4 points of leading. Leading that is smaller than the size of the text can result in a cramped appearance. When you alter the size of your text, the leading automatically adjusts to match the size of the characters to maintain appropriate space between each line. This is known as *auto-leading*. You can increase the leading size to provide more space for your text.

Kerning refers to the spacing between a pair of type characters. For example, when the characters *A* and *V* or *W* and *A* are arranged together, this can create unwanted white space between them, which can be mitigated by reducing the kerning value to tighten the space between them. You can use the shortcut *Alt + left/right arrow* (Windows) or *Option + left/right arrow* (macOS) to adjust the kerning value.

Tracking in typography refers to the consistent spacing between characters within a word or a line of text. It involves adjusting the overall letter spacing to enhance readability and aesthetic appeal. For example, tracking is used in movie posters to space out the name of a production company to match that of the movie's name:

Figure 9.6: Examples of kerning and tracking

All typeface characters rest on a baseline – that is, an invisible line. To move type characters above or below the baseline, you can use a feature known as **baseline shift**. Increasing the baseline shift moves characters higher, while decreasing it lowers characters. An appropriate use of baseline shift would be to separate the type from an underline to make text more legible, or to center numerical values between parentheses. Baseline shift can be found in the **Character** panel or by using the shortcut *Alt + Shift + up/down* (Windows) or *Option + Shift + up/down* (macOS) with the text highlighted:

Figure 9.7: Baseline shift moves characters up or down from the line they rest upon

Fonts are composed of hundreds of characters, referred to as **glyphs**. These range from letters and numbers to symbols and ornaments, such as trademark symbols. You will find several versions of letters designed for specific scenarios, such as superscript, where the letters *S* and *T* combine to create *1st*. *Figure 9.8* provides a selection of just some of the glyph characters available. These include superscript (**1**), subscript (**2**), fractions (**3**), all small caps (**4**), swash (**5**), ligatures (**6**), discretionary ligatures (**7**), registration mark (**8**), trademark (**9**), math symbols (**10**), and the degree sign (**11**):

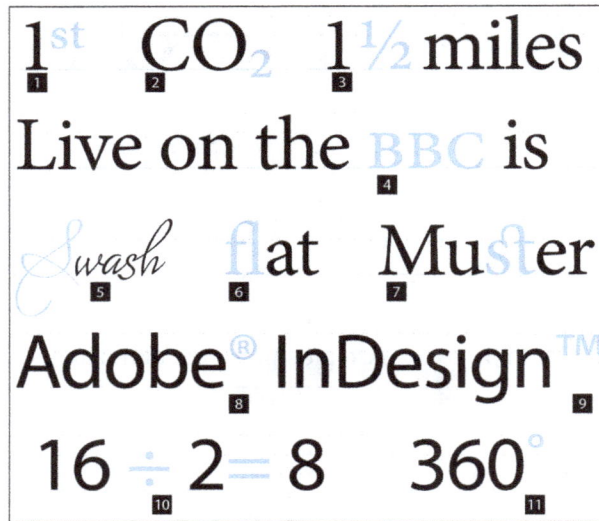

Figure 9.8: Examples of open type characters

In this section, we explored essential typographic terms and principles that will allow you to take granular control of text within Photoshop and across Creative Cloud. Now that we know how to fine-tune type and white space, it's time for some exercises that bring type to life in various visual styles and effects.

Synchronizing Adobe fonts

All the exercises in this chapter use fonts from Creative Cloud. You can "sync" fonts from Creative Cloud by following these steps:

1. Open your preferred web browser and head to `https://fonts.adobe.com`.

2. Enter the font name you wish to find using the **Search all Fonts** bar in the web page's center. In this chapter, you will need to sync (a) **Abril Text, Extra Bold**, (b) **Nimbus Sans Condensed Black**, (c) **Gelato Luxe, Regular**, (d) **Subway New York SC**, and **Regular**.

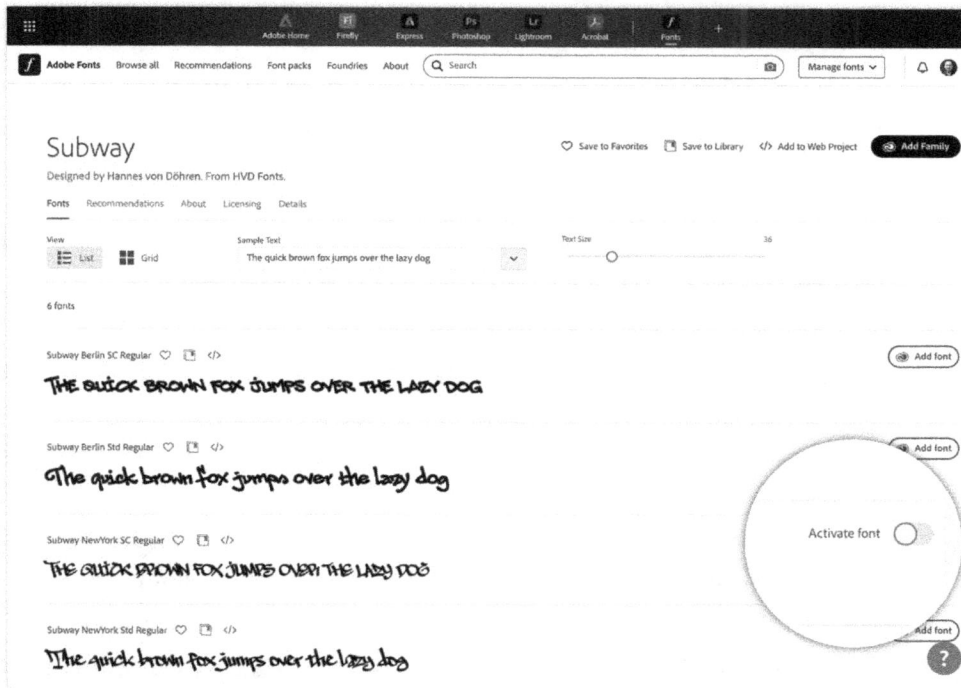

Figure 9.9: Activate one or more fonts to use them in your desktop Adobe apps

3. The search results will preview the closest matches to your query in the form of thumbnails of the font and its name. Click on the appropriate thumbnail to view the corresponding font family page. Click on the **Activate font** toggle adjacent to the relevant font.

4. Once you've activated the desired fonts, the Creative Cloud desktop app will automatically sync and download them to your computer. This process may take some time, depending on the number and size of the fonts.

5. Once the fonts have finished syncing, you can access and use them within Adobe applications such as Photoshop, Illustrator, and InDesign. The synchronized fonts should appear in the Photoshop font menus.

6. Repeat this process until you have installed all the necessary fonts. You can choose different fonts if you prefer, or if you don't have an active internet connection while working through the following exercises, use fonts already installed on your system.

In this section, we described how to install fonts from Creative Cloud. While not mandatory, using the recommended fonts will help you better match the look and feel of the artwork you create in each exercise. Next, you'll start by creating a sliced text effect.

Creating cut and fold effects

In the following exercises, you will slice, tear, and cut out text as though it had been applied to paper, all with the power of **smart objects** and editable type.

Creating sliced text

In the first of our text effect exercises, you will cut an editable text layer in half and apply shadows to the lower half to create the illusion of sliced text running through it:

1. Open `Background.psd` from the `09-Type` folder.

2. Switch to the **Type** tool from the **Tools** panel and click on the center of the canvas to create a point type, intended for a single line of text. You will now see the type cursor flashing in the canvas. Type `& diced` into the text frame and then select all the characters with the **Type** tool.

3. Go to the **Properties** panel and set **Font** to **Myriad Pro**, **Style** to **Black**, **Leading** to **Auto**, **Font Size** to `400` pt, and **Tracking** to `-60`. Then, click on the **Color** preview (**A** in *Figure 9.10*) to open the color picker, enter `dddddd` into the **Hexadecimal** field, and click **OK**.

Figure 9.10: The formatted base type layer

4. When you're finished, click the **Commit Changes** button in the **Options** bar to add the text layer. Switch to the **Selection** tool, ensure **Smart Guides** are enabled (**View → Smart Guides**), and then drag the text to the center of the canvas.

5. Hover your cursor over the BKG layer in the **Layers** panel, then *Shift* and click on the layer's name to make both layers active in the **Layers** panel. Right-click on the **BKG** layer's name in the **Layers** panel and choose **Convert to Smart Object** from the list of commands.

6. Rename the new **Smart Object** layer to Bottom.

7. Next, right-click on the **Bottom** layer's name in the **Layers** panel and choose **Duplicate Layer** from the list. In the dialog box that appears, enter a new name of Top in the **Duplicate As** field and click **OK**:

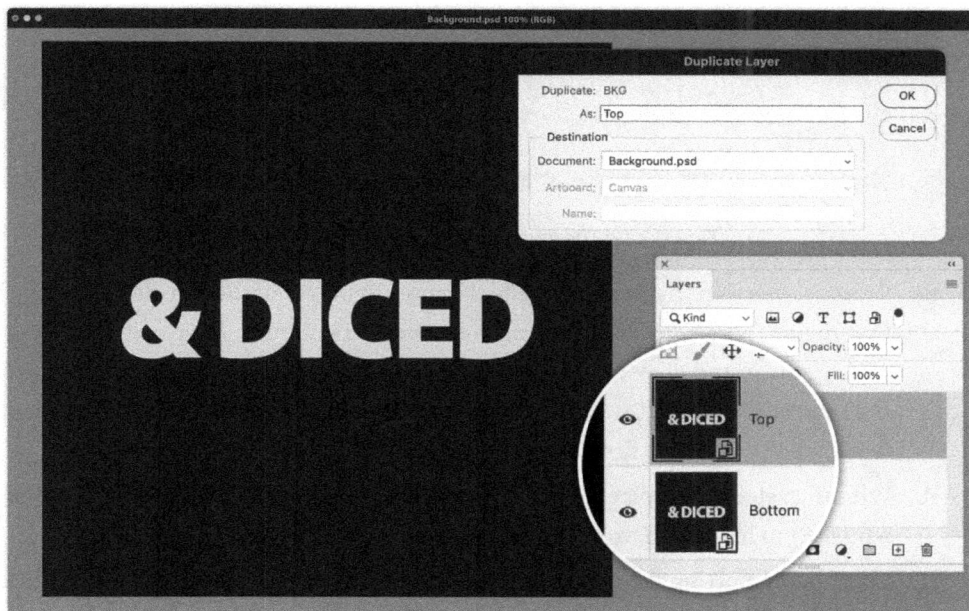

Figure 9.11: Type converted to smart objects

8. With the first stage of the edits complete, save the document as a PSD in the 09-Type folder and keep the document open.

9. Ensure only the **Top** layer is active in the **Layers** panel, then switch to **Polygonal Lasso Tool** (*Figure 9.12*) from the **Tools** panel. From the **Options** bar, set the selection mode to **New** and **Feather** to 0. Hide the **Bottom** layer in the **Layers** panel.

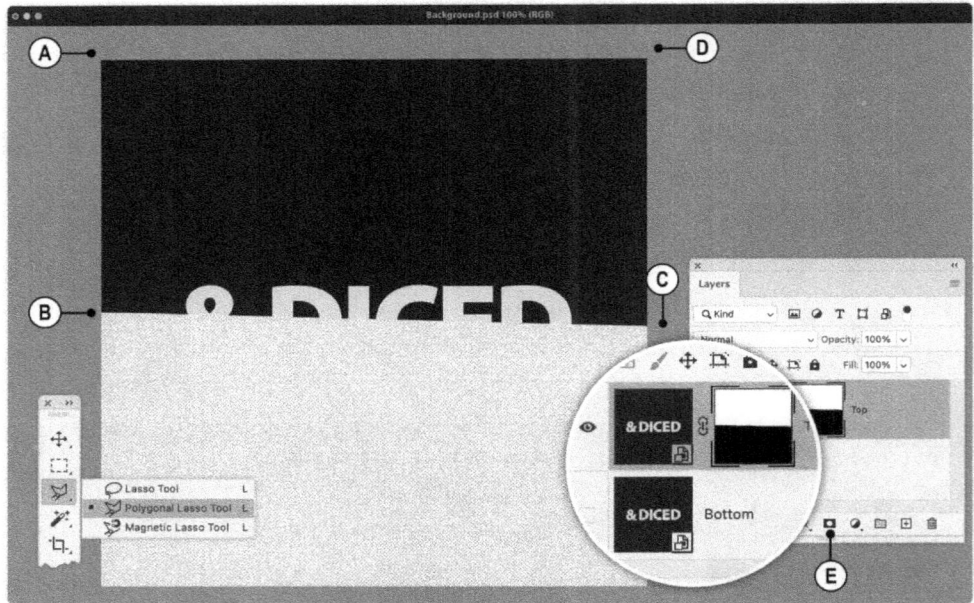

Figure 9.12: The layer mask applied to the top version of the text

10. Create a selection that starts outside the top-left corner of the canvas by clicking once in that region (**A** in *Figure 9.12*). Then, hover your cursor lower down on the outer-left edge of the canvas and click again (**B**). Hover your cursor over the right-hand side, beyond the canvas, and click (**C**). Then, click in the top-right corner beyond the canvas (**D**), and finally click where you first started to generate the selection.

11. With the selection in place, click on the **Add a Mask** button at the bottom of the **Layers** panel (**E**) to hide the bottom region of the layer.

12. Click on the **Bottom** layer to make it active, then turn on its visibility. Then, click on the **New Layer** icon in the **Layers** panel, which will appear immediately above the bottom layer in the stack.

13. Double-click on the new layer's name and change it to Shadows. Then, change **Blend Mode** to **Multiply**.

14. Press the *B* key to switch to the **Brush** tool. In the **Options** bar, set **Brush Tip** to **Soft Round** and lower **Opacity** to 30%. Press the *D* key to reset the colors to black and white.

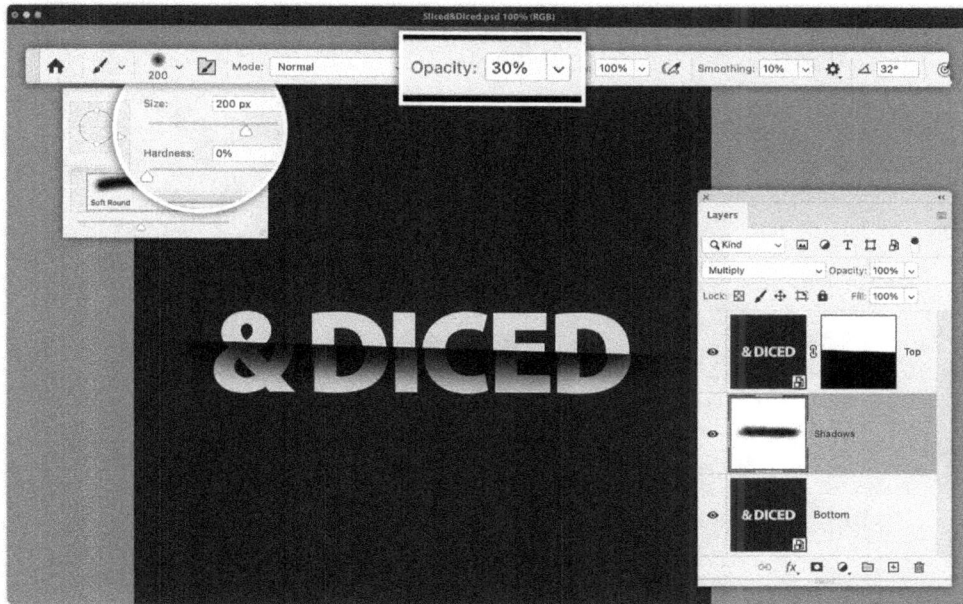

Figure 9.13: Painting with the Brush tool to create the shadow effect across the bottom half

15. Hover the **Brush** tool's cursor just beyond the left edge of the bottom half of the text, then drag to the right-hand side to paint a black paint stroke region that finishes just beyond the right edge of the text. Repeat the same technique to darken the shadow as necessary. Go to **File → Save** when you're done and close the document.

Creating an embossed type

This paper embossing technique is handy for conceptualizing printing effects to demonstrate the final product before it goes to print. Let's get started:

1. Go to **File → Open** and browse to the 09-Type folder. Select Embossed.jpg and then click **Open**.

2. Press the *D* key to reset the colors to black and white, then switch to the **Type** tool from the **Tools** panel.

3. Click and drag across the canvas to create an area type text frame occupying at least half the canvas area. Type Embrace life's little detours and select all characters with the **Type** tool.

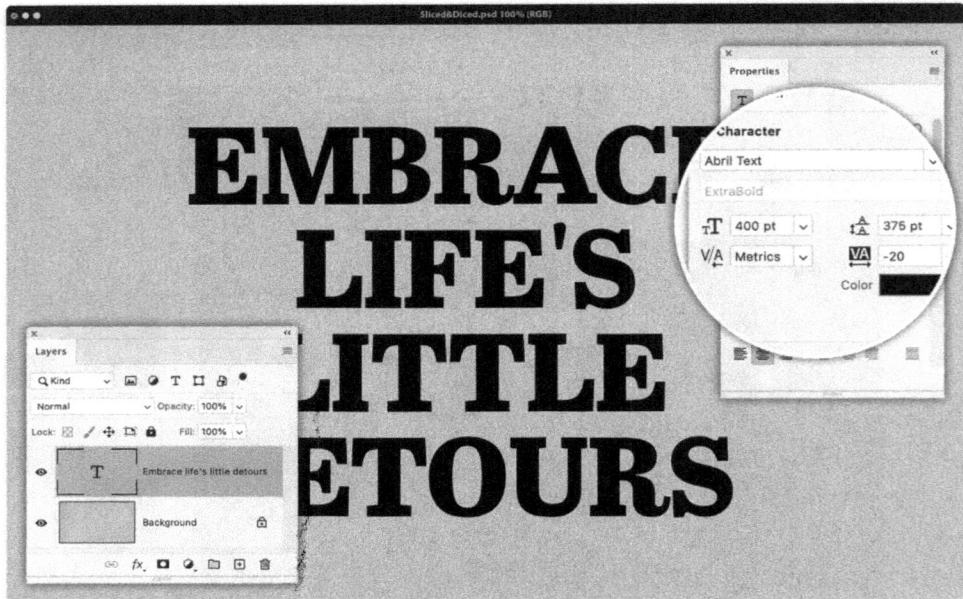

Figure 9.14: The underlying type layer with basic formatting applied

4. Go to the **Properties** panel and set **Font** to **Abril Text**, **Style** to **Extra Bold**, **Font Size** to
    400 pt, **Leading** to 375 pt, and **Tracking** to -20. Set **Alignment** to **Centered**.

5. Resize the text frame so that each line contains one word, resulting in four lines. Click the
    Commit Changes button in the **Options** bar to finish editing the text frame.

6. With the text layer still active, press *Ctrl + G* (Windows) or *Cmd + G* (macOS) to add the
    text to a new layer group. Rename the layer group Logotype.

7. Ensure the layer group is still active in the **Layers** panel, and then click on the **Add a layer
    style** button at the bottom of the **Layers** panel. From the list of options, click on **Blending
    Options**. When the dialog appears, reduce **Fill Opacity** to 0%.

8. Next, click on the **Bevel & Emboss** style from the list on the left-hand side of the dialog to apply the effect and reveal the options. Ensure you click on the name of each style to reveal its options, not just the checkbox, which simply adds the default effect. Click on the **Reset to Default** button at the bottom of the **Layer Style** panel. Then, set **Style** to **Inner Bevel**, **Technique** to **Smooth**, **Depth** to 90%, **Direction** to Down, **Size** to 8 px, and **Soften** to 2 px.

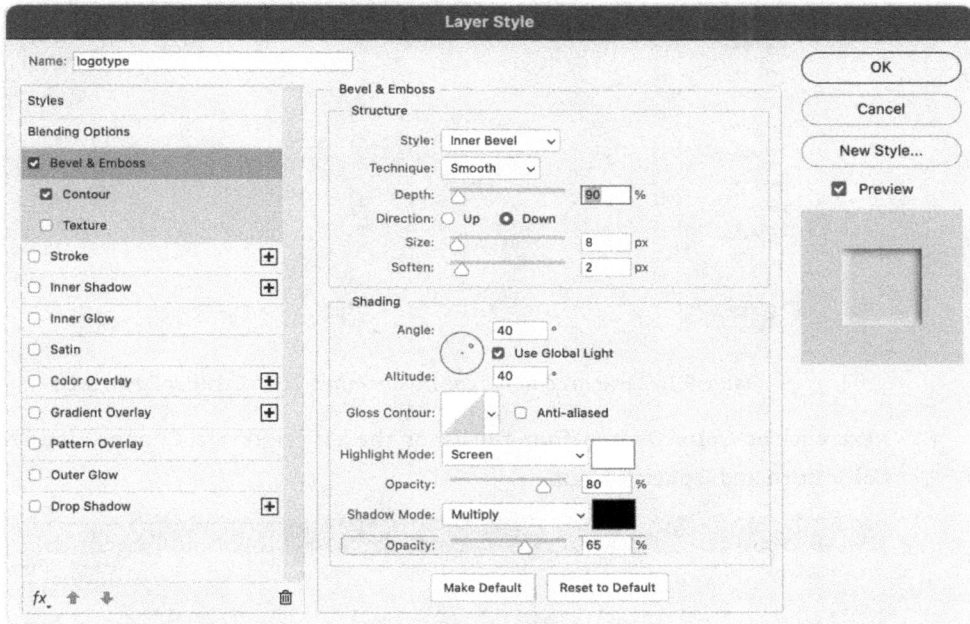

Figure 9.15: Emboss settings

9. From the **Shading** group settings lower down, set **Angle** to 40°, **Altitude** to 40°, **Highlight Mode Opacity** to 80%, and **Shadow Mode Opacity** to 65%.

10. Click on the **Contour** subcategory from the list on the left-hand side. When the options appear, click on the **Contour Editor** thumbnail to open the editor (*Figure 9.16*). Then, click on the center of the line that appears in the grid to add a new point. Change **Input** to 35% and **Output** to 55%. Click **OK** to apply the settings. This will change the shape of the emboss so that it's smoother and shallower.

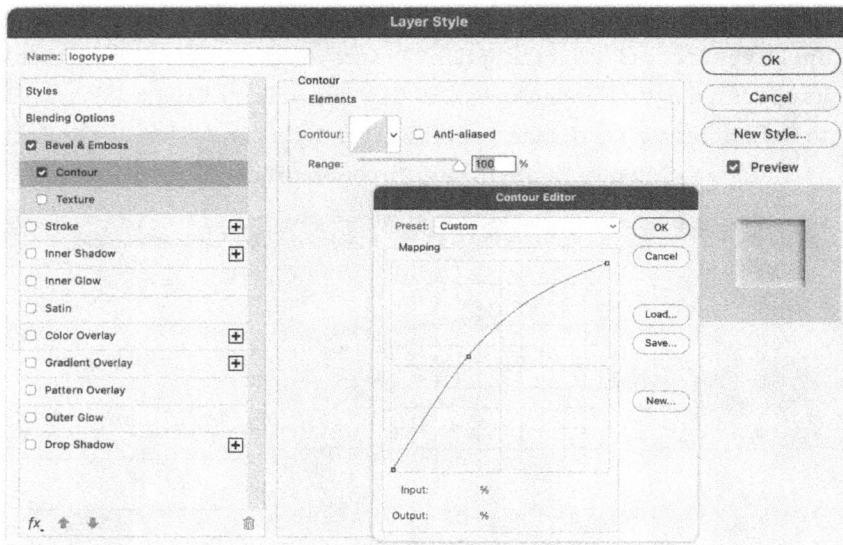

Figure 9.16: Custom contours can be smoothed in the Contour Editor area

11. Next, click on **Color Overlay** from the list on the left-hand side. Change **Blend Mode** to **Color Burn** and **Opacity** to 40%.

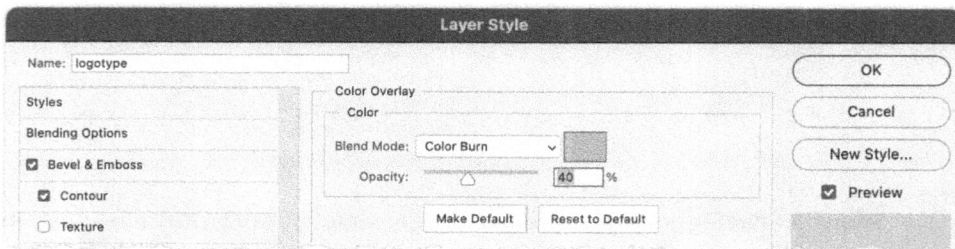

Figure 9.17: Color Overlay helps darken the type characters

Then click on **Set color of overlay** to open the color picker. Hover your cursor over a region away from the text to sample the paper color and click **OK** to close the **Color Picker** dialog. This will subtly darken the embossed region of text to help differentiate it from the other regions of the paper.

12. With the **Layer Style** dialog box still open, click on **Drop Shadow** (*Figure 9.18*) from the list on the left-hand side. Click the **Reset to Default** button at the bottom of the **Drop Shadow** settings. Ensure **Blend Mode** is set to **Multiply**, turn off the **Use Global Light** checkbox, and set **Opacity** to 24%, **Angle** to -145°, **Distance** to 5 px, **Spread** to 0%, and **Size** to 2 px.

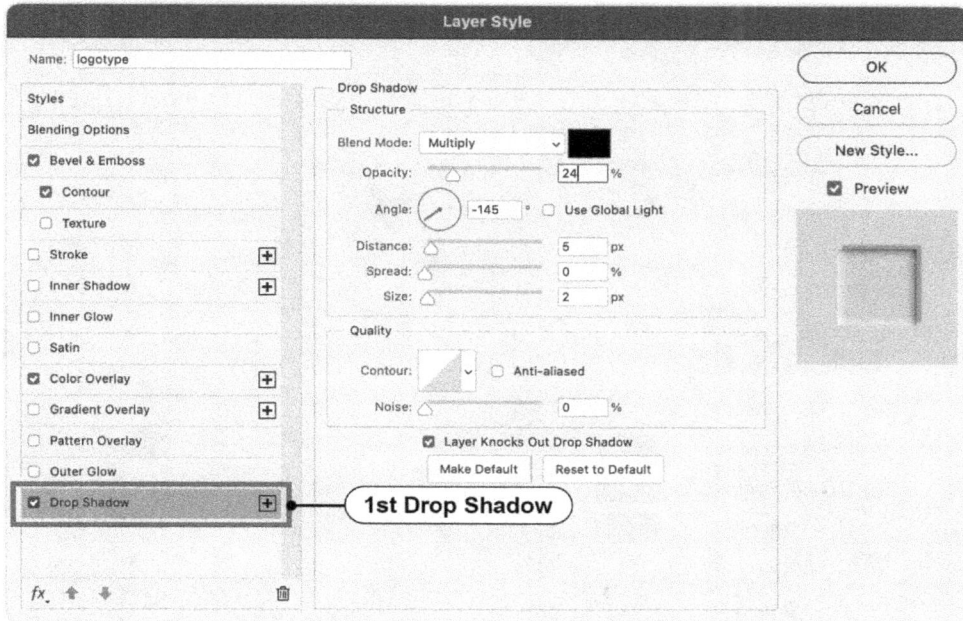

Figure 9.18: Apply the first of four Drop Shadow effects

13. Next, we need to emphasize the shaded regions inside the embossed text. Click on the **Duplicate Style** button, shown as a plus (+) icon, adjacent to the **Drop Shadow** effect you just edited from the list on the left-hand side.

14. Set the newly duplicated **Drop Shadow** options (**2nd** in *Figure 9.19*) – that is, set **Opacity** to 4%, **Angle** to -145°, **Distance** to 26 px, **Spread** to 0%, and **Size** to 65 px.

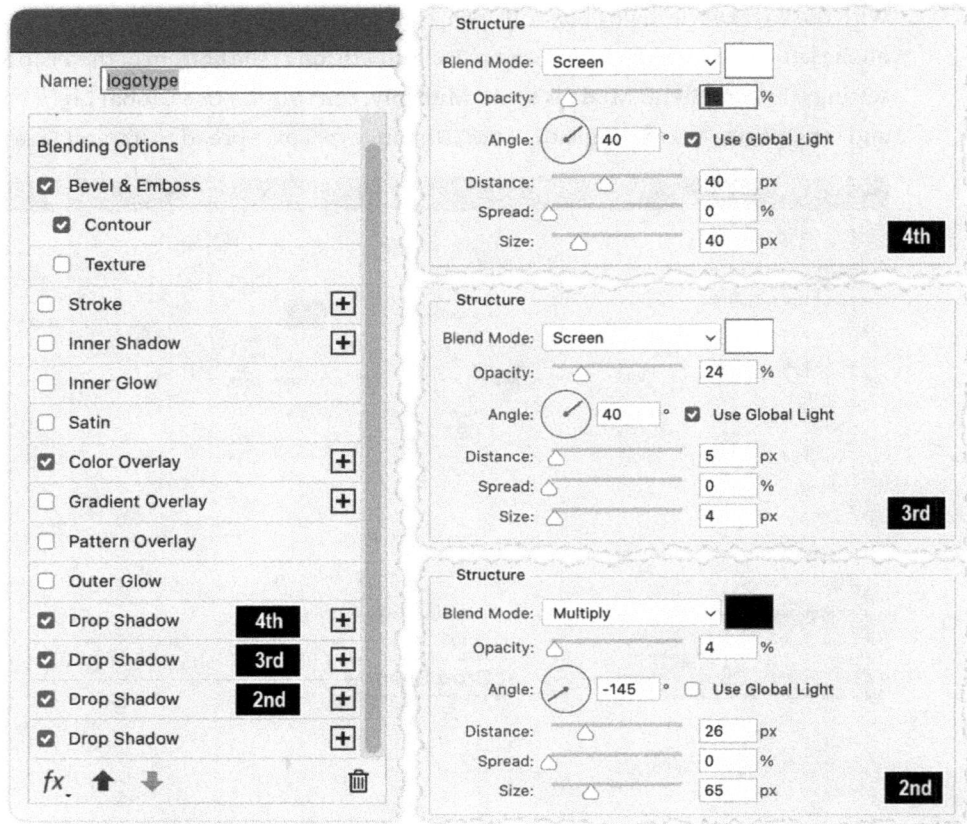

Figure 9.19: Apply the remaining three Drop Shadow effects

15. Repeat the same step to add a third **Drop Shadow** effect by clicking on the **Duplicate Style** button adjacent to the one you just added. However, this time, we need to emphasize the highlighted edges.

16. Set the third **Drop Shadow** effect's options – that is, set **Blend Mode** to **Screen**, **Opacity** to 24%, **Angle** to 40°, **Distance** to 5 px, **Spread** to 0%, and **Size** to 4 px.

17. Finally, add a fourth **Drop Shadow** effect by clicking on the **Duplicate Style** button adjacent to the one you added. This effect will lighten the surface around the text.

18. Set the fourth **Drop Shadow** effect's options – that is, set **Opacity** to 15%, **Angle** to 40°, **Distance** to 40 px, **Spread** to 0%, and **Size** to 40 px. You will be relieved to read that you can now click **OK** to apply all the effects, close the dialog box, and return to the main Photoshop interface.

19. This technique will allow you to add any content to the **Logotype** layer group, after which it will apply the embossed effect, keeping all text editable. Go to **File → Save**, browse to the 09-Type folder, and save the document as a PSD file. Close the document when you're done.

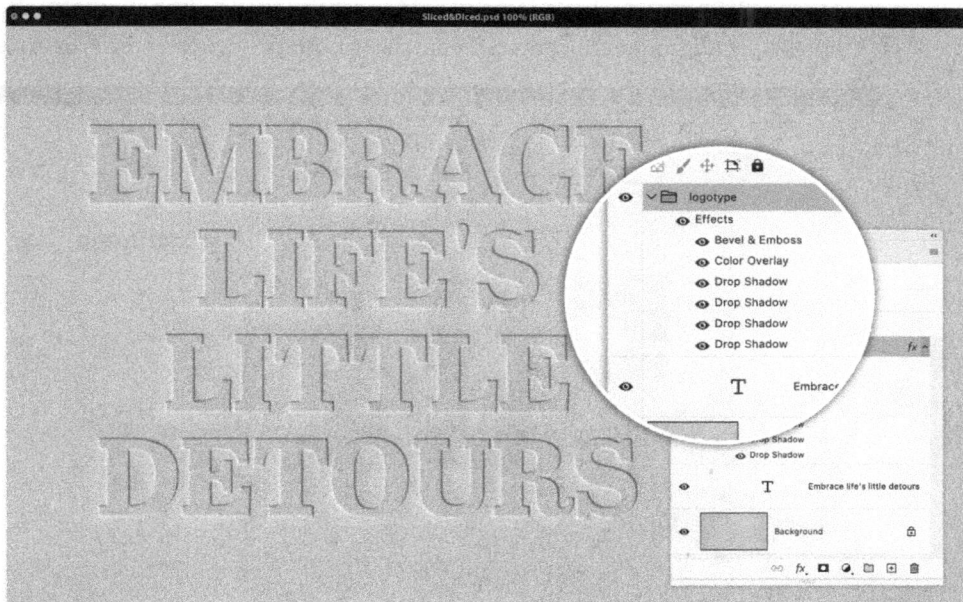

Figure 9.20: The completed embossing effect

Creating cut and fold effects

This 3D text effect is great for grabbing attention in ads or web banners on social media. The technique allows for editable text and doesn't require any 3D tools. Let's take a look:

1. Go to **File → Open** and browse to the 09-Type folder. Select 3DPaper.jpg and then click **Open**.

2. Press the *D* key to reset the colors to black and white and then switch to the **Type** tool from the **Tools** panel.

3. Click and drag across the canvas to create an area type text frame that occupies at least half the canvas area. Type FOLD and then select all characters with the **Type** tool.

4. Go to the **Properties** panel (*Figure 9.21*) and set **Font** to **Nimbus Sans Condensed**, **Style** to **Black**, **Leading** to **Auto**, **Font Size** to 1000 pt, and **Tracking** to 60. Lower down on the same panel, under **Type Options**, turn on **All Caps**. Click on the **Set text color** thumbnail and enter fb920a into the **Hexadecimal** field to set the color to bright orange; then, click **OK**. Finally, set **Alignment** to **Centered** from the **Paragraph** section of the **Properties** panel.

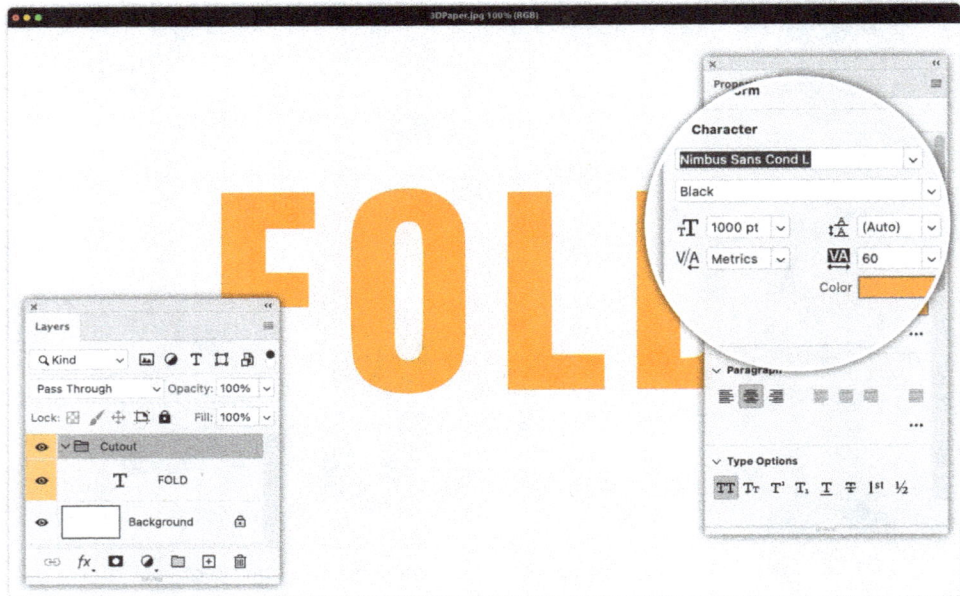

Figure 9.21: The base type layer formatting

5. Resize the text frame so that it is as small as possible, without hiding any characters. Click on the **Commit Changes** button in the **Options** bar to complete the text frame edits. Switch to the **Move** tool and center the text to the canvas.

6. With the text layer still active, press *Ctrl* + *G* (Windows) or *Cmd* + *G* (macOS) to add the text to a new layer group. Rename the layer group Cutout.

7. Ensure that the layer group is still active in the **Layers** panel, and then click on the **Add a layer style** button at the bottom of the **Layers** panel. From the list of options, click on **Inner Shadow**.

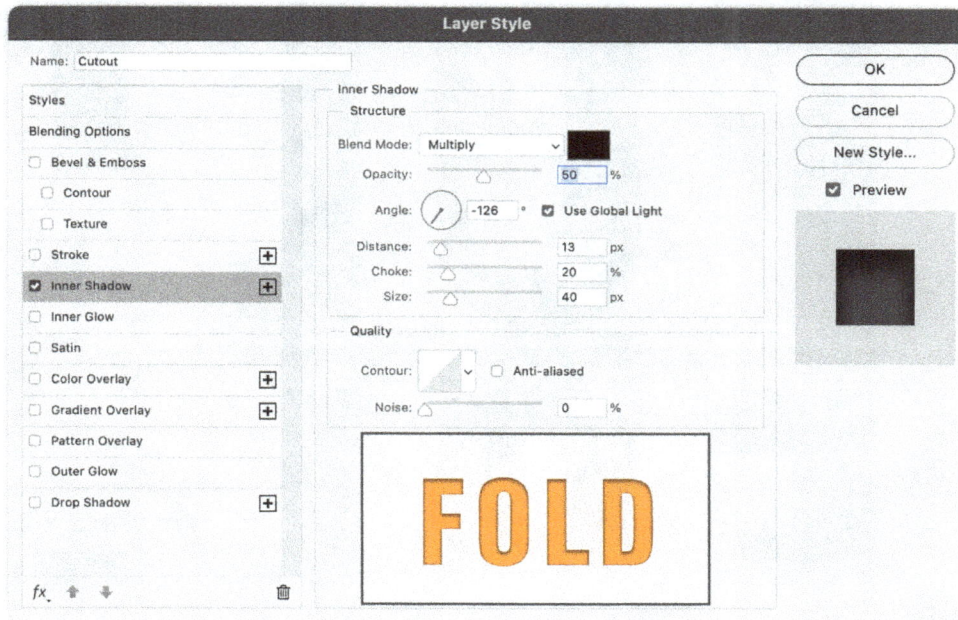

Figure 9.22: Inner shadow settings with the effect shown

8. Click on the **Reset to Default** button at the bottom of the **Inner Shadow** settings. Then, set **Opacity** to 50%, **Angle** to -126°, **Distance** to 13 px, **Spread** to 20%, and **Size** to 40 px. Click **OK** to apply the effect when you're done.

9. Duplicate the FOLD text layer by dragging it onto the **Create new layer** icon at the bottom of the **Layers** panel. Then drag the duplicated text layer to the top of the layer stack, thereby removing it from the Cutout layer group.

10. From the **Properties** panel, click on **Set text color** and change the color of the text to black.

Figure 9.23: Adding guides to the middle of the type and cropping the type in half

11. Right-click on the original text layer name you just duplicated and choose **Convert to Smart Object** from the list of commands. Rename the layer Top. Then, double-click on the Top layer thumbnail to open the contents in a new window.

12. Go to **View → Rulers** if the rulers are not visible in the image window. Then, go to **View → Snap To → Document Bounds,** which will prevent snapping to the center of the canvas. Hover your cursor over the middle of the horizontal ruler and drag a new guide down to the middle of the text, at approximately 365 px.

13. Switch to the **Crop** tool from the **Tools** panel. From the **Options** bar, set **Mode** to **Ratio** and click on the **Clear** button. Turn off the **Delete cropped pixels** and **Content-Aware** checkboxes. Then, go to **View** → **Snap To** to turn snapping back on. Drag the bottom-middle crop handle up the guide you added in a previous step and click on the **Commit** button in the **Options** bar to apply the edit.

14. Go to **File** → **Save** and close the **Top** document when you're done. This should return you to the master file.

15. You will notice that the text has moved because of the crop edit. Switch to the **Move** tool and reposition the cropped text so that it aligns with the top of the original orange text once more.

16. Right-click on the **Top** layer's name, choose **New Smart Object via Copy**, and rename the newly duplicated layer Bottom. Then, drag the **Bottom** layer under the **Top** layer in the **Layers** panel.

17. Next, double-click on the **Bottom** layer's thumbnail to open the contents in a new window. Go to **Image** → **Reveal All**. Switch to the **Crop** tool, drag the top-middle handle of the crop frame down to the guide, and click on the **Commit** button in the **Options** bar to crop the top half of the text. Go to **File** → **Save** and close the **Bottom** document when you're done.

18. Click on the **Top** layer in the **Layers** panel to make it active. Then, click on the **Add a layer style** button at the bottom of the **Layers** panel. From the list of options, click on **Gradient Overlay** and click on the **Reset to Default** button in the **Gradient Overlay** settings.

19. Set **Blend Mode** to **Normal** and **Opacity** to 100%, ensure the **Reverse** checkbox is deactivated, and set **Style** to **Linear**, **Angle** to 90°, **Scale** to 100%, and **Method** to **Perceptual**.

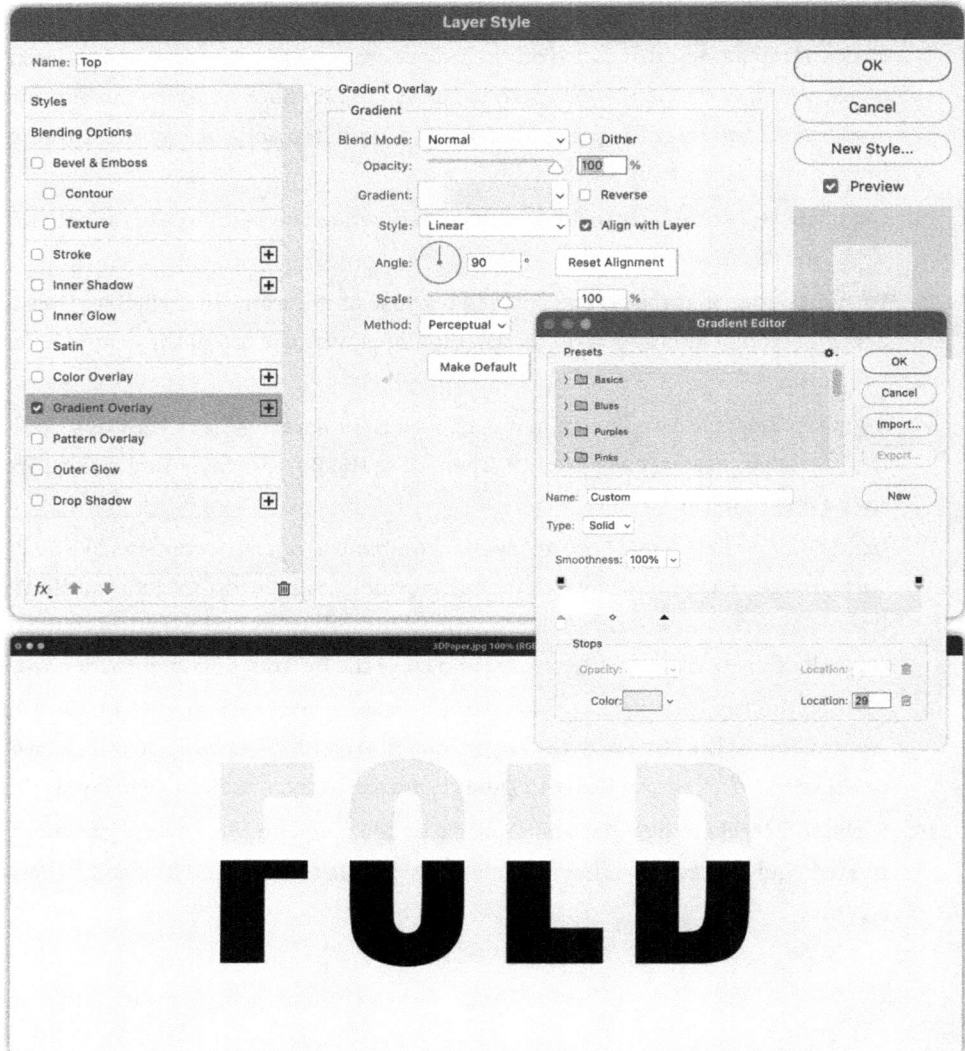

Figure 9.24: Gradient Overlay effects used to create highlights

20. Next, click on the **Gradient** thumbnail to open the **Gradient Editor** area. When the dialog appears, expand the **Basic** folder of presets and select the first preset, called **Foreground to Background**.

21. Click on the left-hand **Color Stop** and change its appearance by clicking on **Change color of selected stop**, the color swatch thumbnail. Enter ffffff into the **Hexadecimal** field to make the color stop white.

22. Then, click on the right-hand **Color Stop** to make it active. Click on **Change color of selected stop**. Enter e8e8e8 into the **Hexadecimal** field to make the color stop light gray. With the right-hand **Color Stop** still active, set **Location** to 30%. Click **OK** when you're done. Then, click **OK** in the **Layer Style** dialog box to apply the overlay.

23. Hover your cursor over the **Fx** icon assigned to the **Top** layer in the **Layers** panel, hold *Alt* (Windows) or *Option* (macOS), and drag the **FX** icon onto the layer named **Bottom** to duplicate the effect.

24. Double-click on the newly duplicated text label, **Gradient Overlay**, that was assigned to the **Bottom** layer in the **Layers** panel to edit it. When the dialog appears, click on the **Gradient** thumbnail to open the **Gradient Editor** area.

25. Click on the left-hand **Color Stop** to make it active, then change its color to fcfcfc. Click **OK** to apply the change and then click on the right-hand **Color Stop** and change its color to f2f2f2. With the right-hand **Color Stop** still active, set **Location** to 75%. Click **OK** when you're done. Then, click **OK** in the **Layer Style** dialog box to apply the overlay:

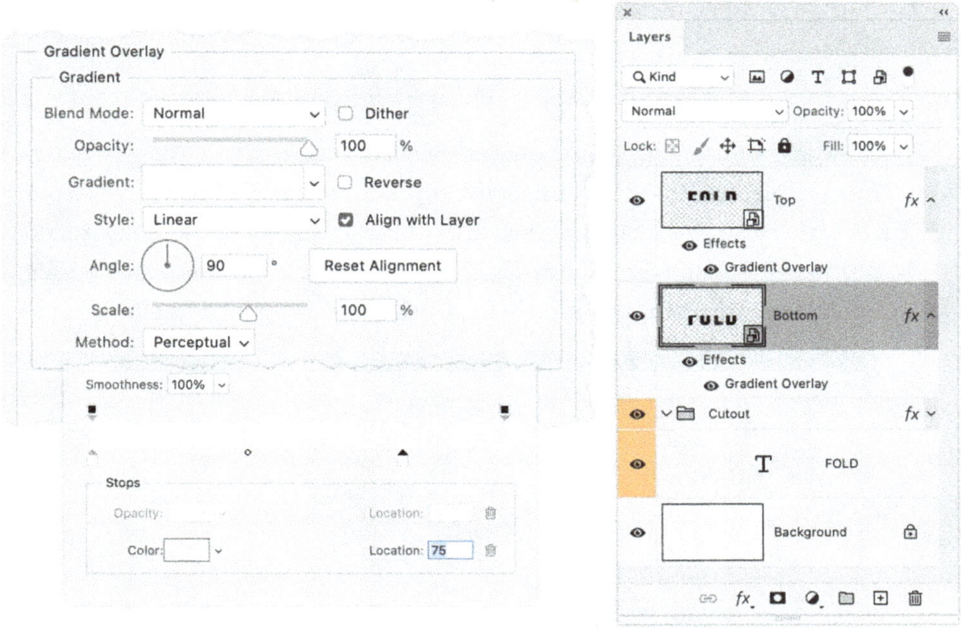

Figure 9.25: The lower-half Gradient Overlay settings

26. Click on the **Top** layer in the **Layers** panel to make it active. Then, go to **Edit → Transform → Distort**. Hover your cursor over the top-middle bounding box point and drag to the right to skew by -12° and then drag upward to make the text look as though the top edge has moved to the right, and upward slightly. Click on the **Commit changes** button in the **Options** bar to apply the edits.

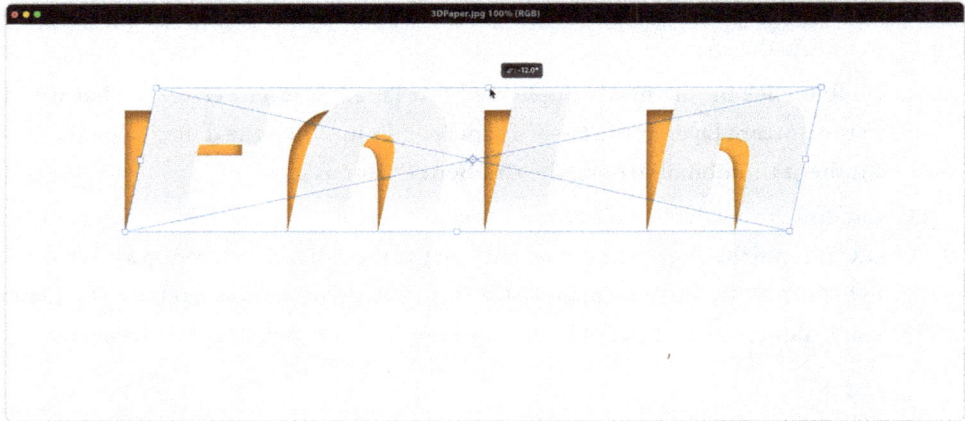

Figure 9.26: The distorted upper-half type characters

27. Click on the **Bottom** layer in the **Layers** panel to make it active. Then, go to **Edit → Transform → Distort**. Hover your cursor over the bottom-middle bounding box point, drag to the right to **Skew** by 10°, and then drag upward to **Skew** by 12°. This should make the text look as though the bottom edge has moved to the right, and upward slightly. Click on the **Commit changes** button in the **Options** bar to apply the edits.

Figure 9.27: The distorted lower-half type characters

28. With the **Bottom** layer still active, hold *Shift* and click on the **Top** layer to make both layers active. Then, press *Ctrl + G* (Windows) or *Cmd + G* (macOS) to add the text to a new layer group. Rename the layer group Letters.

29. Right-click on the **Letters** layer group and choose **Duplicate Group** from the list of commands. When the dialog appears, change the name in the **As** field to **Shadows** and click **OK**.

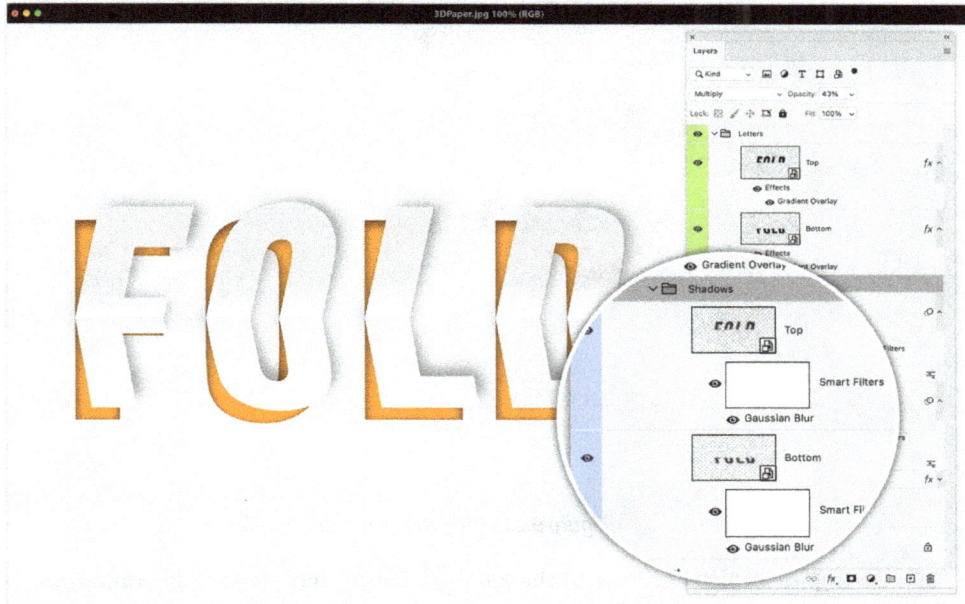

Figure 9.28: Duplicate the text to turn it into type shadows

30. Expand the **Shadows** layer group and make both the **Top** and **Bottom** layers active in the **Layers** panel. Right-click on one of the active layer names and choose **Clear Layers Style** from the list. The text needs to be black for the shadow effect.

31. Make the **Top** layer active in the **Shadows** layer group by clicking on it. Go to **Filter → Blur → Gaussian Blur**. Set **Radius** to 25 px and click **OK**.

32. Next, click on the **Bottom** layer in the **Shadows** layer group to make it active. Finally, go to **Filter → Gaussian Blur** to apply the same effect.

33. To make this design more flexible, collapse all the layer groups in the stack and make them all active. Then, click on the **Letters** group, hold *Shift*, and click on the **Cutout** layer. Right-click on any of the active layer group names and choose **Convert to Smart Object** from the list.

34. You can then move, rotate, and scale as necessary. In the example shown in *Figure 9.29*, the **Letters** Smart Object was rotated by -25°.

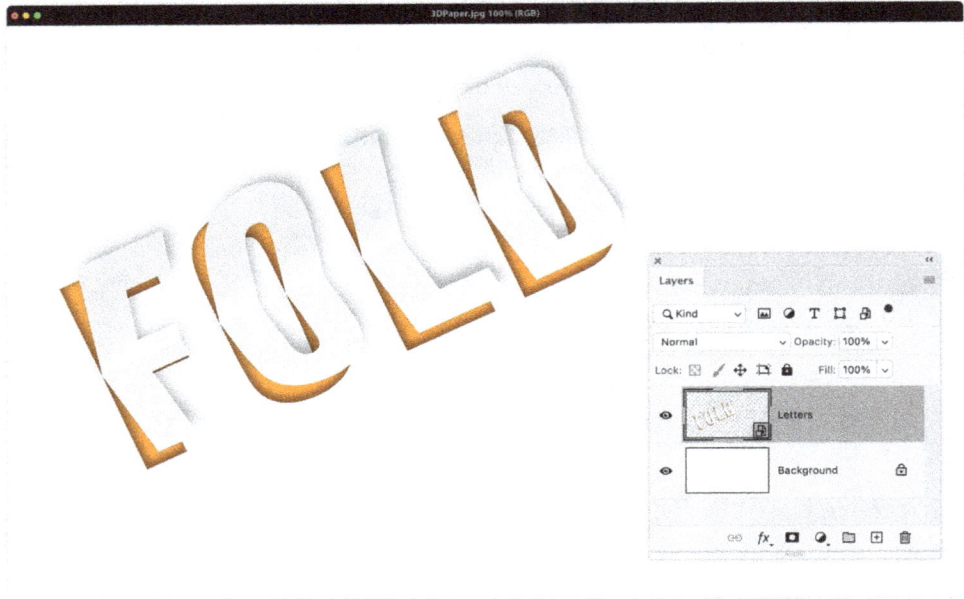

Figure 9.29: The completed faux 3D effects

35. Go to **File → Save**, browse to the 09-Type folder, and save the document as a PSD file. Close the document when you're done.

In this section, we explored a series of effects that create slices, folds, and emboss patterns that can be applied to text. Each technique allows the text to remain editable by combining Smart Objects and layer styles, which are assigned via layer groups. In the next set of exercises, we will explore painterly effects.

Applying ink and paint effects

Infusing type with painterly effects is always a challenge when translating into a digital context, and something is often lost in the process. However, with a sound knowledge of Photoshop filters and layer styles, you can achieve impressive results.

Creating dripping paint

This technique uses displacement maps to distort editable text, giving the impression of paint dripping in a vertical direction. Let's get started:

1. Go to **File → Open** and select `DrippingPaint.jpg` from the `09-Type` folder. Then, click **Open**.

2. Press the *D* key to reset the colors to black and white and then switch to the **Type** tool from the **Tools** panel.

3. Click and drag across the canvas to create an area type text frame that occupies at least half the canvas area. Type `Giuseppe's` and then select all characters with the **Type** tool.

4. Go to the **Properties** panel and set **Font** to **Gelato Luxe**, **Style** to **Regular**, **Font Size** to `900` pt, **Leading** to **Auto**, and **Tracking** to `0`. Set **Alignment** to **Centered**. Click on the **Set text color** thumbnail and enter `26befd` into the **Hexadecimal** field to create a light blue. Finally, click **OK**:

Figure 9.30: The base type formatting when using the Gelato Luxe font

5. Resize the text frame so that it's as small as possible without hiding any characters. Click on the **Commit changes** button in the **Options** bar to complete the text frame edits. Change **Blend Mode** for the text layer to **Linear Burn** to help blend the text in with the white brickwork.

6. Right-click on the text layer's name and choose **Convert to Smart Object** from the list of commands. This will allow the displacement filter to be applied nondestructively as a smart filter.

Creating and applying the paint displacement map

To create the dripping effect, we need to create a displacement map that will pull parts of the text layer down the canvas, imitating paint. Follow these steps:

1. Go to **File → New**. Click on the **Web** text tab at the top of the dialog. Change the name of the document to PaintDisplace. Set its **Width** to 3840 px and **Height** to 2160 px and turn off the **Artboards** checkbox. Set **Background Contents** to **White** and then click on the **Create** button.

2. Right-click on the **Background** layer's name and choose **Convert to Smart Object**. Rename the layer Texture.

3. Press the *D* key to reset the **Foreground** and **Background** colors to black and white, respectively. Then, go to **Filter → Render Fibers**. When the dialog appears, set **Variance** to 15 and **Strength** to 6. Click **OK** when you're done.

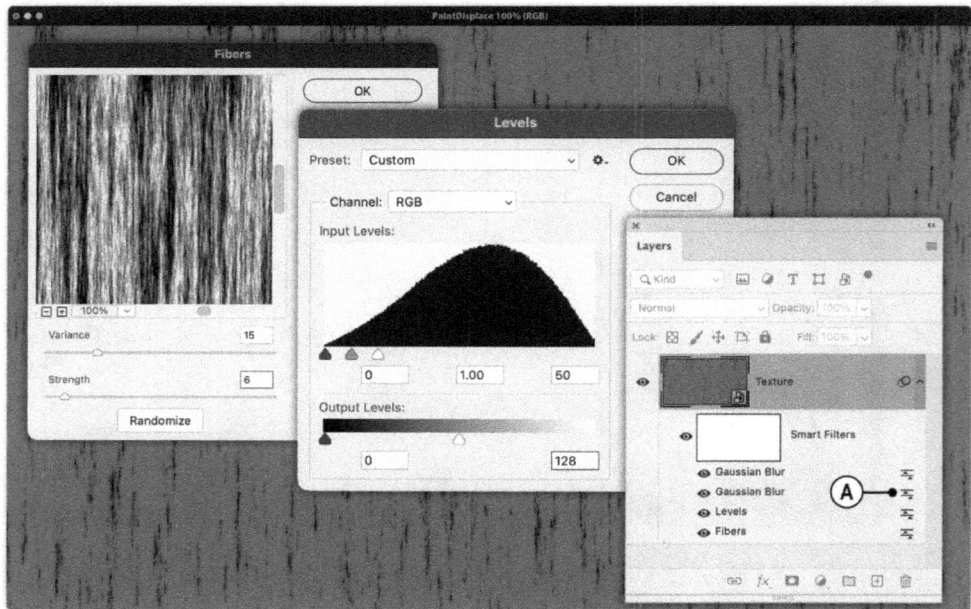

Figure 9.31: Fibers, Levels, and blur effects used to create a displacement map

4. Next, go to **Image → Adjustment → Levels**. You will see three numerical fields below the **Input Levels** graph. Enter 50 into the right-hand field to set the white point to increase the contrast and reduce the amount of black fiber marks. Under the **Output** fields at the bottom, change the white point to 128. We're doing this because displacement maps affect regions of an image that are black and white when applied, but a mid-tone gray will remain unaffected. Click **OK** when you're done to apply the edit.

5. Next, go to **Filter → Blur → Gaussian Blur**. When the dialog appears, set **Radius** to 5.0 px. Click **OK** when you're done. Double-click on the **Gaussian Blur Blend Mode** icon, adjacent to the filter name in the **Layers** panel (*Figure 9.31*, **A**). Change **Blend Mode** to **Darken** and click **OK**.

6. Then, apply a similar edit by going to **Filter → Gaussian Blur**. When the dialog appears, set **Radius** to 1.0 px. Click **OK** when you're done.

7. Go to **File → Save**, browse to the 09-Type folder, and save the document as a PSD file. Close the document when you're done.

8. With the DrippingPaint.jpg document open and active, ensure that the **Giuseppe's** Smart Object layer is active in the **Layers** panel.

9. Then, go to **Filter → Distort → Displace**. When the dialog appears, set **Horizontal Scale** to 0 and **Vertical Scale** to 100. This will ensure that the displacement map pulls pixels in the layer downward only. You can leave the other settings with their defaults. Click **OK** when you're done.

10. You will then be prompted to select an image to use as your displacement map. Choose PaintDisplace.psd and click **OK**. This will apply a subtle drag downward to the editable text.

11. You can use the same technique to intensify the effect by going to **Filter → Displace**, selecting the same document (PaintDisplace.psd), and clicking **OK**. Repeat this as many times as you require. In this example, the displacement was applied five times:

Figure 9.32: The effect of each of the five displacement maps once added

Refining the paint effect

You cannot predict how a displacement filter effect will look before you apply it. In the case of the dripping paint, some portions could be enhanced with a layer mask. Let's do this now.

1. Switch to the **Brush** tool by pressing the *B* key. Click on the **Brush Tip** menu from the **Options** bar. Click on the fly-out menu, shown as a cog icon in the top-right corner of the **Brush Tip** menu, and choose **Legacy** from the list.

2. Expand the **Legacy brush** folder when it appears, then expand the **Default Brushes** folder. Scroll down the list of brushes until you find **Dry Brush**. Click on it to make it active and increase its **Size** value to 100 px.

Figure 9.33: Masking out parts of the paint drips with the Brush tool

3.   Ensure **Opacity** is set to 100% in the **Options** bar and set **Black** under **Foreground Color** in the **Tools** panel. Click on the **Smart Filter** mask in the **Layers** panel that is assigned to the Smart Object you created with your text in it. Then, start to click and drag across the parts of the text in the image window that you wish to reveal.

4.   Save the document as a PSD in the 09-Type folder. Close the document when you're done.

Creating a graffiti typographic effect

This exercise combines several techniques to create a graffiti street art style, allowing you to consolidate some of the techniques we covered in earlier chapters under a different context. Again, the aim here is flexible, editable type effects.

Formatting the underlying type layer

As with previous exercises, we need to start with a type layer as the basis for our document artwork. Let's get started:

1. Open StreetArt.jpg from the 09-Type folder.

2. Press the *D* key to reset the colors to black and white and then switch to the **Type** tool from the **Tools** panel.

3. Click and drag across the canvas to create an area type text frame that occupies at least half the canvas area. Type Art and then select all characters with the **Type** tool.

4. Go to the **Properties** panel and set **Font** to **Subway New York SC**, **Style** to **Regular**, **Font Size** to 1000 pt, **Leading** to Auto, and **Tracking** to 0. Set **Alignment** to **Centered**. Click on the **Set text color** thumbnail, enter ffffff in the **Hexadecimal** field to define white text, and click **OK**:

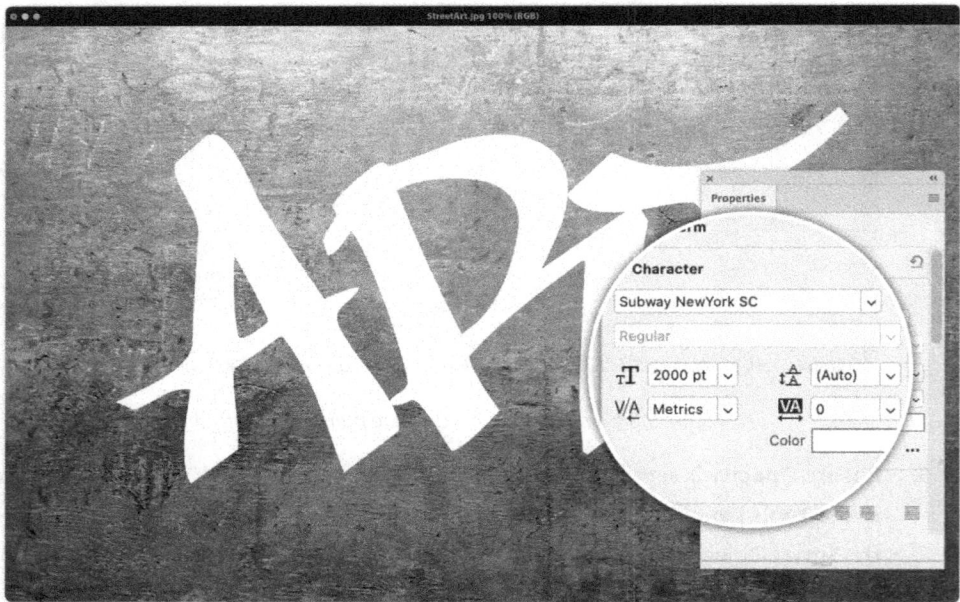

Figure 9.34: The base type formatting, using the Subway New York SC font

5. We need the text to be 2000 pt, but Photoshop doesn't allow a font size this large. The solution is to go to **Edit → Free Transform**, increase **Scale** to 200%, and click on the **Commit changes** button in the **Options** bar.

Creating long shadows

In *Chapter 5*, we utilized the **Actions** panel to record repetitive, tedious steps to save valuable time. Here, we will use it to create a long shadow effect:

1. Open the **Actions** panel by going to **Window → Actions**. Then, click on the **Create new set** icon at the bottom of the panel. Name the set Effects and click **OK** when you're done.

2. Click on the **Create new action** button at the bottom of the **Actions** panel, name it Long Shadow, ensure it is added to the **Effects** set, and click **Record**:

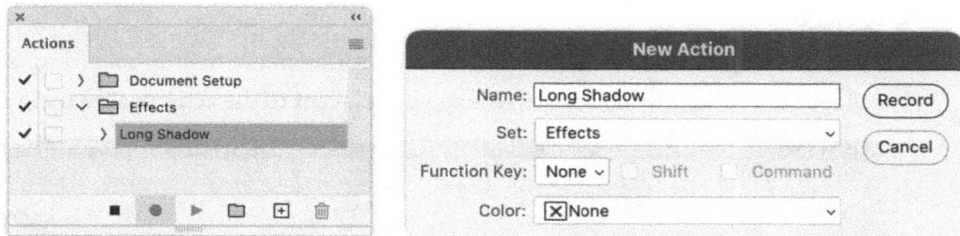

Figure 9.35: Creating a new action to record the long shadow effect

3. Hover your cursor over the **Art** type layer thumbnail and then press *Ctrl* (Windows) or *Cmd* (macOS) and click to select the type.

4. Then, go to **Select → Modify → Expand**, set the **Expand By** value to 20 pixels, and click **OK**.

5. Click on the **Create new layer** icon at the bottom of the **Layers** panel. Then, press *Ctrl + [* (Windows) or *Cmd + [* (macOS) to move the layer down one level in the stack, under the **Art** text layer.

6. Press the *D* key to reset the **Foreground** and **Background** colors, and then press *Alt + backspace* (Windows) or *Option + delete* (macOS) to fill the selection with black. Then, press *Ctrl + D* (Windows) or *Cmd + D* (macOS) to deselect.

7. Switch to the **Move** tool, then press the down arrow key once and the left arrow key once to move the layer one pixel down and one pixel to the left.

8. Create a duplicate of the layer by pressing *Ctrl + J* (Windows) or *Cmd + J* (macOS), then press *Ctrl + [* (Windows) or *Cmd + [* (macOS). After, press the down arrow key once and the left arrow key to extend the shadow effect.

9. Repeat the previous step a further eight times to generate the shadow effect. In total, you should now have 10 shadow layers. Next, we need to merge them into a single layer. Press *Alt + Shift + [* (Windows) or *Option + Shift + [* (macOS) nine times to select each of them in the layer stack. Then, press *Ctrl + E* (Windows) or *Cmd + E* (macOS) to merge them.

10. Create a duplicate of the merged shadow layer by pressing *Ctrl + J* (Windows) or *Cmd + J* (macOS), then press *Ctrl + [* (Windows) or *Cmd + [* (macOS). Then, press the *Shift +* down arrow key once and the *Shift +* left arrow key to extend the shadow effect 10 pixels down and to the left.

11. Repeat the previous step four times to complete the long shadow effect. Then, press *Ctrl + E* (Windows) or *Cmd + E* (macOS) to merge them. Rename the newly merged layer Shadow.

12. Press *Alt + Shift + [* (Windows) or *Option + Shift + [* (macOS) four times to select each of the shadow layers in the layer stack. Then, press *Ctrl + E* (Windows) or *Cmd + E* (macOS) to merge them.

13. Click the **Stop** button at the bottom of the **Actions** panel to stop recording and then collapse the actions by clicking on the toggle adjacent to the action name **Long Shadow**.

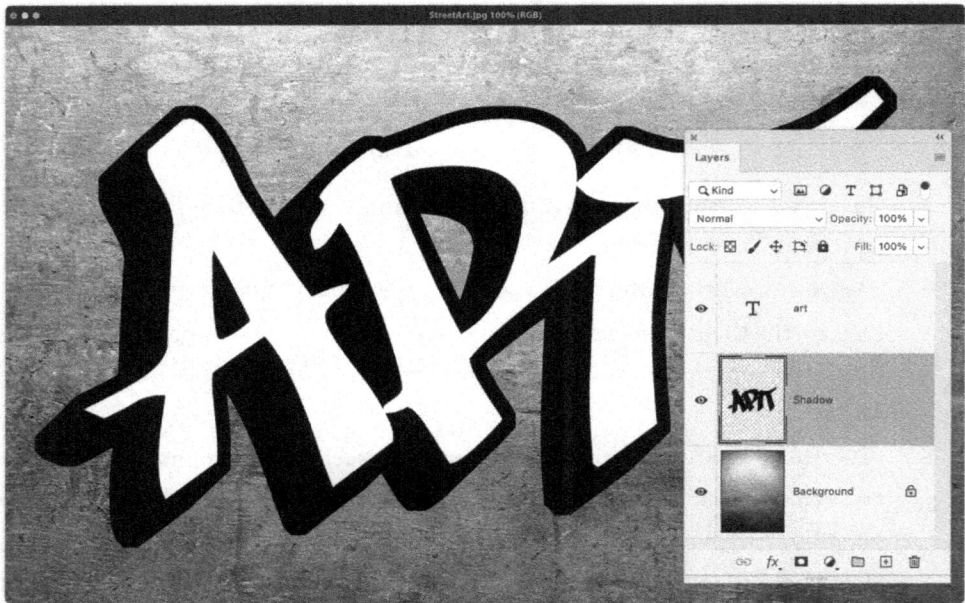

Figure 9.36: The completed long shadow effect

14. With the **Shadow** layer still active in the **Layers** panel, you can test the action you just created by clicking on the action's name and then clicking the **Play selection** button at the bottom of the **Actions** panel. This will create a second long shadow effect, building upon the first.

15. Make both shadow layers active in the **Layers** panel and press *Ctrl + E* (Windows) or *Cmd + E* (macOS) to merge them.

Adding spray paint effects to the text and shadows

Follow the steps given here:

1. Ensure the **Art** type layer is active in the **Layers** panel, then right-click on the layer's name and choose **Convert to Smart Object** from the list of commands. Change the layer's **Blend Mode** to **Dissolve**.

2. With the **Art** layer still active, go to **Filter** → **Blur Gallery** → **Field Blur**. When the **Blur Gallery** interface appears, you will see a single **Blur Widget** in the canvas. Drag the first **Blur Widget** (**A** in *Figure 9.37*) above the letter *R*, then change **Blur** to 60 px from the **Blur Tools** panel:

Figure 9.37: Field Blur combined with the Dissolve blend mode to create a spray paint effect

3. Hover your cursor above the letter *T* and click to add a second **Blur Widget** (**B**). Set the **Blur** value to 50 px.

4. Add a third **Blur Widget** to the right-hand side of the letter *T* (**C**) and set the **Blur** value to 5 px.

5. Add a fourth **Blur Widget** under the middle of all the letters (**D**) and set the **Blur** value to 35 px.

6. Finally, add a fifth **Blur Widget** inside the counter of the letter *R* (**E**) and set the **Blur** value to 10 px. Turn on the **High Quality** checkbox in the **Options** bar, and then click **OK** to apply the blur edits and close the interface.

7. Click on the **Shadow** layer in the **Layers** panel, then right-click on the layer's name and choose **Convert to Smart Object** from the list of commands. Change the layer's **Blend Mode** to **Dissolve**.

8. Next, hover your cursor over the **Smart Filter** mask named **Blur Gallery**, hold *Alt* (Windows) or *Option* (macOS), and then drag the smart filter onto the **Shadow** layer:

Figure 9.38: The Shadow layer with spray paint effects applied

9. Then, double-click on the **Blur Gallery** filter name that was assigned to the **Shadow** layer to open **Blur Gallery**. Change all **Blur Widget** values to 8 px and click **OK** to apply the edits.

10. If you wish to emphasize the spray paint effect on any part of the **Art** text or **Shadow** layer, you can add a layer mask and paint black into the mask. In the example shown, I used a **Soft Round** brush tip with a **Size** value of 600 px, **Hardness** set to 0%, and **Opacity** set to 30%. Focus on painting along the ends of the type characters to create a diffused spray paint effect.

11. Go to **File** → **Save** when you're done to capture all edits, saving it as a PSD file in the 08-Type folder. Close the document when you're done:

Figure 9.39: The completed graffiti effect

In this section, we used a variety of filters to recreate painterly effects such as spray paint and dripping paint. We also used actions to create long shadow effects that can be applied to editable text layers in the future for ease.

Summary

In this chapter, we leveraged Photoshop's powerful layer styles, filters, and effects to create visually arresting type layers. Each used a nondestructive workflow that allows for type to be edited without the need for us to recreate any effects.

First, we converted an editable type layer into a Smart Object, duplicated it, and then, using a layer mask, divided the text into two halves to form a slice effect. This enabled the type to remain editable, with any edits applied to either half automatically updating the other.

Then, we created a classic paper embossed effect with a combination of layer styles. On this occasion, the effects were added to a single layer group, where any content added to the group would be instantly styled with the embossed effects. This technique keeps the styling limited to a single item in the layer stack that can be updated with ease and allows for vector logos and text to be added or removed as required. Once removed from the layer group, the original layer's appearance is reinstated.

After that, we explored a faux 3D effect, which started with the primary text layer as a cutout effect. This was then copied and both layers were converted to Smart Objects. Each half was then distorted to create cut-out letters with gradient overlays to create highlights and shadow effects.

Then, we moved on to displacement maps to create a dripping paint effect. Using a combination of a fiber filter, level adjustments, and blur effects, we created a displacement map that was then applied multiple times to vertically distort the type layer to achieve the dripping paint effect. Again, the type and the distortion effects remained editable.

Finally, we looked at a technique for creating spray paint graffiti type by combining the dissolve blend mode with field blur effects.

In the next chapter, we will explore methods for creating interesting backdrops with patterns, gradients, and filter effects.

Get This Book's PDF Version and Exclusive Extras

UNLOCK NOW

Scan the QR code (or go to packtpub.com/unlock). Search for this book by name, confirm the edition, and then follow the steps on the page.

Note: Keep your invoice handy. Purchases made directly from Packt don't require one.

10

Creating Textures, Patterns, and Backdrops

Sometimes, even an extensive library of stock images can't provide that one special design aesthetic that you're looking for. That's when you can leverage Photoshop's textures, gradients, and patterns to turn a dull image into one that bursts with energy and visual interest.

Textures add a certain feel to the surface, which can be random or consistent. By using them as a subtle backdrop to your visuals, you can avoid the mundane feel of a solid color. Textures range from natural surfaces such as wood and stone to steel mesh. In the first section of this chapter, we will look at techniques to create textures from scratch and apply them to an image as a fill or with a painting tool.

Gradients combine two or more colors, blending them smoothly, like a sunset that transitions from deep blue to warmer orange and red tones on the horizon. Gradients are useful for adding emphasis or atmosphere to an image. We will explore techniques to create gradients using layer styles and the **Gradient** tool.

When we think of patterns, wallpaper is often the first thing that springs to mind – a repeating design with no visible joints or edges. In this chapter, we will create patterns with pixel and vector shapes with the **Pattern Maker**.

You will have the opportunity to integrate backdrops into existing compositions and experiment with a combination of layer styles, painting tools, and filters to create realistic effects such as star fields.

This chapter covers the following topics:

- Creating new textures, gradients, and patterns
- Managing preset assets
- Simulating environments with filters and effects

Technical requirements

The project files for this chapter can be found at https://packt.link/gbz/9781806021710.

Creating new textures, gradients, and patterns

Like most Photoshop projects, creating visually appealing designs begins with high-quality source content. However, in terms of textures, gradients, and patterns, we enjoy more flexibility because each of these can be created from scratch within the application.

Gradients are almost always generated via layer styles, layer overlays, or the Gradient tool. Textures and patterns can be generated from raster graphics or vector graphics.

Creating a texture from scratch

In the first exercise, we will create background artwork that comprises a texture, then a pattern, and finally, a gradient, using a combination of filters, layer overlays, and blend modes without any source imagery:

1. Go to **File → New**, click on the **Web** tab at the top of the dialog. Enter the name Road, then change the document width to 3840 px and the height to 2160 px. Turn off the **Artboards** checkbox and set **Background Contents** to **White**. Then, click on **Create** to generate the file.

2. Then, go to **Edit → Fill**. When the dialog appears, choose **50% Gray** from the **Contents** drop-down menu and click **OK**. This will fill the layer with a neutral gray that enhances the filters you will add in later steps.

3. Right-click on the **Background** layer name and choose **Convert to Smart Object** from the list of commands. Rename the layer Tarmac.

4. With the **Tarmac** layer still active, go to **Filter → Noise → Add Noise**. When the dialog appears, set **Amount** to 340%, set **Distribution** to **Gaussian**, and turn on the **Monochromatic** checkbox. Click **OK** when done:

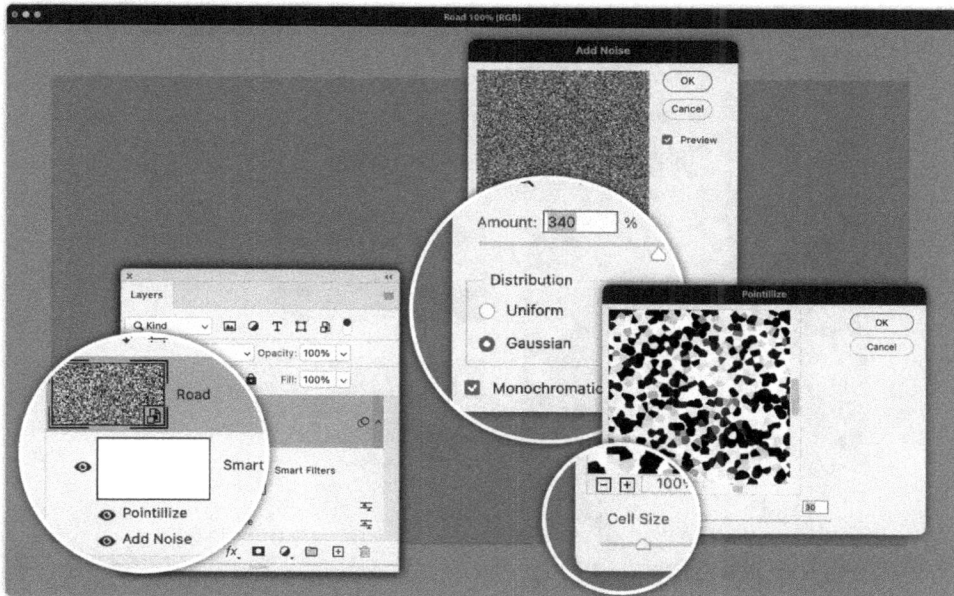

Figure 10.1: The gray layer with the Add Noise and Pointillize filters applied

5. Next, go to **Filter → Pixelate → Pointillize**. When the dialog appears, set **Cell Size** to 30, then click **OK** when done. The **Pointillize** filter turns the active layer content into a series of tiny dots.

6. With the **Tarmac** layer still active, go to **Filter → Filter Gallery**. When the dialog appears, expand the **Sketch** filters, and click on **Reticulation**. Set **Density** to 5, **Foreground Level** to 45, and **Background Level** to 5 to add a grainy effect to the layer:

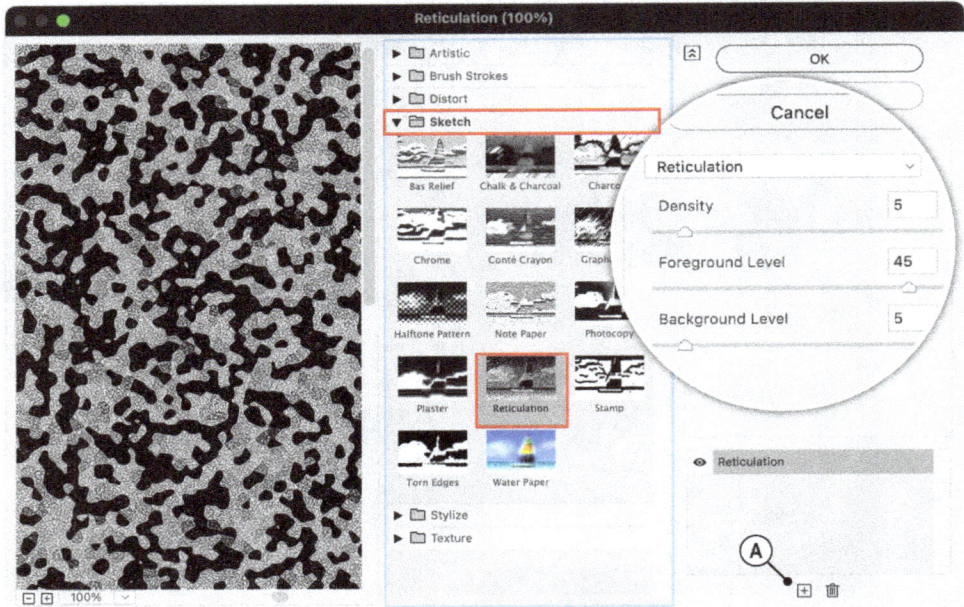

Figure 10.2: Filter Gallery, showing Reticulation settings

7. Click on the **New Effect layer** icon (**A** in *Figure 10.2*) at the bottom of the dialog to duplicate the first effect, replace it by expanding the **Artistic** filters, and then click on **Fresco**. Set **Brush Size** to 2, **Brush Detail** to 8, and **Texture** to 1.

8. Duplicate the effect by clicking on the **New Effect layer** icon at the bottom of the dialog to add an unedited copy to emphasize the original effect.

9. Click on the **New Effect layer** icon for a third time to duplicate the previous effect, replace it by expanding the **Texture** filters, and then click on **Craquelure**. Set **Crack Spacing** to 8, **Crack Depth** to 2, and **Crack Brightness** to 0 to add an irregular cracked surface effect. Finally, click **OK** to apply the edits and exit:

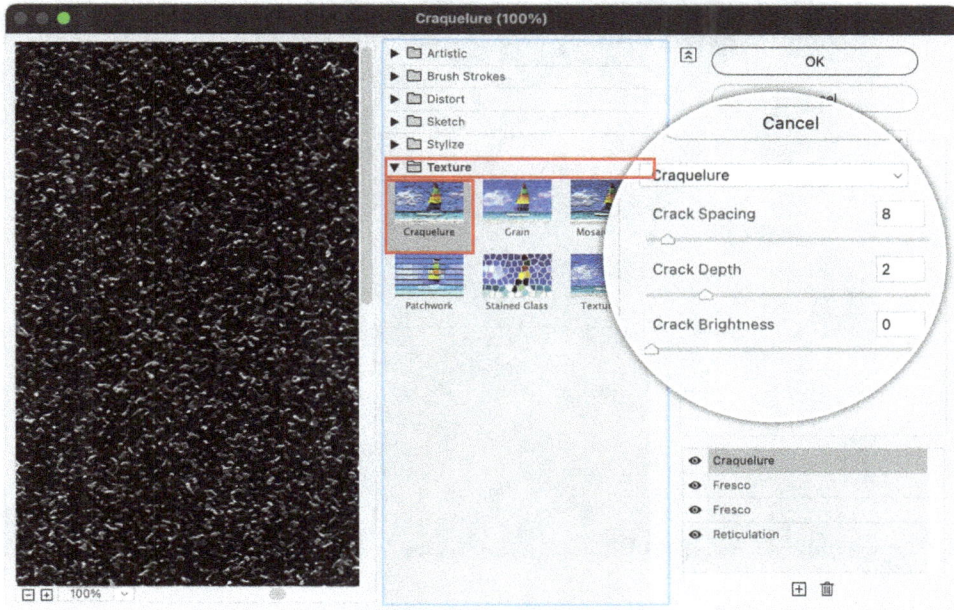

Figure 10.3: Filter Gallery showing the Craquelure settings

10. With the **Tarmac** layer still active, go to **Select** → **All**. Then, go to **View** → **Pattern Preview**. If a warning message appears, click **OK** to proceed to preview mode.

11. Next, open the **Patterns** panel by going to **Window → Patterns**. Then, click on the **New Pattern** icon (**A** in *Figure 10.4*) at the bottom of the **Pattern** panel. When the dialog appears, name the pattern Tarmac, and click **OK**:

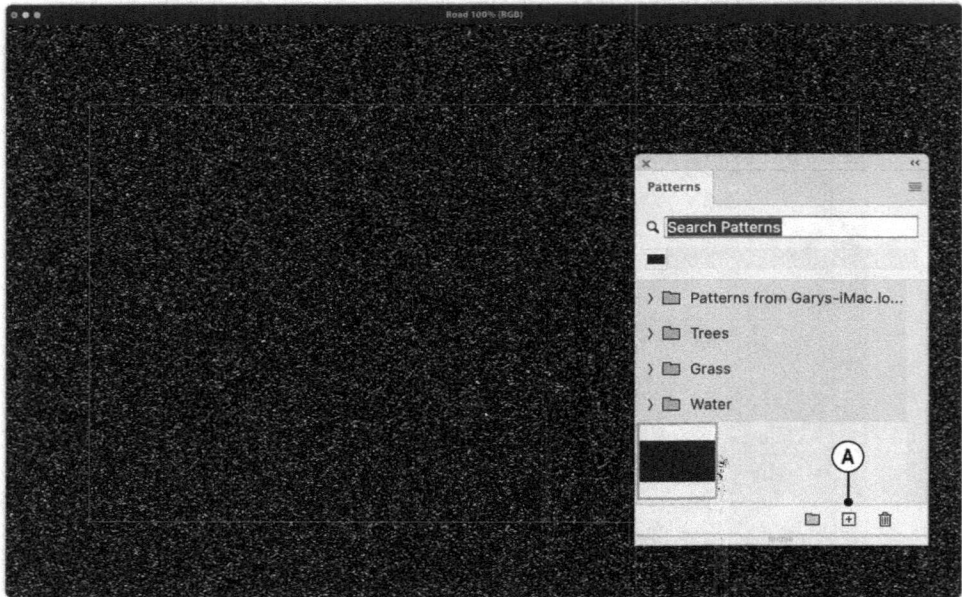

Figure 10.4: Create a tarmac pattern using Photoshop's pattern preview mode

12. Go to **View → Pattern Preview** to deactivate the mode and then go to **Select → Deselect**. You now have a saved pattern that can be applied to any document in the future, so let's test it out.

13. Head to the **Layers** panel and click on the **Create new fill or adjustment layer** icon; from the list of options, choose **Pattern**. When the dialog appears, click on the **Pattern picker** thumbnail to reveal the library, and then click on the **Tarmac** pattern, which will appear at the bottom of the list. Set **Scale** to 85%, and then click **OK**.

14. Next, we need to add a highlight across the surface of the tarmac. To achieve this, click on the **Fx** icon at the bottom of the **Layers** panel and select **Gradient Overlay** from the list of options.

15. When the **Layer Styles** dialog appears, set **Blend Mode** to **Overlay** and **Opacity** to 100%, turn on the **Align with Layer** checkbox, and set **Style** to **Linear**, **Angle** to 76%, and **Scale** to 128%:

Figure 10.5: Add a gradient overlay

16. Then, click on the **Gradient Preview** thumbnail (**A** in *Figure 10.5*) to open the **Gradient Editor** dialog. Click on the bottom-left **Color** stop and then click on the **Color** thumbnail lower down. Change the **Hexadecimal** value to 646464 and click **OK**.

17. Click on the bottom-right **Color** stop and click on the **Color** thumbnail lower down. Change **Hexadecimal** to ffffff and click **OK**.

18. Between the left and right **Color** stops is a midpoint, shown as a diamond symbol (**B**). Click on it to make it active and then change the **Location** value to 70%. Click **OK** to close the **Gradient Editor** dialog, return to **Layer Styles**, and click **OK** to apply the edits and close the dialog.

19. Switch to the **Rectangular Marquee** tool from the **Tools** panel. From the **Options** bar, set **Selection Mode** to **New**, **Feather** to 0 px, and **Style** to **Normal**.

20. Hover your cursor approximately 5% into the left edge of the canvas, but above the top of the canvas edge. Click and hold down the left mouse button to drag down beyond the bottom of the canvas. The widget adjacent to your cursor should inform you that the height of the selection is 2160 px. Drag across to the right-hand side until the width of the selection reads 160 px. Then, release the left mouse button to complete the selection.

21. From the **Options** bar, set **Selection Mode** to **Add**, and then create a second selection of the same size to the right-hand side of the original, leaving a gap of around the same width as the first selection.

22. Head to the bottom of the **Layers** panel and click on the **Create new fill or adjustment layer** icon; from the list of options, choose **Solid Color**. When the **Color Picker** dialog appears, set **Hexadecimal** to c2ad20, creating a deep yellow. Then, click **OK** when done.

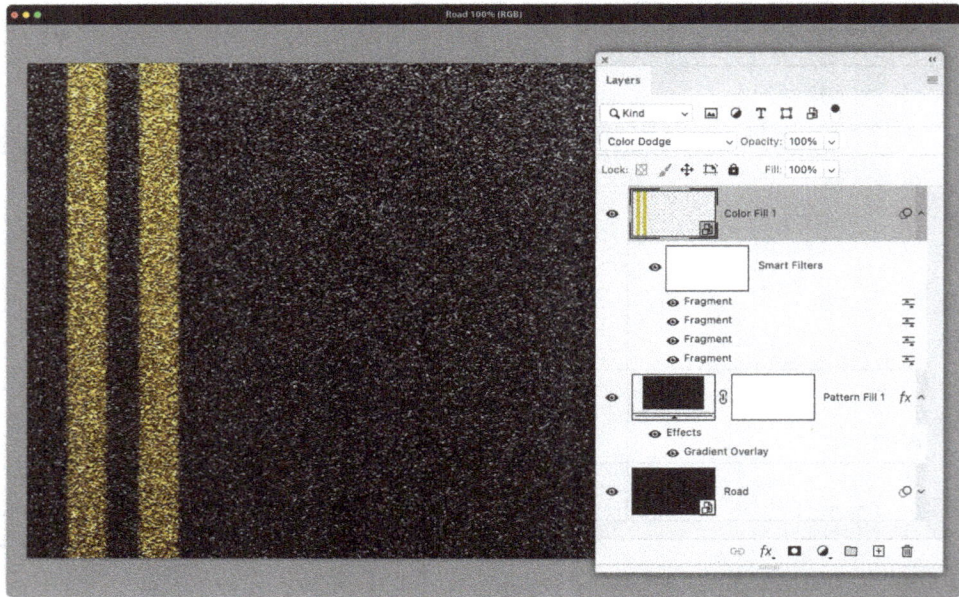

Figure 10.6: The road markings added via a color fill

23. Right-click on the **Color Fill** layer name in the **Layers** panel and choose **Convert to Smart Object** from the list of commands. Rename the layer Markings.

24. To roughen the lines slightly, go to **Filter → Pixelate → Fragment**. You can enhance the effect by duplicating it. Repeat this step until you are happy with the edge details. In our example, the filter was added four times.

25. Finally, change the layer **Blend Mode** to **Color Dodge**, and save the document in the 10-Backdrops folder as a PSD file. Close the document when done.

This form of backdrop can be used to add text to or, if you work with 3D models, provide the basis for a seamless texture that can be applied to your mesh. If you add editable text to images like this, convert the type layer to a Smart Object and use filters such as **Fragment** or a displacement map to make them look as though they are painted on a road surface.

Creating an atmospheric gradient backdrop

Gradients in Photoshop tend to be applied once, in isolation from one another, like the previous exercise. There are, however, ways that you can apply multiple gradients, overlapping them to achieve interesting effects using the **Gradient** tool:

1. Go to **File → New** and click on the **Web** tab across the top of the dialog. Enter the name `Atmospherics` and then change the document width to `3840` px and the height to `2160` px. Turn off the **Artboards** checkbox and set **Background Contents** to **White**. Then, click on **Create**.

2. Switch to the **Gradient** tool by pressing *G* to activate the correct group of tools in the **Tools** panel. If the **Gradient** tool isn't visible, click and long-hold on the active tool, which will be the **Paint Bucket** tool, to reveal the tool popup, and then click on the **Gradient** tool from the list.

3. From the **Options** bar, change **Gradient Mode** to **Classic gradient**. This will ensure you have access to blend modes, which is crucial for this technique. Click on the **Linear Gradient** button (**A** in *Figure 10.7*), which is active by default, select `Difference` from the **Blend Mode** menu, and set **Opacity** to `100%`. Turn off the **Reverse** checkbox but ensure that the **Dither** and **Transparency** checkboxes are active.

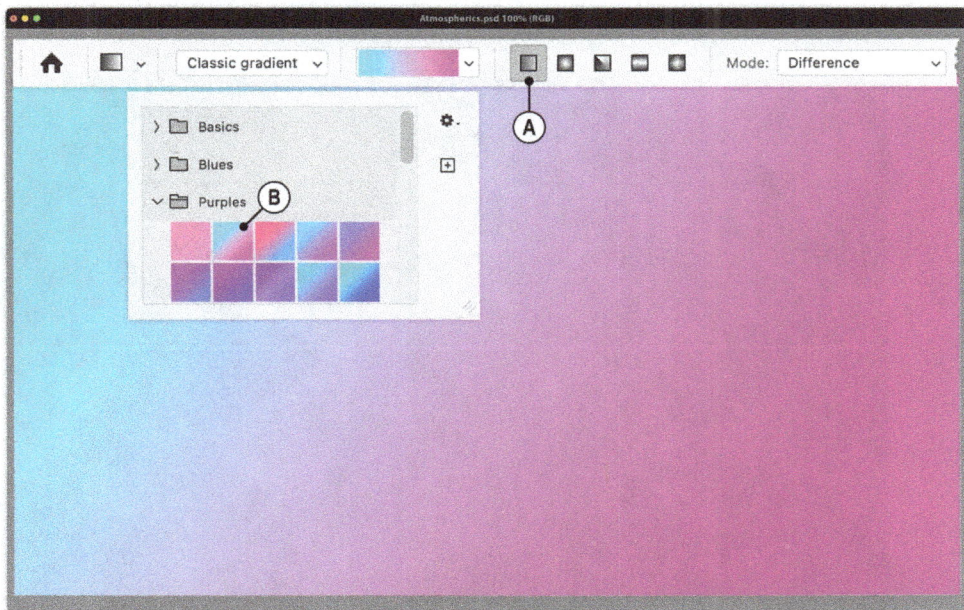

Figure 10.7: Define settings for the Gradient tool

4. Finally, we need to choose a color for our gradient. Click on the arrow adjacent to the gradient thumbnail in the **Options** bar to view **Gradient Presets**. From the folders that appear, expand **Purples**, and then click on the second thumbnail within that group, named Purple 2 (**B**).

5. With the **Background** layer active, hover your cursor over the top-left corner outside the canvas, click and drag down to the lower-right corner of the canvas, and then release the left mouse button to create the gradient. Now that you have color on the canvas, you can start experimenting.

6. Click and drag the **Gradient** tool from the lower-left side of the canvas to the upper-right side of the canvas and release the mouse. Instead of replacing the previous gradient, the active **Blend Mode** of Difference builds on it and inverts the colors, making them green, black, and red. However, if you drag a third time, from right to left, starting and finishing approximately a third of the way into the canvas, the purple and violet hues will be restored.

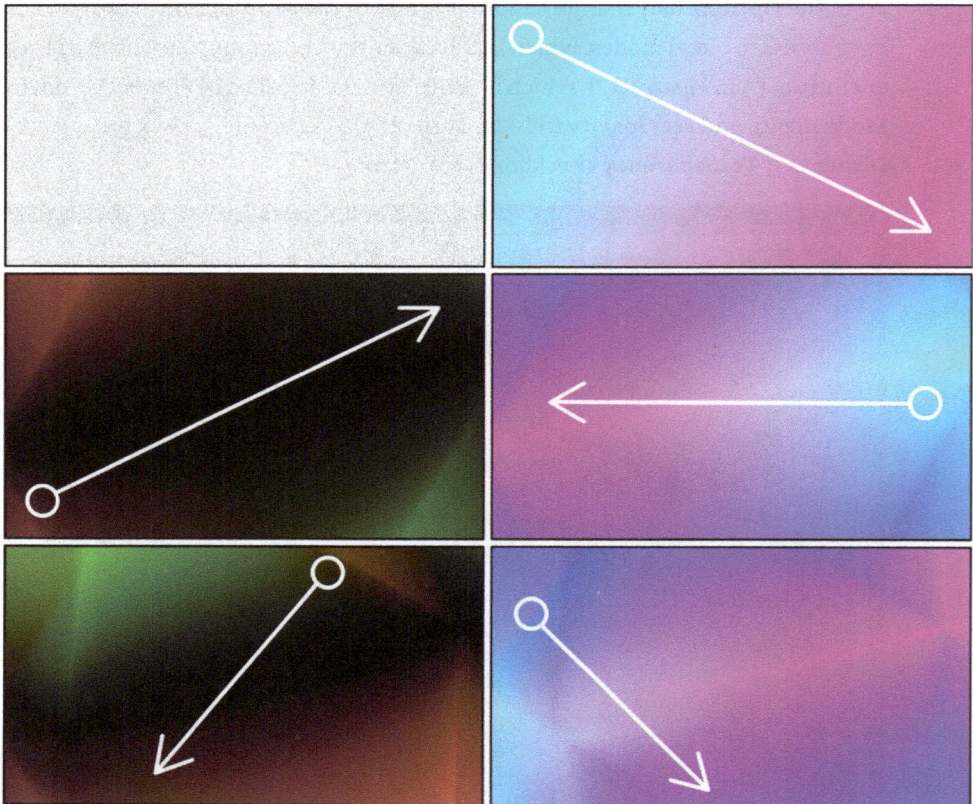

Figure 10.8: The length and direction of each gradient

7. Experiment further by dragging across the image in different directions. Remember that the further you drag across the image, the smoother the gradient will be. However, you can also try dragging over a short distance to add a short but pronounced transition.

8. If you like the effect but want to experiment further, create a new layer and carry on using the same technique. You can also try changing the gradient preset. Save your document in the 10-Backdrops folder when you have finished.

Figure 10.9: The completed gradient backdrop

Creating pop-art-inspired artwork with custom patterns

Roy Lichtenstein's pop art is renowned for its imitation of print material, such as comic books, with vivid primary colors, halftone ink dots, and bold outlines. In this exercise, you will create your own dot patterns and use them to create a pop-art-inspired image:

1. Open Dots.psd from the 10-Backdrops folder. This document contains a series of shape layers, containing circles that have been arranged ready to be turned into a pattern and stored in a layer group.

2. Next, go to **Select → All**. Then, go to **View → Pattern Preview**. If a warning message appears, click **OK** to proceed to preview mode.

3. Next, open the **Patterns** panel by going to **Window → Patterns**. Then, click on the **New Pattern** icon at the bottom of the **Pattern** panel. When the dialog appears, name the pattern Red Dots, and click **OK**.

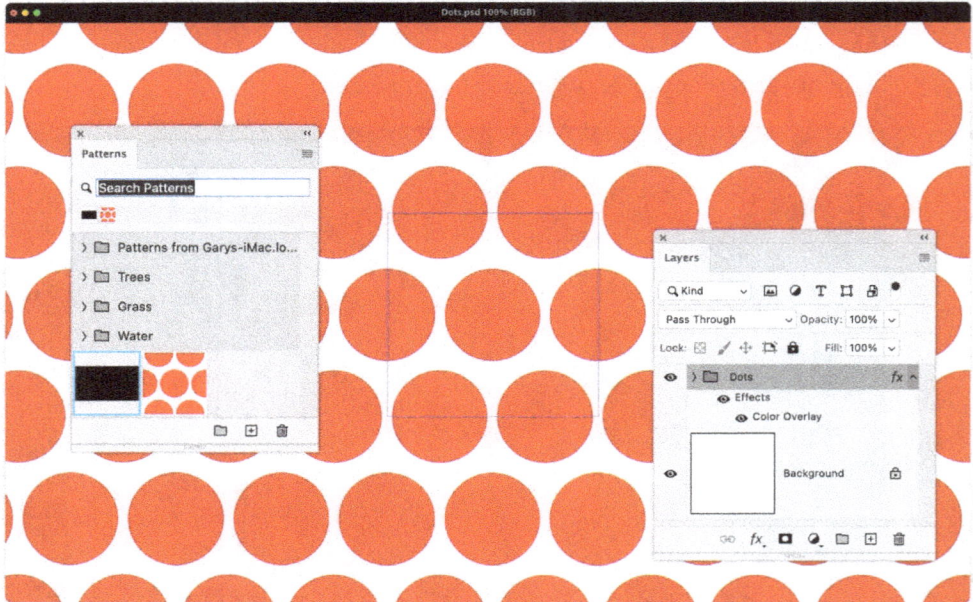

Figure 10.10: The red dotted pattern saved in the Patterns panel

4. Double-click on the **Color Overlay** effect that is assigned to the **Dots** layer group in the **Layers** panel. When the dialog appears, change the color to a yellow **Hexadecimal** value of F8E605. Click **OK** to update the color, and then click **OK** to apply the change to the layer.

5. Then, click on the **New Pattern** icon at the bottom of the **Pattern** panel. When the dialog appears, name the pattern Yellow Dots, and click **OK**.

6. Double-click on the **Color Overlay** effect once more and change the color to a blue **Hexadecimal** value of 3B86C7.

7. Once the change has been made to the color overlay, click on the **New Pattern** icon at the bottom of the **Pattern** panel. When the dialog appears, name the pattern Blue Dots, and click **OK**.

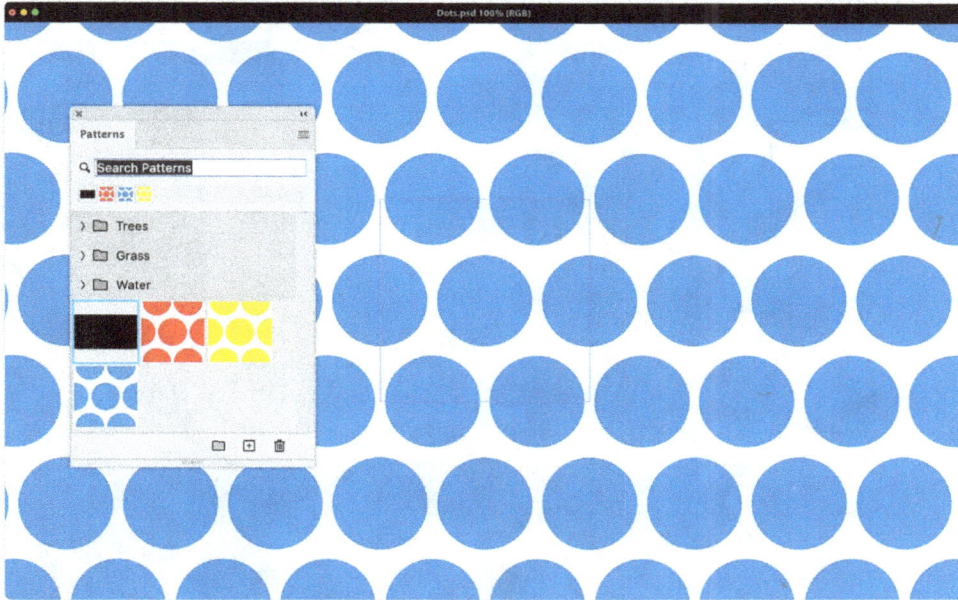

Figure 10.11: The red, yellow, and blue dots saved in the Patterns panel

8. Go to **View → Pattern Preview** to deactivate the mode and then go to **Select → Deselect**. Save and close the Dots.psd document.

9. **Open** PopArt.psd from the 10-Backdrops folder. This document contains several shape layers that need the patterns you've just created applied to the designs.

10. Press *A* to activate the correct group of tools in the **Tools** panel. If the **Path Selection** tool isn't visible, click and long-hold on the active tool, which will be the **Direct Selection** tool, to reveal the tool popout, and then click on the **Path Selection** tool.

11. Click on the Bang 4 shape layer in the **Layers** panel to make it active. From the **Options** bar, click on the **Fill** icon, and then open the **Set fill type** dialog. Click on the **Pattern** icon to change the fill type, and then select the **Red Dots** pattern you created earlier, setting **Scale** to 25%:

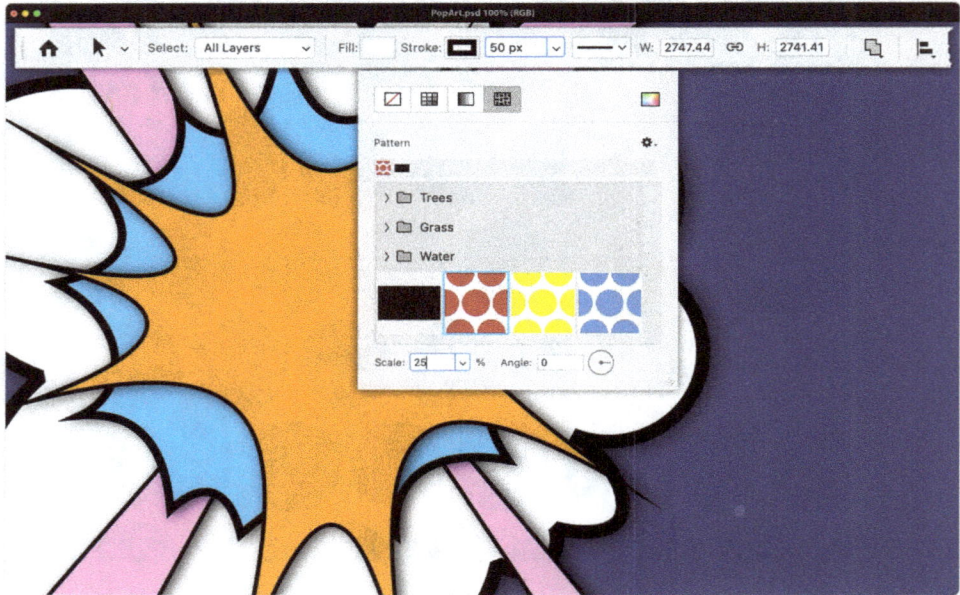

Figure 10.12: Apply the red dots pattern to the shape layer

12. Click on the Bang 2 shape layer in the **Layers** panel. Then, apply the Blue Dots pattern, again setting the scale of the pattern to 25%. Feel free to experiment with other shape layers and patterns. Save and close the document when done.

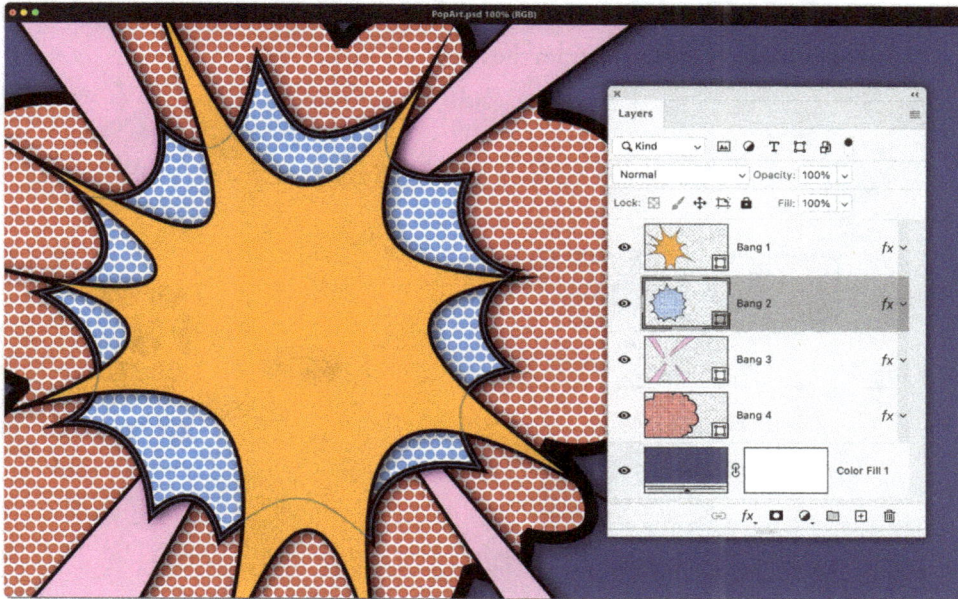

Figure 10.13: The completed pop-art image

In this section, we looked at techniques to create a texture, patterns, and gradients, using methods such as a painting tool, shape fills, and adjustment layers. In the next section, we will integrate backdrops into project files.

Managing backdrop assets

You don't have to create textures, gradients, and patterns every time you need to use them; you can download and import them or store them in Creative Cloud Libraries.

Adding assets with Creative Cloud libraries

Adobe introduced a handy sync feature in Photoshop that allowed users to store presets, such as patterns, brushes, and gradients, making them available in Photoshop when logged into Creative Cloud. Sadly, this feature was removed in February 2025. However, you can add presets such as patterns and gradients to Creative Cloud Libraries using the following technique:

1. Create a new document in Photoshop. In this scenario, I often click on the **Web** tab and select the **Web Large** preset, which is 1920px x 1080px.

2. In the **Layers** panel, click on the **Create new fill or adjustment Layer** icon (**A** in *Figure 10.14*) and select **Pattern...** from the list:

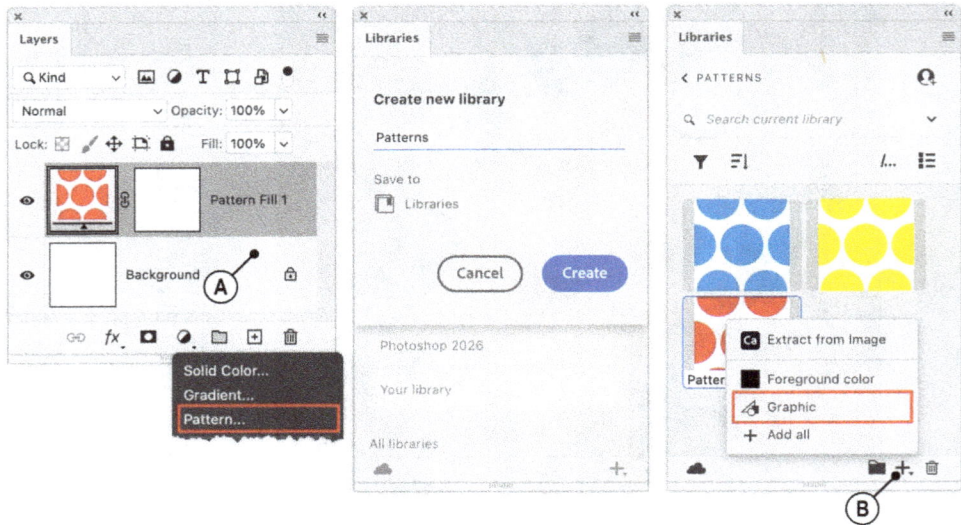

Figure 10.14: Add assets to Creative Cloud Libraries

3. When the dialogue appears, select the pattern you wish to add to a library and click **OK**.

4. From the **Libraries** panel, click **Create new library** and enter a name for the library, such as Patterns.

5. Ensure the **Pattern** layer is active in the **Layers** panel, and then click the **Add Elements** button (**B** in *Figure 10.14*). From the popup, select **Graphic**. This will add the entire layer to the library, including the assigned pattern swatch. Keep adding more assets to your library as needed.

6. To reuse the pattern in the future, hold *Alt* (Windows) or *Option* (macOS) as you drag the asset from the **Libraries** panel onto the layer stack in the active document. This creates a new pattern layer that can be edited just like the original.

Importing and exporting assets

If you prefer to keep a local backup of assets such as patterns and gradients, you can export them as a file. In the following steps, we will examine exporting patterns; however, the process is identical for other asset types.

1. Select the patterns you wish to export in the **Patterns** panel.

2. Click on the **Panel** flyout menu, found at the top right-hand side of the **Patterns** panel. Choose **Export Selected Patterns…**.

3. Browse to the folder where you wish to export the assets and click **Save** when you are done.

4. To import assets such as patterns, click on the **Patterns** panel's flyout menu. Choose **Import Patterns…**:

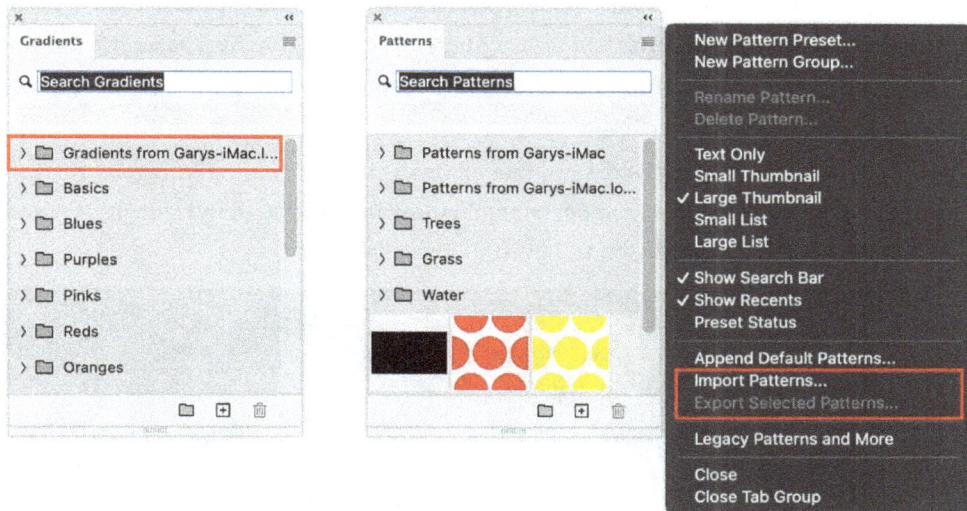

Figure 10.15: Importing and exporting assets such as patterns

5. Browse to the folder where your patterns are stored, select the desired file, and click **Open** when done.

In this section, we examined the process of sharing assets, such as patterns, gradients, and swatches, on Creative Cloud, making them accessible to you wherever you log in with your Adobe ID. We also reviewed techniques for importing and exporting assets to a folder. In the next section, you will create an entire space scene using only filters, effects, and painting tools, without relying on source images.

Simulating environments with filters and effects

In the last exercise of this chapter, you are going to create a space scene using only filters, effects, and brushes. First, we need to create stars, both large and small, as our backdrop, and then add a nebula with the focal point of a starburst:

1. Go to **File** → **New** and click on the **Web** tab at the top of the dialog. Enter the name Atmospherics and then change the document width to 1920 px and the height to 1080 px. Turn off the **Artboards** checkbox and set **Background Contents** to **Black**. Then, click on **Create**.

2. With the **Background** layer still active, right-click on the layer name, choose **Convert to Smart Object** from the list of options, and rename the layer Stars SMALL.

3. Go to **Filter** → **Noise** → **Add Noise**. When the dialog appears, set **Amount** to 25% and **Distribution** to **Gaussian**, and then turn on the **Monochromatic** checkbox. Click **OK** when done.

4. Next, go to **Filter** → **Blur** → **Gaussian Blur**. When the dialog appears, set **Amount** to 0.3 px, and click **OK** when done.

5. We now need to reduce the number of small stars by going to **Image** → **Adjustment** → **Levels**. When the dialog appears, set **Shadow Input** to 86 (**A** in *Figure 10.16*), **Midtone** to 1.00, and **Highlight Input** to 113 (**B**). Then, click **OK**:

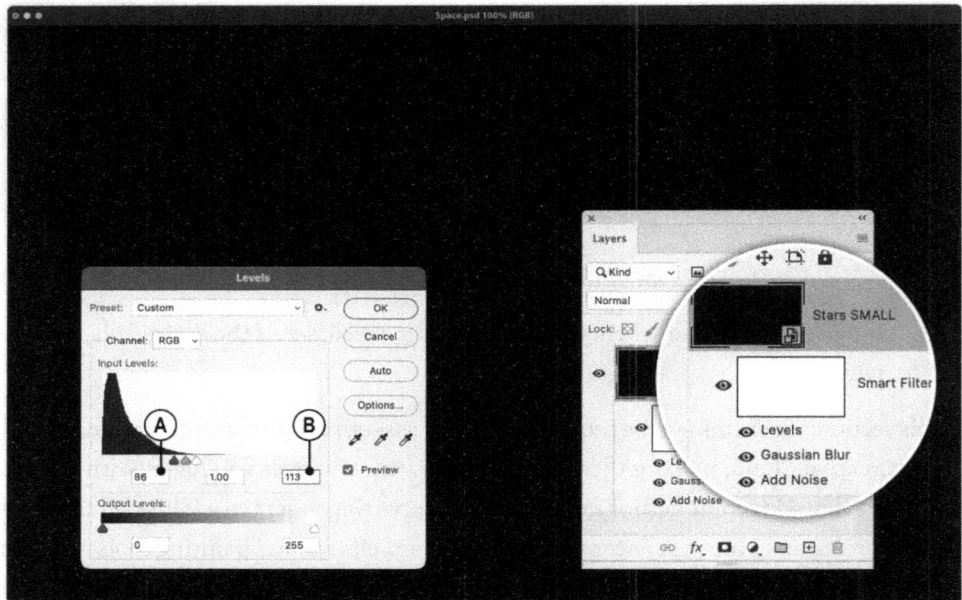

Figure 10.16: Add a noise filter

6. Drag the **Stars SMALL** layer onto the **New Layer** icon at the bottom of the **Layers** panel to duplicate it. Rename the layer Star BUILDER. Right-click on the **Star SMALL** layer visibility icon and color-code the layer red to help differentiate it.

7. Double-click on the **Gaussian Blur** text label, assigned to the newly duplicated **Star BUILDER** layer in the **Layers** panel. When the dialog appears, increase **Amount** to 1.2 px, and click **OK** when done.

8. Double-click on the **Levels** text label assigned to the newly duplicated **Star BUILDER** layer in the **Layers** panel. Set **Shadow Input** to 51, **Midtone** to 1.00, and **Highlight Input** to 57. Then, click **OK**.

9. With the white portions created that form the basis of our **Star BUILDER**, we now need to turn them into a selection so that we can add an outer glow to them. Go to **Window → Channels**, and hover your cursor over the **RGB** composite thumbnail, which combines all color data in the visible image. Hold *Ctrl* (Windows) or *Cmd* (macOS) as you click on the **RGB** thumbnail (**A** in *Figure 10.17*). The selection will now appear around each of the white pixels in the image.

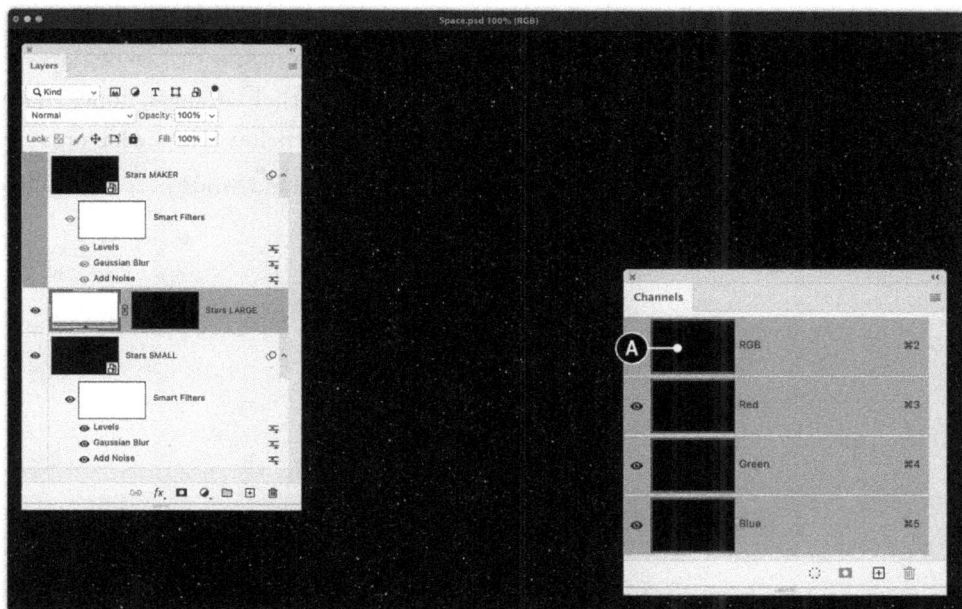

Figure 10.17: Use the Channels panel to select white pixels

10. Go to the bottom of the **Layers** panel, click on the **New fill or adjustment** layer, and select **Solid color** from the list. When the **Color Picker** dialog appears, choose white by entering ffffff into the **Hexadecimal** field, and then click **OK**. Rename the new color fill layer Stars Large.

11. Move the **Star BUILDER** layer up to the top of the **Layers** stack and hide it by clicking on the layer visibility icon. You should now have just three layers in the **Layers** panel.

12. Click on the **Stars Large** layer to make it active, click on the **Fx** icon at the bottom of the **Layers** panel, then select **Outer Glow** from the list. When the **Layer Style** dialog box appears, set **Blend Mode** to **Screen**, **Opacity** to 45%, **Noise** to 0%, **Spread** to 0%, **Size** to 16 px, and **Range** to 29%. Then, click **OK**.

13. Turn on layer visibility for the **Star BUILDER** layer, and rename it Star COLOURS. Drag the **Levels** adjustment assigned to it onto the **Delete** button at the bottom of the **Layers** panel to remove it.

14. Double-click on the **Add Noise** filter assigned to the **Star COLOURS** layer to edit it. When the dialog appears, set **Amount** to 350% and **Distribution** to **Gaussian**, and turn off the **Monochromatic** checkbox to create random colored noise. Then, click **OK**.

15. Double-click on the **Gaussian Blur** filter assigned to the **Star COLOURS** layer to edit it. When the dialog appears, set **Amount** to 1.7 px, and click **OK** when done. This will blur the noise just enough to recolor the stars in the layers below it in the **Layers** stack.

16. With the **Star COLOURS** layer still active, change its **Blend Mode** property to Color from the **Layers** panel.

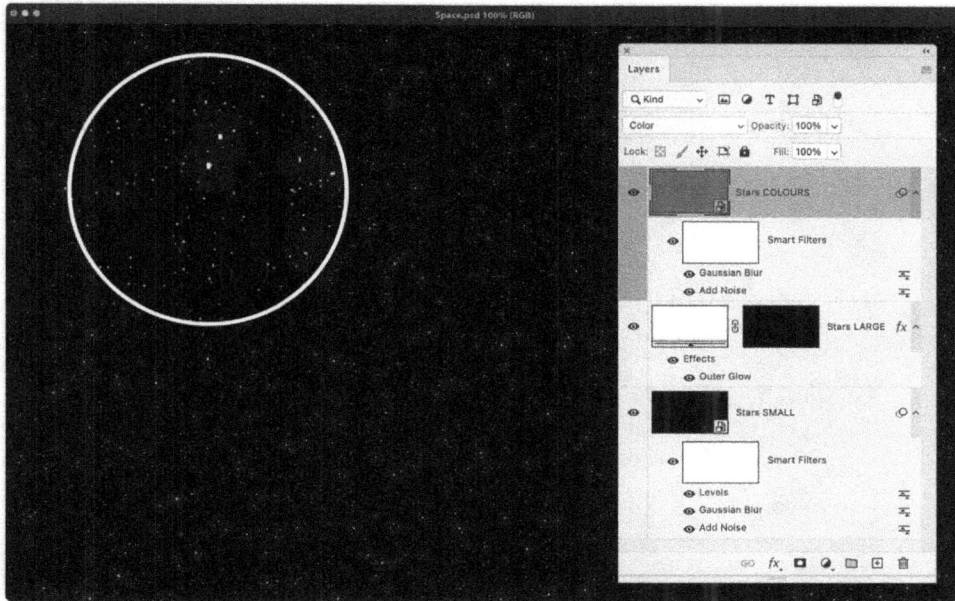

Figure 10.18: The stars with random colors applied

17. Next, go to **Select → All Layers** and press *Ctrl + G* (Windows) or *Cmd + G* (macOS) to add the star layers into a new **Layer** group. Name the new group `Stars`.

18. Add a new layer to the **Layers** panel and name it `Nebula Clouds`. Go to **Edit → Fill**; when the dialog appears, choose **Black** from the **Contents** drop-down menu, and click **OK**. Right-click on the layer name and choose **Convert to Smart Object** from the list of options.

19. Press the *D* key to reset the **Foreground** and **Background** colors in the **Tools** panel so that the clouds we generate will be grayscale. Go to **Filter → Render → Clouds**.

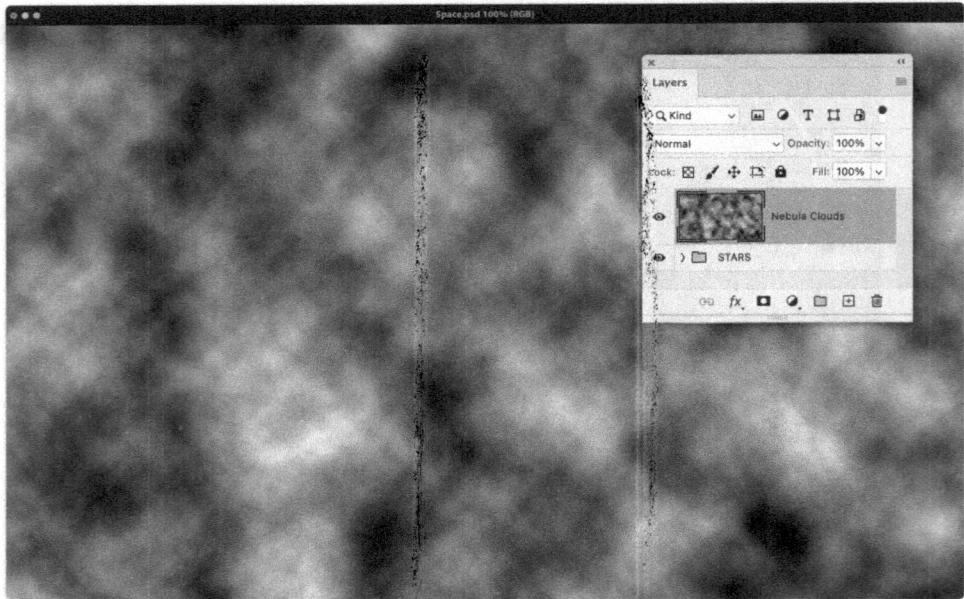

Figure 10.19: The render clouds filter

20. Change the **Blend Mode** property of **Nebula Clouds** to **Color Dodge** from the **Layers** panel. Add another new layer to the **Layers** panel and name it Nebula Colour. Drag it below the Nebula Clouds layer in the **Layer** stack.

21. Switch to the **Brush** tool by pressing the *B* key. Click on the **Brush Tip Preset** menu in the **Options** bar, select **Soft Round brush** from the list. Ensure **Hardness** is set to 0% and **Opacity** is set to 10%.

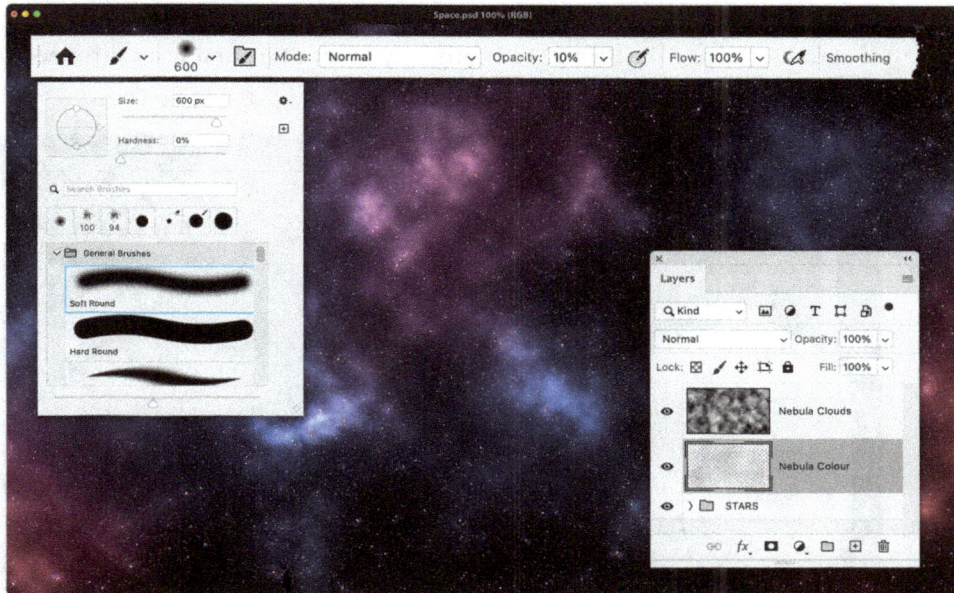

Figure 10.20: Paint blue and red onto the Nebula layer

22. Click on the **Foreground Color** swatch in the **Tools** panel to define the brush color. When the dialog appears, enter 25538b in the **Hexadecimal** field to create a light blue, and click **OK**.

23. Hover your **Brush** tool cursor over the canvas and click in different areas of the image to reveal the blue-colored clouds. Experiment with the placement of your brush clicks to add a nebula cloud.

24. Try changing the **Foreground Color** swatch to f43f4c to create a light red color and click **OK**. Click on random sections of the image with the **Brush** tool.

25. Click on the Nebula Cloud layer to make it active. Add another new layer to the **Layers** panel and name it Starburst. Ensure that it is at the top of the **Layer** stack.

26. Go to **Edit → Fill**; when the dialog appears, choose **Black** from the **Contents** drop-down menu, and click **OK**.

27. Then, right-click on the layer name and choose **Convert to Smart Object** from the list of options. Change the **Blend Mode** property of the **Starburst** layer to **Screen** from the **Layers** panel.

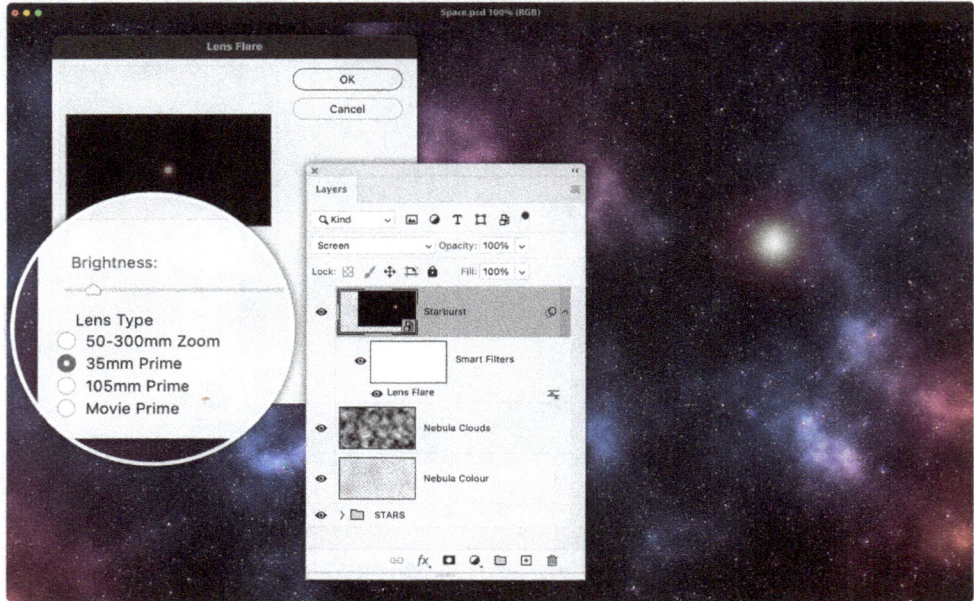

Figure 10.21: The lens flare filter

28. Go to **Filter → Render → Lens Flare**. When the dialog appears, select **35mm prime**. Then, hover your cursor over the center of the preview window and click to set the center of the canvas as the place where it will be added. We need to create the effect of a star; however, clicking around the edges of the preview creates a flare, like those created by the lens of a camera, which is not required in this scenario. Set **Brightness** to 30% and click **OK**.

29. The star will appear in the center of the canvas. You can now move the **Starburst** layer to any part of the image. If you wish to edit the **Lens Flare** properties, simply double-click on the **Lens Flare** text label under the **Starburst** layer in the **Layers** panel.

30. Save the document in the 10-Backdrops folder as a PSD file and close the file when done.

In the final section of this chapter, we have created an entire space scene made from a combination of Photoshop filters, layer styles, blend modes, and the **Brush** tool, all without the need for source photographs.

Summary

In this chapter, we focused on creating backdrops to complement a design, particularly in scenarios where stock images do not meet our needs or when we require greater control over content.

The key features to create backdrops were textures, patterns, and gradients, with the help of Photoshop's filters and effects. We first experimented with a combination of textures, patterns, and gradients to create a road surface backdrop. This provided an opportunity to see how each process works within Photoshop.

We then created abstract artwork using the **Gradient** tool. Changing the blend mode allowed us to combine several gradients to form subtle geometric shapes and lines against a light background.

We then moved on to creating patterns, taking a red dot and turning it into a seamless pattern with the help of Photoshop's **Pattern Preview** feature. These patterns were saved in the **Patterns** panel and used to complete a pop-art-inspired image.

We also looked at methods to import, synchronize, and export assets such as patterns through preference settings, Creative Cloud, and locally stored library files.

Finally, we applied all that we learned to create an entire space scene using only filters, effects, and painting tools, with no source assets. We created a star field by adapting a noise filter and created clouds that could be turned into a colorful nebula by painting with cool and warm colors using the **Brush** tool. The image was given a focal point with the inclusion of a lens flare effect to create a nearby star.

In the next chapter, we will continue exploring brushes as we examine libraries of brush tips, as well as creating our own brush tips and brush effects.

11

Creating and Applying Brushes

Brushes are an integral part of day-to-day editing in Photoshop. Whether it's one of the handful of brush tools themselves, or the **Clone Stamp** or **Healing Brush** tools, the brush tip and style have a profound impact on the results you achieve.

Photoshop ships with an extensive library of brush tips ranging from the default soft and hard round brush tips for general-purpose mark-making to leaf and grass brushes, which are applied randomly to achieve a natural look. With a little adaptation, these brush tips will serve you well. As such, you could be forgiven for just sticking with this default set of brush libraries; however, you can also download and create your own.

The process of creating custom brush tips is relatively quick and simple. As we get started in this chapter, you will first create a flock of birds from custom brush tips from a black and white image. This will allow you to add a focal point to a photo and bring the image to life.

Progressing further, we'll experiment by sampling real-world brush marks as source shapes for our Photoshop brush tips. We'll then apply them to more obscure features, such as the **Art History Brush** tool, and randomize the size, spacing, color, and angle of each individual brush mark.

By the end of this chapter, you will be able to create, edit, import, and export a brush tip preset, apply brush marks for creative effects, and retouch images by adding snowflakes. In this chapter, you will explore the following topics:

- Creating and managing brush tip presets
- Modifying brush properties
- Applying brushes for creative effect
- Using brushes for retouching

Technical requirements

The project files for this chapter can be found at https://packt.link/gbz/9781806021710.

Creating and managing brush tip presets

Most of the brushes you use in Photoshop are derived from a single grayscale image. White regions of the source image become transparent, while darker shades of gray become brush marks that you can change the color of as required.

Photoshop ships with an extensive library of brushes, yet many are relegated to the brush tip preset popup and are challenging to locate, such as the hidden gem called **Legacy Brushes**. You can revive legacy brushes by clicking on the brush preset popup (**A** in *Figure 11.1*). Then, click on the cog icon (**B**) to display the settings menu, and then click on **Legacy Brushes** (**C**). Legacy brushes will appear as a folder at the bottom of the brush preset pop-up list.

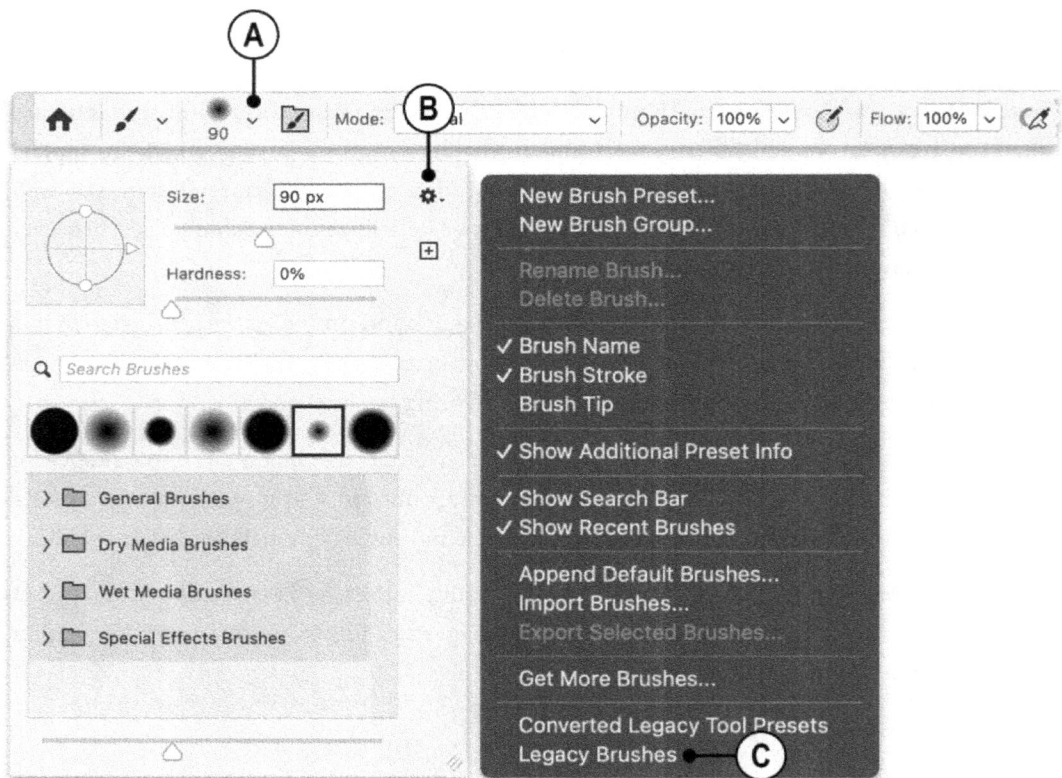

Figure 11.1: Importing brush libraries and restoring Legacy Brushes

Creating a custom bird brush

Let's start with a simple example of creating a custom brush in this first exercise. You'll create a set of custom bird brushes to add visual interest to the source image:

1. Go to **File → Open** and browse to the 11-Brushes folder. Select Flock.jpg and then click **Open**. The image contains a flock of birds.

2. Right-click on the **Background** layer under **Layers** and choose **Convert to Smart Object** from the list of options. Rename the layer to Source.

3. Then, go to **Image → Adjustments Levels**. Set the **Shadow Input** value to 14 and **Highlight Input** to 185. This will turn the background into a bright white. Click **OK** when done:

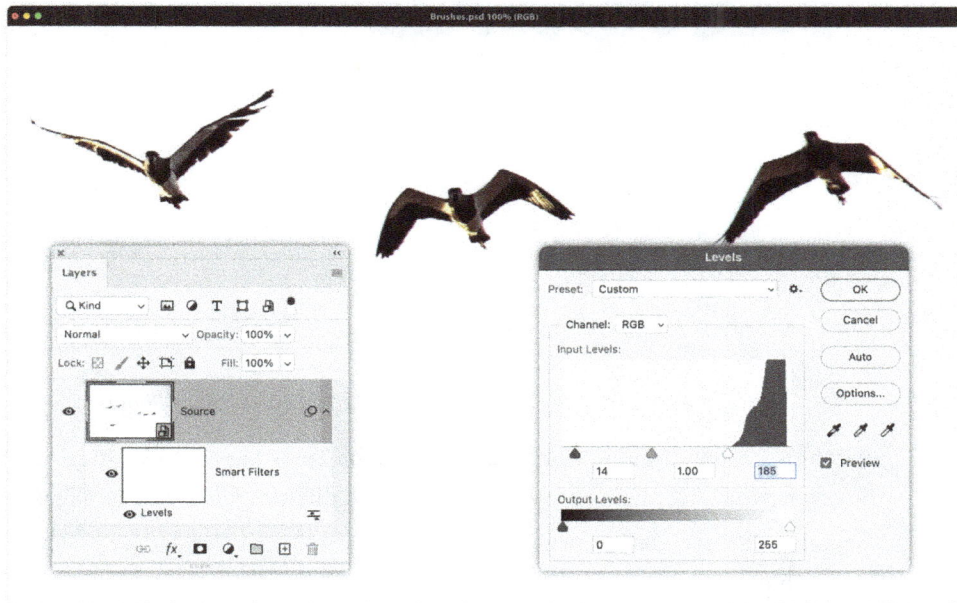

Figure 11.2: Removing any background details to prevent them from appearing in the brush tip

4. Switch to the **Rectangular Marquee** tool from the **Tools** panel. Set the selection mode to **New**, **Feather** to 0, and **Style** to **Normal**. Create a selection around one of the birds in the image, leaving a generous border around it so that when the brush tip is created, it will have a transparent border.

5. Then, go to **Edit → Define Brush Preset**. When the **Brush Name** dialog appears, enter the name bird 1. Click **OK** when done. The brush preset will now be saved to the **Brushes** panel and is ready to use. Select it from the brush tip pop-up menu when a painting tool is active.

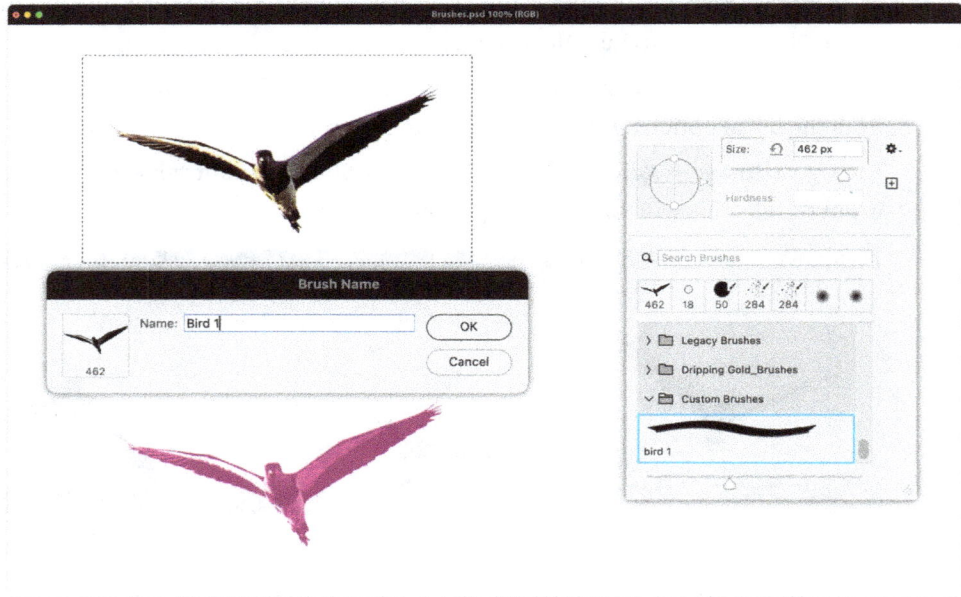

Figure 11.3: The selected artwork captured as a brush tip in Photoshop

6. Switch to the **Rectangular Marquee** tool from the **Tools** panel. Hover your cursor inside the active selection, allowing you to drag it over a different bird with an alternative pose.

7. Then, go to **Edit → Define Brush Preset**. When the **Brush Name** dialog appears, name the brush tip bird 2 and click **OK**.

8. With the **Rectangular Marquee** tool still active, drag the selection over a different bird with a different pose from the previous two.

9. Then go to **Edit → Define Brush Preset**. When the **Brush Name** dialog appears, name the brush tip bird 3 and click **OK**.

10. Save the document in the 11-Brushes folder as a PSD file and close the document when done, as it is no longer required.

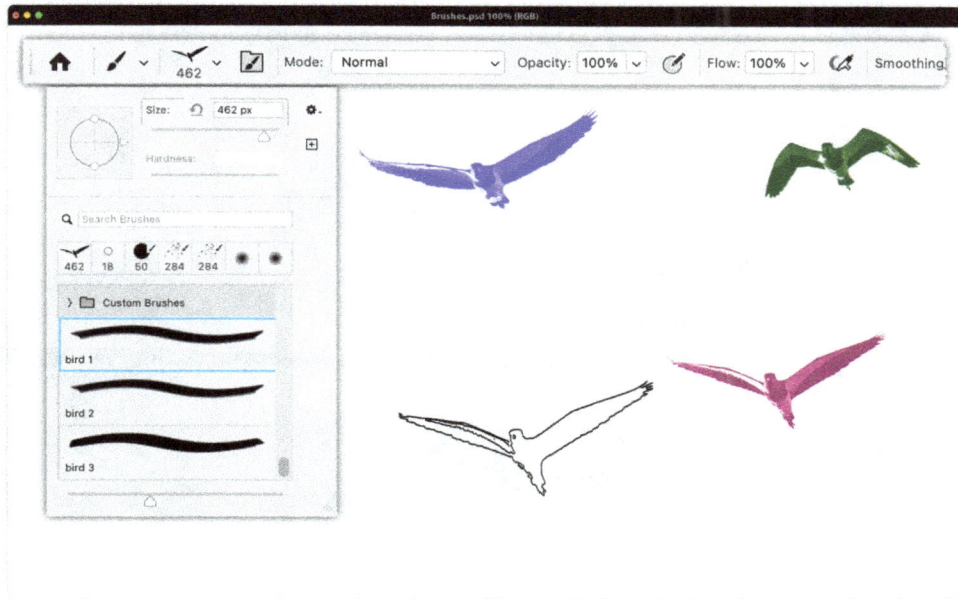

Figure 11.4: An example of the three bird brushes added to Photoshop

11. Open Lake.jpg from the 11-Brushes folder.

12. Click on the **New Layer** icon at the bottom of the **Layers** panel to add a new empty layer and rename it Birds.

13. Switch to the **Brush** tool by pressing the *B* key. From **Options**, click on the **Brush tip** menu and scroll down to the bottom of the list, where you will find your newest brush tips and folders. Click on the **bird 1** brush. Change the **Size** of the brush to approximately 175 px:

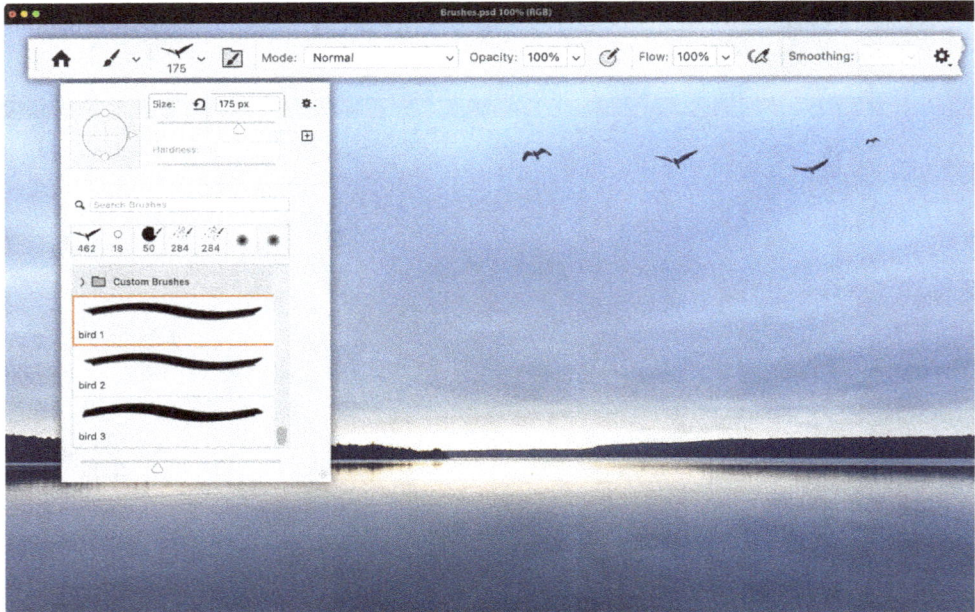

Figure 11.5: The bird brush marks added to the photo

14. Hover your cursor over the dark silhouette of the trees that run along the horizon line. Then, hold *Alt* (Windows) or *Option* (macOS) as you click in the same region to sample the color of the trees. For reference, this should provide a hexadecimal color of **012440**. This color will be ideal to use for the bird brush marks.

15. Hover your cursor in a region approximately 1/3 of the way up the upper right-hand side of the image. Then, click once to paint a bird in the sky.

16. Switch to the **bird 2** brush and set **Size** to approximately 175 px. Then, click to add it to the image in a similar region. Repeat the same step to add 4–6 different birds to the image. Try varying the size of each bird to make some look as though they are positioned further away from the camera.

17. Drag the **Birds** layer onto the **New Layer** icon at the bottom of the **Layers** panel to dupli-cate it. Rename the duplicated layer `Reflections`.

18. Go to **Edit → Transform → Flip Vertical**. The duplicated layer should now appear upside down. Switch to the **Move** tool and drag the **Reflections** layer down the image and over the lake.

19. Change **Blend Mode** of the **Reflections** layer to **Multiply** and reduce **Fill** to **30%**. Reducing the fill will make the layer fainter and, in doing so, a touch more realistic.

20. Save the image as a PSD in the 11-Brushes folder and close the document.

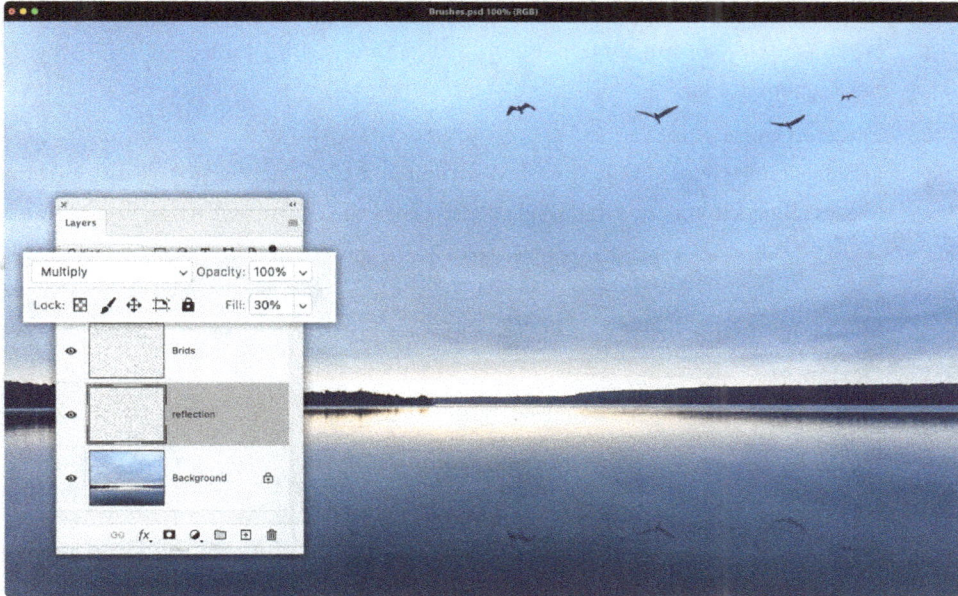

Figure 11.6: The completed image with birds and reflections made from brush marks

In this section, we looked at the process of capturing image content as a brush tip that can be used for painting. In this scenario, three bird images were painted onto an empty sky to provide a focal point. In the next section, you will create brushes from real-world paint marks.

Modifying brush properties

Hidden away at the bottom of a popup in the **Tools** panel is the **Art History Brush** tool. The first time you experiment with this tool, its default brush settings can be off-putting, to say the least. But with a little experimentation, you can produce interesting results.

The Art History Brush tool works in conjunction with the History panel to paint a stylized version of your image. By default, the History panel displays your previous 50 edits, including a snapshot of the document's appearance when it was opened. It's this snapshot that Photoshop uses as a sample to repaint the image through the painterly effects of the Art History Brush tool.

In the following exercises, you'll create several brushes from real paint strokes and use them to make Art History Brush tool presets. The hard work you put into preparing your brushes will be rewarded when you see how effortless the results can be with this technique. Once created, these brushes can be used time and again on any image:

1. Open `Brush-01.jpg`, `Brush-02.jpg`, `Brush-03.jpg`, and `Brush-04.jpg` from the `11-Brushes` folder.

2. I created these paint marks and captured them with my iPhone. I adjusted the levels to achieve a pure white background. With `Brush-01.jpg` active, go to **Edit → Define Brush Preset**. Name it `Brushes-1` and click **OK**. Close the document when you're finished.

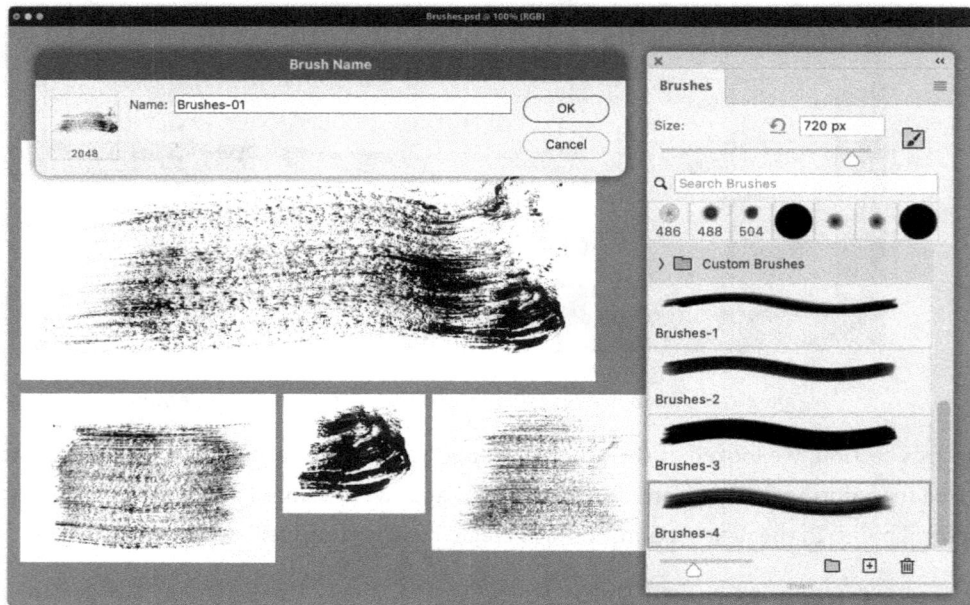

Figure 11.7: Save real brush marks as digital brush tips in Photoshop

3. Repeat the same step for Brushes-2, Brushes-3, and Brushes-4, naming them accordingly. Once complete, close all documents.

4. Open Pattern-Canvas.jpg from the 11-Brushes folder.

5. Go to **Edit** → **Define Pattern**. Name it Canvas and click **OK**. Check that the pattern has been added by going to **Window** → **Patterns**.

6. Go to **Window** → **Brushes**. The **Brushes** panel lists all the default, imported, and user-created brushes in Photoshop. Now that the base shapes for the brushes have been created, they need to be modified and saved as new brushes for the Art History Brush tool.

Creating the large Art History Brush

The Art History Brush tool enables you to create stylized brush marks that sample pixels from your original image content:

1. Press the *Y* key to switch to one of the **History** tools, then make sure you have the **Art History Brush** tool active, as they share the same shortcut.

Figure 11.8: The Art History Brush tool options

2. From the **Options** bar, set **Mode** to **Normal**, **Opacity** to **100%**, **Style** to **Dab**, and **Area** to 200 px.

3. Click on **Brushes-1** in the **Brushes** panel to make it active. Then, go to **Window** → **Brush Settings**. The **Brushes** panel enables you to browse for, activate, and resize a brush tip, while **Brush Settings** allows you to customize the behavior and appearance of the brush.

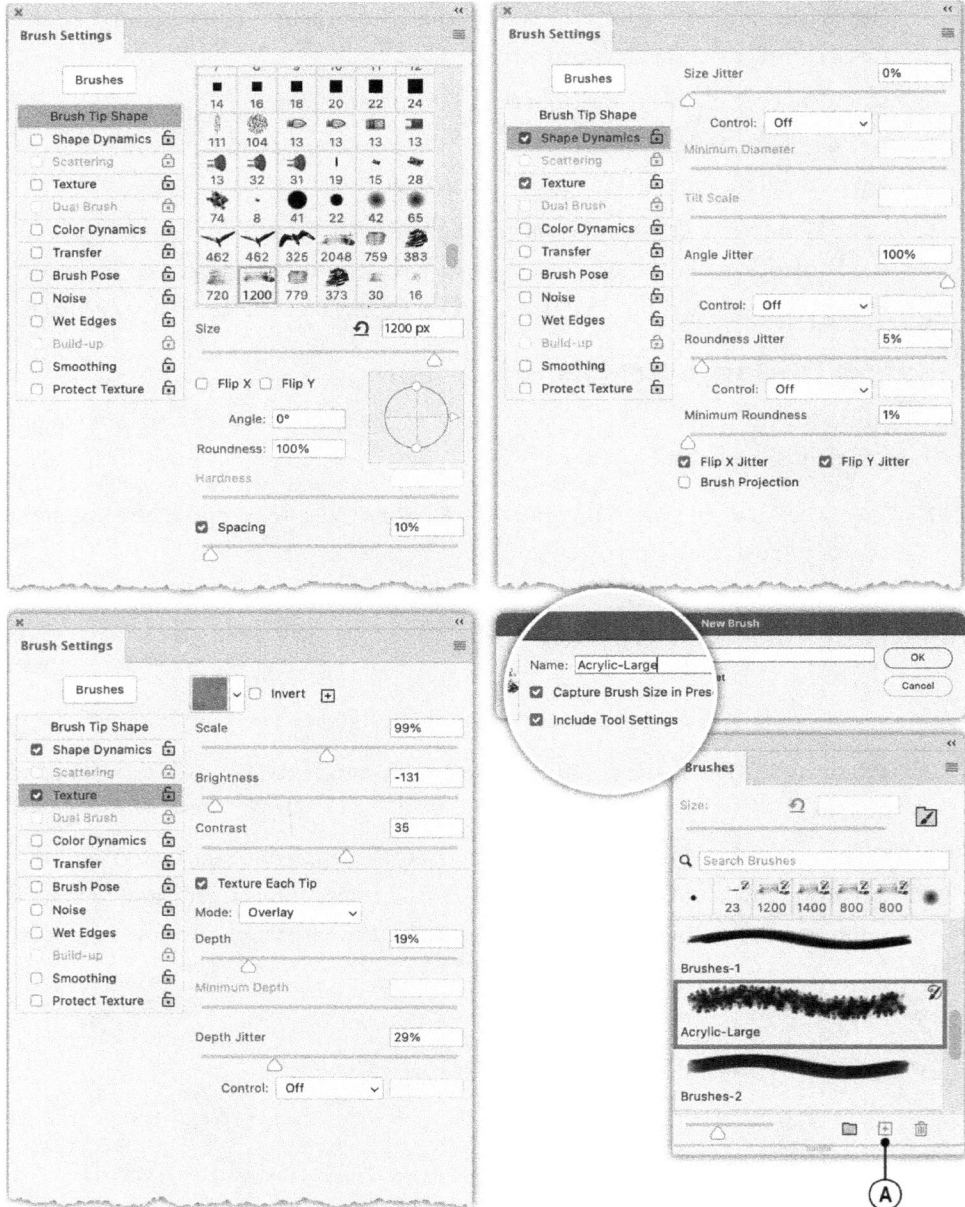

Figure 11.9: Brush-1 used as the basis for a new brush preset named Acrylic-Large

4. With **Brushes-1** active, click on **Brush Tip Shape** from the **Brush Settings** panel on the left-hand side. Set **Size** to 1200 px, **Angle** to 0°, **Roundness** to 100%, and **Spacing** to 10% (*Figure 11.9*).

5. Next, click on **Shape Dynamics** from the left-hand list to activate the adjacent checkbox. Set **Size Jitter** to 0%, **Angle Jitter** to 100%, **Roundness Jitter** to 5%, and **Minimum Roundness** to 1%. Enable the **Flip X Jitter** and **Flip Y Jitter** checkboxes but leave **Brush Projection** unchecked. This will cause the brush tip to rotate randomly.

6. Next, click on **Texture** from the left-hand list. Click on the **Pattern Picker** thumbnail at the top of the panel. Scroll down to the bottom of the list to find the **Canvas** pattern created in a previous step. Set **Scale** to 99%, **Brightness** to -131%, and **Contrast** to 35%. Turn on the **Texture Each Tip** checkbox and set **Mode** to **Overlay**. Set **Depth** to 19% and **Depth Jitter** to 29%. This will add the **Canvas** pattern as a subtle texture to each brush stroke, adding a touch of realism and character.

7. Click on the **Create New Brush** icon (**A** in *Figure 11.9*) at the bottom of the **Brushes** panel to capture the changes as a new preset. Name the brush Acrylic-Large and click **OK**.

Creating the medium Art History Brush

To do so, follow the steps given here:

1. Click on **Brushes-2** in the **Brushes** panel to make it active. Then, from the **Brush Settings** panel, click on **Brush Tip Shape** from the list on the left-hand side. Set **Size** to 700 px, **Angle** to 0°, **Roundness** to 100%, and **Spacing** to 26%.

2. Click on **Shape Dynamics**. Set **Size Jitter** to 0%, **Angle Jitter** to 100%, **Roundness Jitter** to 15%, and **Minimum Roundness** to 25%. Enable the **Flip X Jitter** and **Flip Y Jitter** checkboxes but leave **Brush Projection** unchecked.

3. Click on **Texture** from the left-hand list. Click on the **Pattern Picker** thumbnail and select the **Canvas** pattern again. Set **Scale** to 100%, **Brightness** to 114%, and **Contrast** to 19%. Turn on the **Texture Each Tip** checkbox and set **Mode** to **Overlay**. Set **Depth** to 100% and **Depth Jitter** to 50%.

4.   Click on the **Create New Brush** icon, name the brush `Acrylic-Medium`, and click **OK**.

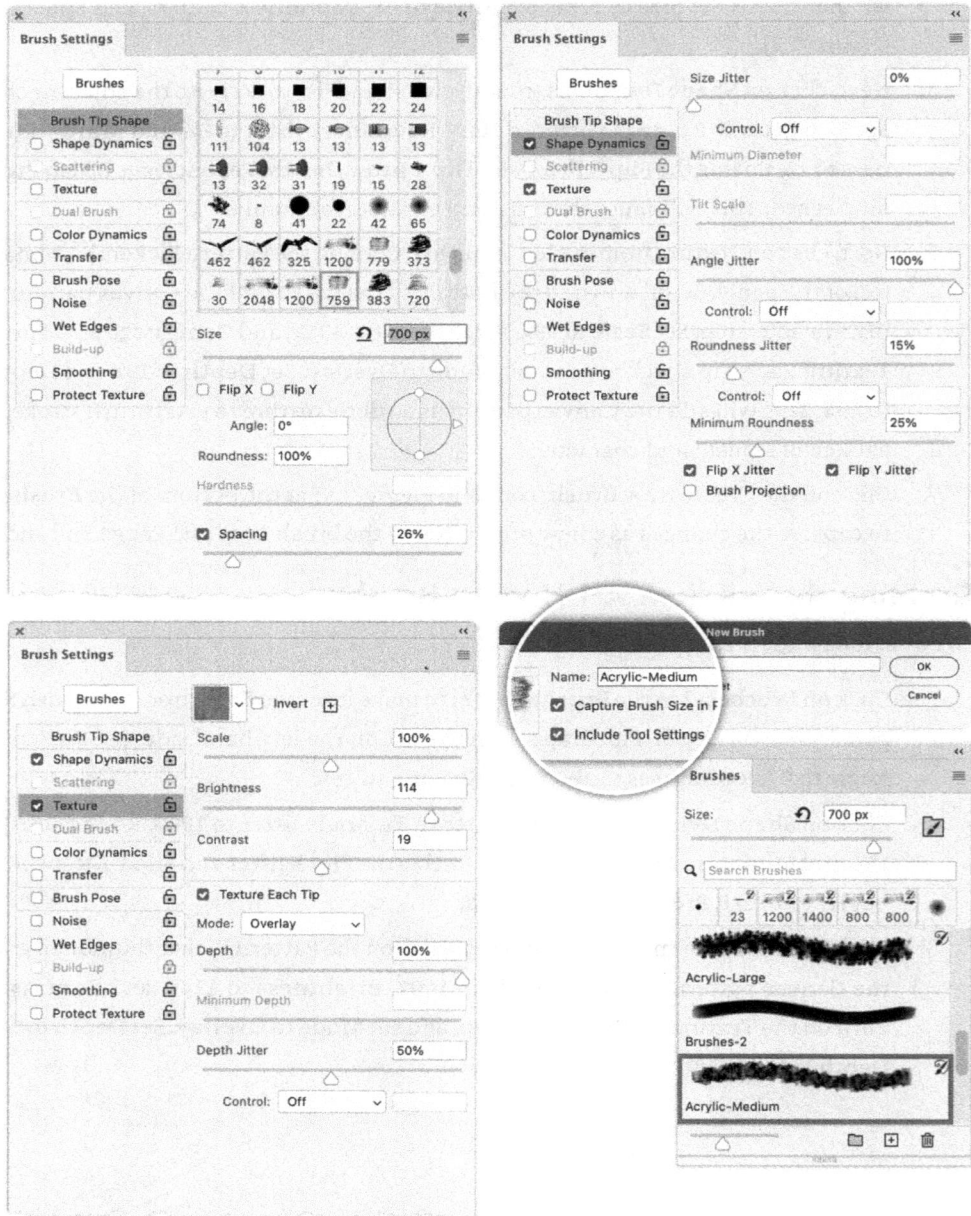

Figure 11.10: Brush-2 used as the basis for a new brush preset named Acrylic-Medium

Creating a small Art History Brush

To do so, follow the steps given here:

1. Click on **Brushes-3** in the **Brushes** panel to activate it. Then, from the **Brush Settings** panel, click on **Brush Tip Shape** from the list on the left-hand side. Set **Size** to 373 px, **Angle** to 0°, **Roundness** to 100%, and **Spacing** to 10%.

2. Click on **Shape Dynamics** from the list on the left-hand side. Set **Size Jitter** to 0%, **Angle Jitter** to 100%, **Roundness Jitter** to 0%, and **Minimum Roundness** to 0%. Turn on the **Flip X Jitter** and **Flip Y Jitter** checkboxes but leave **Brush Projection** unchecked.

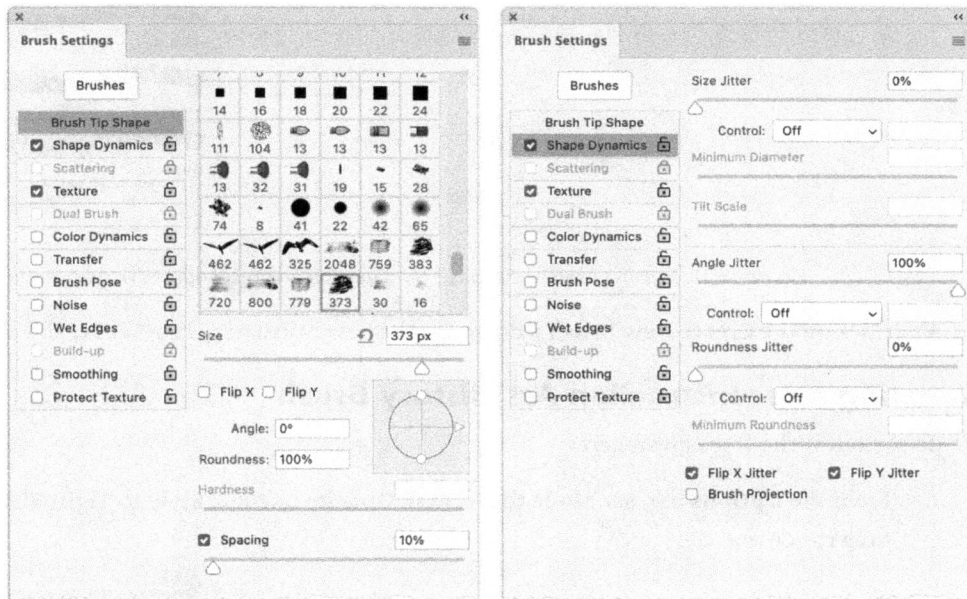

Figure 11.11: Brush-3 tip shape and dynamics

3. Click on **Texture** from the left-hand list. Click on **Pattern Picker** and select the **Canvas** pattern again. Set **Scale** to 100%, **Brightness** to 0%, and **Contrast** to 14%. Turn on the **Texture Each Tip** checkbox and set **Mode** to **Height**. Set **Depth** to 12% and **Depth Jitter** to 28%.

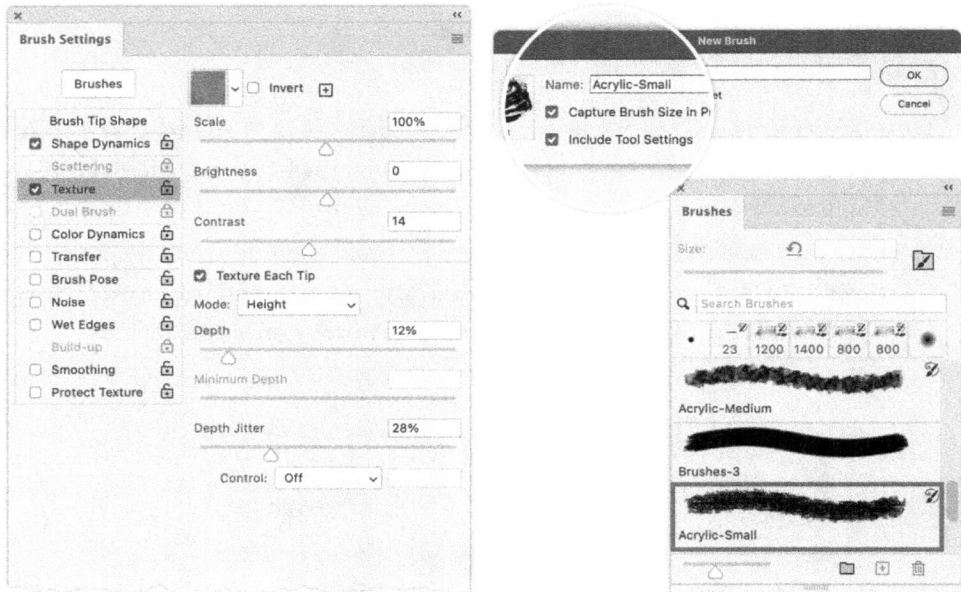

Figure 11.12: Brush-3 used as the basis for a new brush preset named Acrylic-Small

4. Click on the **Create New Brush** icon, name the new brush `Acrylic-Small`, and click **OK**.

Creating a reconstruction Art History Brush

To do so, follow the steps given here:

1. From the **Options** bar, set **Mode** to **Normal**, **Opacity** to 100%, **Style** to **Tight Short**, and **Area** to 500 px.

Figure 11.13: The Art History Brush tool options defined for the reconstruction brush preset

2. Click on **Brushes-4** in the **Brushes** panel to make it active. Then, from the **Brush Settings** panel, click on **Brush Tip Shape** from the list on the left-hand side. Set **Size** to 30 px, **Angle** to 0°, **Roundness** to 100%, and **Spacing** to 50%.

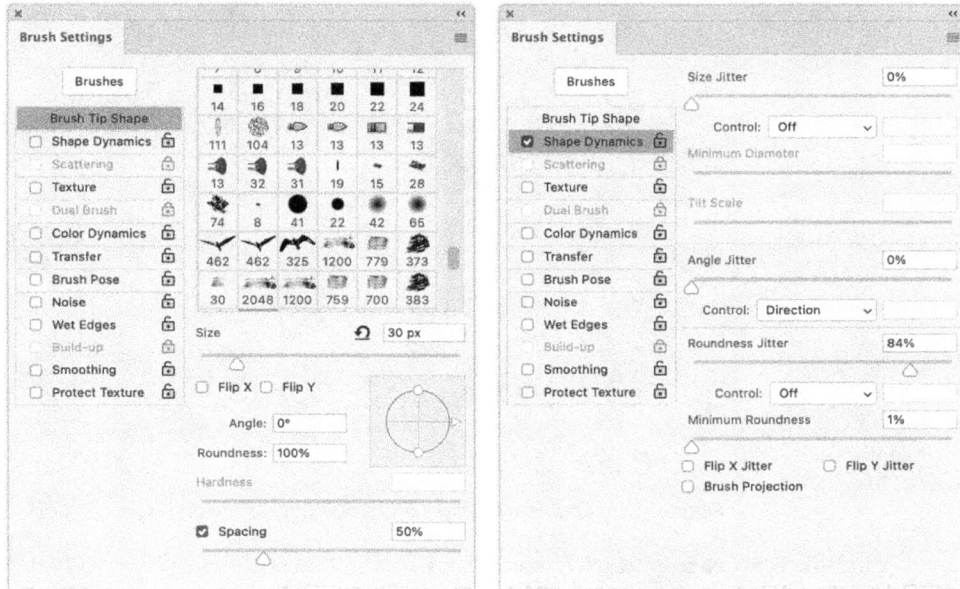

Figure 11.14: Brush-4 tip shape and dynamics

3. Click on **Shape Dynamics** from the list on the left-hand side. Set the **Size Jitter** to 0%, **Angle Jitter** to 0%, **Roundness Jitter** to 84%, and **Minimum Roundness** to 1%. Turn off the **Flip X Jitter**, **Flip Y Jitter**, and **Brush Projection** checkboxes.

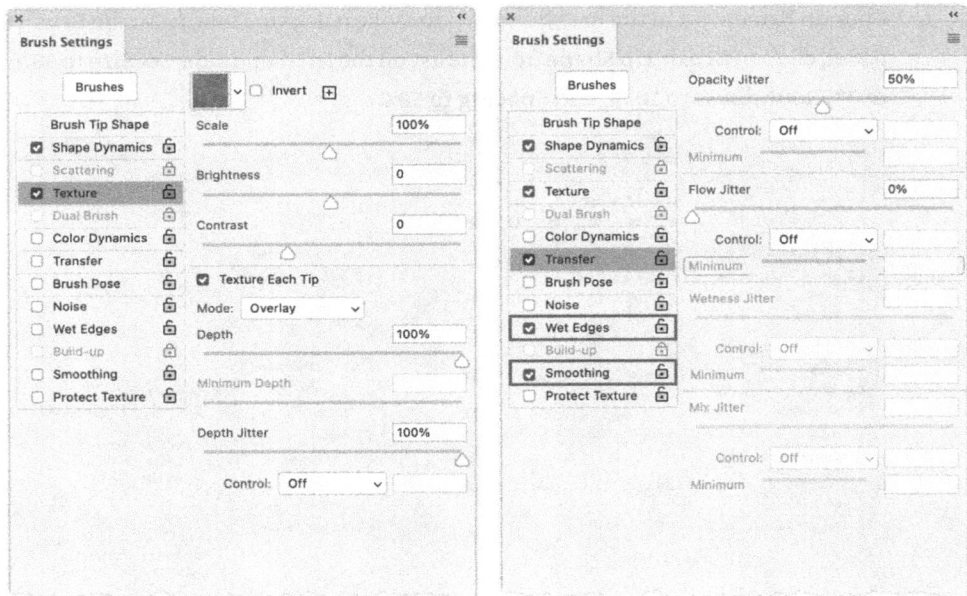

Figure 11.15: Adding wet edges and smoothing to the brush preset

4. Click on **Texture** from the left-hand list. Click on **Pattern Picker** and select the **Canvas** pattern again. Set **Scale** to 100%, **Brightness** to 0%, and **Contrast** to 14%. Turn on the **Texture Each Tip** checkbox and set **Mode** to **Overlay**. Set **Depth** to 12% and **Depth Jitter** to 28%.

5. Click on **Transfer** from the left-hand list. Set **Opacity Jitter** to 50% and **Flow Jitter** to 0%. Finally, turn on the **Wet Edges** and **Smoothing** checkboxes from the list on the left-hand side, neither of which contains settings to define.

6. Click on the **Create New Brush** icon and name the brush `Acrylic-Reconstruct`. Then, click **OK** to save the final acrylic brush.

Creating and backing up a brush preset group

Having created all of the new brushes and presets, it would be a real shame to lose them should your computer be damaged; if you need to use Photoshop on a different computer, you can import them. Like any asset, it is prudent to back up your presets to a separate drive. To do so, follow the steps given here:

1. Click on the **Create a new group** icon at the bottom of the **Brushes** panel. Name the group `Acrylics` and click **OK**.

2. With the new group created, start dragging each of the **Art History Brush** tool presets into it. This should only include the **Acrylic-Large**, **Acrylic-Medium**, **Acrylic-Small**, and **Acrylic-Reconstruct** brush presets.

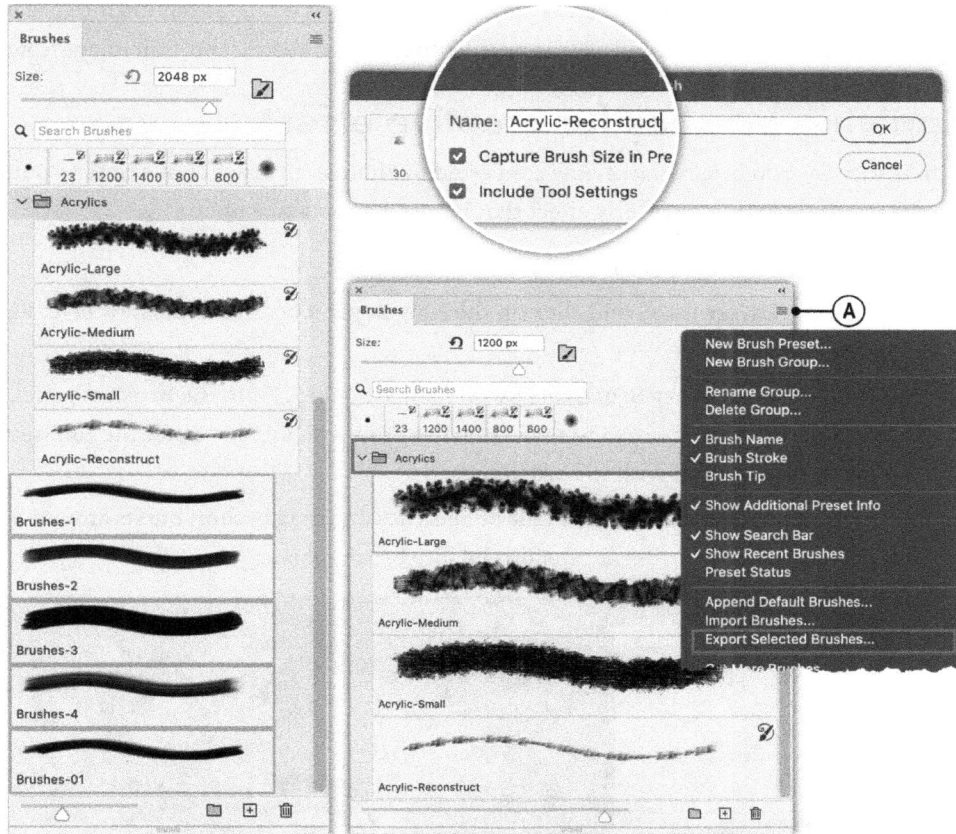

Figure 11.16: Saving the new Acrylic-Reconstruct brush preset

3. The original brushes, **Brushes-1**, **Brushes-2**, **Brushes-3**, and **Brushes-4**, are no longer required and, as such, can be deleted by clicking on them and pressing the **Delete Brush** button at the bottom of the **Brushes** panel.

4. Click on the Acrylics brush group folder in the **Brushes** panel. Go to the **Brushes** panel fly-out menu and choose **Export selected brushes**. Browse to a folder of your choice, name it Acrylics, and choose **Save**.

In this section of the chapter, we created and modified brush tips. Starting with real paint marks, we captured the basic form as a brush tip preset. Then, with the Art History Brush tool, we modified the brush properties specifically for that tool. We added shape dynamics that randomly altered the angle of each brush stroke when applied, as well as built a canvas texture into the brush tip itself. In the next section, you will use the brushes to create an abstract portrait image from a photo.

Applying brushes for creative effect

With the real-world brush marks now converted to Photoshop brushes, it's time to put them to use, creating an abstract painterly effect that is based on a source photo:

1. Open `Portrait.jpg` from the `11-Brushes` folder.

2. Go to the **Layers** panel and click on the **New Layer** icon. Name the new layer `Paint` and ensure it is active.

3. Switch to the **History Brush** tool by pressing the *Y* key. From the **Brushes** panel, click on the `Acrylic-Large` brush to make it active. You won't need to edit the tool settings, as they were captured with the brush preset.

4. Starting from the outer edges of the image, click and drag in short bursts around the image until the edges have been transformed into brush marks:

Figure 11.17: Painting from the edges of the image up to the face

How the Art History Brush tool works

By default, the Art History Brush tool uses the state of the document when it was opened as a reference for color and structure. As you drag across the image, the original photo is sampled and transformed into paint marks.

5. From the **Brushes** panel, click on the **Acrylic-Medium** brush to make it active. Paint over some of the inner brush marks and add some strokes to the center of the image so that the original photo is concealed in paint. Ensure that you click and drag over the image in short bursts to prevent the brush from distorting the color and form too much:

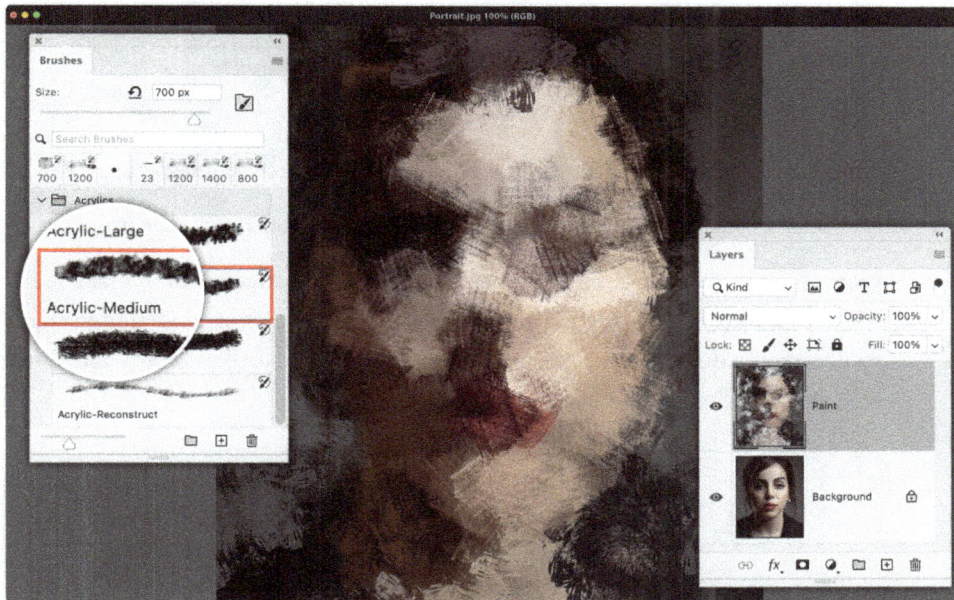

Figure 11.18: Adding medium painterly effects over the original photo

6. From the **Brushes** panel, click on the **Acrylic-Small** brush to make it active. Reduce the brush size to 125 px. Focusing on the subject's features only, paint over the eyes, nose, and mouth. This will add some of the structure back into the image:

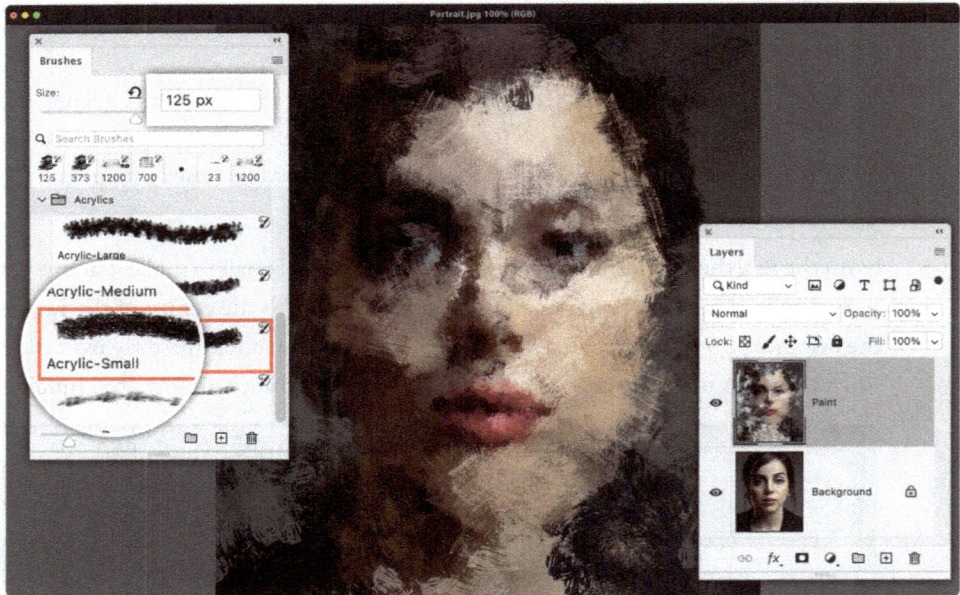

Figure 11.19: Adding small painterly effects over the original photo

7.   From the **Brushes** panel, click on the **Acrylic-Reconstruct** brush to make it active. This brush will look for contrasting edges, only applying paint strokes along them. In doing so, it restores detail to the painting. Focus your brush strokes on the facial features, as well as the neck and jaw:

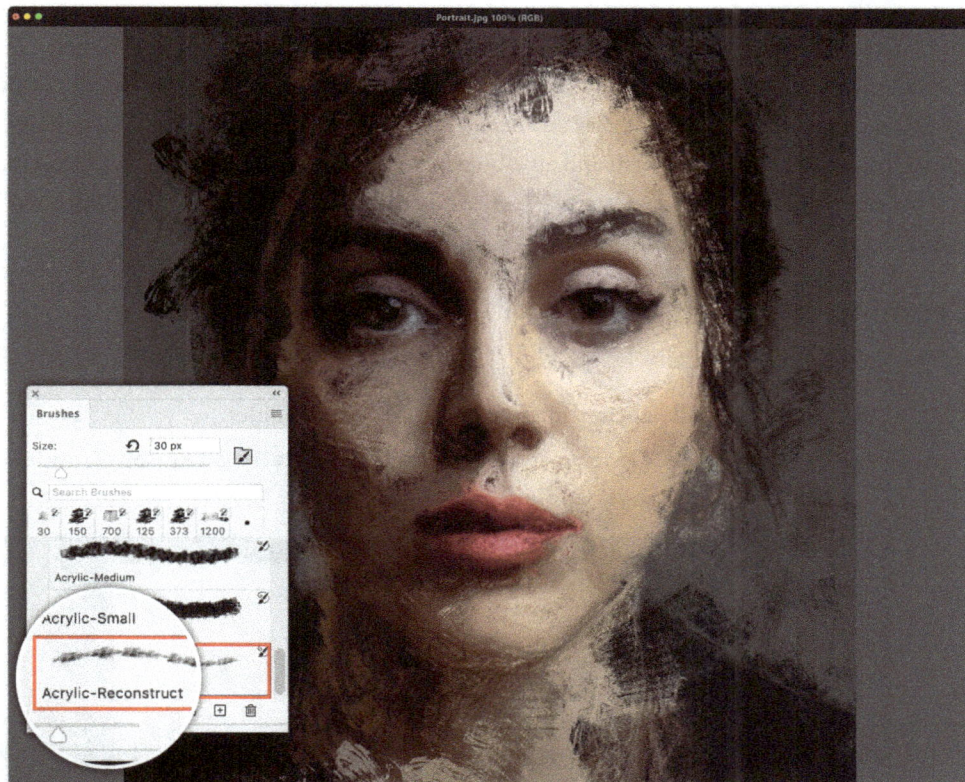

Figure 11.20: The completed image

8. Some regions may require a little touch-up with the **Acrylic-Small** brush to restore the correct colors or paint a clearer jawline, for example. By switching back to the **Acrylic-Reconstruct** brush afterward, you can add more definition and refine the edges once more.

9. Save the image as a PSD in the 11-Brushes folder and then close the document.

In this section, we applied Art History Brush tool paint marks to a photo to create an abstract art piece. First, we added broad strokes around the edges using lower-detail mark-making. Then, as we progressed to the center of the image, the brushes became progressively smaller to capture facial features. We then used a brush to reconstruct fine details and edges, built specifically to paint over regions with contrasting edges in the original photo. Next, you will use brushes for healing and retouching.

Using brushes for retouching

We have already seen the flexibility of brushes in this chapter, adding basic marks or painterly effects to images. However, brushes can also be used for retouching, and in the following exercise, you will create a snowflake brush and a stubble brush. By using settings such as **Angle Jitter** and **Scattering**, we allow the brush tip to rotate and scatter by a predefined amount, making the results appear more convincing.

Creating a snowflake brush

Follow the steps given here:

1. Open Snow.jpg and Winter.jpg from the 11-Brushes folder.

2. With the Snow.jpg document active, go to **Edit → Define Brush Preset**. Name it Snow and click **OK**. Then, close the document.

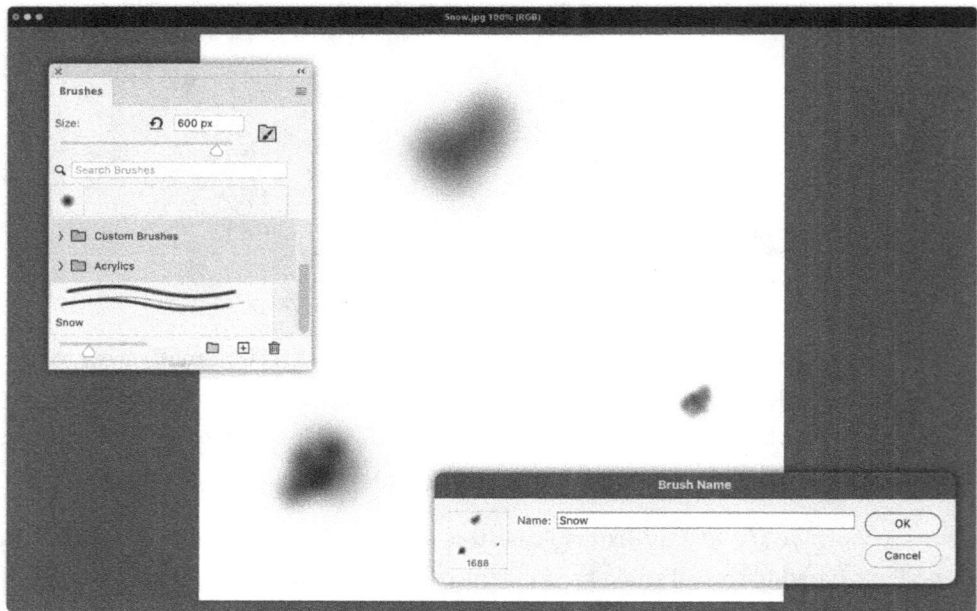

Figure 11.21: The initial Snow brush after capturing from an image

3. Click on the **Snow** brush, located at the bottom of the **Brushes** panel, to make it active. Then, go to **Window → Brush Settings**.

4. Switch to the **Brush** tool from the **Tools** panel. Set **Blend Mode** to **Normal**, **Opacity** to 100%, and **Flow** to 85%:

Figure 11.22: The Brush tool options

5. Click on **Brush Tip Shape** from the **Brush Settings** panel from the list on the left-hand side. Set **Size** to 600 px, **Angle** to 0°, **Roundness** to 100%, and **Spacing** to 104%.

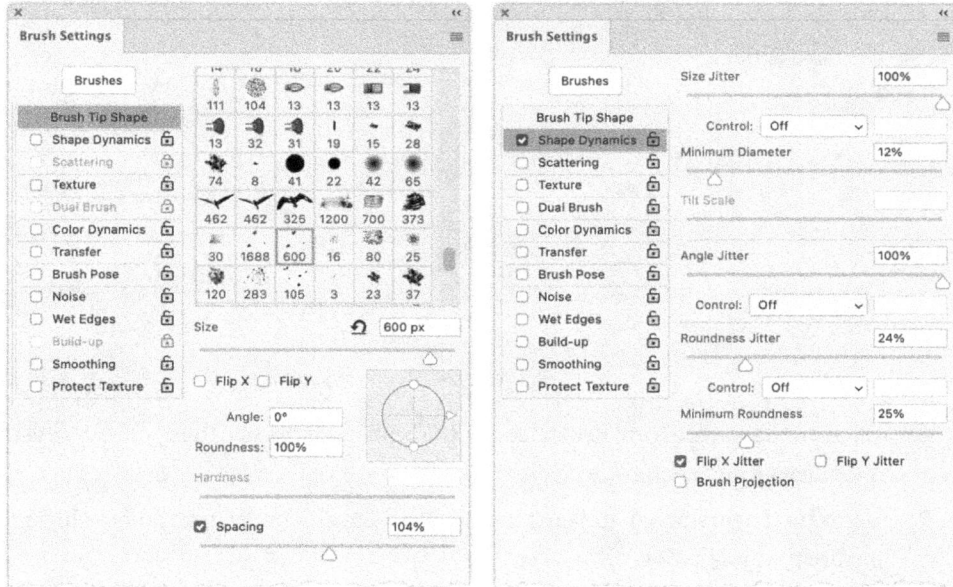

Figure 11.23: The Brush Tip Shape and Shape Dynamics settings

6. Click on **Shape Dynamics** from the left-hand list. Set **Size Jitter** to 100%, **Angle Jitter** to 100%, **Roundness Jitter** to 25%, and **Minimum Roundness** to 2%. Turn off the **Flip Y Jitter** and **Brush Projection** checkboxes.

7. Next, click on **Scattering** from the left-hand list. Turn on the **Both Axis** checkbox at the top of the panel and set the **Scatter** value to 1000%. Set **Count** to 1 and **Count Jitter** to 0%. Finally, turn on the **Smoothing** checkbox from the list on the left side.

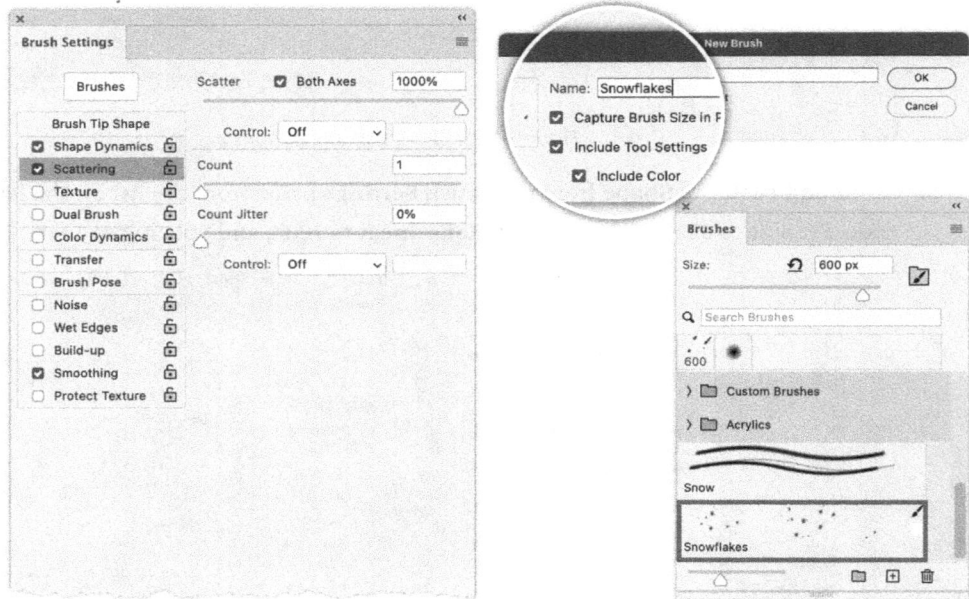

Figure 11.24: Scattering settings

8. Click on the **Create New Brush** icon at the bottom of the **Brushes** panel. Name the brush Snowflakes and click **OK**.

9. Go to the **Layers** panel and click on the **New Layer** icon. Name the new layer Snow and ensure that it is active.

10. Then, click and drag across the image to test the **Snowflakes** brush. For the best results, drag in long arching brush strokes to space out the snowflakes and spread them evenly across the image.

Figure 11.25: The brush mark applied to the original photo

11. Reduce **Brush Size** to at least half its original size, approximately 300 px. Then, repeat the same technique of dragging across the image to add finer snowflakes. Try to avoid adding too many snowflakes in front of the subject's face, as we don't want to obscure it.

12. As a final step, the snow would benefit from some motion. Right-click on the **Snow** layer and choose **Convert to Smart Object** from the list of options.

13. Go to **Filter → Blur → Motion Blur**. Set **Angle** to -35° and **Distance** to 21 px. The **Distance** value controls how intense the blur is; as such, we don't need to add too much blur to the snowflakes. Click **OK** when done. If you need to edit the snow at any point in the future, you can double-click on the **Snow** layer thumbnail in the **Layers** panel to open the smart object.

14. Once complete, save the image as a PSD in the 11-Brushes folder and then close the document.

Figure 11.26: The completed snow image

Creating a stubble brush

In the last exercise of this chapter, you will create a brush based on a simple brush stroke representing a hair to fill in the subject's beard:

1. Go to **File → Open** and browse to the 11-Brushes folder. Select Hair.jpg and Barbour. jpg, then click **Open**.

2. With Hair.jpg active, go to **Edit** → **Define Brush Preset**. Name the brush Single Hair-1 and click **OK**. Close the document:

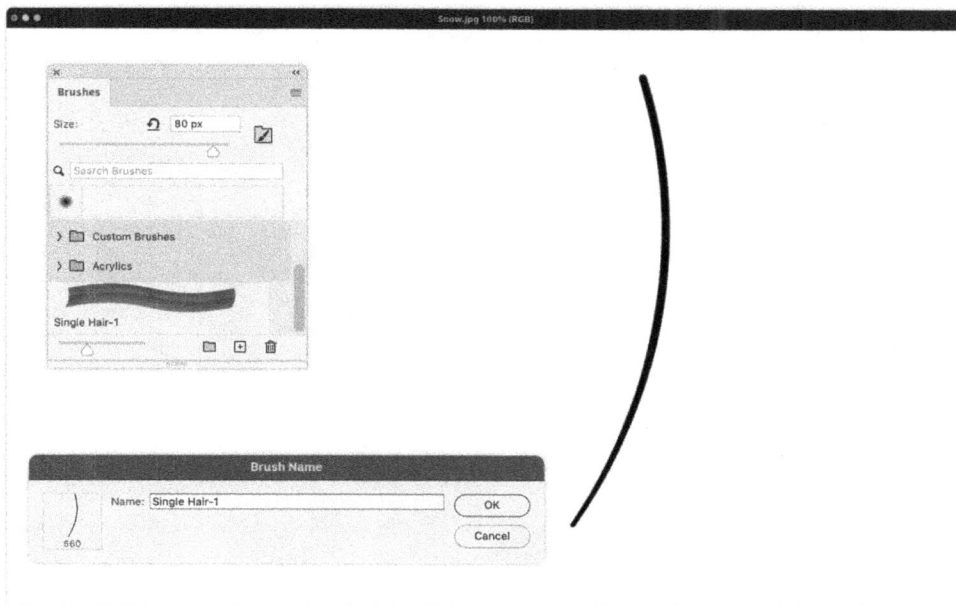

Figure 11.27: The source hair image

3. Click on the **Single Hair-1** brush, located at the bottom of the **Brushes** panel, to make it active. Then go to **Window** → **Brush Settings**.

4. Click on **Brush Tip Shape** from the **Brush Settings** panel from the list on the left-hand side. Set **Size** to 80 px, **Angle** to 86°, **Roundness** to 100%, and **Spacing** to 76%:

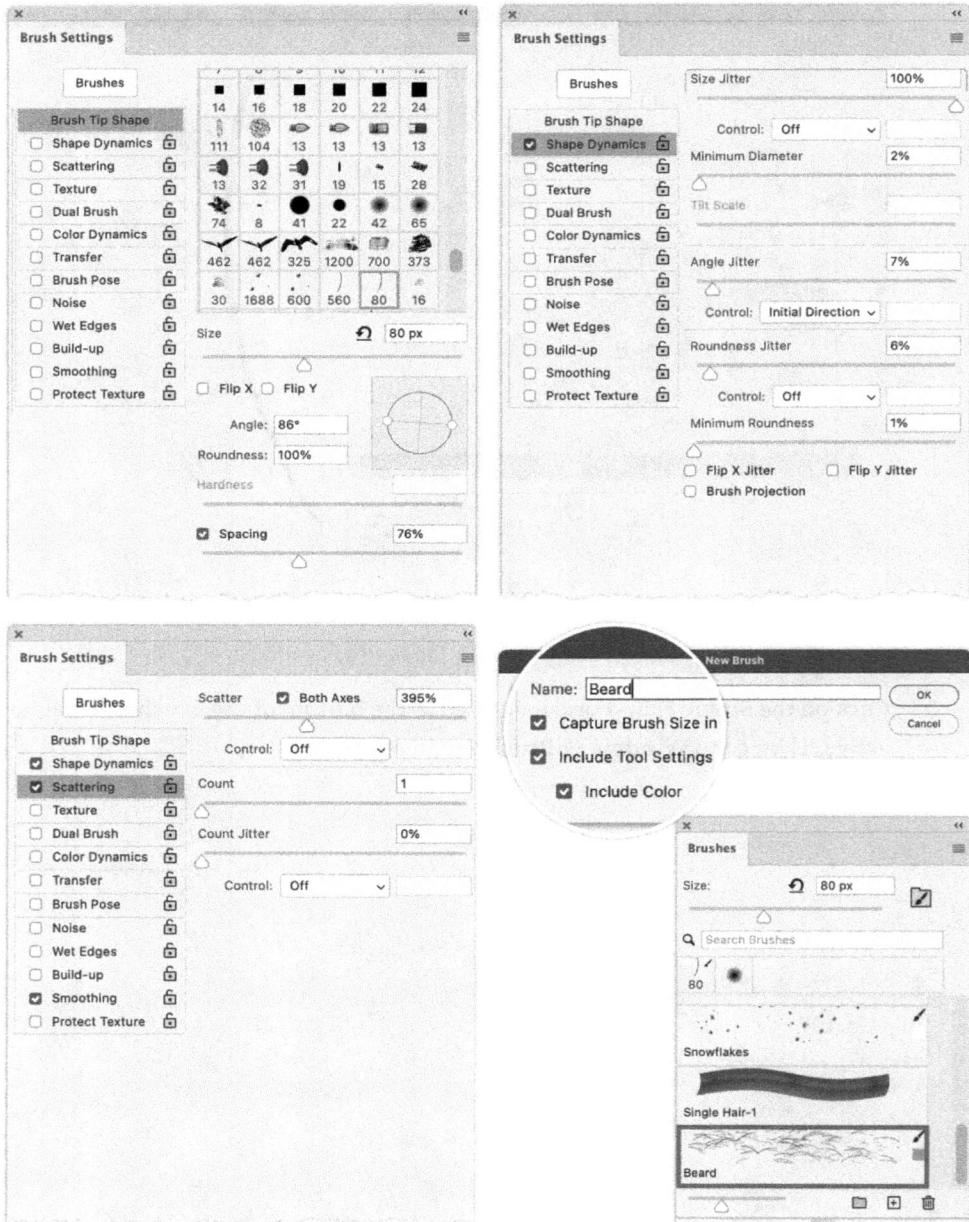

Figure 11.28: The brush settings for the beard brush

5. Next, click on **Shape Dynamics** from the left-hand list. Set **Size Jitter** to 100% and **Minimum Diameter** to 2%. Set **Angle Jitter** to 7% and then change the **Control** dropdown to **Initial Direction**. With this specific brush, controlling the angle of the hairs is tricky, but I find using the direction you first drag in to be reliable. Set **Roundness Jitter** to 6% and **Minimum Roundness** to 1%. Turn off the **Flip X Jitter**, **Flip Y Jitter**, and **Brush Projection** checkboxes.

6. Next, click on **Scattering** from the left-hand list. Turn on the **Both Axes** checkbox at the top and set the **Scatter** value to 395%. Finally, turn on the **Smoothing** checkbox from the list on the left.

7. Click on the **Create New Brush** icon at the bottom of the **Brushes** panel. Name the brush Beard and click **OK**.

8. Go to the **Layers** panel and click on the **New Layer** icon. Name the new layer Hair and ensure that it is active.

9. Switch to the **Brush** tool in the **Tools** panel. From **Options**, set **Blend Mode** to **Normal**, **Opacity** to 100%, **Flow** to 100%, and **Smoothing** to 10%. Set **Foreground Color** to a hexadecimal of 987c67 to match some of the colors in the subject's beard.

10. Then, click and drag across the man's cheek, ensuring that you drag the mouse downwards in the direction that the hairs point. Vary the colors by changing to a lighter brown, such as be9d81. You can also adjust the brush size to enhance the result, especially for the chin and top lip:

> In the **Brush Settings** panel, **Color Dynamics** lets you use the **Foreground** and **Background** colors in the **Tools** panel as samples to vary the color of each brush stroke as you paint, adding greater realism to your edits.

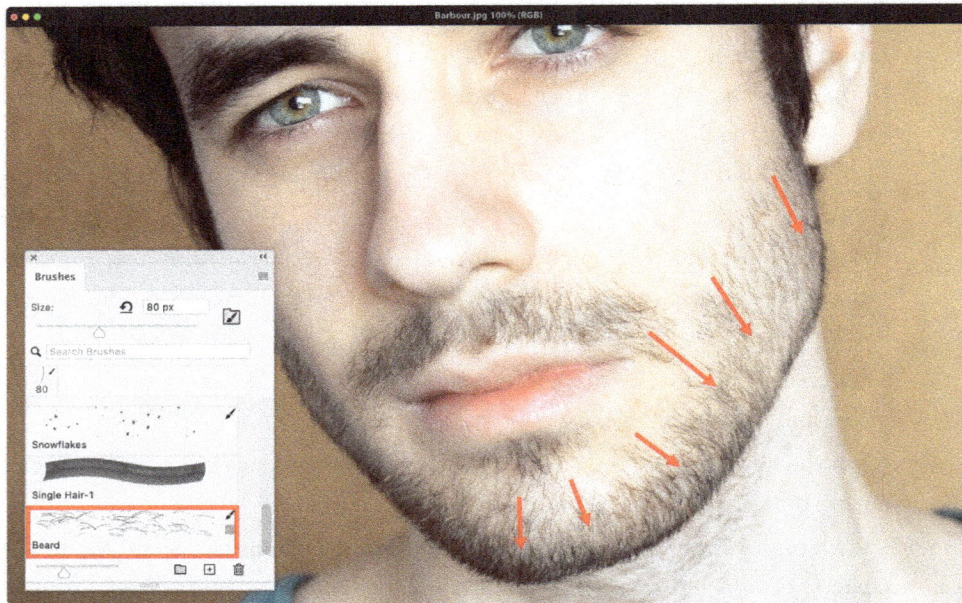

Figure 11.29: Adding brush marks over the existing beard

11. As a final step, switch to the **Blur** tool from the middle of the **Tools** panel. From the **Options** bar, set **Mode** to **Normal**, **Strength** to 50% and ensure that the **Sample All Layers** checkbox is turned off. Click and drag across the hair marks where the shot is out of focus so that the painted hairs match those around them in the original photo.

12. Once completed, save the image as a PSD in the 11-Brushes folder and then close the document.

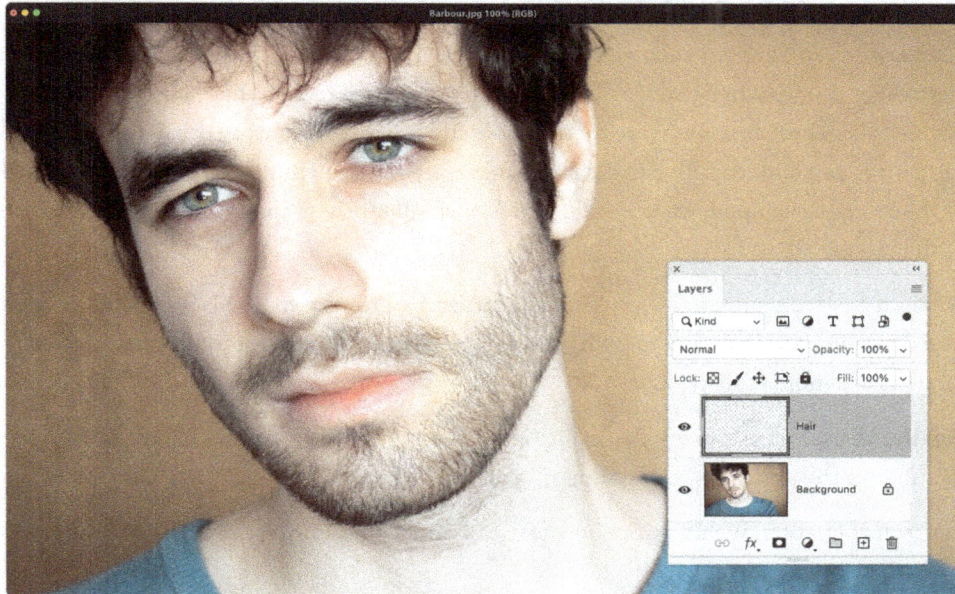

Figure 11.30: The completed image

In this final section, we used brushes to heal and retouch images, first by adding fake snow to emphasize a wintery scene and then by creating a brush for facial hair to fill in gaps in a beard. Due to the flexibility of brushes, if you can think of a use for them, there's probably a solution with a custom brush.

Summary

In this chapter, we focused on creating and editing custom Photoshop brushes. Initially, we captured portions of an existing image within a rectangular selection to create three bird brushes. We saw how a brush is converted into a grayscale image. The white portions of the brush act as transparent areas when painting, and any darker color than white applies a color of your choice, selected from the Color Picker.

The resulting brushes were then used to paint a small flock of birds in an image, providing a focal point. We sampled colors from the original photo to form dark bird silhouettes on a separate layer and duplicated it to create a mirrored version, which would create reflections on the lake's surface.

In the second exercise, we captured real-world brush strokes. Once captured as a basic brush tip shape, we then adapted each of them, adding shape dynamics that allowed the brush angle to change randomly when used, as well as a canvas texture to give that paint-on-canvas feel with each stroke. These brushes were then combined with the Art History Brush tool to sample colors from a portrait and reapplied in dabbed strokes, creating a painterly effect. As the painted version of the image developed, we utilized a series of smaller brush tips to reconstruct the finer details of the image.

We then created a snowflake brush to emphasize a wintery scene. This brush had shape and position dynamics applied to it, allowing the snowflakes to be sized, rotated, and scattered randomly to achieve a more realistic look.

Finally, we used a custom brush to complete the retouching of a model's beard, applying scattering to enhance the appearance of our painted beard hairs.

In the next chapter, we'll explore new features and technology enriched by AI within Photoshop.

Get This Book's PDF Version and Exclusive Extras

UNLOCK NOW

Scan the QR code (or go to packtpub.com/unlock). Search for this book by name, confirm the edition, and then follow the steps on the page.

Note: Keep your invoice handy. Purchases made directly from Packt don't require one.

Part 4

World Building

In the final part of this book, you will put your professional editing skills to test. You will learn essential generative text-prompting techniques to work with AI features in Photoshop and Adobe Firefly. Then, you'll apply all your knowledge to combine multiple assets into a single photomontage. You will work with collage techniques, panoramas, and high dynamic range images. Finally, you will face three challenges to create surrealist compositions. These challenges will push your Photoshop skills to the limit: the best way to solidify what you've learned by putting it into practice.

This part of the book includes the following chapters:

- *Chapter 12, Integrating Artificial Intelligence*
- *Chapter 13, Blending and Collaging Images*
- *Chapter 14, Creating Surrealist Artwork*

12

Integrating Artificial Intelligence

It seems impossible to avoid hearing or reading about **artificial intelligence (AI)** these days.

At the time of writing, Adobe offers over 100 AI features across its applications, with 15 available in Photoshop. These AI-enabled features are powered by a platform called **Adobe Sensei** and range from cable removal to canvas extensions and image background creation.

In this chapter, we'll take a deep dive into Photoshop's most significant AI-powered features and learn how to maximize their benefits while also being aware of the technology's current limitations.

In this chapter, you will explore the following topics:

- Handy tips for text prompts
- Generating images with Firefly
- Generative retouching
- Partner models
- Replace and expand backgrounds

Technical requirements

The project files for this chapter can be found at https://packt.link/gbz/9781806021710.

Handy tips for text prompts

Many of the AI features in Photoshop, such as **Generative Fill**, require you to prompt the AI with a set of commands or instructions. For example, `replace a bowl filled with oranges with a different type of fruit`. This would require you to select the part of the image you want to edit and enter text into a prompt field, such as `red apples`. Photoshop would then replace the original content with images from its library of data on Adobe Stock and public domain content where the copyright has expired. However, the results vary. If you don't get the results you want, you can reword or refine the results, but it costs you to do so.

Each prompt costs you in generative credits: a standard prompt is worth one credit that generates four image variants. The Creative Cloud Pro Plan includes 4,000 monthly credits that expire at the end of each month. Most of the generative features in Photoshop do not use generative credits when using Adobe's Firefly model. Third-party generative models, such as Nano Banana, do use generative credits. While you can purchase additional credits, it would be prudent to utilize the credits included efficiently first. Let's explore how to get better results with high-quality text prompts. Here are a few points to consider:

- Have a clear outcome in mind before you start. Instead of typing `Painting of a dog`, enter exactly what you require, such as `Renaissance oil painting of a Golden Retriever`.
- Use direct language as though you were explaining something to a friend.
- Avoid commands such as `create`, `generate`, `add`, or `fill` as they are too vague to offer value.
- Try to be as specific and descriptive as possible to increase the likelihood that the generative results will meet your expectations.
- Longer descriptions do not guarantee better results. Adobe suggests limiting your prompts to 175 words or fewer.
- Add asterisks around descriptors that you want Photoshop/Firefly to focus on—for example, `a *castle* floating in the clouds`.
- Use punctuation marks such as commas and semicolons to structure and organize your prompts, as it helps the AI engine better understand your prompts.
- The prompt bar is for entering specific instructions to generate images, video, or audio; it is not a chat box like those found on other AI platforms.

How to structure effective prompts

While you might have a clear outcome in mind, it's helpful to start thinking about how you would translate that into a structured text prompt. Of the 10 common descriptors, generally, your prompt should consist of 5 essential descriptors where relevant: a **medium**, a **subject**, an **action**, an **environment**, and **props**.

Medium + Subject + Action + Environment + Props

a painting of a dog standing on a rock in a forest with a ball

Figure 12.1: The suggested structure for prompts

You can vary the number of descriptors you require and their order. However, you are more likely to achieve the desired outcome by adding the subject near the beginning of your prompt. From experience, recent versions of Firefly will produce an image in the style of a photo if the medium is omitted.

Describing the medium and subject

A simple prompt could include just a subject and the medium, such as a `drawing of a dog`. The medium could be reimagined in several ways, such as a photo, graffiti, watercolor, or sculpture. You could include further details in the prompt, such as a `Renaissance oil painting of a dog`. Alternatively, you could specify additional characteristics about the subject, such as a `drawing of a Golden Retriever`. The following examples use a different medium and a subject of dog:

Figure 12.2: Three Firefly prompts of a dog, rendered as a drawing, photo, and sculpture

Describing actions, the environment, and props

Let's now look at adding each of the remaining descriptors to complete the prompt, building on the original concept of a dog in the woods. In reality, you would add all descriptors in the same prompt. In the first example (left in *Figure 12.3*), from the prompt painting of a dog standing on a rock, Firefly generated an image that includes each descriptor, albeit the medium isn't quite a painterly style:

Figure 12.3: Each prompt builds on the previous with more descriptors

The second prompt (center in *Figure 12.3*) includes the environment descriptor, which generates a similar dog pose in the correct setting, but the medium has become more photographic. The third prompt (right in *Figure 12.3*), which includes all five descriptors, positions the prop suitably in relation to the dog, which has been altered slightly in appearance, as well as the angle. Additionally, the medium now appears closer to digital illustration than a painterly style and would require some adjustments to achieve the desired look. As we'll see later in this chapter, details can often be fine-tuned without changing the text prompt, but instead, through the Firefly sidebar, which allows you to specify art styles and reference images.

Going deeper with your prompt

Now that we have a clear idea of how to structure a prompt, let's examine the remaining five descriptors for situations when you need to go more in-depth with a prompting formula.

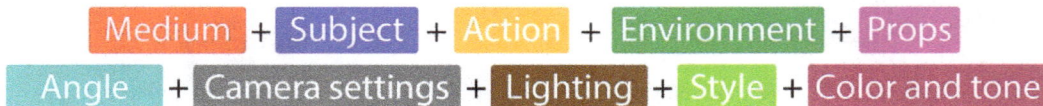

Figure 12.4: Ten common descriptors can be used to generate a detailed prompt

Specify an **angle** for your subject, such as portrait, macro, or shot from above. You can include the **camera settings**, such as lens type, f-stop, and ISO. Include the type of **lighting** in your image, such as HDR, dramatic light, or studio light. **Style** could include descriptors such as atmospheric, hyper-realistic, or cinematic. You can also specify the overall **color and tone** of the image, such as muted, monochromatic, or vibrant.

In the following example, this prompt was used to generate two images, the first in standard quality and the second in high quality: Ultra-macro close-up of a dew-kissed emerald tree frog clinging to the velvety surface of a vibrant moss-covered branch, tiny droplets of water clinging to its skin; the first light of dawn filters through the dense canopy, casting a soft, ethereal glow while warm, dappled sunlight highlights the frog's iridescent skin, revealing intricate pore texture and its large, reflective golden eyes. Shot on a full-frame DSLR, 100mm macro lens, f/5.6, ISO 200, 1/500 s, capturing razor-sharp detail, rich color contrast between deep greens and earthy browns, and a hyper-realistic nature documentary style.

Figure 12.5: An in-depth prompt used in standard quality, Image Model 4 (left), and high quality, Model 4 Ultra (right)

Although not technically one of our aforementioned descriptors, emotion can play a significant role in the prompting process. Try to capture the mood of people or the mood in your images by using words such as love, happy, confident, and excited. If your image includes scenery, you could use phrases such as swirling clouds that envelop distant snow-topped mountains.

Like all new skills, it will take time to adapt and achieve high-quality results that meet your intentions. If you hit a prompting brick wall, you can ask other AI platforms, such as ChatGPT, to help you write your prompts as you build confidence.

In this section, we have explored techniques for effective generative text prompts to create images. We looked at 10 common descriptors for your ideas, 5 essential descriptors for efficient prompting, and, where necessary, up to 10 descriptors with specific criteria, such as the lens type, camera angles, and style. In the next section, we'll look at the Adobe Firefly interface and features.

Generating images with Adobe Firefly

First announced at Adobe MAX in October 2022, **Firefly** enables you to create new, AI-generated images from a text prompt. Since then, Adobe Firefly has helped creatives generate over 22 billion images and undergone several updates that incorporate powerful new features.

In July 2024, Firefly made its way into the desktop version of Photoshop, where it can be accessed under the **Edit** menu (**Edit → Generate Image**). For nine months, the Beta version of Photoshop offered an outstanding update that rivaled the web version but was sadly removed in September 2025. Hopefully, it will return to Photoshop in the near future. This chapter will focus on the web version, but feel free to compare Firefly on the web with **Generate Image**.

About Firefly image models

Firefly's AI capabilities are often referred to as **image models**—the computer science part that enables the creation of structures and colors in generative image creation. Currently, new Firefly models are released every 12 months, and with each release, the results become increasingly impressive.

The default, "standard" image model is currently **Image Model 4** (October 2025). Each Image Model 4 prompt incurs a one-credit cost and generates four image variants. Adobe also offers **Image Model 4 Ultra,** which provides superior image quality and detail. Each Image Model 4 Ultra prompt incurs a 20-credit cost with just one image per generation. This might be an option for a final generation once you've refined it with the standard model, Image Model 4, to save a few credits.

Alternatively, you can select non-Adobe image models such as **Gemini 2.5 Flash Image (Nano Banana)**, **Imagen**, **Flux**, or **GPT** with the same 20-credit cost incurred for a single image variant. Some new image models cost 10 credits for a limited time. As a direct comparison, shown in *Figure 12.6*, an identical text prompt was used with different image models:

Figure 12.6: A comparison of Model 4 (left), 4 Ultra (center), and GPT (right) using an identical prompt

Getting to know the Firefly interface

There are numerous options in the Firefly interface, not all of which are easy to locate. These settings work in combination with the text part of your prompt. If you can become acquainted with them, this will avoid wasting time and credits on subsequent re-prompts.

The Firefly interface has three key components: generative results, controls, and the prompt text field. **Generative results** are the images Firefly creates based on your input, displayed as a set of thumbnail images on the right-hand side of the screen. **Controls**, located on the left side of the interface, work in conjunction with your text prompt to define the image model, aspect ratio, content type, visual intensity, composition, styles, effects, color and tone, lighting, and camera angles.

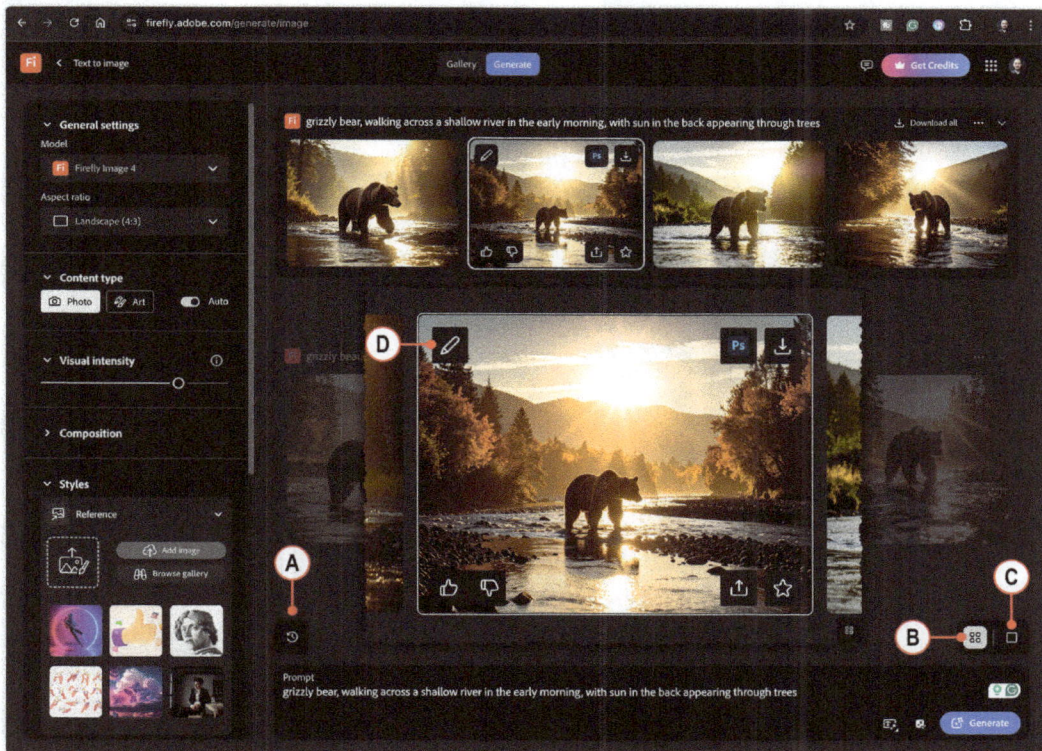

Figure 12.7: The Firefly interface

Above the text prompt field, you will find the **Generation History** button (**A** in *Figure 12.7*), where you can review your recently generated images. In addition, you can click on the small thumbnails (**B**) or the large thumbnails button (**C**). The default is small thumbnails. Hover over a thumbnail to reveal follow-up options to download, generate similar, or from the **Edit** menu (**D**), progress in Photoshop on the web, or Adobe Express.

Choose from five aspect ratios: **Widescreen (16:9)**, **Vertical (9:16)**, **Square (1:1)**, **Portrait (3:4)**, and the default **Landscape (4:3)**. Interestingly, when using third-party image models such as Gemini 2.5, the settings are often limited to aspect ratio or the use of a reference image.

Figure 12.8: Ratio differences between 4:3 (a), 16:9 (b), 3:4 (c), 1:1 (d), and 9:16 (e)

You can choose from **Photo** or **Art** under **Content type**. **Art** will produce a style closer to abstract digital illustration with less photo-realism.

Visual intensity controls the level of detail and the number of points of interest in the generated image. It is presented as a slider with nine levels. In the example shown, the slider was set to no intensity (left in *Figure 12.9*), midway (center), and full intensity (right). It is also fair to say that the higher the visual intensity, the more the image appears to be AI-generated.

Figure 12.9: Different levels of visual intensity

You can use a reference image to specify the **composition** of your prompt, either from the gallery of sample images or by uploading your own. In the example shown in *Figure 12.10*, a source image of the Scottish Highlands was used at 50% strength to influence the generated image.

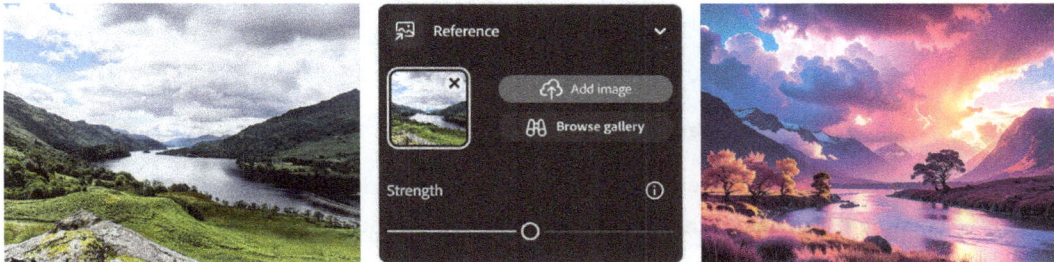

Figure 12.10: Refining the composition with a reference image

Like composition, you can also specify the **style** of your generated image from the available gallery or upload your own reference image. From **Acrylic** and **Watercolor** to **Paper** and **WPAP**, there is something to suit almost any preference. It is worth noting that changes to the style also change the image content.

Figure 12.11: Changing the style of your generated image

Effects allow you to save time and simplify prompting. If you're unsure how to articulate a specific appearance or art movement, chances are, you'll find effects such as **Art Deco, Bauhaus**, and **Vaporwave** useful. Unlike **Styles** and **Composition**, you can't upload a reference image for the effects.

Figure 12.12: Adding effects with your prompt

Although easily overlooked, there are additional options in the Firefly interface when the **Effects** library is expanded. The first of three drop-down menus is **Color and tone**, which allows you to specify an overarching mood for the generated image, such as **Muted**, **Pastel color**, and **Warm tones**. Similarly, **Lighting** offers setups that include **Backlighting**, **Long exposure**, and **Studio light**. Finally, **Camera angles** includes 10 options such as **Closeup**, **Macrophotography**, and **Surface detail**. **Color and tone**, **Lighting**, and **Camera angles** can be helpful if you want to avoid getting bogged down adding them to your prompt text.

Creating an image in Firefly

Let's now put into practice what we've learned so far in this chapter and create a simple generative prompt. Firefly can be found in the Creative Cloud desktop application, alongside your other installed applications, or at `firefly.adobe.com`. The Firefly home screen offers text to *images*, *vectors*, *video*, and *sound effects*:

1. From the Firefly home screen, click on **Text to image**.

2. The **Text to image** interface will now appear. From the controls on the left-hand side, set **Model** as **Firefly Image 4**, and choose the **Aspect ratio** setting of **Landscape (4:3)**. Leave the **Visual intensity** slider at its default value, ¾ to the right-hand side:

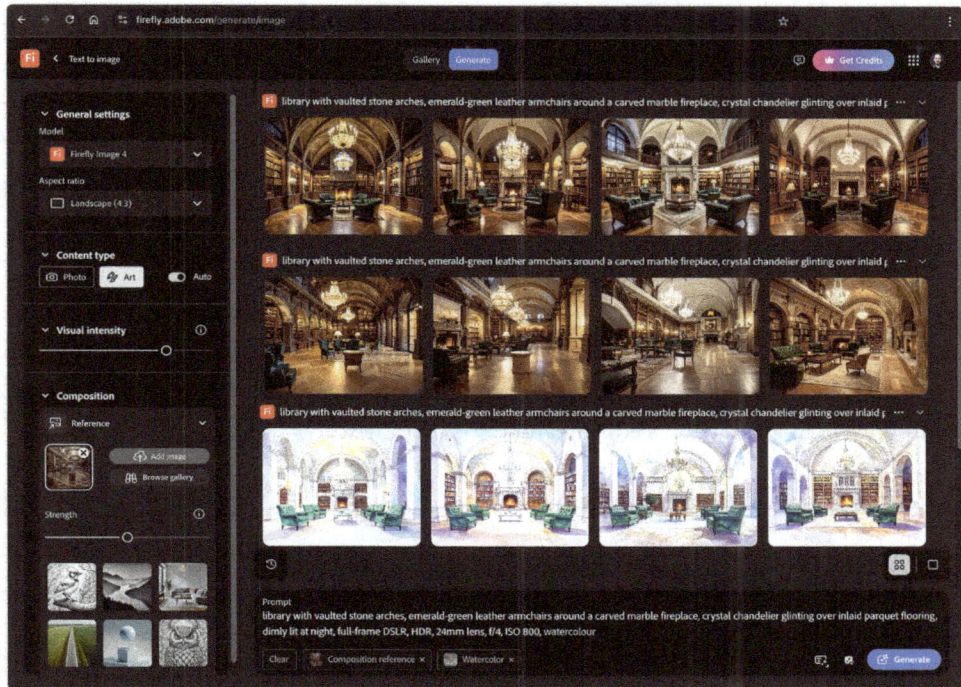

Figure 12.13: Three generated images based on prompt and control settings

3. Next, enter the following text into the text prompt field at the bottom of the page: library with vaulted stone arches, emerald-green leather armchairs around a carved marble fireplace, crystal chandelier glinting over inlaid parquet flooring, dimly lit at night, full-frame DSLR, HDR, 24mm lens, f/4, ISO 800.

4. Click the **Generate** button when ready. The generated image may take up to a minute to appear. You can inspect each image in full-screen mode by clicking on it.

5. Next, click on the **Add image** button under **Composition** settings and select LibraryReference.jpg from the 12-AI folder. Leave the **Strength** slider at its default value, halfway.

6. Click **Generate** once more. Notice the angle and content in the updated image change according to the source photo you uploaded.

7. Scroll down the control settings until you see **Effects**. Click on the **Techniques** button and then click on the **Watercolor** thumbnail.

8. Click **Generate** when ready. Although results will vary, I sometimes find the composition is ignored once an effect is applied. You could remove the watercolor effect by clicking on the **Close** button in the text prompt box. Then, type the word watercolor at the end of the prompt, and generate a new version.

9. Hover your cursor over the image thumbnail to display the download button in the top right corner, then click it. The image will be downloaded as a JPG.

In this section, we have explored the Adobe Firefly interface and settings that help refine AI-generated images. We then looked at a typical workflow for creating an image with specific and in-depth descriptors and reference images to generate an image. In the next section, we will look at AI integration in Photoshop's editing and retouching features.

Generative retouching

Of the 15 AI-powered features in Photoshop, 8 are closely tied to healing and retouching. Not every AI feature in Photoshop is brand-new; some have been enhanced by it. In the following exercises, we'll take a look at the best AI-powered features in Photoshop 2026.

Replacing drab skies

Sky Replacement was introduced to Photoshop in 2021. As the name suggests, Sky Replacement analyzed the active image and superimposed a new sky, either from Adobe's pre-supplied collection or your own. However, the quality of masking often fell short of what was required. Although not a direct update to sky replacement, Photoshop's recent AI-enhanced masking makes this feature worth revisiting. Let's take a look.

1. Open GreatOak.jpg from the 12-AI folder.

2. Go to **Edit → Sky Replacement**. When the dialog appears, ensure the **Preview** checkbox is active:

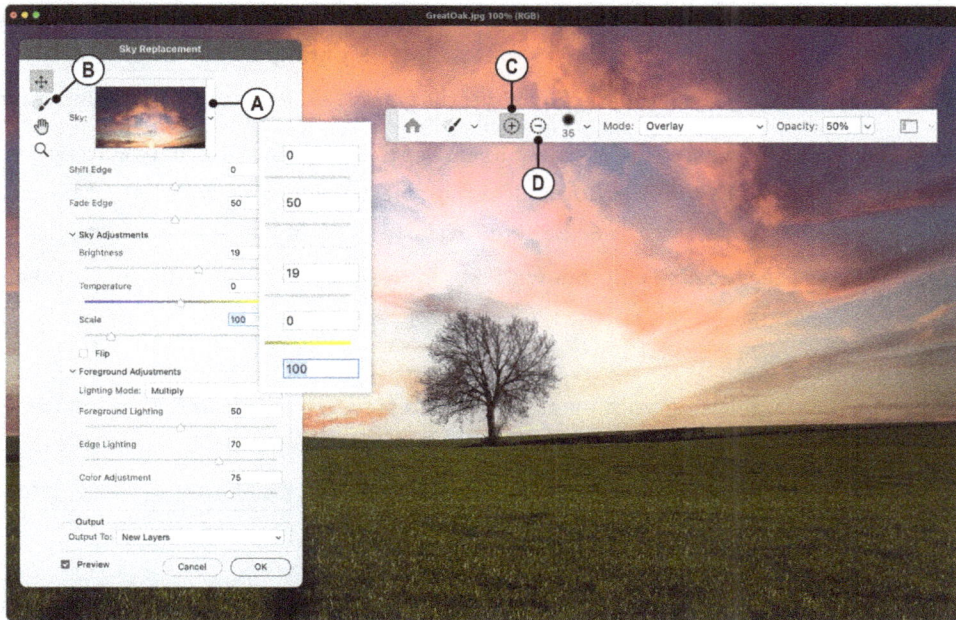

Figure 12.14: The Sky Replacement dialog

3. Click on the **Sky** presets menu (**A** in *Figure 12.14*) and select one of Adobe's pre-supplied sky images. In the example shown, I chose a warm sunset from the Spectacular set.

4. For regions where the mask requires finessing, you can switch to the **Sky brush** tool (**B**). From the **Options** bar, choose an appropriate brush size and hardness; the default is **Soft Round, 35px**.

5. To reveal more of the new sky, choose the **Add** mode (**C**); conversely, hide parts of the sky by selecting the **Subtract** mode (**D**). When you click and drag across the desired region, Photoshop will look for edge details and refine the mask accordingly.

6. To fine-tune the edits further, you can edit the sliders:

    •   Adjust the softness of the mask edges by dragging the **Shift Edge** slider. Positive values expand the mask, while negative values contract the mask edge.

    •   Soften the mask edges by dragging the **Fade Edge** slider. Positive values increase softening, while negative values create a harder mask edge.

    •   I chose to increase the **Brightness** value of the new sky to +19 but left **Temperature** at its default of **0**.

- Expand **Foreground Adjustments** to alter the color and tonal edits. I increased **Foreground Lighting** to +50 and **Edge Lighting** to +70.

- I increased the warm tones over the grassy field by setting **Color Adjustment** to +75.

7. Press the *V* key, then hover your cursor over the image and drag it to suit. By default, the new sky will be scaled at 100%. If you reveal the old sky at the edges of the image, you may need to increase the **Scale** value of the new sky or adjust its position.

8. Ensure the **Output To** dropdown is set to **New Layers**, to add the edits in separate, editable layers.

9. Click **OK** when done.

10. You can toggle the visibility of the edits to view the before and after images. Save the document as a PSD in the 12-AI folder. Close the document when done.

Figure 12.15: A comparison of the image before and after Sky Replacement

Replacing content with Generative Fill

Introduced in Photoshop 2024, **Generative Fill** uses an active selection to replace unwanted content via a text prompt, similar to Firefly. There is currently one notable limitation to be aware of when using this feature. The results are limited to a size of 1024 x 1024 px. However, based on experience, this feature often yields better results than **Content-Aware Fill**. In this exercise, we'll examine a typical workflow:

1. Open Apples.jpg from the 12-AI folder.

2. Switch to the **Rectangular Marquee** tool from the **Tools** panel.

3. From the **Options** bar, set **Mode** to **New Selection**, **Feather** to 0, and **Style** to **Normal**.

4. Create a rectangular selection around the center apple in the active image that includes some of the background.

5. Then, go to **Edit → Generative Fill**. When the dialog appears, type ripe orange into the **Prompt** field and click **Generate**:

Figure 12.16: Generative Fill used to change an apple to an orange

6. When the generated content appears, you will also see all three variations in the **Properties** panel. Click on each thumbnail to view the image itself and select your favorite version.

7. Save the image as a PSD in the 12-AI folder, then close the document.

Removing distractions

For many years, I've resorted to using **Spot Healing Brush Tool** to remove unwanted content from an image. With the addition of **Remove Tool** in May 2023, the process became easier thanks to a simplified workflow. First, we'll experiment with an October 2024 addition to Remove Tool, designed to automatically eliminate distractions, such as people and cables. This feature doesn't count toward your generative credits. Let's see how it works.

1. Open Steps.jpg from the 12-AI folder.

2. Switch to **Remove Tool** from the **Tools** panel.

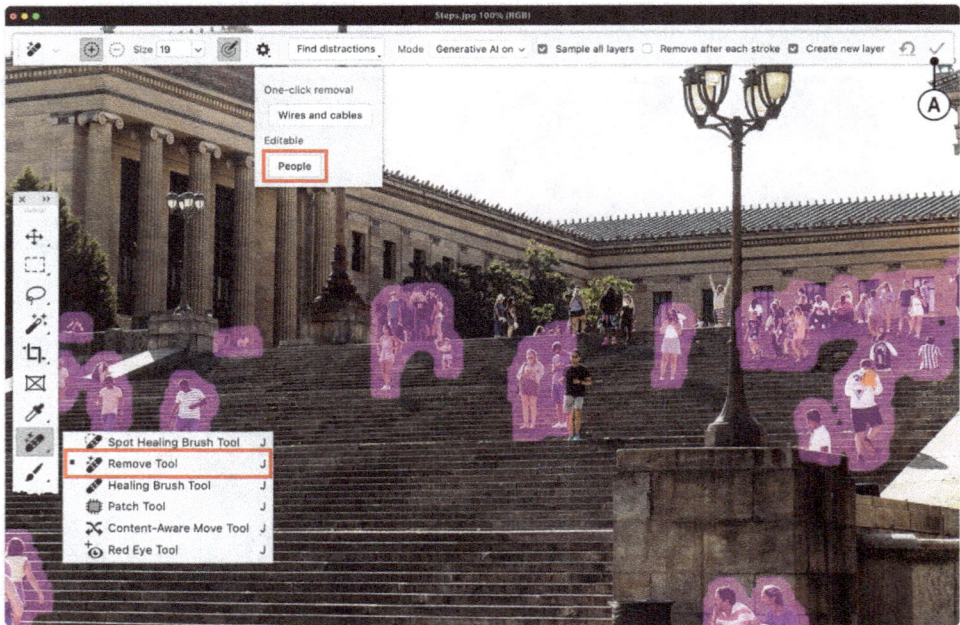

Figure 12.17: Automatically removing distractions such as people

1. First, we need to reduce the number of people in the image. From the **Options** bar, set **Mode** to **Generative AI on**, and turn on the **Sample all layers** and **Create new layer** checkboxes.

2. Then, click on the **Find distractions** button in the **Options** bar, and select **People** from the options. The generative AI process took around 3 minutes to complete when I attempted this, due to the large number of people in the image.

3. Photoshop will display a magenta highlight around all the detected distractions. Click **Apply** in the **Options** bar (**A** in *Figure 12.17*) to conceal the highlighted content.

Figure 12.18: Photoshop detects and removes all detected people with generative AI

1. The generative AI edits will appear in a new layer, named **Remove tool edits**. Keep the document open for the next exercise.

The Remove Tool

The simplicity of Remove Tool lies in the fact that you don't have to concern yourself with a bewildering set of brush tip settings, just the brush tip size. This can also be changed by pressing the open (*[*) and closed (*]*) bracket keys, respectively, to decrease or increase the brush size.

1. From the **Options** bar, turn off the **Remove after each stroke** and **Create new layer** checkboxes. Set the brush tip size to 120 px.

2. Ensure the **Remove tool edits** layer is active in the **Layers** panel.

3.   Click and drag the cursor across the entire region of the shirtless man at the top of the steps.

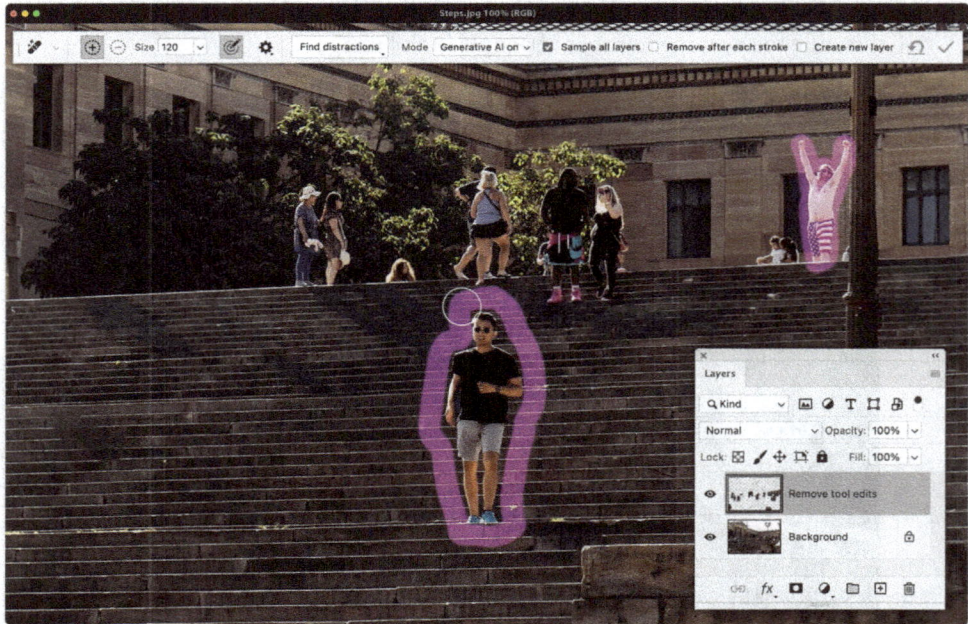

Figure 12.19: Using the Remove Tool to edit regions manually

4.   Then, drag your cursor around the man walking down the steps. You can use a nifty, hidden feature built into **Remove Tool**, which allows you to paint around the perimeter of the subject, rather than dragging across the entire area. Photoshop will fill the region in magenta when you release the mouse.

5.   Then, when you're ready to apply the edits, click on the **Commit** button in the **Options** bar. Photoshop will use generative AI to conceal the people, adding the edits to the **Remove tool edits** layer.

6.   Save the image as a PSD in the 12-AI folder, then close the document.

In this section, we have explored new and enhanced retouching features, empowered by generative AI such as Sky Replacement, Generative Fill, and removing distractions. In the final section of this AI-themed chapter, we will extend and replace backgrounds.

Partner models

Partner AI models are now available in Photoshop, and each has their core strengths depending on the task at hand. Let's first take a look at the new partner models for upscaling images.

Upscaling images with AI

I've lost count of the times I've been supplied pixel-based artwork only to discover it lacks the resolution (quality) needed for printing or on-screen display. Many people turn to the **Image Size** dialog in the belief that simply increasing the image's physical size will solve the problem. While this increases file size and resolution, it doesn't actually improve image quality.

Photoshop has made minor improvements over the years in its ability to upscale images; however, the process still results in a loss of fine details, such as hair. This led people to use third-party software for their upscaling needs, such as Topaz Labs. The good news is that, along with **Firefly Upscaler**, **Topaz** is now available in Photoshop as a partner model in two varieties: **Topaz Gigapixel** and **Topaz Bloom**.

To increase the size of an active image, go to **Edit → Generative Upscale**. When the dialog appears, you can choose your preferred partner model and **2x** or **4x** output size:

Figure 12.20: Upscaling images with Firefly and Topaz

Firefly Upscaler supports an upscaled image size of up to 6144 px, costing 5–10 credits, depending on the original image size. Once applied, Photoshop increases the image size and creates a new layer containing the upscaled version above the background layer, which, incidentally, uses the crude (image size) upscale method and is excellent for comparison. I found Firefly Upscaler produces a faithful rendition of the original image, retaining fine details such as hair and facial features, but not with the same sharpness as Topaz.

Topaz Gigapixel upscales original images up to a maximum of 56 megapixels and costs 10–20 credits. You can turn on the **Facial recovery** checkbox to recover details that would otherwise be lost during upscaling. Topaz Gigapixel generates a faithful rendition of the original image with greater detail in the face than Firefly Upscaler. It can, however, make hair appear straw-like, as though over-sharpened. The results are nevertheless impressive.

Topaz Bloom offers creative upscaling for 35 credits. It's important to note that it can produce results with significant changes to the subject's posture and overall image details. Set to **5** by default, the **Creativity** slider yields results closer to the original at 0, while 10 yields a version that can differ greatly from the original. Topaz Bloom is useful when prioritizing image quality over accuracy. Like all emerging AI features, it will be interesting to see how this feature improves over time.

Everyone is Bananas for Gemini 2.5

On August 26, 2025, Google released Gemini 2.5 Flash Image, aka **Nano Banana**, and it caused quite a stir with breathtaking text-to-image results. The impact has been such that people have begun discussing what it might mean for Photoshop's future development. My personal viewpoint is that until AI combines precision, quality, and predictability, Photoshop will continue to evolve iteratively, as it has for over 35 years. Let's take a look at what all the fuss is about in the following example of Nano Banana.

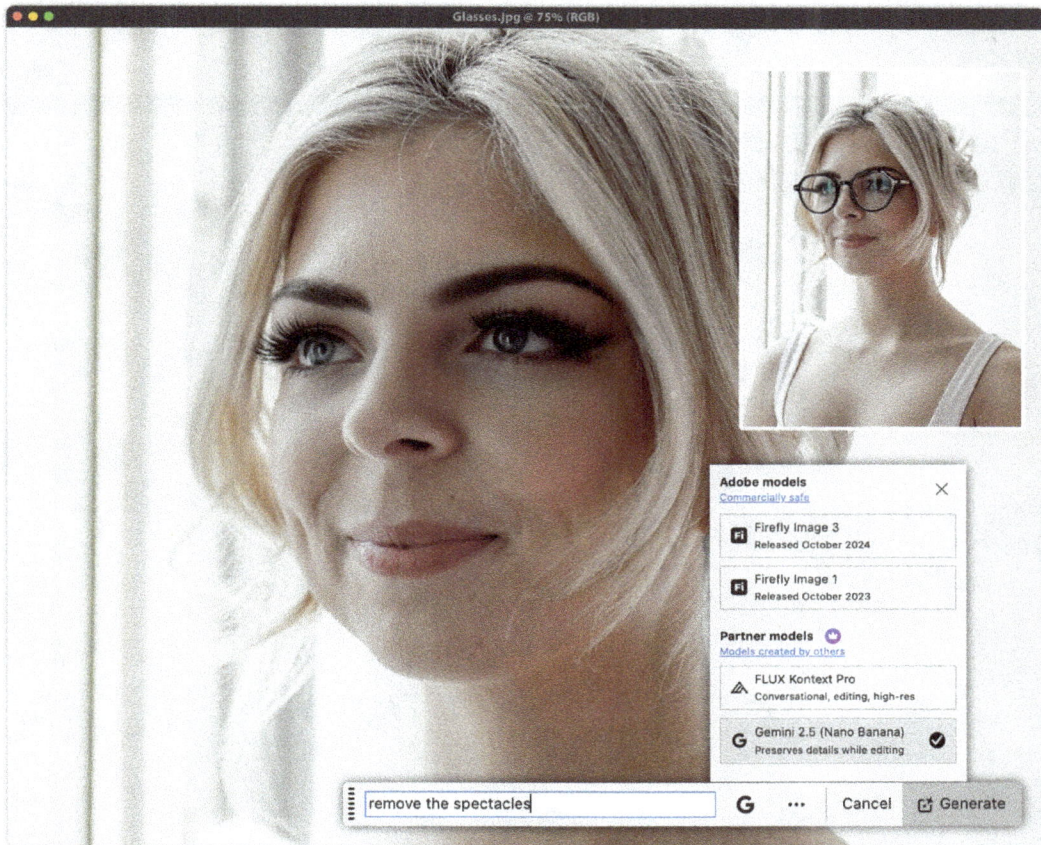

Figure 12.21: Removing details such as spectacles with the Nano Banana image model

The aim here was to remove the spectacles. I created a rectangular marquee selection around the spectacles. Then, from the Contextual Task Bar, I changed the partner model to **Gemini 2.5 (Nano Banana)**, only available with a Creative Cloud Pro plan at the time of writing. I entered remove the spectacles into the generative text field and pressed **Generate**, and after a few seconds, it returned the result in *Figure 12.21*. The image generated is impressive. The only downside was that the generative layer shifted position, requiring repositioning and masking to blend it into the original image, which only took a few minutes.

In contrast to Nano Banana, Adobe's **Firefly Image 3** model didn't fare quite so well, as shown in *Figure 12.22*:

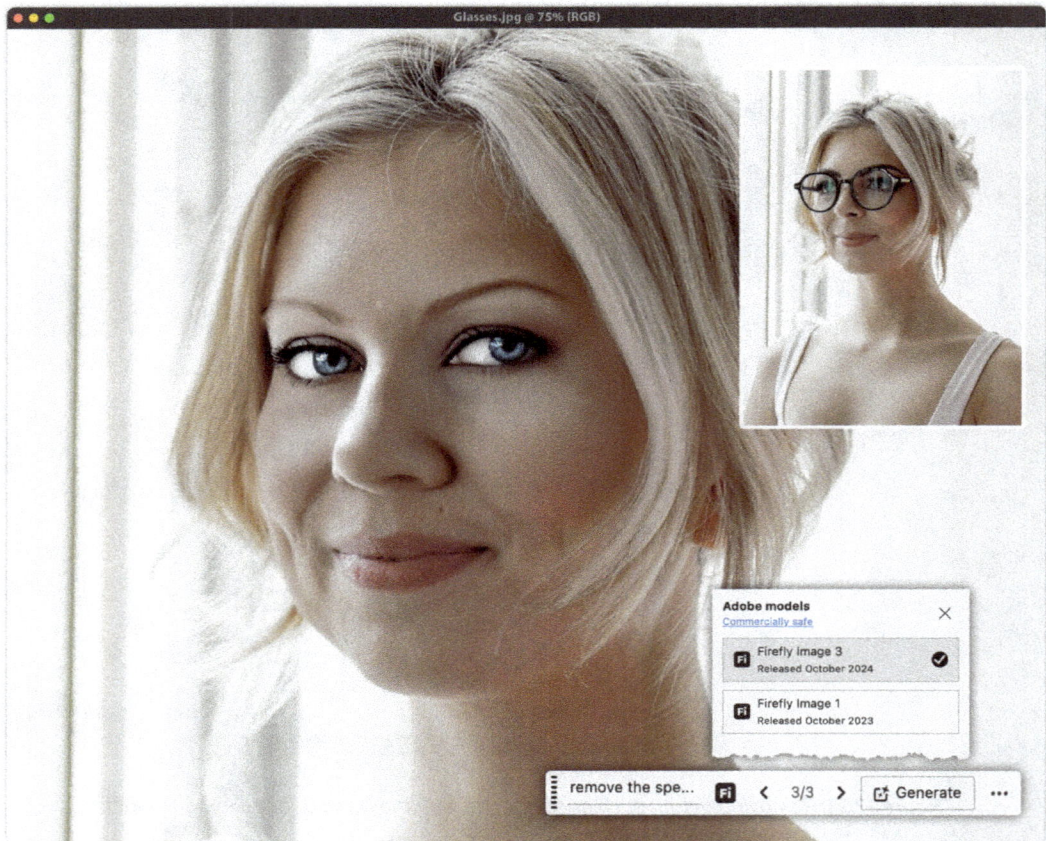

Figure 12.22: Adobe's Firefly 3 Image model doesn't come close to Nano Banana

The positives are that the position of the generative layer remained unchanged, and the results didn't require masking because they blended well with the original image. The quality of the generative image, however, didn't come close to matching Nano Banana. Firefly 3 was released 10 months prior to Nano Banana, and in AI terms, that is a very long time. Perhaps Firefly 4 or Firefly 4 Ultra will deliver better results once integrated into Photoshop on the desktop.

> Nano Banana will accept on-image annotations and reference images when generating prompts. This can be handy when placing new clothing on people or adding content to a scene.

Replacing and expanding backgrounds

The **Crop** tool has been an essential part of Photoshop since its inclusion back in 1991. Over the years, there's been three fundamental updates, including **Content-Aware Extend** and, more recently, **Generative Expand**. Although not related to the **Crop** tool, the new **Generate Background** offers similar benefits to your editing workflow. We'll examine both generative features in this section.

Extending the canvas

The generative canvas extension features added to the crop tool are handy for adapting images to fit social media aspect ratios more effectively. Let's dive in and take a look:

1. Open Beach.jpg from the 12-AI folder.

2. Switch to the **Crop tool** by pressing the *C* key.

3. Then, from the **Options** bar, make sure the **Preset** dropdown is set to **Ratio** and change the **Fill** dropdown to **Generative Expand**.

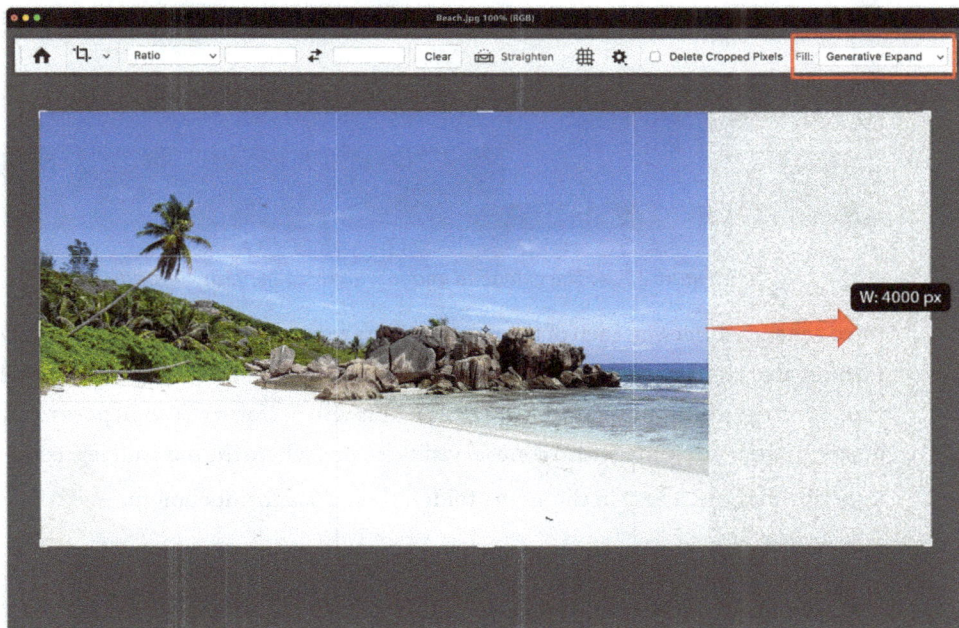

Figure 12.23: Extending the canvas with the Crop tool using Generative Expand

4. Hover your cursor over the center-right handle on the crop frame. Then, drag it to the right until the width reads approximately 4000 px.

5. Press *Enter* (Windows) or *Return* (macOS) on the keyboard to apply the crop, at which point the **Generative Expand** dialog will appear. Leave the **Prompt** field empty and press the **Generate** button.

Figure 12.24: The extended image with three generative variants

6. Once generated, click on each of the three variants to inspect them and decide which is best. I would also suggest clicking on the **Enhance Details** icon in the top-right corner of the chosen image thumbnail (**A** in *Figure 12.24*). This will perform a second pass to match the details of the source image and conceal visible seams where the old and new content meet.

7. Save the image as a PSD in the 12-AI folder, then close the document.

Generating new backgrounds

Generate background combines two recently added features, **Remove background** and **Generative Fill**, into a convenient workflow. In this exercise, you'll create a new background for a project:

1. Open Pottery.jpg from the 12-AI folder.

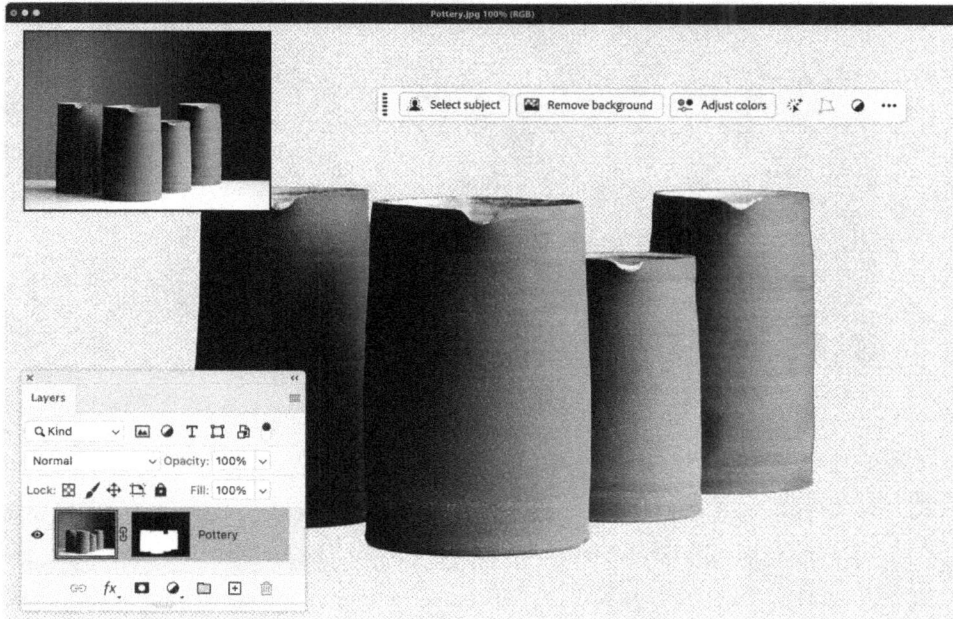

Figure 12.25: Removing the background of the image

2. Go to **Window → Contextual Task Bar** and then press the **Remove background** button. Photoshop will then identify the subject of the image and add a layer mask, concealing anything deemed not to be the subject.

3. The contextual task bar will now display different options with the background removed. At this stage, you can choose to edit the layer mask if necessary. In this example, the layer mask is more than adequate for our purposes and requires no edits. Click on **Generate background**.

Figure 12.26: Creating a new generative-AI background

4. The contextual task bar will now display a **Prompt** field. Enter your prompt text; I chose `modern kitchen, white marble worktop`. Click the **Generate** button when ready.

5. Photoshop references the black, concealed regions of the layer mask in the active layer to generate three variants that fill the empty background. Inspect each of the three variants, then click the **Enhance Details** icon in the top-right corner of the chosen image thumbnail.

    In this example, Photoshop created an impressive backdrop that includes reflections and shadows of the pottery on the marble worktop.

6. Save the image as a PSD in the `12-AI` folder, then close the document.

In this final section of the chapter, we have explored Photoshop's stand-out healing and retouching features, empowered by AI.

Summary

In this chapter, we have taken a deep dive into the AI features in Firefly and Photoshop. We started with the building blocks of most high-quality generative content, converting ideas into text-driven prompts. We examined 10 common descriptors that direct the image model with specific instructions, starting with essential descriptors such as the subject, medium, action, environment, and props, to help generate the desired image. After exploring all 10 descriptors, we crafted an in-depth prompt that included the lens type and f-stop for situations where highly detailed instructions are required.

We also looked at the Adobe Firefly interface, exploring the controls that support the text prompt and define criteria such as the image model, aspect ratio, styles, and effects. We saw how reference images can be used to influence both the structure and visual style of the generated image.

In the final section, we returned to Photoshop, examining AI-empowered features for healing and retouching images and comparing Adobe's own image models to newer partner models such as Nano Banana. We saw how a drab sky could be replaced with the help of auto-generated layer masks and a library of dynamic-looking skies. We also saw how the resulting edits could be added as a set of adjustment layers, which allowed for non-destructive editing.

We examined how **Generative Fill** can be used to replace unwanted content in images, first by transforming an apple into an orange, and then by removing distracting elements, such as cables and people, using **Remove Tool**. Finally, we explored editing and creating backgrounds for existing images. We extended the canvas using **Generative Fill** for a social media post, changing the aspect ratio. Then, we removed the existing background of the product shot using **Remove background**, another AI-powered feature that automatically added a high-quality layer mask. Then, we used a form of **Generative Fill** to create a new backdrop for our products with the **Generate background** feature.

In the final two chapters, we will combine many of the skills covered in this book to tackle more challenging projects, beginning with image collages.

Get This Book's PDF Version and Exclusive Extras

UNLOCK NOW

Scan the QR code (or go to packtpub.com/unlock). Search for this book by name, confirm the edition, and then follow the steps on the page.

Note: Keep your invoice handy. Purchases made directly from Packt don't require one.

13

Blending and Collaging Images

Throughout this book, blending or masking has been a constant theme and an essential skill that allows you to hide unwanted content or combine multiple subjects into one composition. In this chapter, we'll be taking that concept a little further.

First, we will take six photographs of a beach landscape and stitch them seamlessly as a panorama, having Photoshop do the heavy lifting for us, removing vignettes and transparent edges with **Content-Aware Fill**. You'll also practice your healing and retouching skills as you remove all the tourists from the beach with the **Healing Brush** tool and the **Clone Stamp** tool.

We'll then move on to collaging, where you'll take source images of weathered posters, newsprint, and paint to recreate a portrait. This will involve the use of adjustment layers, smart objects, masks, and brushes.

You'll then get the chance to create a double-exposure image, where two photos are combined into a surreal composition. In this exercise, you'll blend a cityscape through the silhouette of a subject, again using various masking techniques.

Finally, you'll create a **high dynamic range** (HDR) image, typically combining three images of the same scene taken at different exposures. The aim is to capture details such as shadows and highlights that would otherwise be lost in a single image. By practicing many of the techniques covered in this book, you will acquire all the skills required to tackle the final chapter, the culmination of all of our learning.

In this chapter, you will explore the following topics:

- Creating seamless panoramas
- Building collages with texture and paint

- Creating double-exposure compositions
- Working with HDR images

Technical requirements

The project files for this chapter can be found at `https://packt.link/gbz/9781806021710`.

This chapter will require you to download and install **Adobe Bridge** for the HDR exercises. In a nutshell, Adobe Bridge is a visually focused file browser and asset management tool that can be used in conjunction with other Adobe applications.

Creating seamless panoramas

Photoshop has a very intuitive photo-merging feature that detects where images should join and seamlessly blends their edges. Here's how to use it:

1. Head to Adobe Photoshop and go to **File → Automate → Photomerge** to launch the **Photomerge** interface.

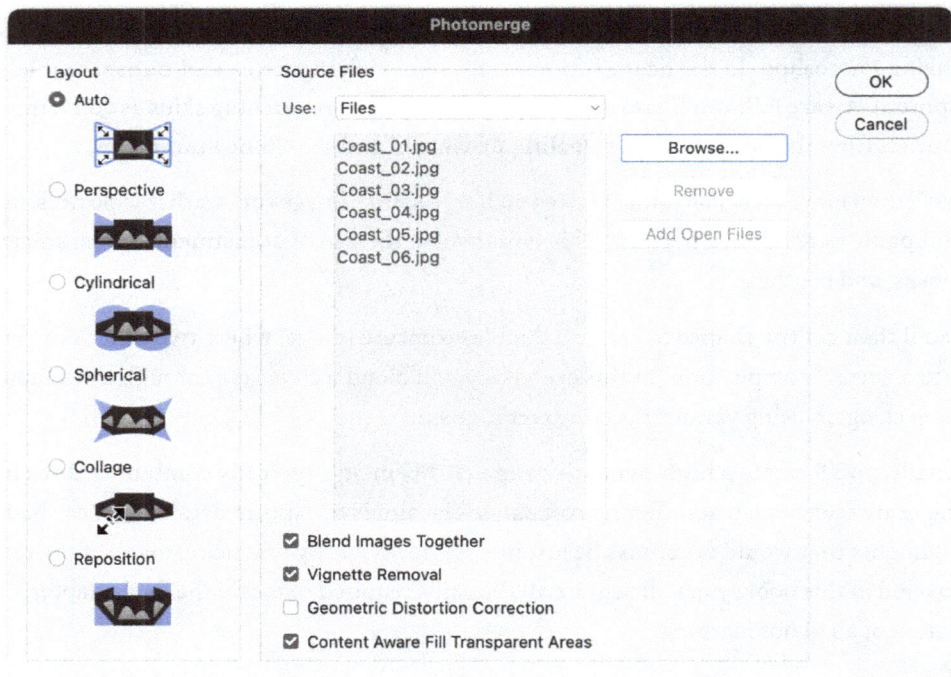

Figure 13.1: Adding images to the Photomerge dialog

2. Click on the **Browse...** button and select Coast_01.jpg to Coast_06.jpg (six files in total) from the 13-Blend folder. Click **Open** when done to add them to **Photomerge**.

3. Set **Layout** mode to **Auto**, which is the default. Then, turn on the checkboxes for **Blend Images Together**, which performs the seamless stitching for us, **Vignette Removal**, to remove darkened edges around each image, and **Content Aware Fill Transparent Areas**. Click **OK** when done.

> **Photomerge source options**
>
> **Geometric Distortion Correction** is beneficial when stitching images that contain structures such as buildings and other manufactured subjects. However, by focusing on maintaining strong visual lines, **Geometric Distortion Correction** can add considerable time to completing the stitching process. My suggestion is to stitch your images without this feature turned on, and if necessary, repeat the process with the option turned on if the initial panorama lacks the quality you require. Vignettes are a phenomenon that darkens or lightens the edges of an image at the point of capture. For a panorama to be seamless, vignettes must be removed; that's where **Vignette Removal** comes in. We are no strangers to **Content-Aware Fill**, having used it several times in this book. It is common that in the process of stitching and distorting each image to build a panorama, the edges will suffer from an uneven "bow-tie" effect. **Content-Aware Fill** simply fills the transparent regions around the edge of the canvas to provide a full image. Prior to **Content-Aware Fill**, images were often cropped down, which resulted in the loss of large portions of image content.

Photoshop will now open each of the six images and merge them into one new document. Each image is stored in a separate layer, named according to its original filename, and these are stitched together to form a seamless panorama with a series of simple yet effective layer masks. Notice that the top layer is a merged version of all the layers in the panorama. The original panorama edges should also have been filled with the help of Content-Aware technology, inside the active selection. You can also hide the top layer and edit the original Photomerge layers if you wish:

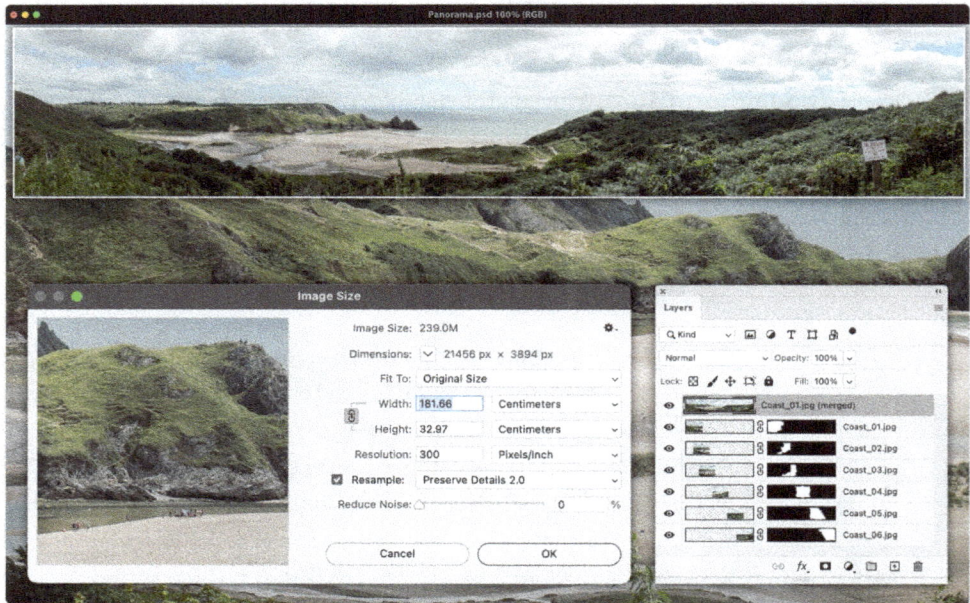

Figure 13.2: The stitched panorama in Photoshop

4. Go to **Select → Deselect** and then head to **Layer → Flatten Image**. This is one of the few occasions when it is prudent to lose additional layers—in this scenario, layers we cannot see—to reduce the file size. After all, this image is 181 cm x 33 cm at a resolution of 300 PPI.

5. Click on the **Create new layer** icon at the bottom of the **Layers** panel and name the layer Retouch. Ensure it is active.

6. Go to **File → Save**. Name the document Panorama as a PSD in the 13-Blend folder. Click **Save** when done and keep the document open.

7. Switch to the **Spot Healing Brush** tool by pressing the *J* key, then click and hold down the left mouse button on the active tool in the **Tools** panel. From the popout, click on the **Spot Healing Brush** tool to make it active.

8. Click on the **Brush Tip** menu and set the brush's **Size** value to 40 px. Set the **Type** option to **Content-Aware** and turn on **Sample All Layers**. Ensure that the **Retouch** layer is active in the **Layers** panel:

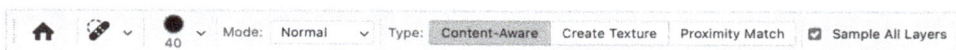

Figure 13.3: The Spot Healing Brush settings in the Options bar

9. Click on as many people and brightly colored tents as you can find on the beach to remove them, leaving an almost-empty beach scene. Remember to drag across the entire subject in a single brush stroke as you attempt to remove it; otherwise, Photoshop tends to smudge the leftover pixels into the surrounding region:

Figure 13.4: Removing distracting elements from the beach

Try to avoid retouching several textures at once, for example, where people are standing in front of the river, with a backdrop (texture) of water, the river edge, and sand. The **Spot Healing Brush** tool can struggle to remove the subject and maintain hard lines, such as the river edge, often smudging or distorting surrounding pixels. You can also try the **Clone Stamp** tool instead. Remove all the tourists from the beach and the sea.

10. Next, zoom into the lower-left corner of the panorama, where you will find a group of people that need to be concealed as they are distracting. This type of edit is often achieved simply by using the **Clone Stamp** tool. Click on the **Brush Tip** menu in the **Options** bar, scroll down the list of brushes, and find the **Chalk 60** brush.

11. Change the brush tip's **Size** value to 150 px, then press *Enter* to close the brush tip pop-out. Set **Mode** to **Normal** and ensure the **Opacity** and **Flow** options are both set to 100%. From the sampling settings, turn on the **Aligned** checkbox and set the **Sample** drop-down menu to **Current & Below**:

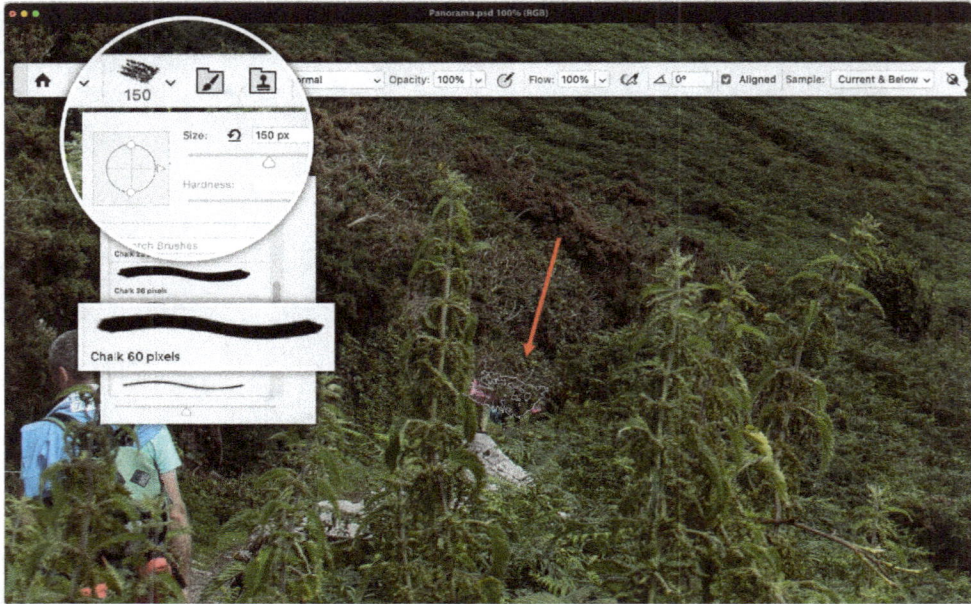

Figure 13.5: Using the Clone Stamp tool to conceal people in the foreground

12. Finally, if you navigate to the right-hand side of the image, you may recognize the sign, which we removed from a similar image in an earlier chapter. If you want to practice further, try removing the sign in this panorama.

13. When done, go to **File → Save** and close the document.

In the first section of this chapter, we used **Photomerge** to combine six images, remove vignettes, and apply automatic layer masks to achieve a seamless panorama. We then applied our knowledge of the **Spot Healing Brush** tool and the **Clone Stamp** tool to remove tourists from the landscape. Next, we'll turn a photo into a collage.

Building collages with texture and paint

In this exercise, you will transform a portrait photo into a collage by dividing the source image into defined bands of grayscale. These will then be turned into selections, within which our collage artwork will appear.

Posterizing the source photo

Follow these steps to posterize the source photo:

1. Open LayeredMan.jpg from the 13-Blend folder.

2. Duplicate the background layer by dragging the layer onto the **New Layer** icon at the bottom of the **Layers** panel. Rename the duplicated layer Subject. Turn off background layer visibility.

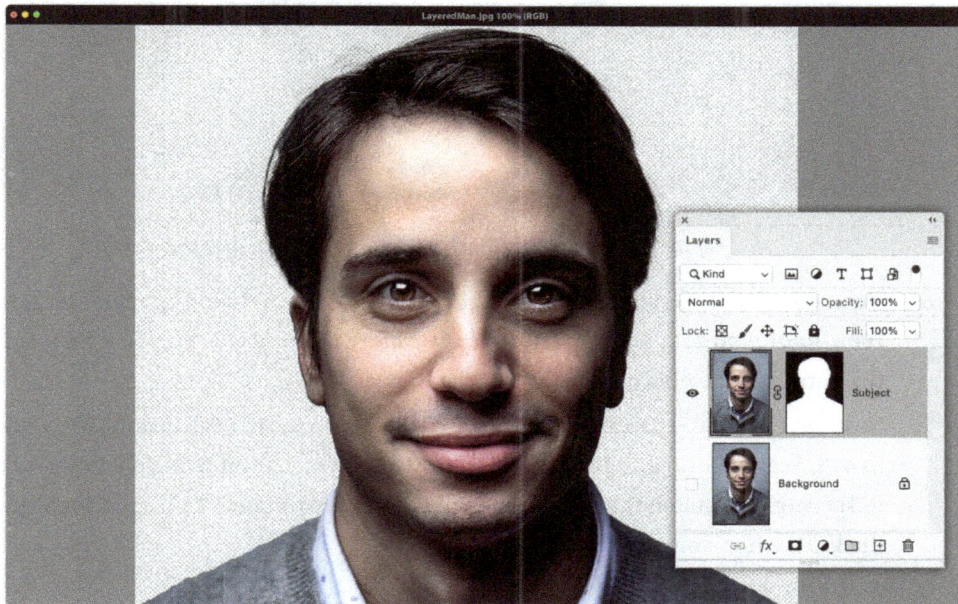

Figure 13.6: Duplicating the background layer and masking the subject

3. With the **Subject** layer active, right-click on the layer name and choose **Convert to Smart Object** from the list of options.

4. Switch to the **Magic Wand** tool and click on **Select Subject** from the **Options** bar. With the selection in place, click on the **Add a mask** button at the bottom of the **Layers** panel to hide the backdrop in the photo.

5. Go to **Image** → **Adjustments** → **Black & White**, and when a dialog appears, click **OK** to apply the default settings:

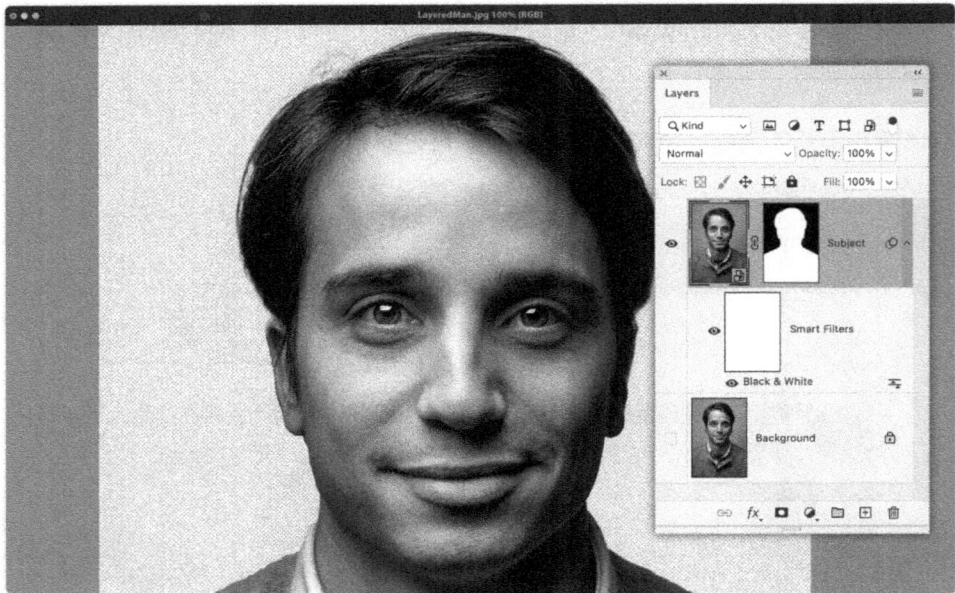

Figure 13.7: Applying a Black & White adjustment as a smart object

6. Next, go to **Filter** → **Sharpen** → **Unsharp Mask**. When a dialog appears, set **Amount** to 100%, **Radius** to 1.0, and **Threshold** to 10 before clicking **OK**. This will help emphasize the details in the photo.

7. Next, go to **Filter** → **Oil Paint**. When a dialog appears, set **Stylization** to 7, **Cleanliness** to 4.3, **Scale** to 0.7, and **Bristle Detail** to 10. Click on the **Lighting** checkbox to activate it, set **Angle** to match the light in the photo at approximately 133°, and set **Shine** to 1.3. Click **OK** when done:

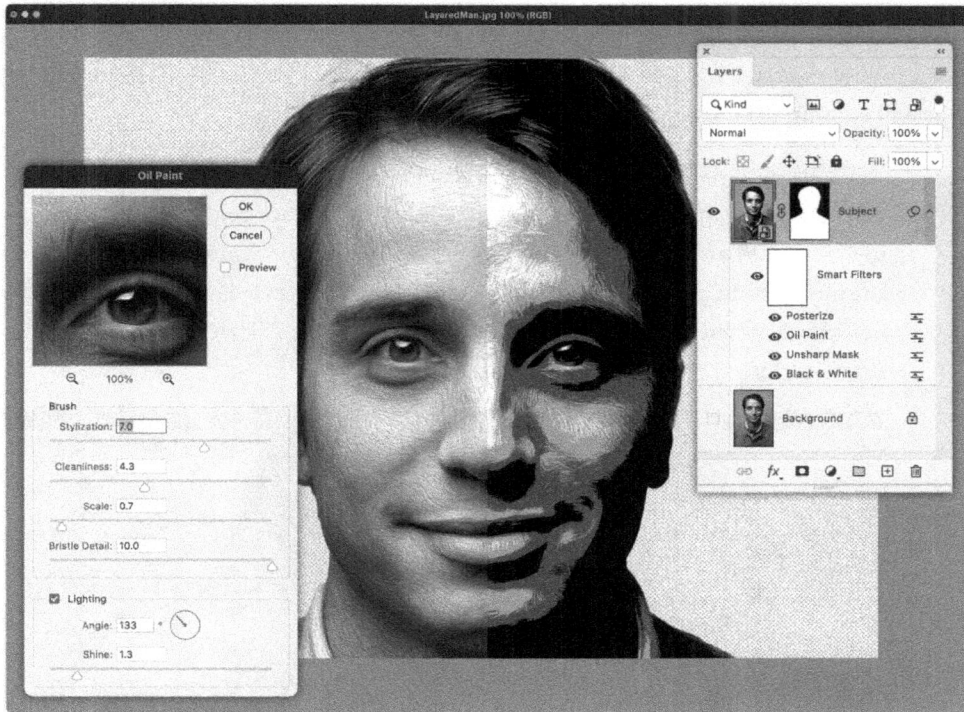

Figure 13.8: Photo with the Oil Paint filter applied (left) and after posterization (right)

The settings used here will help make the source artwork feel less like a photo as we progress it. The idea here is to create pronounced effects of oil paint marks. Depending on the size of the image you apply this to and the nature of the content, you will need to adapt the settings each time to suit.

8. Next, go to **Image → Adjustments → Posterize**. This will reduce the number of colors—or, in this case, shades of gray—from a possible 256 to a new number of our choosing. For this image, just four levels will be sufficient.

9. Save the document in the 13-Blend folder as a PSD. Keep the image open for the next exercise.

Selecting and masking posterized regions

In the following steps, you'll leverage the posterized regions of gray as the basis for four selections that will contain the collage artwork:

1. With the **Subject Source** layer active, go to **Select** → **Color Range**.

2. When a dialog appears, hover your cursor over the black region of the subject's hair (**A** in *Figure 13.9*) and click to define the selection. To ensure you select only black regions of the image, reduce the **Fuzziness** slider to around 24%. A preview of the selected pixels will be shown in white in the dialog's preview thumbnail. Click **OK** when done to generate the selection:

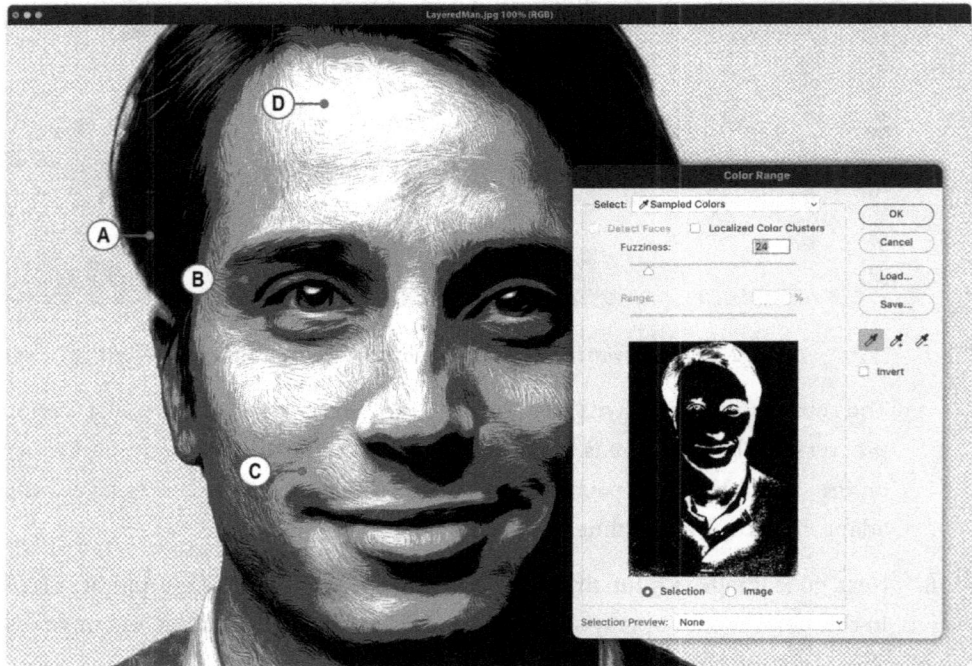

Figure 13.9: Create a selection of each region of gray

3. Go to the bottom of the **Layers** panel and click the **Create a new group** icon. Then, click the **Add a mask** icon at the bottom of the **Layers** panel to apply the mask to the newly created group. Rename the group Shadows.

4. With the **Subject Source** layer active, go to **Select** → **Color Range** and repeat the same technique as before. This time, select the dark gray band of color in the image (**B** in *Figure 13.9*) and adjust the **Fuzziness** slider to suit. In this example, I chose 16.

5. Select the layer group named **Shadows** and then click on the **Create a new group** icon. Rename the newly added group Dark Gray.

6. Using the techniques in this exercise, create two more layer groups for light gray (**C** in *Figure 13.9*) and white (**D**). You should now have four layer-groups named **Shadows**, **Dark Gray**, **Light Gray**, and **Highlights**.

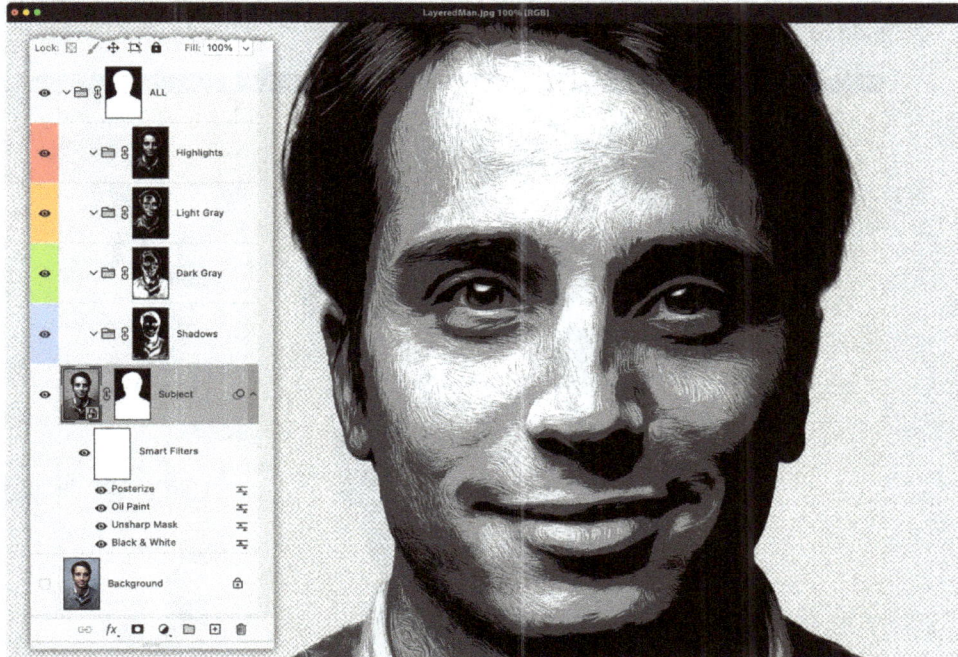

Figure 13.10: From each selection, create a new layer group with an assigned layer mask

7. To help identify each part, color-code the **Shadows** layer group blue, the **Dark Gray** group green, the **Light Gray** group orange, and the **Highlights** group red.

8. Hover your cursor over the **Subject** layer mask thumbnail, hold *Ctrl* (Windows) or *Cmd* (macOS), and click to load the mask as a selection. Click on the **Create a new group** icon. Then, click on the **Add a mask** icon at the bottom of the **Layers** panel to apply the mask to the newly created group. Rename the group ALL.

9. Drag the newly created layer group to the top of the layer stack. Click on the layer group named **Highlights**, then press *Shift* and click on the layer group named **Shadows** to make all four layer-groups active. Then, drag them into the layer group named ALL. This will ensure the edges of the subject are neat and tidy once you add textures to them.

Adding texture and paint to the posterized sections

To add texture and paint, follow these steps:

1. Click on the **Background** layer in the **Layers** panel to make it active. Then, click on the **Create new fill or adjustment layer** icon at the bottom of the **Layers** panel and select **Solid Color** from the list. When the Color Picker appears, enter fcdc00 into the **Hexadecimal** field to create a vivid yellow.

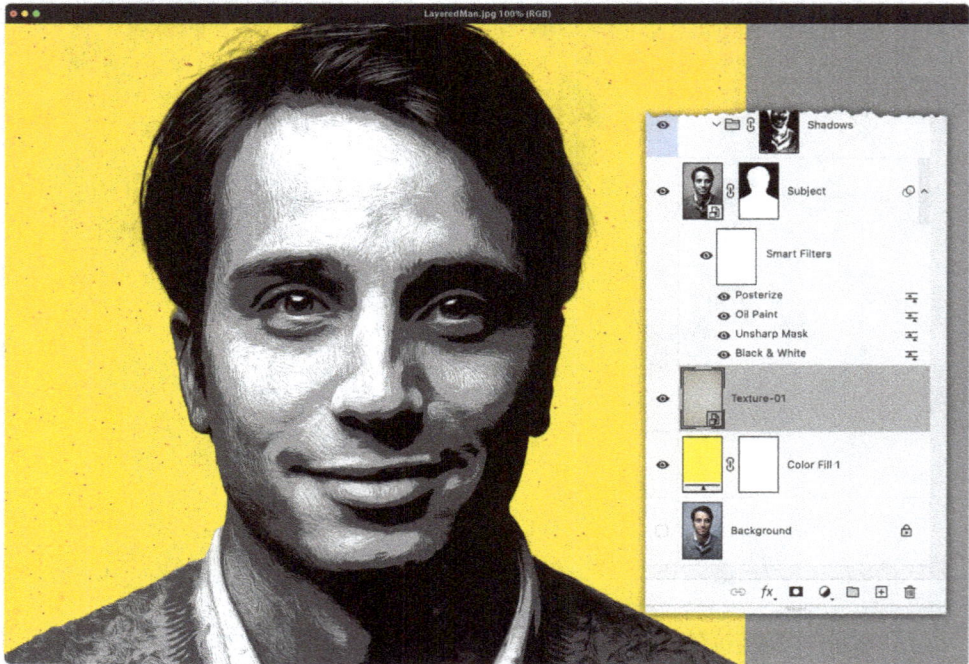

Figure 13.11: Adding a color fill layer and then overlaying the paint spatter texture

2. Next, go to **File → Place Embedded**, browse to the 13-Blend folder, select Texture-01. jpg, then click **Open**. When the image appears, press *Enter* (Windows) or *Return* (macOS) to complete the import. Change the layer's **Blend** mode to Color Burn.

3. Click on the **Dark Gray** layer group, then go to **File → Place Embedded**, browse to the 13-Blend folder, select Paint-01.jpg, and then click **Open**. When an image appears, press *Enter* (Windows) or *Return* (macOS) to complete the import.

4. Ensure the imported artwork is added to the **Dark Gray** layer group by dragging the layer in the **Layers** panel onto the **Dark Gray** layer group folder icon. Switch to the **Move** tool from the **Tools** panel and drag the Paint-01 layer into a position so that it covers the man:

Figure 13.12: Adding the first paint sample to the Dark Gray layer group

5. Click on the **Shadows** layer group and repeat the same technique to import Paint-02.jpg from the 13-Blend folder. Ensure the **Scale** value of the layer is 100% and reposition the artwork to cover the subject. Drag the imported artwork onto the **Shadows** layer group icon to ensure it is added to the group.

6. With the **Paint-02** layer still active, go to **File → Place Embedded**, browse to the 13-Blend folder, select Paint-03.jpg, then click **Open**. Change the **Blend** mode to **Multiply**. This will emphasize dark tones.

Figure 13.13: Adding two paint images to the Shadows layer group

7. Click on the **Light Gray** layer group, go to **File → Place Embedded**, browse to the 13-Blend folder, select Texture-02.jpg, then click **Open**. Ensure the **Scale** value of the layer is 100%. Reposition the artwork to your own preference. Press *Enter* (Windows) or *Return* (macOS) to complete the import.

8. Ensure the imported artwork is added to the **Light Gray** layer group by dragging the layer in the **Layers** panel onto the **Light Gray** layer group folder icon.

9. Click on the **Highlights** layer group, go to **File → Place Embedded**, browse to the 13-Blend folder, select Paint-05.jpg, then click **Open**. Ensure the **Scale** value of the layer is 65%. Reposition the artwork so that it covers all white regions of the artwork. Press *Enter* (Windows) or *Return* (macOS) to apply the edits:

Figure 13.14: Add the concrete photo to the Highlights layer group

10. Ensure the imported artwork is added to the **Highlights** layer group by dragging the layer in the **Layers** panel onto the folder icon for the **Highlights** layer group.

11. Click on the **Paint-01** layer, go to **File → Place Embedded**, browse to the 13-Blend folder, select Paint-04.jpg, then click **Open**.

12. Ensure the **Scale** value of the layer is 60%, set **Angle** to 110°, and reposition the artwork so that it covers the lower section of the image only, with a small portion overlapping the subject's chin. Press *Enter* to apply the edits.

Figure 13.15: Add the remaining collage artwork to the composition

13. Experiment with the **Blend** mode to see which is your favorite. I chose **Overlay**, but you can change the appearance drastically with modes such as **Multiply**. Save the document when done.

In this section, we created accurate selections with the help of **Select Subject**, applied oil-painting brush stroke effects, and posterized artwork to form four regions: highlights, lighter midtones, darker midtones, and shadows. We transformed each region into a selection, which we then filled with paint and texture samples to create a colorful collage effect. All of these can be re-edited, replaced, and transformed in a nondestructive workflow. Next, we will examine double-exposure effects.

Creating double-exposure compositions

A **double exposure** was originally achieved in photography by exposing the same frame of film several times to blend different images on a single negative.

Blending unrelated images

You will first create an accurate selection and mask the street image in the shape of the woman's body. Follow these steps:

1. Open `Exposure-Subject.jpg` from the `13-Blend` folder.

2. Then, go to **File → Place Linked**, browse to the `13-Blend` folder, select `Exposure-Street.jpg`, and click on **Place**.

3. When the artwork appears, click on the **Commit** button in the **Options** bar. Turn off the **Exposure-Street** layer visibility and click on the **Background** layer in the **Layers** panel to make it active.

4. Press the *W* key to switch to any one of the selection tools, either the **Magic Wand** tool, the **Quick Selection** tool, or the **Object Selection** tool. From the **Options** bar, click on the **Select Subject** button to create a selection of the woman.

5. Next, click on the `Exposure-Street` layer to make it active, even though it is currently hidden, and then click on the **Create a new group** icon at the bottom of the **Layers** panel.

6. Ensure the new group is active in the **Layers** panel before clicking the **Add a mask** icon at the bottom of the **Layers** panel. The selection will now be assigned to the layer group.

7. Rename the layer group `Street` and then drag the **Exposure-Street** layer into the layer group. In the example shown in *Figure 13.16*, the layer group was also color-coded red for clarity.

8. Enable visibility for the **Exposure-Street** layer. You should now see that the street image is masked. By adding the street image to a layer group with an assigned mask that is the same shape as the woman's silhouette, we can apply a second layer mask, this time to the **Exposure-Street** layer, and edit it without affecting the first mask.

Figure 13.16: Street photo masked in front of the subject

9. Go to **Select → Reselect**; this will load the previously created selection of the woman. Then, click on the **Background** layer in the **Layers** panel and choose **Layer → New → Layer Via Copy**.

10. When the pasted layer appears above the background in the **Layers** panel, rename it
    `Overlay` and drag the layer to the top of the layer stack:

Figure 13.17: Add a duplicate of the background layer to restore vital details

11. Click on the **Exposure-Street** layer to make it active, and then click on the **Add a layer
    mask** icon at the bottom of the **Layers** panel.

12. Switch to the **Brush** tool by pressing the *B* key. In the **Options** bar, click on the **Brush Tip**
    preset menu and choose the **Soft Round** brush tip.

Figure 13.18: The brush settings

13. Set the brush **Size** value to 900 px and the **Opacity** value to 30% from the **Options** bar. Press the *D* key to reset the **Foreground** and **Background** colors, and then press the *X* key to switch them so that black is the active color for painting.

14. Hover your cursor over the region where the woman's face is and drag across it with the **Brush** tool to fade the street image gradually:

Figure 13.19: Masking the street layer where it covers the woman's face

15. Work from the outside edge of the woman's hair toward the face, concealing the street image. Ensure that not all parts of the street layer are removed from the top and right-hand sides of the woman's hair. You can leave some of the faint glow of the streetlights around the left-hand-side edges of the hair for dramatic effect if you wish.

16. Reduce the **Size** value of the brush tip to 200 px and then conceal the street image around the region of the woman's chin by painting black in that region with the **Brush** tool. A simple, soft fade along the edge of the chin will be sufficient to achieve the desired look:

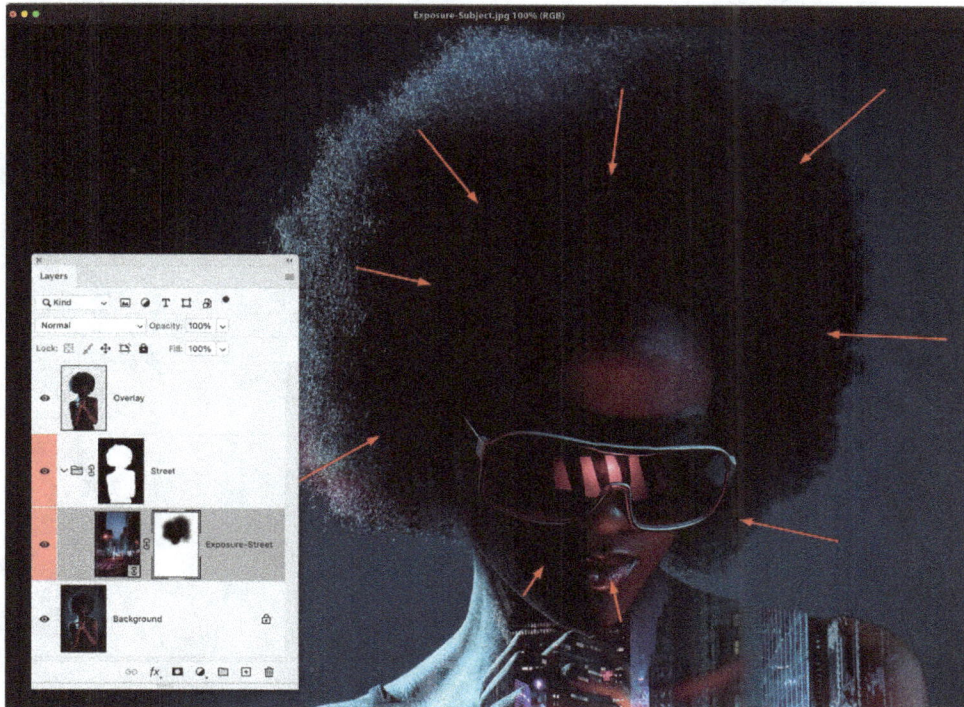

Figure 13.20: Using the Brush tool, concealing sections around the woman's face and hair

17. Save the document in the 13-Blend folder as a PSD with the name SeeingDouble. Then, close the document when done.

Figure 13.21: The completed double-exposure image

Blending two exposures of the same image

In earlier chapters, we reviewed techniques for blending two images, especially when removing unwanted content from the final visual. There are also scenarios where you may need to create separate photos to combine intentionally. In the following exercise, we'll merge two photos using a Photoshop script and combine them using a layer mask to create an abstract visual. Follow these steps:

1. Go to **File → Scripts → Load files into stack**, browse to the 13-Blend folder, and select 01-Hands.jpg and 02-Face.jpg. Leave all checkboxes deactivated and then click on **OK** when done.

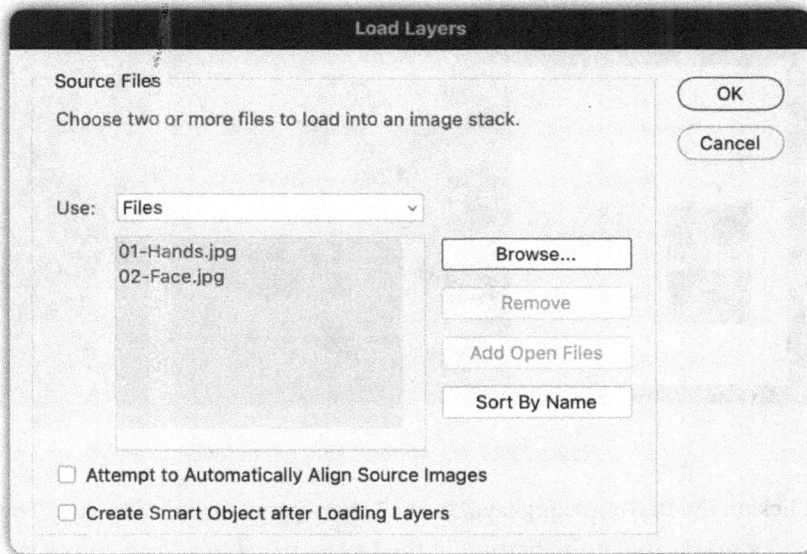

Figure 13.22: Importing both JPG files into a single-layer stack

2. The order of the images listed in the **Load Layers** dialog is how the photos will be layered in Photoshop. In this case, we needed the image of the subject's face at the bottom and the shot of the hands in front of the face at the top of the stack. Hence, the images are numbered 01 and 02 so that Photoshop imports them in the order required. They can, of course, be reordered in Photoshop as well.

Figure 13.23: The imported images as layers in the stack

3. Click on the **01-Hands.jpg** layer in the **Layers** panel to make it active. Then, click on the **Add a mask** icon at the bottom of the **Layers** panel to add an empty layer mask, filled with white.

4. Press the *D* key to reset the **Foreground** and **Background** colors back to black and white, then press the *X* key to switch them so that black is the active color to paint with.

5. Switch to the **Brush** tool by pressing the *B* key. In the **Options** bar, click on the **Brush Tip** preset menu and choose the **Soft Round** brush tip:

Figure 13.24: The brush settings

6. Set the brush **Size** value to 800 px and the **Opacity** value to 12% from the **Options** bar. With this technique, we need to fade the hands very subtly to reveal parts of the underlying face, so having the **Opacity** value set low will help restrain the brush marks.

7. Hover the **Brush** tool over the region where the right eye should be and click repeatedly, which should make them appear gradually. You will also need to ensure that you leave enough of the hands and fingers visible. You can press *X* to switch the **Foreground** and **Background** colors, painting white to reveal the hands and fingers if you go too far with your masking.

8. Repeat the same technique by hovering the **Brush** tool over the region where the left eye should be and click repeatedly to reveal it:

Figure 13.25: The completed image, revealing the face through the hands

9. Save the document in the 13-Blend folder as a PSD file named Visions. Then, close the document when done.

In this section, we combined two images to create a double-exposure effect using blend modes and layer masks. The first mask was applied to a layer group, which allowed us to set an edge for the street layer around the silhouette of the woman's hair and body. The second mask was applied to a specific layer to hide the parts of the street image that obscured the woman's face. In the next section, we will combine five photos to overcome challenging lighting conditions with an HDR image.

Working with HDR images

Single-shot photos with a digital camera can sometimes lack the detail required to show the full luminance range, resulting in deep black shadow areas or blown-out white highlights. Traditional HDR images preserve light data closer to that perceived by the human eye. By combining several shots at different bracketed F-stops (exposures), you can create 32-bit images to keep incredible detail in your photographs.

Advice for shooting HDR source images

Although a growing number of DSLRs offer an HDR feature that captures several shots automatically, called bracketing, many cameras still require you to generate an HDR image by taking several shots of the same scene at different exposures, each capturing different light information. The challenge with this is movement, called **ghosting**, between each shot. To give yourself the best chance of capturing several shots with minimal ghosting, use a tripod. Keep the aperture setting constant throughout all of your shots, or you will risk altering the depth of field. Use a remote cord, as even pressing the capture button for each shot will move the camera.

Installing Adobe Bridge

Earlier in this chapter, I mentioned that Adobe Bridge will be needed for the HDR exercises. While it isn't strictly needed, utilizing Adobe Bridge to combine and edit HDR images or digital negatives certainly does make life easier. Here's how to use it:

1. To check whether you have Bridge installed, go to **File → Open with Bridge**. If Bridge is not installed, the Creative Cloud desktop application will appear and display all the installed apps, along with other apps that you can choose to install, including Bridge.

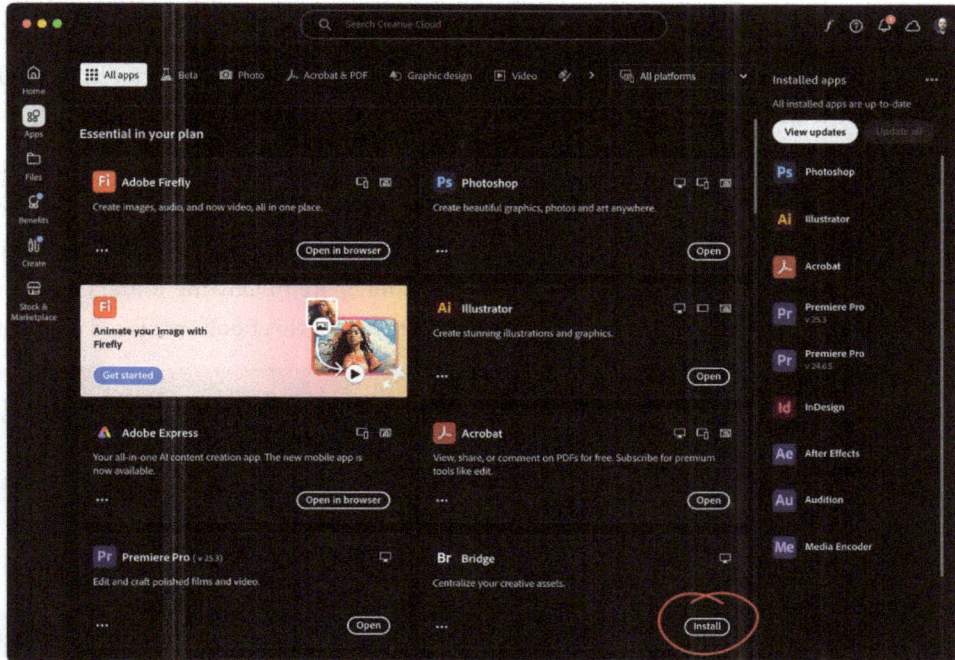

Figure 13.26: Installing Bridge from the Creative Cloud desktop application

2. Click the **Install** button next to **Bridge** to initiate the installation process. Bridge will then appear alongside other installed applications and show the progress of the installation:

3. Once the installation is complete, you can click on the **Open** button in the Creative Cloud desktop application dialog. Bridge should now appear after a couple of minutes. If you are prompted to install components from other Adobe applications, such as Photoshop, choose **Yes**.

You may need to be patient as Bridge connects to other Adobe applications on the first occasion it is launched. If you intend to use the **Open in Bridge** command found in Photoshop, this may not work until you perform a restart of your computer. Once restarted, Bridge should connect to Photoshop accordingly.

Creating an HDR image with HDR Pro

You will combine five photos to create a composite of an architectural interior in which lighting conditions mean a single image cannot capture the full range from shadows to highlights. Here's how to do it:

1. With Bridge open and active, click on the **Folder** panel name, on the upper left-hand side of the interface, to display your locally connected drives. The **Folder** panel functions similarly to a file browser, enabling you to navigate to existing folders. Browse to the 13-Blend folder. In this example, the project files for this book are stored on my desktop:

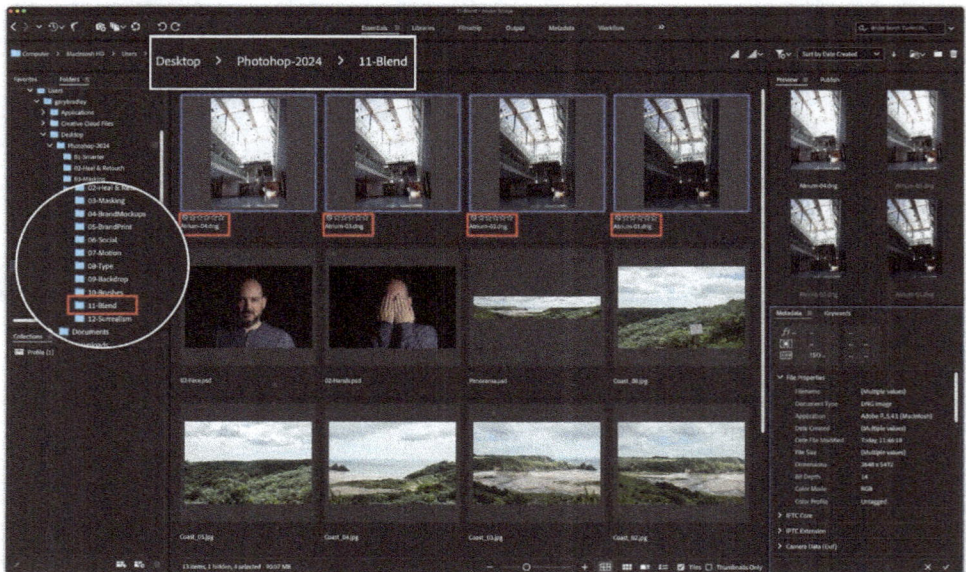

Figure 13.27: Select all the Atrium images for this exercise

2. Once you click on the 13-Blend folder from the **Folder** panel, you will see the files displayed in the central portion of Bridge, called the **Content** panel, the nearest thing to an image window that you would see in Bridge. The **Content** panel is where you interact with your files. Click on Atrium-01.dng and then press *Shift* and click on the other atrium images, four in total.

3. This will place a highlight color around each of the active image thumbnails. Next, right-click on one of the highlighted thumbnails, and from the context menu, choose **Open in Camera Raw**. The images will then appear in **Camera Raw**, displayed at the bottom of the interface in the filmstrip, with one of them shown in the image window. The images now need to be combined into an HDR image.

4. Next, you will again need to select all the photos. Click the far-left-hand-side thumbnail to make it active, then press *Shift* and click the far-right-hand-side thumbnail to select all four images. Hover your cursor over one of the thumbnails to reveal a rollover menu, containing three dots, then click it and choose **Merge to HDR…**:

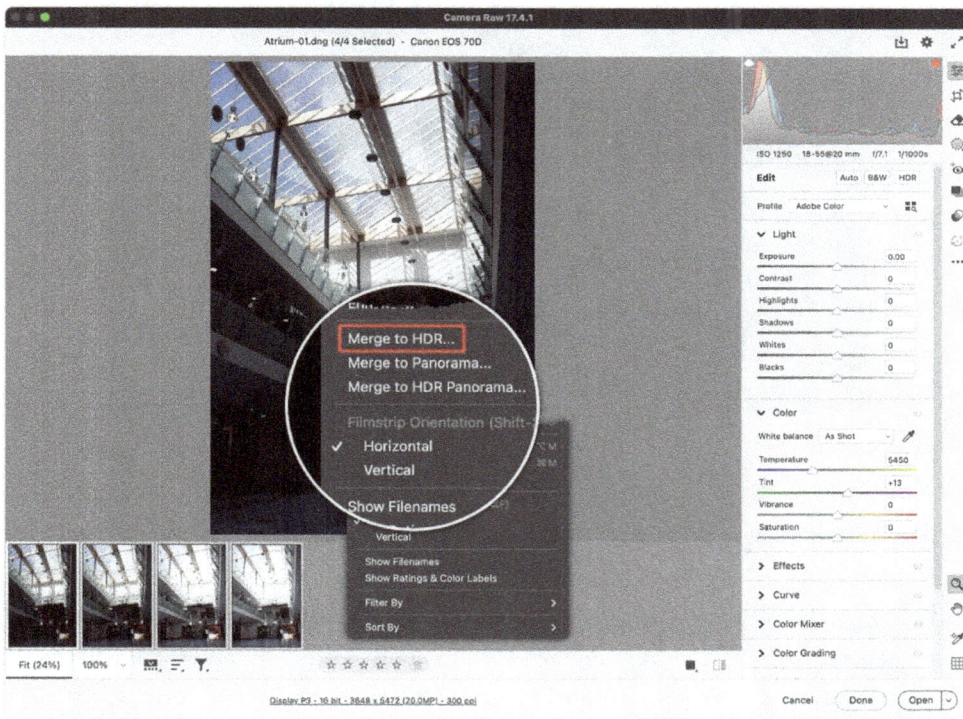

Figure 13.28: The five atrium images open in Camera Raw

5. When the **HDR Merge Preview** dialog appears, turn on the **Align Images** and **Apply Auto Settings** checkboxes and set the **Deghost** dropdown to **Off**. Then, click on the **Merge...** button at the bottom right-hand side of the dialog:

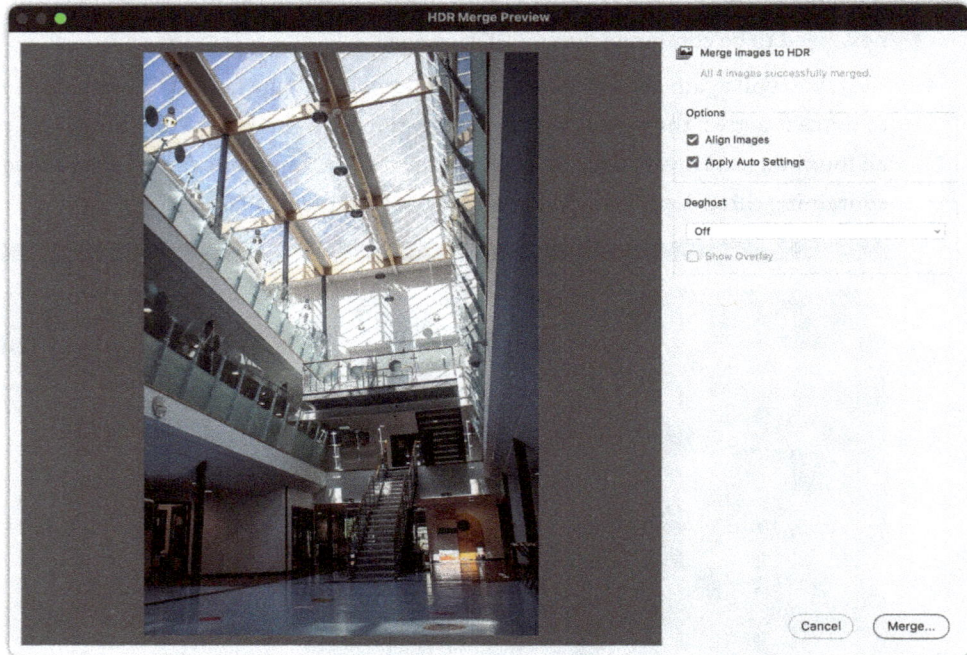

Figure 13.29: The HDR Merge Preview dialog

6. You will then be prompted to save the image as **HDR** in the **Digital Negative (DNG)** format. Save it in the 13-Blend folder as Atrium-HDR.

7. Once the file has been saved, you will be taken back to the **Camera Raw** interface. Click on the **Auto** button (**A** in *Figure 13.30*) to apply basic color and tonal edits to the image. However, it's likely that you will need to fine-tune the settings further:

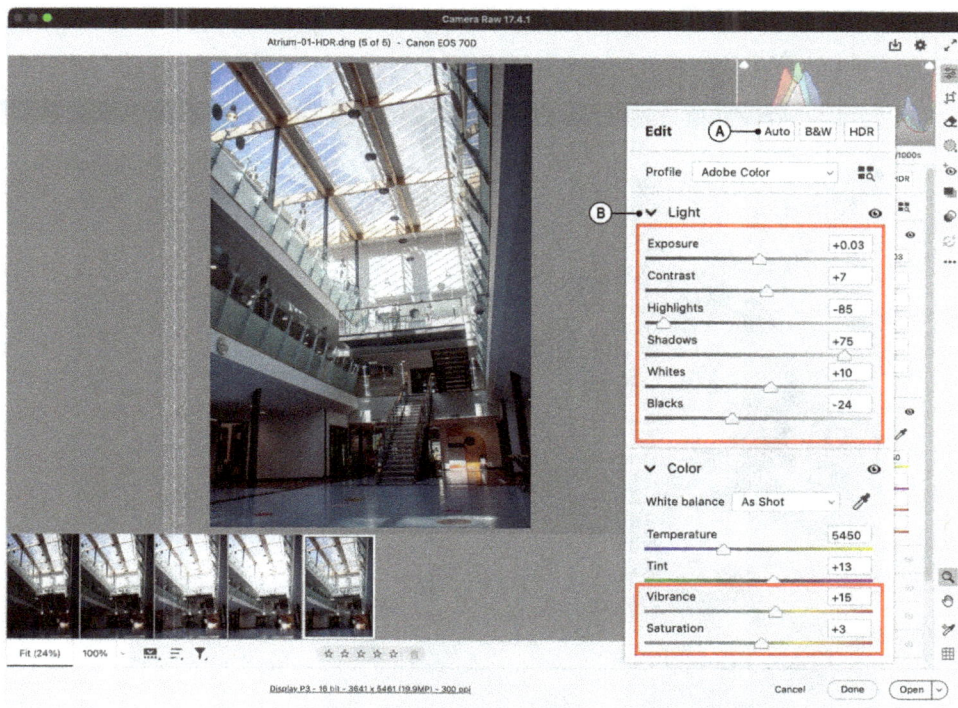

Figure 13.30: Edit the Light and Color settings

8. From the **Basic** settings, set **Exposure** to +0.03, **Contrast** to +7, **Highlights** to -85, **Shad-ows** to +75, **Whites** to +10, and **Blacks** to -24.

9. Leave the **Texture**, **Clarity**, and **Dehaze** sliders set to 0. Then, set **Vibrance** to +15 to boost the warmth of the wood beams in the roof, and boost the color intensity slightly by setting **Saturation** to +3.

10. Under the **Detail** settings, set **Sharpening** to 79. To preview the sharpening in grayscale, hold *Alt* (Windows) or *Option* (macOS) as you drag the slider to the right-hand side.

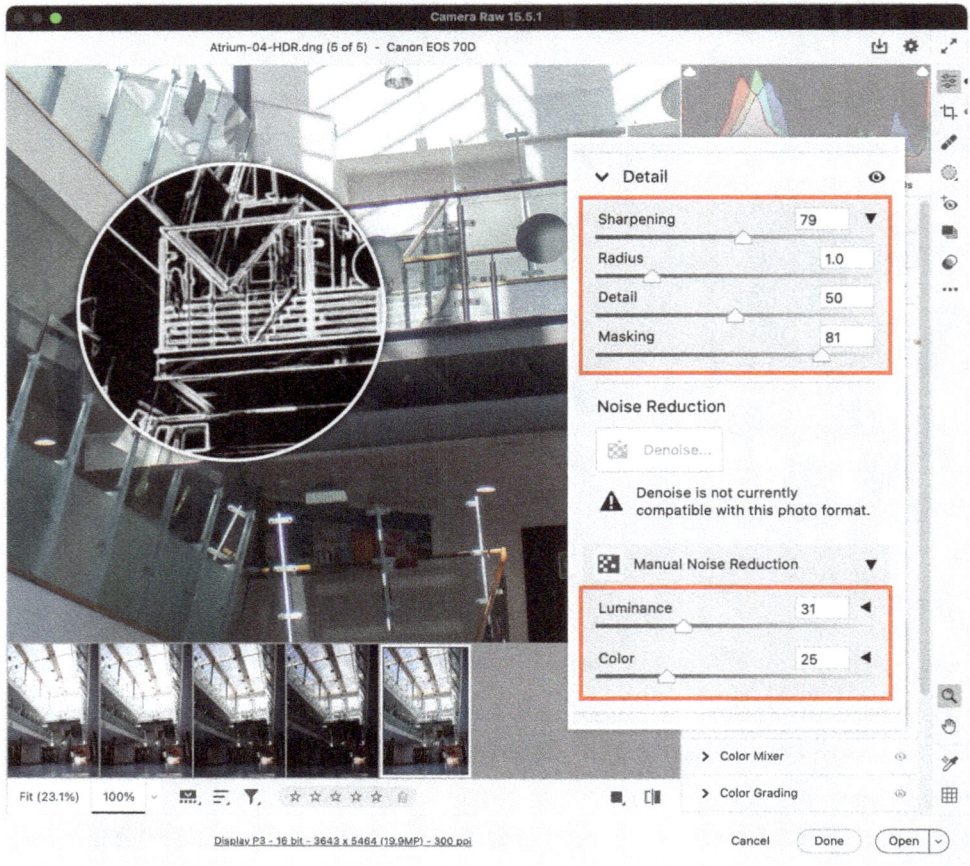

Figure 13.31: Adjust the sharpening options

11. Leave the **Radius** slider set to its default of 1.0. Set the **Detail** slider to 50 by again holding *Alt* (Windows) or *Option* (macOS) and dragging the slider to the right-hand side to visualize the edit in grayscale.

12. Next, reduce the sharpening effect in regions of low detail by holding *Alt* (Windows) or *Option* (macOS) and dragging the **Masking** slider to 81. We need edge details, such as the handrails, to be sharper, but want to avoid adding noise to the image on flat surfaces such as walls.

13. Finally, to reduce the grainy effect of noise that is synonymous with low lighting conditions, expand **Manual Noise Reduction** and set **Luminance** to 31 and **Color** to 25. This should remove any grayscale noise and random colored noise that was present in the image.

14. Click on the **Crop Tool** icon (**A** in *Figure 13.32*). Once the options appear, click on the **Straighten Tool** icon (**B**):

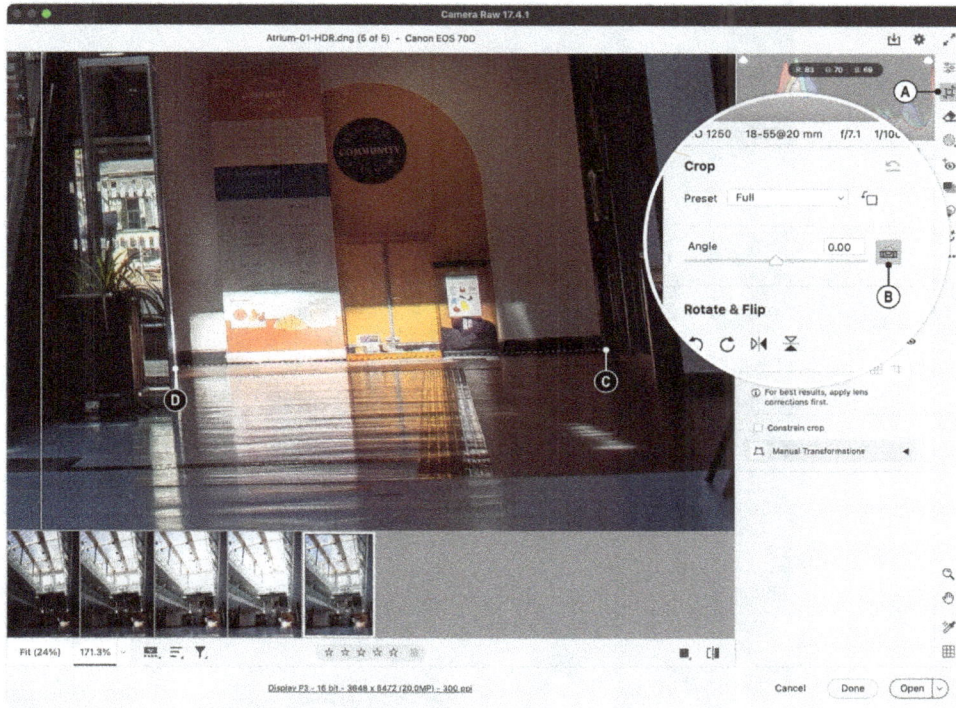

Figure 13.32: Straighten the photo

15. Hover the **Straighten** tool over the right-hand side skirting in the image (**C**), then click and hold the left mouse button down, drag to the far-left edge of the skirting, and release the left mouse button (**D**). By using the skirting in the photo, which should be level, this will straighten the image.

16. Once all the edits have been applied, click **Done** to apply all settings, close **Camera Raw**, and return to Bridge.

Figure 13.33: The completed HDR image

In the final section of this chapter, we took several images shot at different exposures that on their own would not be adequate, but by combining them as an HDR image, we were able to use the data in all five images. The final composite utilizes a far broader range of luminance levels that successfully capture details in shadows, midtones, and highlights.

Summary

In this chapter, we explored various techniques for combining multiple images, starting with a panorama, where six beach photos were stitched seamlessly to create one image.

We then recapped some of the healing and retouching techniques covered in previous chapters to remove tourists and other distracting elements from a beach using the **Spot Healing Brush** tool and the **Clone Stamp** tool. Photoshop also provided a helping hand during the stitching process, allowing us to fill in uneven, empty regions around the edge of the panorama with **Content-Aware Fill**.

We then used two unrelated images to form a double-exposure effect by generating accurate selections and layer masks to overlay the image of an atmospheric nighttime street scene over the figure of a woman.

Using a similar set of techniques, we created an unusual overlay effect that combines two photos: one of my head and shoulders, and another where I held my hands over my face. Once combined and aligned together, we used a layer mask to reveal parts of my eyes, nose, and mouth through my hands.

We then looked at a more artistic method for collaging artwork that combined old posters, paint marks, and newsprint. We created bands of light from the source image and converted them into layer masks, assigning them to layer groups. This enabled us to deposit the source print marks and distressed paper images to form a digital collage.

Finally, we overcame the challenge of inconsistent interior lighting. We took five source images, each captured at a different exposure, and combined them as an HDR image. The final artwork used light data from all five images to capture details in shadows and highlights without them being lost.

In the final chapter, we'll create surreal artwork by combining several images with selections, layer masks, and painting tools.

Get This Book's PDF Version and Exclusive Extras

UNLOCK NOW

Scan the QR code (or go to packtpub.com/unlock). Search for this book by name, confirm the edition, and then follow the steps on the page.

Note: Keep your invoice handy. Purchases made directly from Packt don't require one.

14

Creating Surrealist Artwork

One of the most impressive and undoubtedly challenging kinds of projects you can undertake in Adobe Photoshop is the creation of surreal or abstract compositions. From a house floating in a light bulb through the vacuum of space to rowing boats gliding through clouds, impossible realities and fantastical, illusionary images can look impressive when executed with time and care. The techniques in this chapter are aimed at pushing your Photoshop skills to the limit.

This chapter will approach the creation of surrealistic artwork with two methodologies. Firstly, with a limited budget, I'll show you how to curate and assemble high-quality artwork from stock content. The second approach will focus on planning, capturing, and creating surrealist artwork specifically for the project.

Regardless of the methods you choose to combine separate images to create a montage, lighting is one of the most critical aspects. Achieved with sophistication and impeccable planning, or simply by good luck, consistent lighting will make or break a montage, particularly in terms of the direction of highlights and shadows.

I first want to focus on how you can create relatively simple yet highly effective surrealist images using techniques we have covered in this book. This will allow you to become comfortable with the types of challenges you will face in this type of work and prepare you for the final project.

In the final project of this book, we will undertake our most ambitious challenge yet: combining multiple images through a series of demanding techniques that will take approximately 2 hours to create a visually stunning and professional-looking surrealistic image. To help manage this challenge into more manageable chunks, we will approach the topics in the following sections:

- How to approach a surrealist art project
- Creating simple yet effective surrealist art
- Creating and editing project-specific assets

Technical requirements

The project files for this chapter can be found at `https://packt.link/gbz/9781806021710`.

How to approach a surrealist art project

With its origins in the surrealist art movement in the early 20th century, surrealist art features bizarre, irrational, and fantastical elements to challenge conventional notions of reality and create intrigue for the viewer. Surrealist artists aim to unleash their creative potential through dreamlike imagery, unexpected juxtapositions, and unconventional techniques.

Building these dreamlike, imaginary worlds will require us to implement everything we've learned so far in this book. In previous chapters, we took an in-depth look at masking, healing, retouching, and montages. These will be central to a surrealist workflow, as well as time and patience.

Lighting is a key factor in combining separate images. While it is possible to change the hue of an image to match another, if the sum of the parts doesn't contain consistent lighting, it won't hold the viewers' attention. Low-budget projects that rely on completely unrelated stock content will require you to dedicate serious time scouring the web for images containing the subjects and locations you require and lit in similar ways. The alternative is to pay for a photographer to create source images specifically for your project, which comes at a financial cost far greater than royalty-free stock content. Alternatively, you could, of course, shoot the images yourself if you can. And don't forget, one of the new additions to Photoshop 2026, **Harmonize**, could provide a faster workflow for merging objects into a new background, provided you are willing to give up a little control over the outcome.

If you resort to stock content, I suggest downloading the watermarked version to test whether the images will combine successfully before you purchase the full–quality image. I can't tell you the number of times my initial feeling about the suitability of an image turned out to be no good when "comped" with the other assets. To create a quick proof of concept, copy and paste each of the images together and juxtapose them in the correct positions in your mock–up. This will indicate whether the lighting, angle, and quality meet your needs. You won't know if the resolution of an asset is good enough until you paste it into the composition.

In the first exercise of this chapter, we will combine two stock images using many of the skills learned in previous chapters, such as masks, blend modes, and adjustment layers.

Creating simple yet effective surrealist art

The first exercise uses free stock images that are the best match for a concept I wanted to include of an out-of-place object. In this case, the Moon turns into a balloon that is fastened to a wooden chair. I had to keep my mind open to working very loosely with this concept.

Transferring the Moon artwork

This project requires just two pieces of artwork: an image of the Moon against a night sky, and a studio image of a chair with a balloon tied to it. We'll use the studio image as the "master image" within which the composition will be built. The first step is to transfer the Moon into the master file. Here's how to do it:

1. Open Balloon.jpg and Moon.jpg from the 14-Surreal project folder.

2. With the Moon.jpg document active, switch to the **Elliptical Marquee** tool. From the **Options** bar, set the **Selection Mode** setting to **New**, **Feather** to 0 px, the **Anti-alias** checkbox to **Active**, and **Style** to **Normal**.

3. Click and drag across the Moon in the photo to create a basic selection; don't worry about the accuracy of this selection. With the selection created and active, go to **Select → Transform Selection**.

4. Use the bounding-box frame handles to change the selection scale to match the Moon. Once complete, click on the **Commit** button in the **Options** bar to update the selection.

5.   The **Elliptical Marquee** tool should remain active. Click the **Select and Mask** button from the **Options** bar to open the editor. Under the **Global Refinements** section, set **Smooth** to 4% and **Shift Edges** to approximately -16. This will ensure that the edge of the selection is consistent, eradicating any pixelated regions of the original selection and trimming away any green fringe pixels. Click **OK** when done to close the editor and update the selection.

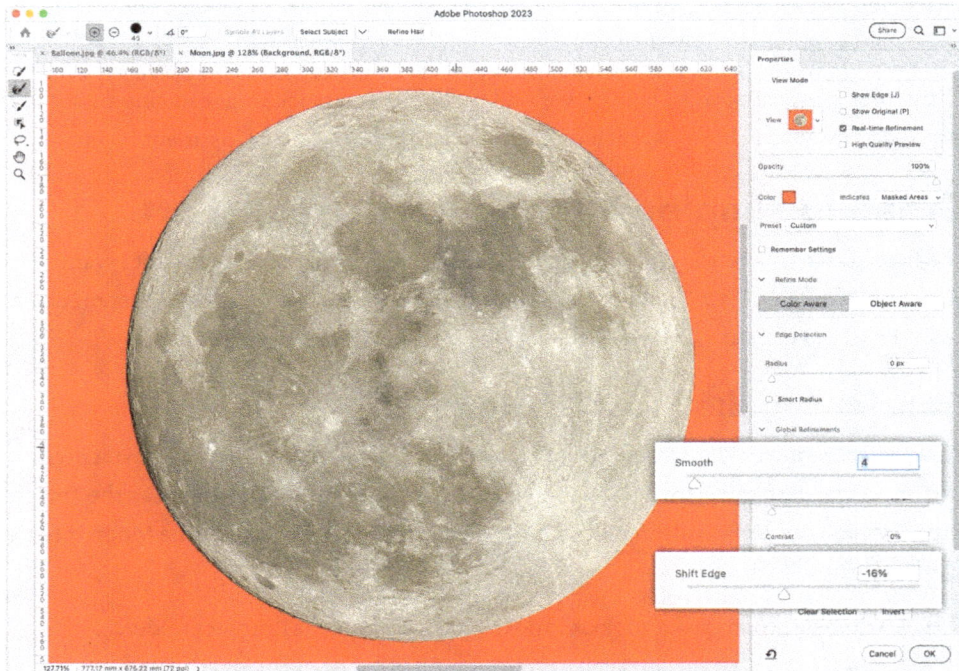

Figure 14.1: The Moon contracted selection with a smoother edge

6.   From the bottom of the **Layers** panel, ensure the **Background** layer is active, then press *Ctrl +J* (Windows) or *Cmd +J* (macOS) to create a copy of the selection as a new layer. We won't require the portion outside of the selection in the background, so a mask is unnecessary.

7.   Right-click on the newly copied layer name and select **Duplicate Layer** from the context menu. When the dialog appears, rename the layer Moon and set **Destination** to Balloon. jpg. Click **OK** when finished.

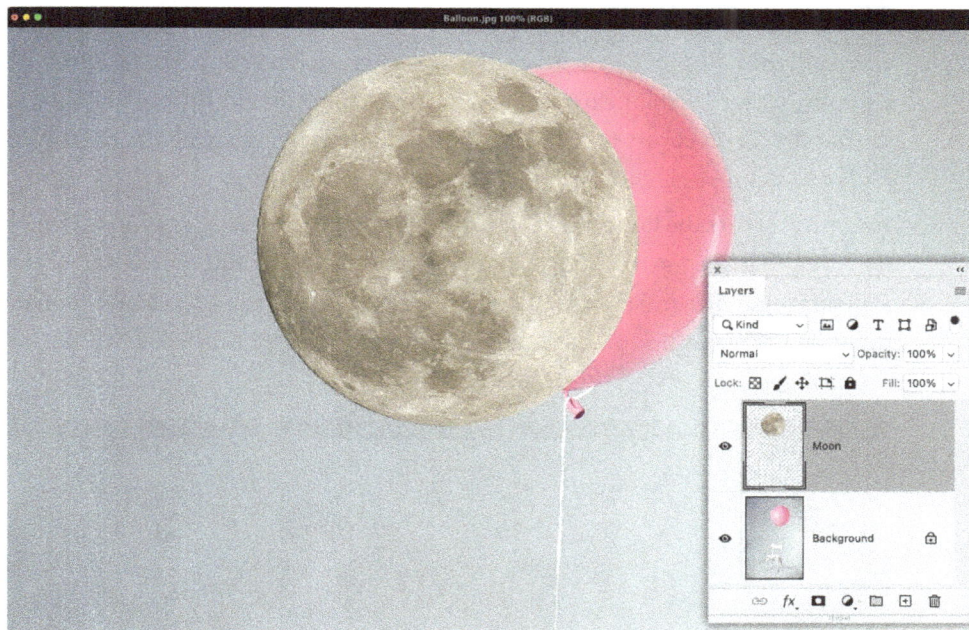

Figure 14.2: The Moon image transferred to the master file

8. Check that the **Moon** layer has been transferred to the `Balloon.jpg` document and then close the `Moon.jpg` file without saving changes.

9. Next, you will need to reduce the Moon's size to be slightly larger than the balloon. To see the balloon and the moon simultaneously, change the **Blend Mode** setting of the **Moon** layer to **Linear Burn**. This blend mode change is only temporary.

Scaling and distorting the Moon

Next, you will shape the Moon to match the balloon as closely as possible. Here are the steps:

1. Go to **Edit → Free Transform**. Hover your cursor over the Moon's center, inside the transform frame, and position it centrally to the balloon.

2. Then, ensure that the **Width** and **Height** fields are linked in the **Options** bar, and drag the opposing corners of the transform frame to scale the Moon down in size. Scale the Moon so that it is still slightly larger than the balloon. I found that approximately 87% was appropriate.

3. With the moon scaled accordingly, right-click on the transform frame and choose **Distort** from the list of modes. Turn off the link between the **Width** and **Height** fields in the **Options** bar for greater flexibility. Pull the bottom-middle transform handle downward so that the Moon covers the bottom of the inflated balloon; avoid the region where it is tied in a knot if possible.

4. You will find that the lower half of the balloon will need to be tapered so that the width is narrower than the top half of the Moon. To do this, drag the bottom-left and bottom-right transform handles inward toward the center while ensuring the moon remains larger than the balloon. Click on the **Commit** button in the **Options** bar when done to apply the changes:

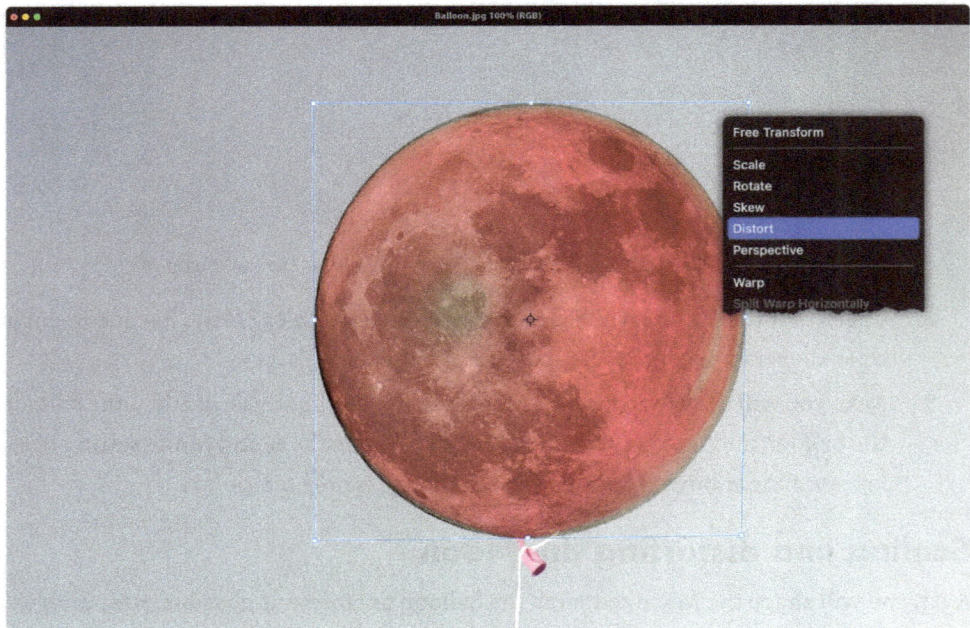

Figure 14.3: Scaling and distorting the Moon to be slightly larger than the balloon shape

5. Change the Moon's **Blend Mode** to **Normal** from the **Layers** panel to see a natural version of the moon artwork.

6. Hover your cursor over the **Moon** layer thumbnail in the **Layers** panel, hold *Ctrl* (Windows) or *Cmd* (macOS), and click on the thumbnail to select all pixels. Then, go to **Select → Inverse**. This will prevent you from adding **Clone Stamp** marks on the original Moon image, so you only add brush marks over the knotted region at the bottom of the balloon.

7. Switch to the **Clone Stamp** tool and set the brush tip to **Soft Round**, at a **Size** value of 35 px. Ensure the **Sample** drop-down menu is set to **Current**, as we don't want to sample the balloon, just the lunar surface.

8. Start by sampling from a darker region of the lunar surface, remembering to press *Alt* (Windows) or *Option* (macOS) and click to set the sample. Ensure the **Moon** layer is targeted, and the selection is still active.

9. Next, hover the brush tip over the top edge of the pink balloon knot and add clone marks to the image. Don't be concerned if you add **Clone Stamp** brush marks beyond the balloon's knot; we'll mask those out later.

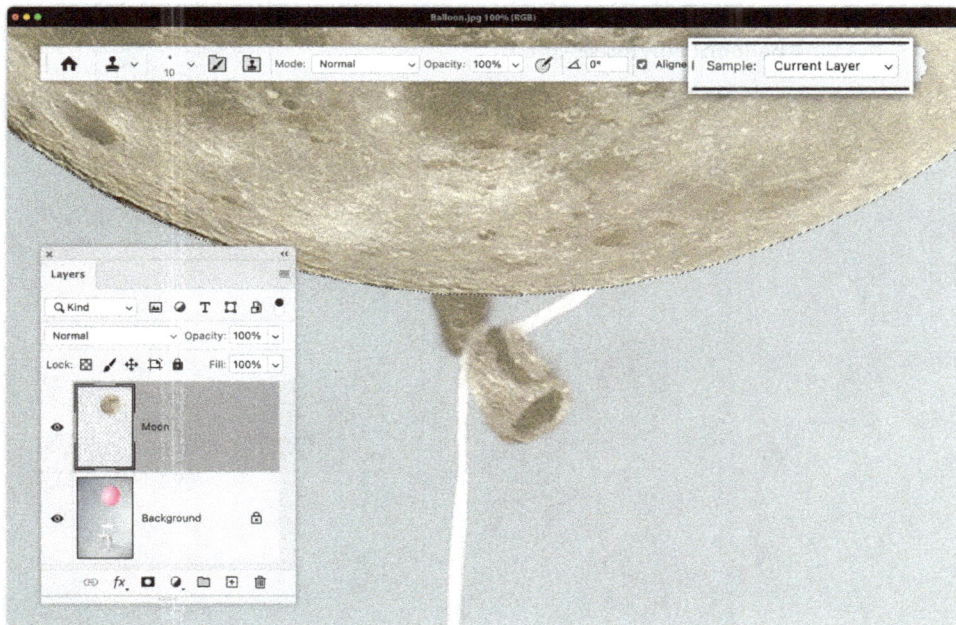

Figure 14.4: Clone Stamp over the balloon knot with samples from the lunar texture

10. Working down the rest of the balloon knot, paint light patches of the lunar surface over highlighted regions of the knot, and darker regions of the lunar surface on shadow areas of the knot until off-pink regions have been concealed. Go to **Select → Deselect**.

Turning the pink balloon into grayscale

For the montage to work seamlessly, the balloon must be converted to grayscale so that highlights and shadows shine through the **Moon** layer without appearing pink. Here's how you can achieve this:

1. Switch to the **Rectangular Marquee** selection tool, then from the **Options** bar, set **Mode** to **New Selection**, **Feather** to 0, and **Style** to **Normal**.

2. Hide the **Moon** layer. Then create a selection that includes the balloon.

3. Next, switch to the **Magic Wand** tool, then from the **Options** bar, set **Mode** to **Subtract Selection** and **Sample Size** to **11 by 11 Average**, to sample an average pixel color of 11 px x 11 px. Set **Tolerance** to 15 and turn on all checkboxes in the **Options** bar.

4. Hover the **Magic Wand** tool inside the active selection, over a region of the background, then click to remove that part of the selection.

5. Repeat the same technique, clicking on the background and the white string until only the pink balloon remains selected:

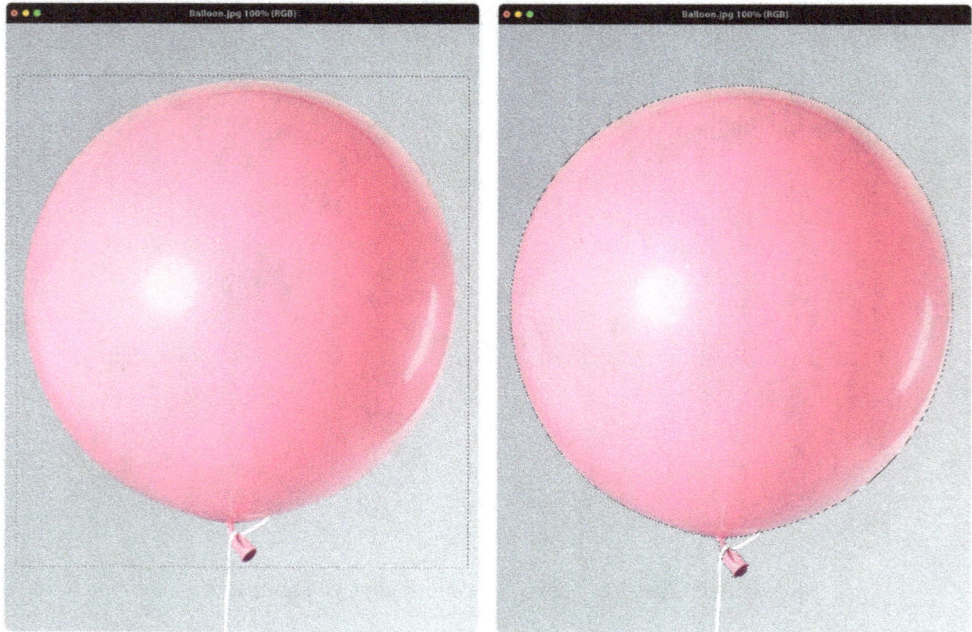

Figure 14.5: The initial rectangular selection (left), then with the background trimmed (right)

6. Next, go to **Select → Modify → Expand**. When a dialog appears, set **Expand By** to 1 px and click **OK**.

7. Go to **Select → Save Selection**. When the dialog appears, ensure the **Document** drop-down is set to Balloon.jpg, **Channel** is set to New, and then name the selection Balloon before clicking **OK**:

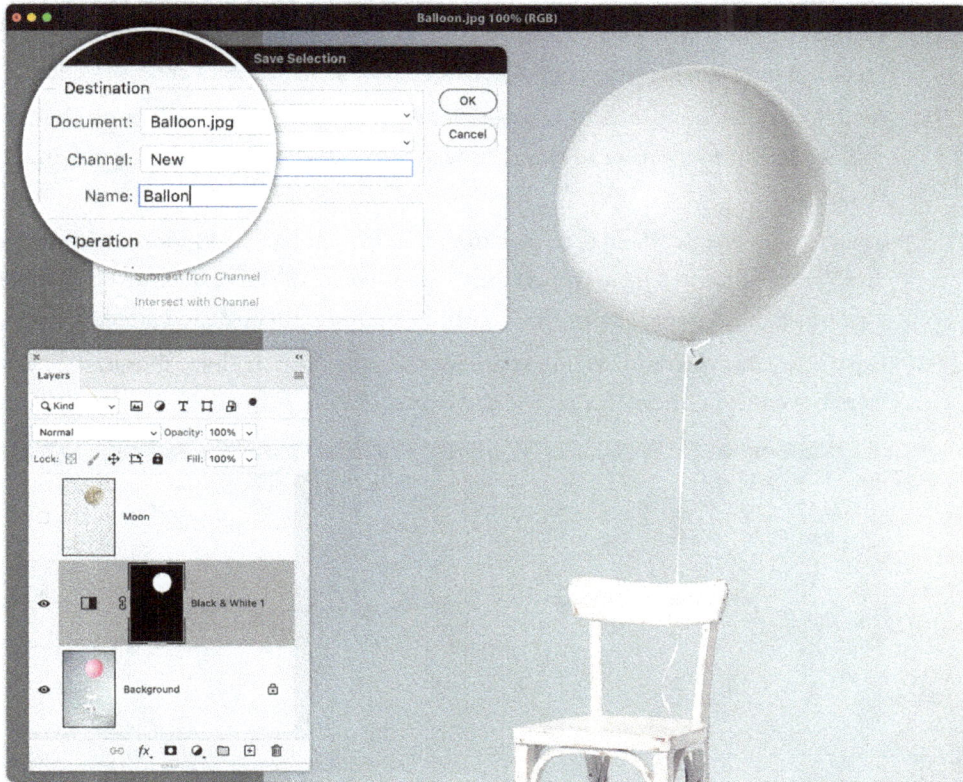

Figure 14.6: Save the active selection

8. Ensure that the **Background** layer is active in the **Layers** panel and click on the **Black & White** adjustment icon in the **Adjustments** panel. This will turn the pink of the balloon into grayscale.

Replacing chair shadows

The Moon will affect the shadows cast across the chair and floor. The existing floor needs to be replaced, which starts by isolating the chair from the background. Let's proceed:

1. The enhanced **Select Subject** feature in Photoshop 2026, which can be found in the contextual task bar, should provide accurate selection results of the chair. Click **Select Subject** to make the selection. If, however, you don't achieve an accurate selection of the chair, try steps 2-5 below. Otherwise, head on to step 6 with an accurate chair selection.

2. Switch to the **Rectangular Marquee** selection tool, then from the **Options** bar, set **Mode** to **New Selection**, **Feather** to 0, and **Style** to **Normal**. Then, create a selection that includes the chair.

3. Switch to the **Magic Wand** tool, then from the **Options** bar, set **Mode** to **Subtract Selection** and **Sample Size** to **3 by 3 Average**. Set **Tolerance** to 10 and turn on all checkboxes in the **Options** bar, except for **Sample all layers**, which should be deactivated.

4. Ensure the **Background** layer is active in the **Layers** panel. Then, click in the background to remove it from the selection (**A–E** in *Figure 14.7*):

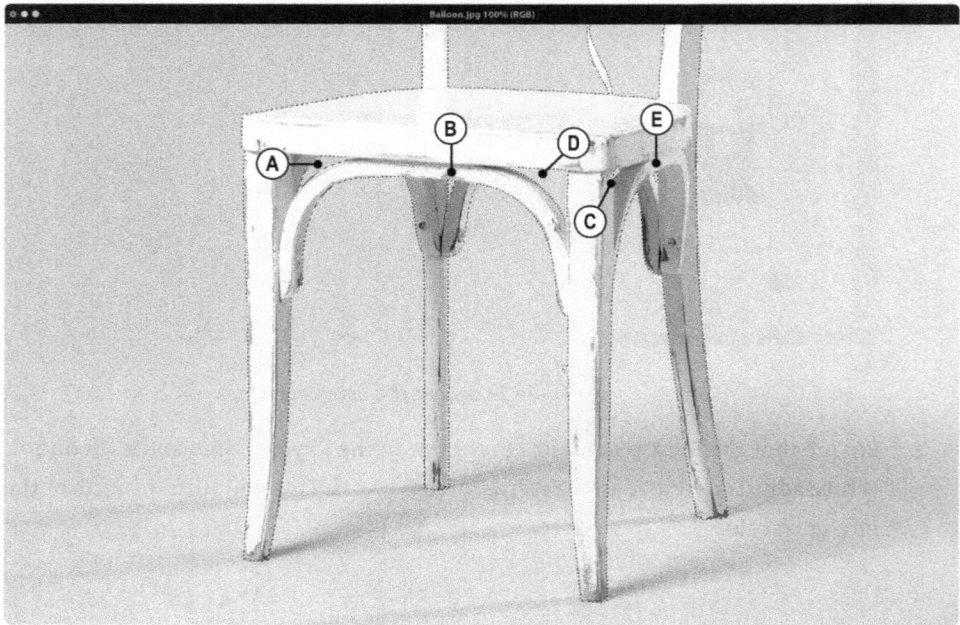

Figure 14.7: Select the background of the image, including portions seen through the chair legs

5. Tidy the selection using any selection tool you prefer, focusing on areas such as shadows under the chair legs and the ribbon, except where it is tied to the top of the chair. Looking closely at the selection edges around the chair legs, I found that they were very uneven and required the **Polygonal Lasso Tool** to create neater, straight edges.

6. Once you have completed the refinements of the base selection, click on **Select and Mask** in the **Options** bar. When a dialog appears, go to **Global Refinements** and change the **Smooth** slider to 4, **Feather** to 2.0 px, **Contrast** to 52%, and **Shift Edges** to -10%, then click **OK**. This should help smooth uneven edges by feathering them and then tightening them with a higher contrast value:

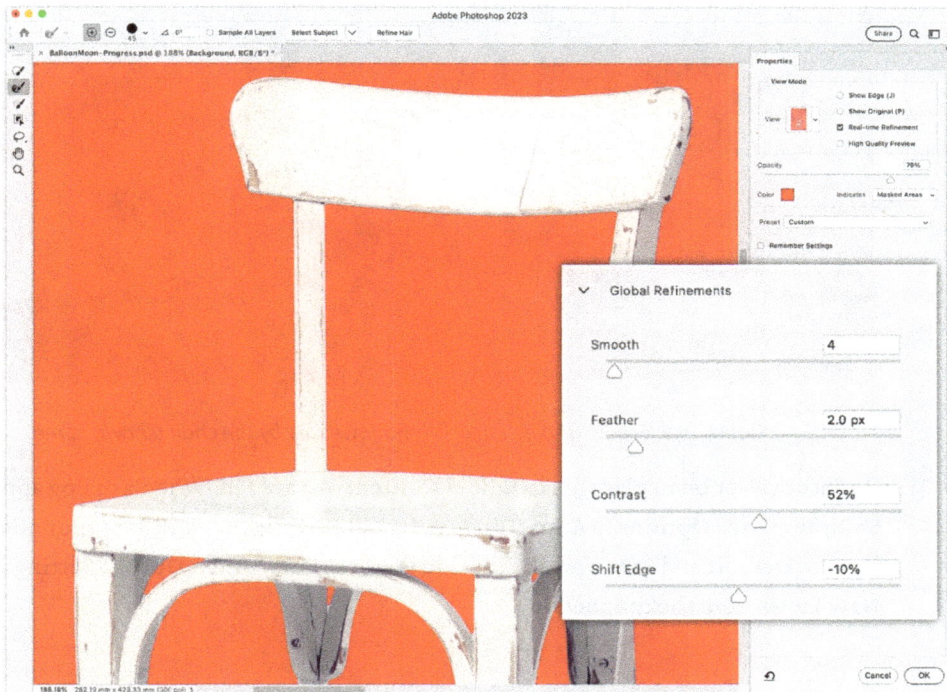

Figure 14.8: The Refine Edge settings applied to the chair selection

7. Go to **Select → Save Selection**. When a dialog appears, ensure the **Document** dropdown is set to Balloon.jpg, **Channel** to **New**, and then name the selection Chair before clicking **OK**.

8. With the selection still active, go to **Layer → New → Layer Via Copy**. The new layer will appear above the **Background** layer in the **Layers** panel. Rename the new layer Chair.

9. Click on the **Background** layer in the **Layers** panel to make it active, then hide all other layers in the stack.

10. Switch to the **Polygonal Lasso Tool**, then from the **Options** bar, set **Mode** to **New Selection**, **Feather** to 0, and leave the **Anti-alias** checkbox turned on. Create a selection around all shadows cast by the chair, which should run across the entire width of the image:

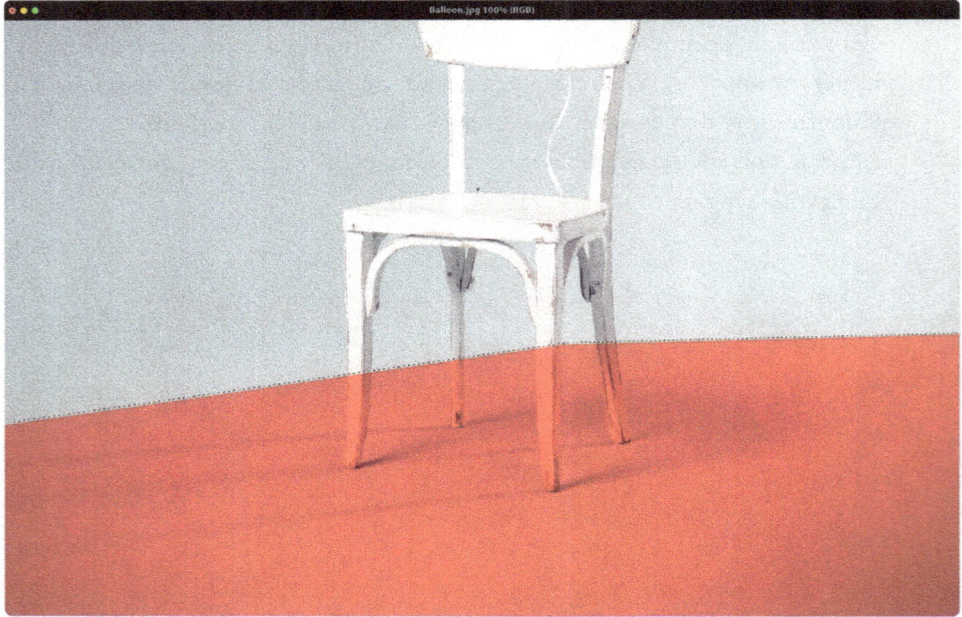

Figure 14.9: Create a selection of all shadows cast by the chair (shown in red)

11. With the selection in place, go to **Edit → Content-Aware Fill**. When a dialog appears, set **Sampling Area Options** to **Auto**. Then, under **Fill Settings**, ensure that **Color Adaptation** is set to **Default** and **Rotation Adaptation** is set to **None**. Under **Output Settings**, choose **New Layer** from the dropdown:

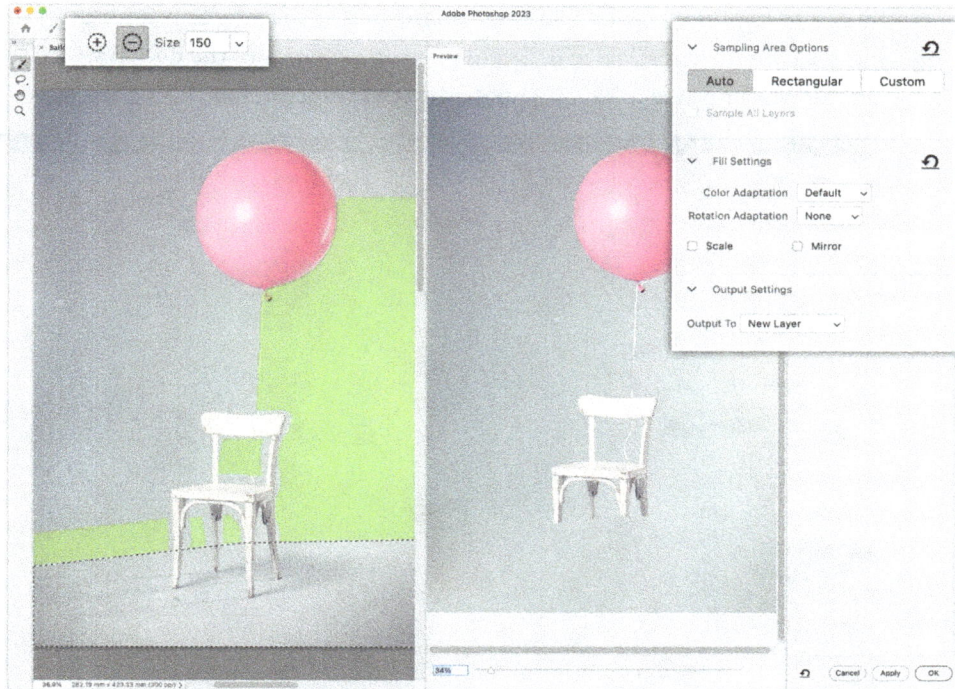

Figure 14.10: Removing sampling from the chair by painting over the green highlights

12. The left-hand window displays the sampling area (*Figure 14.10*), highlighted in green by default. To achieve the desired result, you will need to switch to the **Sampling Brush** tool from the upper left-hand side of the dialog and remove any green sampling from the chair. This should provide a smooth replacement floor.

13. Click **OK** when done to add the edits to a new layer. Then, rename the new layer Floor and hide the **Background** layer's visibility.

14. To prevent hard edges from appearing along the new floor layer, click the **Add a mask** icon at the bottom of the **Layers** panel.

15. Switch to the **Brush** tool. From the **Options** bar, choose the **Soft Round** brush tip, but increase the **Hardness** value to 30% to prevent too much of the floor from disappearing. Set the brush tip **Size** to 25 px, and the **Opacity** value to 100%:

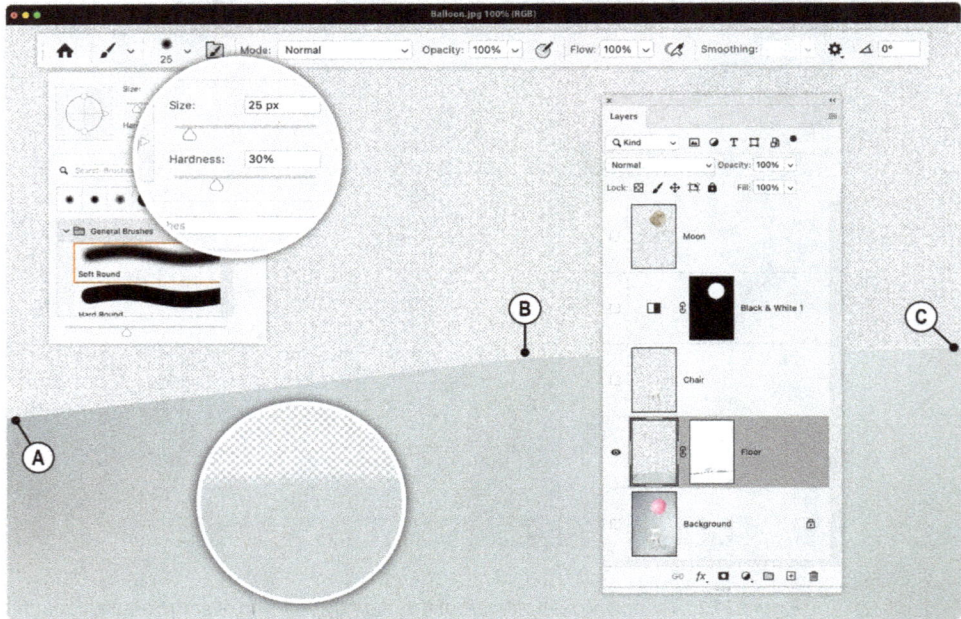

Figure 14.11: Soften the edge of the floor with a layer mask and a soft edge brush tip

16. Ensure the **Foreground** and **Background** colors are reset by pressing the *D* key. Hover your cursor over the left edge of the canvas, level with the edge of the floor pixels added in a previous step (**A** in *Figure 14.11*). Click to add a circular brush mark and release the mouse button. Then, hover your cursor over the center of the image where the floor changes direction (**B**), hold *Shift*, and then click to paint a straight line.

17. Repeat the same technique by clicking in the same place you previously clicked in the center of the image (**B**). Then, hover your brush tip cursor over the far-right edge of the floor pixels where it meets the edge of the canvas (**C**), hold *Shift*, and then click to paint a second straight line. This should now create a soft edge.

18. With the **Floor** layer active in the **Layers** panel, click the **Create a new layer** icon at the bottom of the **Layers** panel. Name the new layer Leg shadows and then change the **Blend Mode** setting to Multiply.

19. Switch to the **Brush** tool, then from the **Options** bar, choose the **Soft Round** brush tip with a **Hardness** value of 30%. Then, set the brush tip **Size** value to 55 px. Next, make the brush tip elliptical by dragging the bottom **Roundness** widget close to the center of the brush preview (**A** in *Figure 14.12*). Then, set the brush **Opacity** to 70%:

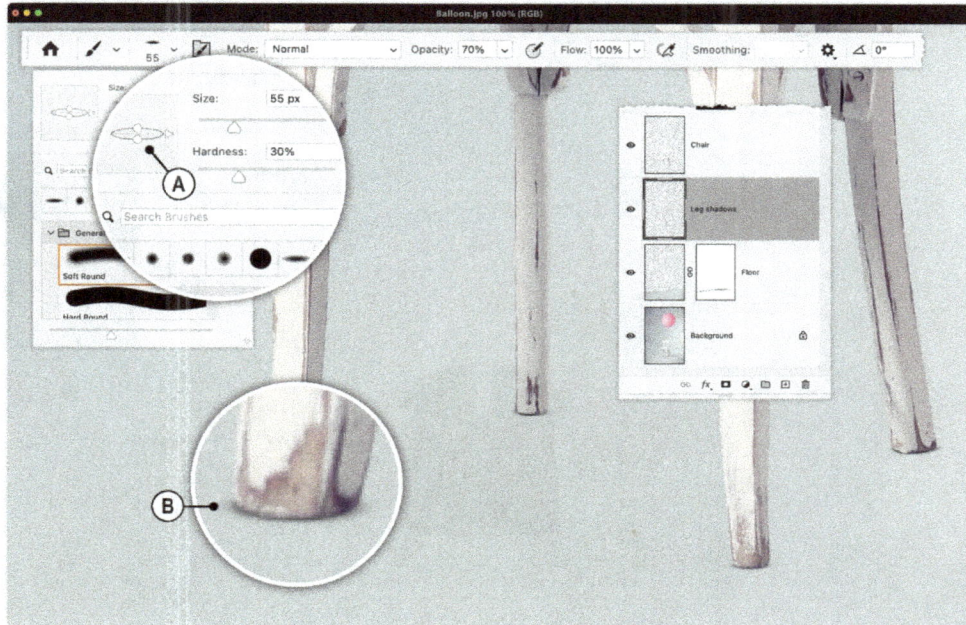

Figure 14.12: Add shadows under the chair legs to make it appear to touch the floor

20. Turn on the **Chair** layer visibility, then click on the **Leg shadows** layer to ensure it is active. Hover your cursor level with the underside of a chair leg (**B** in *Figure 14.12*) and click once to add a pale, soft shadow. I found that clicking four times under each leg provided an appropriate shadow.

21. The final step for replacing the original shadows will be to add a shadow cast under the chair from the Moon. For this, I created a simple shape in Photoshop to represent a loose interpretation of a shadow in a separate file. Click on the **Leg shadows** layer in the **Layers** panel to ensure it is active. Then, go to **File → Place Embedded**. Browse to the 14-Surreal folder and select Seat.psd. Click **Open**.

22. When the artwork appears in the image window, click on the **Commit** button in the **Options** bar to complete the import process. Right-click on the **Seat** layer in the **Layers** panel and choose **Rasterize Layer** from the list of options (**A** in *Figure 14.13*):

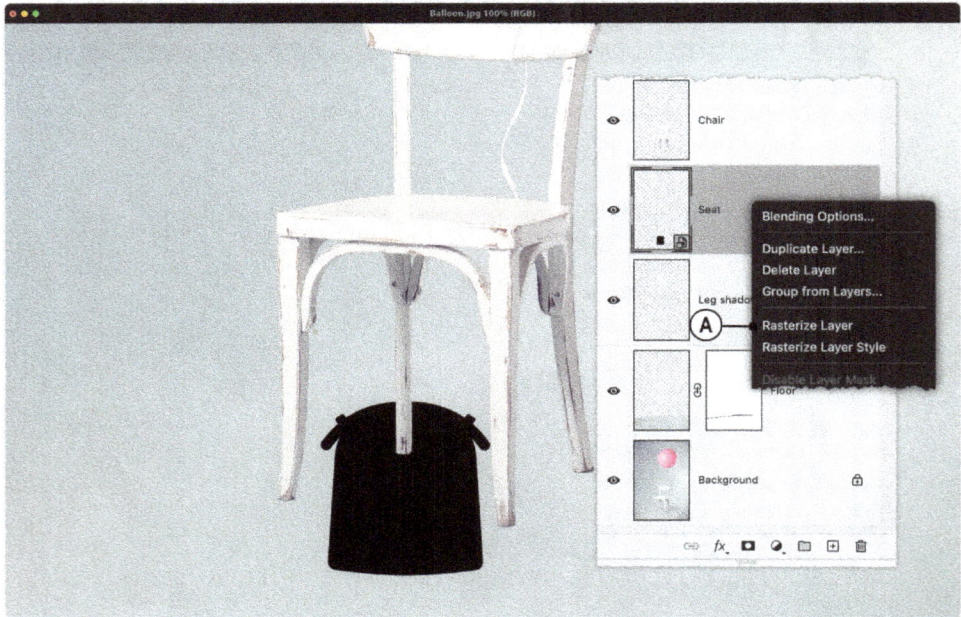

Figure 14.13: Importing the fake seat shadow

23. Go to **Select → All** to create a selection that includes all content on the canvas. Then, go to **Edit → Cut**. Ensure the **Seat** layer is still active, then go to **Filter → Vanishing Point**.

24. When a dialog appears, the **Create Plane** tool is active by default. Click first at the outer edge of the left-hand chair leg (**A** in *Figure 14.14*) and click to add a point. Repeat the same technique to complete the grid by adding a point level with the outer corner of each leg (**B-D**). Finally, click on the first point you added to form a perspective grid:

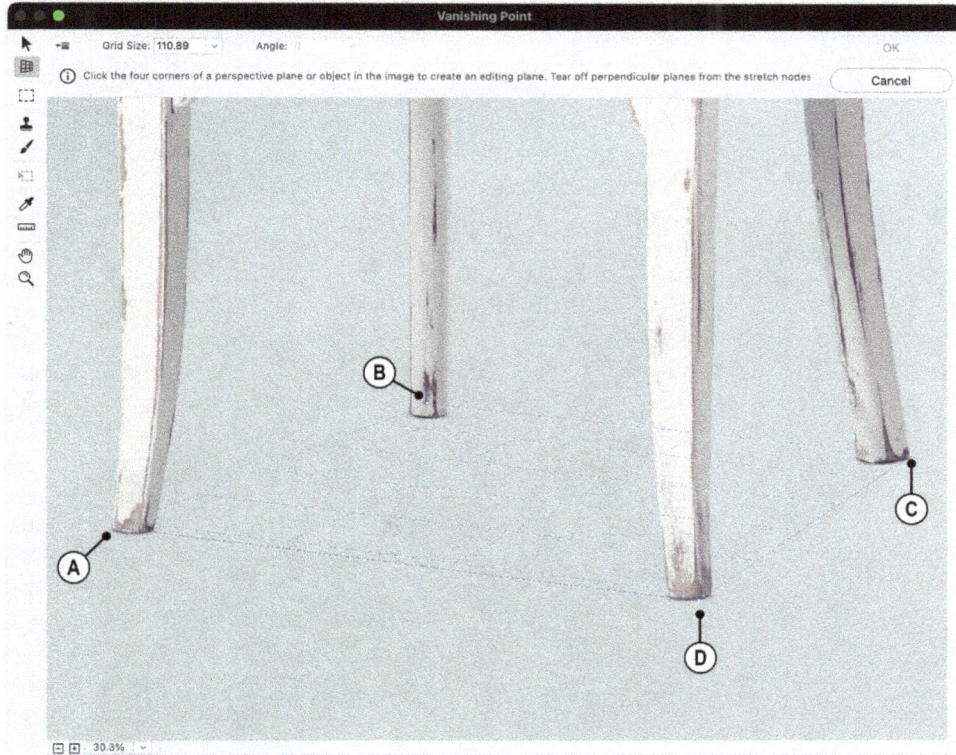

Figure 14.14: Adding a grid point on each of the outer corners of the chair legs (A-D)

25. Enlarge the grid to accommodate the new chair shadow. Hover your cursor over each edge handle on the grid and drag it away from the center of the grid to enlarge it (see *Figure 14.15*):

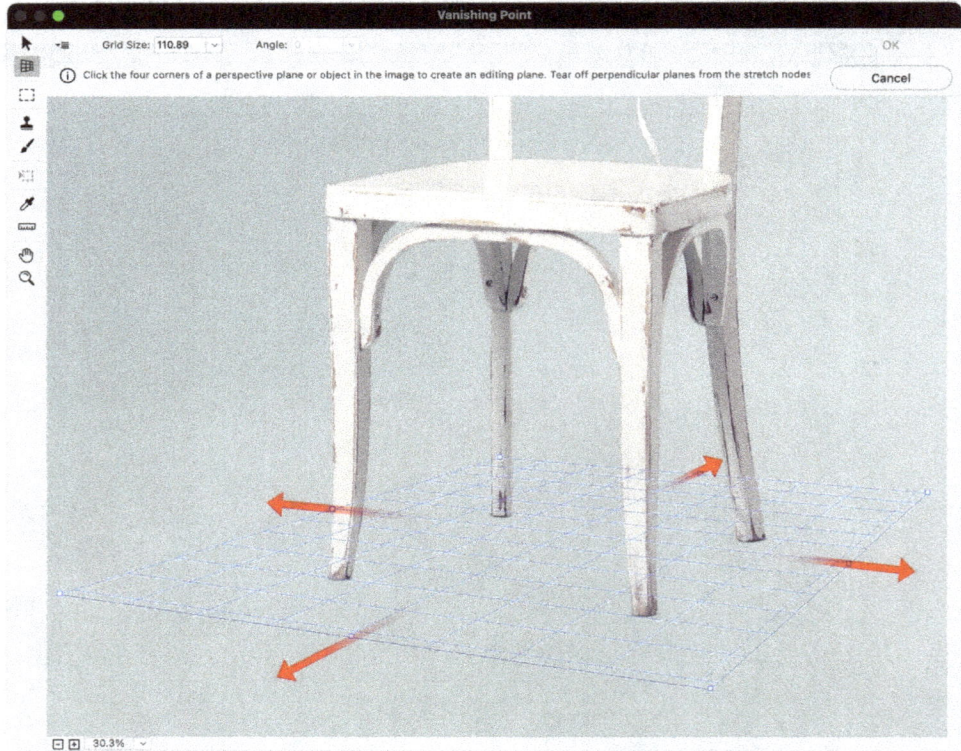

Figure 14.15: Dragging out each edge handle of the grid to increase its size

26. With the grid in place and at the appropriate size, you can press *Ctrl + V* (Windows) or *Cmd + V* (macOS) to paste the artwork into the **Vanishing Point** dialog. Remember that the artwork always appears in the top-left corner of the image window, so if you can't see it, you may need to zoom out.

27. Hover your cursor over the pasted seat image, then drag it onto the perspective grid where it will conform to the plane. Once in place, click **OK**.

28. The artwork will be pasted back into the active layer. Change the **Blend Mode** setting for the seat layer to **Multiply** and reduce the layer **Opacity** value to 12%.

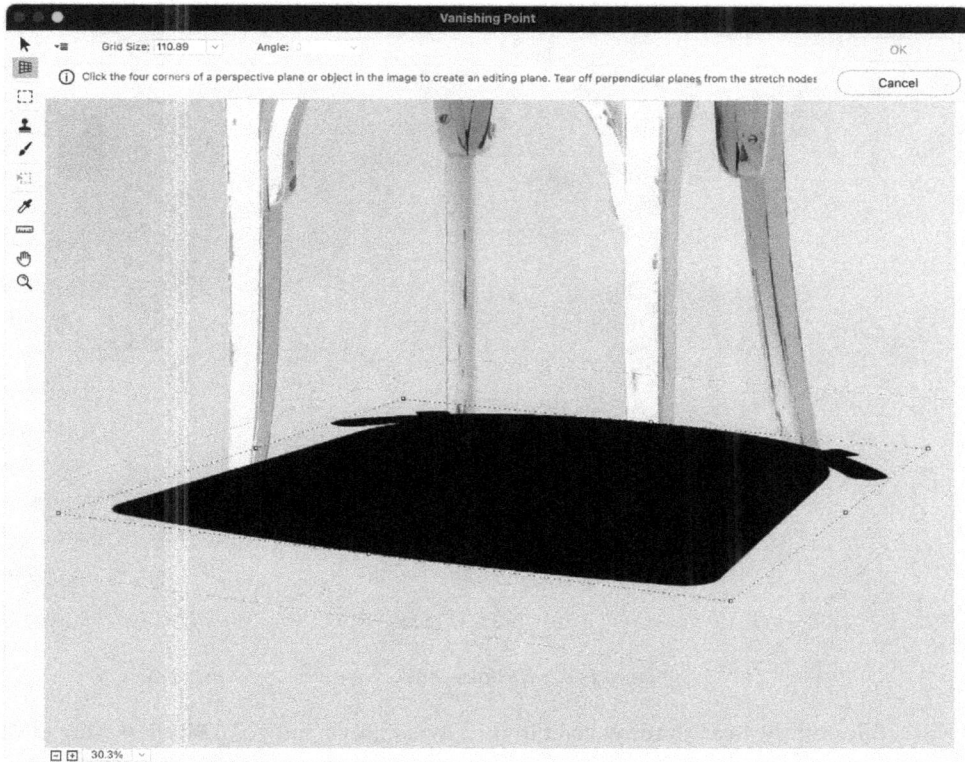

Figure 14.16: Pasting and placing the fake shadow artwork into the grid

29. Click on the **Chair** layer, then hold *Shift* and click on the **Floor** layer to select them both, and any layers between them in the layer stack. Then, press *Ctrl + G* (Windows) or *Cmd + G* (macOS) to add the selected layers into a new layer group.

30. Rename the layer group to Shadows. Then, right-click on the layer group visibility icon and choose **Violet** from the list of available colors. Then, rename the **Seat** layer Seat shadow:

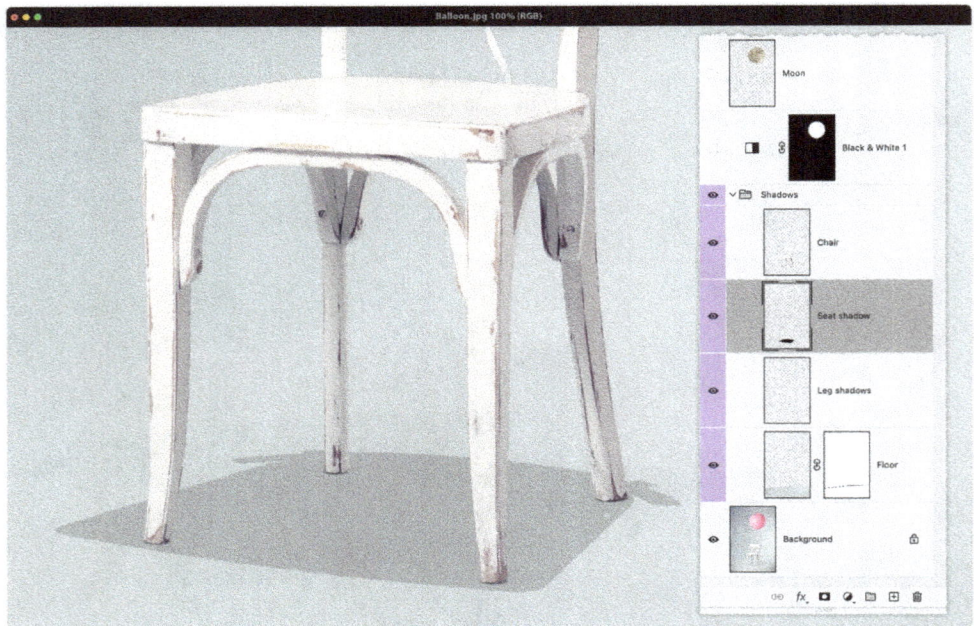

Figure 14.17: The fake shadow in place under the chair

31. Click on the **Seat shadow** layer in the **Layers** panel and go to **Filter → Blur → Gaussian Blur**. Set the **Amount** value to 1.0 px and click **OK**. This will add a slight blur to the shadow based on the distance from the seat to the floor to make it more realistic.

32. Switch to the **Blur** tool, found in the middle of the **Tools** panel. Set the brush tip to **Soft Round, Size** to 100 px, and **Hardness** to 0 px, then from the **Options** bar, set the **Strength** value to 75%. This controls how much blur will be applied as you click and drag over a region.

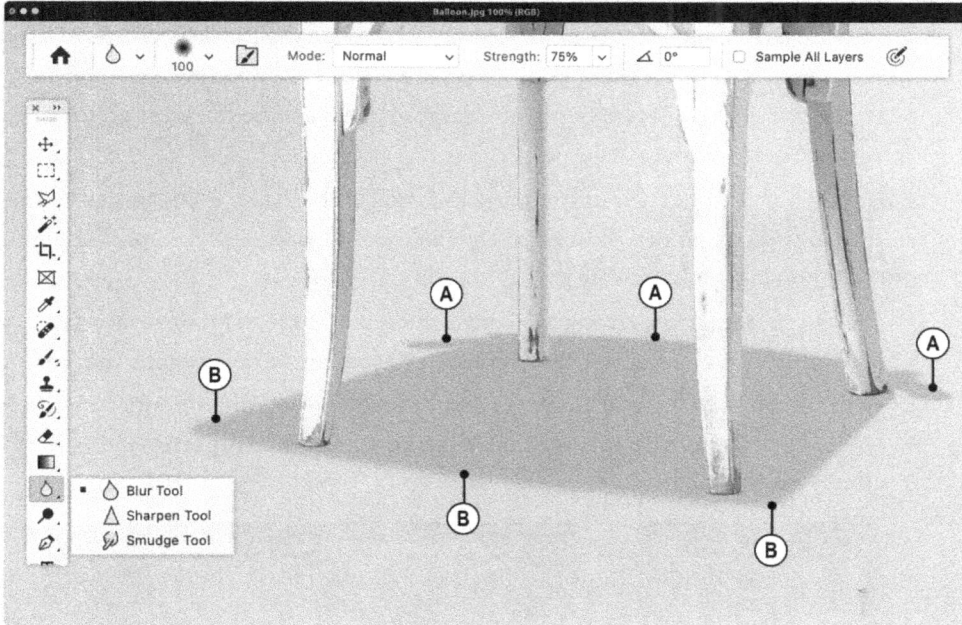

Figure 14.18: Softening the shadow at the back-left and -right edges

33. With the **Seat shadow** layer active, hover your cursor over the back-left edge of the shadow and drag over it to increase the softness of the edge (**A** in *Figure 14.18*). Repeat the same step for the back-right portion of the shadow, also labeled (**A**).

34. From the **Options** bar, adjust the brush **Size** to 200 px and set **Strength** to 100%. We'll need to intensify the effect for the next edit.

35. Hover your cursor over the front edge of the shadow (**B** in *Figure 14.18*). Drag repeatedly across the front edge of the shadow with the **Blur** tool, doubling the softness compared to the rear of the shadow.

36. With all the edits complete for the shadows, you can collapse the **Shadows** layer group in the layer stack.

Creating moonlight effects

The final step for our surreal balloon-Moon image is to turn the studio shot into a nighttime scene, add highlights to the chair, and emit a glow from the Moon. Let's get started:

1. Click on the **Moon** layer, then hold *Shift* and click on the **Black & White** adjustment layer beneath it to select them both. Then, press *Ctrl + G* (Windows) or *Cmd + G* (macOS) to add the selected layers into a new layer group. Rename the layer group `Balloon` and color-code it **Yellow**.

2. Hover your cursor over the layer mask assigned to the `Black & White 1` adjustment layer, then, by pressing *Alt* (Windows) or *Option* (macOS), drag the layer mask thumbnail onto the **Moon** layer to duplicate it.

3. Click on the **Moon** layer to make it active, then change **Blend Mode** to **Overlay**. This will allow the balloon material to show through the Moon while maintaining the Moon's texture.

4. With the **Moon** layer still active, click on **Levels** in the **Adjustments** panel (**A** in *Figure 14.19*). Click on the **Clip to layer** icon at the bottom of the **Properties** panel so that it only affects the **Moon** layer.

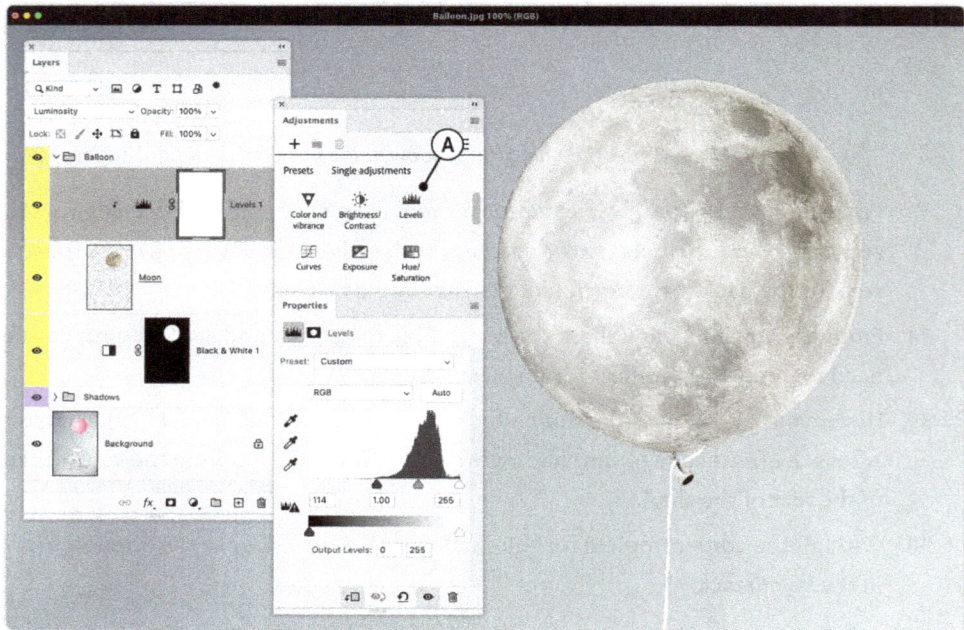

Figure 14.19: Enhancing the contrast of the Moon layer with a Levels adjustment

5. Drag the **Black point** slider in the **Levels** settings to an **Input** value of approximately 114, which should be where the data starts to appear in the graph above in the **Properties** panel. This will enhance the layer's contrast. Then, change the **Blend Mode** setting of the **Levels** adjustment layer to **Luminosity** so that it affects only the light, not the Moon's colors.

6. Next, click on the **Color Lookup** setting in the **Adjustments** panel. When the **Properties** panel appears, choose NightFromDay.CUBE from the **3DLUT File** dropdown (**A** in *Figure 14.20*):

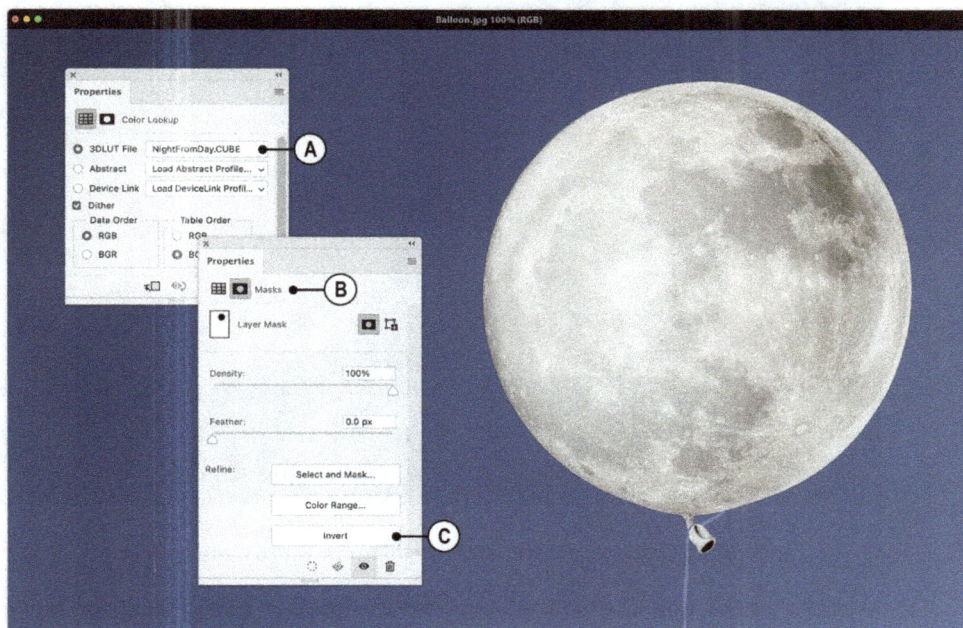

Figure 14.20: Invert the selection

7. Hover your cursor over the **Black & White 1** layer mask, press *Alt* (Windows) or *Option* (macOS) to drag the layer mask thumbnail onto the **Color Lookup** layer.

8. Next, click on the **Masks** icon located at the top of the **Properties** panel to reveal masking options (**B**). Ensure the **Properties** panel is tall enough to reveal all three buttons at the bottom of the panel. Then, click on the **Invert** button (**C**).

9. Ensure the **Color Lookup** adjustment layer resides between the **Shadows** and **Balloon** layer groups in the layer stack. Right-click on the adjustment layer visibility icon and change the layer color tag from the list to **Blue**. Then, finally, change the **Blend Mode** setting of the **Color Lookup** layer to **Multiply**:

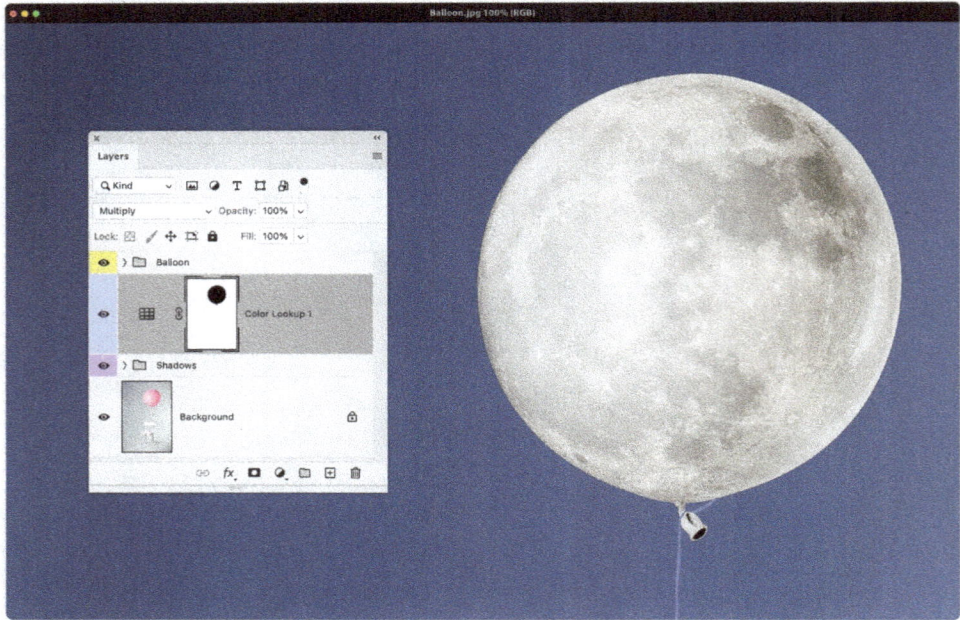

Figure 14.21: Changing the scene from night to day with a Color Lookup adjustment

10. Switch to the **Polygonal Lasso Tool**. From the **Options** bar, set the **Selection Mode** setting to **New** and **Feather** to 0 px. Then, create a selection of the chair backrest (**A** in *Figure 14.22*):

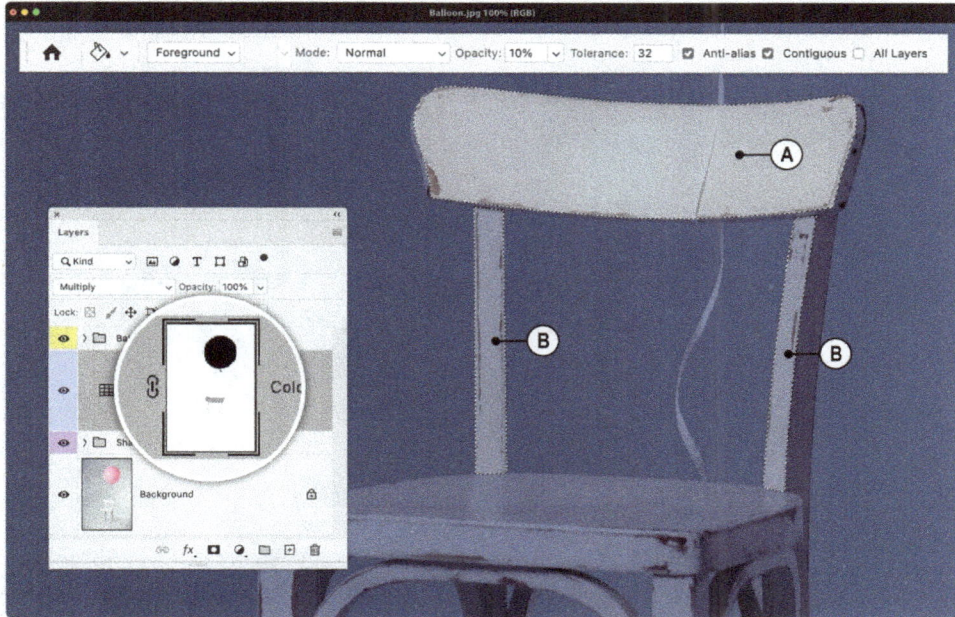

Figure 14.22: Selecting the chair backrest and supports

11. Change the **Selection Mode** setting to **Add to Selection**. Then, create a selection of both the chair support fronts that connect the backrest to the base of the chair (**B**).

12. Switch to the **Paint Bucket Tool** by pressing the *G* key to activate the correct group of tools, then click and hold on the active tool, and from the popout, select the **Paint Bucket Tool**.

13. From the **Options** bar, set the selection **Source** drop-down menu to **Foreground**, **Mode** to **Normal**, **Opacity** to 10%, and **Tolerance** to the default of 32. Turn on all checkboxes except **All Layers**, which should be deactivated. Press the *D* key to reset the **Foreground** and **Background** colors to their defaults of black and white, with black being the foreground color you will paint with.

14. Hover your cursor over any region inside the active selection and click six times. As you do so, you will see the blue hue disappear – in this case, to 40% of its original strength.

15. Go to **Select → Save Selection**. Name the new selection Chair back support and click **OK**. If you decide to experiment with the strength of the blue, it will be quicker to load the selection. Then, go to **Select → Deselect**.

16. Switch to the **Polygonal Lasso Tool**. From the **Options** bar, set **Selection Mode** to **New**. Select the chair seat (**A** in *Figure 14.23*):

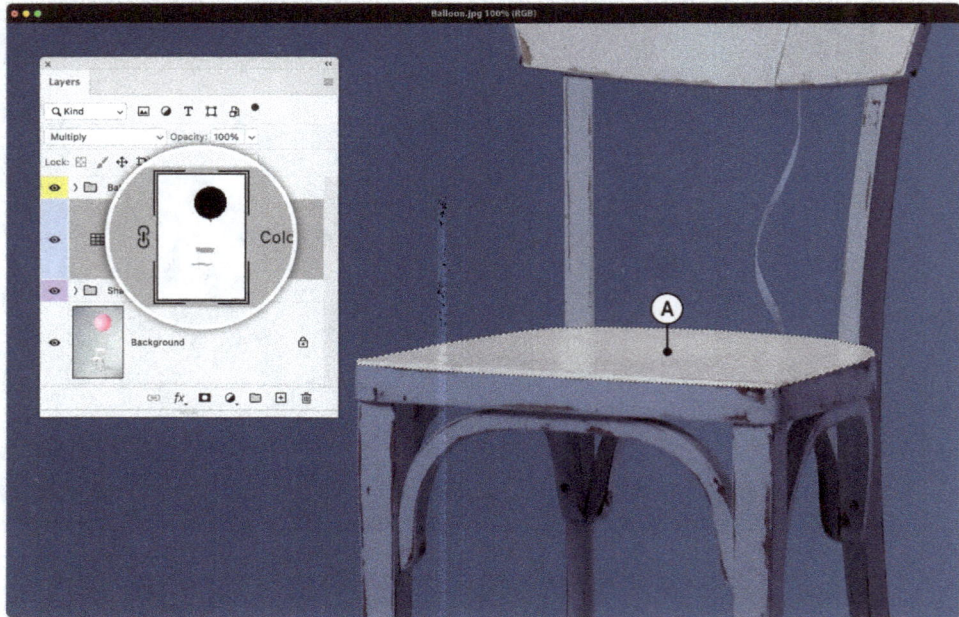

Figure 14.23: Reducing the blue hue on the seat

17. Switch to the **Paint Bucket Tool**. Then, hover your cursor inside the active selection and click eight times to reduce the blue hue and brighten the seat as though lit by moonlight. Again, save the selection if you believe it will be of benefit in the future and save time.

18. Hide all layers in the **Layers** panel except for the **Background** layer.

19. Switch to the **Polygonal Lasso Tool**. Ensure that **Selection Mode** is set to **New**. Create a selection around all the ribbon that ties the balloon to the chair; this will inevitably include some of the background, which you will remove in a later step. Once you have created a selection of one region of the ribbon, make sure you change **Selection Mode** to **Add to Selection**.

20. Now, switch to the **Magic Wand Tool**. From the **Options** bar, set **Mode** to **Subtract from selection**, set **Sample Size** to **3 by 3 Average** and **Tolerance** to **10**, and then turn on the **Anti-alias** and **Contiguous** checkboxes.

21. Hover your cursor inside any part of the selection that includes the background color and click to remove those portions. Continue this for the entire selection until you are left with just the ribbon selected.

22. Click on the **Color lookup** layer mask thumbnail to make it active. Ensure that black is the foreground color in the **Tools** panel. Then, press *Alt + Backspace* (Windows) or *Option + Delete* (macOS) to remove the blue hue completely from the ribbon.

23. Go to **Select → Save Selection**. Name the new selection Ribbon and click **OK**. Then, go to **Select → Deselect**.

24. Go to **Select → Load Selection**. Select Chair from the **Channel** drop-down menu and click **OK**. Then, go to **Select → Inverse** to select everything in the canvas except the chair.

25. Switch to the **Brush** tool, then from the **Options** bar, choose the **Soft Round** brush tip with a **Hardness** value of 0%. Then, set the brush tip **Size** value to 50 px, and the **Opacity** value to 25%.

26. Ensure black is set as the **Foreground** color to paint with and that the **Color Lookup** adjustment layer mask is active. Then, add paint strokes along the regions of the ribbon where it twists and becomes thinner.

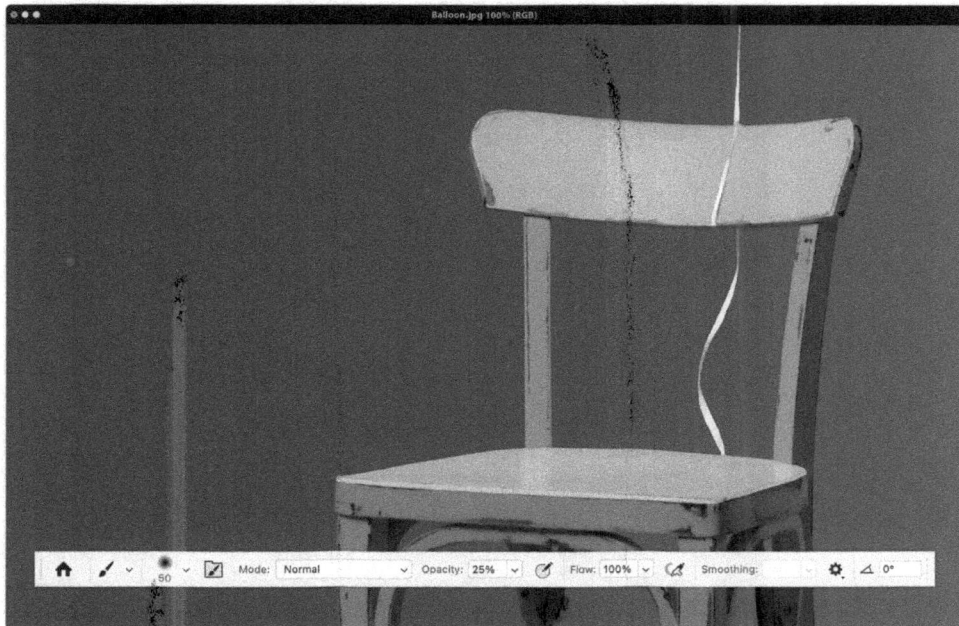

Figure 14.24: Adding a blue hue along the twisted parts of the ribbon for effect

27. Work your way along the entire length of the ribbon to add the blue hue back in where the ribbon twists. When done, go to **Select → Deselect**. As a final touch, click on the **Moon** layer to make it active. From the bottom of the **Layers** panel, click on the **Fx** icon and select **Outer Glow** from the list of effects. When a dialog appears, set **Blend Mode** to **Screen**, **Opacity** to 15%, **Noise** to 0%, and **Size** to 185 px. Click **OK** when done.

28. As an optional step, you can make the lighting more dramatic by duplicating the **Color Lookup** adjustment layer and setting the **Fill** value to 50% at the top of the **Layers** panel.

29. Take a moment to admire all your hard work. Then, go to **File → Save**, browse to the 14-Surreal project folder, save the document as a PSD, and close the document when ready.

Figure 14.25: The completed project

In the first exercise, we examined a workflow that utilized two stock images and the challenges inherent in combining them to create a convincing result. Most of the work required replacing the original shadows. If the source image had been taken specifically for the project, it would have been lit from the balloon's position. Next, we'll examine a workflow that utilizes project-specific shots.

Creating and editing project-specific assets

This project is based on an editorial design on the topic of AI. The three source images have been re-shot for this exercise and feature hands and an iPad.

Isolating the hands from the shot

Although the images for this project were carefully photographed with a specific artistic aim in mind, we still need to mask some portions of the artwork before we can combine them.

1. **Open** AiIpad.jpg from the 14-Surreal project folder.

2. Go to **File → Place Linked**, browse to the 14-Surreal project folder, select Hands.jpg, and click **Open**. Click on the **Commit** button in the **Options** bar.

3. With the **Hands** layer active, switch to the **Object Selection Tool**, and once active, click on **Select Subject** from the **Options** bar to select the hands, while ensuring you don't include the pencil in the selection:

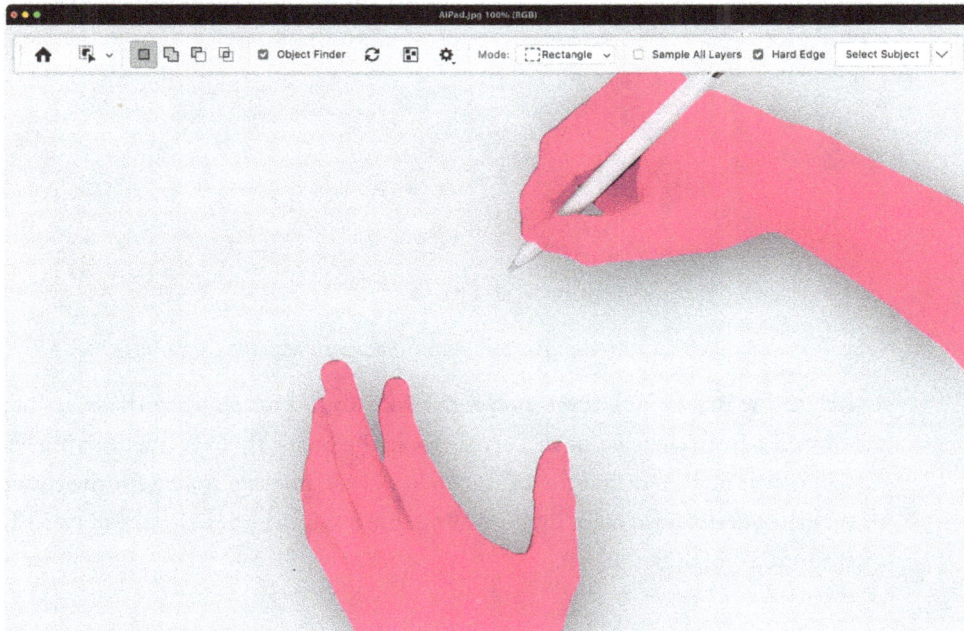

Figure 14.26: Creating a base selection of the hands, then refining its accuracy

4. You may need to fine-tune the selection to tidy the edge details. I found the **Magnetic Lasso Tool** handy for this follow-up step due to the high-contrast background of the photo.

5. Go to **Select → Save Selection**, and when a dialog appears, set **Selection Name** to Hands and click **OK**.

6. Next, create a selection of the pencil only. To achieve this, start by using the **Polygonal Lasso Tool** to match the clean, straight lines. Don't worry too much about including the rounded ends of the pencil at either end.

7. With a base selection in place, click on the **Quick Mask** button at the bottom of the **Tools** panel (**A** in *Figure 14.27*). If you haven't tried it before, it displays selected regions in a light red overlay. You can then paint it black or white to add and remove sections of the selection:

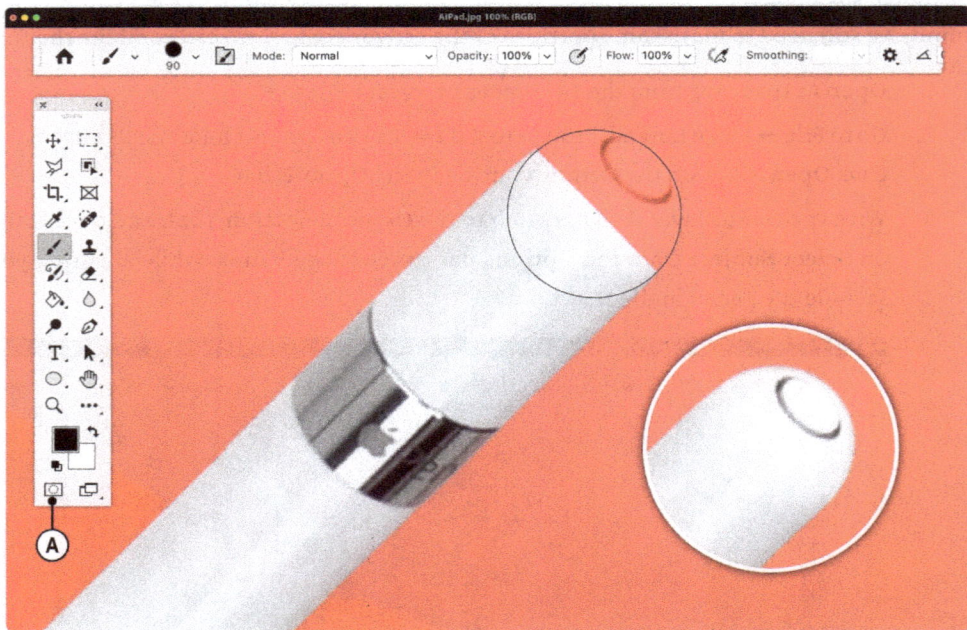

Figure 14.27: Creating a selection of the pencil with the Quick Mask mode

8. Switch to the **Brush** tool, then choose the **Soft Round** brush tip with a **Hardness** value of 96% and a brush **Size** value of 15 px. Hover the brush tip over the drawing end of the pencil; you should find that the brush tip is almost an exact match for the rounded end. Ensure the **Foreground** color in the **Tools** panel is white and click once or twice to match the rounded end of the pencil.

9. Repeat the same technique to add the eraser end of the pencil but increase the brush **Size** value to 90 px. Again, you may find it takes two to three clicks to add the entire rounded section.

10. Go to **Select → Save Selection**. When a dialog appears, set **Selection Name** to Pencil and click **OK**.

Figure 14.28: Two versions of the hands image, with masks applied for the pencil and hands

11. With the selection still active, duplicate the **Hands** layer by dragging the layer onto the **New Layer** icon at the bottom of the **Layers** panel. Rename the duplicate layer Pencil and click on the **Add a mask** icon, also at the bottom of the **Layers** panel.

12. Go to **Select → Load Selection**. When a dialog appears, choose **Hands** from the **Channels** drop-down menu at the top of the screen and click **OK**:

13. Click on the **Background** layer to make it active, then click on the **New fill or adjustment layer** icon at the bottom of the **Layers** panel. Choose **Solid Color** from the list and set the **Hexadecimal** value to b6b6b6, to create a light gray. As we will initially make the original hands disappear, we need something to represent the area where they should be; that's the purpose of the fill layer. Rename the fill layer Guides.

14. Color-code the layer's **Visibility** column green by right-clicking on the **Visibility** icon in the **Layers** panel.

15. Next, click on the **Create a new layer** icon at the bottom of the **Layers** panel. Name the new layer Thick. With the layer active, press *Ctrl + G* (Windows) or *Cmd + G* (macOS) to add it to a new layer group. Rename the layer group Lines and set the color of the **Visibility** column to **Red**.

16. Click on the **Hands** layer, go to the **Layers** panel fly-out menu, and from the list of options, choose **Create Clipping Layer**. This will make the hands disappear in the image window. Next, we'll add them back in, along with sweeping brush strokes.

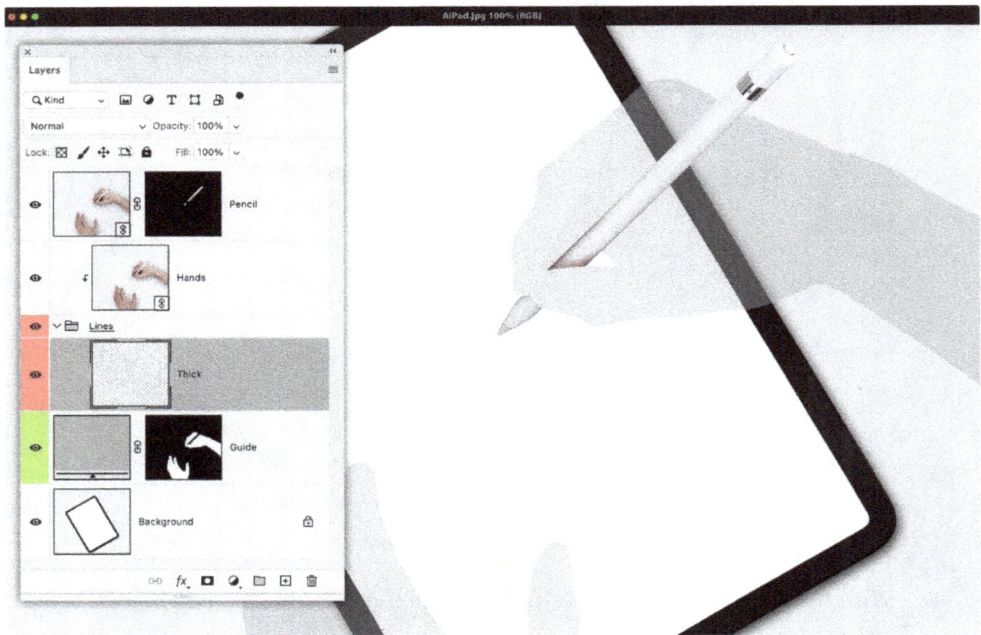

Figure 14.29: Setup layers ready for drawing thick, thin, and fine-painted lines

17. Switch to the **Brush** tool and then go to **Window → Brushes Settings**. We must create a brush that smooths out hand gestures to produce lovely, looping brushstrokes. Choose the **Hard Round** brush preset from the **Brush Tip** menu in the **Options** bar. Set the **Hardness** value to 85%.

18. From the **Brush Settings** panel, click on the **Brush Tip Shape** category from the list on the left-hand side. Set the **Size** value to 4 px and **Spacing** to 1%. From the list on the left-hand side of the panel, turn on the **Smoothing** checkbox (**A** in *Figure 14.30*). This will activate the **Smoothing** field in the **Options** bar. You can then set the **Smoothing** value to 50%:

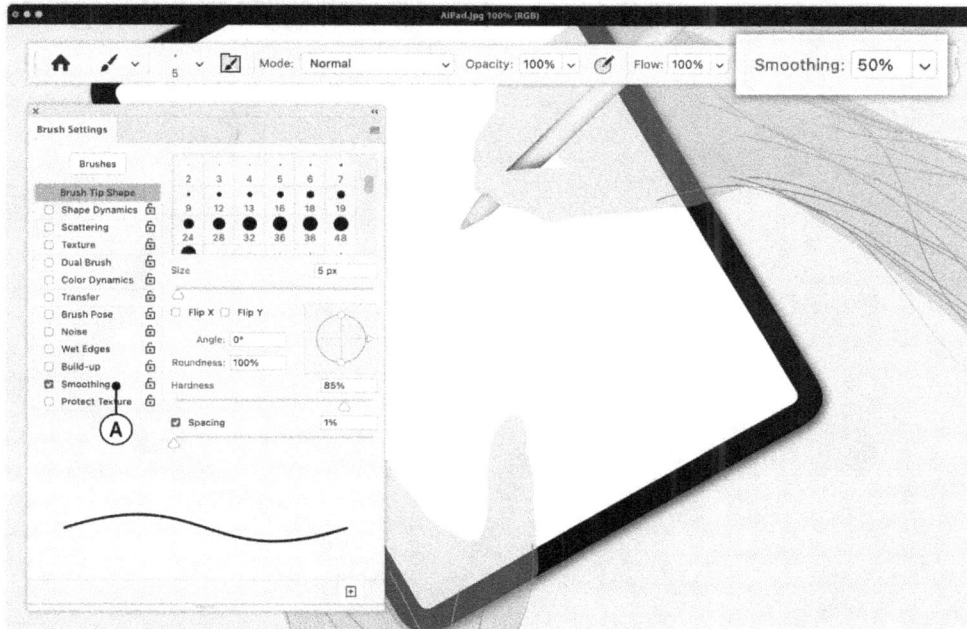

Figure 14.30: Creating a new brush tip

19. With the **Thick** layer active in the **Layers** panel, hover your cursor over the hand holding the pencil, close to a fingertip, and then drag out a long, looping brush stroke along the wrist, staying within the gray region denoted as the hand and beyond the edge of the right-hand side of the canvas. As you do, you will notice the brush stroke is textured with the image of the hand.

20. Repeat this technique for both hands, adding eight to ten brush marks for each hand. We need to give the impression that the hand is made of futuristic cables or nanoparticles. Once you have established some baselines for the hands, you can then add two loose brush strokes that veer away from the hand to make it seem as though they are forming toward the fingertips.

21. Click on the **Create a new layer** icon at the bottom of the **Layers** panel. The new layer should appear immediately above the **Thick** layer in the stack. Rename it Thin.

22. Change the brush tip **Size** value to 3 px. With this layer of thin lines, we need to keep most of the brush marks within the gray guide region of the hands. Try to follow the contour of where you believe fingers are, creating long looping lines. Create some lines that follow the edge of the hands and wrists to give it more form and structure:

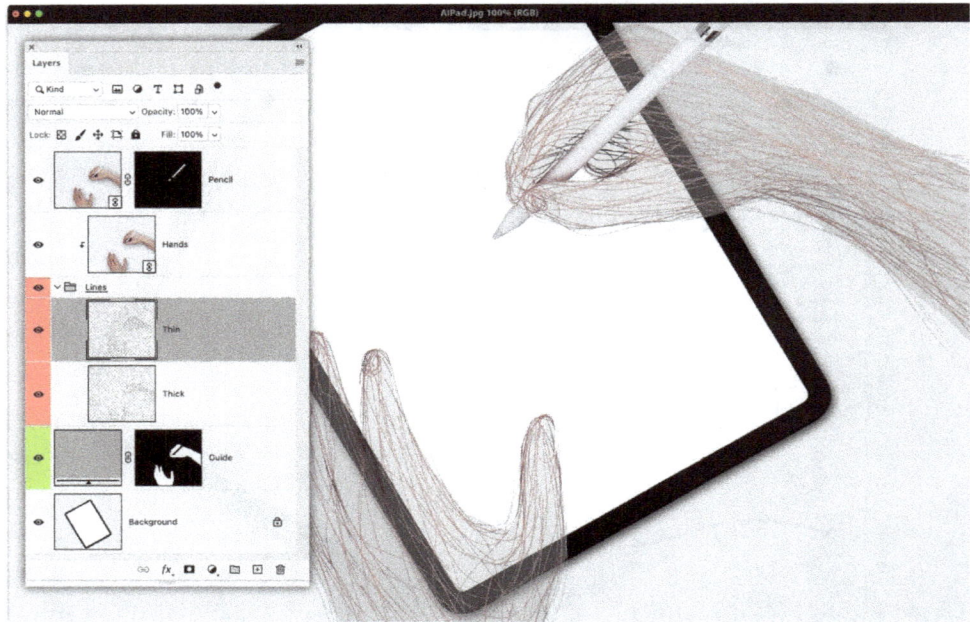

Figure 14.31: Adding thin details to the hands

23. Add more lines in the regions where the nails would be and the curve of the fingers. All of this will help give the lines a 3D effect when combined.

24. Click on the **Create a new layer** icon at the bottom of the **Layers** panel. The new layer should appear immediately above the **Thin** layer in the stack. Rename the new layer Fine.

25. It's painstaking work to paint over the hands and arms, so I have also included a document called FineDetails.psd in the 14-Surreal project folder. You can import it into the master file if you prefer not to follow every step.

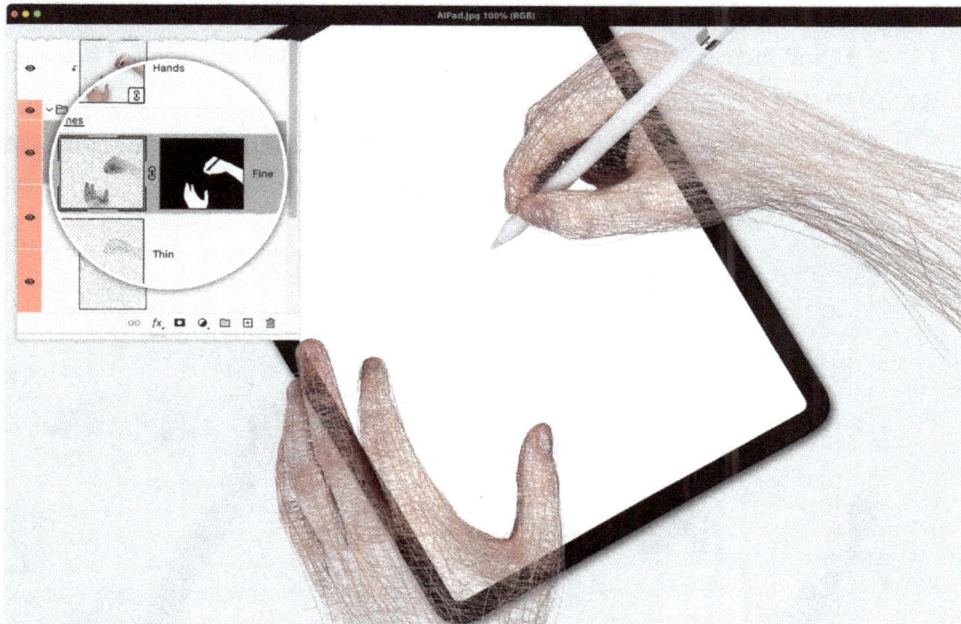

Figure 14.32: Filling in the details along the fingers and knuckles

26. If you want to do this the hard way, with your own brush marks, proceed to scribble in the rest of the details. To keep a neater edge for your scribble lines, go to **Select → Load Selection**, and when a dialog appears, choose **Hands** from the **Channels** drop-down menu and click **OK**.

27. Click on the **Add a mask** icon at the bottom of the **Layers** panel. Then, click on the image thumbnail for the **Fine** layer to ensure you are painting on the layer and not on the mask.

28. Set the brush tip **Size** value to 1 px, then lower the **Smoothing** value in the **Options** bar to 15%. Keep the scribble lines compact near the fingertips, but as you work down the wrist to the arm, loosen the lines to make them look as though they are untangling.

29. Click on the **Hands** layer in the **Layers** panel, then click the **Create a new layer** icon at the bottom of the **Layers** panel. The new layer should appear immediately above the **Hands** layer in the stack. Rename it Dots.

30. From the **Brush Settings** panel, under **Brush Tip Shape**, set the brush tip **Size** value to 4 px and increase the **Spacing** value to 470%. This will create a dotted brush-stroke appearance when applied.

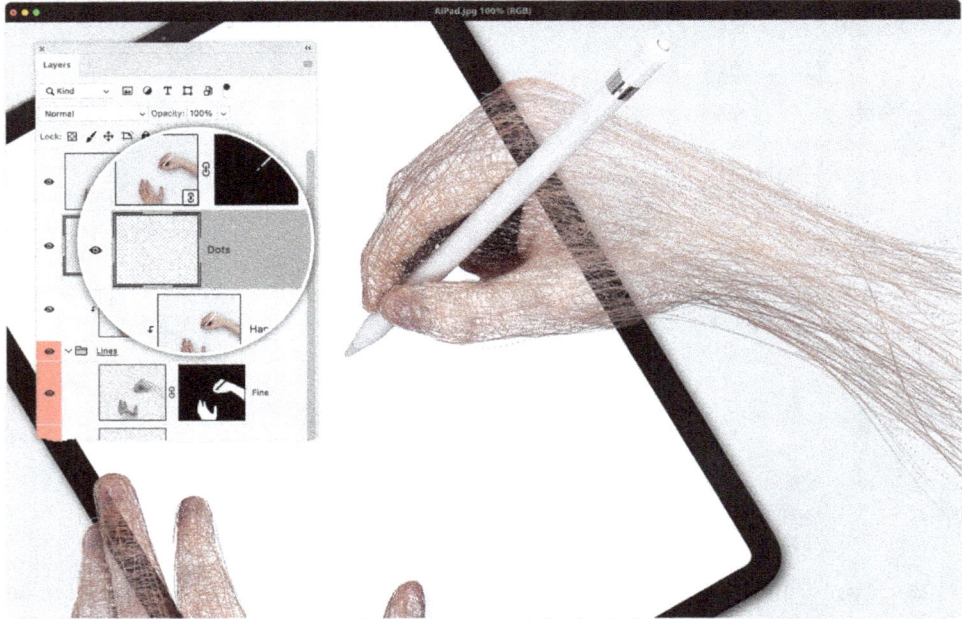

Figure 14.33: Adding dotted lines along the wrist

31. These brush strokes need to be applied from the wrist and down the arm. Click in the **Foreground** swatch in the **Tools** panel and enter 9e6e62 into the **Hexadecimal** field to create a dark brown color. Apply dotted brush marks in long, weaving lines down the arm.

32. The screen on the iPad needs to be replaced. Hide the gray color fill layer named **Guide**. Then, click on the **Background** layer in the **Layers** panel, go to **File → Place Linked**, browse to the 14-Surreal project folder, and select ScreenArt.jpg. Click **Open** when done.

33. When the artwork appears in the image window, click on the **Reference Point** checkbox to activate it, and then pin the top-center point on the reference grid. Hover your cursor over the transform frame in the image window and reposition the artwork so that the top-center point of the transform frame is in the same place as the iPad camera.

Figure 14.34: Add the screen art image

34. From the **Options** bar, change the **Scale** value to 43% and then enter -30° into the **Angle** field. This should center the image over the iPad screen. Click on the **Commit** button in the **Options** bar to complete the import process. Hide the layer you just imported and click on the **Background** layer. Switch to the **Magic Wand Tool**, and from the **Options** bar, set the **Tolerance** value to 10 and turn off the **Sample All Layers** checkbox. Hover your cursor over the white screen of the iPad and click to select it.

35. Turn on the ScreenArt layer's visibility and make it active. Then, click on the **Add a Mask** icon at the bottom of the **Layers** panel.

36. To add depth to the screen, click on the **Fx** icon at the bottom of the **Layers** panel, and from the list of options, choose **Inner Shadow**. Set the **Opacity** value to 46%, **Angle** to 117°, **Distance** to 11 px, **Choke** to 0%, and **Size** to 35 px. Click **OK** when done to apply the effect:

Figure 14.35: The completed image

37. You can now go to **File → Save**, browse to the 14-Surreal project folder, and save the document as AiPad.psd. Close the document when done.

Creating smoke effects with brushes and filters

We've used the Liquify feature throughout this book, utilizing its Face-Aware features to add smiles to faces and to morph a pattern design to match the folds of a cushion. In the final exercise of this book, you will manipulate basic brush strokes with the Liquify filter to create a realistic smoke effect. Let's get started!

1. Open SmokeSkull.jpg from the 14-Surreal folder.

2. Click on the **Create a new layer** icon at the bottom of the **Layers** panel. Name the new layer Smoke.

3. Switch to the **Brush** tool. Click on the **Brush Tip Preset** menu from the **Options** bar and select the **Soft Round** brush tip from the preset list. Adjust the brush **Size** to around 400 px and set **Hardness** to 0%.

4. Reset the foreground and background colors at the bottom of the **Tools** panel to black and white and ensure white is the active color.

5. Then, hover your cursor over the center of the right-hand eye and click and drag to create a wavy brush stroke to the upper right-hand side of the skull. Release the mouse button when done.

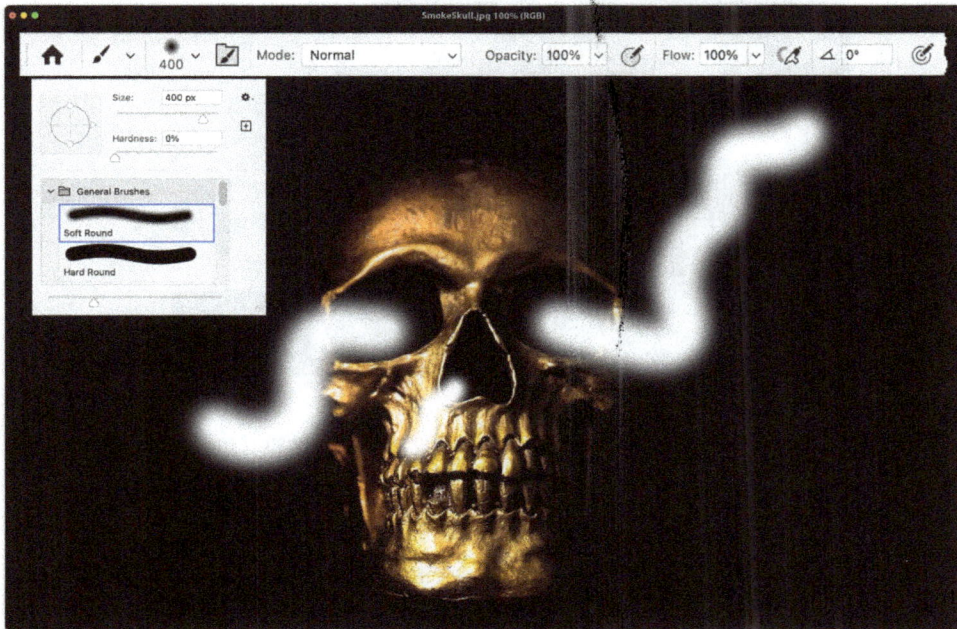

Figure 14.36: Paint three white-colored brush marks

6. Next, create a second brush stroke starting from the center of the left eye downwards to create an S-shaped stroke.

7. Reduce the Brush tip size to 200 px and then create a third and final brush stroke from the nose downwards in a wavy motion.

8. Go to **Filter → Liquify**. To better judge the appearance of the edits you are applying, turn on the **Show Backdrop** checkbox and ensure that the **Use** dropdown is set to **Background**, **Mode** is set to **Behind**, and **Opacity** is set to 100%:

9. Zoom into the image so that all the brushstrokes are visible in the image window. Switch to the **Forward Warp** tool by pressing the *W* key. Set the brush **Size** to 700px, **Density** to 50, and **Pressure** to 60:

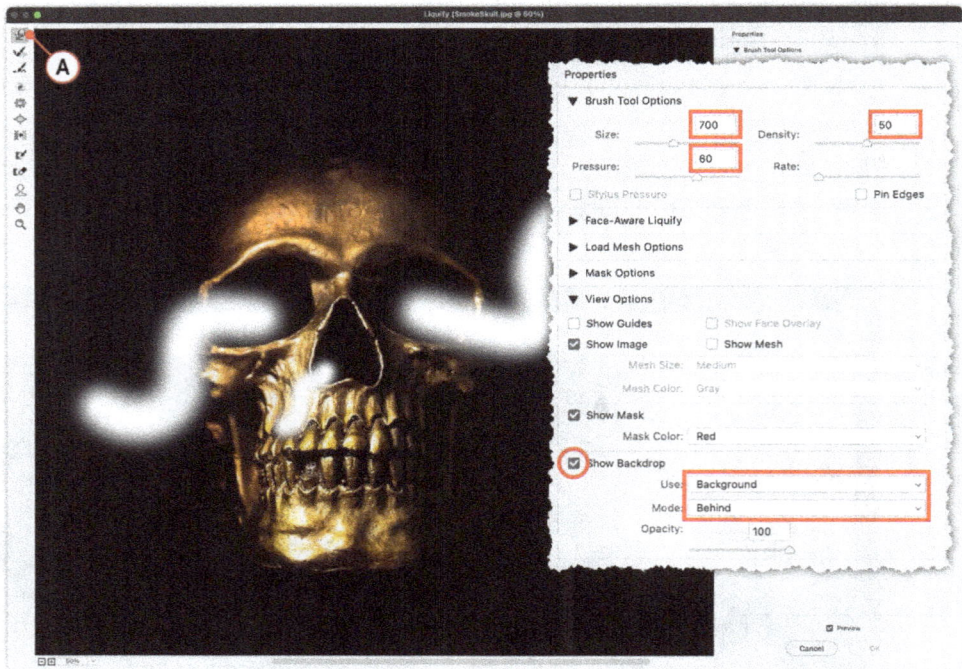

Figure 14.37: Use the Forward Warp tool to distort the brush marks

10. Then drag the **Warp Tool** cursor perpendicular to each of the brush marks to mix and ripple them. Avoid distorting more than one brush mark at a time to simplify the edits. A large brush stroke will gently pull the brush marks; however, you can reduce the brush size using the [and] keys to create more intense pulls through the brush marks.

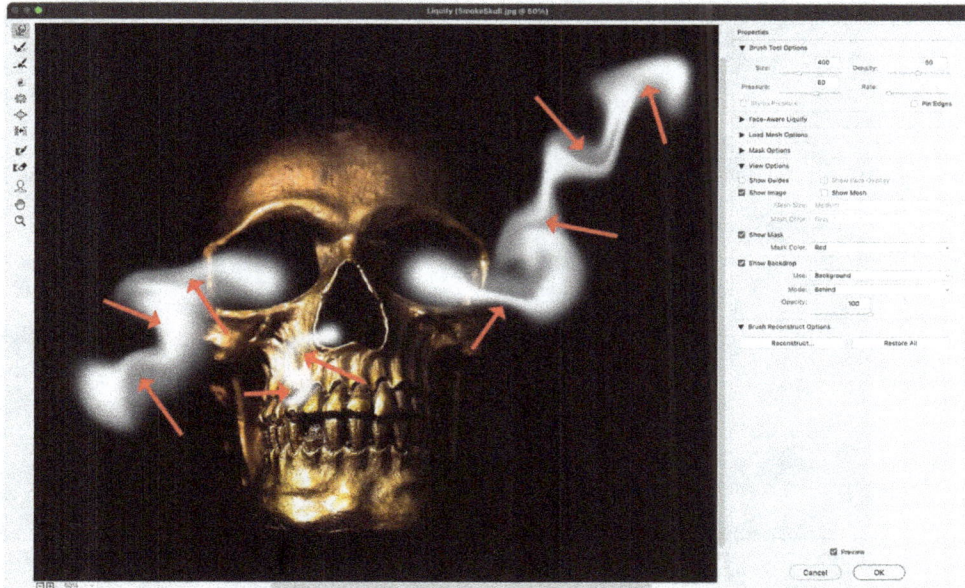

Figure 14.38: Use the Forward Warp tool to distort the brush marks

11. Once the brush marks have been rippled to your liking, click on **OK** to exit the Liquify interface. Unfortunately, you cannot turn the layer into a smart object, as it would not allow us to access the next step and fade the effect.

12. Then, you must go immediately to **Edit → Fade**. When the dialogue appears, change **Opacity** to 50% and click **OK**. This step reduces the impact of your Liquify edit by half, creating the smoke effect.

13.   Then you will need to return to **Filter → Liquify** seven more times to repeat the rippling and distorting of each brush stroke using the same method as before. Remember to fade each Liquify adjustment by going to **Edit → Fade** and lowering **Opacity** to 50%.

Figure 14.39: Edit the brush marks eight times with the Liquify filter

14. Try to pull the ends of the strokes to make it appear as though the smoke is dispersing each time you apply the Liquify effect.

15. Ensure that the **Smoke** layer is active in the **Layers** panel and then click on the **Add a Mask** icon at the bottom of the panel.

16. Switch to the **Brush** tool. Set the brush tip to **Soft Round**, **Size** to 1400 px, **Opacity** to 20% and **Hardness** to 0%. Set the foreground color to black.

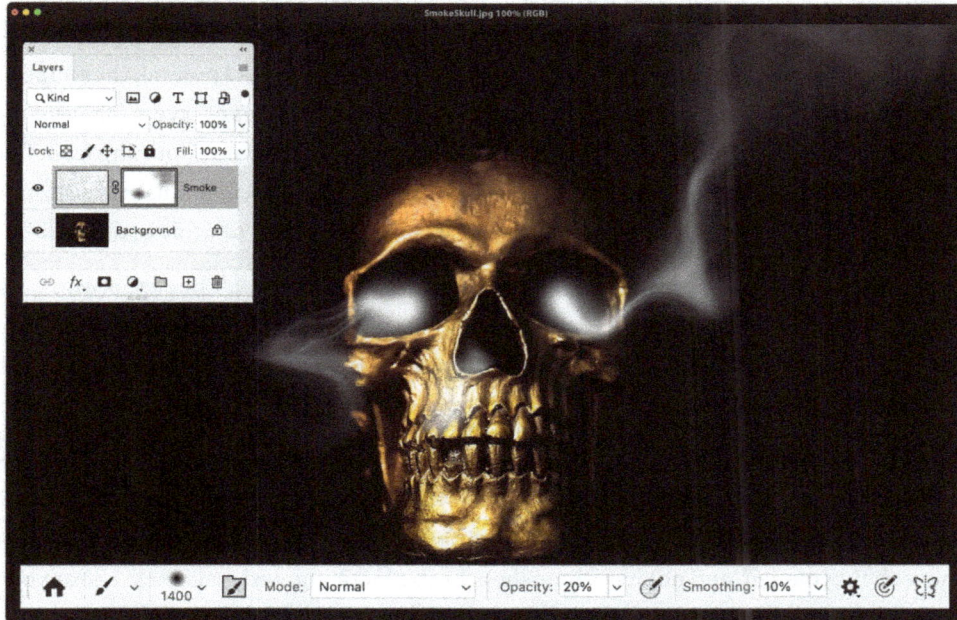

Figure 14.40: Fade the ends of the brush strokes with a layer mask

17. Then click on the ends of the largest brush marks to fade them. This will make the smoke effect more convincing.

18. Save the image as a PSD in the 14-Surreal folder and close the document when done.

In the second half of this surrealism-themed chapter, we used images of an iPad Pro and hands, shot specifically for this project. This gave us more control over the editing process and allowed us to achieve the exact look we were aiming for without compromising with unrelated stock images. We used clipping masks as the method for turning the hands into wire-like fibers from a series of layers filled with custom brush marks. In the final exercise, we used Liquify to distort simple brush marks, turning them into an eerie smoke effect.

Summary

In this final chapter, we examined two techniques for creating surrealist images. The first used a set of curated stock images to turn the Moon into a balloon tied to a chair. We painstakingly replaced the original shadows on the floor with our own. We saw how most of the work involved correcting unwanted details from those stock images.

In the second surrealist project, we started with a series of studio shots taken specifically for the project. Each image was carefully set up to work with each other through post-production editing in Photoshop. We combined a shot of an iPad Pro against a white background, then superimposed a shot of hands, one holding an Apple Pencil. We then used a series of layers to reveal the hands with a clipping-mask technique. This gave the impression of the hands forming from fine cables that assembled at the fingers where the hand was holding the pencil. In this exercise, most of the work involved painting hundreds of lines with custom brush tips to achieve the desired effect.

Congratulations! You've completed the final exercises in this book. I hope that you now have a better understanding of how to approach a variety of Photoshop challenges across print, web, and screen projects. In addition, you should have greater confidence in choosing an appropriate tool for each task and manipulating it to suit your needs, along with other Photoshop features.

Of course, we never truly stop learning, just as Photoshop never ceases to evolve. You'll no doubt find, as I have over the years, that it's only when you undertake your own projects with a different set of challenges that you truly push your abilities to the limit and discover things that you didn't know about yourself, and not just Photoshop. Keep practicing, and good luck. I hope you find the same sense of fun and fulfillment that I have over the years using Photoshop.

Get This Book's PDF Version and Exclusive Extras

UNLOCK NOW

Scan the QR code (or go to packtpub.com/unlock). Search for this book by name, confirm the edition, and then follow the steps on the page.

Note: Keep your invoice handy. Purchases made directly from Packt don't require one.

15

Unlock Your Exclusive Benefits

Your copy of this book includes the following exclusive benefits:

- ☁ Next-gen Packt Reader
- 📄 DRM-free PDF/ePub downloads

Follow the guide below to unlock them. The process takes only a few minutes and needs to be completed once.

Unlock this Book's Free Benefits in 3 Easy Steps

Step 1

Keep your purchase invoice ready for *Step 3*. If you have a physical copy, scan it using your phone and save it as a PDF, JPG, or PNG.

For more help on finding your invoice, visit `https://www.packtpub.com/unlock-benefits/help`.

> **Note:** If you bought this book directly from Packt, no invoice is required. After *Step 2*, you can access your exclusive content right away.

Step 2

Scan the QR code or go to `packtpub.com/unlock`.

On the page that opens (similar to *Figure 15.1* on desktop), search for this book by name and select the correct edition.

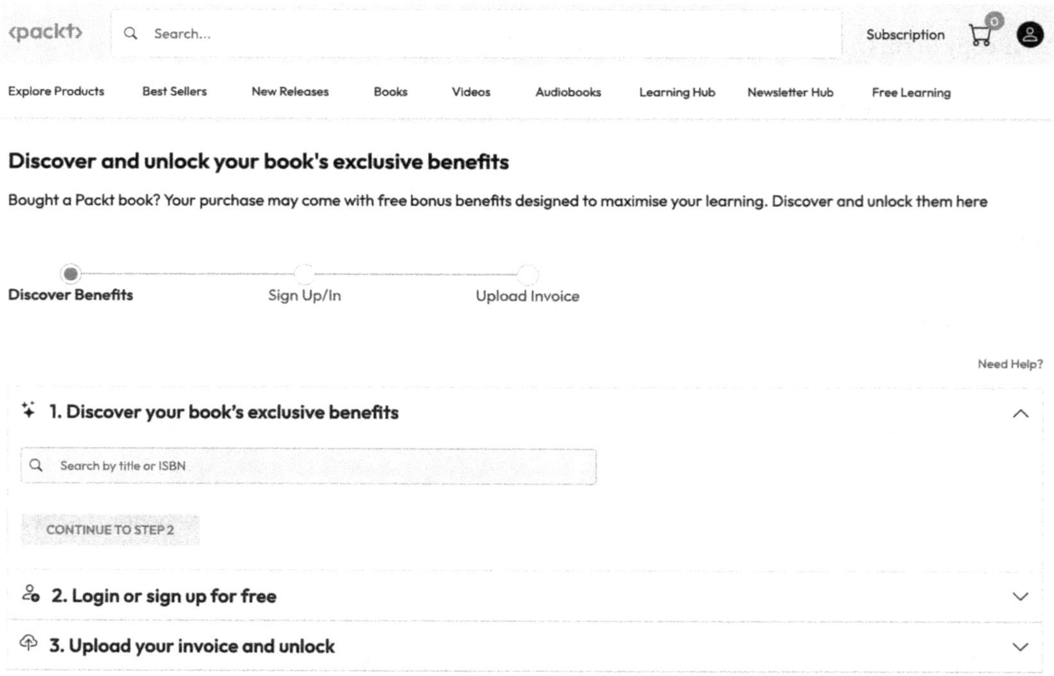

‹packt›   🔍 Search...   Subscription 🛒⁰ 👤

Explore Products   Best Sellers   New Releases   Books   Videos   Audiobooks   Learning Hub   Newsletter Hub   Free Learning

Discover and unlock your book's exclusive benefits

Bought a Packt book? Your purchase may come with free bonus benefits designed to maximise your learning. Discover and unlock them here

●───────────────○───────────────○
Discover Benefits   Sign Up/In   Upload Invoice

Need Help?

✦ **1. Discover your book's exclusive benefits**   ∧

🔍 Search by title or ISBN

CONTINUE TO STEP 2

👥 **2. Login or sign up for free**   ∨

☁ **3. Upload your invoice and unlock**   ∨

Figure 15.1: Packt unlock landing page on desktop

Step 3

After selecting your book, sign in to your Packt account or create one for free. Then upload your invoice (PDF, PNG, or JPG, up to 10 MB). Follow the on-screen instructions to finish the process.

Need help?

If you get stuck and need help, visit `https://www.packtpub.com/unlock-benefits/help` for a detailed FAQ on how to find your invoices and more. This QR code will take you to the help page.

Note: If you are still facing issues, reach out to `customercare@packt.com`.

‹packt›

packtpub.com

Subscribe to our online digital library for full access to over 7,000 books and videos, as well as industry leading tools to help you plan your personal development and advance your career. For more information, please visit our website.

Why subscribe?

- Spend less time learning and more time coding with practical eBooks and Videos from over 4,000 industry professionals
- Improve your learning with Skill Plans built especially for you
- Get a free eBook or video every month
- Fully searchable for easy access to vital information
- Copy and paste, print, and bookmark content

At www.packtpub.com, you can also read a collection of free technical articles, sign up for a range of free newsletters, and receive exclusive discounts and offers on Packt books and eBooks.

Other Books You May Enjoy

If you enjoyed this book, you may be interested in these other books by Packt:

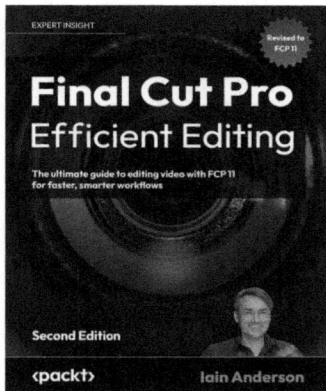

Final Cut Pro Efficient Editing

Iain Anderson

ISBN: 9781837631674

- Organize and manage media from multiple sources with ease
- Edit video using an intuitive interface and powerful tools
- Streamline workflows with customizable workspaces and shortcuts
- Sync multicam interviews and master advanced trimming
- Enhance edits with AI color tools and audio workflows
- Collaborate smoothly with built-in editing tools
- Create visual effects and motion graphics titles
- Export projects in multiple formats for any platform

Procreate for Digital Artists

Mellisa Aning

ISBN: 9781835082980

- Build stunning backgrounds using texture, color, and composition
- Master perspective to create depth, realism, and dynamic scenes
- Control light and shadow using professional techniques tailored for Procreate
- Develop visual storytelling skills to evoke emotion through your art
- Apply color theory to improve your digital coloring skills
- Create character designs that complement your background art
- Explore digital techniques for creating engaging background concepts

Packt is searching for authors like you

If you're interested in becoming an author for Packt, please visit authors.packt.com and apply today. We have worked with thousands of developers and tech professionals, just like you, to help them share their insight with the global tech community. You can make a general application, apply for a specific hot topic that we are recruiting an author for, or submit your own idea.

Share your thoughts

Now you've finished *Mastering Adobe Photoshop 2026*, we'd love to hear your thoughts! Scan the QR code below to go straight to the Amazon review page for this book and share your feedback or leave a review on the site that you purchased it from.

https://packt.link/r/1806021714

Your review is important to us and the tech community and will help us make sure we're delivering excellent quality content.

Index

A

A4 poster document
building 198-201

Adjust colors feature 7, 8

Adjustment Brush Tool 5-7

adjustment layers 88
color cast, removing 90, 91
color matching method 95-97
multiple subjects hue, altering 92-94
subjects matching, to backdrops 97-101
used, for color and tonal editing 88
working 88

adjustment presets
applying 5
creating 4, 5

Adobe Bridge 39
installing 458, 459

Adobe Camera Raw (ACR) 4

Adobe Express
used, for scheduling posts 259, 260

Adobe Firefly 13, 410
image, creating 414-416
image models 410
interface 411-414

Adobe fonts
synchronizing 312, 313
URL 312

Adobe PDF
exporting to 221

Adobe Sensei 405

Adobe Stock 46, 47
reference link 47

animated GIFs
exporting 300-302

animated GIFs creation 271
animation document, defining 271, 272
brand colors, adding 272-275
frame animations, creating 275-277
logos, adding 272-275
text, adding 272-275
tween animations, creating 278-282

artboards 226
batch export artboards 257, 258
duplicating 252-256
header image, adding 244, 245
text, adding to 251, 252
working with 239-242
X post template, creating 245-250

Art History Brush tool 377

artificial intelligence (AI) 405

artwork
adding, to brochure 216-220
importing 205

artwork specs, examining
for Facebook 228-230
for LinkedIn 235, 237
for Pinterest 234, 235
for X 230, 231

atmospheric gradient backdrop
creating 353-355

auto-cropping feature 61

auto-leading 310

AV file formats 268

B

backdrop assets
adding, with Creative Cloud
libraries 359, 360
exporting 361
importing 361
managing 359

backgrounds
generating 429, 430

baseline shift 311

bleed 196

Blend If 106

blend modes 90

brushes
applying, for creative effect 388-391
for retouching 392
snowflake brush, creating 392-395
stubble brush, creating 396-401

brush properties
brush preset group, backing up 386, 387
brush preset group, creating 386, 387
large Art History Brush, creating 379-381

medium Art History Brush, creating 381
modifying 377-379
reconstruction Art History Brush,
creating 384-386
small Art History Brush, creating 383, 384

brush tip presets
creating 372
managing 372

business card design
creating, with vector assets 206-209
font synchronization,
from Creative Cloud 209
paragraph styles, applying 214, 215
paragraph styles, creating 214-216
types, adding to Z-fold brochure 210-213

business card template
creating 201-205

C

Camera Raw 35

canvas
extension 54
extension, with content-aware
cropping 58-60

CC BY license 49

CC BY-NC license 49

CC BY-NC-ND license 50

CC BY-NC-SA license 49

CC BY-ND license 49

CC BY-SA license 49

clipping masks 106

Clone Stamp 65

clothing and soft furnishing mock-ups
creating 180
original designs, applying 180-183
pattern designs, adding 183

collages, with texture and paint
  adding, to posterized sections 444-448
  building 439
  posterized regions, selecting
      and masking 442, 443
  source photo, posterizing 439-441

Color and Vibrance 8

color cast 90

color editing
  with adjustment layers 88

content-aware scaling 63, 64

Contextual Task Bar 15, 16

controls 411

Creative Cloud
  fonts, synchronizing from 209

Creative Cloud libraries
  backdrop assets, adding with 359, 360

Creative Commons licensing 48
  CC0 50
  CC BY 49
  CC BY-NC 49
  CC BY-NC-ND 50
  CC BY-NC-SA 49
  CC BY-ND 49
  CC BY-SA 49
  reference link 50

crooked image
  straightening 54, 56

crop marks 196

cropping 56

custom bird brush
  creating 373-377

cut and fold effects
  creating 323-332

**cyan, magenta, yellow,
    and black (CMYK) 194**

D

daubs 42

Delete Layer Mask 105

device screens
  iPad mock-up, creating 172, 173
  replacing, with artwork 172
  screen reflections, adding 177-179
  smartphone mock-up, creating 174-177

Digital Negative (DNG) format 462

digital single-lens reflex cameras (DSLRs) 39

Disable Layer Mask 105

displacement maps 180

distractions
  removing 420, 421

dots per inch (DPI) 42

double-exposure compositions
  creating 449
  two exposures, blending
      of same image 455-458
  unrelated images, blending 449-454

drab skies
  replacing 416-418

dripping paint effect
  creating 333
  displacement map, creating 334, 335
  refining 336, 337

E

editable vignette
  creating, with vector mask 136, 137

embossed type
  creating 317-323

F

Facebook
artwork specs, examining 228, 229
Firefly Image 3 model 426
Firefly Upscaler 423, 424
Flux 410
folds 196, 197
fonts 312
Freepik
reference link 48
Freeze Mask tool 189

G

Gemini 2.5 Flash Image (Nano Banana) 410
Generate image dialog 13, 14
generative canvas extension 427, 428
Generative Fill 406, 419
generative results 411
generative retouching 416
ghosting 458
GIF limitations
on social media 269
glyphs 312
GPT 410
graffiti typographic effect
creating 337
long shadows, creating 339, 340
spray paint effects, adding
to text and shadows 341, 342
underlying type layer, formatting 338
group masks 145

H

Harmonize 11-13, 470
HDR images
Adobe Bridge, installing 458, 459
advice, for shooting 458
creating, with HDR Pro 460-466
working with 458
HDR Pro
used, for creating HDR image 460-466
header image
adding, to artboard 244, 245
healing and retouching tool 64
cables, removing from photo 66, 67
Clone Stamp tool, using to remove
unwanted content 76-79
glare, eliminating from glasses 83-87
large blemishes, removing with Content-
Aware Fill 68, 69, 70
portrait retouching 81, 82, 83
smiles, adding to portraits
with Face-Aware Liquify 79, 80
subjects, bending with Puppet Warp 71-75
Healing Brush tool 65
high dynamic range (HDR) image 433

I

image creation
with social media, required sizes 238, 239
Image Model 4 410
Image Model 4 Ultra 410
image models 410
Imagen 410
images
creating, in Firefly 414-416
cropping 54-58
straightening 54

images and masks
layer groups, masking 132-135
unlinking 130, 131

image usage and copyright 48

Instagram
artwork, examining 232, 233
examining, for X 232, 233

international copyright
reference link 50

J

JPG
saving as 222

K

kerning 310

L

layer mask 103
applying 104, 105, 106
applying, to adjustment layers 110-112
Blend If settings, masking with 121-124
distressed photo edges, creating 119, 121
editing 104-106
gradient masks, working with 116-119
power shortcuts, masking 107
retouching, with layer mask 113-116
using, to cut out image
backgrounds 107-110

leading 310

liability waiver 50

linked assets 145

LinkedIn
artwork, examining 235-238

Liquify 189

M

Magic Wand tool 92

masking hair 124-127
detailed adjustments, making
to layer mask 128, 129

mock-ups
developing 146, 147

model release 50

moonlight effects
creating 490-497

motion workspace 264

N

Nano Banana 424-426

notable stock resources 48

O

online resources 44
Adobe Stock 46, 47
Creative Commons 48
image usage and copyright 48
model release 50
notable stock resources 48
Pexels 46
property release 50
Unsplash 45

P

painting cursors 36

paper embossing technique 317

partner models 423

Patch tool 82

pattern artwork 191

pattern designs
  adding 183
  cushion displacement map,
      creating 183-185
  pattern artwork, applying 185-187
  rippled surface details, finessing 187-192

Pexels 46
  reference link 46

Photoshop app
  on Android 16-18
  on iOS 16-18

Photoshop Document (PSD) 35

Photoshop grid system
  A4 poster document, building 198-201
  business card template, creating 201-203
  setting up 197
  Z-fold brochure, building 203-205

Photoshop tools and features
  Color Settings, defining 38-40
  creating 20
  custom workspace, saving 28
  keyboard shortcuts and menus,
      modifying 29, 31
  panels, customizing 25, 26
  panels, modifying 21-23
  preferences, modifying 31-38

Photoshop warp transform features 159
  book designs artwork, warping 162-171
  cylinder warp, applying 159-162

Pinterest
  artwork specs, examining 234, 235

pixels 41

pixels per inch (PPI)
  calculating, in Photoshop 43, 44
  quality-first approach 42

plus widgets 227

pop-art-inspired artwork
  creating, custom patterns 355-358

posterized regions
  selecting and masking 442, 443

posterized sections
  texture and paint, adding to 444-448

posts
  exporting 256
  scheduling 256
  scheduling, with Adobe Express 259, 260

print projects
  color 194
  creating 194
  folds 196, 197
  marks 194-196

professional print
  documents, exporting 220
  exporting, to Adobe PDF 221
  saving, as JPG 222, 223
  Tagged Image File Format (TIFF).
      exporting to 221

project-specific assets
  creating 497
  hands, isolating from shot 497-506

prompts
  actions, describing 408
  detailed prompt 408, 409
  effective prompts, structuring 407
  environment, describing 408
  medium, describing 407
  props, describing 408
  subject, describing 407

property release 50

Puppet Warp mesh 75

puzzle post 233

Q

quality-first approach 40, 41
  image quality 41
  pixels per inch (PPI) 42
  pixels per inch (PPI), calculating in
    Photoshop 43, 44
  resolution 42
  vector graphics 42

R

red, green, and blue (RGB) 194
Remove background feature 9, 10
Remove Tool 420-422

S

sans serif 309
screen
  documents, creating 226-228
seamless panoramas
  creating 434-438
serif 309
Sky Replacement 416-418
sliced text
  creating 314-317
smart objects 145, 314
smoke effects
  creating, with brushes and filters 507-511
snowflake brush
  creating 392-395
source photo
  posterizing 439-441
space scene
  creating, with filters and effects 362-368
Spot Healing Brush tool 65

Statista
  reference link 228
stubble brush
  creating 396-401
surrealist art project
  approaching 470, 471
  chair shadows, replacing 478-489
  creating 471
  Moon artwork, distorting 473-475
  Moon artwork, scaling 473, 475
  Moon artwork, transferring 471-473
  moonlight effects, creating 490-497
  pink balloon, turning into grayscale 476, 477

T

Tagged Image File Format (TIFF)
  exporting to 221
text prompts
  handy tips 406
texture
  creating, from scratch 346-352
Timeline panel 264, 265
tonal editing
  with adjustment layers 88-90
Topaz 423
Topaz Bloom 423, 424
Topaz Gigapixel 423, 424
tracking 310
tweening 278
typefaces 309
typographic
  principles 308-311
  terms 308-311
typographic mask effect
  creating 138-141

U

Unsplash 45
reference link 45
Unsplash+ 45
user interface (UI) 31

V

Vanishing Point 147
limitations 151
logo, adding to bag 148-151
mural mock-up, creating 151-158
vector graphics 42
vector mask
editable vignette, creating with 136, 137
typographic mask effect, creating 138-140
working with 136
video 269
exporting 302, 303
video and audio
Adobe Illustrator logo,
   animating in timeline 287-290
document, creating 283, 284
media, adding to timeline 284, 285
soundtrack, adding to timeline 291
transitions, applying to footage 286, 287
working with 283
video groups 266, 268
video limitations
on social media 269
**videos, creating from still
   images and text 292**
duplicate document, setting up 292
image, animating 292-294
image, importing 292-294

keyframes, copying and pasting onto
   second and third clip 294, 295
titles, adding to sequence 297-300

W

web
documents, creating 226-228

X

X
artwork, examining 230, 231
X post template
creating 245-250

Z

Z-fold brochure
type, adding 210-213

www.ingramcontent.com/pod-product-compliance
Lightning Source LLC
Chambersburg PA
CBHW081216220326
41598CB00037B/6793